# ANNUAL EDITIONS

# Gender 10/11

*First Edition*

## EDITOR

**Bobby Hutchison**
*Modesto Junior College*

Bobby Hutchison is a Professor of Psychology and Human Sexualities at Modesto Junior College in California. He graduated from the University of California at Santa Barbara with degrees in psychology and sociology. He also has an academic background in the biological sciences and French language and literature, having completed the equivalent of a major in French. Focusing on gender and sexualities during his graduate studies, Professor Hutchison has taught sex and gender courses at a variety of institutions, from community colleges to public and private universities. He has published numerous articles, essays, and reviews in psychology, sociology, education, and history journals. In addition to serving as editor for *Annual Editions: Gender,* Professor Hutchison is also the editor of *Annual Editions: Human Sexualities.*

 **Higher Education**

Boston   Burr Ridge, IL   Dubuque, IA   New York   San Francisco   St. Louis
Bangkok   Bogotá   Caracas   Kuala Lumpur   Lisbon   London   Madrid   Mexico City
Milan   Montreal   New Delhi   Santiago   Seoul   Singapore   Sydney   Taipei   Toronto

The McGraw·Hill Companies

# Mc Graw Hill **Higher Education**

ANNUAL EDITIONS: GENDER, FIRST EDITION

Published by McGraw-Hill, a business unit of The McGraw-Hill Companies, Inc., 1221 Avenue of the Americas, New York, NY 10020.

Copyright © 2010 by The McGraw-Hill Companies, Inc. All rights reserved. No part of this publication may be reproduced or distributed in any form or by any means, or stored in a database or retrieval system, without the prior written consent of The McGraw-Hill Companies, Inc., including, but not limited to, in any network or other electronic storage or transmission, or broadcast for distance learning.

Some ancillaries, including electronic and print components, may not be available to customers outside the United States.

Annual Editions® is a registered trademark of The McGraw-Hill Companies, Inc.

Annual Editions is published by the **Contemporary Learning Series** group within The McGraw-Hill Higher Education division.

1 2 3 4 5 6 7 8 9 0 QWD/QWD 0 9

ISBN 978–0–07–805052–7
MHID 0–07–805052–9
ISSN 1948–2663

Managing Editor: *Larry Loeppke*
Senior Managing Editor: *Faye Schilling*
Developmental Editor: *Debra Henricks*
Editorial Coordinator: *Mary Foust*
Editorial Assistant: *Cindy Hedley*
Production Service Assistant: *Rita Hingtgen*
Permissions Coordinator: *Lenny J. Behnke*
Senior Marketing Manager: *Julie Keck*
Marketing Communications Specialist: *Mary Klein*
Marketing Coordinator: *Alice Link*
Project Manager: *Joyce Watters*
Design Specialist: *Tara McDermott*
Senior Production Supervisor: *Laura Fuller*
Cover Graphics: *Kristine Jubeck*

Compositor: Laserwords Private Limited
Cover Images: © Getty Images/RF (inset); © Getty Images/RF, © Brand X Pictures/Punchstock, © Fancy Photography/Veer, © Digital Vision/Getty Images/RF (background montage)

**Library in Congress Cataloging-in-Publication Data**
Main entry under title: Annual Editions: Gender 2010/2011.
   1. Gender—Periodicals. LIC info to come I. Hutchison, Bobby, *comp*. II. Title: Gender.
658′.05

www.mhhe.com

# Editors/Academic Advisory Board

Members of the Academic Advisory Board are instrumental in the final selection of articles for each edition of ANNUAL EDITIONS. Their review of articles for content, level, and appropriateness provides critical direction to the editors and staff. We think that you will find their careful consideration well reflected in this volume.

## ANNUAL EDITIONS: Gender 10/11
1st Edition

## EDITOR

**Bobby Hutchison**
*Modesto Junior College*

## ACADEMIC ADVISORY BOARD MEMBERS

**Mary Beth Ahlum**
*Nebraska Wesleyan University*

**Sanjam Ahluwalia**
*Northern Arizona University*

**Katrina Akande**
*University of Kentucky—Lexington*

**Iris Allen**
*University of Maryland—College Park*

**Sine Anahita**
*University of Alaska—Fairbanks*

**Deborah Anderson**
*St. Olaf College*

**Susan Anspaugh**
*Tri-State University*

**Margaret Bader**
*Nunez Community College*

**Emma Bailey**
*Western New Mexico University*

**Janice Baldwin**
*University of California—Santa Barbara*

**Lacy Barnes-Mileham**
*Reedley College*

**Eleen Baumann**
*University of Oregon*

**Cari Beecham-Bautista**
*Columbia College Chicago*

**James Benjamin, Jr.**
*Oklahoma Panhandle State University*

**Christine Bennett**
*University of Northern Iowa*

**Todd Bernhardt**
*Broward College*

**Victoria Bisorca**
*California State University—Long Beach*

**Josephine Bitler**
*Alpena Community College*

**Barbara Bonnekessen**
*New Mexico Tech*

**Lizzie Boyles**
*Valencia Community College—Osceola*

**Leila Brammer**
*Gustavus Adolphus College*

**Mariana Branda**
*College of the Canyons*

**Tristan Bridges**
*Univ of Virginia—Charlottesville*

**Rebecca Bryant**
*Texas Woman's University*

**Gayle Bush**
*Troy State University—Troy*

**Mary Cameron**
*Florida Atlantic University*

**Amy Capwell-Burns**
*University of Toledo*

**Bernardo J. Carducci**
*Indiana University—Southeast*

**Susan Carter**
*Lee University*

**Deena Case-Pall**
*Moorpark College*

**Mathilda Catarina**
*William Paterson University*

**Dianne Catherwood**
*University of Gloucestershire*

**Cheryl Chopard**
*Des Moines Area Community College*

**Lyndie Christensen**
*University of Nebraska—Lincoln*

**Evelyn Christner**
*Columbus College of Art and Design*

**Geraldine Cicero**
*St. Johns University*

**Leigh Clemons**
*Louisiana State University*

**Amber Clifford**
*University of Central Missouri*

**Jodi Cohen**
*Bridgewater State College*

**Herb Coleman**
*Austin Community College*

**Kimberly Coleman**
*Georgia Southern University*

**Carol Conaway**
*University of New Hampshire*

**Don Conway-Long**
*Webster University*

**John A. Cook**
*University of Texas at Brownsville*

**Vanessa Cooke**
*Bowie State University*

**Ann Crawford**
*Lynn University*

**Miki Crawford**
*Ohio University Southern Campus—Ironton*

**Lisa Cuklanz**
*Boston College*

**Gaye Cummins**
*University of Houston—Clear Lake*

**Mitch Darnell**
*Cosumnes River College*

**Lisa Davison**
*Lexington Theological Seminary*

# Editors/Academic Advisory Board continued

Darlene DeFour
*Hunter College*

Vivian Deno
*Butler University*

Liz Desnoyers-Colas
*Armstrong Atlantic State University*

Mary Devitt
*Jamestown College*

Amanda Diekman
*Miami University of Ohio—Oxford*

Rachel Dinero
*Cazenovia College*

Mary Dolan
*California State University—San Bernardino, University of Redlands*

Elizabeth Domangue
*Louisiana State University—Baton Rouge*

MaryAnn Drake
*Mercer University*

Elizabeth Drake-Boyt

Mike Dudley
*Southern Illinois University*

April Dye
*Carson-Newman College*

Donald Dyson
*Widener University*

Belle Edson
*Arizona State University—Tempe*

Tami Eggleston
*McKendree University*

Cheryl Ellis
*Middle Tennessee State University*

Steve Ellyson
*Youngstown State University*

Marina Epstein
*University of Michigan*

Melinda Everman-Moore
*Ohio State University—Marion*

Daniel Farr
*Randolph College*

Susan Farrell
*Kingsborough Community College*

Kathryn Feltey
*University of Akron*

Christopher Ferguson
*Texas A&M International University*

James Ferraro
*Southern Illinois University—Carbondale*

Jorge Figueroa
*University of North Carolina—Wilmington*

Africa Fine
*Palm Beach Community College*

Paul Finnicum
*Arkansas State University*

Juanita Firestone
*University of Texas at San Antonio*

Wm. Michael Fleming
*University of Northern Iowa*

Kristin Flora
*Franklin College*

Kay Foland
*South Dakota State University*

Pamela Forman
*University of Wisconsin—Eau Claire*

Karen Foss
*University of New Mexico*

James Francis
*San Jacinto College—South Campus*

Peter Frecknall

Bill Galic
*Kenai Peninsula College*

Rachel Gillibrand
*University of the West of England*

Sally Gillman
*South Dakota State University*

Teresa Gonya
*University of Wisconsin—Fox Valley*

Teresa Gonzalez
*Queens College*

Kris Gowen
*Portland State University*

Kathryn Grant
*University of North Florida*

Jerry Green
*Tarrant County College Northwest Campus*

Penny Green
*Colorado State University—Pueblo*

Timothy Grogan
*Valencia Community College—Osceola*

Barbara Gryzlo
*North Park University*

Patricia Guth
*Westmoreland County Community College*

Jodi Hallsten
*Illinois State University*

Ellen Hansen
*Emporia State University*

Trudy Hanson
*West Texas A&M University*

Diana Hart
*Arapahoe Community College*

Marta Hartmann
*University of Florida at Gainesville*

Jennifer Helgren
*University of the Pacific*

Bridget Hepner
*Sam Houston State University*

Gilbert Herdt
*San Francisco State University*

Jodie Hertzog
*Wichita State University*

Erin Hightower
*Flagler College*

Danielle Holbrook
*Florida State University*

Debra Hollister
*Valencia Community College East*

Earl Hopper
*Mt. San Jacinto College—Menifee Valley Campus*

Gregory Horne
*Middlesex Community College*

Scott Horton
*Mitchell College*

Hua-Lun Huang
*University of Louisiana—Lafayette*

Rosemarie Hughes
*Regent University*

Gwen Hunnicutt
*University of North Carolina at Greensboro*

Heather Jarrell
*Ohio State University*

Ethel Jones
*South Carolina State University*

Jean Jones
*Edinboro University*

# Editors/Academic Advisory Board continued

**Jennifer Jones**
University of New Mexico—Albuquerque

**Lindsy Jorgensen**
University of Utah

**Vonda Jump**
Utah State University

**Carl Jylland-Halverson**
University of Saint Francis

**Christopher Kacir**
Shawnee State University

**Michael Kimmel**
Stony Brook University

**Katherine Kinnick**
Kennesaw State University

**Jen Krafchick**
Colorado State University

**Cynthia Kreutzer**
Georgia Perimeter College—
Lawrenceville

**Charles Krinsky**
Northeastern University

**Steve Kronheim**
University of Maryland—
University College

**Mary Krueger**
Bowling Green State University

**Elizabeth Kubek**
Benedictine University

**Karen Kunkle**
Youngstown State University

**Sharon Lamb**
Saint Michael's College

**Mary Landeros**
Northern Illinois University

**Sara Levine Kornfield**
Drexel University

**Diane Levy**
University of North Carolina—
Wilmington

**Patricia Levy**
Fort Hays State University

**Joe Lopiccolo**
University Of Missouri—Columbia

**Adrianna Lozano**
Purdue University

**Tammy Mahan**
College of the Canyons

**Jimmie Manning**
Northern Kentucky University

**Amy Marin**
Phoenix College

**Jennifer Martinez**
Chapman University—Yuba City Campus

**Chandra Massner**
Pikeville College

**Christine Mattley**
Ohio University—Athens

**Danielle McAneney**
Southwestern College

**Cecily McDaniel**
North Carolina Agriculture & Technical
State University

**Michael McGee**
Fairleigh Dickinson University

**Karen McKinney**
University of Louisville

**Abigail McNeely**
Austin Community College—
Cedar Park

**Abi Mehdipour**
Troy University

**Sylvia Mendez-Morse**
Texas Tech University

**Melinda Miceli**
Hillyer College

**Eva Mika**
Loyola University

**Abigail Mitchell**
Nebraska Wesleyan University

**Robert Moore**
Marshalltown Community College

**Kelly Morrison**
Michigan State University—
East Lansing

**Tina Mougouris**
San Jacinto College—Pasadena

**Thalia Mulvihill**
Ball State University

**Sue Murray**
Andrews University

**Jill Nealey-Moore**
University of Puget Sound

**Teri Nicoll-Johnson**
Modesto Junior College

**Cynthia Noyes**
Olivet College

**Ingrid Ochoa**
San Francisco State University

**Camille Odell**
Utah State University

**Peggy Ondrea**
Columbia College

**Elizabeth Ossoff**
Saint Anselm College

**David Oxendine**
University of North Carolina—
Pembroke

**Sheila Patterson**
Cleveland State University

**Amanda Paule**
Bowling Green State University

**Keisha Paxton**
California State University—
Dominguez Hills

**Allison Pease**
John Jay College

**Joy Pendley**
University of Oklahoma—Norman

**Zoe Peterson**
University of Missouri—St. Louis

**Jane Petrillo**
Kennesaw State University

**Shea Pezeshk**
Alliant International University

**Mary Pflugshaupt**
Indiana University Northwest

**Catherine Pittman**
Saint Mary's College

**Johna Pointek**
Pace University

**Nancy Porter**
Chestnut Hill College

**Judith Pratt**
California State University—
Bakersfield

**Curtis Proctor**
Wichita State University

**Tina Quartaroli**
Huston-Tillotson University

**Cora Reda-Marmo**
College of DuPage

# Editors/Academic Advisory Board continued

**Doug Rice**
Sacramento State University

**Deb Risisky**
Southern Connecticut State University

**Dennis Roderick**
University of Massachusetts—Dartmouth

**Debra Rodman**
Randolph-Macon College

**Lynn Rose**
Truman State University

**Louise Rosenberg**
University of Hartford

**Judy Rosovsky**
Johnson State College

**Betty Rugg**
Webb Institute

**Josephine Ryan**
University of Texas at Arlington

**Lynn Ryzewicz**
Pratt Institute

**Florence Sage**
Clatsop Community College

**Christa Salamandra**
Lehman College

**Sue Saul**
California State University—Los Angeles

**Shawn Sellers**
Western Oregon University—
Chemeketa Community College

**Marla Selvidge**
University of Central Missouri

**Shawna Shane**
Emporia State University

**Catherine Sherwood**
Indiana University—Bloomington

**Sheida Shirvani**
Ohio University—Zanesville

**Richard Siegel**
Palm Beach Community College

**Allan Simmons**
Jackson State University

**Amy Slater**
Blue River Community College—
Independence

**Cathey Soutter**
Southern Methodist University

**Debbie Sowers**
Eastern Kentucky University

**Colleen Spada**
Loyola University

**George Spilich**
Washington College

**Carolyn Springer**
Adelphi University

**Susanne Sreedhar**
Boston University

**Jade Stanley**
Northeastern Illinois University

**Janice Stapley**
Monmouth University

**Lea Stewart**
Rutgers University—New Brunswick

**Lori Sudderth**
Quinnipiac University

**Sara Sutler-Cohen**
Bellevue Community College

**Becky Talyn**
California State University—San Bernardino

**Sharon Taylor**
Washington-Jefferson College

**Leslie Templeton**
Hendrix College

**Cheryl Terrance**
University of North Dakota

**Ardel Thomas**
City College of San Francisco

**Michael Thomas**
Arkansas State University

**Ronald Thomas**
Embry Riddle Aeronautical
University—Daytona Beach

**Sandra Todaro**
Bossier Parish Community College

**Linda Tollefsrud**
University of Wisconsin—Rice Lake

**Margaret Torrie**
Iowa State University

**Carolyn Turner**
Texas Lutheran University

**Susan Turner**
Front Range Community College

**Eric Vilain**
University of California—Los Angeles

**Kate Waites**
Nova Southeastern University

**J. Celeste Walley-Jean**
Clayton State University

**Esther Wangari**
Towson University

**Elizabeth Weiss**
The Ohio State University Newark

**Casey Welch**
Flagler College

**Maria Wessel**
James Madison University

**Debra Wetcher-Hendricks**
Moravian College

**Amanda White**
St. Louis Community College at Meramec

**Yvonne Wichman**
Kennesaw State University

**Gary Wilson**
The Citadel

**Dow Winscott**
College of DuPage

**Leanna Wolfe**
Los Angeles Valley College

**Patricia Wren**
Oakland University

**David Yarbrough**
University of Louisiana at Lafayette

**Alyson Young**
University of Florida

**Jodi Zieverink**
Central Piedmont Community College

# Preface

In publishing ANNUAL EDITIONS we recognize the enormous role played by the magazines, newspapers, and journals of the public press in providing current, first-rate educational information in a broad spectrum of interest areas. Many of these articles are appropriate for students, researchers, and professionals seeking accurate, current material to help bridge the gap between principles and theories and the real world. These articles, however, become more useful for study when those of lasting value are carefully collected, organized, indexed, and reproduced in a low-cost format, which provides easy and permanent access when the material is needed. That is the role played by ANNUAL EDITIONS.

**W**elcome to the inaugural volume of *Annual Editions: Gender.* Professors and students have responded overwhelmingly in favor of the publication of a gender book in this series. They told us exactly what they wanted, and we have responded with this book in order to meet their course needs. *Annual Editions: Gender* has been a long time coming, and I am personally very excited to be responsible for the editing and writing responsibilities of this book.

When the *Annual Editions* series first began publication, there were few dedicated academic programs for students interested in studying gender. Today, there are undergraduate majors and minors in women's and gender studies as well as a variety of graduate programs. Disciplines such as women's and gender studies, lesbian/gay/bisexual/transgender studies, and ethnic studies have thrived. Gender scholars from diverse academic perspectives make rich and lasting contributions to fields such as psychology, sociology, anthropology, education, history, literature, communication, and the life sciences, to name just a few areas.

Multidisciplinary and interdisciplinary aspects of gender studies are reflected throughout this book. On these pages, you will find articles written by sociologists, psychologists, historians, and journalists among others. Regardless of the backgrounds of the authors, topics such as identities, lived experiences, perspectives, voices, and social worlds are examined through the lens of gender. This book is, therefore, reflective of the diversity of the world today and the people we study, as well as the richness and variety of perspectives in a multidisciplinary, dynamic area of inquiry.

The articles that are included in this volume relate nicely to current gender textbooks as well as important trends in research and teaching today. The organization of this volume is intended to provide the reader with the greatest flexibility possible. This book can be used as either a core text or as a supplement for a variety of courses focusing on gender. This is the kind of flexibility that professors told us they needed. This book was organized with these requirements in mind.

*AE: Gender* is divided into six units to best serve gender courses as they are currently taught at colleges and universities. *Theoretical and Research Perspectives* offers the reader an opportunity to become acquainted with content covering a range of topics from the social construction of gender to quantitative and qualitative approaches to the study of gender. *Gender and Development* examines a variety of gender issues as they relate to different stages of our lives. *Gender and Education* focuses on critical issues students and educators face every day in a variety of educational settings. *Gender, Work, and Health* provides insights into the world of work and the health experiences of men and women. The *Gender and Sexualities* unit looks at diverse topics from transgendered voices and intersexed perspectives to marriages and sexual orientations. The last unit, *Gender and Social Issues,* highlights issues such as sexual assault, sex trafficking, the media, religion, and politics.

The articles are organized by topic in the *Topic Guide.* The up-to-date *Internet References* can be used to explore the many topics presented in this book. You may be surprised by what you will learn about gender just from doing a little bit of browsing on some of these sites.

All articles included in this book have been carefully reviewed and selected for their quality, readability, currency, interest, and usefulness. Some of what you will read you may personally relate to. Some of it you may find hard to understand. Some of what you will read may be upsetting to you. Some points of view you will agree with, some you will not. Whatever your experience with these articles, I hope you will learn from each of them.

Larry Loeppke, Managing Editor, Debra Henricks, Developmental Editor, and Lenny Behnke, Permissions Coordinator at McGraw-Hill, made this book possible. They have been incredibly supportive of this book. Debra Henricks is a dream editor. Her intelligence, vision, and constructive criticism have provided me with the essential guidance I needed as I worked on this project.

Much gratitude and thanks go to Janice Baldwin, Teri Nicoll-Johnson, Danielle McAneney, Dianne Catherwood, and Rachel Gillibrand for their support, encouragement, and critical feedback. I couldn't have done this book without their generous help.

My daughter, Anaïs, is my biggest inspiration. Being a parent, I find that I care even more about each of the topics covered in this book. Everything in life, including this course, takes on so much more meaning than I ever thought possible. This book, even more than prior projects, is for Anaïs.

Many thanks to those who have submitted articles for this anthology. Because of the feedback and guidance we have received from hundreds of professors, this is one of the most useful, flexible, and up-to-date gender books available on the market today.

Please tell us what you think by returning the postage-paid Article Rating Form located on the last page. If you know of a recent article that you think should be considered for the next edition, please note the title, source, and publication information for the article at the bottom of the rating form. We look forward to hearing from you and receiving your feedback!

Bobby Hutchison

Bobby Hutchison
*Editor*

# Contents

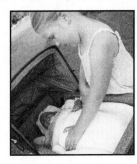

## UNIT 1
## Theoretical and Research Perspectives

The concepts in bold italics are developed in the article. For further expansion, please refer to the Topic Guide.

# UNIT 2
## Gender and Development

# UNIT 3
## Gender and Education

The concepts in bold italics are developed in the article. For further expansion, please refer to the Topic Guide.

# UNIT 4
## Gender, Work, and Health

The concepts in bold italics are developed in the article. For further expansion, please refer to the Topic Guide.

# UNIT 5
## Genders and Sexualities

The concepts in bold italics are developed in the article. For further expansion, please refer to the Topic Guide.

# UNIT 6
## Gender and Social Issues

### Unit Overview    **210**

The concepts in bold italics are developed in the article. For further expansion, please refer to the Topic Guide.

# Correlation Guide

The *Annual Editions* series provides students with convenient, inexpensive access to current, carefully selected articles from the public press. **Annual Editions: Gender 10/11** is an easy-to-use reader that presents articles on important topics such as *gender and development, gender and education, social issues,* and many more. For more information on *Annual Editions* and other *McGraw-Hill Contemporary Learning Series* titles, visit www.mhcls.com.

This convenient guide matches the units in **Annual Editions: Gender 10/11** with the corresponding chapters/parts in two of our best-selling McGraw-Hill Gender textbooks by Disch and Hyde/DeLamater.

| **Annual Editions: Gender 10/11** | **Reconstructing Gender: A Multicultural Anthology, 5/e by Disch** | **Understanding Human Sexuality, 10/e by Hyde/DeLamater** |
|---|---|---|
| **Unit 1:** Theoretical and Research Perspectives | **Part I:** It's Not Just about Gender<br>**Part II:** Gender Socialization | **Chapter 1:** Sexuality in Perspective<br>**Chapter 2:** Theoretical Perspectives on Sexuality<br>**Chapter 5:** Sex Hormones, Sexual Differentiation, Puberty, and the Menstrual Cycle<br>**Chapter 11:** Attraction, Love, and Communication<br>**Chapter 12:** Gender and Sexuality |
| **Unit 2:** Gender and Development | **Part II:** Gender Socialization<br>**Part III:** Embodiment<br>**Part V:** Sexuality<br>**Part VI:** Families | **Chapter 5:** Sex Hormones, Sexual Differentiation, Puberty, and the Menstrual Cycle<br>**Chapter 9:** Sexuality and the Life Cycle: Childhood and Adolescence<br>**Chapter 10:** Sexuality and the Life Cycle: Adulthood |
| **Unit 3:** Gender and Education | **Part VII:** Education | |
| **Unit 4:** Gender, Work and Health | **Part VIII:** Paid Work and Unemployment<br>**Part X:** Health and Illness | **Chapter 1:** Sexuality in Perspective<br>**Chapter 5:** Sex Hormones, Sexual Differentiation, Puberty, and the Menstrual Cycle<br>**Chapter 10:** Sexuality and the Life Cycle: Adulthood<br>**Chapter 14:** Variations in Sexual Behavior<br>**Chapter 18:** Sexually Transmitted Infections |
| **Unit 5:** Genders and Sexualities | **Part IV:** Communication<br>**Part V:** Sexuality<br>**Part XI:** A World That Is Truly Human | **Chapter 9:** Sexuality and the Life Cycle: Childhood and Adolescence<br>**Chapter 12:** Gender and Sexuality<br>**Chapter 13:** Sexual Orientation |
| **Unit 6:** Gender and Social Issues | **Part I:** It's Not Just about Gender<br>**Part IX:** Violence at Home and Abroad | **Chapter 7:** Contraception and Abortion<br>**Chapter 15:** Sexual Coercion<br>**Chapter 16:** Sex for Sale |

# Topic Guide

This topic guide suggests how the selections in this book relate to the subjects covered in your course. You may want to use the topics listed on these pages to search the Web more easily.

On the following pages a number of websites have been gathered specifically for this book. They are arranged to reflect the units of this Annual Editions reader. You can link to these sites by going to *http://www.mhcls.com*.

**All the articles that relate to each topic are listed below the bold-faced term.**

# Internet References

The following Internet sites have been selected to support the articles found in this reader. These sites were available at the time of publication. However, because websites often change their structure and content, the information listed may no longer be available. We invite you to visit http://www.mhcls.com for easy access to these sites.

# Annual Editions: Gender 10/11

## General Sources

**American Psychological Association: Society for the Psychology of Women**
*http://www.apa.org/divisions/div35/*

The Society for the Psychology of Women is an official division of the American Psychological Association, a professional association of academic and applied psychologists. Visit its website for information on its history, news, and resources on a variety of gender topics.

**American Psychological Association: Society for the Psychological Study of Men and Masculinity**
*http://www.apa.org/divisions/div51/*

The Society for the Psychological Study of Men and Masculinity is an official division of the American Psychological Association, a professional association of academic and applied psychologists. Visit its website for information on its history, an official newsletter and various resources available on men and masculinity.

**American Sociological Association: Sex and Gender Section**
*http://www2.asanet.org/sectionsexgend/*

The Sex and Gender section of the American Sociological Association, a professional association of sociologists, is one of the largest divisions within the ASA. Check out its newsletter and links to journals.

**Association for Feminist Anthropology**
*http://www.aaanet.org/sections/afa/*

This organization of feminist anthropologists publishes *Voices,* with some of the issues available in pdf format on its website. If you are interested in feminist anthropology, have a look at this organization's history and some of its resources.

**The Kinsey Institute for Research in Sex, Gender, and Reproduction**
*http://www.indiana.edu/~kinsey/*

This is the official website for Indiana University's Kinsey Institute. This website will be helpful to anyone interested in the scientific study of sex. Check out its latest news and events section as well as its resources. Find out about the history of this important research institute.

**SexInfo**
*http://www.soc.ucsb.edu/sexinfo/*

SexInfo is based out of the University of California at Santa Barbara. The site is run by advanced human sexuality students under the supervision of two UCSB sexuality professors. All aspects of sex and sexuality are covered on this website with great articles and Q&As. There are many topics at this site that will be of interest to students of gender. You do not want to miss this great website.

## UNIT 1: Theoretical and Research Perspectives

**Institute for Gender Research, Stanford University**
*http://www.stanford.edu/group/gender/index.html*

Learn about research on gender through articles and podcasts at Stanford University's gender research site. Be sure to click on "Publications and Podcasts."

**Gender Institute, London School of Economics**
*http://www.lse.ac.uk/collections/genderInstitute/*

For exciting examples of gender research go to this website and click on "working papers" to access numerous papers of interest to students of gender.

**Institute for Women's Policy Research**
*http://www.iwpr.org/index.cfm*

IWPR is a scientific research institute that makes vast amounts of data and information available to researchers and the general public through its published reports. Countless reports are available at this website.

**SocioSite: Feminism and Women's Issues**
*http://www.sociosite.net/topics/women.php*

Visit the University of Amsterdam "Social Science Information System" to gain insights into a number of issues that affect both men and women. It provides biographies of women in history, an international network for women in the workplace, links to family and children's issues, and much more.

**Queertheory.com**
*http://www.queertheory.com/*

This website houses a variety of resources on queer theory and gender studies. There are many exciting links under "Gender Theory." This site is a must for anyone interested in queer theory and/or gender theory.

## UNIT 2: Gender and Development

**Girls, Inc.**
*http://www.girlsinc.org/*

This youth organization maintains an excellent website with many resources, including news feeds, information for parents, and a variety of publications.

**The Boys Project**
*http://www.boysproject.net/*

The Boys Project is based out of the University of Alaska at Fairbanks. Visit the "statistics" section of this website for fascinating data comparing boys and girls on numerous measures from conception to suicide.

**American Association of Retired Persons (AARP)**
*http://www.aarp.org*

The AARP, a major advocacy group for older people, includes among its many resources suggested readings and Internet links to organizations that deal with the health and social issues that impact men and women as they age. There are numerous articles and resources on gender and aging available at this site.

**National Institute on Aging (NIA)**
*http://www.nih.gov/nia/*

# Internet References

The NIA, one of the institutes of the National Institutes of Health, presents this home page to lead you to a variety of resources on aging.

**Parents, Familes, and Friends of Lesbians and Gays**
*http://www.pflag.org*

This is the site of PFLAG: Parents, Families and Friends of Lesbians and Gays. Information and downloadable pamphlets with information and support on a variety of topics including "coming out" can be found here. Many of the resources available through PFLAG relate to developmental issues.

## UNIT 3: Gender and Education

**National Parent Teacher Association**
*http://www.pta.org/*

From student success to diversity and inclusion, the National Parent Teacher Association's website is a source of information on topics related to education that are of interest to gender studies.

**Early Childhood News**
*http://www.earlychildhoodnews.com/*

"The Professional Resource for Teachers and Parents," the Early Childhood News website publishes short articles and information about early childhood education.

**The National Coalition for Women and Girls in Education**
*http://www.ncwge.org/*

Reports, position statements, and wide-ranging information on gender and education are available at this website.

**International Boys' Schools Coalition**
*http://www.theibsc.org/*

The International Boys' Schools Coalition is a group of member institutions promoting boys' issues in education. Check out the conferences, workshops, and publications links.

**The Gay, Lesbian & Straight Education Network**
*http://www.glsen.org*

The Gay, Lesbian & Straight Education Network (GLSEN) provides resources for teachers, parents, and students. It promotes safe school environments for all students regardless of sexual orientation. Be sure to click on the "research" link to access a variety of useful reports.

## UNIT 4: Gender, Work and Health

**Institute for Women and Work, Cornell University**
*http://www.ilr.cornell.edu/iww/*

Access a variety of working papers and full reports on a variety of topics related to gender and work through Cornell University's Institute for Women and Work.

**American Psychological Association: Society for Industrial and Organizational Psychology**
*http://www.siop.org/*

The Society for Industrial and Organizational Psychology is an official division of the American Psychological Association, a professional association of academic and applied psychologists. Visit its website for information on a variety of topics that are important to gender studies.

**National Institutes of Health (NIH)**
*http://www.nih.gov*

Consult this site for links to extensive health information and scientific resources. The NIH is one of eight health agencies of the Public Health Service, which in turn is part of the U.S. Department of Health and Human Services.

**Dr. Susan Love Research Foundation**
*http://www.dslrf.org/*

The Dr. Susan Love Research Foundation website is a wonderful resource on women's health-related issues, including menopause, breast cancer, and bone health. This website provides information that everyone needs to know about women's health.

**World Health Organization: Gender, Women and Health**
*http://www.who.int/gender/en/*

The World Health Organization (WHO) maintains this website to provide educational information on the organization's activities and programs on gender and health. This is a great resource for facts, statistics, reports, and educational materials on gender and health around the world. There are numerous issues on this site of interest to students of gender.

**National Cancer Institute: Breast Cancer**
*http://www.cancer.gov/cancertopics/types/breast*

The National Institutes of Health (NIH) National Cancer Institute runs this Breast Cancer website. Find out more about breast cancer and treatment options here. This site includes information on both male and female breast cancer.

**National Cancer Institute: Ovarian Cancer**
*http://www.cancer.gov/cancertopics/types/ovarian*

The National Institutes of Health (NIH) National Cancer Institute runs this Ovarian Cancer website. Find out more about ovarian cancer and treatment options here. This site includes a wide range of information on ovarian cancer.

**National Cancer Institute: Testicular Cancer**
*http://www.cancer.gov/cancertopics/types/testicular/*

The National Institutes of Health (NIH) National Cancer Institute runs this Testicular Cancer website. Find out more about testicular cancer and treatment options here. This site includes a wide range of information on testicular cancer.

## UNIT 5: Gender and Sexualities

**World Association for Sexology**
*http://www.tc.umn.edu/nlhome/m201/colem001/was/wasindex.htm*

The World Association for Sexology works to further the understanding and development of sexology throughout the world. Access this site to explore a number of issues and links related to gender and sexuality.

**SIECUS**
*http://www.siecus.org*

Visit the Sexuality Information and Education Council of the United States (SIECUS) home page to learn about the organization, to find news of its educational programs and activities, and to access links to resources in sexuality education.

**The Society for the Scientific Study of Sexuality**
*http://www.sexscience.org/*

SSSS is a professional association of sex researchers from a many different scientific disciplines. According to its website, it is "[t]he oldest professional society dedicated to the advancement of knowledge about sexuality." Have a look at its ethics statement as well as the various kinds of publications it sponsors.

# Internet References

## SexInfo

*http://www.soc.ucsb.edu/sexinfo/*

SexInfo is based out of the University of California at Santa Barbara. The site is run by advanced human sexuality students under the supervision of two UCSB sexuality professors. All aspects of sex and sexuality are covered on this website with great articles and Q&As. There are many topics at this site that will be of interest to students of gender.

## Teenwire.com

*http://www.teenwire.com*

This site, by Planned Parenthood, is targeted at teenagers and young adults. Topics range from the body to school and relationships.

## Human Rights Campaign

*http://www.hrc.org/*

The Human Rights Campaign is the largest lesbian, gay, bisexual, and transgender rights organization in North America. Detailed information on LGBT issues, laws, and elections can be found here.

## The Intersex Society of North America (ISNA)

*http://www.isna.org/*

ISNA maintains this resource for anyone interested in the issue of intersex conditions. Physicians, therapists, parents, intersexed individuals, and many others will want to learn more about the problems caused by stigma and lack of knowledge for people who are born intersexed.

## GenderTalk

*http://www.gendertalk.com/*

This "trans-friendly" website offers resources, articles, and programs that can be listened to on topics ranging from transgender at work to transgender health issues.

## UNIT 6: Gender and Social Issues

## Department of State: Human Rights

*http://www.state.gov/g/drl/hr/*

The U.S. State Department's Web page for human rights includes country reports, fact sheets, reports on discrimination and violations of human rights, plus the latest news covering human rights issues from around the world.

## SocioSite: Feminism and Women's Issues

*http://www.sociosite.net/topics/women.php*

Visit the University of Amsterdam "Social Science Information System" to gain insights into a number of issues that affect both men and women. It provides biographies of women in history, an international network for women in the workplace, links to family and children's issues, and much more.

## Planned Parenthood

*http://www.plannedparenthood.org*

Planned Parenthood has an "Abortion Issues" section and provides information on reproductive rights.

## Rape, Abuse and Incest National Network (RAINN)

*http://www.rainn.org/*

RAINN is committed to providing "anti-sexual assault" information and education. Learn about rape, incest, and other kinds of sexual victimization as well as what you can do to make a difference. There are a variety of resources, including *RAINN's 2008 Back-to-School Tips for Students.*

## Child Rights Information Network (CRIN)

*http://www.crin.org*

The Child Rights Information Network (CRIN) is a global network that disseminates information about the Convention on the Rights of the Child and child rights among nongovernmental organizations (NGOs), United Nations agencies, intergovernmental organizations (IGOs), educational institutions, and other child rights experts.

## Child Exploitation and Obscenity Section (CEOS)/U.S. Department of Justice

*http://www.usdoj.gov/criminal/ceos/trafficking.html*

This site introduces the reader to essential information about trafficking and sex tourism. There are links to sex trafficking of minors and child prostitution FAQs in addition to other resources at this site.

# UNIT 1

# Theoretical and Research Perspectives

## Unit Selections

1. **The Social Construction of Gender,** Margaret L. Andersen and Dana Hysock
2. **Framed before We Know It: How Gender Shapes Social Relations,** Cecilia L. Ridgeway
3. **Gender Is Powerful: The Long Reach of Feminism,** Nancy MacLean
4. **The World, the Flesh and the Devil,** Robert W. Thurston
5. **A Case for Angry Men and Happy Women,** Beth Azar
6. **Beauty, Gender and Stereotypes: Evidence from Laboratory Experiments,** James Andreoni and Ragan Petrie
7. **I'm Not a Very Manly Man: Qualitative Insights into Young Men's Masculine Subjectivity,** Richard O. de Visser

## Key Points to Consider

- What is meant by the claim that gender is a social construction?

- How are sex and gender linked? Can we have one without the other? In other words, is sex a necessary component of gender? Why? Why not?

- What do people take for granted about our gender roles, behaviors, and identities?

- People seem to rarely question gender, unless a norm is broken. Why is that?

- How have the contributions of feminism impacted the daily lives of men and women in the Western world?

- Is there a wider range of socially "acceptable" expressions of gender for men or women? If so, why do you think that is? Which behaviors first come to your mind?

- What do we mean when we use words such as "femininity" and "masculinity?"

- Do you anticipate any specific historical shifts in how we view and express gender in your lifetime? Explain your answer.

## Student Website
www.mhcls.com

## Internet References

**Institute for Gender Research, Stanford University**
*http://www.stanford.edu/group/gender/index.html*
**Gender Institute, London School of Economics**
*http://www.lse.ac.uk/collections/genderInstitute/*
**Institute for Women's Policy Research**
*http://www.iwpr.org/index.cfm*
**SocioSite: Feminism and Women's Issues**
*http://www.sociosite.net/topics/women.php*
**Queertheory.com**
*http://www.queertheory.com/*

Gender is usually defined as a social and cultural phenomenon. Sex, on the other hand, tends to be viewed in more biological terms, although some theorists argue that sex, too, is a social construction. We are born a particular sex; male, female, or somewhere in between, with the associated biological characteristics such as xx/xy chromosomes, hormones, and anatomical structures. Gender, though, is about self expression, behaviors, roles, identities, power, social structures, and much more. In this unit, we begin our exploration of gender by examining social structures and institutions, history, biology, individual differences, and lived experiences.

The articles in this unit function as an introduction to the study of gender. The work of psychologists, sociologists, historians, and others is presented, reflecting different theoretical and research perspectives in gender studies. The selections represent various theoretical orientations, as well as different methodological approaches. From laboratory experiments and qualitative research to historical/cultural/literary analysis, we learn something about gender through each of these approaches.

It is important that students of gender gain an understanding of the field of gender studies as rich, diverse, and multifaceted. You are encouraged to read beyond this unit to gain an even greater appreciation of the theories and methods of gender studies scholars. Your research may take you to the works of Eve Kosofsky Sedgwick, Judith Butler, Michel Foucault, Jeffrey Weeks, Ken Plummer or other prominent writers.

As you expand your knowledge, there may be some surprises in your future. Perhaps you will become interested in literary theory, biographical studies, ethnographies, or queer approaches to gender. These new interests may spark not only a passion for studying gender, but possibly a related field as well.

What do you want to know about gender? What approaches speak to your lived experiences? What explanations make the most sense to you? What writings help you to step outside of your comfort zone? What ideas are most challenging to your beliefs and values? These are just a few questions you may wish to consider.

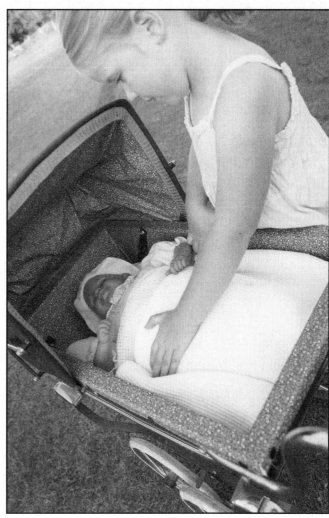

© Punchstock/BananaStock

The following articles hint at the richness and diversity found in gender studies today. The topics that we cover in this unit begin our journey into the fascinating gendered worlds that we inhabit, yet so few of us ever seem to question. In this unit, and throughout this book, we continually *question gender.*

# The Social Construction of Gender

MARGARET L. ANDERSEN AND DANA HYSOCK

## Socialization and the Formation of Gender Identity

The fact that gender is a social, not a natural, phenomenon means that it is learned. Although rooted in institutions, gender is passed on through social learning and is enacted through what sociologists call gender roles. Gender roles are the patterns of behavior in which women and men engage, based on the cultural expectations associated with their gender. Gender roles are learned through the process of socialization. It is through the socialization process that individuals acquire an identity based on gender. **Gender identity** is an individual's specific definition of self, based on that person's understanding of what it means to be a man or a woman. In other words, it is through the socialization process that gender is socially constructed.

### Sanctions and Expectations

Through gender socialization, different behaviors and attitudes are encouraged and discouraged in men and women. That is, social expectations about what is properly masculine and feminine are communicated to us through the **socialization** process. Our family, peers, and teachers, as well as the media and religious groups, act as agents of the socialization process. Although probably none of us becomes exactly what the cultural ideal prescribes, our roles in social institutions are conditioned by the gender relations we learn in our social development.

Some persons become more perfectly socialized than others, and sociologists have warned against the idea of seeing humans as totally passive, overly socialized creatures. To some extent, we probably all resist the expectations society has of us. Our uniqueness as individuals stems in part from this resistance, as well as from variations in the social experiences we have. Studying patterns of gender socialization does not deny individual differences, but it does point to the common experiences shared by girls as they become women and boys as they become men. However much we may believe that we were raised in a gender-neutral environment, research and careful observation show how pervasive and generally effective the process of gender role socialization is. Although some of us conform more than others, socialization acts as a powerful system of social control.

Peter Berger describes social control as something like a series of concentric circles. At the center is the individual, who is surrounded by different levels of control, ranging from the subtle (such as learned roles, peer pressure, and ridicule) to the overt (such as violence, physical threat, and imprisonment). According to Berger, it is usually not necessary for powerful agents in the society to resort to extreme sanctions, because what we think and believe about ourselves usually keeps us in line. In this sense, socialization acts as a powerful system of social control. . . .

The pressure to adopt gender-appropriate behavior is evidence that the socialization process controls us in several ways: (1) it gives us a definition of ourselves; (2) it defines the external world and our place within it; (3) it provides our definition of others and our relationships with them; and, (4) the socialization process encourages and discourages the acquisition of certain skills by gender. . . .

Conformity to traditional roles takes its toll on both men and women, and research shows that those who conform most fully to gender-role expectations experience a range of negative consequences. For example, higher male mortality rates can be attributed to the stress in masculine roles. The cultural association between masculinity and aggression can also help explain the high rates of violence that encourage behaviors in men that put them at risk in a variety of ways.

For women too much conformity to gender expectations also produces many negative consequences. Women who score as "very feminine" on personality tests tend to exhibit more feelings of depression and say they do not feel in control of their lives. The cultural expectations associated with gender and beauty are known to produce a whole range of negative health consequences. The dominant culture promotes a narrow image of beauty for women. Women and young girls who internalize this ideal—one that is generally impossible to achieve—often end up being disturbed about their body image, feeling they are never adequate. Millions then engage in constant dieting, even when they are well within healthy weight standards. Purging themselves of food via eating disorders or cycling through fad diets can all have serious health consequences. Many young women develop a distorted image of themselves, thinking they are "overweight" when they may actually be dangerously thin. And, despite the known risks of smoking increasing numbers of young women smoke and do so not only because they think it "looks cool," but because they think it will keep them from gaining weight. . . .

# Socialization across the Life Course

Socialization begins at birth, and it continues throughout adulthood, even though gender roles are established very early. When we encounter new social experiences, we are socialized to adopt new roles through the expectations others have of us. This section examines the processes and consequences of gender socialization as it occurs throughout the life course.

## Infancy

Beginning in infancy, boys and girls are treated differently. Research on infant socialization shows, in fact, how quickly gender expectations become part of our experience. Studies find that as early as 18 months, toddlers have learned to play mostly with toys judged to be appropriate for their gender. Parents describe their babies differently, depending on their gender—including descriptions rating their male children as more intelligent than female children.

Research continues to show that parents treat their infants differently, depending on the infant's sex. How parents act may even be unintentional or subtle, but it has an effect on later life, nonetheless. In one fascinating series of studies, researchers observed fathers and mothers (in couples) walking young children through public places. Both fathers and mothers were more likely to let boy toddlers walk alone than they were to allow girls to do so. These same observers found that even when the child was out of the stroller, mothers were far more likely to push the empty stroller than were the fathers, demonstrating the attachment of mothers to child care roles. Despite the fact that mothers are much more likely than fathers to engage in and manage child care, research also finds that fathers are more likely to gender-type their children.

Parents are not the only agents of gender socialization, however. Other children have just as important an impact on learning gender roles. Children of all ages notice the sex of infants and use it as a basis for responding to the child. Preschool girls also show more interest in interacting with babies than do preschool boys, a pattern that is most pronounced among children whose parents hold gender-stereotyped attitudes. Peers develop expectations and definitions of gender-appropriate behaviors and use those expectations as the basis for their interaction with others.

## Childhood Play and Games

Research in child development emphasizes the importance of play and games in the maturation of children. Through play, children learn the skills of social interaction, develop cognitive and analytical abilities, and are taught the values and attitudes of their culture. The games that children play have great significance for the children's intellectual, moral, personal, and social development and for their gender identity.

George Herbert Mead, a social psychologist and major sociological theorist in the early twentieth century, described three stages in which socialization occurs: imitation, play, and game. In the *imitation stage,* an infant simply copies the behavior of significant persons in his or her environment. In the play stage, the child begins "taking the role of the other"—seeing himself or herself from the perspective of another person. Mead argues that taking the role of the other is a cognitive process that permits the child to develop a self-concept. Self-concepts emerge through interacting with other people and from learning to perceive how others see us. The other people most emotionally important to the child (e.g., parents, siblings, or other primary caregivers) are, in Mead's term, significant others. In the *play stage,* children learn to take the role of significant others, primarily by practicing others' social roles—for example, "playing Mommy" or "playing Daddy."

In the *game stage,* children are able to do more. Rather than seeing themselves from the perspective of only one significant other at a time, they can play games requiring them to understand how several other people (including more than just significant others) view them simultaneously. Playing baseball, to use Mead's example, involves the roles and expectations of many more people than does "playing Mommy." Eventually, children in the game stage learn to orient themselves not just to *significant others* but to a generalized other, as well. The generalized other represents the cultural expectations of the whole social community. Mead's analysis of the emergence of the self emphasizes the importance of interpretative behavior in the way the child relates to others in the social environment. Early activity, especially through play, places children's experiences in a social environment; therefore, meanings communicated through play help the child organize personal experience into an emerging self. Children's play, then, is a very significant part of the socialization process.

Research reveals the pervasiveness of gender stereotyping as it is learned in early childhood play. The toys and play activities that parents select for children are a significant source of gender socialization. Studies of parents find that they gender stereotype toys for boys and girls of all ages, although toys for infants and toddlers are somewhat less stereotyped. Children also quickly pick this up. As research on preschoolers has found, given a choice between playing with a tool set or a dish set, boys will pick the tool set, saying that their fathers think playing with the dishes would be "bad." Clearly, parents' values influence the gender play of children. Other studies find that parents, especially fathers, are more likely to be involved in physical play with boys than with girls; not surprisingly, then, boys are more likely to play physically than girls, whereas girls engage in more fantasy or "pretense" play. At the same time, parents are more likely to tolerate cross-gender play in girls than in boys.

These patterns are not fixed, however, because changing attitudes among parents are reflected in the values their children learn. Compared to 20 years ago, young girls now express a greater number of occupational aspirations, more so than young boys. Mothers' education and employment also have a significant impact on the gender attitudes of their daughters and sons; in general, there has been some shift in attitudes toward more egalitarian roles—a fact that will influence the gender attitudes of future generations.

Even with these changes, however the world children encounter is laden with gender-stereotypic expectations. Children

3

themselves impart gender expectations to each other. Thus, researchers observing children's activities have found that when girls disregard the ordinary codes for gender behavior and transgress into other activities, higher-status boys react in ways that regulate the transgression. Aside from the behavior of children and adults, young people are also bombarded with gendered images from literature, video games, and television. Even with a greater awareness of the importance of reducing gender stereotypes, studies of children's literature show that males are still overwhelmingly shown as aggressive, argumentative, and competitive, even though publishers have published guidelines for nonsexist portrayals. Female characters are more likely to be depicted using household objects, whereas male characters use nondomestic objects. Girls and women are still depicted as less adventurous and more domestic than boys. In general, there are still more males than females in children's picture books, and males are shown as more potent and active, although, interestingly, more positive adjectives are used to describe female characters. Books written by African Americans are more likely to show girls and women as less dependent and more competitive, but they also show them as more nurturing than do books written by White authors.

In television cartoons, boys are depicted as more violent, girls as more domestic; furthermore, children who watched such cartoons subsequently express more traditional job expectations for themselves and others. Even the Sunday comics communicate these expectations, with researchers finding that, although some stereotypical images have diminished, there is now a return to earlier levels of stereotyping. In video games—one of the major outlets for children's play—traditional gender roles and violence are central themes. Using a sample of Nintendo and Sega Genesis games, researchers found that 41 percent of the games had no female characters at all, 28 percent portrayed women as sex objects, and 80 percent included aggression or violence as the strategy. Half the games included violence directed at others; the other half depicted violence toward women. All told, these sources of socialization send powerful messages to young boys and girls. The numerous examples that can be found in children's play, literature, and other cultural systems demonstrate how gender is socially constructed.

## Socialization and the Schools

Although we tend to think of the family as the primary source of social values and identity, peers, teachers, the media, and additional significant others are important agents of the socialization process. Schools, in particular, exercise much influence on the creation of gendered attitudes and behavior, so much so that some researchers call learning gender the "hidden curriculum" in the schools. In the schools, curriculum materials, teachers' expectations, educational tracking, and peer relations encourage girls and boys to learn gender-related skills and self-concepts.

Within schools, teachers and older children display expectations that encourage children to behave and think in particular ways; moreover, these expectations are strongly influenced by gender. Teachers, for example, respond more often to boys in the classroom. Even when they do so in response to boys'

misbehaving, they are calling more attention to the boys. Differences between boys and girls become exaggerated through practices that divide them into two distinct human groups. In schools, children are often seated in separate gender groups or sorted into play groups based on gender; these practices heighten gender differences, making them even more significant in the children's interactions. In school, boys tend to be the center of attention, even when they are getting attention for disruptive behavior; girls are, in general, less visible and more typically praised for passive and acquiescent behavior.

These gender-typical behaviors have consequences for what boys and girls learn in school. Although boys and girls enter schools with roughly equal abilities, and although overall gender differences in such important areas as math and science are no longer pronounced, girls report liking these subjects less than boys and they express little confidence in their math and science abilities. Those who report liking math and science have higher self-esteem and have higher career aspirations than other girls. Moreover, gender expectations influence other course-taking patterns, so that girls are far more likely to take courses in social sciences, foreign languages, and the arts and humanities—suggesting how patterns of thinking become arrayed along gender lines. These patterns also have profound effects on the extent of gender segregation in the labor market as young men and women become adults.

Families and schools are not the only sources of gender socialization. One of the reasons that gender is so extensive in its influence on our lives is that it is so pervasive throughout all social institutions. Gender expectations are also visible at work, in voluntary organizations, in health care organizations, and in athletics. Religion, also has a significant effect on our concepts of who we are and our consciousness of gender. Families and schools are primary sources for some of the earliest influences of gender socialization, but the process of learning and enacting gender goes on throughout people's lifetimes.

## Adult Socialization and the Aging Process

As we encounter new experiences throughout our lives, we learn the role expectations associated with our new statuses. Although our gender identities are established relatively early in life, changes in our status in society—for example, graduation, marriage, or a new job—bring new expectations for our behavior and beliefs.

Aging is perhaps the one thing about our lives that is inevitable; yet, as a social experience, it has different consequences for men and women. Cross-cultural evidence shows that aging is less stressful for women in societies where there is a strong tie to family and kin, not just to a husband; where there are extended, not nuclear, family systems; where there is a positive role for mothers-in-law (rather than the degrading status attached to it in our society); and where there are strong mother–child relationships throughout life. Even within our own society, racial and ethnic groups attach more value to older persons, thereby easing the transition to later life. Although the elderly in African American and Latino communities experience even greater difficulties with poverty and health than do the White elderly, their valued role in the extended family seems to alleviate some of the stress associated with growing old.

Gender differences in the social process of aging can be attributed in large part to the emphasis on youth found in this culture and, in particular, to the association of youth and sexuality in women. Cultural stereotypes portray older men as distinguished, older women as less desirable. As a woman ages, unlike a man, she will generally experience a loss of prestige; men gain prestige as they become more established in their careers.

The effects of aging for women and men are, however, strongly influenced by factors such as one's class, race, and other social factors. The cumulated inequities that women experience because of gender, race, and class continue into their older years—both in the social and economic value placed on them. And, as we will see further in the chapter on health, these inequities have consequences for the physical and mental health that different groups experience. Research consistently demonstrates that poor women are less likely to receive good-quality health care. In fact, financial resources are one of the best predictors of health for both women and men. Being in a subordinated race, class, or gender group makes some groups more vulnerable to problems of physical and mental health at all stages in the life course, but these can become more acute in old age.

For women, the caregiving responsibilities that mark younger years continue as they grow older. Even during so-called "retirement," women most often do the unpaid labor associated with caring for others. Researchers have found that there can actually be increased differentiation in the gender roles of men and women in their older years because of women's ongoing caregiving responsibilities. And one's well-being as an older person depends a great deal on one's level of education and the resources one has—such as during retirement. Because they have generally had lower levels of earnings during their younger adult years, during retirement, women typically have less retirement pension and receive less in Social Security than men do—even though women are also more likely to be dependent on Social Security and other forms of government assistance during retirement than are men.

Despite these problems for older women, aging also relaxes some of the social pressure experienced by younger people.

How positively one experiences the aging process depends to a large extent on the economic and cultural resources one has available, as well as the social supports received from family and friends. One study of retired African American professional women has documented, for example, the satisfaction that these women experience from their achievements, especially in regard to the social supports they both create and rely on over a lifetime of confronting racism.

There is little doubt that women experience significant disadvantage during the aging process. At the same time, however, the capacities and strengths that women acquire over their lifetimes also give them certain advantages as they grow old. Older women report higher levels of emotional support than do older men, and they tend to have more extensive social contacts and friendships. In general, the fact that women work throughout their lives to maintain social and emotional networks helps them maintain this connection in their older years, whereas men may experience greater social isolation. Better social support also has a known positive effect on people's ability to withstand stressful life events; thus, this learned ability among women helps them face the difficult problems of death, loss, and, perhaps, poor health in their elder years. . . .

## Limitations of the Socialization Perspective

. . . Not all girls and boys grow up in the gender-stereotyped way that the research literature sometimes suggests; nevertheless, research on childhood learning underscores the point that gender socialization is situated within social institutions that tend to value masculine, not feminine, traits. Were values associated with women—such as flexibility, orientation toward others, and cooperation—to be incorporated into dominant social institutions, then we might well produce more gender-balanced boys and girls. As it is, the process of socialization throughout life separates men and women and creates gender differences among children and adults.

---

MARGARET L. ANDERSEN is a professor of sociology and women's studies and vice provost for academic affairs at the University of Delaware.

From *Thinking About Women: Sociological Perspectives on Sex and Gender,* 8/e by Margaret L. Andersen and Dana Hysock, (Allyn & Bacon, 2009). Copyright © 2009 by Allyn & Bacon—Pearson. Reprinted by permission.

# Framed before We Know It
## *How Gender Shapes Social Relations*

CECILIA L. RIDGEWAY

During the past decade, I have made the case that gender is one of our culture's two or three primary frames for organizing social relations (Ridgeway 1997, 2007). I have also argued that unless we take into account how gender frames social relations, we cannot understand how the gendered structure of contemporary society both changes and resists changing. My purpose here is to spell out this argument in more specific detail. I first explain what I mean by gender as a "primary frame" and describe some of the implications of this approach. Second, and just as important, I explain why I believe we must incorporate the effects of gender as a primary frame into our analyses of the gendered structure of society. To do this, I offer two empirical illustrations that demonstrate that we cannot understand the shape the gender structure takes in particular situations without taking into account the background effects of the gender frame on behavior. In the first illustration, I show how the gender frame causes the same organizational logic to have rather different implications for gender inequality in two different types of innovative high-tech firms. In the second illustration, I draw on research that shows how the background effects of the gender frame help us understand why some of the societies that have gone farthest in reducing gender inequality nevertheless have some of the most gender-segregated occupational structures in the advanced industrial world (Charles and Bradley 2009).

In discussing the question of "why it matters" whether we incorporate the effects of the gender frame into our analyses, I also wish to address an unresolved tension among feminist scholars in how best to approach the gendered structure of society. In 1987, West and Zimmerman shook up the world of gender theorizing in sociology with their groundbreaking analysis of gender as a social interactional accomplishment, a performance of difference that one "does" rather than "is" (Fenstermaker and West 2002; West and Zimmerman 1987). This "doing gender, doing difference" perspective continues to wield persuasive power, as attested by the rate at which it is cited. Yet, this micro-interactional account of gender has, in some ways, remained an undigested nugget.

As sociologists, most of us are structuralists who see gender and race inequality as rooted in broad organizational and institutional structures with strong material bases. Many feel a theoretical tension between micro-interactional approaches, evocative as they may be, and more structuralist explanatory leanings. There are lingering questions about how to fit the micro-interactional account into institutional structure and how much weight to give the micro account. Micro accounts are appealing and add richness to our understanding, but do they really matter?

Another major innovation in gender theorizing in sociology has partially assuaged this theoretical tension. This is the recognition that gender is a multilevel structure, system, or institution of social practices that involves mutually reinforcing processes at the macro-structural/institutional level, the interactional level, and the individual level (Acker 1990; Lorber 1994; Ridgeway and Smith-Lovin 1999; Risman 1998, 2004). The remaining difficulty, however, is to explicate how these multilevel processes affect one another, beyond simply saying that they generally but not always reinforce one another.

My argument that gender is a primary frame for social relations is at root a micro-interactional approach that owes much to the "doing gender" account, even though my argument is a bit different in emphasis. To make the case that the gender frame matters, I will focus on the interface of the micro-interactional and the institutional and structural levels of analysis.

My intent is to shed more light on how these multilevel processes work together to shape the gender structures that emerge. In doing so, I hope to contribute toward resolution of the tension between micro-interactional and structural-level explanations.

## Gender as a Primary Frame

What does it mean to say that gender is a primary cultural frame for organizing social relations (Ridgeway 1997, 2006, 2007)? As we know, people depend on social relations with others to attain most of what they want and need in life. Social relations pose a well-known problem, however. To relate to another to accomplish a valued goal, we have to find some way to coordinate our behavior with that other. Classic sociologists such as Goffman (1967) and contemporary game theorists (Chwe 2001) have arrived at the same conclusion about what it takes to solve this coordination problem. For you and me to coordinate effectively, we need shared, "common" knowledge to use as a basis for our joint actions. Common knowledge is cultural knowledge that we all assume we all know. I have argued that actually, we need a particular type of common, cultural knowledge (Ridgeway 2007). We need a shared way of categorizing and defining "who" self and other are in the situation so that we can anticipate how each of us is likely to act and coordinate our actions accordingly.

## Coordination and Difference

Systems for categorizing and defining things are based on contrast, and therefore, difference. Something is this because it is different from that. Defining *self* and *other* to relate focuses us on finding shared principles of social difference that we can use to categorize and make sense of one another. The coordination problem inherent to organizing social relations drives populations of people who must regularly relate to one another to develop shared social-category systems based on culturally defined standards of difference.

To manage social relations in real time, some of these cultural-category systems must be so simplified that they can be quickly applied as framing devices to virtually anyone to start the process of defining *self* and *other* in the situation. In fact, studies of social cognition suggest that a very small number of such cultural-difference systems, about three or so, serve as the primary categories of person perception in a society (Brewer and Lui 1989; Fiske 1998). These primary categories define the things a person in that society must know about someone to render that someone sufficiently meaningful to relate to him or her.

Sex/gender, of course, is a form of human variation that is highly susceptible to cultural generalization as a primary category for framing social relations (Ridgeway 2006, 2007). It yields a cultural-difference system that is relevant to sexuality and reproduction and that delineates a line of difference among people who must regularly cooperate with one another. Thus, the male–female distinction is virtually always one of a society's primary cultural-category systems (Glick and Fiske 1999). In the United States, race and age are also primary categories (see Schneider 2004, 96).

Social-cognition studies show that in fact, we automatically and nearly instantly sex categorize any specific person to whom we attempt to relate (Ito and Urland 2003; Stangor et al. 1992). We do this not just in person but also over the Internet and even imaginatively, as we examine a person's resume or think about the kind of person we would like to hire. Studies show that Americans categorize others they encounter on Black or white race almost instantly as well (Ito and Urland 2003). When we categorize another, we by comparison implicitly make salient our own sex and race categorization as well.

We so instantly sex-categorize others that our subsequent categorizations of them as, say, bosses or coworkers are nested in our prior understandings of them as male or female and take on slightly different meanings as a result (Brewer and Lui 1989; Fiske 1998). This initial framing by sex never quite disappears from our understanding of them or ourselves in relation to them.

Thus, we frame and are framed by gender literally before we know it. Importantly, however, the extent to which this pre-framing by gender shapes what happens in a specific situation depends greatly on what else is going on in that situation. As we will see, this is a point at which the gender frame interacts with institutional context. But first, I need to say more about how the gender frame coordinates behavior.

## Cultural Beliefs about Gender

Primary categories of person perception, including sex category, work as cultural frames for coordinating behavior by associating category membership with widely shared cultural beliefs about how people in one category are likely to behave compared to those in a contrasting category. These cultural beliefs are shared stereotypes, as in "men are from Mars and women are from Venus." Gender stereotypes are our beliefs about how "most people" view the typical man or woman (Eagly and Karau 2002; Fiske 1998; Fiske et al. 2002). We all know these stereotypes as cultural knowledge, whether or not we personally endorse them. But the point is, because we think "most people" hold these beliefs, we expect others to judge us according to them. As a result, we must take these beliefs into account in our own behavior even if we do not endorse them. In this way, these shared cultural beliefs act as the "rules" for coordinating public behavior on the basis of gender (Ridgeway and Correll 2004).

The use of sex or gender as a primary cultural frame for defining *self* and *other* drives the content of gender stereotypes to focus on presumed gender differences. *Difference* need not logically imply inequality. Yet, among groups of people who must regularly deal with one another, difference is easily transformed into inequality through any of a variety of social processes (Ridgeway 2006). Once inequality is established between groups of people, however, it will reshape the nature of the differences that are culturally perceived as characteristic of the higher and lower status groups (Fiske et al. 2002; Jackman 1994). The content of our gender stereotypes shows the characteristic pattern of status inequality in which the higher status group is perceived as more proactive and agentically competent ("from Mars") and the lower status group is seen as more reactive and emotionally expressive ("from Venus"; Conway, Pizzamiglio, and Mount 1996; Glick and Fiske 1999; Wagner and Berger 1997). Thus, difference and inequality codetermine each other in our shared gender beliefs, and coordination on the basis of them produces social relations of inequality as well as difference (Wagner and Berger 1997).

The social importance of gender as a primary frame for making sense of *self* and *other* and the cultural definition of this frame as a difference that implies inequality create two distinct sets of interests for individuals. These interests affect the extent to which individuals actively gender their behavior. As a belief system that privileges men over women, it gives most men and some women who benefit from male dominance an interest in enacting and maintaining that system. In addition, as a fundamental category for understanding the self, it gives almost all women and men a sometimes powerful interest in enacting essentialist expressions of gender difference. Both types of interests can have consequences for the actions individuals take when the constraining social structures around them give them the space to act on their own.

## Hegemonic and Alternative Gender Beliefs

The familiar, widely known gender stereotypes that I have called the rules of gender are not just individual beliefs. They are culturally *hegemonic* beliefs for two reasons. First, these beliefs are institutionalized in media representations, in the images of men and women implied by laws and government policies, and in a wide variety of taken-for-granted organizational practices. Second, the content of these gender beliefs, while they purport to be universal depictions of the sexes, in fact represent most closely the experiences and understandings of gender by dominant groups in society—those who most powerfully shape our institutions. The men and women we see in gender stereotypes look most like white, middle-class heterosexuals. Yet, as Shelley Correll and I have argued, in public places and with strangers, these hegemonic cultural beliefs about gender act as the default rules of gender (Ridgeway and Correll 2004). This makes the public enactment of gender that much more complicated for those who are not white, middle-class heterosexuals.

Although we all know hegemonic gender beliefs, many of us also hold alternative beliefs about gender that we share with a subgroup of similarly minded others—fellow feminists, a racial or ethnic group, or an immigrant group. Some evidence suggests that these alternative cultural beliefs about gender, rather than the hegemonic ones, shape our behavior and judgments most clearly when we are relating to others we believe share those beliefs (Filardo 1996; Milkie 1999). This makes sense if we are using these beliefs to coordinate our behavior with those others. It remains for future research to investigate the contexts in which we systematically rely on alternative gender beliefs, rather than hegemonic beliefs, to guide our behavior.

# How Does the Gender Frame Shape Behavior?

Thus far, I have spoken in general terms about the gender frame and cultural beliefs that shape behavior. Exactly how does this shaping process work, however? Also, what about the fact that in any given context in which we relate to others, much more is going on than just gender? In particular, we typically act in the context of some institutional or organizational framework that suggests specific role identities and role relations. What happens to the gender frame in that context? To address these questions, I first describe how the gender frame itself shapes behavior and judgments and then turn to how it interfaces with the organizational frame within which individuals act.

## Effects of the Gender Frame

Research shows that sex categorization unconsciously primes gender stereotypes in our minds and makes them cognitively available to shape behavior and judgments (Blair and Banaji 1996; Kunda and Spencer 2003). The extent to which they actually do shape our behavior, however, can vary from negligible to substantial depending on the nature of the particular situation and our own motives or interests. What matters is the extent to which the information in gender beliefs is diagnostic for us in that it helps us figure out how to act in the situation. Research shows that some basic principles guide how this works.

When people in the situation differ in sex category, cultural beliefs about gender become effectively salient and measurably affect behaviors and judgments unless something else overrides them (see Ridgeway and Smith-Lovin 1999). Also, in either mixed or same-sex contexts, gender stereotypes implicitly shape behavior and judgments to the extent that gender is culturally defined as relevant to the situation, as, for instance, with a gender-typed task such as math (Ridgeway and Correll 2004; Ridgeway and Smith-Lovin 1999). The effects of gender beliefs on an actor's behavior will also be greater to the extent the actor consciously or unconsciously perceives the game of gender to be relevant to his or her own motives or interests in the situation (Fiske 1998).

Pulling these arguments together, we can see that the way the gender frame brings cultural beliefs about gender to bear on our expectations for self and other, on our behavior, and on our judgments produces a distinctive pattern of effects. In mixed-sex settings in which the task or context is relatively gender neutral, cultural beliefs that men are more agentically competent and more worthy of status will advantage them over otherwise similar women, but only modestly so. In settings that are culturally typed as masculine, gender beliefs will bias judgments and behaviors more strongly in favor of men. In contexts culturally linked with women, biases will weakly favor women except for positions of authority. A wide variety of research supports this general pattern of effects (see Ridgeway and Correll 2004; Ridgeway and Smith-Lovin 1999).

These effects largely describe the way the gender frame introduces implicit biases into expectations and behaviors that affect gender inequality in the setting. The enactment of inequality, however, is accomplished through the enactment of gender difference (e.g., agentic competence vs. reactive warmth) that implies and creates the inequality. The enactment of gender difference or inequality is fed by the interests the gender frame gives people in understanding themselves as appropriately gendered as well as by the way the gender frame causes them to react to and judge the behaviors of others. As institutionalized cultural "rules," gender beliefs about difference and inequality have a prescriptive edge that people enforce by sanctioning explicit violations. Women are typically sanctioned for acting too domineering and men for being too yielding or emotionally weak (Eagly and Karau 2002; Rudman and Fairchild 2004).

## Gender as a Background Identity

How, then, do these contextually varying effects of the gender frame interface with the specific organizational or institutional contexts in which our relations with others occur? People typically confront the problem of coordinating their behavior with another in the context of both a primary person frame (gender, race, and age) and an institutional frame (a family, a university, a place of work). As part of the primary person frame, the instructions for behavior encoded in gender stereotypes are exceedingly abstract and diffuse. For this very reason, they can be applied to virtually any situation, but by the same token, they do not take an actor very far in figuring out exactly how to behave.

In contrast, institutional frameworks, even vague ones such as "the family," are much more specific. They contain defined roles and the expected relations among them. The roles that are embedded in institutional and organizational frameworks are often themselves infused with gendered cultural meanings. Indeed, one of the most powerful ways that the gender frame affects the gendered structure of society is through infusing gendered meanings into the institutional practices, procedures, and role identities by which various organizations operate. For now, however, the point is that these institutional roles, even the gendered ones, provide clearer instructions for behavior in a given context than do the diffuse cultural meanings of the primary gender frame. For individuals, it is these institutional identities and rules that are in the foreground of their sense of who they are in a given context and how they should behave there.

Gender, in contrast, is almost always a background identity for individuals. I have made this point elsewhere, but I wish to emphasize it here because it is essential to understanding how gender shapes social structure (Ridgeway and Correll 2004; Ridgeway and Smith-Lovin 1999). As a background identity, gender typically acts to bias in gendered directions the performance of behaviors undertaken in the name of more concrete, foregrounded organizational roles or identities. Thus, gender becomes a way of acting like a doctor or of driving a car. This, of course, is what West and Zimmerman (1987) meant by "doing gender."

## The Interaction of the Gender Frame and Institutional Structure

The extent to which the gender frame flavors or biases the performance of institutional role identities depends on two general factors. The first is the salience and relevance of the gender frame in the situation. As we can infer from above, this depends on the gender composition of the institutional context and the extent to which the activities and roles in the context are themselves culturally gendered. When organizational activities are gendered, the background gender frame becomes more powerfully relevant for actors, and the biases it introduces shape how people carry out those activities and how they fill in the details not clearly specified by institutional rules. The gendering of institutional tasks or roles, then, empowers the background gender frame in the situation to become a significant part of the process by which people enact their institutional roles. Scholars such as Patricia Martin have given us powerful illustrations of this process (Martin 2003).

A second factor that affects the impact of the gender frame is the extent to which organizational rules and procedures constrain individual discretion in judgments and behavior. The more constrained individuals' actions are, the less scope the gender frame has to implicitly shape their behavior on its own. For this reason, many scholars have recommended formal rules and procedures as

devices to suppress stereotype bias and discrimination in employment (Bielby 2000; Reskin and McBrier 2000). On the other hand, feminist scholars have also long pointed out that apparently neutral formal rules and procedures can embody bias in their application or effect (e.g., Acker 1990; Nelson and Bridges 1999; Steinberg 1995).

The gender-framing perspective suggests that whether formal personnel procedures do more good than bad depends not only on the extent to which bias is built into the procedures but also on how powerfully disadvantaging the gender frame would be for women if actors were not constrained by formal procedures. Thus, there is no simple answer to the "are formal rules best" question. But a consideration of the joint effects of the gender frame and the organizational frame allows us to specify how the answer to this question varies systematically with the nature of the context. One of my empirical examples will illustrate this point.

To the extent that cultural beliefs about gender do shape behavior and social relations in an institutional context, either directly through the gender frame acting on individuals or indirectly through biased procedures, these gender beliefs will be reinscribed into new organizational procedures and rules that actors develop through their social relations in that setting (Ridgeway 1997; Ridgeway and England 2007). In this way, the gendered structure of society can be projected into the future through new organizational procedures and forms that reinvent it for a new era.

My argument suggests that the background gender frame is the primary mechanism by which material, organizational structures become organized by gender. By the same token, these organizational structures sustain widely shared cultural beliefs about gender. To the extent that economic, technological, and political factors change these structures and the material arrangements that they create between men and women, these material changes create gradual, iterative pressure for change in cultural beliefs about gender as well.

## The Explanatory Importance of the Gender Frame

I will illustrate my abstract arguments about how the gender frame interacts with institutional structures with two empirical examples. My purpose in offering these examples is to demonstrate how we have to take into account the background effects of the gender frame to understand the gender structure that emerges in a given context from particular organizational or institutional structures.

### Gender in Innovative, High-Tech Firms

My first example comes from studies of the small, science-focused start-up firms that have become a leading edge of the biotechnology and information technology (IT) industries. As Kjersten Whittington and Laurel Smith-Doerr (2008; Whittington 2007) describe, many of these high-tech firms have adopted a new organizational logic called the network form. Work in these firms is organized in terms of project teams that are often jointly constructed with a network of other firms. Scientists in a firm move flexibly among these project teams, and the hierarchies of control over their activities are relatively flat.

Is this informal, flexible structure advantageous or disadvantageous for women scientists who work in these high-tech firms? Whittington and Smith-Doerr's (2008; Whittington 2007) research suggests that the answer is quite different for biotech firms based in the life sciences than it is for firms based in engineering and the physical sciences, such as IT firms. To understand why the same organizational logic plays out so differently for women scientists in one context compared to the other, we need to take into account how the background frame of gender acts in each context.

The life sciences are not strongly gender-typed in contemporary culture. Women now constitute about a third of the PhDs in the area (Smith-Doerr 2004). Applying our framing account to this situation leads us to expect that because of the mixed gender composition of the workforce in this field, cultural beliefs about gender will be salient in biotech firms, but only diffusely so. Because the field is not strongly gender-typed, we expect these background gender beliefs to create only modest advantages for men in expected competence. Facing only modest biases, women scientists in biotech should have the basic credibility with their coworkers that they need to take effective advantage of the opportunities offered by the flexible structure of innovative firms. They should be able to press forward with their interests, work around "bad actors" if necessary, find projects that match their skills, and excel (Smith-Doerr 2004). As a result, in the biotech context, an informal, flexible organizational form could be more advantageous for women than would a more hierarchical structure.

In fact, Whittington and Smith-Doerr (2008) find women life scientists do better in these innovative biotech firms than they do in more traditionally hierarchical research organizations such as pharmaceutical firms. In comparison to more hierarchical firms, women in these flexible firms achieve more supervisory positions (Smith-Doerr 2004) and attain parity with men in the likelihood of having at least one patent to their name (Whittington and Smith-Doerr 2008). Even in these innovative firms, however, the total number of patents women acquire is less than that of comparable men, as it also is in traditional hierarchical firms. This remaining disadvantage is not surprising if we remember that background gender biases still modestly favor men, even in this innovative biotech context.

In contrast to the life sciences, engineering and the physical sciences are still strongly gender-typed in favor of men in our society. Thus, the background gender frame in the IT context is more powerfully relevant and creates stronger implicit biases against women's competence than in biotech settings. In this situation, the informality and flexibility of the innovative firm is unlikely to be an advantage for women scientists and may even be a disadvantage. Facing strong challenges to their credibility, it will be harder for women to take effective advantage of the flexible structure. Also, in the context of a masculine-typed gender frame, the informal work structure may lead to a "boys club" atmosphere in these innovative IT firms.

Consistent with the above analysis, Whittington (2007), in her study of patenting, found that women physical scientists and engineers were no better off in small, flexible, less hierarchical firms than they were in traditional, industrial research and development firms. In both contexts, they were less likely to patent at all and had fewer patents overall than did comparable men. In another study, McIllwee and Robinson (1992) found that women engineers actually did better in a traditional, rule-structured aerospace firm than in a more informal, flexible IT start-up because in the context of a disadvantaging background gender frame, formal rules leveled the playing field to some extent. This example suggests that we cannot understand the full implications of a particular organizational logic for the gender structure it will produce without considering how that organizational logic interacts with the background effects of the gender frame.

## Sex Segregation of Field of Study in Affluent Societies

My second example comes from Maria Charles' and Karen Bradley's (2009) provocative study of how the sex-typing of fields of higher education varies across societies. The sex-segregation of fields of study such as the humanities or engineering feeds one of the most durable and consequential gender structures of industrial societies, the sex-segregation of occupations (Charles and Grusky 2004). Gender scholars often puzzle over the fact that some of the societies that have achieved the lowest levels of material inequality between men and women, such as the Scandinavian countries, nevertheless have some of the most sex-segregated occupational structures of advanced industrial societies (Charles and Grusky 2004). How does such sex-segregation persist and even flourish in the face of institutional, political, and economic processes that undermine gender inequality?

Charles and Bradley's analysis shows that we cannot answer this question from a purely economic and structural perspective. Structural factors such as the growth of the service and health sectors in postindustrial economies do contribute to the sex-segregation of jobs and fields of study (Charles and Bradley 2009; Charles and Grusky 2004). But to really explain segregation, we have to take into account how the background frame of gender interacts with cultural developments in highly affluent societies.

As Charles and Bradley (2009) note, contemporary affluent societies tend to embrace a "postmaterialist" ethic of self-expression and self-realization. In the context of wealthy societies that free most of their citizens from the fear of dire material want and that value self-expression, Charles and Bradley argue that the background gender frame powerfully influences the fields of study people pursue. If our fundamental understanding of who we are is rooted in our primary identities, including gender, then many of us will implicitly fall back on cultural beliefs about gender to frame what it means to make life choices that "express" ourselves. There will be a tendency on the part of many us to, in Charles and Bradley's (2009) phrase, "indulge our gendered selves." In support of their argument, they find that affluent postindustrial societies have larger gaps between boys and girls in expressed affinity for math ("I like math"), controlling for boys' and girls' relative mathematical achievement. Furthermore, these culturally gendered affinities more strongly predict the sex-segregation of higher education fields in these societies than in less-developed ones.

An irony of the structural freedoms of advanced affluent societies is that they give their citizens greater space to fall back on an old, deeply ingrained cultural frame as they try to make sense of themselves and others and organize their choices and behaviors accordingly. In the context of economic, legal, and political processes that push against gender inequality in such societies, this reanchoring in the gender frame takes the form of reinvestments in cultural ideas of gender difference. But gender difference is culturally defined in terms that imply gender hierarchy. Thus, although the degree of inequality may decline, we are unlikely to fully eliminate the ordinal hierarchy between men and women in a society that intensifies its organization on the basis of gender difference.

## Conclusion

With these examples, I hope I have been convincing that we cannot understand the shape that the gendered structure of society takes without taking into account the background effects of gender as a primary cultural frame for organizing social relations. I hope I have also been convincing that the theoretical tension some feel between micro-interactional and institutional approaches to gender is unnecessary. When it comes to gender, the effects of processes at one level cannot be understood without reference to those at the other level. Although the gender frame acts through the sense-making of individuals as they try to coordinate their behaviors, it does more than add texture and detail to a structural account of gender and society. When considered jointly with an institutional or structural analysis, the effects of the gender frame help us see how gender becomes embedded in new organizational forms and material arrangements. This analysis also suggests that change in the gendered system of a society will be iterative and may not always proceed smoothly. The forces for change come from political, economic, and technological factors that alter the everyday material arrangements between men and women in ways that undercut traditional views of status differences between men and women. The initial impact of such material changes is often blunted because people reinterpret the meaning of these changes through the lens of their existing, more conservative gender beliefs. Yet, even as people do this, the material changes make those more conservative gender beliefs harder and harder to sustain as meaningful representations of men and women in everyday life. If, over time, changes in the material arrangements between men and women continue to accumulate, the traditional content of cultural beliefs about gender will gradually change as well. A single wave does not move a sandbar, but wave after wave does.

## References

Acker, Joan. 1990. Hierarchies, jobs, and bodies: A theory of gendered organizations. *Gender & Society* 4:139–58.

Bielby, William T. 2000. Minimizing workplace gender and racial bias. *Contemporary Sociology* 29:120–28.

Blair, Irene V., and Mahzarin R. Banaji. 1996. Automatic and controlled processes in stereotype priming. *Journal of Personality and Social Psychology* 70:1142–63.

Brewer, Marilynn, and Layton Lui. 1989. The primacy of age and sex in the structure of person categories. *Social Cognition* 7:262–74.

Charles, Maria, and Karen Bradley. 2009. Indulging our gendered selves: Sex segregation by field of study in 44 countries. *American Journal of Sociology* 114, forthcoming.

Charles, Maria, and David B. Grusky 2004. *Occupational ghettos: The worldwide segregation of women and men.* Stanford, CA: Stanford University Press.

Chwe, Michael Suk-Young. 2001. *Rational ritual: Culture, coordination, and common knowledge.* Princeton, NJ: Princeton University Press.

Conway, Michael, M. Teresa Pizzamiglio, and Lauren Mount. 1996. Status, communality, and agency: Implications for stereotypes of gender and other groups. *Journal of Personality and Social Psychology* 71:25–38.

Eagly, Alice H., and Stephen J. Karau. 2002. Role congruity theory of prejudice towards female leaders. *Psychological Review* 109:573–79.

Fenstermaker, Sarah, and Candace West, eds. 2002. *Doing gender, doing difference: Inequality, power, and institutional change.* New York: Routledge.

Filardo, Emily K. 1996. Gender patterns in African American and white adolescents' social interactions in same-race, mixed-sex groups. *Journal of Personality and Social Psychology* 71:71–82.

Fiske, Susan T. 1998. Stereotyping, prejudice, and discrimination. In *The hand book of social psychology, vol. 2,* edited by D. T. Gilbert, S. T. Fiske, and G. Lindzey. 4th ed. Boston: McGraw-Hill.

Fiske, Susan T., Amy J. Cuddy, Peter Glick, and Jun Xu. 2002. A model of (often mixed) stereotype content: Competence and warmth respectively follow from perceived status and competence. *Journal of Personality and Social Psychology* 82:878–902.

Glick, Peter, and Susan T. Fiske. 1999. Gender, power dynamics, and social interaction. In *Revisioning gender,* edited by M. M. Ferree, J. Lorber, and B. B. Hess. Thousand Oaks, CA: Sage.

Goffman, Erving. 1967. *Interaction ritual.* Garden City, NY: Doubleday.

Ito, Tiffany A., and Geoffrey R. Urland. 2003. Race and gender on the brain: Electrocortical measures of attention to the race and gender of multiply categorizable individuals. *Journal of Personality and Social Psychology* 85:616–26.

Jackman, Mary. R. 1994. *The velvet glove: Paternalism and conflict in gender, class, and race relations.* Berkeley: University of California Press.

Kunda, Ziva, and Steven J. Spencer. 2003. When do stereotypes come to mind and when do they color judgment? A goal-based theoretical framework for stereotype activation and application. *Psychological Bulletin* 129:522–44.

Lorber, Judith. 1994. *Paradoxes of gender.* New Haven, CT: Yale University Press.

Martin, Patricia Y. 2003. "Said and done" versus "saying and doing": Gendering practices, practicing gender at work. *Gender & Society* 17:342–66.

McIllwee, Judith S., and J. Gregg Robinson. 1992. *Women in engineering: Gender power, and workplace culture.* Albany: State University of New York Press.

Milkie, Melissa A. 1999. Social comparison, reflected appraisals, and mass media: The impact of pervasive beauty images on Black and white girls' self-concepts. *Social Psychology Quarterly* 62:190–210.

Nelson, Robert, and William Bridges. 1999. *Legalizing gender inequality: Courts, markets, and unequal pay for women in America.* New York: Cambridge University Press.

Reskin, Barbara, and Debra Branch McBrier. 2000. Why not ascription? Organizations' employment of male and female managers. *American Sociological Review* 65:210–33.

Ridgeway, Cecilia L. 1997. Interaction and the conservation of gender inequality: Considering employment. *American Sociological Review* 62:218–35.

———. 2006. Gender as an organizing force in social relations: Implications for the future of inequality. In *The declining significance of gender?* edited by F. D. Blau, M. C. Brinton, and D. B. Grusky. New York: Russell Sage Foundation.

———. 2007. Gender as a group process: Implications for the persistence of inequality. In *The social psychology of gender,* edited by S. J. Correll. New York: Elsevier.

Ridgeway, Cecilia L., and Shelley J. Correll. 2004. Unpacking the gender system: A theoretical perspective on gender beliefs and social relations. *Gender & Society* 18 (4): 510–31.

Ridgeway, Cecilia L., and Paula England. 2007. Sociological approaches to sex discrimination in employment. In *Sex discrimination in the workplace: Multidisciplinary perspectives,* edited by F. J. Crosby, M. S. Stockdale, and A. S. Ropp. Oxford, UK: Blackwell.

Ridgeway, Cecilia L., and Lynn Smith-Lovin. 1999. The gender system and interaction. *Annual Review of Sociology* 25:1991–216.

Risman, Barbara J. 1998. *Gender vertigo: American families in transition.* New Haven, CT: Yale University Press.

———. 2004. Gender as a social structure: Theory wrestling with activism. *Gender & Society* 18:429–50.

Rudman, Laurie. A., and Kimberly Fairchild. 2004. Reactions to counterstereotypic behavior: The role of backlash in cultural stereotype maintenance. *Journal of Personality and Social Psychology* 87:157–76.

Schneider, David J. 2004. *The psychology of stereotyping.* New York: Guilford.

Smith-Doerr, Laurel. 2004. *Women's work: Gender equality vs. hierarchy in the life sciences.* Boulder, CO: Lynne Rienner.

Stangor, Charles, Laure Lynch, Changming Duan, and Beth Glass. 1992. Categorization of individuals on the basis of multiple social features. *Journal of Personality and Social Psychology* 62:207–18.

Steinberg, Ronnie J. 1995. Gendered instructions: Cultural lag and gender bias in the hay system of job evaluation. In *Gender inequality at work,* edited by J. A. Jacobs. Thousand Oaks, CA: Sage.

Wagner, David G., and Joseph Berger. 1997. Gender and interpersonal task behaviors: Status expectation accounts. *Sociological Perspectives* 40:1–32.

West, Candace, and Don Zimmerman. 1987. Doing gender. *Gender & Society* 1:125–51.

Whittington, Kjersten Bunker. 2007. *Employment structures as opportunity structures: The effects of location on male and female scientific dissemination.* Stanford, CA: Department of Sociology, Stanford University.

Whittington, Kjersten Bunker, and Laurel Smith-Doerr. 2008. Women inventors in context: Disparities in patenting across academia and industry. *Gender & Society* 22:194–218.

**CECILIA L. RIDGEWAY** is the Lucie Stern Professor of Social Sciences at Stanford University. Her research addresses the role that social hierarchies in everyday interaction play in gender stratification and social inequality. She is currently working on a book titled *Framed by Gender: How Gender Inequality Persists in the Modern World.*

From *Gender & Society*, April 2009; vol. 23, pp. 145–160. Copyright ©. 2009 by Sage Publications. Reprinted by permission via Rightslink.

# Gender Is Powerful
## *The Long Reach of Feminism*

NANCY MacLEAN

Of all the movements of the Sixties, those involving gender, enlisted the largest number of participants and produced the deepest transformation in American society. Emboldened by the wider activism of the era, especially the black freedom movement, and spurred by seismic changes in the economy and family life, feminists attracted a growing following after 1966 as they set out to end the reign of gender inequality in American institutions and culture. Within a few years, lesbians and gay men too showed new daring in laying claim to the nation's core promises of freedom and equality. Public debate has since raged between supporters and opponents of these movements over a host of specific issues: the Equal Rights Amendment, abortion, affirmative action, gay school teachers, and more. Yet underlying the specific conflicts were profound alterations in political economy and culture that made gender issues matter as never before to activists on all sides—and to millions of ordinary citizens.

As is common with new social movements, early scholarship on second wave feminism took its cue from journalism and its inspiration from personal experience. Authors of the formative studies of the women's movement such as Jo Freeman and Sara Evans had themselves participated in the struggle, and so had intimate knowledge of their subjects. They showed, in the words of Evans' subtitle, "the roots of women's liberation in the civil rights movement and the New Left." Evans, in particular, focused on young women activists' recognition that "the personal is political" and showed how they used consciousness-raising discussion sessions to deepen understanding of the social roots of seemingly personal problems and develop innovative practices to address them, such as rape crisis centers[1]. Yet, rich as these works were, closeness to the events led to greater interest in immediate concerns than in the deep structure of change.

Most textbooks today follow early participants and journalists in taking a short view of the movement. The texts lead students to think that organizing for gender equality stopped after women won the vote in 1920 and suddenly "reawakened," the oft-used word, in the 1960s. Certainly there is some truth to this view: in the late Sixties, the ranks of women activists surged, their supporters multiplied many times over, and the pace of reform accelerated. Within just a few years, women won protection from employment discrimination, inclusion in affirmative action, abortion law

reform, greater representation in media, equal access to athletics, congressional passage of an Equal Rights Amendment, and much more[2]. Yet students are ill-served by the notion that such a powerful force came out of nowhere, or even that its main cause was the youthled movements of the "Sixties."

Forty years have passed since some activists coined the phrase "women's liberation" and others formed the National Organization for Women (NOW), In that time a wealth of new scholarship has revealed the far deeper roots of these movements, both in social changes over generations and in political history reaching back to the early twentieth century. What made some kind of change in the gender order feel necessary to so many was, most immediately, the demise of the family wage system: the male breadwinner/female homemaker model that shaped government policy and employer practices, even though it never described the reality of millions of American households. Just as important, however, were profound demographic changes sweeping every industrial society; infant mortality and birth rates declined, life expectancy surged, and women entered the paid labor force in massive numbers. In this context, popular understanding of marriage and the very meaning of life changed: no longer expecting to die soon after their last child left home, women came to want more from men, marriage, education, and themselves. That is why even countries that had no equivalent upheaval in the 1960s nevertheless generated their own variants of feminism as they sought to cope with these massive changes using the tools of the democratic process, above all, new public policies suited to changing family forms and individual life cycles[3].

While one track of recent history reveals how a seemingly new movement accomplished so much so quickly, another provides a deep context for why so many welcomed feminism. The feminist movement, in other words, was not new at all. The ranks of self-described "feminism" dwindled after 1920, to be sure, as the elite, white National Women's Party made that label anathema to women working for wider social justice thanks to its leaders' single-minded quest for an Equal Rights Amendment, a gender-blind approach that threatened hard-won, gender-conscious reforms like protective legislation[4]. But tens of thousands of others continued to try to improve the lives of women between 1920 and 1965 through their work in the labor movement and in such organizations as the National Consumers League, the National Council of Negro Women, and the YWCA[5].

This grassroots base made possible an ambitious organizing effort after World War II, a broad-based left-led coalition called the Congress of American Women. It joined women's equality to peace and wider social reforms, such as full employment, government sponsored child care facilities, and an end to racial segregation. CAW anticipated all of the agenda of second wave feminism save its sexual politics, and had more black women in leadership positions than any other feminist movement in U.S. history[6]. Such broad advocacy was enabled by changes in the infrastructure of American politics that began in the Progressive Era and expanded in the New Deal and war years. Feminism's goals and accomplishments depended on prior national commitment to a federal regulatory state to advance social citizenship, and on the mass membership organizations that ensured continued government commitment to a welfare state in the face of opposition from northern corporate Republicans and southern white supremacist Democrats.

One reason the Rip van Winkle account of feminism seemed plausible for so long was that the postwar Red Scare hurt organizing among women as it did labor and civil rights activism. CAW was a broad coalition, but communist women had played a key role in bringing it together. Under the harsh glare of investigation by the House Un-American Activities Committee and a demand by the attorney general that the organization must register as a "foreign agent," membership plummeted from a claimed high of 250,000 to just 3,000. Gerda Lerner, who later became a pioneer historian of women and president of the OAH, was then a rank-and-file CAW activist, a Jewish refugee from Nazism, and a Communist Party member herself. She burned all her records in terror of what the Right's new power portended. Most other groups doing innovative work for gender equality in 1940s and 1950s were affected in some way, and individual leaders became much more cautious. But many continued working, forming a human bridge between eras more propitious to activism as they labored quietly but steadily in arenas ranging from the American Civil Liberties Union to the United Auto Workers Women's Commission[7].

This existing infrastructure helps explain how feminists were able to make such stunning headway after the formation of NOW and the take off of women's liberation. The wide array of leaders from earlier groups came together in the President's Commission on the Status of Women, which in turn spurred state-level women's commissions that became organizing centers. In 1963, the PCSW issued its major report calling for wide-ranging reform to end sex discrimination. Textbooks thus get it wrong when they credit Betty Friedan's bestselling 1963 book. *The Feminine Mystique,* for the rise of second wave feminism. What the book did, rather, was name what so many women were already feeling and invigorate those already acting. Friedan developed her expert aim, moreover, in the Popular Front of the 1940s as a labor-left journalist. Her book thus built on far more than her experience as a suburban wife and mother[8].

Similarly, some of feminism's greatest policy victories in the 1960s and 1970s came as a result of using tools won by other movements. By far the most important was the employment section of the Civil Rights Act of 1964, Title VII, won by the black freedom movement to end occupational segregation. Women used it not only to enter good jobs of all kinds long closed to them but also to end pregnancy discrimination and fight sexual harassment. Indeed they raised foundational questions about gender and power with reverberations in every area of American life. Title VII also encouraged new coalitions between feminists and labor and civil rights groups of all kinds that expanded the constituency pushing for gender equity. Without a Title VII, NOW and small women's liberation never would have achieved so many successes so quickly, if they achieved them at all[9].

Part of what made feminism so successful is the way that, almost from the outset, women in different situations developed their own variants and organized for the goals most important to them. As historian Nancy Cott wrote of the first wave, "feminism was an impulse that was impossible to translate into a program without centrifugal results"[10]. The trite caricature of a white middle-class movement obscures this far more interesting history. From the beginning, black women inside and outside the movement put forth their own visions of gender justice, often with a particular focus on how the combined impact of racism and sexism hurt black families and harmed men as well as women. Latina feminists soon advanced a critique of *machismo* and of the constraining role of the Catholic Church in their communities. And so it went: Native American women, working-class women in trade unions, Jewish women. Catholic women, sex workers, older women, and women with disabilities all described what gender equality would mean from their vantage points and worked to achieve it[11]. Initial friction notwithstanding, over time these differences enriched the very definition of feminism while enlisting the commitment of a vast spectrum of Americans[12].

Seen in the light of this older and broader story, the lesbian and gay quest for equality seems almost inevitable. It too responded to changes in family life and gender as it emphasized mutual love as the basis for domestic partnership, regardless of the sex of each partner. Like feminism, this movement built on foundations laid during the New Deal and World War II newly accepted ideas about the rights of citizens and the role of government, newly powerful grassroots movements of labor and the left, massive same-sex armed forces, and a new capacity to enforce rights made possible by an expanded administrative state. It was no accident that the first gay rights group, the Mattachine Society, was founded in the wake of World War II by left-wing activists such as Harry Hay, or that it identified gay rights *with* "our fellow minorities . . . the Negro, Mexican, and Jewish Peoples"[13].

The cold war had subdued this organizing, too, as it encouraged a "lavender scare" that cost more government workers their jobs than did the Red Scare itself. The State Department alone boasted in 1950 that it was firing one suspected homosexual a day[14]. But as in the case of women's equality, the social and cultural changes driving this movement were too powerful for repression to succeed over the long term. Thanks to being held back artificially in the 1950s, the gay liberation movement, like the women's movement, exploded with greater force in the 1960s—most dramatically in the four-night-long Stonewall riot in New York City in 1969. And the gay movement too generated a panoply of different organizations, the division of labor among which enabled the movement to work on various fronts—from creating its own media to changing municipal law, medical knowledge, and the practices of police and employers[15].

For movement opponents, however, open homosexuality dramatized the separation of sexuality and reproduction that traditionalists already feared. It also showed how pliable gender was: its very existence implied there was no "natural" way for men or women to behave and so raised unprecedented questions about gender hierarchy and the meaning of family. Further, what would it mean to grant equal rights for lesbians and gay men? That would require acknowledging the legitimacy of rights enforcement for others, too, beginning with blacks, something that conservatives in the North and South had long resisted. In short, on virtually every front that mattered to the right, this new movement seemed a particular challenge[16].

With a focus on the deeper roots and larger stakes of these movements, it is easier to make sense of the phenomenon of mass antifeminism among women. Mobilized in 1972 by the veteran conservative activist Phyllis Schlafly in a group called STOP ERA, female antifeminism proved powerful enough to defeat the Equal Rights Amendment, which had sailed through both houses of Congress in 1972 after the surge of pro-equality activism. In my experience the paradox of women who fought gender equality is a great hook for teaching; it is hard to imagine, for example, African Americans organizing to fight passage the Civil Rights Act. On the face of it, it is so odd that students who yawn at feminism itself sit up to figure this out.

Solving the puzzle of why some women fought against equal treatment for their sex requires looking at how the family wage system and its breakdown drove gender-conscious politics of all kinds. Different groups of women came up with different answers to the decline of the family wage and the deep alterations in marriage and family because they stood in very different relation to these developments. Women who feel that they have benefited from the changes of recent years often become feminists, who try to further dismantle the old male dominated system in the name of equality and fairness. Yet many women who feel they have lost or will lose from the changes have rallied to the old system's defense[17]. Both reactions are understandable in a society that provides less of a social safety net than any other comparably developed nation. In western Europe, by contrast, which has more public policy supports for family well being and a stronger ethic of social solidarity, antifeminism is far weaker and there is no mass-based or influential analogue to America's religious right[18].

Analysis of the deep structure of gender politics also helps to make sense of the prominent place of issues of masculinity, femininity, family, and sexuality in other movements of the era not ostensibly concerned with gender. For example, historians have recently used gender analysis to reveal new dimensions of civil rights and black nationalism, the Chicano youth movement, and the conflict over the war in Vietnam. Their studies reveal how heated gender rhetoric signaled underlying concerns that influenced conduct once beyond the purview of women's history[19].

This call for a new framework based on "the long women's movement" promises both challenges and opportunities for teachers of the U.S. survey[20]. It demands more of teachers, who will have to supply storyline, analysis, and documents that current textbooks do not. Most texts say little or nothing about women's organizing between 1920 and 1966, and almost none mentions the decisive role of the labor movement and broader progressive organizations, not explicitly feminist, in helping to advance women's equality. Taking the long view may also require sacrificing some of the attention-getting drama that dominates journalistic accounts. Time spent on media magnets like the demonstration at the 1969 Atlantic City Miss America Pageant may have to make room for how older women in the 1940s and 1950s worked for measures that would reduce the burden of the "double day" on working women, when few young people were paying attention. Given the widespread concern among today's students about how they will manage to combine employment and family commitments, that seems a fair trade[21].

Indeed, the concept of a long women's movement offers pedagogical benefits that more than offset its start-up costs. Incorporating the best new scholarship, it introduces students to a cast of activists far more diverse than they meet in the worn-out stereotype of a "reawakened" white, middle-class movement based in the Northeast. The actors in these broader struggles look more like today's student bodies in class, race, religion, and region, if not in age, and therefore are more likely to hold their interest. Perhaps the most enticing advantage of "the long women's movement" framework for teachers, however, is that it reinforces earlier lessons by deepening student understanding of the present-day ramifications of the Progressive Era, the New Deal, the cold war, the civil rights movement, and the rise of political conservatism. It offers, that is, an opportunity for the ever-elusive synthesis. Not least, in a time of rapid worldwide economic restructuring and political disorientation, it provides students a better understanding of how momentous democratic change has really come about in the past.

# References

1. Sara M. Evans, *Personal Politics: The Roots of Women's Liberation in the Civil Rights Movement and the New Left* (New York: Knopf, 1979); Jo Freeman, *The Politics of Women's Liberation: A Case Study of an Emerging Social Movement and Its Relation to the Policy Process* (New York: David McKay, 1975); also Alice Echols, *Daring to Be Bad: Radical Feminism in America, 1967–1975* (Minneapolis: University of Minnesota Press, 1989); Ruth Rosen, *The World Split Open: How the Modern Women's Movement Changed America* (New York: Viking, 2000).

2. For an overview, see Winifred D. Wandersee, *On the Move: American Women in the 1970s* (Boston: Twayne, 1988); Susan M. Hartmann, *From Margin to Mainstream: American Women and Politics since 1960* (New York: Alfred A. Knopf, 1989).

3. Barbara Ehrenreich, *The Hearts of Men: American Dreams and the Flight From Commitment* (New York: Anchor Books, 1983); Nancy MacLean, "Postwar Women's History: From the 'Second Wave' to the End of the Family Wage?" in *A Companion to Post-1945 America,* ed. Roy Rosenzweig and Jean-Christophe Agnew (London: Blackwell, 2002); Stephanie Coontz, *Marriage, a History. From Obedience to Intimacy, or How Love Conquered Marriage* (New York: Viking, 2005); Estelle Freedman, *No Turning Back: The History of Feminism and the Future of Women* (New York: Ballantine, 2003).

4. Nancy F. Cott, *The Grounding of Modern Feminism* (New Haven: Yale University Press, 1987); Leila Rupp and Verta Taylor, *Survival in the Doldrums: The American Women's Rights Movement, 1945 to the 1960s* (New York: Oxford University Press, 1987).

5. Vicki L. Ruiz, *Cannery Women, Cannery Lives: Mexican Women, Unionization, and the California Food Processing Industry, 1930–1950* (Albuquerque: University of New Mexico, 1987); Nancy F. Gabin, *Feminism in the Labor Movement: Women and the United Auto Workers, 1935–1975* (Ithaca: Cornell University Press, 1990); Deborah Gray White, *Too Heavy a Load: Black Women in Defense of Themselves, 1894–1994* (New York: W. W. Norton, 1998); Landon R.Y. Storrs, *Civilizing Capitalism: The National Consumers' League, Women's Activism, and Labor Standards in the New Deal Era* (Chapel Hill: University of North Carolina Press, 2000); Bruce Fehn, *Striking Women: Gender, Race and Class in the United Packinghouse Workers of America* (Iowa City: University of Iowa Press, 2003); Dorothy Sue Cobble, *The Other Women's Movement: Workplace justice and Social Rights in Modern America* (Princeton: Princeton University Press, 2005), An excellent documentary that makes this case, is *Step by Step: Building a Feminist Movement* (Videocassette, Wisconsin Public Television, 1998; distributed by Women Make Movies).

6. Amy Swerdlow, "The Congress of American Women: Left-Feminist Peace Politics in the Cold War" in *U.S. History as Women's History: New Feminist Essays,* ed. Linda K. Kerber, Alice Kessler-Harris, and Kathryn Kish Sklar (Chapel Hill: University of North Carolina Press, 1995).

7. Gerda Lerner, *Fireweed: A Political Autobiography* (Philadelphia: Temple University Press, 2002); also Landon R.Y. Storrs, "Red Scare Politics and the Suppression of Popular Front Feminism: The Loyalty Investigation of Mary Dublin Keyserling," *Journal of American History* 90 (Sept. 2003): 491–524; Susan Lynn, *Progressive Women in Conservative Times: Racial Justice, Peace, and Feminism, 1945 to the 1960s* (New Brunswick: Rutgers University Press, 1992); Joanne Meyerowitz, *Not June Cleaver. Women and Gender in Postwar America* (Philadelphia: Temple University Press, 1994); Susan M. Hartmann, *The Other Feminists: Activists in the liberal Establishment* (New Haven: Yale University Press, 1998).

8. Cynthia Harrison, *On Account of Sex: The Politics of Women's Issues, 1945–1968* (Berkeley: University of California Press, 1988); Daniel Horowitz, *Betty Friedan and the Making of "The Feminine Mystique": The American Left, the Cold War, and Modern Feminism* (Amherst: University of Massachusetts Press, 1998).

9. Hartmann, *The Other Feminists;* Nancy MacLean, *Freedom Is Not Enough: The Opening of the American Workplace* (Cambridge: Harvard University Press and the Russell Sage Foundation, 2006); also Cobble, *The Other Women's Movement.*

10. Cott, *Grounding of Modern Feminism,* 282.

11. For a sample, see Nancy Seifer, *"Nobody Speaks for Me!": Self-Portraits of American Working Class Women* (New York: Simon and Schuster, 1976); Asian Women United of California, *Making Waves: An Anthology of Writings By and About Asian American Women* (Boston: Beacon Press, 1989); Beverly Guy-Sheftall, ed. *Words on Fire: An Anthology of African-American Feminist Thought* (New York: The New Press, 1995); Alma M. Garcia, *Chicana Feminist Thought: The Basic Historical Writings* (New York: Routledge, 1997).

12. Freedman, *No Turning Back;* Sara M. Evans, *Tidal Wave: How Women Changed America at Century's End* (New York: Free Press, 2003); Benita Roth, *Separate Roads to Feminism: Black, Chicana, and White Feminist Movements in America's Second Wave* (New York: Cambridge University Press, 2004); Kimberly Springer, *Living for the Revolution: Black Feminist Organizations, 1968–1980* (Durham: Duke University Press, 2005).

13. Quote from "Statement of Purpose" in Van Gosse, *The Movements of the New Left, 1950–1975: A Brief History with Documents* (Boston: Bedford Books, 2005), 40; Allan Berube, *Coming out under Fire: The History of Gay Men and Women in World War Two* (New York: Free Press, 1990); Leisa D. Meyer, *Creating GI Jane: Sexuality and Power in the Woman's Army Corps during World War II* (New York: Columbia University Press, 1996); John D' Emilio, *Sexual Politics, Sexual Communities: The Making of a Homosexual Minority in the United States, 1940–1970,* 2nd ed, (Chicago: University of Chicago Press, 1998); Martin Meeker, "Behind the Mask of Respectability: Reconsidering the Mattachine Society and Male Homophile Practice, 1950s and 1960s," *Journal of the History of Sexuality* 10 (Jan. 2001): 78–116.

14. David K. Johnson, *The Lavender Scare: The Cold War Persecution of Gays and Lesbians in the Federal Government* (Chicago: University of Chicago Press, 2004).

15. John D'Emilio, "After Stonewall," in his *Making Trouble: Essays on Gay History, Politics, and the University* (New York: Routledge, 1992), 234–74; *Creating Change: Sexuality, Public Policy, and Civil Rights,* ed. John D'Emilio, William B. Turner, Urvashi Vaid (New York: St. Martin's Press, 2000).

16. On the import of the separation of sexuality and reproduction, see John D'Emilio and Estelle B. Freedman, *Intimate Matters: A History of Sexuality in America* (New York: Harper & Row, 1988): on conservatives and civil rights, see MacLean. *Freedom Is Not Enough,* esp. chaps, 2, 7, and 9.

17. Kristin Luker, *Abortion and the Politics of Motherhood* (Berkeley: University of California Press, 1984); Jane J. Mansbridge, *Why We Lost the ERA* (Chicago: University of Chicago Press, 1986): MacLean, "Postwar Women's History."

18. The best source of up-to-date information is the Institute for Women's Policy Research: <http://wvvw.iwpr.org/>. For U.S. distinctiveness and its roots, see Barry D. Adam, "The Defense of Marriage Act and American Exceptionalism: The 'Gay Marriage' Panic in the United States," *Journal of the History of Sexuality* 12 (April 2003): 259–76, esp. 265–66.

19. Vicki L Crawford, et al, eds., *Women in the Civil Rights Movement: Trailblazers and Torchbearers, 1941–1965* (Bloomington: Indiana University Press, 1990); Scot Brown, *Fighting for US: Maulana Karenga, the US Organization, and Black Cultural Nationalism* (New York: New York University Press, 2003); Ramon A. Cutierrez, "Community, Patriarchy and Individualism: The Politics of Chicano History and the Dream of Equality." *American Quarterly* 45 (March 1993): 44–72; Joshua B. Freeman, "Hardhats: Construction Workers, Manliness, and the 1970 Pro-War Demonstrations," *Journal of Social History* (Summer 1993): 725–44; Robert D. Dean, *Imperial Brotherhood: Gender and the Making of Cold War Foreign Policy* (Amherst: University of Massachusetts Press, 2001): Justin David Suran, "Coming out against the War. Antimilitarism and the Politicization of Homosexuality in the Era of Vietnam," *American Quarterly* 53 (Sept., 2001): 452–488.

20. On "the long civil rights movement," see Jacquelyn Dowd Hall, "The Long Civil Rights Movement and the Political Uses of the Past," *Journal of American History* (March 2005): 1233–63; also *Time Longer than Rope: A Century of African American Activism, 1850–1950,* ed. Charles M. Payne and Adam Green (New York: New York University Press, 2003).

21. For a model from the civil rights movement of how much is gained by changing the vantage point in this way, see Charles Payne, *I've Got the Light of Freedom: The Organizing Tradition and the Mississippi Freedom Struggle* (Berkeley: University of California Press, 1995).

---

**NANCY MACLEAN** professor of history and African American studies and chair of the history department at Northwestern University. She is author of *Freedom Is Not Enough: The Opening of the American Work Place* (Harvard University Press, 2006) and *The Modern Women's Movement: A Brief History with Documents* (Bedford Books, forthcoming , 2007)

From *OAH Magazine of History*, October 2006, pp. 19–23. Copyright © 2006 by Organization of American Historians. Reprinted by permission via the Copyright Clearance Center.

# The World, the Flesh and the Devil

## Robert W. Thurston looks at the politics of demonology and rethinks attitudes to witches and women between 1400 and 1700.

ROBERT W. THURSTON

*All wickedness is but little to the wickedness of a woman . . . [She is] an evil of nature . . . [Women] are more credulous; and since the chief aim of the devil is to corrupt faith, therefore he rather attacks them . . . Women . . . are intellectually like children . . . [A woman] always deceives.*

As the Dominican monk Heinrich Kramer (c.1430-c.1505) sat down to write about witches in early 1486, he must have felt desperate. He had recently been sentenced to prison for theft, blocked by other clerics as he tried to convict women of witchcraft, and scorned and threatened by a bishop. Kramer (known as Institoris in some sources) needed to recoup the respect appropriate to a papal inquisitor, his position in 'Upper Germany', a swathe of present day Germany, France and Austria.

This was the inauspicious background to the creation of the *Malleus Maleficarum* ('Hammer of Witches'). First printed in 1486, the *Malleus* is often considered to be the pivotal work for the study of both the witch hunts, which lasted roughly from the 1420s to the 1690s, and the era's commentaries on women.

The book owes much of its fame to late nineteenth- and early twentieth-century scholars who were certain that superstition and fanaticism produced the hunts, while the Enlightenment's breakthrough to reason ended them. In 1878 the President of Cornell University, Andrew Dickson White, showed an early edition of the *Malleus* to 'his shuddering class', saying that it had 'caused more suffering than any other [work] written by human pen'. The narrator of Dan Brown's *The Da Vinci Code* (2004) echoes this claim:

> The Catholic Inquisition published the book that argu- ably could be called the most blood-soaked publication in human history. *Malleus maleficarum*—or *The Witches' Hammer*—indoctrinated the world to 'the dangers of free- thinking women' and instructed the clergy how to locate, torture, and destroy them. . . . During three hundred years of witch hunts, the Church burned at the stake an astound- ing five million women.

Not astounding but absurd—the old guesses of up to nine million victims have been revised downwards: recent esti- mates suggest 30-40,000 executions. Nor did 'the Inquisi- tion' itself publish the *Malleus*. Germany, particularly along the Rhine, was the worst killing ground. France was a distant second, while England and even Scotland lagged far behind. Italy, Spain, and Portugal contributed relatively few victims to the pyres.

For all that estimates of the death toll have fallen recently, it still appears that females typically comprised about 75 percent of the victims. However, commentators on witchcraft between 1400 and 1700 divide sharply on three key points: whether or not women are intrinsically wicked; whether demons could per- form real actions or simply create illusions; and whether witch- craft was truly practised. These divisions go far to explain why the witch-hunts were so erratic.

The reasons for the high proportion of female victims must be sought in more mundane factors than the demonologists advanced: the tasks that women performed, giving birth, suck- ling babies, preparing food, caring for children, and washing the dead, were just the ones that contemporaries suspected could provide opportunities and substances for evil acts.

The story of the *Malleus* and its author open the way to rethinking demonology in general. In the last decade studies of European demonology have focused more on widespread anxi- ety about heresy than on obsessions with women. When Kramer's work is seen in the context of the wider politico-religious struggles of the era, the *Malleus* appears less an assault on women than an attempt to use them—or stock images of them—to make points about correct belief.

Kramer had been arrested in 1482 for allegedly stealing sil- verware and money in the course of his inquisitorial duties. The Inquisition had arisen in the late twelfth century as the Church focused on combating heresy. Managed by the papacy and the Dominican and Franciscan Orders in its early phases, the Inqui- sition later developed various 'Holy Offices', for example in Portugal and Rome. Kramer, operating under the Pope and his own Dominican Order, was responsible in Upper Germany for investigating, arresting, and ordering the torture of suspected heretics, which by now included witches.

Before Kramer could actually be gaoled, the Archbishop of Craynensis (Albania) issued a call for a new Church council. Kramer seized this moment to write a strong defence of papal authority in opposition to conciliarism, the movement which argued that councils possessed higher authority than the Pope. Pope Sixtus IV, recognizing that Kramer's pen could be an important force on his side, dropped all charges against the monk and returned him to his inquisitorial post.

But Sixtus died in 1484, to be replaced by Innocent VIII. At this juncture Kramer, possibly supported by his inquisitorial partner Jakob Sprenger, complained to the new pontiff that ecclesiastical officials were hampering their efforts to combat heresy. Innocent responded by issuing the Bull *Summis desiderantes affectibus* ('Desiring with supreme ardour') in 1484, in which he enjoined all secular and Church authorities in Upper Germany to aid the two inquisitors.

Armed with this Bull, Kramer arrested some fifty women on the charge of witchcraft and put several on trial in Brixen, east of Innsbruck. He denied his prisoners legal counsel and had them tortured immediately, both gross violations of inquisitorial rules. His actions provoked strong opposition from officials appointed by the Bishop of Brixen, Georg Golser. These clerics finally agreed to try the women, but the case led to Kramer's downfall. When he questioned a defendant about her sexual practices and moral standing in her community, the judges found his query irrelevant and overruled him. The trial was quickly ended and the women released, as episcopal members of the court decided that Kramer had abused his position.

Golser wrote to a priest named Nikolaus criticizing Kramer for his 'completely childish' behaviour, a result of 'his advanced age' (he was about fifty-five). Kramer 'still wants perhaps to mix in women's affairs', the bishop continued, but 'I am not letting him do that, as formerly he erred almost completely in his trial'. Instead he advised him to return to his monastery in Innsbruck. But in the autumn of 1485, Golser informed Kramer that he had now become unwelcome in Innsbruck, warning him that a popular uprising against his witchcraft cases might develop. No ruch revolt occurred, but after a second threatening letter from Golser in early 1486, Kramer departed for Salzburg.

He then set to work on the *Malleus,* perhaps in the hope that a new book could salvage his standing. Hastily written by Kramer alone, and with glaring lapses in presentation of the argument and grammar, the text was printed late in the year. Sprenger's name became attached to the work in a later reprinting, which may have been a ploy by Kramer to give his book more scholarly weight.

While the *Malleus* offered little new on the theory of witchcraft, it did argue vehemently that witches existed, that women were particularly drawn to witchcraft and sex with demons, and that with demons' help, witches performed evil deeds. The book also presented sensational stories. For example, Kramer reported that in a certain city beset by plague, a dead 'woman was gradually eating the shroud in which she had been buried'. The pestilence would continue until she consumed the entire cloth. When the body was exhumed, half the shroud had been eaten. Aghast, an official cut the head from the corpse and threw it out of the grave; 'at once the plague ceased'.

After the *Malleus* appeared, Kramer continued his dubious or outright criminal behaviour. He implied that the book had direct papal approval by inserting Innocent VIII's Bull as the preface to an edition printed in 1487. But Innocent had merely written a standard directive reaffirming the authority of his inquisitors. The Bull repeats the conventional wisdom of the day on the sexual depravity of heretics, but not witches—it does not mention nocturnal flight and refers to the sabbat only indirectly. It did not single out women as Satan's whores.

Nevertheless, the *Malleus* has retained a leading role in studies of the witch persecutions because of its vitriolic condemnation of women. The most important reason for the Devil's appeal to females, Kramer argued, is that a woman is 'more carnal than a man, as is clear from her many carnal abominations'. The Dominican obsessively reiterated this point, concluding that 'all witchcraft comes from carnal lust, which is in women insatiable'. He did mention 'chaste and honest women', but the remark paled beside his overall misogyny. Clearly he feared women, as shown by the many references to impotence caused by witches and even to their removal of penises.

Kramer's career after 1486 demonstrates that by no means everyone agreed with him on witchcraft. He undermined his own cause by having a forgery endorsing his book inserted among letters from the theology faculty at the University of Cologne, which had offered only limited support for his ideas. Kramer then bribed a notary to label all the letters as true documents. The letters, along with the papal Bull of 1484, were bound with the *Malleus* in some reprintings, in an attempt to give it maximum authority. When this forgery became known, Kramer's reputation plummeted, and his ex-partner Sprenger opened prosecution against him for the forgery.

Kramer then moved on to the Mosel district, where he angered his superiors by approving a local community's effort to create counter-magic against dark forces by erecting a large crucifix. The Church could not openly approve such quasi-pagan measures.

Kramer's behaviour in Brixen had so discredited the concept of diabolical witchcraft that no further witch trials took place there. In 1490, the Dominican Order condemned him for excesses in his work. Although in 1491 the Nuremberg city council requested Kramer's assistance in witch trials and he obliged by writing a treatise denouncing laxity in the pursuit of witches, the city aldermen refused to publish it, perhaps because they had finally been informed about his past. He moved yet again, this time to Bohemia, where he died in about 1505.

While the *Malleus* represents an extreme strain in late fifteenth-century male attitudes toward women, it does not support the notion that misogyny was the pre-eminent factor behind the witch hunts. To begin with, the extent of the book's influence is far from clear. While some later works on witches drew heavily on the *Malleus,* its publication history was erratic. It appeared in two waves (sixteen editions were published between 1486 and 1520, and about the same number between 1574 and 1621), but none in the intervening fifty years, a crucial period in the rise of the witch trials. In 1526 the Spanish Inquisition denounced the *Malleus* as worthless. Nor were there further editions during another great round of hunts between 1620 and 1665.

The book's appeal is often explained in terms of its completeness in guiding witch-hunters, down to how to lead the witch into a courtroom (backwards). Yet, especially in view of the sensationalist qualities of the *Malleus,* it cannot be assumed that readers always accepted Kramer's arguments.

Sigismund, Count of Tyrol, had been so disturbed by Kramer's conduct at the Brixen trial in 1484 that he commissioned the jurist Ulrich Molitor to clarify the issues. Molitor's *De lamiis* [or *laniis*] *et phitonicis mulieribus* ('On Female Witches and Fortunetellers', 1489) reached the traditional conclusion that while demons exist they can only create illusions, and cannot interact physically with humans. While Molitor agreed that women were more likely than men to enlist in Satan's service and should be tried for making a pact with him, he explained female attraction to demons by referring to specific circumstances such as poverty, hatred or other unspecified temptations, rather than to general female characteristics such as lust or defective character.

A stronger counter-attack against Kramer, Johann Weyer's *De praestigiis daemonum* ('On Demonic Illusions' or 'On Witchcraft'), appeared in numerous editions beginning in 1563. Weyer too maintained that Satan could only produce illusions; violent phenomena such as sudden illnesses or hailstorms had natural, not diabolic, causes. Evidence obtained under torture was worthless, and old women's voluntary confessions of witchcraft resulted from 'melancholy'.

Reading Kramer's work within the broad context of demonology makes it clear that the genre's primary goal was to defend the reality of demons and humans' physical interaction with them. This argument underscored the need for mainstream Christianity to engage in a sharper struggle against evil. The *Malleus* begins, 'Question the First. Whether the belief that there are such beings as witches is so essential a part of the Catholic faith that obstinately to maintain the opposite opinion manifestly savours of heresy'. No wonder Kramer argued for the existence of witches.

He sought a vivid means of supporting the notion that Satan could easily recruit some humans. Sex sells, and emphasizing purported female sexual transgressions was for Kramer a way of drawing on existing negative stereotypes to make demonic activity more plausible. Since women were traditionally considered the weaker sex and the Devil was definitely male, demonic copulation had to be overwhelmingly with females. Thus *incubi,* or demons who insert a sexual member into a human body, appear about nine times as often in demonological works as *succubi,* which are sexually receptive creatures.

In this and other respects, Kramer borrowed heavily from earlier works on witchcraft, especially Johann Nider's *Formicarius* ('The Ant Heap', 1435-37). The *Malleus* cites Nider at least fifty times. Though Nider had never been a witch-hunter, he was deeply concerned with heresy, particularly with the Hussite movement. A negotiator with the Hussites at the Council of Basel in 1433, he wavered between seeking their return to the fold and urging their destruction.

Nider noted that both sexes could be witches but argued that women's sexual 'weakness' often led them into the Devil's arms. Yet in contrast to Kramer, he was unwilling to break completely with the old doctrine that insisted Satan produced illusions, not acts, on Earth: two of the five books in *Formicarius* are concerned with 'false visions' and dreams.

Nider considered that demons posed a grave problem for true Christianity, because they allied with opponents of reform within the Church. He quoted St Paul in 1 Corinthians 11:19: 'For there must be also heresies among you, that they which are approved may be made manifest among you.' Heretics of all sorts were useful to the Church by demonstrating what *not* to believe and how not to act—and this included their reported copulation with demons. As this argument unfolds in *Formicarius* amid discussion of such topics as the importance of growing rye, it becomes clear that Nider's anxiety about wanton women is a small part of his larger concerns.

Although most witch-hunts occurred in German-speaking lands, the most developed demonology arose, surprisingly, in France during the mid- to late sixteenth century. Yet the many French treatises on demons by no means sparked large-scale witch persecutions. Indeed, trials in Francophone regions occurred mostly in eastern borderlands not then under the crown, especially Franche Comté and Lorraine. Normandy, long an integral part of the realm, did witness numerous cases, but there male witches far outnumbered females.

Lambert Daneau (1564), Jean Bodin (1580), Henri Boguet (1602), Martin Del Rio (1603 and 1611), and Pierre de Lancre (1612) were the leading French experts on witchcraft. Some of these men did think women were especially drawn to Satan. But, paralleling new work on Nider, historians such as Michael Bailey have seen these writers as preoccupied above all with political-cum-religious battles. Except for the Protestant Daneau, who fled to Geneva to write, the French authors were all zealous Catholics, writing in the wake of the Council of Trent (1545-63), which had adopted a host of new policies to strengthen the Church in the face of the Protestant challenge. They produced copious propaganda directed at the enemies of Tridentine reform: Catholic *politiques* (compromisers) as well as Protestants. How best to smear these opponents and solidify one's own ranks? Simple: by linking these enemies of the true faith to Satan.

The French demonologists directed particular fire at the Paris *parlement,* an appeals court whose jurisdiction covered a large part of the kingdom. The *parlement,* dominated for most of this period by religious moderates, was stubbornly sceptical toward the evidence for witchcraft accepted in lower tribunals. Unlike them, the Paris court used torture half-heartedly at best; of 185 appellants the court had tortured, only one confessed. The tribunal did not use physical duress in any witchcraft case after 1593. In 1624, the *parlement* required an automatic appeal to it from lower courts for all witch trials; by the 1640s the Parisian magistrates rejected witchcraft accusations altogether and even ordered that lower-court judges who tortured prisoners accused of the crime be punished themselves. The witch-hunters charged that these developments suggested the *parlement* had succumbed to diabolical influence.

Like Kramer, the French demonologists insisted that demons were real, flew about the earth and had intercourse with humans. Again like Kramer, they identified females as the likely candidates for diabolical connections. Yet they did not exhibit misogyny anything like Kramer's; most were rather even-handed about the sex of witches. In maligning all women, the *Malleus* occupied a special, perhaps unique, niche within demonology.

Since the existence of witches would confirm the earthly activities of demons, the concern to find them was, at root, related to a fear of atheism. More than a few observers argued that, if there were no witches, then the Devil might not be real either, which could mean that even God might be an unnecessary concept. Giordano da Bergamo may have been the first to say publicly that a belief in witchcraft was essential to true Christian faith. He wrote in 1470, well ahead of Kramer, and possibly he provided a stimulus for the Dominican's arguments.

The dread of atheism and its connection to discussions of witches appeared especially strongly in England. Clergyman Joseph Glanvill fulminated in 1668 against those who thought witches not real but merely 'creatures of melancholy and superstition'. To him, this was a notion fostered by 'ignorance and design'. And even though Meric Casaubon's *Of Credulity and Incredulity*, published in the same year, was sceptical regarding evidence of witchcraft, the author still believed in witches, or said he did, because to doubt was a step toward atheism. The Platonist Henry More evinced a similar concern. But as the belief that God intervened continually in the daily round of the natural world gave way in the late seventeenth century to the idea that he was the divine watchmaker, it became less important to believe that evil forces daily stalked good Christians.

The politics of belief in witches must also be seen against the background of a literary and theological debate on women known as the *querelle des femmes,* which ran from the late Middle Ages into the eighteenth century. This centred at first on the *Roman de la Rose,* a rambling poem begun by Guillaume de Lorris and completed by Jean de Meun around 1278. The poem is an allegory of courtly and carnal love but also a guide to manners, clothing, and the conquest of friends and lovers. Along the way, several characters deliver scathing attacks on women. Jealous Husband offers the worst tirade; he complains that a married woman reveals 'her evil nature'. His own wife is an 'evil bitch'. Husband defies anyone who says, 'I am overconfident in my attacks on all women'. Husband is sure that, 'All women get themselves laid', for the wish of each one 'is always to do it'.

A century later, Christine de Pizan replied to the misogyny she saw in the *Rose,* in her poem *The God of Love's Letter* (1399) and particularly in *The Book of the City of Ladies* (1404-05). She sparked a debate that dominated literary Paris in 1400-02, from which some twenty related treatises, letters, and sermons survive. Prominent men arranged themselves on both sides; one of de Pizan's foremost supporters was Jean Gerson, provost of the University of Paris.

The new demonology followed closely upon the *Rose* debate and in key respects was closely intertwined with it. Thus Nider's *Formicarius* of 1435-37 and Martin Le Franc's *Le Champion des Dames* (1440-42) contributed to a new stereotype of the witch as female, sexually assertive, and eager to be in league with Satan. But neither book is essentially misogynistic. Le Franc's main character is Defender (of women), who refers to the 'valiant Christine'. Le Franc describes how evil persons greet the Devil as their leader, proceed to have sex with him or each other, and receive lethal powders from him. For all that,

Defender maintains that women are essentially good and easily wins the debate.

Gianfresco Pico's *Strix, sive de ludificatione daemonum* ('Strix or The Deceptions of Demons', 1523), features a character who until the last page is sceptical that demons recruit humans. And in *De venificis* (1564), translated in 1575 into English as *A Dialogue of Witches,* Lambert Daneau's Theophilus also succeeds only after much talk in convincing his friend Anthony of the reality of witchcraft. These works do not insist that women are generally vile.

Alfonso de Spina, writing in 1458-60, qualified the issue of gender and demons by indicating that only old women became Satan's lovers. In 1584, Reginald Scot's influential *Discoverie of Witchcraft* all but denied the existence of demons on earth. Scot attacked the *Malleus* on logical grounds and was almost completely unconcerned with what women might or might not do. Other important voices directly defended women; Signor Magnifico in Baldesar Castiglione's *The Book of the Courtier* (1528) praises women and forgoes any mention of witchcraft.

The thorough-going misogynistic sentiments of the *Malleus* were largely discarded. While James VI of Scotland insisted in *Daemonologie* (1597), that there were twenty female witches for every male, the only reason he cited for the disproportion was women's greater frailty. After assuming the English throne in 1603, he refused to promote hunts and even stopped them on occasion.

Even as the witch-hunts intensified, powerful arguments continued to refute the idea that females were naturally evil. In the doleful story of the witch persecutions, misogyny by no means triumphed completely. Europeans could choose among competing views of the nature of women and their purported attraction to Satan. Political and religious questions often hovered just behind those debates.

# For Further Reading

Richard Golden, (ed.), *Encyclopedia of Witchcraft: The Western Tradition* (ABC-CLIO, 2006); Michael Bailey, *Battling Demons: Witchcraft, Heresy, and Reform in the Late Middle Ages* (Pennsylvania State University Press, 2003); Stuart Clark, *Thinking with Demons: the Idea of Witchcraft in Early Modern Europe* (Oxford University Press, 1997); Dylan Elliot, *Fallen Bodies: Pollution, Sexuality, and Demonology in the Middle Ages* (University of Pennsylvania Press, 1999); Jonathan L. Pearl, *The Crime of Crimes: Demonology and Politics in France, 1560-1620* (Wilfrid Laurier University Press, 1999); Eric Wilson, 'Institoris at Innsbruck: Heinrich Institoris, the Summis Desiderantes and the Brixen Witch-Trial of 1485', in Bob Scribner and Trevor Johnson, eds. *Popular Religion in Germany and Central Europe, 1400-1800* (St Martin's Press, 1996).

**ROBERT W. THURSTON** is Phillip R. Shriver Professor of History at Miami University, Oxford, Ohio. His new book *The Witch Hunts* is published by Pearson early next year.

This article first appeared in *History Today*, November 1, 2006, pp. 51–57. Copyright © 2006 by History Today, Ltd. Reprinted by permission.

# A Case for Angry Men and Happy Women

**Observers are quicker to see anger on men's faces and happiness on women's. A simple case of gender stereotyping, or something more deeply rooted?**

BETH AZAR

It might not be surprising that people find it easier to see men as angry and women as happy. Women do tend to be the nurturers and men—well—men do commit 80 to 90 percent of all violent crimes. More surprising, perhaps, is new research suggesting that the connection between men and anger and women and happiness goes deeper than these simple social stereotypes, regardless of how valid they are.

Our brains automatically link anger to men and happiness to women, even without the influence of gender stereotypes, indicate the findings of a series of experiments conducted by cognitive psychologist D. Vaughn Becker, PhD, of Arizona State University at the Polytechnic Campus, with colleagues Douglas T. Kenrick, PhD, Steven L. Neuberg, PhD, K.C. Blackwell and Dylan Smith, PhD. They even turned it around to show that people are more likely to think a face is masculine if it's making an angry expression and feminine if its expression is happy. In fact, their research, published in February's *Journal of Personality and Social Psychology* (Vol. 92, No. 2, pages 179–190), suggests that the cognitive processes that distinguish male and female may be co-mingled with those that distinguish anger from happiness, thereby leading to this perceptual bias.

Becker proposes that this bias may stem from our evolutionary past, when an angry man would have been one of the most dangerous characters around, and a nurturing, happy female might have been just the person to protect you from harm. Evolutionary psychologist Leda Cosmides, PhD, agrees.

"If it's more costly to make a mistake of not recognizing an angry man, you would expect the [perceptual] threshold to be set lower than for recognizing an angry female," says Cosmides, of the University of California, Santa Barbara (UCSB).

## More than a Stereotype

Becker first noticed that people find it easier to detect anger on men and happiness on women a couple years ago while working on his dissertation at Arizona State. He was testing whether viewing an angry or happy expression "primes" people to more quickly identify a subsequent angry or happy expression. Becker confirmed his initial hypothesis, but when he ran an additional analysis to test whether the gender of the person making the facial expression affected his results, he found that gender was, by far, the biggest predictor of how quickly and accurately people identified facial expressions.

Becker couldn't find any mention of this gender effect in the literature. So he set out to confirm that people more quickly link men to anger and women to happiness and figure out why that might be.

In the first of a series of studies, 38 undergraduate participants viewed pictures of faces displaying prototypical angry and happy expressions. They pressed "A" or "H" on a computer keyboard to indicate whether the expression was angry or happy, and the researchers recorded their reaction times. As expected, participants were quicker to label male faces "angry" and female faces "happy."

The researchers then used a version of the "Implicit Association Test" to uncover unconscious biases that study participants may have linking men to anger and women to happiness. The well-documented test allows researchers to examine the strength of connections between categories, which lead to unconscious stereotypes. Becker tested whether study participants unconsciously linked male names with angry words and female names with happy words. Most did.

However, 13 students showed the opposite association (male-happy, female-angry), implying that their unconscious gender stereotypes run counter to those of the general public. It was an ideal opportunity to determine whether gender stereotypes are at the heart of the emotion/gender bias. They weren't: Just like the main group of participants, this subgroup more quickly and accurately categorized male faces as angry and female faces as happy.

"While gender stereotypes clearly influence perception, the implicit association test results made us think the effect is not solely a function of stereotypes," says Becker.

# Overlapping Signals

Since gender stereotypes don't seem to be the culprit, Becker looked toward more deeply rooted causes.

For example, perhaps we see more men with angry faces—on television, in movies—than we see women with angry faces, so our brains are well practiced at recognizing an angry expression on a man. To investigate this possibility, one of the co-authors, Arizona State University graduate student K.C. Blackwell, suggested they flip the experiment around. Instead of asking people to identify facial expressions while the experimenters manipulated gender, they asked them to identify whether a face was male or female while manipulating facial expressions.

"While you can argue that the majority of angry faces we see are male, it's tough to argue that the majority of male faces we see are angry," says Becker. So, if the relationship between emotional expression and gender is simply a matter of how frequently we see anger on men and happiness on women, the effect should disappear when researchers flip around the question. What they found, on the contrary, was that people were faster to identify angry faces as male and happy faces as female.

To follow-up on this finding, they conducted another study in which they used computer graphics software to control not only the intensity of facial expressions, but also the masculinity and femininity of the facial features, creating faces that were just slightly masculine or feminine. As predicted, people were more likely to see the more masculine faces as angrier, even when they had slightly happier expressions than the more feminine faces.

These findings suggest that the brain begins to associate emotions and gender very early in the cognitive process, says Becker. One possible explanation is that the brain has an "angry male detection module" enabling fast and accurate detection of what would have been one of the most dangerous entities in our evolutionary past. But Becker thinks there's a more parsimonious explanation.

"I'm more inclined to think that we've got a situation where the signals for facial expressions and those for masculinity and femininity have merged over time," he says.

In particular, features of masculinity —such as a heavy brow and angular face—somewhat overlap with the anger expression, and those of femininity—roundness and soft features—overlap with the happiness expression.

To test this hypothesis, Becker and his colleagues used computer animation software to individually manipulate masculine and feminine facial features of expressively neutral faces. As predicted, a heavier brow caused participants to see faces as both more masculine and more angry, implying that the mental processes for determining masculinity and anger may be intertwined.

"These results make a lot of sense," says University of Pittsburgh behavioral anthropologist and facial expression researcher Karen Schmidt, PhD. "Faces have always had gender, so if we're always activating gender and affect at the same time then the processing is likely highly coordinated."

The paper raises new and interesting questions about gender, says UCSB postdoctoral student Aaron Sell, PhD, who studies the evolution of gender. "Specifically," he says, "why do male and female faces differ, and what is the nature of emotion detection?"

The data appear to suggest that the anger expression has evolved to make a face seem more masculine, says Sell. Even female faces may communicate anger more effectively the more masculine they appear, says Becker. Future studies will have to tackle questions about the intentions expressed by the angry face and why looking more male would be an evolutionary advantage in communicating these intentions.

"I see this article as opening the book on a new research topic more than having the final say on the issue," says Sell.

---

BETH AZAR is a writer in Portland, Ore.

From *Monitor on Psychology* by Beth Azar, April 2007, pp. 18–19. Copyright © 2007 by American Psychological Association. Reprinted by permission. No further distribution without permission from the American Psychological Association.

# Beauty, Gender and Stereotypes: Evidence from Laboratory Experiments

JAMES ANDREONI AND RAGAN PETRIE

## 1. Introduction

It is well known from labor market studies that beauty and gender can have big effects on earnings. Hamermesh and Biddle (1994) have shown a significant premium to beauty, with attractive people earning more money than unattractive people. There is also a significant and persistent male–female wage gap. Even when controlling for age and experience, men earn about 25% more than women (O'Neill, 1998, 2003). While some of these differences can be attributed to labor market factors, much of the beauty premium and wage gap remains unexplained.

With labor market studies as inspiration, we look at the returns to beauty and gender in an economic laboratory experiment where there are benefits to group cooperation. Typically economic experiments take great pains to shield the identities of subjects from each other, and as such have nothing to say about how appearances may affect earnings.[1] Instead, we reveal the identities of players to one another by showing their digital photos in the experiment. We find that beauty and gender have significant and sometimes unexpected affects on earnings. Furthermore, the behaviors and apparent stereotyping we find may provide some clues into why gender and beauty are so important in the labor market.

The experimental setting we consider is a repeated linear public goods game. While not a direct test of the beauty premium or the wage gap found in the labor market, a public goods game is nonetheless an interesting institution for exploring how such wage differences can emerge in an employment setting. People often work in teams where shirking cannot always be perfectly monitored. This allows for stereotyping to color evaluations of and reactions to both free riding and generosity, and to affect the productivity of the team. A repeated public goods game offers a setting where stereotyping is possible (in groups of more than two) and people have an opportunity to see if their expectations of behavior mesh with actual behavior. When effort is observable, certain people can "set the tone" for the work group. Gender and beauty may affect which people in the group may be emulated by others, how much retribution people take against shirkers and how much cooperation is used to reward generosity. In the end, the beauty and gender of the individuals in the group will affect the cooperation and success of the group as a whole, and the earnings of its individual members.

In our experiment we show each player the digital photos of all other members of their group each round. We have two conditions, one in which only total group contributions are revealed, and another in which information on each player's contribution is revealed.

Our experiments find evidence for a beauty premium. This premium, however, disappears once people know exactly what each group member contributed to the public good. When only the total group contribution is observable, attractive people make more money than unattractive people, even though they are no more or less cooperative, on average, than unattractive people. When individual contributions are observable, the reward to being beautiful disappears. People seem to expect beautiful people to be more cooperative than others, and when their behavior does not meet expectations, people are less cooperative with them. There is also a difference in payoffs for men and women, but not always favoring men.

Women make more money than men when only group contributions are known. This can be attributed primarily to the stereotype that women are more helpful. Men, however, do best when individual contributions to the group are clearly identified. Men earn 15% more when individual contributions are known, compared to when only group contributions are known. Interestingly, women's payoffs do not change. This effect can be attributed entirely to men being better "leaders." They contribute their full endowment more often, and others follow their good example by contributing more in later rounds.

With these results, we begin to see some of the underlying factors that could generate both a beauty premium and a wage gap, especially in team work environments. People give beautiful people the benefit of the doubt in groups and cooperate more with them, thereby enhancing group welfare. Women earn more than men when individual contributions to group output are unknown because they are stereotyped overall to be more helpful. However, once individual contributions are known with certainty, the beauty premium disappears and a male premium replaces it. This appears to be due to people being more willing to follow the lead of generous men. When a man's generous contribution is observed, it engenders more cooperation than a similar contribution by a woman. This effect is amplified when the proportion of men in the group is higher, suggesting a kind of generosity-competition among men. As a result, men earn more money in the experiment when individual contributions to group output are known. In our data, the male premium is almost equal in size to the beauty premium.

Why are these results important? They illustrate how easily subtle sex and beauty stereotypes can influence economic outcomes, and suggests that further study on the role of stereotypes in economics could yield important insights.

## 2. Background

In our experiment subjects see the digital photos of their partners on the computer screen when they make their decisions. In half of our sessions we also tell subjects what each member contributed in the prior round. There are three ways this could have an effect. Simply showing faces could matter, gender and beauty could matter, and finally the information on amounts given could matter.

There is good reason to expect that simply seeing the faces of partners will affect play. Bohnet and Frey (1999a, 1999b) find that visual identification increases cooperation in one-shot Prisoner's Dilemma and Dictator games, and Burnham (2003) reports that giving more than doubles in Dictator games when at least one of the partners sees the other's photograph. Scharleman, Eckel, Kacelnik, and Wilson (2001) see slightly more cooperation when subjects are faced with a photograph of smiling bargaining partners, and Wilson and Eckel (2006) find subjects are more trusting when they see their partner. Solnick and Schweitzer (1999) report a significant effect of attractiveness on offers received and responses made in ultimatum bargaining games.

Gender also has been shown to have an important effect on behavior and payoffs. Eckel and Grossman (1998) find groups of women to be more generous than groups of men in Dictator games, while Andreoni and Vesterlund (2001) find women more equalitarian than men in Dictator Games. Buchan, Croson, and Solnick (2003) report that

women are less trusting but more trustworthy than men in an investment game. Gneezy, Niederle, and Rustichini (2003) find women to be more productive in competitive-pay environments when in same-sex groups, rather than mixed-sex groups. [2] Mobius and Rosenblat (2006) use a labor market experiment to decompose the beauty premium. Castillo, Petrie, and Torero (2007) find that attractive people are more likely to be chosen as group members.

There is also experimental evidence from the sociology and psychology literature that beauty carries a premium. In Prisoner's Dilemma games, people are more cooperative with attractive partners (Mulford, Orbell, Shatto, & Stockard, 1998). Indeed, in a comprehensive review of the literature on beauty, Langlois et al. (2000) find that attractive people are not only judged and treated more favorably but they also behave differently.

Finally, simply knowing what each other player has chosen can also have an impact. For instance, Andreoni and Petrie (2004) find that cooperation is highest when actions can be linked to the actor. Sell and Wilson (1991) also find positive effects when information is available. But, information may also help adjust judgements. Social expectancy theory predicts that if people have different expectations of how, for instance, attractive and unattractive others will behave, then they may have totally different reactions to the same observed behavior depending on which person they are facing (Darley & Fazio, 1980; Zebrowitz, 1997). Furthermore, psychologists suggest that people come to the table with prejudices and stereotypes. However, after meeting someone and gaining more information, these prejudices are often revised or washed away (Devine, 1989). Related to this are issues of similarity and familiarity. People tend to favor those similar to themselves (McPherson, Smith-Lovin, & Cook, 2001), and working with familiar others can reduce transaction costs, as familiarity can enhance trust (Glaeser, Laibson, Scheinkman, & Soutter, 2000).

This suggests that people may behave differently with others when they know their decisions, rather than just their appearance, and that people may want to emulate the choices of "similar" others. Also, people can use their choices to signal information to others in order to establish a link later (such as getting a date). Identification may not only serve to help form impressions before actions, but people may also use identification as a guideline for judging actions and formulating a response.

## 3. Methodology

Our experiments use a linear public goods game. The game is repeated, and subjects make their decisions on a computer. Each session has 20 subjects, and they are randomly divided into 4 groups of 5 subjects. In each round a subject is endowed with 20 tokens that could be invested in a private good or a public good. The private good pays $0.02 per token invested by the individual, and the public good pays $0.01 per token invested by the entire group. Therefore, the marginal return to investing in the public good is 0.5. Each subject is paid based on his investment in the private good and the total group investment in the public good. Subjects play with the same group of 5 people for 8 rounds, then are randomly re-matched to new groups for another 8 rounds, until they play with five different groups, each for 8 rounds. So, subjects play 40 rounds in total in each session.[3]

A digital passport-style photograph is taken of each subject at the beginning of the experimental session. The photo is from the shoulders up and is displayed on top of the screen while subjects make decisions. At the end of each round, the total amount contributed to the public good by all group members is reported. There are two treatments: No Information and Information.[4] In the Information treatment, both the photo and the contribution of that group member from the previous round are displayed. The contribution is listed below each photo, and the photos are rearranged each round with the highest contributor on the left and the lowest on the right. In the No Information treatment, only the photos of each group member are displayed on the screen and no information on individual actions is given.

All treatments were conducted twice. This gives us 80 subjects in total. Subjects were recruited from economics and business classes at the University of Wisconsin–Madison. There were 39 female subjects and 41 male subjects in total, ranging in age from 18 to 29 years (mean 20.3 years old, std dev 1.7 years). Each experimental session took about an hour and a half, and the average subject payment was $26.46 (standard deviation $3.13).

Subsequently, people not involved in the experiments rated each photo as to the person's physical attractiveness or how helpful-looking he/she appears. In total, the raters saw 140 photographs. These photos were of the 80 subjects in the No Information and Information treatments and 60 other photos of subjects in two other public goods game treatments.[5] These other treatments were not used here as they do not allow a clear test of beauty and gender effects.

We chose to have the raters view the 80 subjects randomly mixed among the other 60 photos to get a "global" measure of physical attractiveness and helpfulness. We want to know if a subject is considered physically attractive among his or her peers, not only among the subjects in the session. Drawing on this broader distribution of 140 photographs gives us more information and confidence in our classification and subsequent results.

Each rater rates all 140 photographs along one dimension, physical attractiveness or helpfulness.[6] The raters view the photos on the computer in a random order, assign a rating, and have the ability to move back to previously rated photos to change or check ratings. Raters know they can do this before they begin rating. The raters use a 9-point scale, with 1 indicating "not at all" and 9 indicating "very much so." Raters are told to think of the number 5 as average. There are 15 raters in total. Four women and four men rated each photo in terms of physical attractiveness, and four women and three men rated each photo in terms of helpfulness. The raters were all undergraduates of the University of Wisconsin–Madison, with an average age of 20.7. The raters were paid a flat fee of $15 to rate 140 photographs, and the rating task took 30–45 min to complete.

## 4. Beauty Classification

In this section we discuss our beauty classification methodology, the reliability across those rating beauty, and explain how we define attractiveness.

First, we assume the raters use all 140 photos as a frame of reference. When discussing consensus among raters, therefore, we consider the consensus for all 140 photos. Also, when defining attractiveness, we use all 140 photos as the entire frame of reference.[7]

Turning to the consensus among raters, the inter-rater reliability for physical attractiveness is 0.86, and for helpfulness it is 0.82.[8] These reliability measures compare well with previous research on attractiveness and suggest a strong consensus among raters. Our reliability measures also compare well with previous research on attractiveness, where the range of reliability measures is between 0.85 and 0.95 (Langlois et al., 2000).[9]

There is some variability in the spread and average rating any given rater gave. Some raters use the entire range from 1 to 9, but others truncate the range between 3 and 8. Therefore, each rater's ratings of all photos are standardized by the rater's mean and standard deviation, resulting in mean zero and standard deviation of one. The standardized rating is then transformed back to a one to nine scale.[10] Finally, for each subject, we average the transformed ratings across all raters to give a value of physical attractiveness and helpfulness for each subject. These averaged transformed ratings are used throughout the paper.

Overall, women are rated significantly higher in attractiveness than men. Women receive an average transformed rating of 4.87 and men 3.78. The same holds for helpfulness. Women were rated, on average, at 5.12 and men at 4.30. That is, women are considered more attractive and more helpful-looking than men.

## Table 1  Distribution of Attractiveness

|  | Women | Men |
|---|---|---|
| Attractive | 15 | 3 |
| Middle | 19 | 25 |
| Unattractive | 5 | 13 |
| Total | 39 | 41 |

## Table 2  Average Payoff

|  | No Information | Information |
|---|---|---|
| Attractive | $26.81 ($3.43) | $26.58 ($2.06) |
| Middle | $25.04 ($3.19) | $27.19 ($3.00) |
| Unattractive | $23.91 ($1.65) | $28.83 ($2.03) |
| p-value [a] | 0.0718 | 0.2005 |

[a] Joint Kruskal-Wallis rank sum test for equality of payoffs across the three categories. Standard deviation of the mean in parentheses.

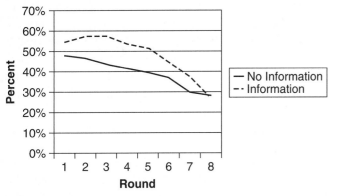

**Figure 1**  Average percent of endowment contributed to the public good.

There are, obviously, many ways of defining an attractive person. We classify someone as attractive if his attractiveness rating lies in the top quartile of the distribution of attractiveness, and we classify someone as unattractive if his attractiveness rating lies in the bottom quartile of the distribution of attractiveness. Anyone in the middle of the distribution was classified as middle attractive. For robustness, we repeated our analysis with both more and less exclusive definitions, with nearly identical results.[11] This classification of subjects is also within the range used by Hamermesh and Biddle (1994), where between 25% and 34% of their samples were classified as above average or higher in attractiveness.[12]

The distribution for the 80 subjects considered here is shown in Table 1.[13] Of the 18 attractive people, 15 are women, and of the 18 unattractive people, 13 are men.[14] We show the full distribution of beauty classifications by group and gender inAppendix Table A1.

# 5. Results

We first discuss average contributions, then the beauty premium and gender differences in payoffs, and finally the interaction of beauty and gender.

## 5.1. Average Contributions

Figure 1 shows average contribution behavior combining all five 8-round sequences for the two treatments.[15]

Contributions are significantly higher in the Information treatment for all rounds except the last two rounds.

## 5.2. Does Beauty Pay?

First consider the No Information treatment. The left-hand side of Table 2 shows that there are positive returns to beauty. Attractive people make 7% more than middle attractive people and 12% more than unattractive people. The returns to beauty are similar to those found by Hamermesh and Biddle (1994), where above average-attractive people earned about 5% more than average-attractive people. The differences across the three attractiveness categories are significant.[16]

While there is evidence for a beauty premium in the No Information treatment, it disappears in the Information treatment and becomes a beauty penalty. The right-hand side of Table 2 illustrates this. In the Information treatment, comparing across all groups, payoffs are statistically independent of beauty. Although, in pair-wise comparisons, unattractive people make 8% more than attractive people. This difference is significant.[17]

We see that returns to beauty are significant, but only when performance cannot be observed. We explore the returns to gender in Section 5.2. Next, we ask why the beauty premium might exist.

### 5.2.1. Behavior of Attractive People

Why do attractive people make more money? Two possible explanations are that they are either more selfish or that they engender more cooperation from others. The first explanation is explored in Table 3. For the No Information treatment, the left-hand side of the table shows that attractive people and unattractive people are, on average, less selfish than middle attractive people. Both attractive and unattractive people contribute between 39% and 44% of their endowment to the public good, and middle attractive people contribute 36%. However, there is no significant difference in contributions across any two groups in pair-wise comparisons.

If higher earnings are due to more selfishness, then middle attractive people should make more money than

**Table 3**  Average Percent Contributed per Round

|  | No Information | Information |
|---|---|---|
| Attractive | 44.2 (19.6) | 35.0 (12.3) |
| Middle | 36.4 (19.5) | 47.2 (16.9) |
| Unattractive | 39.1 (26.2) | 56.8 (21.5) |
| p-value[a] | 0.6743 | 0.1685 |

[a]Joint Kruskal-Wallis rank sum test for equality of contributions across the three categories. Standard deviation of the mean in parentheses.

**Table 4**  Average Percent Contributed by Nonattractive People in Groups of Attractive People, All Rounds

| # of Attractive People in Group | No Information | Information | All |
|---|---|---|---|
| 0 | 30.5 | 56.3 | 47.2 |
| 1 or more[a] | 41.8 | 41.5 | 41.7 |
| p-value | 0.0060 | 0.0001 | 0.1062 |

[a]In the No Information treatment, there are 7 groups with one attractive person, 12 with two attractive people, 7 with three attractive people, 2 with four attractive people, and 1 with five attractive people. In the Information condition, there are 15 groups with one attractive person, and 5 with two attractive people.

unattractive and attractive people since they contribute less on average. But, they do not. Indeed, while there is no significant difference between the average contribution of an attractive and unattractive person, an attractive person makes $2.90 more than an unattractive person. Selfish behavior is *not* an explanation for why attractive people make more money.

For the Information treatment, the right-hand side of Table 3 shows that attractive people contribute less than middle attractive and unattractive people. It seems that cooperation, not beauty, pays. Unattractive people contribute about 62% more than attractive people, and they earn $2.25 more. The difference in contributions and payoffs are significant.[18]

We do not find evidence that the beauty premium observed in the No Information treatment is due to more selfish behavior by attractive people. Indeed, there are no clear trends in contribution behavior and payoffs. Attractive people are no more cooperative than unattractive people, but they still make more money. This suggests that the difference in payoffs may be due to how others respond to beauty. We explore this next.

## 5.2.2. Favoritism and Beauty Stereotypes

Could the observed beauty premium be due to favoritism towards attractive people? If favoritism exists, then we would expect people to react more cooperatively with attractive people than with people who are not attractive. Table 4 explores this hypothesis. We compare the average contribution of nonattractive people (those who are classified as middle and unattractive) in groups with no attractive people and in groups with at least one attractive person. We concentrate on the contributions of nonattractive people because we want to isolate the effects of beauty in a group on the behavior of others.

Table 4 shows that the contributions of nonattractive people depend on the beauty of the other groupmembers. In the No Information treatment, the presence of beauty in

the group does engender more cooperation. The average percent contributed in groups with no attractive people is 30.5%, but in groups with at least one attractive person, the average increases to 41.8%.[19] This difference is significant and suggests the presence of beauty may engender more cooperation. In the Information treatment, however, it is the absence of beauty that engenders more cooperation. The average contribution in groups with at least one attractive person is 41.5%, but in groups with no attractive people, it increases to 56.3%. This difference is also significant, but it contradicts favoritism.

Why do nonattractive people reverse their behavior from one treatment to the next? One hypothesis is rooted in beauty stereotypes and reciprocity. That is, people are more cooperative with attractive people because they believe attractive people are helpful. Langlois et al. (2000) found, in a comprehensive review of the beauty literature, that attractive people are consistently judged and treated more positively. We also find this in our ratings data. Thirty-nine percent of attractive subjects are also judged helpful-looking, 16% of middle attractive people are also judged helpful-looking, but only 6% of unattractive people are judged helpful-looking. This is remarkable because these ratings are by people who did not observe the decisions of the individuals in the photos and they did not rate the subjects in terms of attractiveness. This suggests that people independently *expect* attractive people to be more cooperative.

While there may be reason to believe such a stereotype exists, it is a bit tricky to tease apart because people may hold stereotypes but not act upon them. However, Devine (1989) argues that if people hold stereotypes, once they meet a stereotyped individual and gain more information, they revise or eliminate the stereotype. That is, without information, they act upon the stereotype, but with information, behavior changes. How behavior changes depends on how people revise or react to behavior that does not coincide with the stereotype.

If people hold the stereotype that attractive people are cooperative and people wish to reciprocate cooperation, then we should see changes in behavior in two-ways. First, without information, people should be more cooperative with attractive people. Evidence for this behavioral change can be found in Table 4. Without information, we see that nonattractive people are more cooperative in groups with attractive people than in groups with no attractive people, even though we know that attractive people contribute the same, on average, as unattractive people. This result also holds across rounds. There is higher cooperation in groups with attractive people in *every* round of the 8-round sequence, with the difference increasing over the rounds. In round one, the difference in cooperation is 12 percentage points, and in round eight, it is 17 percentage points.

Second, with information, we should see differences in behavior in groups with attractive people and in groups without attractive people because people can now compare how the actions of attractive people differ from their expectations. How behavior changes depends on whether deviations from expectations are rewarded or punished.[20] In Table 4, we see that with information, on average, nonattractive people are more cooperative in groups with no attractive people. They contribute 36% more.

Could this be punishment of behavior that does not meet expectations? We think so. Looking at behavior in the early rounds of the experiment, when people do not have any information on actual behavior, we see that average contributions are *higher* in groups with at least one attractive person compared to groups with no attractive people. Contributions are 56% and 46% respectively in the very first round. This pattern holds for the first three rounds. By round four though, contributions in groups with at least one attractive person start to decline, and by round 6, contributions are 44% in groups with at least one attractive person and 60% in groups with no attractive people. Contributions remain higher in groups with no attractive people for the remainder of the 40 rounds of the experiment.

What is remarkable about this result is that if people base reciprocity solely on met or unmet expectations on behavior, then there should be no difference in Table 4. The presence of an attractive person in the group should not matter. That it does suggests that people react differently to the same actions of attractive and unattractive people.[21]

In sum, it appears that people discriminate based on beauty stereotypes. Attractive people are given the benefit of the doubt when group members do not see performance, even though they contribute amounts similar to unattractive people. Indeed, the presence of beauty

engenders more mutual cooperation, and this may explain the beauty premium. However, when group members can evaluate performance, the presence of beauty engenders less cooperation. People seem to expect attractive people to be more cooperative than average. When they are not, others are less cooperative with them, and the beauty premium disappears.

### 5.2.3. Gender Differences in Beauty Stereotypes

Does favoritism differ by gender? In the No Information treatment, it does not. Both nonattractive men and women are significantly more cooperative in groups with attractive people than in groups with no attractive people.

In the Information treatment, only men significantly decrease their contributions in groups of attractive people compared to groups with no attractive people. In groups with no attractive people, men contribute 60.7%, but this declines to 39.8% in groups with at least one attractive person. Women decrease their contributions, from 50.0% to 44.1%, but this is not significant.[22] This may mean that nonattractive men and women hold different beauty stereotypes. Or, they may hold the same stereotype, but only men act upon it.

These results suggest that there are no gender differences in favoritism, but there may be in beauty stereotypes. In the No Information treatment, both men and women are more cooperative with an attractive person in the group. Men and women, however, react differently to information and attractive people in the group. In the Information treatment, the reduction in contributions in groups of attractive people is driven by the actions of men.[23]

## 5.3. Does Gender Pay?

We now move the focus from beauty to gender. Overall, men and women make the same amount of money. Table 5 shows that both men and women make around $26.50 over both treatments. However, women make $1.67 more than men in the No Information treatment, and men make $1.38 more than women in the Information treatment. The former difference is significant at the 10% level, and the latter is not.

Within gender, women make about the same across treatments. They make $26.22 in No Information and $26.80 in Information. By contrast, the payoff for men is 15% higher in the Information treatment compared to the No Information treatment. This difference is significant.

There is a gender difference, but that switches from favoring women to men when actions are known. There are large benefits to information, but only men reap them. Again, there are two possible explanations. Women could be more selfish than men, or men may engender more

## Table 5 Average Payoff

| | Women | Men | p-value[a] |
|---|---|---|---|
| Both treatments | $26.50 | $26.41 | 0.9463 |
| No Information | $26.22 | $24.55 | 0.0962 |
| Information | $26.80 | $28.18 | 0.1162 |
| p-value[a] | 0.5273 | 0.0002 | |

[a]Pair-wise Wilcoxon test for equality of payoffs across the two treatments/genders.

## Table 6 Average Contribution, Zero Tokens, and All Tokens Both Treatments

| | Men | Women | p-value |
|---|---|---|---|
| Average contribution (%) | 46.7 | 40.7 | 0.1938 |
| % of times zero tokens | 27.7 | 16.3 | 0.0594 |
| % of times all tokens | 22.1 | 9.4 | 0.0012 |

cooperation with their performance than women. We discuss these possibilities next.

### 5.3.1. Behavior of Men and Women

Are women more selfish than men? Table 6 shows that, on average, women are no more or less cooperative than men–men give roughly 15% more than women, but this is not significant. However, men play the extremes significantly more than women.[24] Men contribute zero tokens 27.7% of the time, but women do so only 16.3% of the time. Women also contribute all of their tokens only 9.4% of the time, compared to men who do so 22.1% of the time. Similar results hold for each treatment separately.

This suggests that the gender premium to women is not due solely to more selfishness on their part. Women seem to be benefiting from a combination of their slightly lower contributions and their beauty. While they are not significantly more selfish, they are more beautiful, and returns to beauty are high. We return to the interaction of beauty and gender in Section 5.4. First, we address the question of why men do better in the Information treatment than women.

### 5.3.2. "Good Examples" and Sex Stereotypes

Are people more cooperative with men than with women? Table 7 reports the results of linear regressions showing how the average individual contribution to the group is affected by the gender composition of the group.[25] The regressions include individual fixed effects.[26] Model 1 shows that, over both treatments, as the number of men in the group increases,[27] the average individual contribution

## Table 7 OLS Regression Coefficients Dependent Variable: Average Contribution to the Group Pooled Data

| | Model 1 | Model 2 |
|---|---|---|
| Constant | 6.36 (0.0002) | 8.41 (0.0001) |
| % Men in group other than self | 3.07 (0.0011) | −0.36 (0.7970) |
| % Men in group other than self * Info | | 6.06 (0.0011) |
| Individual fixed effects | Yes | Yes |
| $R^2$ | 0.62 | 0.63 |

Note: p-values in parentheses, n = 400.

## Table 8 Tobit Regression Coefficients Dependent Variable: Average Probability of Contributing Full Endowment Men Only

| | Model 1 | Model 2 |
|---|---|---|
| Constant | −0.29 (0.1683) | 0.04 (0.8543) |
| % Men in group other than self | 0.38 (0.0221) | −0.15 (0.5533) |
| % Men in group other than self * Info | | 0.87(0.0076) |
| Individual fixed effects | Yes | Yes |
| Log-likelihood | −87.20 | −83.75 |

Note: p-values in parentheses, n = 205.

of group members increases as well.[28] These effects are significant. This suggests that people cooperate more with men than with women, even though Table 6 showed that men give no more on average than women.

When we consider treatment effects, Model 2 shows that, with information, the cooperation effect of more men in the group increases two fold.[29] Without information, the effect is not significantly different from zero. That is, people are more cooperative in groups with more men only when performance is observable.[30] For example, the average individual contribution to a group where half of the group, other than oneself, is comprised of men will be about 3 tokens higher in the Information treatment than in the No Information treatment.

Could this significant increase in cooperation with information be explained by favoritism based on sex stereotypes? If people expect attractive people to be more cooperative, could they also expect women to be more cooperative, especially since they are rated higher in attractiveness? From our ratings data on helpfulness, indeed, more people expect women to be helpful than men, but, perhaps more importantly, more people expect men to be more *unhelpful* than women.[31] Thirty-nine percent of men are rated as unhelpful, but only 13% of women are rated as such.

**Table 9** OLS Regression Coefficients Dependent Variable: Total Individual Payoff (Sum Across All 8 Rounds) with a Group

| | Pooled ($n = 400$) | Women ($n = 195$) | Men ($n = 205$) |
|---|---|---|---|
| Constant | **3.91** (0.44) | **4.21** (0.80) | **4.19** (0.60) |
| ln(Attractive) | **0.37** (0.23) | 0.26 (0.37) | 0.28 (0.34) |
| # Attractive people in group other than self | **0.28** (0.10) | **0.30** (0.12) | **0.21** (0.12) |
| % Men in group other than self | 0.63 (0.44) | 0.47 (0.64) | 0.30 (0.61) |
| Info | **1.54** (0.65) | 0.81 (1.17) | 0.88 (0.86) |
| ln(Attractive) * Info | **− 0.59** (0.36) | − 0.51 (0.58) | − 0.33 (0.51) |
| # Attractive people in group other than self * Info | **− 0.56** (0.19) | **− 0.56** (0.23) | **− 0.44** (0.24) |
| % Men in group other than self * Info | 0.30(0.62) | 1.00(0.88) | 1.23(0.90) |
| Individual and group random effects | Yes | Yes | Yes |
| $\overline{R}^2$ | 0.14 | 0.10 | 0.21 |

Note: Standard errors in parentheses, and significant values (*p*-value ≤ 10%) in bold.

This would suggest that people are more cooperative as the number of men in the group increases because they discover that men are not as unhelpful as they expected. So, even though men give no more on average than women, men may be able to engender more cooperation because they exceed expectations.

Perhaps a stronger explanation of men's ability to engender cooperation may come from the "good example" that they set. As noted earlier, men are more likely than women to contribute nothing or contribute their full endowment, but as the number of men in the group increases, the probability of contributing zero declines. A Tobit regression on the average probability of contributing zero in a group shows a significant decline in this probability as the percent of men in the group increases.[32] This holds for pooled data, for men only, and for women only.[33]

While the probability of contributing the "bad" extreme declines with the presence of more men, the probability of contributing the "good" extreme increases, but only for men. Table 8 shows how the average probability that a man will contribute the full endowment to the group changes as the percent of men in the group increases.[34] The results for women are similar, but insignificant. Model 1 shows that men are more likely to contribute all of their tokens as the percent of men in the group increases, and Model 2 shows that, when performance is known, men are almost twice as likely to contribute the full endowment.[35]

This suggests that the reason that men make more money when performance is known is because they put on a better performance, especially in the presence of other men. Moreover, their performance may engender more cooperation from others.[36] While men free ride more than women, they also set a "good example" more than women. As the composition of the group changes from women to men, both men and women free ride less, but men set the

"good example" even more.[37] This significantly increases the contributions of others in the group, and men make more money.

## 5.4. The Combined Effects of Beauty and Gender

Do the effects of beauty and gender hold when we control for them together? Table 9 shows the effects of beauty and gender on individual payoff in each group.[38]

We use the continuous measure for beauty, rather than the dummy variables of attractive and unattractive, because in the Information treatment there is not one man classified as attractive. To account for nonlinearities, we use the natural log transformation of beauty.[39] The regressions control for individual and group effects.[40]

In the pooled data, the beauty premium holds, even when controlling for the beauty and gender composition of the group. The returns to beauty increase at a decreasing rate. Looking at men and women separately, the beauty premium is not significant. Also, the beauty premium disappears when individual performance is known and becomes a beauty penalty.

Interestingly, even when controlling for individual beauty, both men and women earn more money when the number of attractive people in the group increases. The premium to being in the presence of beauty, however, only holds when individual performance is unknown. Once the group knows what each individual member contributes, the premium disappears.[41]

Table 10 shows the effects of beauty and gender on average contributions in each group.[42] As with the payoff regressions, these control for individual and group effects.

Looking at contributions, we see that average contributions are lower in groups with more attractive people

**Table 10** OLS regression Coefficients Dependent Variable: Average Contribution to the Group

| | Pooled | Women | Men |
|---|---|---|---|
| | (n = 400) | (n = 195) | (n = 205) |
| Constant | **7.87** (2.73) | 5.27 (4.83) | **6.51** (3.65) |
| ln(Attractive) | 0.38 (1.63) | 1.06 (2.69) | 1.61 (2.51) |
| # Attractive people in group other than self | 0.51 (0.41) | 0.67 (0.48) | 0.26 (0.48) |
| % Men in group other than self | − 2.25 (2.14) | − 0.56 (2.58) | − 1.12 (2.49) |
| Info | 3.49 (4.15) | 5.68 (7.09) | 2.23 (5.42) |
| ln(Attractive) * Info | − 2.80 (2.60) | − 4.58 (4.15) | − 1.19 (3.78) |
| # Attractive people in group other than self * Info | **− 1.36** (0.84) | − 0.94 (0.96) | **− 1.82** (0.95) |
| % Men in group other than self * Info | **6.12** (2.96) | **6.33** (3.52) | **4.84** (3.57) |
| Individual and group random effects | Yes | Yes | Yes |
| $\overline{R}^2$ | 0.09 | 0.08 | 0.09 |

*Note:* Standard errors in parentheses, and significant values (*p*-value ≤ 10%) in bold.

when individual contributions are revealed. As we saw previously, this change in behavior is driven by men. We also see that people are more cooperative in groups with more men when contributions are known, confirming earlier results.[43]

In sum, when controlling for individual beauty and gender and for the beauty and gender composition of the group, our main results still hold. There is a premium to beauty, but that premium disappears when performance is known. Others also benefit from being in the presence of beauty because people are more cooperative. This monetary return, however, disappears when group members can clearly identify individual contributions. People are far less cooperative as the number of attractive people in the group increases. Being in a group with more men does increase average contributions, but only when individual contributions are observed.

# 6. Discussion and Conclusions

We used laboratory experiments to examine the returns to beauty and gender in a public goods game. Group members were identified with digital passport-style photographs. In one treatment, group members knew only the total amount contributed to the public good by the group, while in the other treatment they also knew the exact contribution of each group member. Subjects' photos were later independently rated in terms of physical attractiveness and how helpful-looking the subject appears.

In general, our results show significant and surprising effects of beauty and gender on earnings. When performance is unknown, people tend to reward beauty and females. And, when performance is known, the beauty

premium disappears and the female premium switches to a male premium. These results appear to be rooted in beauty and sex stereotypes and have three main components.

First, relative beauty is rewarded. Attractive people make more money than middle attractive people, who in turn make more money than unattractive people. This premium to beauty mirrors Hamermesh and Biddle's (1994) results and can be quite large. Attractive people earn 12% more than unattractive people. This premium disappears and becomes a penalty when actions are known. We find the beauty premium is not due to the actions of attractive people, but seems to be due to the expectations of how attractive people will behave, as suggested by psychologists' social expectancy theory. People expect beautiful people to be more cooperative, and thus behave more cooperatively toward them when they are in the same group. But when information on decisions reveals that attractive people are no more or less cooperative than others, contributions decline relative to groups with no attractive people. This seems to reflect disappointed stereotypes of attractive people.

Second, women benefit for being stereotyped as helpful. Women make 7% more than men when contributions are not known. Looking more closely, we find the higher payoff enjoyed by women is not due to more selfishness on their part but, rather, may be a consequence of their beauty and sex stereotypes. Women are rated significantly higher in attractiveness than men, and their higher payoff seems to be the reward to their beauty. Also, because women are stereotyped to be more helpful than men, people are more cooperative in groups of women than in groups of men when performance is unknown.

Third, when performance is known, the gender premium switches from a female premium to a male premium. That is, while women gain the benefits of beauty, men gain the benefits of information. The payoff for men is 15% higher when performance is known. The payoff for women does not change. Indeed, this benefit to information for men is comparable in value to the attractiveness premium for women. Why do men attain this information benefit and women do not? With information on actions, groups with more men are able to engender more cooperation from others. That is, they set good examples that are followed by others. Free riding declines in groups with more men, and, in apparent male-competition, men are more likely to contribute their full endowment as the proportion of men in the group increases.

There are obvious implications of these results for experimental methodology. Indeed, this work justifies the extreme measures experimenters take to protect the identities of subjects. But are there implications of the beauty and gender effects we found for the real world?

The most striking result from this research is that, on average, men and women did not behave very differently, and attractive people did not behave appreciably differently than unattractive people. Nonetheless, beauty and gender had significant effects on earnings. This happened because beauty and gender affect the way people were treated by others.

Hamermesh and Biddle (1994) found that there is some sorting of beautiful people into occupations in which employers report that looks may increase productivity, such as in sales, but that this is not strong enough to explain much of the premium to beauty. This leaves social effects rather than productivity effects as the natural place to look for explanations. Our research suggests one effect of beauty is rooted in stereotypes. Beautiful people tend to be in more successful teams because other team members are more cooperative in the presence of beautiful people. This is true when effort is not observable, and suggests that a beauty premium may be more likely to exist when productivity is not perfectly observed, implying that beautiful people may also sort into occupations where individual productivity is difficult to measure. This hypothesis could be examined with labor market data.

The gender gap can also possibly be explained by a different stereotype for men. While beautiful people benefit from a stereotype of being more cooperative team members, men in our experiment benefit from exceeding the low expectations others have for them. People seem to expect men to be less helpful than they are. When they see men exceeding expectations, they respond by following their lead. Men may be seen as better leaders despite the expectation that they are more selfish. In addition, when men are in groups together, they benefit from a kind of male competitiveness for contributing to the public good. In the end, men are more likely to be in successful groups when information on contributions is known, and the more men in the group the greater the advantage to men. This again suggests hypotheses that can be tested with labor market data. Professions where effort can be verified more easily may favor men, and male-dominated professions may also have a bigger wage gap.

This paper illustrates the possibility for subtle stereotypes to have major economic impacts. However, economists are only beginning to consider seriously causes and consequences of stereotypes. Further work–including theory, policy and experiments–could fruitfully shed light on this important issue.

# Notes

1. An important exception to this is research by Mobius and Rosenblat (2006) who use a labor market experiment to decompose the beauty premium. In their experiment, an employer receives a precise measure of a worker's productivity from a practice round and decides a wage to pay the worker. The interaction between the employer and worker is one shot, so the employer cannot verify if a beautiful worker was as productive as originally thought.

2. See Eckel and Grossman (forthcoming) for a review of gender differences in laboratory experiments.

3. Very few subjects knew other subjects in the experiment (87% of the subjects had "never met" any other subject in the experiment).

4. Note that, in Andreoni and Petrie (2004), the No Information treatment is called "Photos" and the Information treatment is called "Information-and-Photos."

5. The photos of the 60 other subjects come from the same cohort as the 80 subjects in the No Information and Information treatments. They were recruited at the same time as the 80 other subjects from economics and business school classes at the University of Wisconsin – Madison. Of the 60 subjects, 33 are male and 27 are female, ranging in age from 18 to 28 years (mean: 20.1 years old).

6. We do not define either "attractive" or "helpful" for the raters, but let them apply their own definitions. This is done so that the views of our raters are more similar to those of the actual subjects. The instructions state, "You will be shown a series of photographs of ordinary people. For each photograph, you are asked to judge how physically attractive (helpful) you think the person is."

7. Note that similar, yet not as strong, results hold if we define the frame of reference to be only the 80 photos of the subjects in the Information and No Information treatments. So, it appears that the frame of reference is important in defining who is attractive. We opt to base the analysis of this paper on the larger frame of reference because it improves the accuracy and predictive power of our ratings.

8. We use the Cronbach coefficient alpha for standardized variables (Cortina, 1993; SAS Institute Inc., 1988). This measures the correlation between all raters and adjusts for

rater specific mean and variance. While this rating raises automatically as the number of raters increases (we thank Daniel Hamermesh for pointing this out), we report it in order to compare with other studies using attractiveness ratings. Using an alternative measure of reliability, an intra-class correlation coefficient (two-way random effects model), we find similar results. The ICC coefficient is 0.7506. We also find strong agreement among men and women in terms of who is attractive.

9. Langlois et al. (2000) report an acceptable range of reliability measures is between 0.85 and 0.95. The fact that our measures fall on the lower end of this range may reflect our 9-point scale. Most scales were 5-point or 7-point.

10. Let $x_{ij}$ be the standardized rating for person $i$ by rater $j$. Then the transformation is $(x_{ij} - \min_k(x_{kj}) * 8)/(\max_x(x_{kj}) - \min_k(x_{kj})) = 1)$. This preserves the ordinal ranking and gives us a rating between 1 and 9. This transformation will prove useful when looking at the combined effects of beauty and gender.

11. We also classified subjects as attractive and unattractive by using the 20th-percentile and the 30th-percentile. Results using the 20th-percentile cut-off are strikingly similar to those using the quartile cut-off. Results using the 30th-percentile cut-off follow similar trends to those using the quartile cut-off, however some results that are statistically significant with the quartile cut-off are not with the 30th-percentile cut-off.

12. Note that Hamermesh and Biddle (1994) did not use the same range of their data to classify people as unattractive. Between 7% and 17% of their samples were classified as below average or lower in attractiveness.

13. The distributions of attractiveness are similar across the 140 subjects and the sample of 80 subjects. The hypothesis of independence across the two distributions cannot be rejected by a Chi-Square test ($p$-value = 0.5098).

14. We have also done the analysis in the paper using a gender-conditional attractiveness measure. With this measure, a person was classified as attractive if he or she fell in the upper quartile of the distribution of attractiveness for his or her respective gender. Using this classification, there are an equal number of men and women classified as attractive. All the results presented in the paper hold if we use the gender-conditional measure.

15. This means that Round 1 in Figure 1 is rounds 1, 9, 17, 25, and 33.

16. In pair-wise tests using the Wilcoxon rank sum test, attractive people almost make significantly more than middle attractive people ($p$-value = 0.1030) and do make significantly more than unattractive people ($p$-value = 0.0357). Middle attractive people do not make significantly more than unattractive people.

17. Using a Wilcoxon rank sum test, unattractive people make significantly more than attractive people ($p$-value = 0.0662), and there are no significant differences across other groups.

18. Using a Wilcoxon rank sum test, the $p$-value for the difference in the contributions of attractive and unattractive people is 0.0498.

19. Similar results hold if we include the contributions of attractive people. In this case, contributions increase to 42.9% in the No Information treatment and decrease to 41.5% in the Information treatment. This suggests that it is not merely nonattractive people who are affected by the presence of attractive people in the group.

20. Bosman and van Winden (2002) find that subjects that expected their partners to share more of the pie than they actually did were more likely to punish in a power-to-take game.

21. In the very first round of the experiment, before any experience is gained with attractive people, there is no significant difference across treatments in the average contribution of nonattractive people in groups with attractive people. This suggests that subjects start out with the same beliefs across treatments over the actions of attractive people.

22. Strikingly similar results hold if attractive men and women are included in the average.

23. Fershtman and Gneezy (2001) also find that men are more apt to hold and act on stereotypes. Using trust experiments, they find that men in Isreali society are more likely to act on ethnic stereotypes than women.

24. Men are found to have higher variance in behavior relative to women in other research. Andreoni and Vesterlund (2001) find that men are more likely to be completely selfish or completely altruistic. Pinker (2002) finds higher variance in the IQ scores of men relative to women.

25. The dependent variable is the average amount a subject contributed to a group over the 8 rounds he played with that group. That is, the average that individual i contributes to group $j$ is defined as $\bar{g}_{ij} = \sum_{t=1}^{8} g_{ijt}/8$. Each subject plays with 5 different groups, so in total, there are 400 observations for the 80 subjects.

26. These are captured with identification dummy variables. Note that these variables also capture the treatment effects of information.

27. This is the percent of men in the group other than the subject himself. So, for a group with three men and two women, each man would have 50% of the group as men, and each woman would have 75% of the group as men.

28. The dependent variable, average contribution to the public good, is censored at zero and 20 since subjects are only endowed with 20 tokens in each round. Although the models in Table 7 were run as OLS linear regressions, very similar results hold if the models are run as a double-truncated Tobit.

29. Across treatments, there is no significant difference in the distribution of the gender composition of groups. The $p$-value for a Fischer Exact test is 0.522. Thus, the significant treatment effects are not due to one treatment having more groups with more men than the other treatment.

30. Note that this effect also holds for both men and women separately.

31. Twenty-three percent of women are rated in the upper quartile of helpfulness compared to 15% of men.

32. The dependent variable is the average probability that a subject contributed zero tokens to a group over the 8 rounds he played with that group. That is, the average probability that individual i contributes zero tokens to group j is defined as $\bar{p}_{ij} = \sum_{t=1}^{8} I(1|g_{ijt} = 0)/8$, where $I(\cdot)$ is an indicator function that equals 1 when the contribution was 0 tokens. The coefficient on the variable "% men in group other than self" is, $\beta = -0.24$ ($s.d = 0.07$).

33. When performance is known, as in Model 2 in Table 8, the probability of free riding declines even further, but the effects are insignificant.

34. The dependent variable is the average probability that a subject contributed his full endowment to a group over the 8 rounds he played with that group. That is, the average probability that individual i contributes his full endowment to group $j$ is defined as $\bar{p}_{ij} = \sum_{t=1}^{8} I(1|g_i = 20)_{ijt} / 8$, where $I(\cdot)$ is an indicator function that equals 1 when the contribution was 20 tokens.

35. Marginal effects of the percent of men in the group on contributing the full endowment are 0.10 in the No information treatment and 0.24 in the Information treatment.

36. This result is consistent with Camerer, Ho, Chong, and Weigelt's (2002) idea of "strategic teaching." A person, recognizing that others learn in a repeated game, would make choices to maximize long-run payoffs. This would suggest that men set a good example to ensure cooperation, and higher earnings, in the future.

37. This male competitiveness for contributing to the public good also fits well with evidence from biology, i.e. Zahavi's (1975, 1977) theory of costly signaling. Zahavi, Zahavi, Zahavi-Ely, and Ely (1997) finds that alpha male Arabian babbler songbirds compete over altruistic acts. While most experimental work on altruism in groups suggests that men are less generous than women (Dufwenberg & Muren, 2006; List, 2004), our results are consistent with returns to competitiveness in the labor market. Browne (1998) looks at biological differences, such as male competitiveness and risk taking, and links these with different labor market outcomes.

38. The dependent variable is the total payoff a subject earned in a group over the 8 rounds he played with that group. Each subject plays with 5 different groups, so in total, there are 400 observations for the 80 subjects.

39. We also tried other specifications of the beauty measure and got similar results. Other specifications include beauty and beauty squared, an exponential transformation of beauty, negative of the inverse of beauty, and an arcsin transformation of beauty. We report the results with the natural log transformation for ease of interpretation.

40. To address unobservable correlation across individuals and across individuals in the same group, the estimates use a two-way random effects error correction model.

41. If we control for the interaction between the number of attractive people in the group and the percent of men in the group, the same qualitative results hold. However, the returns to being in a group with attractive people is no longer significant.

42. The dependent variable is the average contribution a subject makes in a group over the 8 rounds he played with that group. Each subject plays with 5 different groups, so in total, there are 400 observations for the 80 subjects.

43. If we interact the number of attractive people in the group and the percent of men, the same qualitative results hold. However, contributions are no longer significantly lower in groups with attractive people.

# References

Andreoni, J., & Petrie, R. (2004). Public goods experiments without confidentiality: A glimpse into fund-raising. *Journal of Public Economics, 88*(7–8), 1605–1623.

Andreoni, J., & Vesterlund, L. (2001). Which is the fair sex? Gender differences in altruism. *The Quarterly Journal of Economics, 116*(1), 293–312.

Bohnet, I., & Frey, B. (1999a). The sound of silence in prisoner's dilemma and dictator games. *Journal of Economic Behavior and Organization, 38,* 43–57.

Bohnet, I., & Frey, B. (1999b). Social distance and other-regarding behavior in dictator games: Comment. *American Economic Review, 89*(1), 335–339.

Bosman, R., & van Winden, F. (2002). Emotional hazard in a power-to-take experiment. *The Economic Journal, 112,* 147–169.

Browne, K. R. (1998). An evolutionary account of women's workplace status. *Managerial and Decision Economics, 19*(7/8), 427–440.

Buchan, N., Croson, R., & Solnick, S. (2003). Trust and gender: An examination of behavior, biases, and beliefs in the investment game. Working Paper, The Wharton School, University of Pennsylvania.

Burnham, T. (2003). Engineering altruism: A theoretical and experimental investigation of anonymity and gift giving. *Journal of Economic Behavior and Organization, 50,* 133–144.

Camerer, C., Ho, T., Chong, J.-K., & Weigelt, K. (2002). Strategic teaching and equilibrium models of repeated trust and entry games, Working Paper, California Institute of Technology.

Castillo, M., Petrie, R., & Torero, M. (2007). Social barriers to cooperation: Experiments on the extent and nature of discrimination in Peru. EXCEN Working Paper 2007-1, Georgia State University.

Cortina, J. M. (1993). What is coefficient alpha? An examination of theory and applications. *Journal of Applied Psychology, 78,* 98–104.

Darley, J. M., & Fazio, R. H. (1980). Expectancy confirmation processes arising in the social interaction sequence. *American Psychologist, 35,* 867–881.

Devine, P. (1989). Stereotypes and prejudice: Their automatic and controlled components. *Journal of Personality and Social Psychology, 56*(1), 5–18.

Dufwenberg, M., & Muren, A. (2006). Gender composition in teams. *Journal of Economic Behavior and Organization, 61,* 50–54.

Eckel, C., & Grossman, P. (Forthcoming). Differences in the economic decisions of men and women: Experimental evidence. In C. Plott & V. Smith (Eds.), *Handbook of Experimental Economic Results.* New York: Elsevier.

Eckel, C., & Grossman, P. (1998). Are women less selfish than men? Evidence from dictator experiments. *Economic Journal, 108*(448), 726–735.

Fershtman, C., & Gneezy, U. (2001). Discrimination in a segmented society: An experimental approach. *Quarterly Journal of Economics, 116*(1), 351–377.

Glaeser, E., Laibson, D., Scheinkman, J., & Soutter, C. (2000). Measuring trust. *The Quarterly Journal of Economics, 115*(3), 811–846.

Gneezy, U., Niederle, M., & Rustichini, A. (2003). Performance in competitive environments: Gender differences. *Quarterly Journal of Economics, 118*(3), 1049–1074.

Hamermesh, D., & Biddle, J. (1994). Beauty and the labor market. *American Economic Review, 84*(5), 1174–1194.

Langlois, J., Klakanis, L., Rubenstein, A., Larson, A., Hallam, M., & Smoot, M. (2000). Maxims or myths of beauty? A meta-analysis and theoretical review. *Psychological Bulletin, 126*(3), 390–423.

List, J. (2004). Young, selfish and male: Field evidence of social preferences. *The Economic Journal, 114,* 121–149.

McPherson, M., Smith-Lovin, L., & Cook, J. M. (2001). Birds of a feather: Homophily in social networks. *Annual Review of Sociology, 27,* 415–444.

Mobius, M., & Rosenblat, T. (2006). Why beauty matters. *American Economic Review, 96*(1), 222–235.

Mulford, M., Orbell, J., Shatto, C., & Stockard, J. (1998). Physical attractiveness, opportunity, and success in everyday exchange. *American Journal of Sociology, 103*(6), 1565–1592.

O'Neill, J. (1998). The trend in the male–female wage gap in the United States, Ferber, Marianne (Ed.), *Women in the Labour Market. Volume 1, Elgar Reference Collection. International Library of Critical Writings in Economics, 90* (pp. 520–545).

O'Neill, J. (2003). The gender gap in wages, circa 2000. *American Economic Review, 93*(2), 309–314.

Pinker, S. (2002). *The blank slate: The modern denial of human nature.* New York: Viking Press.

SAS Institute Inc. (1988). SAS Procedures Guide: Release 6.03 Edition, Cary, NC: SAS Institute, Inc.

Scharleman, J., Eckel, C., Kacelnik, A., & Wilson, R. (2001). The value of a smile: Game theory with a human face. *Journal of Economic Psychology, 22*(5), 617–640.

Sell, J., & Wilson, R. (1991). Levels of information and contributions to public goods. *Social Forces, 70*(1), 107–124.

Solnick, S., & Schweitzer, M. (1999). The influence of physical appearance and gender on ultimatum game decisions. *Organizational Behavior and Human Decision Processes, 79*(3), 199–215.

Wilson, R., & Eckel, C. (2006). Judging a book by its cover: Beauty and expectations in the trust game. *Political Research Quarterly, 59*(2), 189–202.

Zahavi, A. (1975). Mate selection: A selection for a handicap. *Journal of Theoretical Biology, 53,* 205–214.

Zahavi, A. (1977). Reliability in communication systems and the evolution of altruism. In B. Stonehouse & C. Perrins (Eds.), *Evolutionary Ecology.* London: MacMillan.

Zahavi, A., Zahavi, A., Zahavi-Ely, N., & Ely, M. P. (1997). *The handicap principle: A missing piece of Darwin's puzzle.* Oxford: Oxford University Press.

Zebrowitz, L. A. (1997). *Reading faces: Window to the soul?* Boulder, CO: Westview Press.

**Acknowledgements**—We are grateful to Terence Burnham, Marco Castillo, Rachel Croson, Daniel Hamermesh, and Bart Lipman for helpful comments. We also thank the National Science Foundation for financial support.

# Appendix A

## Table A1 Distribution of Attractive and Unattractive Men and Women Across All Groups

| Treatment | Session | Group | Attractive Men | Unattractive Men | Attractive Women | Unattractive Women |
|---|---|---|---|---|---|---|
| No Info | 1 | 1 | 0 | 1 | 0 | 1 |
| No Info | 1 | 2 | 1 | 2 | 0 | 0 |
| No Info | 1 | 3 | 0 | 0 | 3 | 0 |
| No Info | 1 | 4 | 0 | 1 | 0 | 1 |
| No Info | 1 | 5 | 0 | 1 | 0 | 1 |
| No Info | 1 | 6 | 0 | 2 | 0 | 0 |
| No Info | 1 | 7 | 0 | 0 | 2 | 0 |
| No Info | 1 | 8 | 1 | 1 | 1 | 1 |
| No Info | 1 | 9 | 0 | 1 | 0 | 1 |
| No Info | 1 | 10 | 1 | 2 | 1 | 0 |
| No Info | 1 | 11 | 0 | 1 | 2 | 0 |
| No Info | 1 | 12 | 0 | 0 | 0 | 1 |
| No Info | 1 | 13 | 0 | 1 | 2 | 0 |
| No Info | 1 | 14 | 0 | 2 | 0 | 1 |
| No Info | 1 | 15 | 0 | 0 | 0 | 1 |
| No Info | 1 | 16 | 1 | 1 | 1 | 0 |
| No Info | 1 | 17 | 1 | 1 | 1 | 0 |
| No Info | 1 | 18 | 0 | 0 | 0 | 1 |
| No Info | 1 | 19 | 0 | 1 | 2 | 0 |
| No Info | 1 | 20 | 0 | 2 | 0 | 1 |
| No Info | 2 | 1 | 1 | 0 | 2 | 0 |
| No Info | 2 | 2 | 1 | 1 | 2 | 0 |
| No Info | 2 | 3 | 0 | 0 | 1 | 0 |

*(continued)*

**Table A1** Distribution of Attractive and Unattractive Men and Women
Across All Groups *(continued)*

| Treatment | Session | Group | Attractive Men | Unattractive Men | Attractive Women | Unattractive Women |
|-----------|---------|-------|----------------|------------------|------------------|--------------------|
| No Info | 2 | 4 | 0 | 1 | 2 | 0 |
| No Info | 2 | 5 | 1 | 0 | 1 | 0 |
| No Info | 2 | 6 | 0 | 1 | 1 | 0 |
| No Info | 2 | 7 | 0 | 1 | 1 | 0 |
| No Info | 2 | 8 | 1 | 0 | 4 | 0 |
| No Info | 2 | 9 | 0 | 0 | 1 | 0 |
| No Info | 2 | 10 | 0 | 1 | 1 | 0 |
| No Info | 2 | 11 | 2 | 1 | 1 | 0 |
| No Info | 2 | 12 | 0 | 0 | 4 | 0 |
| No Info | 2 | 13 | 0 | 1 | 0 | 0 |
| No Info | 2 | 14 | 2 | 0 | 1 | 0 |
| No Info | 2 | 15 | 0 | 0 | 3 | 0 |
| No Info | 2 | 16 | 0 | 1 | 3 | 0 |
| No Info | 2 | 17 | 0 | 1 | 1 | 0 |
| No Info | 2 | 18 | 2 | 0 | 2 | 0 |
| No Info | 2 | 19 | 0 | 0 | 2 | 0 |
| No Info | 2 | 20 | 0 | 1 | 2 | 0 |
| Info | 1 | 1 | 0 | 1 | 0 | 0 |
| Info | 1 | 2 | 0 | 1 | 0 | 2 |
| Info | 1 | 3 | 0 | 1 | 2 | 0 |
| Info | 1 | 4 | 0 | 1 | 0 | 1 |
| Info | 1 | 5 | 0 | 2 | 0 | 2 |
| Info | 1 | 6 | 0 | 0 | 1 | 0 |
| Info | 1 | 7 | 0 | 0 | 1 | 0 |
| Info | 1 | 8 | 0 | 2 | 0 | 1 |
| Info | 1 | 9 | 0 | 0 | 2 | 1 |
| Info | 1 | 10 | 0 | 1 | 0 | 1 |
| Info | 1 | 11 | 0 | 1 | 0 | 1 |
| Info | 1 | 12 | 0 | 2 | 0 | 0 |
| Info | 1 | 13 | 0 | 1 | 1 | 0 |
| Info | 1 | 14 | 0 | 2 | 0 | 1 |
| Info | 1 | 15 | 0 | 1 | 0 | 1 |
| Info | 1 | 16 | 0 | 0 | 1 | 1 |
| Info | 1 | 17 | 0 | 1 | 0 | 0 |
| Info | 1 | 18 | 0 | 1 | 1 | 1 |
| Info | 1 | 19 | 0 | 1 | 0 | 2 |
| Info | 1 | 20 | 0 | 1 | 1 | 0 |
| Info | 2 | 1 | 0 | 0 | 2 | 0 |
| Info | 2 | 2 | 0 | 1 | 0 | 0 |
| Info | 2 | 3 | 0 | 2 | 1 | 0 |
| Info | 2 | 4 | 0 | 0 | 0 | 0 |
| Info | 2 | 5 | 0 | 1 | 1 | 0 |
| Info | 2 | 6 | 0 | 0 | 1 | 0 |
| Info | 2 | 7 | 0 | 1 | 1 | 0 |
| Info | 2 | 8 | 0 | 1 | 0 | 0 |
| Info | 2 | 9 | 0 | 1 | 1 | 0 |
| Info | 2 | 10 | 0 | 0 | 1 | 0 |
| Info | 2 | 11 | 0 | 1 | 0 | 0 |

*(continued)*

**Table A1** Distribution of Attractive and Unattractive Men and Women Across All Groups *(continued)*

| Treatment | Session | Group | Attractive Men | Unattractive Men | Attractive Women | Unattractive Women |
|---|---|---|---|---|---|---|
| Info | 2 | 12 | 0 | 1 | 1 | 0 |
| Info | 2 | 13 | 0 | 1 | 0 | 0 |
| Info | 2 | 14 | 0 | 2 | 2 | 0 |
| Info | 2 | 15 | 0 | 0 | 1 | 0 |
| Info | 2 | 16 | 0 | 0 | 0 | 0 |
| Info | 2 | 17 | 0 | 1 | 0 | 0 |
| Info | 2 | 18 | 0 | 2 | 0 | 0 |
| Info | 2 | 19 | 0 | 0 | 1 | 0 |
| Info | 2 | 20 | 0 | 0 | 2 | 0 |

From *Journal of Economic Psychology*, vol. 29(1) February 2008, pp. 73–93. Copyright © 2008 by Elsevier Ltd. Reprinted by permission via Rightslink.

# I'm Not a Very Manly Man
## Qualitative Insights into Young Men's Masculine Subjectivity

RICHARD O. DE VISSER, PHD

In recent years I have been conducting qualitative research into the links between masculine identity and health-related behavior. One important influence on this work has been studies of masculinities published in the last fifteen or so years—particularly the links between hegemonic masculinity and subordinated, marginalized, or resistant forms of masculinity (Connell 1995; Frosh, Phoenix, and Pattman 2002; Kimmel and Messner 1995). A second important influence has been Courtenay's (2000) theory of gender and health, which emphasizes the importance of healthy and unhealthy behaviors as a means for reinforcing or resisting hegemonic masculinity.

My research has involved group discussions and individual interviews with an ethnically and socioeconomically diverse group of eighteen- to twenty-one-year-old men living in London, England. Some reports of the links between masculinity and health-related behavior have already been published (de Visser and Smith 2006, 2007a, 2007b). In the course of the analysis, the accounts of two men struck me as particularly salient to discussions of masculinity. However, because these accounts did not relate specifically to health-related behavior, I have been unable to present them in other research articles. In this article I present a discussion of these two men and how what they said fits with existing understandings of masculinity and masculine identity.

The two men I will discuss are "John" (nineteen years old) and "Andy" (twenty years old), both white university students. These two interviews were not chosen to be representative of other men in the sample or of other young men. Rather, they were chosen because both men spontaneously referred to themselves as not being a "manly man" or a "man's man." Consideration of what these men said provides interesting insights into the links between discourses of masculinity and subjective experiences of masculinity, particularly whether masculinity is perceived in binary or pluralistic terms.

John's description of himself as "not a very manly man" was an interesting focal point for the analysis of the links between discourses of masculinity and subjective experiences of masculinity:

I'm not a very manly man, really. Like . . . it doesn't really grab me. It just seems a bit ludicrous to me, frankly. Um . . . not that I'm saying . . . you know, it is just another

choice that people make, but I wouldn't make that choice myself.

*Yeah. It's interesting that you said, "I'm not a manly man."*

Yeah.

*I mean, how would you describe a manly man?*

Um [two seconds pause] I don't, I'm not, I'm not an alpha male, really, like the just, sort of, really loud and dominating man. I am quite thoughtful and quite intuitive. And I have quite a lot of feminine attributes. Ah . . . rather than being . . . highly dominant, macho . . . keen to assert myself, and those things . . . like being competitive.

John acknowledged the existence of more than one discourse of masculinity: hegemonic masculinity (personified by the "alpha male") and alternative masculinities. He described hegemonic masculinity as "ludicrous": it is anathema to him. John described the decision to endorse and embody a particular form of masculinity as relatively simple ("just another choice"). However, this is not a simple choice because of the strong fundamental links to identity—behavior that is not hegemonically masculine is immediately judged to be nonmasculine or feminine (e.g., McQueen and Henwood 2002).

The content of John's description of a "manly man" and his embodiment of masculinity was interesting, and so too was the way in which this content was expressed. In terms of content, John described a manly man as embodying a masculinity characterized by dominance, machismo, leadership, and competitiveness. He made a clear contrast between this ideology and his masculinity, which is characterized by "feminine" characteristics such as being thoughtful, quiet, and intuitive rather than macho and competitive. It is noteworthy that John used a binary categorization with masculine attributes at one pole in contrast with feminine attributes at the other pole. Having considered the content of John's comparison and contrast of masculine and feminine characteristics, it is also interesting to consider the language John used to describe these contrasts. John's descriptions of masculine characteristics were accompanied by strong adjectives such as "highly" and "really," whereas his feminine characteristics were accompanied by the moderate adjective "quite." John's comparison of his masculine identity with dominant ideologies presented strong masculine characteristics in clear contrast with moderate feminine characteristics.

John focused on behavioral aspects of masculinity and mentioned choice. In contrast, Andy noted the importance of characteristics that are less easy to change, such as physical appearance. Andy said that because of his short stature and slight physique he was not stereotypically masculine:

> I'm like not very—I mean I'm not, I suppose I'm not what you might call a "man's man" just going by height, the way that I look and everything.

The implicit other in Andy's contrast of himself and a "man's man" is a man with a tall, strong, powerful physique. However, masculinity is not just defined by one's physical appearance: what one does is also important. Thus, Andy noted with relief that his sporting competence (a masculine activity) compensated for his slight physique and his success in the nonmasculine area of academic performance:

> I went to a pretty rough school. Both of my schools were rough—primary and secondary—and it was like . . . I was quite, I suppose I was kind of academically gifted—I mean I was good at school, yeah, especially in the environment that I was in.

*Right.*

> Um . . . and the fact that I played football, made, and that I was captain of the school team, made sure that I wasn't like branded as a geek, you know, "Steal his dinner money!" kind of thing [both laugh]. So there was always that element of which was good, definitely. But, um . . . yeah, it was all—The thing is though, I really enjoy it. It wasn't like "right, I'd better play football to kind of like avoid any hassle." I was . . . I enjoyed, I mean I really did enjoy it, and I really do enjoy it.

In Andy's school, physical prowess was admired, but academic success was not. He noted that he was able to use his skill at football (a hegemonically masculine activity) to counter the negative impact of his small physique and academic ability on his perceived masculinity. His athletic ability meant that—unlike other small studious boys—he was not a target for disdain and/or victimization as a "geek." Elsewhere in the interview he noted the importance of drinking and heterosexual behavior (particularly having an attractive girlfriend) to his masculine identity. Thus, although he was not hegemonically masculine in all domains, he was competent in other domains of hegemonic masculinity. Andy's indication that competence in some masculine domains can compensate for lack of competence in other masculine domains is in accordance with the reports of other men (de Visser and Smith 2006, 2007a; Messerschmidt 2000). Fortunately for Andy, football was something that he enjoyed: he did not have to engage in an unpleasant "masculine" activity for the sake of protecting his identity.

The quotes from John and Andy presented here provide some support for Bem's (1974) notion of androgyny—the idea that it is possible, and indeed preferable—to embody both masculine and feminine characteristics. Despite possessing several feminine characteristics, John still considered himself to be a man—but not a "manly man." However, there was also a clear sense that in these young men's minds, masculinity and femininity are not orthogonal, that masculinity and femininity are not truly independent. John suggested that one cannot be very masculine *and* very feminine, because the characteristics and intensity of hegemonic masculinity are incompatible with what he described as his "feminine attributes": hence his self-definition as "not a very manly man."

Andy's description of himself and his experiences presented a slightly different conceptualization of masculine identity formation. His description of his experiences suggested that rather than masculinity being unitary within a man, it is modular and cumulative: a coherent masculine identity can be constructed by accumulating masculine competence to counter any perceived femininity. Thus, the "gaps" in his masculinity because of his small physique and his intellect were countered through his "successes" in the domains of sports, drinking, and heterosexuality. This conceptualization of masculinity is in accordance with the findings of other recent studies of masculinity, which have shown that young men can compensate for some masculine behavior by accruing masculine "credit" in other social domains (de Visser and Smith 2006, 2007a; Messerschmidt 2000).

The material presented here was selected from a larger corpus of interviews about young men's health. These two interviews were chosen because John and Andy offered—without prompting—a comment on their masculinity and how it relates to a manly/man's man. The other study participants did not offer such descriptions and could not, therefore, be included in this analysis. Although it is not possible to generalize from this study to all young men, their accounts give an interesting insight into non-hegemonic masculine subjectivity. It is interesting that these two men positioned themselves as not a manly/man's man in quite different ways: John by not engaging with hegemonic masculinity at all, Andy by engaging with a masculinity complicit with hegemonic masculinity.

The two cases presented here indicate how young men's conceptualizations of masculinity and femininity as independent characteristics made it possible for them to embody non-hegemonic masculinities. However, it was interesting that although masculinity and femininity per se were not irreconcilable, there was evidence that within particular behavioral domains, masculinity and femininity were seen as oppositional. This reflects the conceptualization of masculinity in which behavior that is not hegemonically masculine is immediately non-masculine or feminine (e.g., McQueen and Henwood 2002). The comments given by John and Andy suggest that although masculinity and femininity are not bipolar opposites, neither are masculinity and femininity truly orthogonal. In line with previous research (Connell 1995; de Visser and Smith 2006, 2007a; Messerschmidt 2000), this study has also shown that men are active in the construction of the masculine identities, and that their behavior is influenced by their understanding of how their own behavior relates to hegemonic masculinity.

The experiences of John and Andy also give hope to young men who reject hegemonic masculinity but still desire a clear sense of being a man.

# References

Bem, S.L. 1974. The measurement of psychological androgyny. *Journal of Consulting & Clinical Psychology* 42:155–62.

Connell, R.W. 1995. *Masculinities.* Sydney: Allen & Unwin.

Courtenay, W. H. 2000. Constructions of masculinity and their influence on men's well-being: A theory of gender and health. *Social Science & Medicine* 50:1385–1401.

de Visser, R. O., and J. A. Smith. 2006. Mister in between: A case study of masculine identity and health-related behavior. *Journal of Health Psychology* 11:685–95.

de Visser, R. O., and J. A. Smith. 2007a. Alcohol consumption and masculine identity among young men. *Psychology & Health* 22:595–614.

de Visser, R. O., and J. A. Smith. 2007b. Young men's ambivalence toward alcohol. *Social Science & Medicine* 64:350–62.

Frosh, S., A. Phoenix, and R. Pattman. 2002. *Young masculinities.* London: Palgrave.

Kimmel, M. S., and M. A. Messner. 1995. *Men's lives.* Needham Heights, MA: Allyn & Bacon.

McQueen, C., and K. Henwood. 2002. Young men in "crisis": Attending to the language of teenage boys' distress. *Social Science & Medicine* 55:1493–1509.

Messerschmidt, J.W. 2000. Becoming "real men": Adolescent masculinity challenges and sexual violence. *Men and Masculinities* 2:286–307.

**RICHARD O. DE VISSER,** PhD, teaches in the Psychology Department and Medical School at the University of Sussex (Brighton, England). He has used both qualitative and quantitative methods to conduct research into sexual health and the links between gender and health.

From *Men and Masculinities*, January 1, 2009, pp. 367–371. Copyright © 2009 by Sage Publications. Reprinted by permission via Rightslink.

# UNIT 2
# Gender and Development

## Unit Selections

## Key Points to Consider

- In what ways do group processes impact gender role socialization?

- Can biological processes impact gender role behaviors? Explain.

- What myths and stereotypes exist about older men and women?

- What impact do the media have on the developing identities and self-concepts of boys and girls?

- Discuss the assumptions we make about parenthood and how these are culturally based.

- Discuss what we know about the gender differences observed in autism spectrum disorders.

## Student Website
www.mhcls.com

## Internet References

**Girls, Inc.**
   *http://www.girlsinc.org/*
**The Boys Project**
   *http://www.boysproject.net/*
**American Association of Retired Persons (AARP)**
   *http://www.aarp.org*
**National Institute on Aging (NIA)**
   *http://www.nih.gov/nia/*
**Parents, Familes, and Friends of Lesbians and Gays**
   *http://www.pflag.org*

This unit is about the importance of gender in child, adolescent, and adult human development. Development is a lifelong process. Gender socialization is a significant part of our development across the lifespan. At birth, we enter a gendered world. From the words used to describe boy and girl newborn babies (e.g., pretty, sweet, strong, active), to the ways in which we are dressed, we are introduced to a world of constraints and limits placed on us by a society that cares deeply about "appropriate" gender roles.

There are many agents of socialization—from parents to peers to social institutions such as schools and the media. During the preschool years, parents and other close family members are extremely influential. What gender role choices are given to children within a family context? Are the choices unnecessarily restrictive? What is available to children is influenced by prevailing attitudes and cultural beliefs about gender. In many families, strict limits are placed on how gender may be expressed. More often than not, boys face stricter gender "rules" than girls. Even if parents are determined to allow a child to express his or her gender in ways that are free from unnecessary constraints, siblings and peers send messages about what is considered appropriate or inappropriate gender role behavior.

During the school years, with exposure to peers, the media, and various social institutions, the developing child receives countless messages—many subtle—about gender roles, behaviors, norms, and social expectations. Most children dutifully incorporate the many messages about gender they receive into their identities and behavioral repertoires. As they internalize what they see and hear; they pass these same messages along to others.

Some children cannot seem to master this process to the extent that their peers do. Gender nonconforming children may become the target of teasing, bullying, and abuse. When the teasing and bullying is done by peers, school may become an especially painful place to be. Some children are able to retreat into the safety of their homes at the end of the school day. Others, for a variety of reasons, cannot. For some children, the abuse continues at home. Children who are targeted as "different" are considered by school counselors as at risk. Research has shown that they are more likely to suffer from depression, experience academic problems, and attempt suicide. As this book went to press, a smart, talented, and sensitive 11-year-old boy in Massachusetts, Carl Joseph Walker-Hoover, hanged himself because of such bullying and harassment.

The high school years continue the pattern already set in elementary and middle school. Some students report that pressures to conform intensify. At university, many people find greater freedom to express their gender in ways that may be

© Getty Images/Digital Vision

experienced as liberating. Colleges and universities are places where young adults can explore and further develop who they are or want to be.

Our gender socialization continues throughout our lives in the worlds of work and families. As we age, we continue to develop and, over time, many people become a little bit freer from some of the more rigid gender constraints imposed on young people. This can be seen in the nurturing behaviors of grandfathers who now delight in pretend tea parties, dolls, and fancy dresses, and who have tears come to their eyes when they are told "I love you" by an adoring grandchild.

# Gender and Group Process
## *A Developmental Perspective*

Until recently, the study of gender development has focused mainly on sex typing as an attribute of the individual. Although this perspective continues to be enlightening, recent work has focused increasingly on children's tendency to congregate in same-sex groups. This self-segregation of the two sexes implies that much of childhood gender enactment occurs in the context of same-sex dyads or larger groups. There are emergent properties of such groups, so that certain sex-distinctive qualities occur at the level of the group rather than at the level of the individual. There is increasing research interest in the distinctive nature of the group structures, activities, and interactions that typify all-male as compared with all-female groups, and in the socialization that occurs within these groups. Next steps in research will surely call for the integration of the individual and group perspectives.

ELEANOR E. MACCOBY

Among researchers who study the psychology of gender, a central viewpoint has always been that individuals progressively acquire a set of behaviors, interests, personality traits, and cognitive biases that are more typical of their own sex than of the other sex. And the individual's sense of being either a male or a female person (*gender identity*) is thought to be a core element in the developing sense of self. The acquisition of these sex-distinctive characteristics has been called *sex typing,* and much research has focused on how and why the processes of sex typing occur. A favorite strategy has been to examine differences among individuals in how sex typed they are at a given age, searching for factors associated with a person's becoming more or less "masculine" or more or less "feminine" than other individuals. In early work, there was a heavy emphasis on the family as the major context in which sex typing was believed to take place. Socialization pressures from parents were thought to shape the child toward "sex-appropriate" behaviors, personality, and interests and a firm gender identity.

On the whole, the efforts to understand gender development by studying individual differences in rate or degree of sex typing, and the connections of these differences to presumed antecedent factors, have not been very successful. The various manifestations of sex typing in childhood—toy and activity preferences, knowledge of gender stereotypes, personality traits—do not cohere together to form a cluster that clearly represents a degree of sex typing in a given child. And whether or not a given child behaves in a gender-typical way seems to vary greatly from one situation to another, depending on the social context and other conditions that make an individual's gender salient at a given moment. Only weak and inconsistent connections have been found between within-family socialization practices and children's sex-typed behavior (Ruble & Martin, 1998). And so far, the study of individual variations in sex typing has not helped us to understand the most robust manifestation of gender during childhood: namely, children's strong tendency to segregate themselves into same-sex social groups. Although work on gender development in individual children continues and shows renewed vigor, a relatively new direction of interest is in children's groups. This current research and theorizing considers how gender is implicated in the formation, interaction processes, and socialization functions of childhood social groupings.

In some of this work, the dyad or larger group, rather than the individual child, is taken as the unit of analysis. Through the history of theoretical writings by sociologists and social psychologists, there have been claims that groups have emergent properties, and that their functioning cannot be understood in terms of the characteristics of their individual members (Levine & Moreland, 1998). Accumulating evidence from recent work suggests that in certain gender configurations, pairs or groups of children elicit certain behaviors from each other that are not characteristic of either of the participants when alone or in other social contexts (Martin & Fabes, 2001). Another possibility is that the group context amplifies what are only weak tendencies in the individual participants. For example, in their article "It Takes Two to Fight," Cole and his colleagues (1999) found that the probability of a fight occurring depended not only on the aggressive predispositions of the two individual boys involved, but also on the unique properties of the dyad itself. Other phenomena, such as social approach to another child, depend on the sex of the approacher and the approachee taken jointly, not on the sex of either child, when children's sociability is analyzed at the level of the individual (summarized in Maccoby, 1998). It is important, then, to describe and analyze children's dyads or larger groups as such, to see how gender is implicated in their characteristics and functioning.

# Gender Composition of Children's Groups

Beginning at about age 3, children increasingly choose same-sex playmates when in settings where their social groupings are not managed by adults. In preschools, children may play in loose configurations of several children, and reciprocated affiliation between same-sex pairs of children is common while such reciprocation between pairs of opposite sex is rare (Strayer, 1980; Vaughan, Colvin, Azria, Caya, & Krzysik, 2001). On school playgrounds, children sometimes play in mixed-sex groups, but increasingly, as they move from age 4 to about age 12, they spend a large majority of their free play time exclusively with others of their own sex, rarely playing in a mixed-sex dyad or in a larger group in which no other child of their own sex is involved. Best friendships in middle childhood and well into adolescence are very heavily weighted toward same-sex choices. These strong tendencies toward same-sex social preferences are seen in the other cultures around the world where gender composition of children's groups has been studied, and are also found among young nonhuman primates (reviewed in Maccoby, 1998).

# Group Size

Naturally occurring face-to-face groups whose members interact with one another continuously over time tend to be small—typically having only two or three members, and seldom having more than five or six members. Some gender effects on group size can be seen. Both boys and girls commonly form same-sex dyadic friendships, and sometimes triadic ones as well. But from about the age of 5 onward, boys more often associate together in larger clusters. Boys are more often involved in organized group games, and in their groups, occupy more space on school playgrounds. In an experimental situation in which same-sex groups of six children were allowed to utilize play and construction materials in any way they wished, girls tended to split into dyads or triads, whereas boys not only interacted in larger groups but were much more likely to undertake some kind of joint project, and organize and carry out coordinated activities aimed at achieving a group goal (Benenson, Apostolaris, & Parnass, 1997). Of course, children's small groups—whether dyads or clusters of four, five, or six children—are nested within still larger group structures, such as cliques or "crowds."

Group size matters. Recent studies indicate that the interactions in groups of four or more are different from what typically occurs in dyads. In larger groups, there is more conflict and more competition, particularly in all-male groups; in dyads, individuals of both sexes are more responsive to their partners, and a partner's needs and perspectives are more often taken into account than when individuals interact with several others at once (Benenson, Nicholson, Waite, Roy, & Simpson, 2001; Levine & Moreland, 1998). The question of course arises: To what extent are certain "male" characteristics, such as greater competitiveness, a function of the fact that boys typically interact in larger groups than girls do? At present, this question is one of active debate and study. So far, there are indications that group size does indeed mediate sex differences to some degree, but not entirely nor consistently.

# Interaction in Same-Sex Groups

From about age 3 to age 8 or 9, when children congregate together in activities not structured by adults, they are mostly engaged in some form of play. Playtime interactions among boys, more often than among girls, involve rough-and-tumble play, competition, conflict, ego displays, risk taking, and striving to achieve or maintain dominance, with occasional (but actually quite rare) displays of direct aggression. Girls, by contrast, are more often engaged in what is called collaborative discourse, in which they talk and act reciprocally, each responding to what the other has just said or done, while at the same time trying to get her own initiatives across. This does not imply that girls' interactions are conflict free, but rather that girls pursue their individual goals in the context of also striving to maintain group harmony (summary in Maccoby, 1998).

The themes that appear in boys' fantasies, the stories they invent, the scenarios they enact when playing with other boys, and the fictional fare they prefer (books, television) involve danger, conflict, destruction, heroic actions by male heroes, and trials of physical strength, considerably more often than is the case for girls. Girls' fantasies and play themes tend to be oriented around domestic or romantic scripts, portraying characters who are involved in social relationships and depicting the maintenance or restoration of order and safety.

Girls' and boys' close friendships are qualitatively different in some respects. Girls' friendships are more intimate, in the sense that girl friends share information about the details of their lives and concerns. Boys typically know less about their friends' lives, and base their friendship on shared activities.

Boys' groups larger than dyads are in some respects more cohesive than girls' groups. Boys in groups seek and achieve more autonomy from adults than girls do, and explicitly exclude girls from their activities more commonly than girls exclude boys. Boys more often engage in joint risky activities, and close ranks to protect a group member from adult detection and censure. And friendships among boys are more interconnected; that is, friends of a given boy are more likely to be friends with each other than is the case for several girls who are all friends of a given girl (Markovitz, Benenson, & Dolenszky, 2001). The fact that boys' friendships are more interconnected does not mean that they are closer in the sense of intimacy. Rather, it may imply that male friends are more accustomed to functioning as a unit, perhaps having a clearer group identity.

# How Sex-Distinctive Subcultures Are Formed

In a few instances, researchers have observed the process of group formation from the first meeting of a group over several subsequent meetings. An up-close view of the formation of gendered subcultures among young children has been provided by Nicolopoulou (1997). She followed classrooms of preschool children through a school year, beginning at the time they first entered the school. Every day, any child could tell a story to a teacher, who recorded the story as the child told it. At the end of the day, the teacher read aloud to the class the stories that were recorded that day, and the child author of each story was invited to act it out with the help of other children whom the child selected to act out different parts. At the beginning of the year, stories could be quite rudimentary (e.g., "There was a boy. And a girl. And a wedding."). By the end of the year, stories became greatly elaborated, and different members of the class produced stories related to themes previously introduced by others. In other words, a corpus of shared knowledge, meanings, and scripts grew up, unique to the children in a given classroom and reflecting their shared experiences.

More important for our present purposes, there was a progressive divergence between the stories told by girls and those told by boys. Gender differences were present initially, and the thematic content differed more and more sharply as time went on, with boys increasingly focusing on themes of conflict, danger, heroism, and "winning," while girls' stories increasingly depicted family, nonviolent themes. At the beginning of the year, children might call upon others of both sexes to act in their stories, but by the end of the year, they almost exclusively called upon children of their own sex to enact the roles in their stories. Thus, although all the children in the class were exposed to the stories told by both sexes, the girls picked up on one set of themes and the boys on another, and two distinct subcultures emerged.

Can this scenario serve as a prototype for the formation of distinctive male and female "subcultures" among children? Yes, in the sense that the essence of these cultures is a set of socially shared cognitions, including common knowledge and mutually congruent expectations, and common interests in specific themes and scripts that distinguish the two sexes. These communalities can be augmented in a set of children coming together for the first time, since by age 5 or 6, most will already have participated in several same-sex groups, or observed them in operation on TV, so they are primed for building gender-distinct subcultures in any new group of children they enter. Were we to ask, "Is gender socially constructed?" the answer would surely be "yes." At the same time, there may well be a biological contribution to the nature of the subculture each sex chooses to construct.

# Socialization within Same-Sex Groups

There has long been evidence that pairs of friends—mostly same-sex friends—influence one another (see Dishion, Spracklen, & Patterson, 1996, for a recent example). However, only recently has research focused on the effects of the amount of time young children spend playing with other children of their own sex. Martin and Fabes (2001) observed a group of preschoolers over a 6-month period, to obtain stable scores for how much time they spent with same-sex playmates (as distinct from their time spent in mixed-sex or other-sex play). They examined the changes that occurred, over the 6 months of observation, in the degree of sex typing in children's play activities. Martin and Fabes reported that the more time boys spent playing with other boys, the greater the increases in their activity level, rough-and-tumble play, and sex-typed choices of toys and games, and the less time they spent near adults. For girls, by contrast, large amounts of time spent with other girls was associated with increasing time spent near adults, and with decreasing aggression, decreasing activity level, and increasing choices of girl-type play materials and activities. This new work points to a powerful role for same-sex peers in shaping one another's sex-typed behavior, values, and interests.

# What Comes Next?

The recent focus on children's same-sex groups has revitalized developmental social psychology, and promising avenues for the next phases of research on gender development have appeared. What now needs to be done?

1. Investigators need to study both the variations and the similarities among same-sex groups in their agendas and interactive processes. The extent of generality across groups remains largely unexplored. The way gender is enacted in groups undoubtedly changes with age. And observations in other cultures indicate that play in same-sex children's groups reflects what different cultures offer in the way of materials, play contexts, and belief systems. Still, it seems likely that there are certain sex-distinctive themes that appear in a variety of cultural contexts.

2. Studies of individual differences need to be integrated with the studies of group process. Within each sex, some children are only marginally involved in same-sex groups or dyads, whereas others are involved during much of their free time. And same-sex groups are internally differentiated, so that some children are popular or dominant while others consistently occupy subordinate roles or may even be frequently harassed

by others. We need to know more about the individual characteristics that underlie these variations, and about their consequences.

3. Children spend a great deal of their free time in activities that are not gender differentiated at all. We need to understand more fully the conditions under which gender is salient in group process and the conditions under which it is not.

# References

Benenson, J. F., Apostolaris, N. H., & Parnass, J. (1997). Age and sex differences in dyadic and group interaction. *Developmental Psychology, 33,* 538–543.

Benenson, J. F., Nicholson, C., Waite, A., Roy, R., & Simpson, A. (2001). The influence of group size on children's competitive behavior. *Child Development, 72,* 921–928.

Cole, J. D., Dodge, K. A., Schwartz, D., Cillessen, A. H. N., Hubbard, J. A., & Lemerise, E. A. (1999). It takes two to fight: A test of relational factors, and a method for assessing aggressive dyads. *Developmental Psychology, 36,* 1179–1188.

Dishion, T. J., Spracklen, K. M., & Patterson, G. R. (1996). Deviancy training in male adolescent friendships. *Behavior Therapy, 27,* 373–390.

Levine, J. M., & Moreland, R. L. (1998). Small groups. In D. T. Gilbert, S. T. Fiske, & G. Lindzey (Eds.), *Handbook of social psychology* (Vol. 2, pp. 415–469). Boston: McGraw-Hill.

Maccoby, E. E. (1998). *The two sexes: Growing up apart, coming together.* Cambridge, MA: Harvard University Press.

Markovitz, H., Benenson, J. F., & Dolenszky, E. (2001). Evidence that children and adolescents have internal models of peer interaction that are gender differentiated. *Child Development, 72,* 879–886.

Martin, C. L., & Fabes, R. A. (2001). The stability and consequences of young children's same-sex peer interactions. *Developmental Psychology, 37,* 431–446.

Nicolopoulou, A. (1997). Worldmaking and identity formation in children's narrative play-acting. In B. Cox & C. Lightfoot (Eds.), *Sociogenic perspectives in internalization* (pp. 157–187). Hillsdale, NJ: Erlbaum.

Ruble, D. N., & Martin, D. L. (1998). Gender development. In W. Damon & N. Eisenberg (Eds.), *Handbook of child psychology* (5th ed., Vol. 3, pp. 933–1016). New York: John Wiley & Sons.

Strayer, F. F. (1980). Social ecology of the preschool peer group. In W. A. Collins (Ed.), *Minnesota Symposium on Child Psychology: Vol. 13. Development of cognitions, affect and social relations* (pp. 165–196). Hillsdale, NJ: Erlbaum.

Vaughn, B. E., Colvin, T. N., Azria, M. R., Caya, L., & Krzysik, L. (2001). Dyadic analyses of friendship in a sample of preschool-aged children attending Headstart. *Child Development, 72,* 862–878.

**ELEANOR E. MACCOBY** Department of Psychology, Stanford University, Stanford, California

Address correspondence to Eleanor E. Maccoby, Department of Psychology, Stanford University, Stanford, CA 94305-2130.

From *Current Directions in Psychological Science*, April 2002, pp. 54–58. Copyright © 2002 by the Association for Psychological Science. Reprinted by permission of Wiley-Blackwell.

# Gender Bender

**New research suggests genes and prenatal hormones could have more sway in gender identity than previously thought.**

SADIE F. DINGFELDER

"It's a boy!" announces the doctor to the exhausted mother, a determination the physician makes instantly. And most of the time, the observed sex of an infant does match the genetic sex—with two X chromosomes producing a girl, and an X plus a Y resulting in a boy.

But in the rare cases where they do not, when prenatal development goes awry and genetic boys are born looking more like girls or vice versa, physicians and parents generally assign the newborn a sex. Most often the child becomes female, because female genitals are easier to construct, says William G. Reiner, MD, a child psychiatrist and urologist at the University of Oklahoma health services center.

The prevailing theory behind this long-standing practice, says Reiner, has been that a person reared as a girl will eventually embrace that category. Now, however, new research by Reiner suggests that perhaps such assumptions ought not to be made. A study by Reiner and John Gearhart, MD, of Johns Hopkins University, finds that biology—in particular the hormonal influences on developing infants' brains—programs children to eventually identify as either male or female, almost regardless of social influences, at least in the case of the children he's studied.

"It's fair to say that some people in the world of psychology have held that [gender] is socially derived, learned behavior," says Reiner. "But our findings do not support that theory."

However, other researchers, such as Sheri Berenbaum, PhD, a psychologist at Pennsylvania State University, maintain that determinates of gender identity may be more complex than that.

"Genetic and hormonal factors are just two of the many influences on gender identity and gender-typical behavior—social influences are certainly very important as well," she says. "And all of these factors seem to interact throughout a child's development."

## New Findings

This isn't the view of Reiner and Gearhart though, who point to the findings of their study, published in the Jan. 22 issue of the *New England Journal of Medicine* (Vol. 350, No. 4). The study found that some infants whose brains were exposed to male hormones in utero later identified as male even though they were raised as female and underwent early-childhood operations. Reiner says that indicates that prenatal sex differentiation can at least sometimes trump social influences.

The study followed 16 genetic males with a rare disorder called cloacal exstrophy. Children with this disorder are born without penises, or with very small ones, despite having normal male hormones, normal testes and XY-chromosome pairs. Fourteen of these children underwent early sex-reassignment surgery and were raised as girls by their parents, who were instructed not to inform them of their early medical histories.

The researchers assessed the gender identities and behaviors of these children when they were anywhere from 5 to 16 years old using a battery of measures including the Bates Child Behavior and Attitude Questionnaire and the Child Game Participation Questionnaire. Researchers also asked the children whether they categorized themselves as boys or girls.

> **"Obviously, gender is both a biological and social phenomenon," says Ruble. "Researchers now really need to look carefully at the unfolding of biologically driven processes in interaction with social influences during the first three years of life and beyond."**
>
> Diane Ruble
> New York University

Of the 14 children raised as females, three spontaneously declared they were male at the initial assessment. At the most recent follow-up, six identified as males, while three reported unclear gender identity or would not talk with researchers. The two participants raised as males from birth continued to identify as male throughout the study.

All of the participants exhibited male-typical behavior, such as rough-and-tumble play and having many male friends.

"If you are looking at the genetic and hormonal male, [sexual identity may be] not plastic at all," says Reiner. "And it appears to be primarily influenced by biology."

Some researchers, such as Kenneth J. Zucker, PhD, a psychologist and the head of the child and adolescent gender identity clinic at Toronto's Centre for Addiction and Mental Health, applaud Reiner's study for renewing interest in the biological determinants of gender and calling into question the notion of some that gender identity is mainly socially constructed and determined by socialization.

That's not to say, however, that socialization isn't still a major or important factor, Zucker emphasizes. "The debate is still up in the air because there are other centers who have studied kids with the same diagnosis, and the rate of changeover from female to male is nowhere near what Reiner is reporting," he explains. "It must be something about their social experience that is accounting for this difference."

## Contradictory Evidence

Backing Zucker's belief that socialization still plays a major role—and biology is only part of the story—is research by Sheri Berenbaum, PhD, a psychologist at Pennsylvania State University, and J. Michael Bailey, PhD, a psychologist at Northwestern University.

In a study published in the March 2003 issue of the *Journal of Clinical Endocrinology & Metabolism* (Vol. 88, No. 3), they investigated the gender identity of genetic girls born with congenital adrenal hyperplasia (CAH). Girls with this disorder do not produce enough of the hormone cortisol, which causes their adrenal glands to produce an excess of male sex hormones. As a result, they develop in a hormonal environment that's between that of typical boys and typical girls. These girls tend to have ambiguous genitals, and like the infants with cloacal exstrophy, they generally undergo surgery to remake their bodies in the mold of typical females.

The researchers recruited 43 girls with CAH ages 3 to 18 and assessed their gender-typical behaviors and gender identities using a nine-item questionnaire. One question, for example, asks the child if she would take the opportunity to be magically turned into a boy.

In comparison with a control group of normal girls, those with CAH answered questions in a more masculine way. However, when compared with hormonally normal girls who identified

as tomboys, they scored closer to typical girls. And few, says Berenbaum, actually identified as male.

"They behave in some ways more like boys, but they self-identify as girls," she explains.

According to Berenbaum, this shows that prenatal hormones, while important determinates of gendered behavior, aren't the only ones.

"Social influences are also pretty important," she says. "I think the interesting question is how biological predisposition affects our socialization experiences."

Diane Ruble, PhD, a New York University psychologist specializing in early childhood gender identity, agrees.

"In Sheri's work, the hormonal exposure has some masculinizing influence on their play behavior," says Ruble. "That may feed into difficulties that children have even if the hormonal exposure prenatally did not actually directly affect their identities as girls or boys."

For example, she says, a girl who discovers that her behavior is slightly masculine may feel more like a typical boy than girl. She may then primarily socialize with boys, leading to even more male-typical behavior.

"Obviously, gender is both a biological and social phenomenon," says Ruble. "Researchers now really need to look carefully at the unfolding of biologically driven processes in interaction with social influences during the first three years of life and beyond."

## Further Readings

Berenbaum, S.A., & Bailey, J.M. (2003). Effects on gender identity of prenatal androgens and genital appearance: Evidence from girls with congenital adrenal hyperplasia. *Journal of Clinical Endocrinology and Metabolism, 88,* 1102–1106.

Martin, C.L., & Ruble, D.N. (in press). Children's search for gender cues: Cognitive perspectives on gender development. *Current Directions in Psychological Science.*

Martin, C.L., Ruble, D.N., & Szkrybalo, J. (2002). Cognitive theories of early gender development. *Psychological Bulletin, 128*(6), 903–933.

Reiner, W.G., & Gearhart, J.P. (2004). Discordant sexual identity in some genetic males with cloacal exstrophy assigned to female sex at birth. *The New England Journal of Medicine, 350*(4), 333–341.

Zucker, K. J. (1999). Intersexuality and gender identity differentiation. *Annual Review of Sex Research, 10,* 1–69.

From *Monitor on Psychology* by Sadie F. Dingfelder (staff), April 2004, pp. 48–49. Copyright © 2004 by American Psychological Association. Reprinted by permission. No further distribution without permission from the American Psychological Association.

# The Secret Lives of Single Women

**Are unattached women sad, lonely, and financially troubled—as the stereotype would have it? In a myth-busting survey, thousands told us that despite some very real hardships, they've never been happier.**

SARAH MAHONEY

It is often said that females are complex and mysterious creatures, hard to understand and completely unpredictable. But older single women seem to have a mythology all their own. They are lonely, they long for love, they are terribly afraid of dying destitute. When Bella DePaulo, Ph.D., a psychology professor at the University of California, Santa Barbara, and author of the forthcoming book *Singled Out* (St. Martin's Press, 2006), asked 950 college students to describe married people, they used words like "happy, loving, secure, stable, and kind." The descriptions of singles, on the other hand, included "lonely, shy, unhappy, insecure, inflexible, and stubborn."

Are the stereotypes true? Is the picture that bleak? Or are these women in fact loving their independence and having the time of their lives? What really goes on behind the closed doors of the millions of single women in America? To find out, AARP recently polled more than 2,500 women ages 45 and older for its landmark "AARP Foundation Women's Leadership Circle Study." Though this group is large and diverse, the results, presented on the following pages, may surprise you.

Mind you, these are not rare birds: of the 57 million American women 45 and up, nearly half—25 million—are unmarried (outnumbering entire populations of countries such as North Korea, Taiwan, and Australia). There are several reasons for this: American women marry later, their divorce rate is high, and, not to put too fine a point on it, those who are married are likely to outlive their mates. As a result, American women are now likely to spend more years of their lives single than with a significant other, according to DePaulo. Instead of having some single stretches in between relationships, she says, "the reality is relationships are now what happens between longer periods of singleness."

Nor are these singles birds of a feather. Is today's typical older unwed female a lot like Carrie Bradshaw, *Sex and the City's* free-spirited patron saint of the deliberately single? Or is she more like Dorothy Zbornak, the wisecracking 50-ish Golden Girl who left her cheating husband to live with a pair of ditzy roommates and her acid-tongued mother? Could she even be Thelma or Louise—two baby-boomer heroines who couldn't decide if they'd be better off dead or single and, in the end, chose both? The answer: a little of this and a little of that, and in some cases, all of the above.

Whatever their type, it's clear that words like *lonely, shy,* and *insecure* no longer apply. Fully half the women in our study say they are happier than they've ever been. Are they sad now and then? Sure—aren't we all? Do they occasionally lose sleep worrying about the future? Yes, and with good reason: being a single older woman comes with its own economic challenges. But that doesn't stop the majority from believing that midlife offers an opportunity for growth, for learning, and the chance to do the things they've always wanted to do. In fact, says DePaulo, "many single women are living lives of secret contentment."

Now, let's take a closer look at the facts and fiction about single older women in the United States today.

**Myth #1: All single women are desperate to find a mate.**
**Reality: Open to a nice relationship? You betcha. But obsessed with finding a partner? Hardly.**

Given the option, many single women wouldn't mind a committed relationship with a cuddly, caring partner—preferably someone with minimal emotional baggage and the kind of income to support a nice summer house, facts supported by an AARP survey, "Lifestyles, Dating & Romance: A Study of Midlife Singles." It finds that 31 percent of single women 40 through 69 are in an exclusive relationship, and another 32 percent are dating nonexclusively. But it also finds that a surprising number couldn't care less. About one in 10 have no desire to date at all, and another 14 percent say that while they'd date the right guy if he came along, they aren't going to knock themselves out trying to find him. (The remaining 13 percent are, indeed, looking.)

In fact, most of those who aren't dating seem disinclined to change that situation anytime soon. Among 40-plus women who hadn't been on a date in the past three years, 68 percent say they just aren't interested in dating or being in a romantic relationship, though 61 percent of them would reconsider if they met someone interesting. Those who do date say it requires a philosophical balance between putting on a game face on Saturday night and not getting stressed if nothing develops. "I'm dating, and I'd like to find a good relationship," says Flo Taylor, 54, a TV producer in Pittsburgh. "But if it doesn't happen for me, I'm fine with that, too."

**Myth #2:** **Single women are lonely.**

**Reality:** **Everyone is lonely sometimes—even married people. But most single women (as well as women with spouses) actually enjoy their solitude.**

Living alone can be lonely. AARP's "Sexuality at Midlife and Beyond" survey found that 28 percent of single women said that within the past two weeks they had felt lonely occasionally or most of the time, compared with only 13 percent of married women in the same category. Slightly more single women (93 percent) than their married sisters (87 percent), however, said they felt their independence was important to their quality of life. "I love the freedom, and the fact that I know so many other single women I can network with," says Flo.

The key, says Brenda Bufalino, 68, a dancer and choreographer who lives in New York City, is to accept that some days will be lonely—no matter who you are. "The other day my granddaughter asked me, 'Nana, don't you ever get lonely?'" Bufalino, who's been divorced since 1973, answered her, "Sure, but I got lonely sometimes when I was married, too."

**Myth #3:** **Older women are clueless about finances and don't know how to invest.**

**Reality:** **Women are more timid investors than men are, but they're the opposite of clueless and actually make fewer investing mistakes than men do.**

It's true that women—both married and single—are more risk-averse and less knowledgeable about investing than men: in a recent Oppenheimer Funds survey, 63 percent of women, versus 41 percent of men, admitted they didn't know how a mutual fund worked.

For single women part of the explanation may be that they have too little money to buy funds. About 39 percent of unmarried women 45 and older are classified by the Census Bureau as "low-income," versus just 20 percent of all women in that age group. But even when they have some money to save, women who have the sole responsibility for household investment decisions invest less in mutual funds than do male decision makers or males and females who make decisions jointly. The Investment Company Institute reports that in households where women are making the investment choices, the mutual fund assets are smaller and less diverse—that is, women investors tend to invest less money and own fewer funds than do the other two groups.

If there is some truth to the cash-under-the-mattress stereotype, it's out of fear rather than an unwillingness to learn, says Ginita Wall, founder of the Women's Institute for Financial Education in San Diego and coauthor of the book *It's More Than Money, It's Your Life* (Wiley, 2004). "Especially for widows, who often get a sum of life insurance, and divorced women, who often get a portion of their ex's retirement account, it can be very hard for them to make decisions. They procrastinate and keep thinking, 'This is the last money I'm ever going to have, so I have to be careful with it.'"

More promising is the fact that women are more likely than men to rely on advice from finance professionals, a finding that is replicated in surveys from brokerage houses Oppenheimer and Merrill Lynch. And because they ask for advice, women investors actually have an edge over men in at least one respect: a recent Merrill Lynch study found that while women knew and cared less about investing than men did, they also made fewer investing mistakes—such as holding a losing stock too long or failing to

research the tax implications of an investment—than men did, and didn't repeat them as often.

"Women are more likely to seek information than men are," says Wall. "But just because single women know something intellectually, it doesn't mean it's easy for them emotionally."

**Myth #4:** **Unlike their female counterparts who were born before the women's movement, baby-boomer career women have it made financially.**

**Reality:** **Many single women—particularly those under age 60—carry dangerously high levels of debt.**

Once again, credit famously single TV character Carrie Bradshaw for drawing attention to a phenomenon that Esther M. Berger, a Beverly Hills certified financial planner and money manager, calls "the *Sex and the City syndrome*." Berger specializes in high-income women, a number of whom work long hours and earn big bucks "but have more or less invested their entire net worth in clothing and shoes. They often live, quite literally, from paycheck to paycheck."

It's not ignorance, exactly—these are women who manage big corporate budgets. "Part of it is a sense of entitlement," says Berger. "They work hard and feel they deserve to spend lavishly on trips and clothes. They tend to trade immediate gratification for long-term planning." Case in point: some 60 percent of the 45-plus single women in the AARP Foundation women's study haven't figured out how much money they'll need in retirement, and 68 percent don't even have a long-term spending plan.

Debt makes everything worse. While women over 60 tend to shy away from debt, baby-boomer women embrace it. Experian, one of the three premier credit-reporting agencies, notes that the average female in the age range of 45 through 59 carries $11,414 in revolving debt, compared with the $6,521 that 60-plus women carry. And, according to the AARP Foundation's women's study, divorced women and women ages 45 through 49 were the least likely to pay off their credit cards each month.

As a result, many single baby-boomer women live with plenty of financial fear: some 27 percent of the single women in the AARP Foundation women's study admit that if they were hit with an unexpected bill of a few thousand bucks—like a leaky roof or a sudden medical emergency—they would have no idea how to pay for it. Patty Leeson, 47, for example, who works for a real-estate association in Kansas City, Kansas, wound up with uncovered medical expenses of $1,000 last year and is still struggling to catch up. "It's scary that I can't pay," says Patty, who has never been married and doesn't date. "I do feel that I don't have the security married people do, and there are plenty of times I wish I had someone to help me with the bills." And when she thinks ahead to the future? "Sometimes I panic," she admits.

**Myth #5:** **Retirement is a time for single women to slow down and get a few more cats.**

**Reality:** **Often it's an exciting chance for reinvention.**

It's true that in terms of happy-right-now measurements, single women, overall, don't fare as well as married women or those with a live-in partner. Though 50 percent of single women say they are happier now than they have ever been, as mentioned earlier, an even greater 75 percent with partners say the same thing, according to the AARP Foundation women's study.

Despite the challenges, though, mature unmarried women are starting to build a culture all their own. And as the proud-to-be-me baby boomers begin to swell their ranks, attitudes are changing. "Single women are starting to realize how much time they have to create a meaningful life," says author Suzanne Braun Levine, who spoke to hundreds of women for her book *Inventing the Rest of Our Lives: Women in Second Adulthood* (Viking, 2005). "If you figure that the first adulthood lasts from 25 to 50, you have statistically at least that much time ahead of you until you're 75, and many women live much longer."

Indeed, some 63 percent of single women who live alone say their older years are the time to pursue their dreams and do things they've always wanted to do. And 80 percent of single women agree that as they've gotten older, they're more free to be themselves. As women reinvent themselves, the results can be surprising. When Carol Wheeler's husband died—just nine days before she would have been eligible to collect his Social Security—she was stunned. They had met and married while she was in her 60s. They had enjoyed the best of city life: a rent-controlled apartment in Manhattan, season tickets to the opera, plenty of time with their grown children. Now, on a Social Security check of just $1,000, Carol had to face facts: "I said to myself, 'I can't go on pretending I'm living the same life without him.'"

So she took a trip to Mexico, checking out the charming mountain town of San Miguel de Allende as a possible retirement destination. Using some money her husband had left her, she bought "an absolute wreck" of a house, which cost far less than anything she could have found in the States, and then renovated it. Now she gets by quite nicely on her Social Security income. And she loves almost everything about Mexico—the way walking on the charming cobblestone streets keeps her fit, her new friends (mostly American women), and how she has been able to fill her little home with brightly colored masterpieces from local artisans. "I lived my whole life with white walls," says Carol, now 70. "Here, everything is bright—I painted my house in mango and rose colors, and the people are so friendly. I'm enchanted."

**Myth #6: When it comes to their appearance, older single women say "the heck with it."**
**Reality: To the contrary, women without partners are keenly aware that appearances matter in our society. But most don't go to extremes to look younger than they really are.**
Turns out those stereotypes about single women desperately trying to hang on to their looks as they age—remember Blanche DuBois, shrinking from bright lights in *A Streetcar Named Desire?*—are a bunch of hooey. Nancy Etcoff, Ph.D., a psychology instructor at Harvard Medical School, studied 3,200 women in 10 countries and found that women's perception of how good-looking they are doesn't erode (or improve) as the years roll by. Just as many women (16 percent) think of themselves as attractive at 65 as at 18, says Etcoff, author of *Survival of the Prettiest* (Anchor, 2000). The same goes for women who regard themselves as average (72 percent) or less physically attractive than others (13 percent). "But single women do pay more attention to appearance," she says. "In the dating world physical appearance is always important. You are judged in part by how you look."

With men and women of all ages flocking to plastic surgeons, it's thus no surprise that older single women are getting their share of nips and tucks as well. The American Society of Plastic Surgeons doesn't track the marital status of patients, but surgeons say

there are definitely a fair number of single older women who feel surgery can give them an advantage with men. "When women in their 60s come to me for neck- and face-lifts, most are single," says Jeannette Martello, M.D., a plastic surgeon with a busy practice in South Pasadena, California.

Take Annette Bilobran, a 62-year-old retired nurse in Schenectady, New York, who recently had a neck- and face-lift. Long divorced, she believes surgery helps her get dates. "You always see guys gathered around the younger women," she says. "Now I feel like I have a bit more of an advantage." Darrick Antell, M.D., the New York City plastic surgeon who worked on Annette, says he's even seen cases where women demanded that money for a face-lift be written into a divorce settlement.

But women are sprucing themselves up for other reasons, too—it's not all about men. Now that they are working longer, "most women are just engaging in defensive aging," says Antell. In other words, they are taking active measures to slow the signs that they are getting older. For patients 51 to 64—most of whom are women—eyelid surgery, liposuction, and nose reshaping are the most common procedures; the 65-plus group tends to opt for eyelid surgery, face-lifts, and hair transplants, according to the American Society of Plastic Surgeons. June Benedict, a 73-year-old widow from New Wilmington, Pennsylvania, recently had a face-lift with her identical twin, Joan. "At this age," says June, "some people would say, why should we bother? It's not that I have an interest in dating—I don't. I just wanted a little improvement. Now I look like me, only better."

**Myth #7: A single woman's worst fear is that she'll wind up old, sick, and alone.**
**Reality: Winding up alone, with no partner to care for them late in life, is increasingly likely for all women, married or single. But it's not something they lose sleep over.**
The majority of single women (81 percent) aren't overly concerned about the prospect of growing old alone, according to the AARP Foundation women's study. Among those who do worry, divorced women (25 percent) fret more than widows (19 percent) and married women (17 percent). And in fact some single women recognize that their single status will actually protect them from the heart-breaking (and often health-breaking) ordeal of caring for a sick husband in his declining years.

For older women, married or single, life can prove challenging whether they fret about it or not. "Married women may enter their 60s better off than women who are single, divorced, or widowed," says Cindy Hounsell, executive director of the Women's Institute for a Secure Retirement. "But through divorce or death, they lose their husbands and many financial benefits of being married. By age 85 the majority are single. That's the astonishing thing—most of us are going to be single."

The truth is that with no spouse to help care for them, women are more likely than men to wind up in nursing homes. And they are also more likely to get chronic illnesses than men are, says Heidi Hartmann, Ph.D., a labor economist and president of the Institute for Women's Policy Research. If the abstract fear of winding up alone doesn't worry single women, the concrete threat of becoming dependent on caregivers does. According to the AARP Foundation women's study, some 41 percent of women who live alone worry that they might lose their independence in a health crisis, versus 35 percent of women who live with a spouse or other adults. A related fear, shared equally by married and single women alike, is imposing on their children at some point in the future. About 31 percent of women who live alone, and 30 percent of women who live with others, say they are at least moderately worried about eventually becoming a burden to their family.

**Myth #8:** **The older they get, the more single women regret the lack of family ties.**
**Reality:** **Unmarried women have strong family relationships, and many have stronger social support systems than married women do.**
"It always surprises me when people say, 'Don't you wish you had a family?' " says Michele Horon, 57, a corporate-communications coordinator who lives in Bethlehem, Pennsylvania, and has never been married. "I do have a family. My mother lives with me, and I've got siblings and tons of nieces and nephews, and we're very close," she says. Even beyond blood family, contented single women knit together their own support systems of friends, colleagues, neighbors, and other people, says E. Kay Trimberger, Ph.D., a sociologist and author of *The New Single Woman* (Beacon Press, 2005), who tracked 27 single women for almost a decade. "Community really means a lot to these women and gives them geographical stability," she says. "In some cases, women in my study even turned down significant career opportunities because they didn't want to move away from these connections."

Among women living alone, 88 percent of the women in the AARP Foundation women's study say they have friends they can depend on in times of crisis. Experts like Trimberger expect women, especially those in the baby-boomer age group (42 through 60), to keep up those connections as they age. The study also found, for example, 41 percent of single women 45 through 59 said that as they got older they would be open to living with women friends.

**Myth #9:** **Single women are sex-starved.**
**Reality:** **They may be hungry at times, certainly, but most have a greater appetite for other forms of sustenance in their lives.**
When it comes to sex, single women have all kinds of ways of dealing with—and without—it. A relatively low number, just 22 percent, of the 45-plus single women in AARP's "Sexuality at Midlife and Beyond" study were sexually active in the past six months, and only 18 percent had a regular sex partner. But either way, they weren't hung up about it. "After age 50 a number of single women want fun sex," says author Levine. "This is a no-holds-barred period of their lives—they're more sexually adventurous and easygoing, and while sex isn't the biggest deal in the world, they're more willing to take pleasure when it comes." Of the single women in AARP's sexuality study, 15 percent had watched adult films with a partner, 14 percent had used sex toys, 10 percent had had phone sex, and 7 percent had exchanged frisky notes or e-mails. And in the past six months 26 percent had masturbated.

But sexual urges aren't the main driving force for older women dating, at least in the same way they are for men. Some 11 percent of the men in the AARP lifestyles, dating, and romance survey, for instance, said the main reason they date is to fulfill their sexual needs, versus a mere 2 percent of the women. And 24 percent of single women in the same survey agreed that they could be happy never having sex again. "Since menopause, I don't feel the need," says Michele Horon. Her last relationship ended five years ago. "That's not to say I wouldn't be turned on. I certainly could be, but sex is just last on my list."

**Myth #10:** **Single women aren't as healthy as married women.**
**Reality:** **Generally true, but now single women are taking charge of their health just as they're taking control of other parts of their lives.**
For decades health researchers have consistently found that married women are healthier than single women. But the most negative health outcomes for women have been associated with those who are divorced or widowed. Very little attention has been paid to the long-term health outcomes of women who are contentedly single. One surprising finding to come out of the AARP Foundation women's survey, however, is that single women tend to think of themselves as healthy—46 percent said their health is excellent or very good. In addition, 90 percent of the single women in the study said they're very or somewhat confident that they're doing all they can to keep themselves healthy. "These findings seem promising," says Jean Kalata, AARP research analyst and principal researcher for the AARP Foundation women's study, "but we need more research into single women and the effects of happiness on health."

So, is being single the new happy ending for American women? Of course not. But it doesn't mean life is over. As more unmarried women embrace the challenges and opportunities that come with living alone, they are writing new chapters in self-discovery, says Florence Falk, Ph.D., a psychotherapist in New York City and author of *On My Own: The Art of Being a Woman Alone* (Harmony Books), due out in January 2007. "Many women are surprised at how learning to be alone, in the best sense of the word, opens them up to a bigger world. Even with the speed bumps, being single can lead them to better relationships, more creativity, new friendships, and a deeper sense of self and community."

Writer **Sarah Mahoney** lives in Durham, Maine. Her last story for AARP The Magazine was *"10 Secrets of a Good, Long Life"* (July–August 2005).

Reprinted from *AARP The Magazine*, May/June 2006, pp. 62, 64–66, 68–69, 104–106. Copyright © 2006 by Sarah Mahoney. Reprinted by permission of the author.

# Goodbye to Girlhood

**As pop culture targets ever younger girls, psychologists worry about a premature focus on sex and appearance.**

STACY WEINER

Ten-year-old girls can slide their low-cut jeans over "eye-candy" panties. French maid costumes, garter belt included, are available in preteen sizes. Barbie now comes in a "bling-bling" style, replete with halter top and go-go boots. And it's not unusual for girls under 12 to sing, "Don't cha wish your girlfriend was hot like me?"

American girls, say experts, are increasingly being fed a cultural catnip of products and images that promote looking and acting sexy.

"Throughout U.S. culture, and particularly in mainstream media, women and girls are depicted in a sexualizing manner," declares the American Psychological Association's Task Force on the Sexualization of Girls, in a report issued Monday. The report authors, who reviewed dozens of studies, say such images are found in virtually every medium, from TV shows to magazines and from music videos to the Internet.

While little research to date has documented the effect of sexualized images specifically on *young* girls, the APA authors argue it is reasonable to infer harm similar to that shown for those 18 and older; for them, sexualization has been linked to "three of the most common mental health problems of girls and women: eating disorders, low self-esteem and depression."

Said report contributor and psychologist Sharon Lamb: "I don't think because we don't have the research yet on the younger girls that we can ignore that [sexualization is] of harm to them. Common sense would say that, and part of the reason we wrote the report is so we can get funding to prove that."

Boys, too, face sexualization, the authors acknowledge. Pubescent-looking males have posed provocatively in Calvin Klein ads, for example, and boys with impossibly sculpted abs hawk teen fashion lines. But the authors say they focused on girls because females are objectified more often. According to a 1997 study in the journal Sexual Abuse, 85 percent of ads that sexualized children depicted girls.

Even influences that are less explicitly erotic often tell girls who they are equals how they look and that beauty commands power and attention, contends Lamb, co-author of "Packaging Girlhood: Rescuing Our Daughters from Marketers' Schemes" (St. Martin's, 2006). One indicator that these influences are reaching girls earlier, she and others say: The average age for adoring the impossibly proportioned Barbie has slid from preteen to preschool.

When do little girls start wanting to look good for others? "A few years ago, it was 6 or 7," says Deborah Roffman, a Baltimore-based sex educator. "I think it begins by 4 now."

While some might argue that today's belly-baring tops are no more risque than hip huggers were in the '70s, Roffman disagrees. "Kids have always emulated adult things," she says. "But [years ago] it was, 'That's who I'm supposed to be as an adult.' It's very different today. The message to children is, 'You're already like an adult. It's okay for you to be interested in sex. It's okay for you to dress and act sexy, right now.' That's an entirely different frame of reference."

It's not just kids' exposure to sexuality that worries some experts; it's the kind of sexuality they're seeing. "The issue is that the way marketers and media present sexuality is in a very narrow way," says Lamb. "Being a sexual person isn't about being a pole dancer," she chides. "This is a sort of sex education girls are getting, and it's a misleading one."

## Clothes Encounters

Liz Guay says she has trouble finding clothes she considers appropriate for her daughter Tanya, age 8. Often, they're too body-hugging. Or too low-cut. Or too short. Or too spangly.

Then there are the shoes: Guay says last time she visited six stores before finding a practical, basic flat. And don't get her started on earrings.

"Tanya would love to wear dangly earrings. She sees them on TV, she sees other girls at school wearing them, she sees them in the stores all the time. . . . I just say, 'You're too young.'"

"It's not so much a feminist thing," explains Guay, a Gaithersburg medical transcriptionist. "It's more that I want her to be comfortable with who she is and to make decisions based on what's right for her, not what everybody else is doing. I want her to develop the strength that when she gets to a point where kids are offering her alcohol or drugs, that she's got enough self-esteem to say, 'I don't want that.'"

Some stats back up Guay's sense of fashion's shrinking modesty. For example, in 2003, tweens—that highly coveted marketing segment ranging from 7 to 12—spent $1.6 million on thong underwear, Time magazine reported. But even more-innocent-seeming togs, toys and activities—like tiny "Beauty Queen" T-shirts, Hello Kitty press-on nails or preteen make-overs at Club Libby Lu—can be problematic, claim psychologists. The reason: They may lure young girls into an unhealthy focus on appearance.

Studies suggest that female college students distracted by concerns about their appearance score less well on tests than do others. Plus, some experts say, "looking good" is almost culturally inseparable for girls from looking sexy: Once a girl's bought in, she's hopped onto a consumer conveyor belt in which marketers move females from pastel tiaras to hot-pink push-up bras.

Where did this girly-girl consumerism start? Diane Levin, an education professor at Wheelock College in Boston who is writing an upcoming book, "So Sexy So Soon," traces much of it to the deregulation of children's television in the mid-1980s. With the rules loosened, kids' shows suddenly could feature characters who moonlighted as products (think Power Rangers, Care Bears, My Little Pony). "There became a real awareness," says Levin, "of how to use gender and appearance and, increasingly, sex to market to children."

Kids are more vulnerable than adults to such messages, she argues.

The APA report echoes Levin's concern. It points to a 2004 study of adolescent girls in rural Fiji, linking their budding concerns about body image and weight control to the introduction of television there.

In the United States, TV's influence is incontestable. According to the Kaiser Family Foundation, for example, nearly half of American kids age 4 to 6 have a TV in their bedroom. Nearly a quarter of teens say televised sexual content affects their own behavior.

And that content is growing: In 2005, 77 percent of prime-time shows on the major broadcast networks included sexual material, according to Kaiser, up from 67 percent in 1998. In a separate Kaiser study of shows popular with teenage girls, women and girls were twice as likely as men and boys to have their appearance discussed. They also were three times more likely to appear in sleepwear or underwear than their male counterparts.

## Preteen Preening

It can be tough for a parent to stanch the flood of media influences.

Ellen Goldstein calls her daughter Maya, a Rockville fifth-grader, a teen-mag maniac. "She has a year's worth" of Girls' Life magazine, says Goldstein. "When her friends come over, they pore over this magazine." What's Maya reading? There's "Get Gorgeous Skin by Tonight," "Crush Confidential: Seal the Deal with the Guy You Dig," and one of her mom's least faves: "Get a Fierce Body Fast."

"Why do you want to tell a kid to get a fierce body fast when they're 10? They're just developing," complains Goldstein. She also bemoans the magazines' photos, which Maya has plastered on her ceiling.

"These are very glamorous-looking teenagers. They're wearing lots of makeup. They all have very glossy lips," she says. "They're generally wearing very slinky outfits. . . . I don't think those are the best role models," Goldstein says. "When so much emphasis is placed on the outside, it minimizes the importance of the person inside."

So why not just say no?

"She loves fashion," explains Goldstein. "I don't want to take away her joy from these magazines. It enhances her creative spirit. [Fashion] comes naturally to her. I want her to feel good about that. We just have to find a balance."

Experts say her concern is warranted. Pre-adolescents' propensity to try on different identities can make them particularly susceptible to media messages, notes the APA report. And for some girls, thinking about how one's body stacks up can be a real downer.

In a 2002 study, for example, seventh-grade girls who viewed idealized magazine images of women reported a drop in body satisfaction and a rise in depression.

Such results are disturbing, say observers, since eating disorders seem to strike younger today. A decade ago, new eating disorder patients at Children's National Medical Center tended to be around age 15, says Adelaide Robb, director of inpatient psychiatry. Today kids come in as young as 5 or 6.

## Mirror Images

Not everyone is convinced of the uglier side of beauty messages.

Eight-year-old Maya Williams owns four bracelets, eight necklaces, about 20 pairs of earrings and six rings, an assortment of which she sprinkles on every day. "Sometimes, she'll stand in front of the mirror and ask, "Are these pretty, Mommy?"

Her mom, Gaithersburg tutor Leah Haworth, is fine with Maya's budding interest in beauty. In fact, when Maya "wasn't sure" about getting her ears pierced, says Haworth, "I talked her into it by showing her all the pretty earrings she could wear."

What about all these sexualization allegations? "I don't equate looking good with attracting the opposite sex," Haworth says. Besides, "Maya knows her worth is based on her personality. She knows we love her for who she is."

"Looking good just shows that you care about yourself, care about how you present yourself to the world. People are judged by their appearance. People get better service and are treated better when they look better. That's just the way it is," she says. "I think discouraging children from paying attention to their appearance does them a disservice."

Magazine editor Karen Bokram also adheres to the beauty school of thought. "Research has shown that having skin issues at [her readers'] age is traumatic for girls' self-esteem," says Bokram, founder of Girls' Life. "Do we think girls need to be gorgeous in order to be worthy? No. Do we think girls' feeling good about how they look has positive effects in other areas of their lives, meaning that they make positive choices academically, socially and in romantic relationships? Absolutely."

Some skeptics of the sexualization notion also argue that kids today are hardier and savvier than critics think. Isaac Larian, whose company makes the large-eyed, pouty-lipped Bratz dolls, says, "Kids are very smart and know right from wrong." What's more, his testing indicates that girls want Bratz "because they are fun, beautiful and inspirational," he wrote in an e-mail. "Not once have we ever heard one of our consumers call Bratz 'sexy.'" Some adults "have a twisted sense of what they see in the product," Larian says.

"It is the parents' responsibility to educate their children," he adds. "If you don't like something, don't buy it."

But Genevieve McGahey, 16, isn't buying marketers' messages. The National Cathedral School junior recalls that her first real focus on appearance began in fourth grade. That's when classmates taught her: To be cool, you needed ribbons. To be cool, you needed lip gloss.

Starting around sixth grade, though, "it took on a more sinister character," she says. "People would start wearing really short skirts and lower tops and putting on more makeup. There's a strong pressure to grow up at this point."

"It's a little scary being a young girl," McGahey says. "The image of sexuality has been a lot more trumpeted in this era. . . . If you're not interested in [sexuality] in middle school, it seems a little intimidating." And unrealistic body ideals pile on extra pressure, McGahey says. At a time when their bodies and their body images are still developing, "girls are not really seeing people [in the media] who are beautiful but aren't stick-thin," she notes. "That really has an effect."

Today, though, McGahey feels good about her body and her style.

For this, she credits her mom, who is "very secure with herself and with being smart and being a woman." She also points to a wellness course at school that made her conscious of how women were depicted. "Seeing a culture of degrading women really influenced me to look at things in a new way and to think how we as high school girls react to that," she says.

"A lot of girls still hold onto that media ideal. I think I've gotten past it. As I've gotten more comfortable with myself and my body, I'm happy not to be trashy," McGahey says. "But most girls are still not completely or even semi-comfortable with themselves physically. You definitely still feel the pressure of those images."

---

STACY WEINER writes frequently for Health about families and relationships. Comments: health@washpost.com.

From *The Washington Post*, February 20, 2007. Copyright © 2007 by Stacy Weiner. Reprinted by permission of the author.

# Teenage Fatherhood and Involvement in Delinquent Behavior

TERENCE P. THORNBERRY, PhD, CAROLYN A. SMITH, PhD, AND SUSAN EHRHARD, MA

The human life course is composed of a set of behavioral trajectories in domains such as family, education, and work (Elder, 1997). In the domain of family formation, for example, a person's trajectory might be described as being in the following states: single, married, divorced, remarried, and widowed. Movement along these trajectories is characterized by elements of both continuity and change. Continuity refers to remaining in a certain state over time (such as being married) while change refers to transitions to a new state (such as getting divorced).

The life course is expected to unfold in a set of culturally normative, age-graded stages. In American society, for example, the culturally accepted sequence is for an individual to complete his or her high school education prior to beginning employment careers and getting married, and all the former, especially marriage, are expected to precede parenthood. Despite these expectations, there is, in fact, a great deal of "disorder" in the life course (Rindfuss, Swicegood, & Rosenfeld, 1987). That is, many life-course transitions are out of order (i.e., parenthood before marriage) and/or off-time (i.e., either too early or too late).

A basic premise of the life-course perspective is that off-time transitions, especially precocious transitions that occur before the person is developmentally prepared for them, are likely to be disruptive to the individual and to those around the individual. Precocious transitions are often associated with social and psychological deficits and with involvement in other problem behaviors. Precocious transitions may also lead to additional problems at later developmental stages. This paper focuses on one type of precocious transition—teenage fatherhood—and investigates whether it is related to various indicators of deviant behavior.

## Teen Fatherhood

Until recently, the study of teen parenthood has focused almost exclusively on becoming a teen mother, and relatively little attention has been paid to teenage fatherhood (Parke & Neville, 1987; Smollar & Ooms, 1988). Nevertheless, teen fatherhood appears to be associated with negative consequences, both to the father and child, that are similar to those observed for teen mothers (Lerman & Ooms, 1993). These consequences include reduced educational attainment, greater financial hardship, and less stable marriage patterns for the teen parent, along with poorer health, educationally, and behavioral outcomes among children born to teen parents (Furstenberg, Brooks-Gunn, & Morgan, 1987; Hayes, 1987; Irwin & Shafer, 1992; Lerman & Ooms, 1993). Given these negative consequences, both to the young father and his offspring, it is important to understand the processes that lead some young men to become teen fathers while others delay becoming fathers until more developmentally normative ages.

One possibility is that becoming a teen father is part of a more general deviant lifestyle. If so, we would expect teen fatherhood to be associated with involvement in other problem behaviors, such as delinquency and drug use. There is some evidence for this hypothesis; teen fathering has been found to be associated with such problem behaviors as delinquency, substance use, and disruptive school behavior (Elster, Lamb, & Tavare, 1987; Ketterlinus, Lamb, Nitz, & Elster, 1992; Resnick, Chambliss, & Blum, 1993; Thornberry, Smith, & Howard, 1997). Some researchers suggest a common problem behavior syndrome underlying all these behaviors (Jessor & Jessor, 1977), a view consistent with Anderson's ethnographic data (1993). In the remainder of this paper, we explore the link between teen fatherhood and other problem behaviors, addressing two core questions:

1. Are earlier delinquency, drug use, and related behaviors risk factors for becoming a teen father?
2. Does teen fatherhood increase the risk of involvement in deviant behavior during early adulthood?

## Research Methods

We examine these questions using data from the Rochester Youth Development Study, a multi-wave panel study in which adolescents and their primary caretakers (mainly mothers) have been interviewed since 1988. A representative sample from the population of all seventh- and eighth-grade students enrolled in the Rochester public schools during the 1987–1988 academic year was selected for the study. Male adolescents and students living in census tracts with high adult arrest rates were oversampled based on the premise that they were more likely than other youth to be at risk for antisocial behavior, the main concern of the original study. Of the 1,000 students ultimately selected, 73% were male and 27% were female.

Because the chances of selection into the panel are known, the sample can be weighted to represent all Rochester public school students, and statistical weights are used here. The Study conducted 12 interviews with the sample members, initially at 6-month intervals and later at annual intervals. This analysis is based on the 615 men in the study who were interviewed in Wave 11, when their average age was 21. Twenty percent of these individuals are White, 63% are African American, and 17% are Hispanic. The interviews, which lasted between 60 and 90 minutes, were conducted in private, face-to-face settings with the exception of a small number of respondents who had moved away from the Northeast and were interviewed by telephone. Overall, 84% (615/729) of the total male sample was interviewed at Wave 11. Due to missing data generated by cumulating data across interview waves, the number of cases included in the models for the analysis varies from 551 to 611. There is no evidence of differential subject loss [see Thornberry, Bjerregaard, & Miles (1993), and Krohn & Thornberry (1999) for detailed discussions of sampling and data collection methods.]

## Measurement of Teen Fatherhood

In Wave 11, respondents were asked to identify all of their biological children, including the name, birth date, and primary caregiver of each child. If the respondent fathered a child before his 20th birthday, he is designated a teen father. The validity of the respondent's self-reported paternity is suggested by the 95% agreement with the report provided by the respondent's parent in their interview at Wave 11.

## Problem Behavior Variables

In predicting teen fatherhood, we examine the effects of delinquent beliefs, gang membership, and three forms of delinquent behavior. These measures are based on data from early waves of the study, generally between Waves 2–5, covering ages 13.5 to 15.5, on average. As such, these indicators of problem behaviors precede the age at which fatherhood began for this sample, and they can be considered true risk factors for teen fatherhood.

Delinquent beliefs asks the respondent how wrong it is to engage in each of eight delinquent acts, with responses ranging from "not wrong at all" to "very wrong." The measure used here is a dichotomous variable denoting whether the respondent was above or below the median value on the scale. Gang membership is a self-reported measure of whether or not the respondent reported being a member of a street gang (see Thornberry, Krohn, Lizotte, Smith, & Tobin, 2003).

Three variables are used to measure deviant behavior: drug use, which is an index of the respondent's use of 10 different substances; general offending, which is an index based on 32 items reflecting all types of delinquency; and violent offending,

which is based on 6 items measuring violent crimes. For the risk factor analysis, all three indices are based on self-reported data and are trichotomized to indicate no offending, low levels of offending (below the median frequency), and high levels of offending (above the median).

These three indicators of offending are also measured during early adulthood (ages 20–22) in order to determine the effects of teen fatherhood on deviant behavior later in life. At this stage, they are simple dichotomies indicating offending versus non-offending.

# Results

We present the results in three sections. The first examines the prevalence of teen fatherhood, and the second examines whether delinquency and related behaviors are significant risk factors for becoming a teen father. The final section focuses on whether the young men who became teen fathers, as opposed to those who did not, are more likely to engage in criminal behavior during early adulthood.

## Prevalence of Teen Fatherhood

In the Rochester sample, 28% of the male respondents reported fathering a child before age 20. The age distribution at which they became fathers is presented in Figure 1. Seven subjects (1%) became fathers at age 15, truly a precocious transition. The rate of fatherhood increased sharply from that point on. At 16, 3% of the sample became fathers; at 17, 6% did; and at both 18 and 19 years of age, 9% entered the ranks of the young fathers.

## Risk Factors

The link between delinquent behavior and becoming a teen father is evident from the results presented in Figure 2. One-third (34%) of the high-level delinquents during early adolescence fathered a child before age 20, as compared to 21% of the low-level delinquents and only 13% of the non-delinquents.

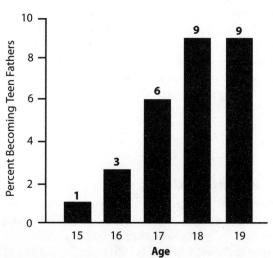

**Figure 1** Relationship Between Age and Teenage Fatherhood.

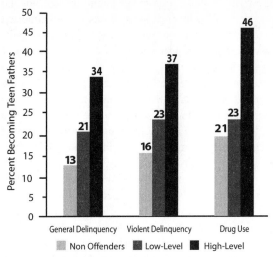

**Figure 2** Relationship Between Early Delinquent Behavior and Teenage Fatherhood.

The same dose-response relationship can be seen for violent behavior: the prevalence of teen fatherhood increases from 16%, to 23%, to 37% across the three groups. The pattern is a little different for drug use. The prevalence of teen fatherhood for the non-users and the low-level users is about the same, 21% and 23% respectively, but the rate for the high-level drug users is substantially higher, 46%. All three of these relationships are statistically significant.

In Figure 3 we present bivariate results for two variables closely related to delinquency, holding delinquent beliefs and being a member of a street gang. Both relationships are statistically significant. Younger adolescents who have higher levels of pro-delinquent beliefs are more likely (27%) to become teen fathers than those who do not (20%). Finally, gang members are more likely (38%) to become teen fathers than non-members (19%).

To this point, we have simply investigated bivariate associations, that is, the link between delinquency, say, and teen fatherhood, without holding the effect of other potential explanatory variables constant. In a fuller investigation of this

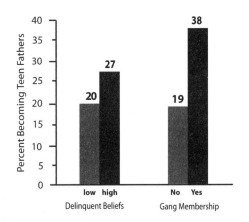

**Figure 3** Relationship Between Delinquent Beliefs and Teenage Fatherhood and Between Gang Members and Teenage Fathers.

issue, Thornberry et al., (1997) examined these relationships when the following variables were controlled: race/ethnicity, neighborhood poverty and disorganization, parent's education and age at first birth, family poverty level, recent life stress, family social support, parent's expectations for son to attend college, CAT reading achievement, early onset of sexual intercourse, and depression. When this was done, delinquent beliefs were no longer significantly related to teen fatherhood, but gang membership remained a significant and sizeable predictor of becoming a teen father. These two variables—delinquent beliefs and gang membership—were then added to the above list of controls when early adolescent delinquency, drug use, and violence were considered. General delinquency was no longer significantly related to the risk of teen fatherhood, but drug use and violent behavior were (figure not included).

Overall, it appears that early problem behaviors are a risk factor for teen fatherhood. This appears to be the case especially for the more serious forms of these behaviors—violence, high-level drug use, and gang membership.

## Later Consequences

The final issue we investigate is whether becoming a teen father is associated with higher rates of criminal involvement during early adulthood, ages 20–22. The results are presented in Figure 4. Teen fathers, as compared to males who delayed the onset of parenthood until after age 20, are not significantly more likely to be involved in general offending or in violent offending during their early 20s. However, there is a significant bivariate relationship between teen fatherhood and later drug use. Of the teen fathers, 66% report some involvement with drug use as compared to 47% of those who delayed fatherhood. This relationship is not statistically significant once adolescent drug use is held constant (results not shown), however. The latter finding indicates that early adult drug use is more a reflection of continuing use than a later consequence of becoming a teen father.

## Conclusion

This article investigated the relationship between teenage fatherhood and involvement in delinquency and related behaviors. Based on data from the Rochester Youth Development Study, it appears that an earlier pattern of problem behaviors significantly increases the risk of later becoming a teen father. This relationship is evident bivariately for the five indicators used in this analysis. Also, three of the relationships—violence, drug use, and gang membership—remain significant when the impact of a host of other important risk factors is held constant.

While earlier involvement in deviant behavior and a deviant lifestyle is related to the odds of becoming a teen father, teen fatherhood is not significantly related to later involvement in criminal conduct. At least during their early 20s, teen fathers are not more likely than those who delayed parenthood to be involved in general offending or in violent crime. They are more likely to use drugs, although that relationship is not maintained once prior drug use is controlled.

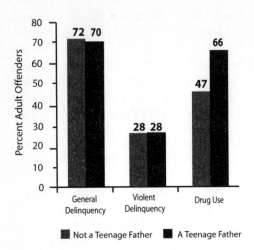

**Figure 4**  Relationship Between Teenage Fatherhood and Adult Offending.

There is a clear link between teen fatherhood and earlier involvement in other deviant behaviors. Two kinds of explanations have been suggested for these effects. The first is that adolescent males immersed in a deviant lifestyle have many opportunities to develop a set of values and behaviors conducive to risky, adult-like adventures, some involving conquest and domination over others, including young women. This notion is supported by some ethnographic research (Anderson, 1993) and some gang studies (for example, Covey, Menard, & Franzese, 1992). Second, research has also documented that about one-fifth of teenage males feel that impregnating a young woman would make them feel "more like a man" (Marsiglio, 1993). There may be so few avenues for positive identity formation, particularly among poor adolescents and adolescents of color, that having a child is no deterrent to potential goals. Involvement in deviant behaviors, including early fatherhood, may at best be a means of achieving adult status and positive recognition or at least a means of making a mark in a world where even survival is in doubt (Burton, 1995).

## Implications

It seems evident that becoming a teen father is not an isolated event in the lives of these young men. It is systematically related to involvement in a deviant lifestyle and, in a broader analysis of these data (Thornberry et al., 1997), to a variety of other deficits. These results have a number of implications for prevention programs designed to delay the transition to fatherhood and to improve the lot of these young men and their offspring. First, these programs need to be prepared to deal with this constellation of behavior problems and how teen fatherhood is intertwined with them. Focusing simply on reducing teenage fatherhood, absent a consideration of the broader context in which it occurs, may not be very effective. Second, prevention programs should include, or at least be prepared to provide access to, services to reduce involvement in antisocial behaviors for these adolescent males. Third, programs to improve the parenting skills of these young fathers need to take into account their higher level of involvement in delinquency, drug use, and related behaviors. All of these behaviors have been shown to be related to less consistent, more erratic styles of parenting (Patterson, Reid, & Dishion, 1992) and efforts to improve effective parenting need to address these risk factors. Finally, programs and policies that try to maximize the teenage father's involvement in the rearing of his children need to be aware of the higher level of antisociality on the part of many of these young fathers. Insuring that risk to the young child is not elevated seems to be the first order of business.

Although there is a pronounced relationship between earlier antisocial behavior and the likelihood of becoming a teen father, we end on a somewhat more positive note. Not all antisocial adolescent males become teen fathers and not all teen fathers have a career of involvement in antisocial behavior. This relationship should not be painted with too broad a brush. Policies need to realistically assess the magnitude of the relationship and realistically take it into account when working with these men and their children.

## References

Anderson, E. (1993). Sex codes and family life among poor inner-city youths. In R.I. Lerman & T.J. Ooms (Eds.), *Young Unwed Fathers: Changing Roles and Emerging Policies* (pp. 74–98). Philadelphia: Temple University Press.

Burton, L.M. (1995). Family structure and nonmarital fertility: Perspectives from ethnographic research. In K.A. Moore (Ed.), *Report to Congress on Out-of-Wedlock Childbearing* (pp. 147–166). Hyattsville, MD: U.S. Department of Health and Human Services.

Covey, H.C., Menard, S., & Franzese, R.J. (1992). *Juvenile Gangs.* Springfield, IL: Charles C. Thomas.

Elder, G.H., Jr. (1997). The life course and human development. In W. Damon (Ed.-in-Chief) & R.M. Lerner (Ed.), *Handbook of Child Psychology, Vol. 1: Theoretical Models of Human Development* (pp. 939–991). New York: Wiley.

Elster, A.B., Lamb, M.E., & Tavare, J. (1987). Association between behavioral and school problems and fatherhood in a national sample of adolescent fathers. *Journal of Pediatrics, 111,* 932–936.

Furstenberg, F.F., Brooks-Gunn, J., & Morgan, S.P. (1987). *Adolescent Mothers in Later Life.* New York: Cambridge University Press.

Hayes, C.D. (1987). *Risking the Future: Adolescent Sexuality, Pregnancy and Childbearing* (Vol. 1). Washington, DC: National Academy Press.

Irwin, C.E., Jr., & Shafer, M.A. (1992). Adolescent sexuality: Negative outcomes of a normative behavior. In D.E. Rodgers & E. Ginzberg (Eds.), *Adolescents at Risk: Medical and Social Perspectives* (pp. 35–79). Boulder, CO: Westview Press.

Jessor, R., & Jessor, S.L. (1977). *Problem Behavior and Psychosocial Development.* New York: Academic Press.

Ketterlinus, R.D., Lamb, M.E., Nitz, K., & Elster, A.B. (1992). Adolescent nonsexual and sex-related problem behaviors. *Journal of Adolescent Research, 7,* 431–456.

Krohn, M.D., & Thornberry, T.P. (1999). Retention of minority populations in panel studies of drug use. *Drugs & Society, 14,* 185–207.

Lerman, R.I., & Ooms, T.J. (1993). Introduction: Evolution of unwed fatherhood as a policy issue. In R.I. Lerman & T.J. Ooms (Eds.), *Young Unwed Fathers: Changing Roles and Emerging Policies* (pp. 1–26). Philadelphia: Temple University Press.

Marsiglio, W. (1993). Contemporary scholarship on fathers: Culture, identity, and conduct. *Journal of Family Issues, 14,* 484–509.

Parke, R.D., & Neville, B. (1987). Teenage fatherhood. In S.L. Hofferth & C.D. Hayes (Eds.), *Risking the Future: Adolescent Sexuality, Pregnancy, and Childbearing, Vol. 2* (pp. 145–173). Washington, DC: National Academy Press.

Patterson, G.R., Reid, J.B., & Dishion, T.J. (1992). *Antisocial Boys.* Eugene, OR: Castalia Publishing Company.

Resnick, M.D., Chambliss, S.A., & Blum, R.W. (1993). Health and risk behaviors of urban adolescent males involved in pregnancy. *Families in Society, 74,* 366–374.

Rindfuss, R.R., Swicegood, C.G., & Rosenfeld, R. (1987). Disorder in the life course: How common and does it matter? *American Sociological Review, 52,* 785–801.

Smollar, J., & Ooms, T. (1988). *Young Unwed Fathers: Research Review, Policy Dilemmas, and Options: Summary Report.* U.S. Department of Health and Human Services, Washington, DC: U.S. Government Printing Office.

Thornberry, T.P., Bjerregaard, B. & Miles, W. (1993). The consequences of respondent attrition in panel studies: A simulation based on the Rochester Youth Development Study. *Journal of Quantitative Criminology, 9,* 127–158.

Thornberry, T.P., Krohn, M.D., Lizotte, A.J., Smith, C.A., & Tobin, K. (2003). *Gangs and Delinquency in Developmental Perspective.* New York: Cambridge University Press.

Thornberry, T.P., Smith, C.A., & Howard, G.J. (1997). Risk factors for teenage fatherhood. *Journal of Marriage and the Family, 59,* 505–522.

**TERENCE P. THORNBERRY,** PhD, is Director of the Research Program on Problem Behavior at the Institute of Behavioral Science and Professor of Sociology, University of Colorado. He is the Principal Investigator of the Rochester Youth Development Study, an ongoing panel study begun in 1986 to examine the causes and consequences of delinquency, drug use, and other forms of antisocial behavior. Professor Thornberry is an author of *Gangs and Delinquency in Developmental Perspective* and an editor of *Taking Stock of Delinquency: An Overview of Findings from Contemporary Longitudinal Studies.* **CAROLYN A. SMITH,** PhD, is Professor in the School of Social Welfare, University at Albany. She holds an MSW from the University of Michigan, and a PhD from the School of Criminal Justice at the University at Albany. She has international social work practice experience in child and family mental health, and in delinquency intervention. Her primary research interest is in the family etiology of delinquency and other problem behaviors, and most recently the impact of child maltreatment on the life course. **SUSAN EHRHARD** holds an MA in Criminal Justice and is currently a doctoral student at the School of Criminal Justice, University at Albany, as well as a Research Assistant for the Rochester Youth Development Study. Her research interests include the sociology of crime, restorative justice, and capital punishment.

From *The Prevention Researcher,* 11(4), November 2004, pp. 10–13. Copyright © 2004 by Integrated Research Services, Inc. Reprinted by permission.

*Ethnography*

# How Many Fathers Are Best for a Child?

**After 40 years of visiting the Barí Indians in Venezuela, anthropologists have discovered a new twist on family values.**

Meredith F. Small

Anthropologist Stephen Beckerman was well into his forties before he finally understood how babies are made. He had thought, as most people do, that a sperm from one man and an egg from one woman joined to make a child. But one summer day, as he and his colleague Roberto Lizarralde lounged around in hammocks, chatting with Rachel, an elderly woman of the Barí tribe of Venezuela, she pointed out his error. Babies, she explained, can easily have more than one biological father. "My first husband was the father of my first child, my second child, and my third child," Rachel said, recalling her life. "But the fourth child, actually, he has two fathers." It was clear that Rachel didn't mean there was a stepfather hanging around or a friendly uncle who took the kid fishing every weekend. She was simply explaining the Barí version of conception to these ignorant anthropologists: A fetus is built up over time with repeated washes of sperm—which means, of course, that more than one man can contribute to the endeavor. This interview changed not only the way Beckerman and Lizarralde viewed Barí families but also brought into question the very way that anthropologists portray human coupling. If biological fatherhood can be shared—an idea accepted by many indigenous groups across South America and in many other cultures across the globe—then the nuclear family with one mom and one dad might not be the established blueprint for a family that we have been led to expect. If so, the familiar story of traditional human mating behavior, in which man the hunter brings home the bacon to his faithful wife, loses credibility. And if the Barí and other groups work perfectly well with more flexible family styles, the variety of family structures that are increasingly common in Western culture these days—everything from single-parent households to blended families—may not be as dangerous to the social fabric as we are led to believe. People in this culture may simply be exercising the same family options

that humans have had for millions of years, options that have been operating in other cultures while the West took a stricter view of what constitutes a family.

## Women grow fat during a pregnancy, while men grow thin from all their work.

Stephen Beckerman folds his 6-foot-4-inch frame into a chair and turns to the mountainous topography of papers on his desk at Pennsylvania State University. Once he manages to locate a map under all the piles, he points to a spot on the border between Venezuela and Colombia where he spent 20 years, off and on, with the indigenous Barí Indians. The traditional Barí culture, Beckerman explains, has come under attack by outside forces, starting with the conquistadors who arrived in the early 16th century. Today Catholic missionaries interact with the Barí, coal and oil companies are trying to seize their land, and drug traffickers and guerrillas are threats. Western influences are apparent: Most families have moved from traditional longhouses to single-family dwellings, and everyone wears modern Western clothes and uses Western goods. However, the Barí continue to practice their traditions of manioc farming, fishing, and hunting, according to Roberto Lizarralde, an anthropologist at the Central University of Venezuela who has been visiting the Barí regularly since 1960. Lizarralde also says that the Barí still have great faith in traditional spirits and ancestral wisdom, including their notion that a child can have multiple biological fathers. The Barí believe that the first act of sex, which should always be between a husband and wife, plants the seed. Then the fledgling fetus must be nourished by repeated anointings of semen; the woman's body is viewed as a vessel where men do all the work. "One of the reasons women give you for taking lovers is that they don't want to wear out their husbands," Beckerman says. "They claim it's hard work for men to support a pregnancy by having enough sex, and so lovers can help." Just look, the Barí say. Women grow fat during a pregnancy, while men grow thin from all their work.

Anthropologists study a culture's ideas about conception because those ideas have a profound impact on the way people run their lives. In our culture, for example, conceiving children incurs long-term economic responsibility for both the mother and father. We take this obligation so seriously that when a parent fails to provide for a child, it is usually a violation of law. In the Barí system, when a man is named as a secondary biological father he is also placed under an obligation to the mother and the child. In addition, he is expected to give gifts of fish and game. These gifts are a significant burden because the man must also provide for his own wife and primary children. Beckerman and his colleagues have discovered that naming secondary fathers has evolutionary consequences. A team of ethnographers led by Beckerman, Roberto Lizarralde, and his son Manuel, an anthropologist at Connecticut College who has been visiting the Barí since he was 5 years old, interviewed 114 Barí women past childbearing years and asked them about their full reproductive histories. "These interviews were a lot of fun," Beckerman says, laughing. "Randy old ladies talking about their lovers." In total, the researchers recorded claims of 916 pregnancies, an average of eight pregnancies for each woman. But child mortality was high—about one-third of the children did not survive to age 15. Naming secondary fathers was a critical factor in predicting which babies made it to adulthood. Secondary fathers were involved in 25 percent of pregnancies, and the team determined that two fathers were the ideal number. Children with one father and one secondary father made it to their teens most often; kids with only one father or those with more than two fathers didn't fare as well. The researchers also found that this decrease in mortality occurred not during the child's life but during fetal development: Women were less likely to have a miscarriage or stillbirth if they had a husband and an additional male contributing food. This result was a surprise because researchers had expected that help during childhood would be more important. "The Barí are not hungry; they are not close to the bone. But it must be the extra fat and protein that they get from secondary fathers during gestation that makes the difference," Beckerman explains as he points to photographs of Barí women who look well nourished, even downright plump. Barí women seem to use this more flexible system of paternity when they need it. Within families, some children have secondary fathers, while their siblings belong to the husband alone. The team discovered that mothers are more likely to take on a secondary father when a previous child has died in infancy. Manuel Lizarralde claims the strategy makes perfect sense, given the Barí belief that the best way to cure a sick child is for the father to blow tobacco smoke over the child's body. "It is easy to imagine a bereaved mother thinking to herself that if she had only provided a secondary father and so more smoke for her dead child, she might have saved

him—and vowing to provide that benefit for her next child." Beckerman says extra fathers may have always been insurance for uncertain times: "Because the Barí were once hunted as if they were game animals—by other Indians, conquistadors, oilmen, farmers, and ranchers—the odds of a woman being widowed when she still had young children were one in three, according to data we gathered about the years 1930 to 1960. The men as well as the women knew this. None of these guys can go down the street to Mutual of Omaha and buy a life insurance policy. By allowing his wife to take a lover, the husband is doing all he can to ensure the survival of his children." Barí women are also freer to do as they wish because men need their labor—having a wife is an economic necessity because women do the manioc farming, harvesting, and cooking, while men hunt and fish. "The sexual division of labor is such that you can't make it without a member of the opposite sex," says Beckerman. Initially, the researchers worried that jealousy on the part of husbands would make Barí women reticent about discussing multiple sexual partners. "In our first interviews, we would wait until the husband was out of the house," says Beckerman. "But one day we interviewed an old couple who were enjoying thinking about their lives; they were lying in their hammocks, side by side, and it was obvious he wasn't going anywhere. So we went down the list of her children and asked about other fathers. She said no, no, no for each child, and then the husband interrupted when we got to one and said, 'That's not true, don't you remember, there was that guy . . .' And the husband was grinning." Not all women take lovers. Manuel Lizarralde has discovered through interviews that one-third of 122 women were faithful to their husbands during their pregnancies. "These women say they don't need it, or no one asked, or they have enough support from family and don't require another father for their child," Lizarralde says. "Some even admit that their husbands were not that happy about the idea." Or it may be a sign of changing times. Based on his most recent visits to the Barí, Lizarralde thinks that under the influence of Western values, the number of people who engage in multiple fatherhood may be decreasing. But his father, who has worked with the Barí for more than 40 years, disagrees. He says the practice is as frequent but that the Barí discuss it less openly than before, knowing that Westerners object to their views. After all, it took the anthropologists 20 years to hear about other fathers, and today the Barí are probably being even more discreet because they know Westerners disapprove of their beliefs. "What this information adds up to," Beckerman says, "is that the Barí may be doing somewhat less fooling around within marriage these days but that most of them still believe that a child can have multiple fathers." More important, the Barí idea that biological paternity can be shared is not just the quirky custom of one tribe; anthropologists have found that this idea is common across South America. The same belief is shared by indigenous groups in New Guinea and India, suggesting that multiple paternity has been part of human behavior for a long time, undermining all previous descriptions of how human mating behavior evolved.

## As the Barí and other cultures show, there are all sorts of ways to run a successful household.

Since the 1960s, when anthropologists began to construct scenarios of early human mating, they had always assumed that the model family started with a mom and dad bonded for life to raise the kids, a model that fit well with acceptable Western behavior. In 1981 in an article titled "The Origin of Man," C. Owen Lovejoy, an anthropologist at Kent State University, outlined the standard story of human evolution as it was used in the field—and is still presented in textbooks today: Human infants with their big brains and long periods of growth and learning have always been dependent on adults, a dependence that separates the humans from the apes. Mothers alone couldn't possibly find enough food for these dependent young, so women have always needed to find a mate who would stick close to home and bring in supplies for the family. Unfortunately for women, as evolutionary psychologists suggest, men are compelled by their biology to mate with as many partners as possible to pass along their genes. However, each of these men might be manipulated into staying with one woman who offered him sex and a promise of fidelity. The man, under those conditions, would be assured of paternity, and he might just stay around and make sure his kids survived. This scenario presents humans as naturally monogamous, forming nuclear families as an evolutionary necessity. The only problem is that around the world families don't always operate this way. In fact, as the Barí and other cultures show, there are all sorts of ways to run a successful household. The Na of Yunnan Province in China, for example, have a female-centric society in which husbands are not part of the picture. Women grow up and continue to live with their mothers, sisters, and brothers; they never marry or move away from the family compound. As a result, sisters and brothers rather than married pairs are the economic unit that farms and fishes together. Male lovers in this system are simply visitors. They have no place or power in the household, and children are brought up by their mothers and by the mothers' brothers. A father is identified only if there is a resemblance between him and the child, and even so, the father has no responsibilities toward the child. Often women have sex with so many partners that the biological father is unknown. "I have not found any term that would cover the notion of father in the Na language," writes Chinese anthropologist Cai Hua in his book *A Society Without Fathers or Husbands: The Na of China.* In this case, women have complete control over their children, property, and sexuality. Across lowland South America,

family systems vary because cultures put their beliefs into practice in different ways. Among some native people, such as the Canela, Mehinaku, and Araweté, women control their sex lives and their fertility, and most children have several fathers. Barí women are also sexually liberated from an early age. "Once she has completed her puberty ritual, a Barí girl can have sex with anyone she wants as long as she doesn't violate the incest taboo," Beckerman explains. "It's nobody's business, not even Mom's and Dad's business." Women can also turn down prospective husbands. In other cultures in South America, life is not so free for females, although members of these cultures also believe that babies can have more than one father. The Curripaco of Amazonia, for instance, acknowledge multiple fatherhood as a biological possibility and yet frown on women having affairs. Paul Valentine, a senior lecturer in anthropology at the University of East London who has studied the Curripaco for more than 20 years, says, "Curripaco women are in a difficult situation. The wives come into the village from different areas, and it's a very patrilineal system." If her husband dies, a widow is allowed to turn only to his brothers or to clan members on his side of the family for a new husband. The relative power of women and men over their sex lives has important consequences. "In certain social and economic systems, women are free to make mate choices," says Valentine. In these cultures women are often the foundation of society, while men have less power in the community. Sisters tend to stay in the same household as their mothers. The women, in other words, have power to make choices. "At the other extreme, somehow, it's the men who try to maximize their evolutionary success at the expense of the women," says Valentine. Men and women often have a conflict of interest when it comes to mating, marriage, and who should invest most in children, and the winners have sometimes been the men, sometimes the women. As Beckerman wryly puts it, "Anyone who believes that in a human mating relationship the man's reproductive interests always carry the day has obviously never been married." The Barí and others show that human systems are, in fact, very flexible, ready to accommodate any sort of mating system or type of family. "I think that human beings are capable of making life extremely complicated. That's our way of doing business," says Ian Tattersall, a paleoanthropologist and curator in the division of anthropology at the American Museum of Natural History in New York City. Indeed, such flexibility suggests there's no reason to assume that the nuclear family is the natural, ideal, or even most evolutionarily successful system of human grouping. As Beckerman says, "One of the things this research shows is that human beings are just as clever and creative in assembling their kin relations as they are putting together space shuttles or symphonies."

From *Discover*, April 2003, pp. 54–61. Copyright © 2003 by Meredith F. Small. Reprinted by permission of the author.

# What Autistic Girls Are Made Of

EMILY BAZELON

Caitlyn and Marguerite sat knee to knee in a sunny room at the Hawks Camp in Park City, Utah. On one wall was a white board with these questions: What's your favorite vacation and why? What's your favorite thing about yourself? If you could have any superpower, what would it be?

Caitlyn, who is 13, and Marguerite, who is 16 (I've used only their first names to protect their privacy), held yellow sheets of paper on which they had written their answers. It was the third day of the weeklong camp, late for icebreakers. But the Hawks are kids with autistic disorders accompanied by a normal or high I.Q. And so the main goal of the camp, run on a 26-acre ranch by a Utah nonprofit organization called the National Ability Center, is to nudge them toward the sort of back and forth—"What's your favorite video game?"—that comes easily to most kids.

Along with Caitlyn and Marguerite, there were nine boys in the camp between the ages of 10 and 18. They also sat across from one another in pairs, with the exception of one 18-year-old who was arguing with a counselor. "All I require is a purple marker," the boy said over and over again, refusing to write with the black marker he had been given. A few feet away, an 11-year-old was yipping and grunting while his partner read his answers in a monotone, eyes trained on his yellow paper. Another counselor hurried over to them.

Marguerite was also reading her answers without eye contact or inflection. "My favorite vacations were to India and Thailand my favorite thing about myself is that I'm nice to people if I could choose any superpower I'd be invisible," she said in an unbroken stream. She looked up from her paper and past Caitlyn, smoothing her turquoise halter top over the waist of a pair of baggy cotton pants. Caitlyn was also staring into the middle distance. She has gold-streaked hair, which was bunched on top, and wore a black T-shirt with a sunburst on the front and canvas sneakers with skulls on the tops. The girls didn't look uncomfortable, just unplugged.

A counselor noticed their marooned silence and prodded Caitlyn to take her turn. At first, she ran quickly through her answers, too. But Caitlyn loves fantasy—she is an avid writer of "fan fiction," spinning new story lines for familiar characters from "Pokémon" and "Harry Potter"—and the superpower question grabbed her. She looked at Marguerite. "If I could have any power, I'd want to be able to transform into an animal like a tiger," she said, smiling and putting her hands in front of her face, fingers tensed as if they were claws. Marguerite smiled and tentatively mirrored the claw gesture. Caitlyn smiled back. "I like tigers," she said, her eyes bright behind her glasses. "Do you?"

It was a small, casual encounter and also an exceedingly rare one—a taste of teenage patter shared by two autistic girls.

Autism is often thought of as a boys' affliction. Boys are three or four times as likely as girls to have classic autism (autism with mental retardation, which is now often referred to as cognitive impairment). The sex ratio is even more imbalanced for diagnoses that include normal intelligence along with the features of autism—social and communication impairments and restricted interests; this is called Asperger's syndrome (when there is no speech delay) or high-functioning autism or, more generally, being "on the autistic spectrum." Among kids in this category, referral rates are in the range of 10 boys for every girl.

According to the Centers for Disease Control, there are about 560,000 people under the age of 21 with autism in the United States. (Adults aren't included because there is no good data on their numbers.) If 1 in 4 are female, the girls number about 140,000. The C.D.C. estimates that about 42 percent of them are of normal intelligence, putting their total at roughly 58,000 (with the caveat that these numbers are, at best, estimates).

Because there are so many fewer females with autism, they are "research orphans," as Ami Klin, a psychology and psychiatry professor who directs Yale's autism program, puts it. Scientists have tended to cull girls from studies because it is difficult to find sufficiently large numbers of them. Some of the drugs, for example, commonly used to treat symptoms of autism like anxiety and hyperactivity have rarely been tested on autistic girls.

The scant data make it impossible to draw firm conclusions about why their numbers are small and how autistic girls and boys with normal intelligence may differ. But a few researchers are trying to establish whether and how the disorder may vary by sex. This research and the observations of some clinicians who work with autistic girls suggest that because of biology and experience, and the interaction between the two, autism may express itself differently in girls. And that may have implications for their well-being.

The typical image of the autistic child is a boy who is lost in his own world and indifferent to other people. It is hard to generalize about autistic kids, boys or girls, but some clinicians who work with high-functioning autistic children say they often see girls who care a great deal about what their peers think. These girls want to connect with people outside their families, says Janet Lainhart, a professor of psychiatry and pediatrics at the University of Utah who treats Caitlyn and Marguerite. But often they can't. Lainhart says that this thwarted desire may trigger severe anxiety and depression.

Other specialists are not sure that girls struggle more in these ways. "This is a profile of both boys and girls," Klin says of the wish to connect that some people with autism have. But he agrees with Lainhart that it is easier for Asperger's boys to find other boys—either on or off the autistic spectrum—who want to spend hours on their Game Boys or in a realm of Internet fantasy. Klin and Lainhart also say they think that the world is a more forgiving place for boys with the quirks of Asperger's because, like it or not, awkwardness is a more acceptable male trait.

This gender dynamic doesn't necessarily affect girls with Asperger's when they are very young; if anything, they often fare better than boys at an early age because they tend to be less disruptive. In 1993, Catherine Lord, a veteran autism researcher, published a study of 21 boys and 21 girls. She found that when the children were between the ages of 3 and 5, parents more frequently described the girls as imitating typical kids and seeking out social contacts. Yet by age 10, none of the girls had reciprocal friendships while some of the boys did. "The girls often have the potential to really develop relationships," says Lord, a psychology and psychiatry professor and director of the Autism and Communication Disorders Center at the University of Michigan. "But by middle school, a subset of them is literally dumbstruck by anxiety. They do things like bursting into tears or lashing out in school, which make them very conspicuous. Their behavior really doesn't jibe with what's expected of girls. And that makes their lives very hard."

No doubt part of the problem for autistic girls is the rising level of social interaction that comes in middle school. Girls' networks become intricate and demanding, and friendships often hinge on attention to feelings and lots of rapid and nuanced communication—in person, by cellphone or Instant Messenger. No matter how much they want to connect, autistic girls are not good at empathy and conversation, and they find themselves locked out, seemingly even more than boys do. At the University of Texas Medical School, Katherine Loveland, a psychiatry professor, recently compared 700 autistic boys and 300 autistic girls and found that while the boys' "abnormal communications" decreased as I.Q. scores rose, the girls' did not. "Girls will have more trouble with social networks if they're having greater difficulty with communication and language," she says.

And so girls with autism and normal intelligence may end up at a particular disadvantage. In a new study published in May, a group of German researchers compared 23 high-functioning autistic girls with 23 high-functioning boys between the ages of 5 and 20, matching them for age, I.Q. and autism diagnosis. Parents reported more problems for girls involving peer relations, maturity, social independence and attention.

The difficulty may continue into adulthood. While some men with Asperger's marry and have families, women almost never do, psychiatrists observe. A 2004 study by two prominent British researchers, Michael Rutter and Patricia Howlin, followed 68 high-functioning autistics over more than two decades. The group included only seven women, too small a sample to reach solid conclusions about gender differences, Rutter and Howlin caution. But 15 men—22 percent of the sample—rated "good" or "very good" for educational attainment, employment, relationships and independent living, while no women did. Two women rated "fair," compared with 11 men, and the other five women were counted as "poor" or "very poor." None had gone to college. None reported having friends or living on their own. Only one had a job. Undermined by anxiety and depression, women with autism appear to be more often confined to the small world of their families.

When Caitlyn started kindergarten and didn't play normally with other kids, her mother, Juli, thought it was because she hadn't gone to preschool. The first warning of real trouble came from the first-grade gym teacher, who told Juli that Caitlyn exposed herself to the class. Caitlyn is overweight, and she has always been private about her body. Juli couldn't imagine her daughter taking off her clothes in public, and when she asked what had happened, Caitlyn said another girl had pulled down her pants. "Caitlyn stood there mortified," Juli says. "But she couldn't express that to the teacher."

Caitlyn lives with her mother, her older sister, the girls' great-grandparents and a pair of poodles in Farmington, outside of Salt Lake City. (Her father died before she was 2.) Until second grade, Caitlyn had a neighborhood friend with whom she went to school. Other than that, she was often alone in class. Her teachers were frequently frustrated with her inability to work and play in groups. But she connected with a few adults—in fifth grade, one class aide took her horseback riding, and the school librarian gave Caitlyn her own copy of "Spindle's End," a retelling of "Sleeping Beauty," "because she said I helped her so much," Caitlyn remembers.

Contrary to the Asperger's stereotype, Caitlyn struggles in math but tests in the highly gifted range in reading and writing. This is another sex difference that Lord sees among her patients. "I don't have any real data, but a lot of high-functioning girls are real readers—not great on subtleties, but they like fantasies and the 'Baby-Sitters' series," she says. "The boys are much less so."

In elementary school, Caitlyn went to special-education classes for math and social skills. At 11, as other girls began to slip out of reach, Asperger's was diagnosed. The shift a year later to junior high for seventh grade was a jolt. By the second week of school, a few boys were mocking Caitlyn's weight and calling her weird while other kids laughed. "No one would sit by me at lunch," Caitlyn says. Girls told her that they didn't want her to be in their reading group. Caitlyn did her homework, but she was too anxious to walk to the front of the room to turn it in. At home, her neighborhood friend no longer came out to play.

In the winter, Caitlyn switched from a special-education math class into a mainstream one, and the kids in her new class made her miserable. For days she refused to go to school. She told Lainhart: "No one likes me at lunch. I'm very sad." (With Juli's and Caitlyn's permission, I read Lainhart's notes on Caitlyn's treatment.) After a huge outburst of anger at home, Caitlyn told her mother that she wanted to die. At her next appointment with Lainhart, she said: "I listen to people's conversations during free time in science. They talk about live games, R-rated movies, outfits. I feel left out." Caitlyn told Lainhart about two dreams. In one, her school had a bridge running through it, and she kept falling off. In the second, she was in the lunchroom throwing a party; no one came. Lainhart says that while boys are aware of rejection and bullying, in her experience they are not hurt by it to the extent that some girls are. "I have rarely had a male patient with autism become suicidal or express such intense emotional pain," she says.

Caitlyn has never hit another child. But at school, her retorts to her peers—"I yelled at a . . . little bimbo. They yelled at me," she told Lainhart during one appointment—pushed them further away. With Lainhart's help, Juli persuaded the school to let her daughter eat lunch in a classroom rather than in the cafeteria. Still, Caitlyn's grades dropped from A's and B's to D's and F's. Her anxiety level spiked, and her sadness bloomed into depression.

Lainhart has seen the same blend of anxiety and depression in other female patients. Like Caitlyn, Marguerite's serious problems date from middle school. In sixth grade, she moved to Salt Lake City and away from a couple of strong friendships, and she couldn't replace them. "She found it increasingly difficult to do the things necessary to maintain friendships with 'normal' kids," her father says. Last fall, at 15, she withdrew further. An olive-skinned girl with thick brown hair—she was adopted from Guatemala as a baby—Marguerite has always liked to go shopping and wear pretty things (not a typical trait for a girl with autism, though not unique either). But she stopped dressing herself, washing her hair and going to school. For months, Marguerite spiraled into one of the worst bouts of depression Lainhart has ever seen.

Since 1990, when she was recruited to work with autistic children by Susan Folstein, a prominent Johns Hopkins researcher, Lainhart has been interested in the relationship between autism and depression. In a 1994 paper, Lainhart and Folstein pointed out that despite the 4-to-1 male-female ratio for autism, females made up half the autistic patients with mood disorders described in the medical literature. The case reports may not represent the population as a whole; still, the overrepresentation is suggestive. Lainhart is currently looking at the relationship between autism and depression in boys and girls and the potential link to depression in their parents and siblings. "We know that anxiety and depression are comorbid," meaning that they occur together, Lainhart says. "And we know that depression is worse for women in the general population. But what's the link to autism? And is it worse for girls?"

Social anxiety affects Lainhart's female patients into adulthood. Liz Lee, who is 43, is studying for her master's degree in electrical engineering, yet she cannot cope with going to lunch with the other graduate students at the lab where she works. Ash Baxter, who is 22, spends hours making art, sewing dolls with wild yarn hair and macramé-edged suits; she created an extraordinary blue-and-gold octopus mask out of a three-foot gourd she found in the garage. She is talented and would like to attend art school, but Baxter can't master her anxiety well enough to learn to drive or live in a dorm, so college art classes remain out of reach. Another patient, Charlotte (she asked that I not use her last name) is 23 and goes to a social-skills class that Lainhart runs for her patients in their late teens and early 20s. Because of the dearth of females, the class is mostly male, and Charlotte often leaves in the middle saying she's "stressed out." "She can only take so much," her mother told me. Lainhart says, "You see these incredible areas of anxiety in Liz and Charlotte and Marguerite that don't seem to have a parallel in the boys and men."

There is preliminary evidence that girls and women also vary from the male Asperger's profile in terms of their interests, as Catherine Lord suggests. David Skuse, a psychiatry professor at the Institute of Child Health at University College London, has analyzed data from 1,000 children, 700 of them on the autistic spectrum. "Girls with autism are rarely fascinated with numbers and rarely have stores of arcane knowledge, and this is reflected in the interests of females in the general population," Skuse explains. "The girls are strikingly different from the boys in this respect."

With her high aptitude for reading and writing and her difficulties with math, Caitlyn fits Skuse's model. Even as she was failing school last year, she kept up her fan fiction, posting stories she had written on the Web site Gaia Online. On the 40-mile drive home from camp, she told me about her plan to write an original eight-book fantasy series about a werewolf, to be called "Midnight Wind."

One of the best-known theorists on sex difference and autism, Simon Baron-Cohen, comes at these questions from another angle. A psychology professor and director of the Autism Research Centre at Cambridge University, Baron-Cohen has characterized autism as a condition of the "extreme male brain." His research shows that in the general population men are more likely than women to score low on a test of empathy and high on a test of recognizing rules and patterns, or "systemizing." High systemizing together with low empathy correlates with social and communication deficits and, at the extreme end of the scale, with autism. Baron-Cohen is currently studying whether elevated levels of fetal testosterone—a prime driver of masculinity—are linked to autistic traits.

Baron-Cohen says that he believes that autistic girls are strong systemizers. That quality may manifest itself in letters rather than numbers. But in his view, the thought processes for Asperger's girls mirror those of boys. He explains, "These females often feel more compatibility with typical males simply because typical males may be more willing to adhere to the linear, step-by-step form of thinking and conversation—more like debating or playing chess or doing logic."

To Lainhart, Baron-Cohen's extreme-male-brain theory is an apt description for a subset of her female patients, for example Liz Lee, who in pursuing electrical engineering is training for a classic Asperger's profession. Lee is socially aloof: she usually sits on the floor with her back to Lainhart during their sessions, twirling the propeller of a toy helicopter. Eye contact makes Lee angry, and she says she would like to live alone in the desert.

But based on their clinical experience, Lainhart and also Skuse see autism as a heterogeneous disorder. Its profile may change and expand as more is understood about girls, whose autism, they worry, often goes undiagnosed. That is partly, Skuse posits, because girls' general aptitude for communication and their social competence helps some Asperger's girls "pass"—they pick up on their difference and carefully mask it by mimicking other girls' speech and manner and dress. In a sense, their femaleness allows some girls to seem less autistic. It is as if they start off with a social advantage—Skuse sees this as a 20-point bonus on a scale of 100—that helps counter the disorder. This idea isn't necessarily at odds with the findings that show girls to be more seriously affected by autism, Skuse says, because the girls who succeed in masking their deficit wouldn't be included in studies. And so they are missing from the picture. "There is no doubt in my mind that the way we have defined autism currently biases our assessments strongly in the direction of identifying a male stereotype," he says. The C.D.C. agrees and says that as a result the estimate for the number of girls with autism and normal intelligence may be low.

W hy would autism express itself differently depending on sex? The short answer is that no one knows. Genetic researchers, however, have just begun to hint at possibilities. In the last two years, new data-pooling efforts have yielded two major genetic-linkage studies—attempts to link autism to specific chromosomes—that suggest that some of the genes underlying autism may be different in males and females. By isolating sex as a variable, scientists are seeing potential genetic hot spots for autism. "By comparing males and females, we will have a much better chance of discovering the causes of autism," says Geraldine Dawson, a psychology professor and director of the University of Washington Autism Center, who was a co-author of one of the studies.

Studies that use the latest brain-scanning tools—magnetic resonance imaging and diffusion tensor imaging—generally focus on boys. But a single study of M.R.I.'s of both boys and girls found differences in their brain anatomy. Published in April in *The Journal of the American Academy of Child and Adolescent Psychiatry,* the study compared nine girls and 27 boys who were matched for age, I.Q. and severity of autism. Other research has established some correlation between abnormally large brain size and autism; the April paper reported that the brain volume of the autistic girls deviated from the norm more than the volume of the autistic boys. Lainhart, who is a member of the University of Utah's Brain Institute, has measured head circumference as a proxy for brain volume. (The two are linked.) In a 1997 paper, she reported that the mean head circumference of eight autistic girls at birth was significantly

greater than the norm, whereas the mean head size of 37 autistic boys was not.

These are small and preliminary studies, but their findings may relate to a puzzle of autism: while overall, there are more mentally retarded autistic boys than girls, a greater proportion of autistic girls are retarded—58 percent compared with 42 percent for boys, according to the C.D.C. As for Asperger's girls, Lainhart, who continues to conduct brain research, says she hopes eventually to shed light on the deficits of girls like Caitlyn and Marguerite and suggest new treatments for them. "In children with dyslexia, scientists identified where the basic cognitive deficits were," she says. "Then they intervened to go after those deficits, and they saw the brain change in those areas."

In the meantime, girls with autism and normal I.Q.'s pose a particular challenge for schools. Though mainstreaming has its benefits, autistic kids risk becoming outcasts in a regular classroom. Yet if girls go to a special-education program or a separate school, they are often swimming in a sea of boys. Lord pointed to this as a factor in girls' lack of friendships in her 1993 study. When the girls in her sample were shifted to specialized programs, "their opportunities to meet girls and women with some common interests were even more limited than those of the boys and men," she wrote.

The Harbour School in Baltimore has tried to address this predicament. The school has 120 students, all with learning disabilities, speech impairments, attention-deficit disorders and autistic-spectrum disorders. Only 19 of them are girls, which leaves one or two in each class from first to 12th grade. (More boys than girls are also diagnosed with the hyperactive form of A.D.D. and some learning disabilities.) Along with the playful Baltimore street scenes that decorate the walls of the hallways at Harbour, the predominance of gangly male bodies and loud voices was the first thing I noticed on a recent visit. The school felt like a haven—for boys.

And so I wondered whether the girls would feel overwhelmed, as Charlotte often is at her mostly male social-skills class. In the school auditorium at about 9 a.m., there were 13 sixth graders—12 boys and a single girl, Krissy, whose clinical designation is pervasive developmental disorder on the autistic spectrum. She was sitting on the floor playing Connect Four with one of the boys. She won her game, smiled without looking at her opponent, then got up and walked across the room to another of her classmates.

"Hi, Michael," she said. He didn't look up. Krissy sat down next to him and watched him play on his Game Boy. They talked quietly about his progress; she knew the game. A few minutes later, she found her Connect Four partner again, and they decided to play Operation. They talked about the rules, but when Krissy tripped the buzzer, he let her finish taking out the body parts she was maneuvering. Krissy declared victory and moved on again, this time to lie on the floor next to a boy who was building with metal rods and blue glass balls.

"Do you need help?" she asked him.

"No," he answered.

"Can I at least play with you?" Krissy persisted. The boy grunted. Without talking more, they each built a structure.

Krissy has been at Harbour since first grade, and the small size of her class means that she knows the boys well. Her teachers say she is at ease with them because she shares their Game Boy enthusiasm and watches the same movies. But sometimes Krissy's interests seem entirely girlish. She was excited about straightening her hair and then styling it into corkscrew curls for her interview with me and showed off pictures she had drawn of princesses, covered with hearts.

Harbour makes a concerted effort to give its girls the chance to develop relationships with one another. The girls' lunch periods coincide to give them time together. A social worker, Kelli Remmel, runs a regular "girls club" for a group of about half a dozen. "There are some things the girls don't want to discuss in front of their male peers," she says. "It's a chance for them to talk about boys, how to handle hormonal changes, other girls, their bodies, dating."

Krissy seems to be getting the social opportunities and support that Lord and Lainhart want for the girls they treat. Salt Lake City has good schools for kids with Asperger's, Lainhart says, but the catch is money. School districts in Maryland, Washington and Virginia pay Harbour's tuition for more than 95 percent of the students. But districts in many parts of the country—including Utah—don't pay for private-school placements for kids with Asperger's. Caitlyn doesn't go to a school like Harbour because her family can't afford it; her experience, not Krissy's, is typical.

Lord and Lainhart try to help by setting up social-skills groups for their patients. But families must pay for the classes out of pocket because medical insurers generally don't pay for treatment and services that focus on autism—a terrible problem for her patients, Lainhart says. So the groups tend to meet only a couple of times a month for a few hours. Charlotte doesn't know the boys in her group the way Krissy knows her classmates. At the University of Michigan, Lord runs co-ed groups for younger children and then tries to put together groups of older girls that mix autistic and nonautistic kids. As the girls get older, it is harder to find normally developing girls who want to participate. Twenty years ago, as a clinical psychologist in Canada, Lord started a group of four Asperger's girls who stayed in touch into adulthood. They called themselves the highest-functioning autistic women in Canada, she remembers, and treasured their solidarity. "It's striking how much girls with

autism can care about each other and other people and develop friendships that are really a source of joy for them," Lord says. "But when I think of the teenage girls I know, many of them have no shot at forming those relationships."

At the Hawks Camp in Utah, Caitlyn and Marguerite didn't become friends. A week earlier, Marguerite and Lainhart had made a list of conversation starters, but Marguerite didn't really use them. Caitlyn didn't try to talk to her much, either. The camp lasted only a week; for these girls, not long enough for bonding. Still, Caitlyn said it was the best week of her year. One day after lunch, the Hawks campers drove in two minivans to a nearby lakefront to go tubing and Jet Skiing. Caitlyn changed into her bathing suit, then wrapped herself in a towel despite the strong hot sun. "Do I look O.K.?" she asked a counselor. "It's just that there are so many people."

But the other kids were paying Caitlyn no mind. This wasn't a group that Caitlyn had to fear. She balled her hands into fists, visibly holding her anxiety at bay. "Sometimes I feel like I'm weird and ugly," she said, "but I'm not going to today. I'm confident!" She strode out to Jet Ski and later returned with a description that she planned to use in a future story: "It was like riding a dragon through the storm."

Back at camp, the Hawks poured onto the playground. During the school year, Caitlyn had been excused from gym class because she was so nervous about changing her clothes and running around in front of her classmates. As she sat on a swing and watched kids play tag, a counselor named Claire came over. As she and Caitlyn talked, Caitlyn did all the tiny things that people do to engage one another, smiling, laughing, gesturing, looking Claire in the eye. Claire urged her to join the game and called out, "Caitlyn's playing!" Caitlyn protested. But Claire persisted, and finally Caitlyn yelled, "O.K., where's the base?" A teenage boy pointed to the monkey bars, and Caitlyn ran for it. Her glasses slipped off her nose, and her shorts slipped a bit, too. She hiked them up and kept running, surrounded by other kids. Sweating and laughing, she yelled, "Safe!"

**EMILY BAZELON** is an editor of the online publication *Slate*. Her last article for the magazine was about the grass-roots pro-life movement.

From *The New York Times Magazine*, August 5, 2007. Copyright © 2007 by Emily Bazelon. Distributed by The New York Times Special Features. Reprinted by permission.

# UNIT 3
# Gender and Education

## Unit Selections

## Key Points to Consider

- In what ways can we talk about educational institutions as *gendered?*

- What does research indicate regarding the importance of play for boys and girls?

- In what ways do schools enforce "gender rules" and gender norms?

- Imagine if teachers asked students to line up by race, the way they do with gender. What are your thoughts on this?

- Discuss female and male achievement gaps in math, science, and reading.

- In what ways can educational institutions be (re)created to be "gender-friendly"?

- What challenges do female faculty members face in male-dominated fields? Are their challenges different from the ones that male faculty members encounter? Why? Why not?

- In what ways has legislation impacted women's status, experiences, and opportunities in higher education settings?

- What kinds of legislative changes would you like to see enacted regarding gender and education? Why?

## Student Website
www.mhcls.com

## Internet References

**National Parent Teacher Association**
   *http://www.pta.org/*
**Early Childhood News**
   *http://www.earlychildhoodnews.com/*
**The National Coalition for Women and Girls in Education**
   *http://www.ncwge.org/*
**International Boys' Schools Coalition**
   *http://www.theibsc.org/*
**The Gay, Lesbian & Straight Education Network**
   *http://www.glsen.org*

This unit focuses on gender and educational institutions. You may notice that many of the topics covered here overlap with Unit 2. We spend significant amounts of time in educational settings from kindergarten through secondary school and beyond, so it follows that significant growth and development also occurs during this time. As far as social institutions go, schools play a unique role in our socialization and development. In this unit, we will focus more directly on educational institutions as we explore gender.

As social institutions, schools socialize students according to the needs of the institution. In other words, the functioning of the institution takes priority over what is best for the individual. Students learn to behave in ways that further the interests of the institution. Schools are far from unique in doing this. It is certainly true of other social institutions. Goffman found this to be the case with mental institutions. In order to function, this seems to be a necessity, at least to some extent. When interests collide within educational settings, it should come as no surprise that conflicts and controversies can arise.

Schools have long been enforcers of "gender rules." The rules of appropriate conduct vary by gender, as found in student handbooks detailing a range of expectations and standards, such as what is considered "appropriate" dress. Prohibiting "cross-dressing" or attending a prom with a date of the same sex are just two examples of conflicts that have arisen in school settings as schools enforce social norms. Stories of institutions and individual students at odds make their way into the news cycle, often at fairly predictable intervals, such as the beginning of a new academic year and prom time. However, a gender-related controversy can certainly crop up at other times, whether it is a parent complaining about gender "inappropriate" content in books or gender role reversals associated with Sadie Hawkins events.

The selections in this unit explore a number of issues and problems in the area of gender and education. However, a good amount of progress has been made over the past few decades. This unit takes that progress into account and in doing so, highlights some potential solutions, such as instructional strategies that address the needs of both boys and girls. Becoming sensitized to both gender diversity and the needs of individuals will

© Jon Feingersh/Blend Images/Getty Images

help us overcome at least some of the problems encountered in educational settings today.

# Learning and Gender

**By paying attention to the differences between boys and girls, schools can gain new perspectives on teaching all children.**

MICHAEL GURIAN

On the day your district administrators look at test scores, grades, and discipline referrals with gender in mind, some stunning patterns quickly will emerge.

Girls, they might find, are behind boys in elementary school math or science scores. They'll find high school girls statistically behind boys in SAT scores. They might find, upon deeper review, that some girls have learning disabilities that are going undiagnosed.

Boys, they'll probably notice, make up 80 to 90 percent of the district's discipline referrals, 70 percent of learning disabled children, and at least two-thirds of the children on behavioral medication. They'll probably find that boys earn two-thirds of the Ds and Fs in the district, but less than half the As. On statewide standardized test scores, they'll probably notice boys behind girls in general. They may be shocked to see how far behind the boys are in literacy skills; nationally, the average is a year and a half.

The moment an administrator sees the disparity of achievement between boys and girls can be liberating. Caring about children's education can now include caring about boys and girls specifically. New training programs and resources for teachers and school districts are opening cash-strapped school boards' eyes, not just to issues girls and boys face but also to ways of addressing gender differences in test scores, discipline referrals, and grades.

In the Edina School District, outside Minneapolis, Superintendent Ken Dragseth and district staff implemented a gender initiative that has helped close achievement gaps and improve overall education for students. In 2002, Dragseth and his staff analyzed district achievement data. They found that girls were doing much better than boys on most academic indicators, showing that they needed to address this achievement gap. They discovered areas of need for girls as well.

Edina officials decided to work on gaining greater knowledge on how boys and girls learn differently. Over the last three years, the district has seen qualitative and quantitative improvement in student performance.

Dragseth says that the gender-specific techniques and gender-friendly instructional theory he and his staff learned at the Gurian Institute helped the district significantly improve student achievement. For example, he says, they have seen higher seventh- and 10th-grade state reading and math mean scores for both boys and girls.

"We have also found that teacher- and parent-heightened awareness of gender differences in learning styles and appropriate strategies has been well received by students themselves," he says.

## Brain Research

Gender training and resources used by Edina and other districts rely on information gained from PET, MRI, and other brain scans. This brain-based approach to gender was conceived in the early 1990s when it became clear that teachers were leaving college, graduate school, and teacher certification programs without training in how boys and girls learn differently. Educational culture was struggling to serve the needs of children—the needs of girls were most publicly discussed in the early 1990s—without complete knowledge of the children themselves.

When I wrote *The Wonder of Boys* in 1996, I hoped to bring a brain-based approach to gender issues into a wider public dialogue. In 1998, I joined the Missouri Center for Safe Schools and the University of Missouri-Kansas City in developing a two-year program to academically test the links among brain science, gender, and teacher education.

In six school districts in Missouri, teachers and staff integrated information from various fields and technologies and developed a number of strategies for teaching boys and girls. Gender disparities in achievement began to disappear in these districts. After one year, the pilot elementary school in the St. Joseph School District finished among the top five in the district after testing at the bottom previously. Discipline referrals diminished as well. In Kansas City's Hickman Mills School District, discipline referrals were cut by 35 percent within six months.

In the five years following the Missouri pilot program, more than 20,000 teachers in 800 schools and districts have received training in how boys and girls learn differently. More and more teachers are using this knowledge in the classroom.

Increasingly, universities and teacher certification programs are training young teachers in the learning differences between boys and girls.

## Different Learning Styles

As with so many things of value in life, a teacher's innovations on behalf of children begins with an epiphany. A fourth-grade teacher recently told me, "When I saw the brain scans and thought about my class, I just went 'aha.' So much made sense now. The boys and their fidgeting; the girls and their chatting; the girls organizing their binders colorfully; the boys tapping their pencils; the girls writing more words in their essays than the boys; even the way the boys end up in the principal's office so much more frequently than the girls. We were all told long ago that every child should be taught as an individual, so gender didn't matter—but it really matters! Knowing about it has completely changed the way I teach, and the success my students are having."

On your way home this afternoon, stop by your local elementary school and see some of these differences for yourself. Walk down the hallway and find a classroom in which the teacher displays students' written work. Stand for a moment and look at the stories.

With all exceptions noted, you will probably find that the girls on average write:

- More words than the boys,
- Include more complex sensory details like color and texture, and
- Add more emotive and feeling details ("Judy said she liked him" "Timmy frowned").

If you could look with X-ray glasses into the brains of the boys and girls who wrote those stories, you would see:

- More blood flow in the verbal centers (in the cerebral cortex) of the girls' brains;
- More neural connections between the verbal centers and emotive centers in the limbic systems of the girls' brains; and
- More blood flow in sensorial centers (for instance in the occipital lobe), with more linkage between those centers and the verbal centers in the girls' brains.

## A Visual Link to Learning

My example of the differences in boys and girls writing has a visual link. The female visual system (optical and neural) relies more greatly than the male on P cells. These are cells that connect color variety and other sensory activity to upper brain functioning. Boys rely more on M cells, which make spatial activity and graphic clues more quickly accessible.

This difference is linked significantly to a gender-different writing process for boys and girls. Boys tend to rely more on pictures and moving objects for word connections than girls. Girls tend to use more words that describe color and other fine,

sensory information. Not surprisingly, gender gaps in writing are often "detail" gaps.

Girls use more sensorial detail than boys, receiving better grades in the process. However, when elementary school teachers let boys draw picture panels (with colored pens) during the brainstorming part of story or essay writing, the boys often graphically lay out what their story will be about. After that, they actually write their "word brainstorming" because they can refer to a graphic/spatial tool that stimulates their brains to greater success in writing.

Watch a fourth-grade classroom led by a teacher untrained in male/female brain differences. You'll probably see the teacher tell students to "take an hour to write your brainstorming for your paper." Five to 10 of the boys in a classroom of 30 kids will stare at the blank page.

But when teachers are trained in male/female brain differences, they tell students to draw first and write later. Students who need that strategy will end up writing much more detailed, organized, and just better papers.

## The Rest State and Discipline Problems

Another area where you'll see gender differences is classroom behavior. Boys tend to fidget when they are bored. In a boy's brain, less of the "calming chemical," serotonin, moves through the pre-frontal cortex (the executive decision-maker in the brain). Boys thus are more likely to fidget, distract themselves and others, and become the objects of the teacher's reprimands.

Furthermore, the male brain naturally goes into a rest state many times per day and is not engaged in learning. Thus the boy "zones out," "drifts off," or "disappears from the lesson."

Sometimes he begins to tap his pencil loudly or pull the hair of the kid in front of him. He's not trying to cause trouble; in fact, he may be trying to wake up and avoid the rest state. Girls' brains do not go to this severe rest state; their cerebral cortices are always "on." They more rarely need to tap, fidget, or talk out of turn in order to stay focused.

Teachers can learn how to organize classrooms so that any boys (and girls) who need it can physically move while they are learning and keep their brains engaged. The rest state and boredom issues begin to dissolve. Discipline referrals decrease exponentially.

## Brains on Math

Both boys and girls can do math and science, of course, but their brains perform these tasks differently. Girls fall behind boys in complex math skills when their lesson plans rely solely or mainly on abstract formulations specified in symbols on the blackboard.

However, when words, essay components, and active group work are added to the toolbox of teacher strategies, girls reach a parity of performance. Brain-based innovations to help girls in math and science over the last decade have brought more verbal elements into math and science teaching and testing: more words, more word-to-formula connections, and more essay answers in math tests.

The results in both math and science achievement have been stunning, with girls closing the math/science gap in many school districts.

# Different Reactions to Competition

Because of neural and chemical differences in levels and processing of oxytocin, dopamine, testosterone, and estrogen, boys typically need to do some learning through competition. Girls, of course, are competitive too, but in a given day, they will spend less time in competitive learning and less time relating successfully to one another through "aggression-love"—the playful hitting and dissing by which boys show love.

The current emphasis on cooperative learning is a good thing, and the basis of a diversity-oriented educational culture. However, because they are not schooled in the nature of gender in the brain, teachers generally have deleted competitive learning, and thus de-emphasized a natural learning tool for many boys. We've also robbed girls of practice in the reality of human competitiveness.

When teachers receive training on how competitive learning can be integrated into classrooms (without chaos ensuing)

they actually come to enjoy seeing both boys and girls challenge one another to learn better. Many girls who avoided leadership before now step forward to lead.

# Learning to Their Potential

Our children are children, of course—but they are also girls and boys. This is something we all know as parents. When a school board makes the decision to focus on how the girls and boys are doing, all children gain. Students learn more, teachers are more productive, test scores and behavior improve, and parents and the community are happier.

A school board member in North Carolina told me, "Ten years ago, it was almost scary to talk about hard-wired gender differences. There were a lot of Title IX concerns, fears of reprisal. Now it's not scary, the brain research has caught up, and now it's so necessary. In fact, it just feels right."

It does indeed feel right to help boys and girls learn to their potential. Ten years ago, our girls were behind our boys in math and science; now, we see that our boys are far behind our girls in literacy. Neither of these gaps need exist anymore, as we engage in best practices on behalf of both boys and girls.

---

**MICHAEL GURIAN,** co-founder of the Gurian Institute, is author of 2 books, including *The Minds of Boys* (with Kathy Stevens), *The Wonder of Girls*, and *Boys and Girls Learn Differently* (with Patricia Henley and Terry Trueman).

From *American School Board Journal*, October 2006, pp. 19–22. Copyright © 2006 by National School Board Association. Reprinted by permission.

# Educating Girls, Unlocking Development

**"Compelling evidence, accumulated over the past 20 years . . . , has led to an almost universal recognition of the importance of focusing on girls' education as part of broader development policy."**

RUTH LEVINE

One of the most important public policy goals in the developing world is the expansion and improvement of education for girls. Vital in its own right for the realization of individual capabilities, the education of girls has the potential to transform the life chances of the girls themselves, their future families, and the societies in which they live. Girls with at least a primary school education are healthier and wealthier when they grow up and their future children have much greater opportunities than they otherwise would; even national economic outcomes appear to be positively influenced by expanded girls' education.

Unlike some development outcomes that depend on multiple factors outside the control of policy makers (either in developing countries or among donor nations), significant improvement in girls' education can be achieved through specific government actions. Expansion of basic education, making school infrastructure and curriculum more girl-friendly, and conditional cash transfers and scholarships to overcome household barriers have all been used to improve key outcomes, with demonstrable success. Lessons from regions that have made rapid advances with girls' education, and from programs that have introduced successful financing and teaching innovations, can be applied to accelerate progress.

While public policy can make the difference, policies that ignore important gender-related constraints to education at the primary and, particularly, at the postprimary educational levels can have the opposite effect, reinforcing existing patterns of gender discrimination and exclusion. Those patterns are often deep-seated. Families in many societies traditionally have valued schooling less for girls than for boys. In most households, the domestic workload falls more to females than to males, leaving less time for school. If families are struggling to find income, the demand for girls' help around the house (or in wage labor) may increase. Many parents believe that the return on educational investments varies according to gender—particularly if girls, when they marry, leave their parents' households to join the husbands'.

When girls in developing countries do enroll in school, they frequently encounter gender-based discrimination and inadequate educational resources. Large numbers of girls in sub-Saharan Africa drop out, for example, when they reach puberty and the onset of menstruation simply because schools lack latrines, running water, or privacy. Parental concerns about girls' security outside the home can limit schooling where girls are vulnerable in transit and male teachers are not trusted. And in some countries, cultural aversion to the education of girls lingers. Afghanistan's Taliban insurgents, who believe that girls' education violates Islamic teachings, have succeeded in closing numerous schools, sometimes by beheading teachers. Afghanistan is an extreme case, but a reminder nonetheless of the challenges that remain on the path toward achieving the high payoffs from girls' education.

## The Benefits

Why is the schooling of girls so critical? Education in general is among the primary means through which societies reproduce themselves; correspondingly, changing the educational opportunities for particular groups in society—girls and minority groups—is perhaps the single most effective way to achieve lasting transformations. A considerable body of evidence has shown that the benefits of educating a girl are manifested in economic and social outcomes: her lifetime health, labor force participation, and income; her (future) children's health and nutrition; her community's and her nation's productivity. Most important, education can break the intergenerational transmission of poverty.

Female participation in the formal labor market consistently increases with educational attainment, as it does for males. In at least some settings, the returns to education of girls are superior to those for boys. Several studies have shown that primary schooling increases lifetime earnings by as much as 20 percent for girls—higher than for their brothers. If they stay in secondary school, the returns from education are 25 percent or higher.

The inverse relationship between women's education and fertility is perhaps the best studied of all health and demographic phenomena. The relationship generally holds across countries and over time, and is robust even when income is taken into account. Completion of primary school is strongly associated with later age at marriage, later age at first birth, and lower lifetime fertility. A study of eight sub-Saharan countries covering the period from 1987 to 1999 found that girls' educational attainment was the best predictor of whether they would have their first births during adolescence.

Another study examined surveys across the developing world to compare female education and fertility by region. The higher the level of female education, the lower desired family size, and the greater the success in achieving desired family size. Further, each additional year of a mother's schooling cuts the expected infant mortality rate by 5 to 10 percent.

Maternal education is a key determinant of children's attainment. Multiple studies have found that a mother's level of education has a strong positive effect on daughters' enrollment—more than on sons and significantly more than the effect of fathers' education on daughters. Studies from Egypt, Ghana, India, Kenya, Malaysia, Mexico, and Peru all find that mothers with a basic education are substantially more likely to educate their children, especially their daughters.

Children's health also is strongly associated with mothers' education. In general, this relationship holds across countries and time, although the confounding effect of household income has complicated the picture. One study, for instance, compared 17 developing countries, examining the relationship between women's education and their infants' health and nutritional status. It found the existence of an education-related health advantage in most countries, although stronger for postneonatal health than for neonatal health. (In some countries the "education advantage" did appear to be eliminated when controlling for other dimensions of socioeconomic status.)

Other studies have found clear links between women's school attainment and birth and death rates, and between women's years of schooling and infant mortality. A 1997 study for the World Bank, which focused on Morocco, found that a mother's schooling and functional literacy predicted her child's height-for-age, controlling for other socioeconomic factors.

Although the causal links are harder to establish at the macrolevel, some researchers have made the attempt, with interesting results. For example, in a 100-country study, researchers showed that raising the share of women with a secondary education by 1 percent is associated with a 0.3 percent increase in annual per capita income growth. In a 63-country study, more productive farming because of increased female education accounts for 43 percent of the decline in malnutrition achieved between 1970 and 1995.

In short (and with some important nuances set aside), girls' education is a strong contributor to the achievement of multiple key development outcomes: growth of household and national income, health of women and children, and lower and wanted fertility. Compelling evidence, accumulated over the past 20 years using both quantitative and qualitative methods, has led to an almost universal recognition of the importance of focusing on girls' education as part of broader development policy.

# The Trends

Given the widespread understanding about the value of girls' education, the international community and national governments have established ambitious goals for increased participation in primary education and progress toward gender parity at all levels. The Millennium Development Goals (MDG), approved by all member states of the United Nations in 2000, call for universal primary education in all countries by 2015, as well as gender parity at all levels by 2015.

There is good news to report. Impressive gains have been made toward higher levels of education enrollment and completion, and girls have been catching up rapidly with their brothers. As primary schooling expands, girls tend to be the main beneficiaries because of their historically disadvantaged position.

The rate of primary school completion also has improved faster for girls than for boys, again in large part because they had more to gain at the margins. Across all developing countries, girls' primary school completion increased by 17 percent, from 65 to 76 percent between 1990 and 2000. During the same period, boys' primary completion increased by 8 percent, from 79 to 85 percent. Global progress is not matched, however, in every region. In sub-Saharan Africa, girls did only slightly better between 1990 and 2000, with primary completion increasing from 43 to 46 percent. (The primary completion rate for boys went in the opposite direction, from 57 to 56 percent.)

The overall good news about girls' progress must be tempered by realism, and a recognition that the goal is not to have boys' and girls' educational attainment "equally bad." Today, a mere nine years from the MDG deadline, it is clear that the important improvements over the past several decades in the developing world—in many instances, unprecedented rates of increase in primary school enrollment and completion—still leave a large number of poor countries very far from the target. While girls are making up ground rapidly, in many of the poorest countries the achievements on improved gender parity must be seen in the context of overall low levels of primary school completion.

An estimated 104 million to 121 million children of primary school age across the globe are not in school, with the worst shortfalls in Africa and South Asia. Completion of schooling is a significant problem. While enrollment has been increasing, many children drop out before finishing the fifth grade. In Africa, for example, just 51 percent of children (46 percent of girls) complete primary school. In South Asia, 74 percent of children (and just 63 percent of girls) do so.

Low levels of enrollment and completion are concentrated not only in certain regions but also among certain segments of the population. In every country completion rates are lowest for children from poor households. In Western and Central Africa, the median grade completed by the bottom 40 percent of the income distribution is zero, because less than half of poor children complete even the first year of school.

The education income gap also exacerbates gender disparities. In India, for example, the gap between boys and girls from the richest households is 2.5 percent, but the difference for children from the poorest households is 24 percent.

## Girls are catching up quickly in most countries, but the level they are catching up to is still quite low.

In some countries the main reason for low educational attainment is that children do not enroll in school. In Bangladesh, Benin, Burkina Faso, Ivory Coast, India, Mali, Morocco, Niger, and Senegal, more than half of children from the bottom 40 percent of the income distribution never even enroll. Elsewhere, particularly in Latin America, enrollment may be almost universal, but high repetition and dropout rates lead to low completion rates. In both cases poor students are much more likely not to complete school.

In many countries the rural/urban education gap is a key factor explaining education differentials. In Mozambique, the rural completion rate is 12 percent, while at the national level 26 percent of children complete school. Burkina Faso, Guinea, Madagascar, Niger, and Togo all demonstrate a similar pattern. In rural areas, the gender gap in completion is pronounced in Africa: in Benin, Burkina Faso, Guinea, Madagascar, Mozambique, and Niger, a mere 15 percent of girls who start primary school make it to the end.

Policy makers increasingly are recognizing the importance of addressing the special needs and vulnerabilities of marginal populations, even in relatively well-off countries with education levels that, on average, look quite good. As my colleagues Maureen Lewis and Marlaine Lockheed at the Center for Global Development highlight in a forthcoming book, girls who are members of marginalized groups—the Roma in Eastern Europe, the indigenous populations in Central America and elsewhere, the underprivileged castes and tribes in India—suffer a double disadvantage. Low educational attainment for girls is an obvious mechanism through which historical disadvantage is perpetuated. In Laos, for example, more than 90 percent of men in the dominant Laotai group are literate, while only 30 percent of the youngest cohort of women belonging to excluded rural ethnic groups can read and write.

Beyond the primary school enrollment and completion trends, a complex problem is the quality of education. Although measurement of learning outcomes is spotty at best, analyses of internationally comparable assessments of learning achievement in mathematics, reading, and science indicate that most developing countries rank far behind the industrialized nations. This is all the more of concern because the tests are taken by the children in school who, in low-enrollment countries, are the equivalent in relative terms to the top performers in the high-enrollment developed nations. The data on national examinations is equally alarming. Student performance on national exams in South Asian and African countries shows major gaps in acquisition of knowledge and skills.

Thus, the picture of progress and gaps is a complex one: rapid improvements relative to historical trends, but far off the ideal mark in the poorest countries. Girls are catching up quickly in most countries, but the level they are catching up to is still quite low. In many nations, the "lowest hanging fruit" has already been reached; for all children, and for girls in particular, the ones now out of school come from the most economically and socially disadvantaged backgrounds, and will be the hardest to reach. Finally, even among those children in school, evidence about poor learning outcomes should be cause for alarm.

## The Challenges

The central imperative for improving educational opportunities and outcomes for girls in the low enrollment countries, including in sub-Saharan Africa and parts of South Asia, is to improve overall access and the quality of primary schooling. In doing so, planners and policy makers should ensure that they are not perpetuating barriers to girls' participation.

Getting to universal primary education (either enrollment or the more ambitious goal of completion) in sub-Saharan Africa and South Asia will require large-scale expansion in physical infrastructure, the number of teachers, and teaching/learning materials. Moreover, it will require fundamental improvements in the education institutions: more attention to learning outcomes rather than enrollment numbers, greater incentives for quality teaching, and more responsiveness to parents. This is a huge agenda. The donor and international technical community can support it, but it must be grounded in the political commitment of national and subnational governments.

Secondary to the "more and better education for all" agenda, and of particular relevance in countries that have already made significant progress so that most children go to school, is the need to understand and address the needs of particular disadvantaged groups, where gender differentials are especially pronounced. Beyond the efforts to reach children from poor and rural households, public policy makers need to understand and pay attention to ethnic and linguistic minorities, reaching them with tailored approaches rather than simply an expansion of the types of educational opportunities provided to the majority population. In addressing this challenge, policy makers must accept that reaching these key populations implies higher unit costs, as well as the adoption of potentially controversial measures, such as bilingual curriculum.

Finally, success in moving close to universal primary school enrollment generates its own new challenges. As more children complete primary school, the private benefits, in higher wages, decline (though the social benefits remain high). Private rates of return—perceived and real—cease to be seen as much of a reason for sending children to primary school, unless there is access to postprimary education. In addition, both the expansion of the existing education systems in many developing countries and the "scaling-up" of other public sector functions (such as health services, water management, and general public administration) require a larger cadre of educated and trained workers, the products of postprimary education. For these reasons, attention must be given to expanded opportunities for girls at the secondary level.

While international attention and goal-setting have been directed almost exclusively at the primary level, and the donor community has been persuaded by arguments about greater economic returns from primary education and the potentially regressive effects of investments at the secondary level, a large agenda remains unattended. It is at the secondary level that many of the microeconomic, health, and fertility outcomes of girls' education are fully realized. And common sense alone suggests that the large (and growing) cohort of children moving through primary schooling will create unsustainable pressures for postprimary education opportunities. If those are severely rationed, as they are in much of sub-Saharan Africa, the negative feedback to parents who sacrificed to send their children through primary school may be profound. Sorting out the design, financing, and institutional arrangements for effective secondary schooling—that is also responsive to labor market demand—is an essential part of good policy making today.

## The Way Forward

Beyond general expansion of enrollment, governments can get out-of-school children into school by crafting specific interventions to reach them, and by increasing educational opportunities (formal and informal) for girls and women. In designing these initiatives, success depends on understanding and taking into account powerful demand-side influences that may constrain girls' school participation.

Specific interventions have been shown, in some settings, to get hard-to-reach children into school. These include eliminating school fees, instituting conditional cash transfers, using school feeding programs as an incentive to attend school, and implementing school health programs to reduce absenteeism. Several interventions have proved particularly successful where girls' participation is low. These include actions that increase security and privacy for girls (for example, ensuring that sanitation facilities are girl-friendly), as well as those that reduce gender-stereotyping in curriculum and encourage girls to take an active role in their education.

While few rigorous evaluations have been undertaken, many experts suggest that literacy programs for uneducated mothers may help increase school participation by their children. Adult literacy programs may be particularly useful in settings where there are pockets of undereducated women, such as ethnic or indigenous communities.

It is tempting for policy makers to focus on specific programmatic investments. But sustained improvements in education are impossible to achieve without improving the way in which key institutions in the sector function, and without increasing parental involvement in decisions affecting their children's education. Many countries with poorly performing educational systems suffer from institutional weaknesses, including low management capacity, nontransparent resource allocation and accounting practices, and substandard human resources policies and practices. Incentive structures that fail to reward good performance create and reinforce the most deleterious characteristics of weak institutions.

Parents who are well informed of policies and resource allocations in the education sector and who are involved in decisions regarding their children's schooling exert considerable influence and help contribute solutions. Involved communities are able to articulate local school needs, hold officials accountable, and mobilize local resources to fill gaps when the government response is inadequate.

**In Benin, Burkina Faso, Guinea, Madagascar, Mozambique, and Niger, a mere 15 percent of girls who start primary school make it to the end.**

## A Modest Proposal

Donor agencies have been at the leading edge of the dialogue about the importance of girls' education, often providing the financial support, research, and political stimulus that may be lacking in countries that have more than their hands full with the basics of "Education for All." There is a broad consensus in the international donor community about the value of girls' education, and innovations have been introduced through donor-funded programs under the auspices of UNICEF, the World Food Program, the US Agency for International Development, and other key agencies. These have been valuable contributions, and have supported the work of champions at the national and local levels.

The donor community could come together now to accelerate progress in a very particular way. Working with both governments and nongovernmental organizations in countries where specific excluded groups—ethnic and/or linguistic minorities—have much poorer education outcomes, donors could finance the design, introduction, and rigorous evaluation of targeted programs to improve access to appropriate educational opportunities, with a particular emphasis (if warranted by the baseline research) on the needs and characteristics of girls. While different bilateral and multilateral donors could take the lead in funding specific types of programs or working in particular countries on the challenge of the "doubly disadvantaged," a shared learning agenda could be coordinated across agencies to generate much more than the spotty anecdotes and case studies on which we currently depend.

The learning agenda would include three components: first, the enduring questions to be examined—for example, determining the most effective strategies to improve learning outcomes among children who come from households where the language spoken is not the language of instruction; second, the use of methods that permit observed results to be attributed to the program; and third, the features that will ensure maximum credibility of the evaluations, such as independence, dissemination of results (whether the findings are favorable or not), and wide sharing of the data for reanalysis.

Just as education can transform individuals' lives, learning what works can transform the debates in development policy. The beneficiaries in developing countries would include not only girls who receive the education they deserve and need, but also families and communities and future generations thereby lifted over time out of poverty.

**RUTH LEVINE** is director of programs and a senior fellow at the Center for Global Development.

From *Current History*, March 2006, pp. 127–131. Copyright © 2006 by Current History, Inc. Reprinted by permission.

# Boys and Girls Together
## *A Case for Creating Gender-Friendly Middle School Classrooms*

DAVID KOMMER

## Are Boys and Girls Really Different?

Close your eyes and picture an average grade school class. Watch the boys and girls as they learn, interact, and deal with problems. Do they look alike in your mind's eye? Do they learn the same way? Do they interact with you and with one another similarly? Do they solve problems—both relationship and academic—in the same ways? Not likely. No, there appears to be a very real difference between boys and girls.

What is the nature of that difference, and from where does it come? Moreover, if there is such a striking difference, are there things we should be doing in the classroom to accommodate for these differences? These are all significant questions that might affect the academic growth of our students.

As young people move into adolescence, they begin to explore gender roles. Finding their way through this potential minefield is complicated and challenging for middle school students. The process of determining the variations in masculinity and femininity is largely a social function, not a biological one (Rice and Dolgin 2002). What it means to be a man, and what it means to be a woman, are communicated to children by all the adults in a child's life, including teachers.

"Peers may play a particularly important role in the development of children's gender identities" (Rice and Dolgin 2002, 195). Boys and girls create very distinct cultures; when they are in same-gender groups they act and play very differently. Girls are talkative and cooperative, boys are competitive and physical (Rice and Dolgin). Teachers need to understand these differences and be purposeful in the treatment of each so as to send the healthiest messages to adolescents.

Looking closely at middle schools, two questions surface: Are boys and girls treated differently from one another? *should* boys and girls be treated differently?

In 1992, the American Association of University Women (AAUW) published a groundbreaking study about how schools were not meeting the needs of young girls. Their schools shortchanged girls in many ways: when questioned in class, girls were less likely to receive a prompt to clarify thinking if they answered incorrectly; boys were more regularly called on, and if not, they were just as likely to shout out an answer, leaving girls to sit quietly; and girls were not encouraged to take advanced math and science classes (AAUW 1992). Perhaps not surprisingly, then, in their middle school years, girls stopped being successful in math and science.

A large concern that must be addressed by middle level educators is the decrease in confidence that girls experience throughout middle school. One recent study shows that just prior to their entry into pre-adolescence, 60 percent of girls had positive feelings about themselves and their ability. Only 29 percent of high school girls felt the same confidence. (This compares with 67 percent of young boys feeling confident, and 46 percent of high school-aged boys having the same confidence.) Confidence fell during middle school (Santrock 2001). I am not suggesting that there is something toxic about middle school, but I am suggesting that while students are on our watch, we can and must do better.

The AAUW (1992) study focused our attention on the issue of educational equity. It was difficult to argue with the findings, and teachers all over the country began to reevaluate their teaching in light of the study. Several years later, the AAUW found that significant progress was made, as evidenced by gains in girls' success in math and science (AAUW 1998). Nevertheless, the story is not yet finished, for it appears now the boys were also often the victims of our educational system. Consider the following gender questions:

1. Who is more likely to drop out of high school?
2. Who is more likely to be sent to the principal's office for a disciplinary referral?
3. Who is more likely to be suspended or expelled?
4. Who is more likely to be identified as a student needing special education?
5. Who is more likely to need reading intervention?

The answer to all of the above questions is "boys" (Taylor and Lorimer 2003). Clearly, the educational system is discouraging some of them. However, even that conclusion is too simple;

this is not a problem that can be solved with a quick fix. Looking again at the questions above, you might also add, "Not all boys are being discouraged/exhibiting behavior problems." And you would be correct: some girls also show these behaviors and problems. The evidence seems to show that, although there are differences in general, it is not possible to put all the boys on one side and all the girls on the other. In fact, there seems to be some type of spectrum with "maleness" on one end and "femaleness" on the other. Everyone exists somewhere in the spectrum, and generally boys cluster toward one end, and girls toward the other. This also has ramifications for classrooms. But perhaps there is an effective way to address gender differences.

So what do we do? The first thing is to become aware of the differences between genders. Once these differences are explained and accepted, educators must be proactive in the way boys and girls are treated in schools. This is not a call for separate schools, for we do not live in a gender-segregated world. Indeed, there are distinct advantages to educating boys and girls together appropriately, for in doing so, each gender will begin to see how the other thinks, feels, responds, and reacts. Such understanding is in itself a major goal for gender-friendly classrooms.

We should also consider the nature of the differences between boys and girls. The question of nature versus nurture is always an intriguing one, but is similarly enigmatic as the one about the chicken and the egg. Most psychologists agree that gender differences may be a function of biological forces, but that they are also shaped by the environments in which our children grow up (Rice and Dolgin 2002). When studying this it is helpful to observe some of the factors and looking more closely at each.

# Brain Theory

As you scan the room in which students are supposed to be reading silently, you see that most of the girls are engaged with their books. Because the reading is student selected, the girls have chosen the books that focus on relationships. The boys seem to be more easily distractible and are not, as a rule, focusing their full attention on the text. Some read for a while, then gaze about the room. If they are reading, they are more likely to have selected action books or sports magazines.

Boys and girls have slightly different brain chemistry that may cause each to think differently. While not yet conclusive, research has uncovered many intriguing possibilities that might provide some explanations.

In addition to having slightly different chemistry, the structure of the male and female brain is actually different (Gurian 2001; Sax 2005; Sousa 2001). As most of us have learned, girls mature more quickly than boys, but what does this mean exactly? Gurian suggests that as the individual grows there is an increase in myelin, a coating that transmits electrical impulses through the nervous system. This accumulating coat of myelin occurs earlier in females.

The most striking difference, Gurian and others suggest, is the system of nerves, the corpus callosum, which connect the right and left hemispheres of the brain. In females this structure is, on average, 20 percent larger than it is in males (Gurian, 2001; Sousa 2001; Walsh 2004). Is this why females seem to be able to use both sides of the brain in processing information and are able to multitask more efficiently than males?

Studies on boys and girls also point out some interesting differences in both hearing and seeing (Sax 2005). Studies reported by Sax indicate that girls hear at different levels—in effect, better—than boys. Other studies show that girls are able to read facial expressions more astutely than boys, and this difference is related to a different chemistry in the eye and corresponding receptor in the brain (Sax).

Girls "tend to take in more sensory data than boys" (Gurian 2001, 27). Boys are more likely to engage in physically risky behaviors as a result. Although the effects of testosterone on the adolescent brain spark some controversy, there seems to be wide acceptance of the fact that testosterone leads males into more aggressive and risky actions than estrogen does with girls (Walsh 2004). "Girls and boys assess risk differently, and they differ in their likelihood of engaging in risky behaviors" (Sax 2005, 41). Might there be ramifications for this in the classroom? You bet. Walsh suggests that the initial burst of hormones that come earlier for girls gives their brains a head start in developing the prefrontal cortex, or rational part or the brain. This allows girls to engage in more complex rational thought than boys. By the end of adolescence, boys have caught up with girls.

Girls tend to be less hemisphere dominant than boys, who seem to be largely right hemisphere dominant. As a result, boys are better at spatial tasks, which gives them an advantage in areas such as mathematics, graphs, and maps. Girls seem to use both sides of the brain and tend to be better at literacy-related activities (Gurian and Stevens 2004; Sax 2005).

In addition to the structural differences, there may be differences caused by the hormones that each gender receives. While this is somewhat more controversial, there is some evidence that the progesterone that girls receive is a bonding hormone, and the testosterone of boys is much more aggressive (Gurian 2001; Sax 2005). It appears that boys receive about a half-dozen spikes of testosterone each day: these spikes may result in boys becoming more anxious, moody, and even aggressive. Estrogen and progesterone, the female hormones, rise and fall throughout the female cycle. Girls experience an increase in mood swings, as well, but they tend to be spread over time rather than the intense change that boys experience. Interestingly, there is evidence that during these hormone infusions in girls, they actually have an increased academic upsurge (Gurian 2001). In short, they are smarter during this peak.

There are many more aspects to this emerging information on brain development and function. However, it should also be noted that although much of what we are learning about the brain is intriguing and may offer keys to helping both genders become more academically successful, perhaps there are other reasons that boys and girls are different.

# Social Differences

As the school day begins, students are all congregated in class. They are not really moving to their workplaces as you would like, but are engaged with each other, seemingly oblivious to the fact that you have an educational agenda ready. So what is their agenda, you wonder? The girls all seem to be huddled in groups whispering and looking about to see who might be paying attention to them. The boys are much more physically active as four boys play a game of trying to slap the other's hand before the other moves it away. Others are playing "basketball" with clean sheets of paper rolled up and tossed at the wastebasket.

Perhaps the issue does not lie in nature, but in nurture—that is, in the way we socialize our young people. "Society prescribes how a male ought to look and behave, what type of personality he ought to have, and what roles he should perform" (Rice and Dolgin, 2002, 193). Girls receive these messages equally as strongly. All adolescents receive messages from adults as they grow; from teachers who encourage and discourage in word and deed; from signals sent by peers; and from the media that also contribute to their developing gender identification.

Boys seem to present the most problems in the academic setting. They often are detached from the learning objective and would prefer to goof off—or so it seems. Why do boys seem ready to respond to any problem by either silence or lashing out? In *Raising Cain: Protecting the Emotional Lives of Boys*, Kindlon and Thompson (2000) argue that boys have been miseducated. Boys get very conflicting messages from everyone: parents, peers, teachers, coaches, and the media. Boys do, in fact, feel they are told not to show emotions; they are told, "Big boys don't cry." And when they hurt, they are told to walk it off. Boys receive strong messages that they must be in control and that any show of emotion is unacceptable, with the result that boys are trying to put their feelings someplace where they will not be betrayed by their own emotions.

What we are beginning to see is that boys, like girls, have many of the same feelings of inadequacy. Boys, however, seem ill-prepared to deal with these feelings, and often, the response from those who might guide them is that boys should "suck it up." Pollack refers to this as "boy code" which society teaches all young males as they grow up (1998). Indeed, the feeling that boys can handle the slings and arrows of adolescence with resilience and fortitude is a myth that has come to hurt boys. Given both lack of an emotional vocabulary and permission to deal with their feelings, boys have difficulty understanding and controlling their emotions. The result is that we see both stoic and self-destructive behaviors (Kindlon and Thompson 2001; Pollack).

Girls also encounter a constant stream of messages, ones that have a strong influence on the way they succeed in school, deal with others, and feel about themselves as people of worth. As educators we must be mindful of these messages and head off the negative ones as much as we can.

In *Reviving Ophelia: Saving the Selves of Adolescent Girls*, Pipher (1994) relates how young girls have an almost effervescent quality and a feeling that they can do anything. Somewhere in early adolescence this buoyancy begins to erode. Is it the demands that girls begin to fit into the roles our society has carved for them that extinguishes that exuberance? Those demands are powerful influences.

Girls begin to judge themselves relative to how they are perceived by the opposite gender. In the attempt to become what they feel others expect them to be, girls quickly lose their own. They hide their true selves to their friends and family (Pipher 1994; Powell 2004). Girls are "sugar and spice and everything nice." But during adolescence, this message is lost in a bewildering array of swirling images. They must "[b]e beautiful, but beauty is only skin deep. Be sexy, but not sexual. Be honest, but don't hurt anyone's feelings. Be independent, but be nice. Be smart, but not so smart that you threaten boys" (Pipher, 35–36).

Most girls like being at school, but there is strong evidence that, as a social institution, schools can damage girls at the same time that they educate them (Sax 2005). One reason might be that girls recognize that schools can be male oriented and male dominated; the books they read are most frequently written by men; they know the hierarchy of the school district is dominated by men; science classes frequently focus on male achievements; and math is presented as a male domain. Although our schools are becoming more aware of the sexist nature of education, there is still a great deal to do (AAUW 1998; Pipher 1994).

As a social institution, schools can do a great deal to educate both boys and girls about the messages they receive every day. For example, media literacy should be taught in all schools, so the culture of appearance is laid bare for all to see. Also, sexual harassment must be eliminated from school hallways and classrooms. Teachers need to be trained in gender issues so they can recognize the features that are detrimental to boys, girls, or both genders.

# Making Classrooms Appropriate for Both Genders

The students are all in groups and they have projects each group has selected. You have carefully arranged the groups to allow for as much diversity as you can, and you told the students that is why they are placed that way. Within each project are a number of tasks which use several multiple intelligence strategies and learning preferences. It is your hope that each student can contribute to this project using his or her strength.

The goal is not to treat boys and girls equally, but to create equity by purposefully addressing the particular needs of each gender. If you believe that education causes the brain to develop and change, then there are things we can do to offset the gender influences whether they are biological or sociological

(Sousa 2001). In the process, we can encourage students to develop more sensitivity and greater academic character than we are currently seeing. Our goal is not to try to make boys and girls the same; we tried that several decades ago. We might have more success if we teach boys and girls to respond to each other as people (Santock 2001).

Creating a gender-friendly classroom does not mean that you create gender-specific activities, divide your classroom, or even insist on single-sex classes. Remembering that everyone lives in a bigendered world makes it necessary to teach your students ways to be successful in that world. Students should at some times have an opportunity to work in a gender-matched activity, while at other times they should learn to function in a more typical gender-mismatched one. This allows students to experience instructional times that are more comfortable for students when the activities are matched to their nature. But they also learn to function outside that comfort area when they are in a mismatched situation, and thus strengthen weaker areas.

For teachers the imperative is to learn about the differences in gender. Teachers need to accept that learning occurs differently for each gender, and to measure out activities and experiences that favor one some of the time, and the other some of the time. Keep in mind that although some girls may be more linguistically advanced than boys, some boys are just as advanced, although some boys manipulate objects well and see patterns better than girls, some girls are headed toward engineering school. So, to teach only one way for each gender would do a disservice to the boys and girls who do not fit the stereotype.

When teachers plan learning experiences that favor one gender, they are also doing a great thing for the other. For as boys see girls appropriately modeling relationship behaviors, the boys learn how to be more sensitive and open. Likewise, when girls see the appropriate use of assertiveness that boys learn early, the girls see that this can be used to their advantage as well.

Students appreciate knowing the reasons for classroom activities. Teach them the differences between genders and explain why you teach things a certain way (Caskey and Ruben 2003). It has amazed me over the last several decades as we learn more about the brain how much we keep from our students. Teachers understand Bloom's Taxonomy, Gardner's Multiple Intelligences, and other theories, but do not let the students in on the secret. Teaching young adolescents about the brain and brain chemistry helps them through these confusing times.

Keep the parents of your students in the information loop as well. By educating them about these differences, they can support your activities at home. This entire concept would make a great parent education evening sponsored by a team.

Begin exploring various gender-friendly strategies in your classrooms. Maintain a balance between competitive and cooperative activities, use gender as a consideration when you regroup, provide movement and energy release activities, build in character education lessons, call on students equally, be aware that some content may be intimidating to one gender or the other, use graphic organizers, provide effective notetaking strategies, provide gender role models, teach students how to be media literate, and provide a positive environment that is gender neutral—these are all ways to make your classroom gender friendly.

# Conclusion

In the past decade or so, much progress has been made in understanding the human brain, both physiologically and environmentally. We are now beginning to see that there may even be gender implications in the way the brain receives and uses information. These differences have implications for teachers striving to make learning more effective and efficient for students.

Whether the differences are genetic, or social, or both is not as important to us as the fact that boys and girls do learn in different ways. The quest is not to create classrooms that focus on one or the other gender. Instead, it is to purposefully structure our classroom so that some activities favor one gender's learning style and some favor the other's. Specifically, it is critical that teachers know the differences and structure the learning environment so that the students work sometimes reinforces individuals' stronger area, and sometimes strengthens a weaker one.

We can use this new and exciting information to make students more academically successful and to make classrooms more gender-friendly.

# References

AAUW. 1992. *How schools shortchange girls*. New York: American Association of University Women.

_____. 1998. *Gender gaps: Where schools still fail our children*. New York: American Association of University Women.

Caskey, M. M., and B. Ruben. (2003). Awakening adolescent brains. *Middle Matters* 12 (1): 4–5.

Gurian, M. 2001. *Boys and girls learn differently! A guide for teachers and parents*. San Francisco: Jossey-Bass.

Gurian, M., and A. C. Ballew. 2003. *The boys and girls learn differently action guide for teachers*. San Francisco: Jossey-Bass.

Gurian, M., and K. Stevens. 2004. With boys and girls in mind. *Educational Leadership* (62)3:21–26.

Kindlon, D., and M. Thompson. 2000. *Raising Cain: Protecting the emotional life of boys*. New York: Ballantine.

Pipher, M. 1994. *Reviving Ophelia: Saving the selves of adolescent girls*. New York: Ballantine.

Pollack, W. 1998. *Real boys: Rescuing our sons from the myths of boyhood*. New York: Random House.

Powell, K. C. 2004. Developmental psychology of adolescent girls: Conflicts and identity issues. *Education* 125 (1):77–87.

Rice, F. P., and K. G. Dolgin. 2002. *The adolescent: Development, relationships and culture.* 10th ed. Boston: Allyn and Bacon.

Santrock, J. W. 2001. *Adolescence.* 8th ed. Boston. McGraw-Hill.

Sax, L. 2005. *Why gender matters: What parents and teachers need to know about the emerging science of sex differences.* New York: Doubleday.

Sousa, D. A. 2001. *How the brain learns.* 2nd ed. Thousand Oaks, CA: Corwin Press.

Taylor, D., and M. Lorimer. 2003. Helping boys succeed: Which research-based strategies curb negative trends now facing boys? *Educational Leadership* 60 (4):68–70.

Walsh, D. 2004. *Why do they act that way?* New York: Free Press.

**DAVID KOMMER** is an associate professor at Ashland University.

From *The Clearing House*, July/August 2006, pp. 247–251. Reprinted by permission of the Helen Dwight Reid Educational Foundation. Published by Heldref Publications, 1319 Eighteenth St., NW, Washington, DC 20036-1802. Copyright © 2006. www.heldref.org

# Female Faculty in Male-Dominated Fields: Law, Medicine, and Engineering

LaWanda Ward

Studies have documented the increased number of women faculty in the academy; however, in areas that are historically male dominated—law, medicine, and engineering—the numbers remain dismal. For example, in the legal academy, "Women constitute only sixteen percent of full professors, however, they constitute almost fifty percent of law school students nationwide" (Farley, 1996, p. 333). More recently, that figure has improved. In 2007–2008, women constituted almost 30 percent of full professors in law schools while still constituting about half of all students (Abdullina, 2008) Yet when women are hired as law faculty, they "receive less pay, are denied tenure at higher rates, and are disproportionately concentrated in lower-ranked schools" (Farley, 1996, p. 333). Even in the most recent statistical report of the Association of American Law Schools, only 30 percent of women law school faculty hold tenured or tenure-track positions compared with 70 percent of the male faculty (Abdullina, 2008). Because the "myths of neutrality and universality—that the perspectives of privileged White males are the embodiment of science, medicine, law or literature—are rarely challenged," subtle sex discrimination continues to permeate educational institutions (Benokraitis, 1998, p. 19). According to Benokraitis, "One of the assumptions has always been that once women had access to education, salary disparities would decrease. In fact, racial and gender inequalities become greater as one goes up the educational hierarchy" (p. 22). Only 20 percent of law school deans are women, yet women constitute 65 percent of instructors and 61 percent of lecturers—both nontenure-track categories that represent the lowest status of academic appointments in law schools (Abdullina, 2008). Research conducted by Ash, Carr, Goldstein, and Frieman (2004) suggests that "the most recent female graduates start with salaries similar to those of their male colleagues, but by three to eight years after a degree is earned, salary disparities appear and then increase with greater seniority" (p. 212).

The women "firsts" in these selected fields endured challenges based solely on their gender. Myra Bradwell,

the first female attorney in the United States in 1869, "was denied admission to the Illinois bar because the court declared that women, because they are delicate and timid biologically, are unfit for the rude world of law practice" (Farley, 1996, p. 349). Similarly, the first woman to obtain a medical degree in 1849, Elizabeth Blackwell, was denied admission to the major medical schools. The one school to accept Blackwell presented her application to the male student body to determine admittance, which was granted under the guise that it was a practical joke. Despite resistance from students, professors, and even community members, Blackwell graduated first in her class. Unfortunately possessing stellar credentials was not sufficient; she was unable to secure a position with hospitals and decided to establish her own infirmary (National Women's Hall of Fame, n.d.).

While challenges of the firsts were mainly blatant acts of sexual discrimination, today the occurrences tend to be subtle and often go unnoticed, especially those who are unaffected by the discrimination. "Subtle sex discrimination is often not noticed because most people have internalized subtle sexist behavior as normal, natural, or acceptable" (Benokraitis, 1998, p. 5). Today access to higher education is not an issue for females; however, male-dominated disciplines rarely provide welcoming or accepting environments compared to other disciplines, such as education or social work. The transition from student to professor status in these male-dominated areas has not met with any less resistance. "The articulated requirements for tenure are scholarship, teaching, and service, but what matters even more importantly, is not spoken. That requirement is the ability to fit in and for a woman in a male-dominated environment, this is a difficult task" (Farley, 1996, p. 347).

## Law

"In legal academia, women are congregated in lower-ranking, lower-paying, lower-prestige positions" (Levit, 2001, p. 778). The perception of women as law professors has had a significant impact on their success and advancement. "Female faculty have entered legal education since the early 1980s but are leaving at greater rates than any other group outside of people of color" (Dusky, 1996, p. 88). Negative and sexist feedback from students in hostile classroom environments, criticism of scholarship, and generally not fitting into the "law professor" mode are factors that have an impact on female law professors.

"One of the main issues for women faculty in law is the presumption of competence. Student evaluations reveal that female law professors are judged on being a woman first and foremost and as not being well suited to teach law" (Farley, 1996, p. 336). Many law students enter law school possessing an image of a white, older, male professor sitting at a podium with a stern demeanor, questioning their competence and undermining their confidence. "The image of the paradigmatic law professor is still Professor Kingsfield from *The Paper Chase*," a movie in which the stereotype of what a law professor is—a stern white male—continues to exist (Farley, 1996, p. 343). Since women do not mirror that image, they are treated with hostility. According to Farley (1996), female professors "report that the classroom is often hostile and students are disrespectful" (p. 341). This type of environment is labeled "a 'prove it' class dynamic where women are required to prove that they are qualified to teach law" (p. 341). Challenges, mostly from male students, have been observed by even male colleagues, who were "most struck by this atmosphere" (p. 341). Levit's 2001 portrait shows that these student perceptions and actions persist over time.

Law schools reinforce gender differences in teaching. "Female law professors are much more likely than male professors to teach substantive courses addressing familial issues, as well as skills courses that demand labor intensive student nurturing" (Levit, 2001, p. 781). In addition, female faculty take on additional responsibilities from "student advising, attending student and community functions, planning law school programs to hosting or participating in colloquium series, reviewing manuscripts for colleagues, and serving on law school, university, and public service committees," which are not factored into the tenure evaluation process (p. 781).

"The main excuse that law faculties use to deny tenure is that the women's scholarship has been found lacking" (Dusky, 1996, p. 104). According to law professor Eleanor Swift, who was not offered tenure at Berkeley, female faculty are provided comments such as, "Your scholarship fails—it's 'unsuccessful,' 'unpersuasive,' 'overly ambitious,' or 'makes no contribution'" (p. 105). Due to this type of ambiguous and unconstructive feedback, many female professors have made their situations public and filed sexual discrimination grievances against law schools. Other accounts of denial of tenure include females being told they "didn't make enough friends of the male faculty" (p. 108). A professor denied tenure at Harvard Law School was informed that "some professors were miffed that she didn't seek them out to chat them up" (p. 108).

There are strategies that individuals and institutions can employ to welcome female law professors. First, women can serve as a catalyst to change the law schools where they teach. Our society is one that debunks myths and stereotypes by demonstrating flawed reasoning and logic. Qualified females graduate from law schools with as stellar credentials to teach and conduct research as their male counterparts do. Female law professors should thus not internalize stereotypes about inferiority, but should strive to maintain self-confidence and align themselves with people who believe in them. Second, essential changes in the law school environment include "institutionalizing the expectation of mentoring" (Levit, 2001, p. 803). Mentoring by women and men in the legal academy is needed to guide those seeking tenure and acceptance. Finally, "what is absolutely required is the recognition that the legal system, the legal reasoning structure, and the law school are gendered institutions" (Farley, 1996, p. 352). According to Acker (1992), "The term 'gendered institutions' means that gender is present in the processes, practices, images and ideologies, and distributions of power. The law was historically created by men, currently dominated by men, and symbolically interpreted from the standpoint of men in leading positions, both in the present and historically" (p. 567). Moreover, Farley (1996) asserts, "We need to confront and reappraise the paradigms of legal education. We need to question ourselves, our colleagues, and our students about our assumptions about what law is and how law should be taught" (p. 7). Institutional change in law schools should address the acceptance of various research interests of females, especially those labeled as "nonmainstream," and should insist on the use of nonsexist criteria to determine tenure.

# Medicine

In the medical field, studies have confirmed that "academic rank and career success of women in academic medicine lags behind that of their male colleagues" (Lewis-Stevenson and others, 2001). "In medicine, 40% of graduates are women, and, until recently, women have entered academia in higher proportions than males" (Ash, Carr, Goldstein, and Frieman, 2004, p. 12). Speculations for the recent decline of female professors are attributed to resident and fellow awareness of the challenges facing women who choose academia. Lewis-Stevenson and others (2001) found that "despite the observation that women are more likely to pursue academic careers, women are more likely to remain at lower rungs on the academic ladder" (p. 459). One justification for this difference has been that "women may place different levels of value on some of the processes associated with achieving promotion and tenure in academic environments" (p. 459). For example, reports have shown that women tend to participate in "teaching and clinical activities over research because they find the former items more satisfying" (p. 459). In a 1997 study of 113 U.S. medical schools with family medicine departments, data collected revealed that "faculty in departments of family medicine were more likely to be female, 41% versus 21%, compared with all academic medicine disciplines. However, women in full-time positions were less likely than men, to be either an associate or full professor" (p. 461). In 2003, women in medical schools constituted only 11 percent of full professors and 13 percent of associate professors (Association of American Medical Colleges, 2003).

Similarly, another study showed that "women in academic emergency medicine spent a greater percentage of time in clinical and teaching activities, published less in peer-reviewed journals, and were less likely to achieve senior academic ranks in their medical schools" (Cydulka and others, 2000, p. 1006). Although the academic preparation is the same for men and women, differences exist in the advancement process: "Women were offered fewer academic resources at the time of their initial appointments, spent longer periods at lower ranks, and even after adjustment for productivity factors, were less likely to be promoted to associate or full professor" (Cydulka and others, 2000, p. 999). Ironically, the study revealed mentoring in an unfavorable light, observing at the turn of the century the following condition:

> Networks of women faculty have not been effective as those of their men colleagues, as networks for women faculty tend to include fewer faculty of high rank and few associates from previous institutions. This problem is certainly true in emergency medicine, where very few women hold leadership positions and only two women are chairs of academic departments [p. 1005].

Another factor discovered in the study is that "women are younger than their male counterparts, spend more time on teaching and patient care activities, and are less likely to reach senior academic ranks than are men"(p. 1002).

Ash, Carr, Goldstein, and Frieman's review (2004) of research shows that in addition to "simple discrimination," female full professors are scarce for several reasons, including "lower motivation, their lack of mentorship, sexual harassment, greater family responsibilities, and less institutional support" (p. 11). In sharp contrast, a study regarding the promotion and salary of female versus male medical school full-time faculty at randomly selected U.S. medical schools revealed that "women had similar motivation, and similar mentoring as male faculty, and gender bias or sexual harassment had noticeably affected academic productivity" (p. 11). Not surprisingly, "Family responsibilities did differentially weigh on female faculty, affect their academic productivity, and contribute to greater time to attaining senior rank" (p. 11). Overall, these studies shed light on a disturbing fact that "despite an adequate pipeline in academic medicine and sufficient years for women to achieve full professor ranks, there is less advancement to full professor rank and lower salaries for women" (p. 12).

Fortunately, there are examples of medical schools that not only recognize the importance of achieving equality by creating policies but by action. The Johns Hopkins Department of Internal Medicine implemented a program beginning in 1990 to address the mentoring of female faculty. A faculty development position was created and was responsible for working "with all levels of staff personnel to analyze problems and mediate solutions" (Cydulka and others, 2000, p. 1005). In addition, faculty members were educated on gender discrimination, and a "reduction of isolation" program was implemented. Proponents of gender equality in higher education assert that a commitment from high-level university officials and department heads who recognize a need for improvement is essential. In support of this assertion, "Johns Hopkins' program success resulted primarily because the chair of the department of medicine was also very interested in seeing this program be successful" (p. 1005).

Medical schools should carefully "examine their environment for gender equity in promotion and compensation" (Ash, Carr, Goldstein, and Frieman, 2004, p. 12). For their success, academic women faculty in medicine "should be encouraged to focus on their goals and objectives and actively steered toward pathways that will help achieve them rather than toward avenues that don't lead to academic promotion" (Cydulka and others, 2000, p. 1005). Strategies designed to retain female faculty in medicine and enhance their professional growth include "mentoring and research relationships developed, creative time planning that includes the consideration of time required for childbearing and child rearing, which would alleviate the pressure of forcing women to decide between career and family and thus potentially decrease the loss of many emerging academicians" (p. 1006). Efforts to include women on projects and committees that may assist in their career development and academic promotion are essential.

# Engineering

According to Horning (1984), "Historically, women's low representation in science and engineering was said to be due in large part to their lack of 'ability, interest, or both'" (p. 30). Today this notion is no longer the case because of programs as early as elementary school promoting math and sciences to girls. Yet a more effective way of attracting females into the sciences, and specifically engineering, would be to increase the number of female faculty who can serve as mentors and role models. "Qualified women applicants are not given the opportunity to become engineering faculty because it is presumed that women will not have the time to serve as effective members of the professoriate given their family obligations" (Baum, 1989, p. 557). The model of the ideal worker in sciences and engineering, says Williams (2006), assumes a work week of more than fifty hours a week, which continues to exclude women who have child care obligations. Xie (2006) finds that women with children are less likely to pursue careers in science and engineering and less likely to be promoted. He states, "Although some of the gender differences are attributable to the advantages that marriage and parenthood bestow upon men, they clearly suggest that being married and having children create career barriers that are unique to women—as opposed to men—scientists." (p. 172). Societal views have constructed the engineering profession as one of prestige and status that is associated with white males. "Historically, women have not been extended opportunities to possess that same status and power" (Aisenberg and Harrington, 1988, p. 4). Similar to women in law, "Female faculty in engineering endure a 'double-bind' in which they attempt to redefine the 'male' image of professor as well as of engineer and are, oftentimes, the lone woman surrounded by a cadre of male academics" (Baum, 1989, p. 557). The "lone woman" image persists: women currently constitute only 11.8 percent of tenured or tenure-track faculty in engineering (Gibbons, 2008).

In a study of female engineering faculty, McKendall (2000) found that "the experiences of women engineering faculty are not unique to the professoriate, but their experiences have more impact because of their low representation. Most of the study participants endure environments that do not consider the problems and issues they encounter" (p. 32). The participants with families "must perform a balancing act between the roles of mother/wife and professor. This provides another source of anxiety that is not unique to the professoriate; however, as the only woman in the department, some may feel inclined to be a 'superwoman' in terms of publishing, teaching, obtaining grants, and service in their quest to prove themselves worthy of their position" (p. 34). McKendall indicates that the majority of males in this field do not have to consider the role of primary caregiver to children because of stay-at-home wives or professional child care providers who take on that responsibility. High levels of burnout and leaving the academy are often the results of taking on the superwoman role.

McKendall (2000) offers these recommendations for how institutions and individuals can take the initiative to change institutional and departmental climates for women in engineering:

- The dean should visit faculty meetings periodically in order to assess the departmental dynamics.

However, this would be effective only if the dean is free from biased, sexist, stereotypical perceptions.

- Create a listserv or discussion group that could foster dialogue among female faculty to discern how others deal with some of the differences and share some of the problems specific to women in engineering and the sciences.
- Create sensitivity classes to make men aware of the differences that affect them not only in working with their colleagues but also with students in the classroom.
- Diversify the faculty and administration.
- Provide a formal setting where women across campus can interact (possibly a monthly seminar series or luncheon)
- Provide day care services.
- Increase the number of women in engineering [p. 34].

Another well-publicized account of female faculty engineers focused on the Massachusetts Institute of Technology (MIT). A group of female and male faculty in the School of Science analyzed the status of women faculty in the department. This committee was created by the dean of science after inequalities were identified by female faculty and brought to his attention. The dean also conducted "a quick study and immediately recognized that a serious problem existed. He became a strong champion of the women's cause" (Committee on Women Faculty in the School of Science at MIT, 1999, p. 6). According to the Committee on Women Faculty in the School of Science at MIT, findings demonstrated that "many tenured women faculty feel marginalized and excluded from a significant role in their departments. Marginalization increases as women progress through their careers at MIT. Data in support of their views are differential pay, space, awards, resources, and response to outside offers between men and women faculty with women receiving less despite professional accomplishments equal to those of their male colleagues" (p. 4). In contrast, "Junior women faculty feel well supported within their departments and most do not believe that gender bias will impact their careers differently from those of male colleagues" (p. 4). Perhaps their positive views expressed were in fear of being viewed as "complainers" or "it is quite possible they have been socialized by the male-dominated paradigm" (McKendall, 2000, p. 33). Alarmingly, the committee discovered that "the percent of women faculty in the School of Science (8%) had not changed significantly for at least 10 and probably 20 years" (Committee on Women Faculty in the School of Science at MIT, 1999, p. 4).

The committee learned that in order to address issues and concerns of female faculty in departments, it was necessary to conduct "meaningful review which is twofold: (1) It is essential to review primary rather than processed data, and (2) It is essential that the review be done by senior women faculty who are deeply knowledgeable about the particular department, discipline, and area of research" (p. 7).

MIT's Committee on Women Faculty (1999) proposed more detailed recommendations to the administration than participants in the McKendall study. The suggestions included specific, action-oriented ways to address each item. Initiatives submitted include "the establishment of the women's committee as a standing committee, review annually the compensation system, replace administrators who knowingly practice or permit discriminatory practices against women faculty, and address family-work conflict realistically and openly" (pp. 14–15). A follow-up report from MIT (Hopkins, Bailyn, Gibson, and Hammonds, 2002) details the similarities in situation between engineering and science schools and other units of the campus. It also highlighted changes that had begun to occur since the 1999 report, such as increases in the representation of women in engineering and science administration.

# Conclusion

Common themes throughout the three disciplines discussed include lower pay for female faculty with the same credentials as male counterparts, longer time to tenure due to various factors, and performing a disproportionate share of stereotypical "nurturing" tasks such as teaching clinical courses, advising students, and serving on committees. Studies reveal that a commitment from department chairs and upper-level administrators, mentoring programs, and consideration of family circumstances all have a positive impact on the environment, treatment, and success of female faculty. Ultimately the eradication of sexist policies and norms has to be recognized and addressed in order to have equity in teaching law, medicine, and engineering.

More important, those who want to help improve the situation of women in nontraditional fields should be inspired to conduct additional research that supports and validates the gender equality effort that has to be continually championed by all. "As students, faculty, administrators, and alumni, we can speak up individually about 'just below the surface' discriminatory behavior that many women (and some men) experience on a daily basis" (Benokraitis, 1998, p. 31).

# References

Abdullina, P. "2007–2008 AALS Statistical Report on Law Faculty: Association of American Law Schools Statistical Report on Law School Faculty and Candidates for Law Faculty Positions."

2008. Retrieved July 4, 2008, from http://aals.org.cnchost.com/statistics/2008dlt/titles.html.

Acker, J. "From Sex Roles to Gendered Institutions." *Contemporary Sociology,* 1992, *21*(5), 565–569.

Aisenberg, N., and Harrington, M. *Women of Academe.* Amherst: University of Massachusetts Press, 1988.

Ash, A. S., Carr, P. L., Goldstein, R., and Frieman, R. H. "Compensation and Advancement of Women in Academic Medicine: Is There Equity?" *Annals of Internal Medicine,* 2004, *141*(3), 205–212.

Association of American Medical Colleges. "Women in American Academic Medicine Statistics 2002–2003." Retrieved July 4, 2008, from http://www.ama-assn.org/ama/pub/category/12919.html.

Baum, E. "Why Are So Few Women in Engineering?" *Engineering Education,* 1989, *74*(5), 556–557.

Benokraitis, N. V. "Career Strategies for Women in Academe." In L. Collins (ed.), *Working in the Ivory Basement: Subtle Sex Discrimination in Higher Education.* Thousand Oaks, Calif.: Sage, 1998.

Committee on Women Faculty in the School of Science at MIT. "A Study of the Status of Women Faculty in Science at MIT." *MIT Faculty Newsletter,* 1999, *11*(4), 1–17.

Cydulka, R. K., and others. "Women in Academic Emergency Medicine." *Academic Emergency Medicine,* 2000, *7*(9), 999–1007.

Dusky, L. "Tenure Travails." In L. Dusky (ed.), *Still Unequal: The Shameful Truth About Women and Justice in America.* New York: Crown, 1996.

Farley, C. H. "Confronting Expectations: Women in the Legal Academy." *Yale Journal of Law and Feminism,* 1996, *8,* 333–358.

Gibbons, M. T. "Engineering by the Numbers." American Society for Engineering Education. 2008. Retrieved July 5, 2008, from http://www.asee.org/publications/ profiles/upload/2007ProfileEng.pdf.

Hopkins, N., Bailyn, L., Gibson, L., and Hammonds, E. "Reports of the Committees on the Status of Women Faculty." Massachusetts Institute of Technology. 2002. Retrieved July 5, 2008, from http://web.mit.edu/faculty/reports/pdf/overview.pdf.

Horning, L. S. "Women in Science and Engineering." *Technology Review,* 1984, *87,* 30–41.

Levit, N. "Keeping Feminism in Its Place: Sex Segregation and the Domestication of Female Academics." *Kansas Law Review,* 2001, *49,* 775–807.

Lewis-Stevenson, S., and others. "Female and Underrepresented Minority Faculty in Academic Departments of Family Medicine: Are Women and Minorities Better Off in Family Medicine?" *Family Medicine,* 2001, *33*(6), 459–465.

McKendall, B. S. "The Woman Engineering Academic: An Investigation of Departmental and Institutional Environments." *Equity and Excellence in Education,* 2000, *33,* 26–35.

National Women's Hall of Fame. "Women of the Hall." N.d. Retrieved Mar. 31, 2007, from http://www.greatwomen.org/women.php?action=viewoneandid=20.

Williams, J. C. "Long Time No See: Why Are There Still So Few Women in Academic Science and Engineering?" Workshop report from the Biological, Social, and Organizational Components of Success for Women in Academic Science and Engineering, National Academies, 2006. Retrieved July 5, 2008, from http://books.nap.edu/open book.php?record_id=11766&page=149.

Xie, Y. "Social Influences on Science and Engineering Career Decisions." Workshop report from the Biological, Social, and Organizational Components of Success for Women in Academic Science and Engineering. National Academies, 2006.

Retrieved July 5, 2008, from http://books.nap.edu/openbook.php?record_id=11766&page=166#p2000fdd89970166001.

**LaWanda Ward** is the director of pro bono and public interest at the Indiana University School of Law-Indianapolis. She is pursuing a doctorate in higher education and student affairs at Indiana University.

From *New Directions for Higher Education,* Fall 2008, pp. 63–72. Copyright © 2008 by John Wiley & Sons. Reprinted by permission.

# Scaling the Ivory Towers

## Title IX has launched women into the studies, professions and administrative jobs of their dreams.

CARYN MCTIGHE MUSIL

I walked onto campus for my first tenure-track faculty position in 1971, the year before Title IX was passed. I was one of only 12 full-time women faculty members on my campus, and the only one in my department. For much of my first year of teaching, I felt like someone with a day pass at a men's club—but so did the women students, who had only gained admission to the school the year before. Numbering just 20 percent of the student body, they used to gather in the women's bathroom to form a protective cluster before daring to walk into the sea of men in the cafeteria.

Anticipating women's arrival in 1970, the college ordered mirrors for the dorms and yogurt for the cafeteria. The passage of Title IX two years later made it clear that full equality was going to demand far more extensive changes than that.

This year, the 35th anniversary of Title IX, my younger daughter, Emily, became a visiting professor at Trinity College in Connecticut, where 42 percent of the faculty are women—just above the national average. Among Emily's generation, just under 50 percent of doctorates have been awarded to women; in my generation, it was 14 percent. She can also draw upon three decades of robust feminist scholarship and women's-studies courses; my generation was just beginning to invent the field.

The contrast between her academic landscape and mine could not be more dramatic. And Title IX is the primary cause for the seismic shifts.

The law's impact has been elemental. Not only has it helped eliminate blatant discriminatory practices across educational institutions, but it has helped root out subtler methods of holding women back by closing the gap between men's and women's financial aid packages, improving housing opportunities for women students (a lack of women's dorms was once used to restrict women's admissions) and combating sexual harassment.

Just before Title IX was signed into law, women were underrepresented as undergraduates, at just over 40 percent of all students. And it wasn't that easy for them to get into those ivied halls. Young women typically had to make higher grades and SAT scores than young men to gain college admission, and often faced quotas limiting the number of women admitted.

Once they got on campus, there were few women role models—less than one in five faculty members were women, and a mere 3 percent of college presidents. In some fields, even the women students were barely visible: About 1 percent of master's degrees in engineering, 1 percent of doctoral dental degrees, and under 2 percent of master's degrees in mathematics were awarded to women in 1970.

The barriers were formidable, and sex discrimination unashamedly open and normative.

In the years since Title IX, however, all of those numbers have risen tremendously. Take college enrollment, for starters:

By 2005, women students comprised almost three out of five undergraduates, with some of this growth due to increased access for women of color (who have more than doubled their share of degrees since 1977, when they earned just over 10 percent). Women have not simply increased their numbers in academia, though: They have also moved into fields formerly dominated by men, particularly business and the sciences. These are the sorts of fields that lead women into higher-paying jobs after graduation.

Bucking the rising trend, however, are computer and information science, where numbers peaked in 1984 before declining, and engineering and engineering technologies, in which the numbers of women grew and then leveled off. Certain fields have continued to be women-dominant from 1980 until 2005—health professions other than physicians and related clinical sciences (currently more than 86 percent women) and education (about 79 percent women), but this isn't the best news for economic equity, since wages tend to stay low in fields with few men.

**The law's impact has been elemental. Not only has it helped eliminate blatant discriminatory practices, but it has helped root out subtler methods of holding women back.**

In graduate and professional schools, too, young women have enjoyed far greater access thanks to Title IX. In 1970, women earned only 14 percent of doctoral degrees, but today earn nearly half. Yet women's doctorates are still not distributed evenly across disciplines: They range from a low of about 19 percent in engineering and engineering technologies to a high of about 71 percent in psychology.

**In 1970, women earned only 14 percent, but today earn nearly half of doctoral degrees.**

The most dramatic gains are in the professional schools. In 1971, just about 1 of 100 dental school graduates were women, while in 2005 that number grew nearly fortyfold. In medical schools the numbers jumped from less than 10 percent to nearly 50 percent, and law school numbers from about 7 percent to nearly 49 percent.

There's been quite a psychological benefit, too. As my older daughter, Rebecca, says of her experience at New York University Law School, "Women were more than half of the students, so sex discrimination was not something we ever worried about. . . . It's not that we don't think about equality, but that we don't *have* to think about it as much because of what's already been done."

Armed with their professional degrees in medicine and law, women have entered those professions at steadily increasing rates. Yet their numbers—and in law firms, their advancement—still lag behind. In 2006, women made up 33 percent of lawyers but just 16 percent of partners in law firms. Similarly, in medicine only 27 percent of doctors are women, and they're unevenly spread across specialties, the top three choices being internal medicine, pediatrics and general family medicine.

The news is also mixed about women in academic leadership. By 1986 the number of women college presidents had tripled from 1970 to almost 10 percent, and by 2006 reached 23 percent, with a large proportion serving as presidents of community colleges. But most of the progress occurred between 1986 and 2001 and now has slowed considerably. Furthermore, today's presidents remain much less diverse by race, gender and ethnicity than the students, faculty or administrators who report to them: Only 4 percent of the respondents in a recent survey of college presidents identified as "minority women." Women also tend to be more qualified and make more sacrifices than men in order to gain leadership; they're far less likely than men presidents to be married and have children, and significantly more likely to hold an advanced degree.

On faculties, women have increased across every rank but continue to move up more slowly than men. In 2006 they accounted for nearly 40 percent of full-time faculty and nearly 50 percent of part-timers. Young women benefit extraordinarily from all these women role models. As my daughter Emily says, "Women professors looked out for me the whole time . . . and that is where I got my career counseling."

But women professors are not employed equally across institutional types—they're just over half the faculty at institutions offering associate degrees, but only 34 percent at doctoral institutions. While women are increasing their numbers in tenure-*track* positions (nearly 45 percent), they still face the accumulated disadvantages of sex discrimination over time and represent only about 31 percent of currently tenured faculty.

"People change faster and more easily than institutions," explains Yolanda T. Moses, associate vice chancellor for diversity at the University of California, Riverside. While the most blatant violations have been eliminated, Moses argues that the next level of work is even more complicated: "Systems can undermine progress . . . and we need to unearth those behaviors that sabotage even our best intentions." A search committee in physics or engineering, for example, may profess to be seeking more women, but make no efforts to break out of all-men, frequently all-white, networks to identify strong women candidates.

These are the sorts of challenges that still remain, yet Title IX has gone a long way toward making campuses more hospitable. By offering legal protection from hostile work and learning environments, it helped draw attention to sexism in the classroom and opened the door for change. The fields of science, technology, engineering and math were among the most chilly toward women, so Title IX helped usher in a period of serious self-study that has led to the adoption of more women-friendly teaching practices and programs, and thus a rise in women taking courses formerly dominated by men.

Finally, Title IX has helped women fight sexual harassment in academia—something for which there was no language in 1970. As a young professor then, I complained in a rage to my department chair about a professor who had just wrapped his arms around one of his students at a reception, a gesture that her frightened face revealed had been unwanted and intimidating. My colleague simply brushed it off and said, "That's just Jim" (not his real name). Spurred by Title IX, my institution eventually established sexual-harassment grievance procedures that allowed a student to file a grievance against this same professor a few years later. Sexual harassment continues to haunt women and girls, but Title IX has helped set behavioral standards and offer institutional safeguards.

## Title IX has helped women fight sexual harassment in academia—something for which there was no language in 1970.

Despite its extraordinary, liberating impact on the lives of girls and women, Title IX remains threatened. Through anti-affirmative-action lawsuits or state referendums that oppose affirmative action in public institutions, a well-funded right-wing movement has led a relentless assault on such elite public institutions as the University of Texas, Austin; the University of Washington; the University of Michigan; and the University of California system. Unfortunately, referenda opposing affirmative action have succeeded in Washington, California and Michigan, and the effect has been the lowering of numbers of women faculty and women students entering certain fields. In the University of California system, for example, women made up 37 percent of new faculty hires in 1994, but in 1999—three years after the passage of anti-affirmative-action Proposition 209, the percentage of new women hires had dropped to 25 percent.

So we must remain vigilant. I can't help wondering what it will be like for my granddaughter Catherine—born as I researched this article—when she reaches college age. Says Rebecca, her optimistic mother, "There is so much already in place that as long as we continue the practices that have gotten us to this point, I feel pretty confident that Catherine will have the same opportunities as a man would have."

Perhaps I should surrender to such optimism, but I will also teach Catherine how to counter forces that try to set her generation back. I want to be sure she is never fooled into believing that mirrors in the dorms and yogurt in the cafeteria are enough.

**CARYN McTIGHE MUSIL** is senior vice president at the Association of American Colleges and Universities (AAC&U). Kathryn Peltier Campbell, who provided research assistance, is editor of *On Campus with Women* for AAC&U.

From *Ms.*, by Caryn McTigue Musil, Fall 2007. Copyright © 2007 by Ms. Magazine. Reprinted by permission of Ms. Magazine and Caryn McTigue Musil.

# UNIT 4

# Gender, Work, and Health

## Unit Selections

## Key Points to Consider

- Do women and men today share equal opportunities in the corporate world?

- Does a "glass ceiling" still exist? If so, for whom and what kinds of opportunities are limited?

- How do the media depict the following: working mothers, stay-at-home mothers, working fathers, and stay-at-home fathers?

- Do gender differences impact health outcomes? Can you imagine both negative and positive influences gender may have on men's and women's health?

- How might the media influence self-esteem and body image?

- What impact can the social construction of masculinity have on health outcomes for men? What impact can the social construction of femininity have on the health outcomes for women?

## Student Website
www.mhcls.com

## Internet References

**Institute for Women and Work, Cornell University**
*http://www.ilr.cornell.edu/iww/*

**American Psychological Association: Society for Industrial and Organizational Psychology**
*http://www.siop.org/*

**National Institutes of Health (NIH)**
*http://www.nih.gov*

**Dr. Susan Love Research Foundation**
*http://www.dslrf.org*

**World Health Organization: Gender, Women and Health**
*http://www.who.int/gender/en/*

**National Cancer Institute: Breast Cancer**
*http://www.cancer.gov/cancertopics/types/breast*

**National Cancer Institute: Ovarian Cancer**
*http://www.cancer.gov/cancertopics/types/ovarian*

**National Cancer Institute: Testicular Cancer**
*http://www.cancer.gov/cancertopics/types/testicular/*

In this unit, we explore some of the ways in which work and health are gendered. The topics of health and work have long been of interest to gender studies scholars. Inequalities in work and healthcare have certainly decreased over the past few decades, but only to a degree. The phrase "the more things change, the more they stay the same" rings true here. Although there have been important improvements and feminist activists have helped create positive social change, we still lack full equality in many areas of our lives. This is especially true in these two areas.

The work section of this unit focuses on articles that discuss topics of importance to men and women in the world of work. Not only is there still a pay gap between men and women, work is heavily gendered in a variety of ways. Compare, for instance, vocational and career opportunities. Think about the work of dental hygienists versus the building trades and whom you might expect to find working in these industries. There are, by far, more dental hygienists who are women. Likewise, construction workers are mostly male. Commercial airline pilots (mostly male) are generally assisted by (mostly female) flight attendants. Corporate chief executive officers, presidents, and executive vice presidents (mostly male) supervise (mostly female) secretarial and administrative support staff. And on this pattern goes. You may ask yourself if the inequalities described here are simply due to the personal preferences of men and women in the types of employment they pursue. Generally, women are more likely to be found in lower-status and lower-paying jobs than men. The higher the social status, and the higher the pay, the more likely we find men occupying those jobs. There are exceptions, to be sure. However, the general trend is what is of interest. Can this trend be fully explained by personal preferences? Or, are there important social and structural influences that impact opportunities for men and women differently? Despite major successes and movement toward a more equal work force, we still find that there is much progress to be made.

The articles in the health section of this unit focus on a range of health topics, including health outcomes, menstruation, and sexual health. Health, including sexual health, now receives a significant amount of attention in the mainstream media. Over the past two decades, the general public's awareness of, and interest and involvement in, their own healthcare has dramatically increased. We want to stay healthy and live longer, and we know that to do so, we must learn more about our bodies,

© Photodisc/Getty Images

including how to prevent problems, recognize danger signs, and find the most effective treatments. In order to become fully empowered, we need to understand how gender can play a significant role in our health. The articles in this section point to some surprising findings about the links between gender and health.

# The Emperor's New Woes

**Man is no longer king of his domain. He's now supposed to be an equal partner—and a good listener, too. Blindsided by the escalating emotional demands of marriage, guys wonder how love became a no-win proposition.**

Sean Elder

Last year I was asked by the editor of a men's magazine to write a story about intimacy in relationships. His was one of those publications that advise the American man how to flatten his stomach and increase his chest size—that look, in other words, like a lot of women's magazines. I spoke to the requisite marriage experts: psychologists and sociologists who had stared into the murk of modern male-female relations. Though I tried to steer my sources toward simple declarative sentences and do-it-yourself answers, the editor was not happy.

"Couldn't you just give it to us in bullet points?" he asked. "We want a step-by-step guide on how to be emotionally intimate with your woman."

Therein lies a précis of the principal dilemma in marriage today. Men have come to accept—even celebrate—their wives' careers and paychecks while learning, step-by-step, how to bathe the baby and baste the turkey. But there is no Julia Child-style primer on closeness, no chart with diagrams: Insert A into slot B, and there you go. Intimacy achieved. Let's go have a cold one.

It would be funny if it weren't so painful. "It's probably the real cause of half of all divorces," according to Sam Margulies, a divorce mediator in Greensboro, North Carolina, and author of several books on the subject of marital breakups. The changes in women's lives—their roles, ambitions, opportunities—have been considered from every angle. But men's lives have changed too, in ways that are more confusing, more contradictory and often less welcome. Men did not ask to have their roles redefined. Now, they're looking for an instruction manual complete with fine print—and a translator's guide as well.

"Very few women could compare their lives to their mothers' and say, 'We look pretty similar,'" says Steven Nock, a professor of sociology at the University of Virginia who has studied what marriage means to men. "Women have so many dramatically different options in their lives. But where are men taking their cues about what it means to be a husband or a father? There is much less discussion in our society about that."

The guidelines for being a good husband used to be simple: provide, protect, maybe trim the hedges now and then. Now wives still want all that in a mate—and more. Today's wife wants a confidante and soul mate as well.

The requirements changed with no warning, and many husbands feel blindsided. Most men were raised with the idea that making it in the outside world is how you score points at home. For many women that also still holds true. It's not as though they want men to be less goal-oriented or less interested in money. They're asking for a breadwinner *and* a best friend.

But the skills needed to be a successful soldier or CEO are literally antithetical to the caring-sharing sort. Success and even heroism are still measured by a man's ability to compartmentalize, desensitize, act decisively and sacrifice himself. "The essence of masculinity is that what it takes to get love makes us distant from love," says Warren Farrell, San Diego-based author of *Why Men Earn More* and *Why Men Are the Way They Are.* "That is the male dilemma in a nutshell."

"Men are beside themselves," Farrell continues. "There is a fundamental contradiction: If [a man] is successful at work he has really prepared himself to be unsuccessful at home. He's damned if he does and damned if he doesn't."

## Marriage Changes Everything

Most men accept that and even welcome the transition. Men recognize that marriage requires compromise and sacrifice—but their beliefs about what's most important are surprisingly traditional, and not necessarily in line with women's beliefs. In his sociological research, Nock followed more than 6,000 young men for decades, gathering data on their social lives, careers and habits. His conclusion is that most men undergo a profound personal transformation when they marry. It is a passage into manhood in an era when the very definition of manhood is in flux. "Marriage changes men because it is the venue in which adult masculinity is developed and sustained," he writes in *Marriage in Men's Lives.*

A married man works longer hours, moves up the career ladder faster and earns more money than his single peers. He spends more time with his relatives. He donates less to charity; he spends less time hanging out with his buddies and more time in formal social organizations like business and civic associations.

A husband even *thinks* differently. "The way men view the world and their place in it changes in the act of marrying," says Nock. "Marriage makes people more conventional. If they are religious, they become more devout. They acquire the trappings of property owners, which makes them more conservative. They're less likely to engage in risky or deviant behaviors. Entering into this traditional arrangement has the effect of making men more traditional." A wedding is more than an expression of love; it's a public declaration that a man plans to abide by a set of social expectations about male adulthood. The seriousness with which men approach marriage and the lengths they are willing to go in order to be better husbands are some of the best evidence we have that men take commitment seriously and are willing to do what is expected of them to make marriage work.

## For a lot of husbands trying to rise to the demands of their 21st-century wives, the lessons of intimacy are worse than rocket science. They're poetry.

But there's a catch. Nock believes that since he conducted his research in the 1990s, women's expectations have expanded to include greater intimacy. While conducting his research, he says, "I was focused more on ordinary expectations." He believes that emotional expectations may now be the most central part of marriage.

"Even a generation ago, if a man was a good breadwinner and he had no profoundly negative attributes, if every night he came home, had a martini and watched TV all night, then went to bed, he was fine," says marriage and family therapist Terry Real, author of *How Do I Get Through to You? Closing the Intimacy Gap Between Men and Women.* Now the job description has been expanded to include listening and that least measurable of skills, empathizing. Today, simply not cheating on your wife or beating your kids doesn't make you a good husband and father.

Real says he counsels a lot of men who would prefer the bullet-point version of how-to-achieve-intimacy-now. "I say to them, 'She wants you to be more relationship-skilled than you were raised to be. You're a smart guy—this isn't rocket science.'" But for a lot of husbands trying to rise to the demands of their 21st-century wives, the lessons of intimacy are worse than rocket science. They're *poetry.*

When husbands realize what their wives are asking for, the reaction isn't " 'I didn't know that you wanted that, too,'" says Margulies. "It's more like 'I don't understand what the hell you're talking about.' " It's not a question of miscommunication, of Mars and Venus. It's a matter of new specifications, of women wanting something more than a traditional husband who, by definition, was removed and even remote. "In a nutshell, women want their husbands to act like girlfriends," Margulies says.

"I wish it were that simple," says Nock. "I don't think we can say, 'Okay, men, here's what you need to do to become better husbands.' " A lot of men would prefer such clear coordinates—even if it meant acting like a girlfriend.

While the conflicted desires of women have created some of this tension, society sends its own mixed signals. Time and feminism have chipped away at the granite facade of traditional masculinity, but old monuments don't fall easily. The last presidential election, after all, was in part a referendum on what kind of father or husband we want for our country. And did not the simple, stubborn, somewhat unintelligible fellow with the apparently traditional marriage best the more nuanced, flexible, loquacious gent with the strong, independent wife? John Kerry was chastised for windsurfing on Nantucket while George Bush was off whacking weeds in the hot Texas sun.

"What's so ludicrous about windsurfing?" asks Real. "It's effete—which is another way of saying it's feminine." Yet guys are forced to contend with such inane stereotypes. (Have you ever tried windsurfing? It's about as easy as riding a shark.)

Worst of all, women are often complicit in the stereotyping. If a single woman goes to a party, says Farrell, her friends don't push her toward the sensitive schoolteacher—they urge her to chat up the banker. "People don't say, 'Look at that man, he's really listening to a woman, asking her questions and drawing her out,' " says Farrell. "You don't get introductions like that, even though you would be introducing the woman to the type of man who would be a wonderful husband and father. Instead the host will say, 'That fellow is an intern at Mt. Sinai Hospital.' "

## For men, actual physical proximity is often as good as intimacy ("I'm here, aren't I?"), while women want something more demonstrative.

So we end up with men wary of the shifting rules of marriage, wondering what's in it for them. The weary white-collar salaryman, having worked his 60-hour week while making time for his daughter's piano recital, may well wonder about the poetry lessons his wife is threatening him with. Suddenly an evening of video games or ESPN doesn't sound so bad, even if it means eating a TV dinner. Hungry-Man meals have gotten a lot better over the years—and they're still nicely compartmentalized, with clear bullet-point instructions on the back of the box.

For the most part, our parents and grandparents did not worry much about the emotional content of marriage. My parents lived through the Great Depression and the second World War. When their marriage ended in divorce in the 1960s, I doubt either of them thought, "If only we had achieved greater intimacy!" It's not that they were stronger or better than we are today, or that our demands and complaints aren't legitimate. The lack of emotional connection certainly killed many marriages, and the right to personal fulfillment was part of what drove the women's movement—which in turn changed marriage for the better.

But on the communication score, most men are still playing catch-up with women. To care about someone else's feelings you have to be in touch with your own, and getting in touch with your feelings is not something we've been raised to think of as essential, or even admirable. Collectively, we don't have a lot of positive examples of an open, questioning, emotional hero. Hamlet, who was certainly introspective, was neither husband nor father; he died, quite conveniently, before facing either of those hurdles.

"It's not so much that men can't provide the emotional support that women want as that men and women define emotional support differently," according to Nock. "As marriages become more focused on emotion and happiness, men and women are defining closeness in somewhat different terms." For men, actual physical proximity is often as good as intimacy ("I'm here, aren't I?"), while women want something more demonstrative.

Just look at how men and women communicate with members of their own gender. I have seen my wife sit down knee-to-knee with one of her close friends and unload, with no preamble or pretext of doing anything else besides perhaps drinking a glass of wine or cup of tea. Guys, for the most part, need some distraction in order to talk about feelings.

Two summers ago, while visiting some old friends in France (and how is that for effete?), my wife marveled at how my longtime pal Randy and I reconnected after not seeing each other for years. We sat knee-to-knee as well—with our iBooks linked, swapping music files. But what she did not hear was us comparing notes on aging—his mother had passed away, mine was ailing—or our marriages, topics we would not have easily broached otherwise. It's as though men need something to do with their hands.

Having established that some men are willing to try to meet women halfway, it's safe to ask what women can do for men. Sex is seriously underrated as a passport to that communicative country a lot of wives want to explore. While some women seem to resent the fact that their husbands want them, and want to be wanted back, the very act (as opposed to talk) allows a lot of men to be more emotionally available. And it, too, gives us something to do with our hands.

"The complaints I hear from men are about their spouses not taking their sexual needs seriously enough," says Mark Epstein, a psychiatrist in private practice in New York and author of *Open to Desire: Embracing a Lust for Life.* "Men become vulnerable when they are sexually engaged. Maybe if women didn't feel demeaned or objectified by male sexuality they wouldn't have to push it away so much. They could start to feel it as more of a form of communication." He acknowledges that many women may see it as more work—but isn't that what they're asking of their men? Sex is one area where men and women can explore differences without yielding their individual identities. "One thing that has to happen in a couple is that each one has to make room for the other's desire," says Epstein, "which is different from the way you experience it. You can approach it but never totally understand it."

Women can cut men a bit of slack, and try to empathize with these rough creatures (remember *Beauty and the Beast?*) rather than change them. They can also adjust their expectations. As Farrell says, "If you expect a man to be a killer and be home on time for dinner, you will end up feeling depressed about your partnership."

After all, men have quickly become masters at another kind of intimacy: fatherhood. Many contemporary fathers feel that they are an upgrade from the previous version. Warm, loving, generous fathers are lionized in the culture rather than scorned, points out Terry Real. "The current generation of men is much better as fathers than their fathers were," he says, "but it's not clear to me that we're much better husbands than our fathers were." The difference is that much less risk is involved in being vulnerable or intimate with your child than there is with your mate. The relationship of parent and child is not that of equals, and while we may have a lot of expectations of our children, we generally don't look to them for complete emotional fulfillment.

Truth be known, most men want the same thing from their mates that their wives are looking for in their husbands. They want to be understood by them, even if it means understanding themselves first. There is plenty of evidence that men want and need marriage as much as women do and are willing to learn new dance steps. Just put them in bullet points, and let us lead sometimes.

From *Psychology Today,* March/April 2005, pp. 42, 44, 46. Copyright © 2005 by Sussex Publishers, LLC. Reprinted by permission.

# The Media Depiction of Women Who Opt Out

ARIELLE KUPERBERG AND PAMELA STONE

Women leaving careers to pursue full-time mothering have generated considerable media attention. Faludi (1991) was among the first to note the extensive coverage given to this group of women, whom she termed "new traditionalists." A stream of articles since the 1980s has kept alive the notion that heterosexual women are forsaking the contemporary role of working mother, which is associated with economic independence, self-reliance, and self-actualization, to return to the more traditional, economically dependent role of full-time stay-at-home mom. Shortly after the publication of Faludi's best-selling book, the influential business publication *Barron's* heralded "a women's revolution" and "exodus" of women from the workforce (Mahar 1992). A decade later, this exodus was given the label that stuck—the "opt-out revolution"—in a high-profile article by the work-life columnist of the *New York Times* (Belkin 2003). A year after that, major newsweekly *Time* published a cover story entitled "The Case for Staying Home: Why More Young Moms Are *Opting Out* [emphasis added] of the Rat Race" (Wallis 2004). Stay-at-home mothers have been deemed fashionable by *New York* magazine (Gardner 2002) and status symbols by *The Wall Street Journal* (Swasy 1993); they are the subject of hit television shows (e.g., *Desperate Housewives*) and best-selling books (e.g., *I Don't Know How She Does it* [Pearson 2002]). Through these and other images, the professional woman who chooses family over career is fast becoming a recognizable cultural type, a development noted by several prominent feminist analysts (e.g., Barnett and Rivers 1996; Williams 2000). Despite this, the way the media portray the phenomenon of opting out has received little systematic scholarly attention.

In this article, we fill this research gap with a content analysis of articles on opting out that appeared in leading print media outlets over a recent 16-year period. We begin by reviewing previous research on the media depiction of women, especially mothers. Next, we present the results of our content analysis, identifying major themes in the imagery surrounding opting out and describing the types of publications and articles in which such imagery appeared. Finally, we further situate the coverage of this phenomenon by first reviewing related research on women's labor force participation trends and presenting new analyses of actual trends in women's opting-out behavior during the period covered by our content analysis.

## The Depiction of Women in Print Media

While no previous research has focused specifically on women who opt out, there is a considerable body of literature on the more general representation of heterosexual women's work and family roles in print media. This research shows that prevailing media images of women often support adherence to patriarchal notions of femininity (Lowe 2003). One of the first studies, and arguably still the most influential, was Friedan's analysis in *The Feminine Mystique* (1983). She found that women with careers were virtually absent from the pages of women's magazines of the 1950s and 1960s and that women with jobs were frequently portrayed as giving them up. Media portrayals of women evolve but display a persistent emphasis on women's home roles. Brown (1978) found that depictions of working women increased during most of the twentieth century (1900–74) but lagged behind changes in women's labor force participation. Demarest and Garner (1992) found a decrease in the depiction of traditional roles in women's magazines between 1954 and 1982, a period that witnessed a particularly dramatic increase in women's labor force participation. Examining women's magazines from 1955 to 1975, Geise (1979, 55) found similarly that support for the traditional male-breadwinner/female-homemaker division of labor declined; however, "at no time" was a woman's career portrayed as more important to her than marriage and family.

In contrast, research on the depiction of motherhood, especially for working mothers, reflects what Hays (1996) has termed "cultural contradictions." Smith (2001), for example, noted a shift in ideology between 1987 and 1997, with women's magazines running an increasing number of negative articles about working mothers and child care options, including several day care horror stories. In a study that took an even longer view, looking at the depiction of mothers and work in women's magazines from the 1950s to 1980s, Keller (1994) found a persistently traditional depiction, with the dominant image of motherhood changing little from the traditionalist stay-at-home mother of the 1960s to the "neotraditionalist" of the 1980s. Consistent with this trend toward a greater focus on full-time motherhood, Douglas and Michaels (2004) surveyed popular media (including but not limited to print media) from the 1970s to the present and identified an emergence of "the new momism," which was exemplified by increasing attention to intensive mothering (Hays 1996) and illustrated primarily by ubiquitous images of stay-at-home moms.

Attention to motherhood is identified with class and race privilege. Advertisements in women's magazines in the late 1990s were dominated by images of white at-home mothers (Johnston and Swanson 2003). Smith (2001) found that the mass-market magazine portrayal of women between 1987 and 1997 perpetuated a view of white middle- and upper-class women as workers and especially mothers, while poor minority women were presented solely in their role as workers and not mothers. Studies also find that the messages conveyed in print media aimed at adolescent girls are traditional, emphasizing women's subordination to men, the centrality of heterosexual relationships, and the reinforcement of gender-segregated occupational stereotypes (Massoni 2004; Milkie 1999; Peirce 1993, 1997).

Reviewing a broad range of media portrayals of women in the decade from the mid-1980s to mid-1990s, Walters identified the dominant ideology as "postfeminism" (1995, 117). Postfeminism encompasses the backlash phenomenon identified by Faludi (1991) as well as what Walters calls a "more complex phenomenon" of antifeminism. While couched in the language of liberation ("choice"), the media images that emerged during "an historical period marked by the rise of the New Right and by the governments of Reagan and Bush," were, she argued, "clearly anti-feminist" (1995, 139). Williams (2000) also noted the ascendance of what she called the "rhetoric of choice" in the media depiction of women, as did Crittenden (2001, 234–35), who commented that today's rhetoric about "choosing" motherhood resembles the 1950s' feminine mystique about "happy women."

During the past two decades, the media depiction of *women in general,* while in some ways reflecting the reality of changes in their labor force participation, continues to focus on traditional roles and is increasingly pervaded by an individualistic rhetoric of choice. The media depiction of *motherhood* remains highly traditional. It is against this backdrop that we explore images about women whose actions signify a return to the traditional family form of male breadwinner–stay-at-home mother.

Previous research is limited, however, in that its conclusions are based on publications (typically magazines) that are aimed specifically at a female audience, many of whom are stay-at-home mothers (MRI 2004). Although this provides an excellent understanding of the rhetoric and imagery reaching a predominately female readership, it raises the question of whether these images are reaching a broader, mixed readership. Insofar as women who opt out are, by their actions, reverting from a dual-earner to a male breadwinner family, it is important to study the reach of such imagery not only among women but also among men. To the extent that these images are "controlling images" (Collins 1991, 68), that is, images that are designed to reinforce sexism and make traditional gendered roles appear natural and normal, they reinforce the ideal of the male breadwinner model and put pressure on men as husbands and fathers to live up to its dictates. In the workplace, where men disproportionately occupy positions of leadership and authority, exposure to opting-out imagery may lead to the assumption that having children will end women's commitment to their careers, which may in turn influence hiring and promotion decisions (Williams 2000, 69). For these reasons, we make a point of expanding our analysis beyond women's magazines to also include a broader set of publications that are aimed at both men and women.

In this article, we fill a gap by providing a systematic assessment of opting-out imagery. Our study extends existing research on media depiction of women by focusing on the relatively new and heretofore unexamined imagery surrounding the subject of opting out as well as by looking at a range of publications that target a large and diverse audience, including women and men. We seek to answer two sets of questions. The first focuses on the *content* of coverage: Who is profiled in these stories, and what are the major themes How are women in these stories described and characterized How consistent is the imagery surrounding women who opt out The second looks at the *context* of coverage by examining the types of media in which these articles appear to see if articles are "ghettoized" into historically female magazines or sections of newspapers aimed at women (style section, etc.) or purveyed to a larger and more diverse readership. We also examine the types of articles that are written about opting out, for example, straight reportage versus editorials. Finally, we further contextualize media imagery by examining actual trends in labor force participation and opting out among the kinds of women depicted in these articles.

## Data and Method

Our research addresses these questions primarily through a content analysis of articles specifically about heterosexual women who left the work force and became stay-at-home mothers. For the textual analysis, we used quantitative and qualitative techniques (viz. Massoni 2004), which allowed us to identify themes based both on their frequency and meaning. We examine the text of articles (omitting pictures but including their captions) published in the 16-year period between 1988 and 2003. We begin our analysis in 1988 because of the availability of easily searchable electronic databases from that year, which allowed us to systematically identify and sample articles for analysis. This time period is also of special historical interest, covering the end of the decade in which the "new traditionalists" were first identified (Faludi 1991) through the Belkin (2003) article that coined the term *opting out*.

Using the search engines LexisNexis, Readers' Guide, and Academic Premier, we searched a variety of publications using a strategy akin to purposive sampling. Because our primary goal was to understand the full array of imagery and themes being conveyed by opting-out coverage rather than to describe the frequency or characteristics of its distribution, we wanted to ensure that we searched publications across a large and diverse readership. We did not select a representative sample in the probabilistic sense but rather searched publications using criteria that would result in a cross section of publications with respect to two major criteria: type of publication (and implicitly, audience) and region of publication. Using the lists of publications in U.S. regions defined by LexisNexis, we selected newspapers in major metro areas with populations of one million or more in 2003. In addition, we included leading business publications such as *Business Week* and *Barron's,* as well as national newsweeklies such as *Time* and *Newsweek.* We made a point of searching special interest magazines such as those for women of color (e.g., *Essence,* which is aimed at Black women) and also searched major women's magazines including *Redbook, Working Woman,* and *Ladies Home Journal.* By design, because we wanted to examine imagery that was widely disseminated, our methods resulted in a sample that favors publications with relatively large circulations (i.e., national or large urban markets) and underrepresents articles appearing in small-town outlets.

To identify relevant articles in these publications, we experimented with several keywords, finding that *stay-at-home mom* was most useful and efficient for our purposes (recall that *opting out* was not coined until 2003). We read brief summaries or, in some cases, the full text of articles identified using this keyword, and included only those that were clearly about women who had "opted out" as this characterization is typically understood, that is, women who had quit paid work and were now at-home mothers. We excluded articles that did not specifically address the issue of opting out. During the period covered by our study, two highly visible women, then–PepsiCo-North America CEO Brenda Barnes in 1998 and then–White House counselor Karen Hughes in 2002, quit to go home, each occasioning significant media coverage. We excluded from the study the many articles about them that were strictly news reportage of their resignations. Otherwise, our sample of articles would have been skewed toward these women's experiences, potentially biasing our results. Using these procedures, we identified 51 articles in 30 publications, the list of which is given in

Appendix A. The procedures used to select publications and articles within them result in a diverse representation of texts, which reflect a comprehensive spectrum of opting-out imagery, potentially reaching a variety of audiences.

Guided by the critique of leading media analysts, as well as by work-family literature, we carried out a pilot study on a subset of articles to identify recurring themes. On the basis of this pretest, we developed two coding guides, one for features of articles and the other for features of women depicted in them. Thus, we use two units of analysis in this article—articles and women. We coded 10 characteristics of articles ($N = 51$), including the section in which they appeared, the type of publication in which they were found, and aspects of their overall depiction of opting out. For women ($N = 98$), we coded the characteristics of those who were described in three or more sentences in an article. This criterion ensured that there was sufficient information on each woman to code her characteristics reliably, although not all characteristics could be coded for every woman. Coded for women were the reasons mentioned for opting out, demographic characteristics, former occupation, husband's occupation, activities at home, and sentiments about quitting. Coding was carried out by three evaluators. To ensure high levels of intercoder agreement, a series of pretests was conducted, and code guide instructions (available from authors) were clarified to reduce inconsistencies (Altheide 1996), resulting in greater than 85 percent agreement among coders. On the basis of the frequencies of these coded characteristics, we identified several recurring themes. We then reanalyzed the articles to identify particular quotations related to the themes determined through quantitative coding.

# Results

## *Imaging Opting Out: The Content of Opt-Out Imagery*

We discovered three broad themes in the opt-out texts, which we identify as (1) "Family First, Child-Centric," (2) "The Mommy Elite," and (3) "Making Choices." Each is described below. In content, these themes are consistent with the feminist critique and past research in their emphasis on motherhood instead of wifehood and their focus on white, upper-middle-class women, as well as in their embodiment of postfeminist, so-called choice feminism. However, we also find evidence of inconsistency in aspects of the portrayal of women who have opted out that paints a more complicated picture about the imagery surrounding these women.

## *Family First, Child-Centric*

In line with prior research, which detects a shift in the portrayal of women to emphasize their role as mothers (Douglas and Michaels 2004), we find that imagery surrounding opting out focuses almost exclusively on women as mothers rather than wives, and on family rather than work. Although the decision to opt out involves consideration of both the work and family sides of the equation (see, e.g., Boushey 2005; Stone 2007), the overall message of the majority of articles (28 of 51) represents it as being primarily about family rather than work, with two articles focused exclusively on family and making no mention of work. These articles were dominated by family- and child-centric rhetoric. An article illustrative of this rhetoric featured a 48-year-old stay-at-home mom with four children who "wanted me to stay home. It meant security for them." Another article featured a mother of children in the 8th and 10th grades who quit because she "and her husband thought their family needed more."

When we turn to an examination of the 98 women depicted in these articles, we find more evidence of child-focused themes attached to opting out. Women had an average of 1.49 children when they left the work-force, with one-third reporting having had an additional child after they were home. At the time of quitting, 82 women had at least one pre-schooler; the remainder had school-age children. Consistent with this profile, taking care of children (rather than spouses or the house) was by far the most frequently given reason for going home, mentioned by 92 women, for most of whom it was also the most important reason.

Further demonstrating the ascendance of the motherhood role, husbands were a minor presence in these accounts. When husbands were mentioned, it was often to reinforce their support for their wives' full-time motherhood role, as in the quote above. Coupled with the pervasive presence of children, the absence of husbands adds to accumulating evidence from the research reviewed earlier that the role of mother is displacing that of wife as women's primary domestic role in media messages about heterosexual women. Only four of the 98 women mentioned husbands in connection with reasons for quitting paid work and for none was a husband the most important reason. Two women described husbands who *discouraged* them from quitting (one motivated by a concern for family finances; another because he wanted his wife to have a career). The decision to go home appears to be women's alone to make, and it is a decision predicated largely on their parenting responsibilities rather than wifely or homemaking ones.

In media accounts, the specific reasons women gave for quitting work invariably focused on motherhood, rather than the constraints of the work-place. This contrasts with more academic research involving interviews with women themselves, which finds workplace obstacles, including long work hours and inflexible schedules, are central reasons for women opting out (Hewlett and Luce 2005; Stone 2007). The media focus on motherhood was linked to essentialist tastes and preferences often expressed in emotionally laden language. Typical was the woman who talked of "longing" and "regret:" "No one admits the longing for a newborn left behind every morning, or the regret at having to leave a child in the hands of a nanny or day care worker." Another commented, "Before my daughter was born, I never had any

doubt that I was going to be a working mom. Of course, my resolve weakened the first time I had to leave my baby in the arms of a babysitter." As one woman explained, she "planned to go back to work shortly after the baby was born," but "the first time I held my daughter in my arms, my priorities completely changed: I knew I couldn't put her in day care to go back to work." Five women specifically cited the lack of high-quality and affordable child care as an important reason in their decision to opt out. Few women, however, offered work-related reasons for leaving. Only seven cited workplace constraints such as the pressures and demanding nature of professional jobs. Nine pointed to the difficulties of juggling work and family.

At home, women's activities were portrayed as revolving almost exclusively around children. Child care was the most frequently mentioned activity, cited by almost all women. Other activities were mentioned much less often and included (in order of frequency) part-time employment (21 women), housekeeping (16 women), volunteer work (11 women), free-lance and consulting work (eight women), and education (two women). The emphasis on child care rather than housekeeping, husband tending, or community involvement further underscores the increasing centrality of motherhood to the depiction of women who opt out and its ascendance over other aspects of the domestic role.

### The Mommy Elite

In the media accounts we analyzed, women who opted out were highly educated and had worked in especially high-status professional jobs. One woman described her incredulity at being ignored during a dinner party, as she had been a magazine editor before deciding to stay at home. Another opened her article about why she quit with a discussion of winning the Pulitzer Prize. Many articles showcased stay-at-home moms' impressive credentials. Three-quarters had completed a college degree, compared to only about one-quarter of all American women (U.S. Bureau of the Census 2005), and an additional one-quarter had gone to graduate or professional school. Only five women were identified as having completed less than a college education.

These women's elite status was also demonstrated by their former careers and their husbands' current ones. Of the 80 women whose prior jobs were identified, 16 had the words *manager, executive, director,* or *administrator* in their job titles; 11 had worked as lawyers; four as vice presidents of corporations; four were former journalists at major newspapers; one had been a corporate CEO; and another a member of the U.S. House of Representatives. Other professional jobs included economist, engineer, college lecturer, broker, magazine editor, network television producer, computer programmer, social worker, and technical writer. Conversely, nonprofessional jobs were sparsely represented and included only child care worker, retail worker, dental assistant, and hairdresser. Not surprisingly, given that opting out requires women to relinquish paid employment, the women featured in these articles were married to men who could support their stay-at-home lifestyle. Husbands' jobs included such high-earning ones as lawyer, doctor, corporate executive, physicist, and U.S. Representative.

## Making Choices

Joan Williams (2000) was one of the first to single out and question the choice rhetoric that surrounds women's decisions to quit jobs and head home. Other recent studies of the opt-out phenomenon also challenge the degree to which women's decisions represent the element of discretion and preference that the word *choice* implies (Boushey 2005; Stone and Lovejoy 2004; Stone 2007). Our results make clear that the media frames the decision to opt out almost exclusively in terms of the rhetoric of choice, with virtually no mention of barriers, constraints, or lack of options. Belkin's (2003) *New York Times Magazine* article is probably the most explicit in its use of such imagery. The lead-in for the article asked: "Q: Why don't more women get to the top" and answered: "A: They *choose* not to" [emphasis added], thereby framing not only the decision to go home as a choice or preference but implicitly attributing women's failure to get to the top to their own choices. In the articles we analyzed, choice imagery also appeared in titles such as "Why can't you respect my *choice*," "More couples *choose* a one-job lifestyle: Mothers *trade* paycheck for time at home," and "Top PepsiCo executive *picks* family over job" [emphasis added]. One woman profiled had worked as an economist before leaving her job to stay home with two children, age 18 months and five years at the time of interview. Her account of her decision emphasized the facility and agency associated with choice; for her, "it was an easy decision to become a stay-at-home-mom."

The choice rhetoric in articles' titles was amplified by women's other comments. Most did not mention feminism or the women's movement at all, but when they did, it was typically in the context of choice. This was the construction put forward by a former publisher: "Women today, if we think about feminism at all, we see it as a battle fought for 'the choice.' For us, the freedom to choose work if we want to work is the feminist strain in our lives." A former teacher with two children under the age of three who had been out of the workforce for three years expressed her gratitude: "I considered myself to be a feminist . . . thanks to the women's movement, I'm happy to have the choice." Thus, consistent with the postfeminist account (Walters 1995), women articulated a view of feminism in which choice and the individualistic discretion it implies figured prominently. It should be noted that very few articles contained explicit antifeminist sentiments. One that did featured a woman who opined, "Feminists want us to believe that these 'other women' [stay-at-home moms] are an extinct species or that when they encounter them, their lives are being wasted," reflecting her understanding of feminism as antifamily or antimotherhood.

## Challenges and Inconsistencies

In analyzing the major themes of these articles, we find that they paint a fairly monolithic portrait of women who opt out. However, a close reading of women's comments hints at inconsistencies. While affirming that the decision to become at-home mothers was their choice, only half of the 98 women expressed exclusively positive sentiments about quitting work. The other half shared either exclusively negative or mixed sentiments about having given up jobs. A 29-year old mother of three young children quit her job as a dental assistant but remarked on feeling lonely with so many of her female friends continuing to work. She admitted that "I'm kind of jealous they get to work," quickly offsetting this with "but they're probably jealous of me getting to be here." A former magazine journalist expressed her regrets: "I would think of the newsroom, crackling with gossip and inside jokes, and then Emma would start crying again: I traded that for *this*"

With regard to their feelings about staying home, half (49) expressed only positive reactions, 34 had mixed sentiments, and 15 reported only negative reactions. Specific problems with staying home included isolation (mentioned by 24 women) and lack of respect, recognition, or low status (25 women). One woman "felt isolated, and found her new career choice did not earn as much respect in society." Women struggled to reconcile the dissonance created by their own decision; on the one hand affirming their choice, on the other, recognizing that their decision put them in a culturally devalued role. A stay-at-home mother for three years reported a long period of acclimation to the perceived loss of status in being home: "It takes 2 1/2 years learning not to be sensitive to people saying: 'You don't work" A 37-year-old mother of a 14-year-old daughter had recently decided to return to work because "I didn't feel good about myself." Complaints about the nature of household work were numerous, made by 27 women, and included the stress of taking care of children, boredom, and lack of structure. One woman, a former graphic designer with two children age three years and nine months, remarked, "Everything you do at home gets undone." Perhaps not surprisingly, given their privileged background, very few women (12) mentioned financial problems as a downside to their having opted out.

Another area of inconsistency has to do with women's paid work *at home*. Although women were repeatedly represented as stay-at-home mothers, more than one-third of them said they were engaged in some sort of paid work once they were home, such as part-time jobs, freelance consulting, or starting their own businesses. Work involvement, in fact, was much more common than volunteering, another traditional pursuit of at-home mothers. A magazine editor with a daughter, while identified as a stay-at-home mother, actually worked part-time from home. Another stay-at-home mom worked at home doing data entry four to eight hours a day, while two other women profiled created a Web-based business.

With regard to working in the future, although most women made no mention of it, 20 women planned to return to work, and only five women volunteered that they would definitely not. Thus, while these portrayals seem to cast women exclusively as stay-at-home mothers, a closer reading indicates that even these so-called at-home mothers have a more fluid relationship with work, with a significant number actually engaged in paid employment and others contemplating returning to it.

## Opt-Out Imagery in Context

We examine various characteristics of the publications in which articles on opting out appeared and of the articles themselves to contextualize our findings and suggest the nature and extent of the audiences reached by this imagery. An examination of the frequency of publication of articles during the 16-year study period finds considerable year-to-year variation in the number of articles on opting out, with a pronounced increase in frequency after 1993 (see Appendix B). Articles were fairly lengthy, averaging 950 words, indicating that they were not cursory treatments. In comparison, only 10.5 percent of articles in daily metro newspapers (the modal type in this study) have more than 750 words (Journalism.org 2006). Articles on opting out appear to reach a broad and diverse audience. The great majority of articles, 45 of 51, were found in general interest newspapers and magazines, which enjoy a large and mixed readership, as opposed to the relatively small, highly specialized, and single-sex audience of women's magazines. Within the publications in which they appeared, and further reflective of a broad general readership, 23 articles were found in general interest/news sections, 18 articles in a lifestyle or living section (which are often targeted to a female audience), and four in business or financial sections (more likely to enjoy a predominately male readership).

When we examined articles by type, we found that just more than half the articles (29 of 51) were commentary in the form of editorials, opinion pieces, advice, and how-to's, and first-person accounts with titles such as "Why I Quit," "Survival Skills on One Salary," and "Why Can't You Respect My Choice" The preponderance of commentary highlights how highly personalized and contested the topic is, with the authors, typically stay-at-home moms, trying to justify their own decision, generate approval for it, or convince others to follow their lead. Authors of this type of article often set themselves up as authorities or role models, or are positioned as such by virtue of their name recognition or a record of prior accomplishment.

Twenty-two articles were general information or straight reportage with titles such as "More Couples Choose a One-Job Lifestyle." Many of the articles, similar to "The Opt-Out Revolution," use words such as *trend* or *revolution* to describe what they claim to be the increasing rate of opting out, but their claims are typically supported only by anecdotal evidence, for example, "Among her *friends* [emphasis added], more women from all professions are opting to stay home with their children."

## Situating Opting-Out Imagery against Actual Trends

Several recent studies (e.g., Boushey 2005; Cohany and Sok 2007; Goldin 2006) present analyses of trends in women's labor force participation that refute the notion that there has been a sustained and sizeble increase in opting out, much less a "revolution." Cohany and Sok (2007) found that there was a decrease in the labor force participation of married mothers of infants in the late 1990s and that the trend was slightly more pronounced among college-educated women—a nine percent drop between 1997 and 2000 versus eight percent for those with less than a college degree. After 2000, however, labor force participation rates of these women showed little change. When these trends were adjusted for changes in demographic characteristics and labor market conditions from 1984 to 2004, Boushey (2005, 10) found them unchanged for highly educated women in their thirties. In fact, after adjustments, this group was "more likely than other educational groups to be in the labor force if they have children at home—even young children." A longitudinal study by Goldin (2006, A27) further illustrates the disconnect between the rhetoric of opting out and the reality. Examining the work histories of women who graduated from highly selective colleges and universities during the early 1980s, she found that "fully 58 percent were never out of the job market for more than six months total" over a roughly 25-year period.

These studies raise questions about the existence of an actual trend in opting out, but to further situate these articles' claims, in Figure 1 we present trends in what we believe is a more direct measure, whether or not a woman stayed home last year to take care of family, focusing specifically on the demographic profiled in these articles, heterosexual married white, non-Hispanic women aged 30–45 who are mothers of young children.[2] Although the two rates (staying home and being in the labor force) track each other quite closely, they are not mirror images of one another, because women can be out of the labor force for other reasons, such as schooling or disability. As Figure 1 shows, despite the articles' trumpeting of trends, even revolution, the rates at which mothers are staying at home (or opting out) remain fairly constant, showing a decrease across all women between 1988 and 2003. The trend, however, is not straightforward. After first decreasing from a high of 32 percent in 1988 to a low of 25 percent in 1994, rates of staying at home increased to 31 percent in 2003—an increase from the low mid-90s levels to be sure, but still lower than the level in 1988.

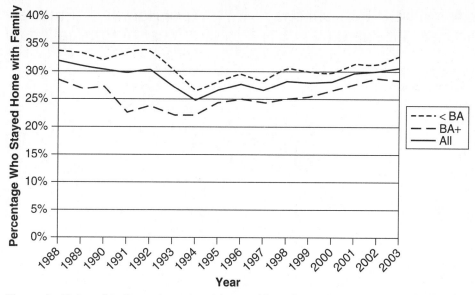

**Figure 1** Rates of opting out among white non-hispanic married women age 30–45 with child younger than 6:1988–2003.

Note. BA = bachelor's degree.

Turning to the highly educated mothers who are the focus of media coverage, rates of staying at home conform to the larger pattern, first decreasing and then increasing, with the result that the proportion at home in 2003, 28.4 percent, was virtually identical to the proportion in 1988, 28.5 percent. Throughout this period, only a distinct minority of mothers are home, with the remainder—approximately three-quarters—engaged in other activities, primarily paid employment. For less educated mothers, rates of staying home also decline before rising again, but do not quite reach their 1988 levels.

Thus, media claims of an upward trend in opting out receive mixed support, showing an increase in the short term but not in the long term. However, inconsistent with the media depiction, a close examination of the data shows that throughout the period studied, the large majority of women portrayed in these articles, that is, college-educated mothers of preschoolers, are working and opting out at levels consistently *lower* than those of their less-educated counterparts.

## Conclusion

Our systematic assessment of opting-out imagery adds to the considerable body of research on the media depiction of women and extends past findings. The sustained publication during a 16-year period of articles on opting out is consistent with prior research showing that the media promulgates traditional images of heterosexual women. The focus in these articles on motherhood as the primary counterpoint to, and reason for forsaking, careers continues the larger trend documented in past research on the media depiction

of women, which emphasizes motherhood over other home roles. Further underscoring motherhood as women's defining role in these stories is the virtual absence of husbands. The omission of husbands is particularly notable since it is their earnings that make it possible for women to opt out by quitting their jobs (Stone 2007). Women in these articles are presented as mothers rather than wives or workers or individuals with their own interests and needs. These portrayals of motherhood are consistent with Hay's (1996) discussion of intensive mothering, in which she notes that contemporary ideologies of child rearing are increasingly child-centric rather than mother-centric. Lareau (2003) calls this form of intense parenting behavior "concerted cultivation," that is, a form of parenting that relies on organized activities and finds that this method of child rearing is more common among middle-class parents, like the women portrayed in these articles, than among parents of lower socioeconomic status.

The characteristics of the women profiled, especially their high-status educational and occupational backgrounds, also illustrate another pattern documented in the research literature: the association of motherhood with class and race privilege. Although we were unable to identify the race of the women profiled in the articles, it seems fairly safe to conclude that the vast majority are white. In addition, all women identified were part of heterosexual couples, reinforcing a heteronormative conception of motherhood. We also find, confirming the feminist critique, that the articles position women's decision to quit careers as reflective of their exercise of choice, as well as exaggerate the extent of opting out. We further extend previous research by showing that such images are not confined to the pages of women's magazines

## Appendix A  List of Publications in Which Articles Appeared (*N* = 51)

The Associated Press State and Local Wire (4)
The Atlanta Journal and Constitution (1)
The Baltimore Sun (1)
The Boston Globe (3)
The Buffalo News (2)
Business Week (1)
Chicago Sun-Times (1)
Chicago Tribune (1)
The Courier-Journal (2)
The Denver Post (2)
Essence (1)
The Indianapolis Star (1)
The Kansas City Star (1)
Ladies' Home Journal (3)
The Los Angeles Times (1)
Money (1)
New York Times (4)
New York Times Magazine (2)
Pittsburgh Post-Gazette (1)
The Plain Dealer (2)
Redbook (1)
The San Francisco Chronicle (1)
St. Louis Post-Dispatch (2)
The Tampa Tribune (1)
The Times-Picayune (1)
The Toronto Sun (1)
The Wall Street Journal (2)
The Washington Post (5)
Washington Post Magazine (1)
Working Woman (1)

Note. The number of articles from each publication is indicated in parentheses.

## Appendix B  Frequency of Articles by Year of Publication (*N* = 51)

| Year | Frequency |
| --- | --- |
| 1988 | 1 |
| 1989 | 1 |
| 1990 | 0 |
| 1991 | 0 |
| 1992 | 2 |
| 1993 | 0 |
| 1994 | 7 |
| 1995 | 6 |
| 1996 | 3 |
| 1997 | 5 |
| 1998 | 10 |
| 1999 | 1 |
| 2000 | 1 |
| 2001 | 4 |
| 2002 | 3 |
| 2003 | 7 |

but appear in a wide variety of publications reaching a large and diverse audience. Men as well as women may perceive opting out as a larger trend, which might affect their own conceptions of role-appropriate behavior, both for themselves and for their partners.

In its portrayal of professional women seemingly rejecting their careers in favor of a return to the traditional domestic role, elements of the depiction of opting out can be interpreted as signaling the emergence of a new feminine mystique, an updated version of what Betty Friedan first identified in 1963. According to the tenets of the feminine mystique (Friedan 1983, 43), women "find fulfillment only in sexual passivity, male domination, and nurturing maternal love," fulfillment realized in the 1950s and 1960s through the role of housewife. In this new mystique, as our results illustrate, the role of mother has displaced that of wife (Douglas and Michaels 2004), and the decision to stay at home is distinguished from the old version by being couched in a discourse of choice and feminism (Crittenden 2001; Williams 2000). The new mystique seems more progressive than the old one because, thanks to feminist gains, college-educated elite women today appear to have more options than women of earlier eras and are now able to *choose* to stay at home, free of overt patriarchal pressure and subjugation.

In portraying opting out as the province of the privileged, educated elite, the media confers status and legitimacy, even desirability, on the decision to stay home. By virtue of their own educational backgrounds and former professional status, the women who are depicted as opting out today are further reminiscent of the women Friedan portrayed and reinforce the idea that opting-out imagery is promulgating a new feminine mystique. The positioning of opting out as a trend, however, is a depiction that is at odds with the more complicated reality of the lives of the educated women who are portrayed as its messengers and are presumably its target. Although the college-educated professional women featured in these articles are, in fact, less likely than other women to opt out of the labor force, they are more likely than less-educated women to read newspapers and magazines in which these articles appear. This disconnect between rhetoric and reality generates new "cultural contradictions" (Hays 1996). Those least likely to opt out are more likely to read that women like themselves are doing so, which may in turn suggest to them that they are deviant for carrying on with their careers.[3] In its singular emphasis on individual choices, the opt-out narrative creates further contradictions in which the "choice" of these women to quit their careers is depicted as a victory of the feminist movement, thereby masking very real structural barriers professional women face in trying to combine work and family, such as the long hours and the lack of flexible options (e.g., part-time or job sharing) (Hewlett and Luce 2005; Stone 2007).

When Friedan wrote about educated women at home, the feminine mystique characterized a relatively large group of women and was a far better-fitting depiction of the women it portrayed than is the case today. In 1960, roughly two-thirds of married women with children under 18 were out of the labor force; in 2000, less than one-third were (Hesse-Biber and Carter 2005). Unlike the women Freidan studied, many stay-at-home mothers today have had careers, allowing them to look to that experience in assessing life at home, and identify more closely with working women as peers or role models. Women who opt out are a minority, albeit a significant minority; Friedan's women were not. This disjuncture between the rhetoric of opting out and the reality of women's lives allows for the possibility that the new feminine mystique will not be as powerful as the old.

## Notes

1. What Belkin (2003) termed "opting out" is known by various names, such as Faludi's (1991) "new traditionalists," Keller's (1994) "neotraditionalism," and Douglas and Michaels' (2004) "new momism," but all refer to the movement of educated women from careers to family or from career combined with family to a family-only focus.

2. For this analysis, we use data from the March supplement of the Current Population Survey (CPS). Staying at home and opting out are used interchangeably. CPS data are cross-sectional and do not enable us to follow women across their lives, nor do they provide information on prior work histories for women who are currently out of the labor force. The results we present give a yearly assessment of the proportion of women fitting the media's opt-out demographic who are at home, enabling us to assess trends thereof.

3. On the other hand, it is worth noting anecdotally that in response to Belkin's (2003) article, the *New York Times* reported an unusually large volume of letters to the editor, many of which were highly negative and challenging of her interpretation.

## References

Altheide, David L. 1996. *Qualitative media analysis.* Thousand Oaks, CA: Sage Publications.

Barnett, Rosalind C., and Caryl Rivers. 1996. *She works/he works.* New York: HarperCollins.

Belkin, Lisa. 2003. The opt-out revolution. *New York Times Magazine* 26 (October): 42–47, 58, 85–86.

Boushey, Heather. 2005. *Are women opting out Debunking the myth.* Briefing paper. Washington, DC: Center for Economic and Policy Research.

Brown, Bruce W. 1978. Wife-employment and the emergence of egalitarian marital role prescriptions: 1900–1974. *Journal of Comparative Family Studies* 9:5–17.

Cohany, Sharon R., and Emy Sok. 2007. Trends in labor force participation of married mothers of infants. *Monthly Labor Review,* February, 9–16.

Collins, Patricia Hill. 1991. *Black feminist thought: Knowledge, consciousness, and the politics of empowerment.* New York: Routledge.

Crittenden, Ann. 2001. *The price of motherhood.* New York: Metropolitan Books.

Demarest, Jack, and Jeanette Garner. 1992. The representation of women's roles in women's magazines over the past 30 years. *Journal of Psychology* 126:357–369.

Douglas, Susan J., and Meredith Michaels. 2004. *The mommy myth: The idealization of motherhood and how it has undermined women.* New York: Free Press.

Faludi, Susan. 1991. *Backlash: The undeclared war against American women.* New York: Crown.

Friedan, Betty. 1983. *The feminine mystique.* New York: Dell.

Gardner, Ralph Jr. 2002. Mom vs. mom. *New York,* October 21.

Geise, L. Ann. 1979. The female role in middle class women's magazines from 1955 to 1976: A content analysis of nonfiction selections. *Sex Roles* 5:51–62.

Goldin, Claudia. 2006. Working it out. *New York Times,* March 15, A27.

Hays, Sharon. 1996. *The cultural contradictions of motherhood.* New Haven, CT: Yale University Press.

Hesse-Biber, Sharlene N., and Gregg L. Carter. 2005. *Working women in America.* New York: Oxford University Press.

Hewlett, Sylvia Ann, and Carolyn Buck Luce. 2005. Off ramps and on ramps: Keeping talented women on the road to success. *Harvard Business Review* 83:43–53.

Johnston, Deirdre D., and Debra H. Swanson. 2003. Invisible mothers: A content analysis of motherhood ideologies and myths in magazines. *Sex Roles* 49:21–33.

Journalism.org. 2006. The state of the news media 2006: An annual report on journalism. *Project for Excellence in Journalism.* http://www.stateofthenewsmedia.org/2006/ (accessed April 11, 2008).

Keller, Kathryn. 1994. *Mothers and work in popular American magazines.* Westport, CT: Greenwood.

Lareau, Annette. 2003. *Unequal childhoods: Class, race and family life.* Berkeley: University of California Press.

Lowe, Melanie. 2003. Colliding feminisms: Britney Spears, "tweens," and the politics of reception. *Popular Music and Society* 26(2): 123–140.

Mahar, Maggie. 1992. A change of place: Reversing a decades-long trend, young women are opting out of the job market and staying home, with major implications for the economy. *Barron's,* March 21.

Massoni, Kelley. 2004. Modeling work: Occupational messages in *Seventeen* magazine. *Gender & Society* 18:47–65.

Milkie, Melissa A. 1999. Social comparisons, reflected appraisals and mass media: The impact of pervasive beauty images on Black and white girls' self-concepts. *Social Psychology Quarterly* 62:190–210.

MRI. 2004. Demographic profile: Women. *Ladies Home Journal.* http://www.meredith.com/mediakit/lhj/print/reader.html (accessed February 13, 2004).

Pearson, Allison. 2002. *I don't know how she does it.* New York: Knopf.

Peirce, Kate. 1993. Socialization of teenage girls through teen-magazine fiction: The making of a new woman or an old lady *Sex Roles* 29:59–68.

———. 1997. Women's magazine fiction: A content analysis of the roles, attributes, and the occupations of main characters. *Sex Roles* 37:581–93.

Smith, Anna M. 2001. Mass-market magazine portrayals of working mothers and related issues, 1987 and 1997. *Journal of Children and Poverty* 7:101–19.

Stone, Pamela. 2007. *Opting out? Why women really quit careers and head home.* Berkeley: University of California Press.

Stone, Pamela, and Meg Lovejoy. 2004. Fast track women and the "choice" to stay home. *Annals of the American Academy of Political and Social Science* 596:62–83.

Swasy, Alecia. 1993. Status symbols: Stay at home moms are fashionable again in many communities. *Wall Street Journal,* July 23, A1.

U.S. Bureau of the Census. 2005. American Fact Finder Website. http://factfinder.census.gov (accessed August 8, 2005).

Wallis, Claudia. 2004. The case for staying home. *Time,* March 22, 51–59.

Walters, Suzanna Danuta. 1995. *Material girls: Making sense of feminist cultural theory.* Berkeley: University of California Press.

Williams, Joan. 2000. *Unbending gender.* New York: Oxford University Press.

**ARIELLE KUPERBERG** is a doctoral candidate in the sociology and demography programs at the University of Pennsylvania. She is the recipient of a National Science Foundation Graduate Research Fellowship. Her current research focuses on union transitions and marital intentions among cohabiters, and educational differences in the meaning of marriage. **PAMELA STONE** is a professor of sociology at Hunter College and The Graduate Center of the City University of New York and author of *Opting Out? Why Women Really Quit Careers and Head Home* (University of California, 2007). In current research, she is studying long-term trends in opting out and cross-national differences in the use of flexible work options.

**Author note**—An earlier version of this article was presented at the 2005 meetings of the Eastern Sociological Society. We would like to acknowledge and thank the following research assistants: April Boykin, Carmen Delcid, Jonathan DeBusk, Hal Weiss, Heidi Ho, and Lori Fisher. We are grateful to Professor Emeritus Cordelia Reimers, Hunter College, City University of New York, who carried out the analysis of recent trends in opting out. This article benefited greatly from the thoughtful comments of anonymous reviewers, as well as those of former Gender & Society editor Christine Williams and current editor Dana Britton. This study was funded by a Hunter College Presidential Student-Faculty Research Fellowship. Arielle Kuperberg is supported under a National Science Foundation Graduate Research Fellowship.

From *Gender & Society,* August 2008, pp. 497–517. Copyright © 2008 by Sage Publications. Reprinted by permission via Rightslink.

# Great Expectations

**Women now hold half of all management jobs in America. Business books and magazines tout their superior leadership style. What's really changing in the country's corner offices?**

JUDITH M. HAVEMANN

On July 17, 1975, less than a year after President Richard M. Nixon resigned in the Watergate scandal, *Washington Post* publisher Katharine Graham threw open the doors of her Georgetown mansion for one of her trademark dinners, with strolling violinists and elegant cuisine. Along the right-hand wall of the foyer, a wheel of tiny envelopes held the table numbers of the 58 guests. On the terrace, Graham, in a pink hostess outfit, greeted people from five different levels of the paper's management by name, introducing each newcomer flawlessly. Then everybody sat down for a gourmet dinner served on her mother's hand-painted china.

It was a virtuoso performance by one of the masters of gracious entertaining. But Graham was applying her formidable social skills to a different arena: her company's business. Although the *Post* was then at the height of its influence and glamour, several of its 13 unions were fighting for their lives. Union contracts were up for negotiation, and Graham, who had become an instant corporate president 12 years earlier on the suicide of her husband, was preparing for trouble. She fretted that the newspaper's managers, on whom she would have to rely to publish the paper in the event of strikes, didn't think of themselves as a team. She wanted her staff to work together and get along. So on a hot July night, Katharine Graham did a stereotypically female thing: She threw a party.

Today her management method is called "transformational" or cooperative—as opposed to the "transactional," or authoritarian, manner then supposedly employed by the men who ran America's biggest companies. But her style was just that—a style. When it came to making decisions, Graham was as tough as any man. She fired former secretary of the Navy Paul Ignatius when he disappointed her as president of the company, hustled his successor upstairs, and ousted a subsequent replacement. When the pressmen's union went on strike in the middle of the night three months after her garden party, she got the paper out with a crew of managers and volunteers. When the pressmen turned down her contract offer, she replaced them with nonunion workers.

True, she talked stirringly about women's issues—sensitized by a friendship with Gloria Steinem, no less. But the *Post* implemented little of the feminist's agenda. It had no daycare center and offered only a bare-bones maternity leave. Part-time schedules to accommodate child rearing were a rare privilege, and part-time employees were ineligible for raises. Although the paper was often generous in family tragedies, it had to issue checks to its female news employees to settle an Equal Employment Opportunity Commission sex discrimination suit over hiring, pay, promotions, and leave. Graham was sympathetic to women, but the pay, benefits, and day-to-day operations of the nation's most famous female-led company broke no feminist ground. Today, Graham's longtime executive editor, Ben Bradlee, cannot think of a single decision that she made because she was a woman.

The corporate world of Graham's era was a men's club, by and large, staffed with female worker bees. Little had changed since William H. Whyte wrote his classic midcentury dissection of corporate conformity and bureaucratic culture, *The Organization Man* (1956). Whyte's index includes a single entry for women: "slenderness progression." But under pressure from a growing women's movement and the federal government, by the 1970s businesses were promoting a few women, although it wasn't at all clear how they would fare when they took charge. At the beginning of the decade, Dr. Edgar Berman, a Democratic national committeeman and close confidante of Vice President Hubert Humphrey, created a minor uproar when he opined that "raging hormonal imbalance" rendered women too unstable to hold top jobs, such as president of the United States.

But Berman's view was not all that unusual, at least among men. Women held only a tiny fraction of supervisory jobs, a category that included management of secretarial pools and other ghettoized occupations. They were simply excluded from elite downtown clubs, golf courses, and other institutions.

Leading companies ran advertising campaigns portraying women as playthings—and they worked. The National Organization for Women was outraged by the 1971 "I'm Cheryl, Fly Me" ads for National Airlines, but the number of passengers grew 23 percent in the first year of the campaign.

Today's corporations are as different from their predecessors as 45-rpm records are from iPods. Women hold half of all management, professional, and related jobs in the United States, and—although some of their companies are small—nearly one-quarter of all CEO positions: Between 1997 and 2002 women started an average of 424 new ventures each day, and by 2004 about 6.7 million privately held businesses were majority owned by women, says *The Journal of Small Business Management*. At the very top of the corporate heap, among the country's Fortune 500 companies, women hold 15.6 percent of corporate officer positions (defined as board elected or board appointed), according to Catalyst, a business research institute in New York. They occupy 14.6 percent of the seats on boards of directors. And they run 13 of the corporations.

That's not the revolution many had hoped for, but it's a significant change. The leadership positions held by women are not only in the corporate world but in the nonprofit sector, the military, higher education, and other fields. They sit on boards and campaign for public office. One of them even stands a good chance of making Edgar Berman's worst nightmare come true. In fact, now the shoe is sometimes on the other foot. A handful of management gurus in the business world are proclaiming that possessing a pair of X-chromosomes equips a person to be a superior leader.

In books such as *Enlightened Power* (2005), *Why the Best Man for the Job Is a Woman* (2000), and *The Female Advantage: Women's Ways of Leadership* (1990), to say nothing of *Secrets of Millionaire Moms* (2007), writers are advancing what some call the "great woman school of leadership" Magazines now assure women that their feminine style will give them an edge in the new "transformational" corporation. *BusinessWeek* has declared that women have the "right stuff" and, even more sensationally, that a "new gender gap" might leave men as "losers in a global economy that values mental powers over might."

After several decades of experience and enough studies to fall a sizable hard drive, there ought to be answers to some basic questions about women's leadership: Does difference make a difference? Are women more effective leaders, producing more successful companies? Are female-led firms better places to work?

Increasingly, research shows that women—surprise!—are indeed different from men. They do a better job, on average, of collaborating, coaching, teaching, and inspiring others to be creative. Yet it is far from clear that gender in the corner office makes a momentous difference. Evidence that female-led organizations produce superior results is scant. A leadership style that works well in certain fields may bomb in others. And as people climb closer to the top of an organization, gender-related styles of management seem to matter less than other factors in determining who wins the race and what they do as leaders.

Alice H. Eagly, chair of the department of psychology at Northwestern University and perhaps the most commonly cited scholar on gender-based leadership differences, finds in a recent overview of many studies in the field that superiors, peers, and subordinates generally rate women better leaders than men. Women are more "interpersonally oriented," a key ingredient in the transformational leadership style, now the *modus du jour* in the American corporation. Transformational leaders lead by example, empower their subordinates, and focus on the future. They stress cooperation, mentoring, and collaboration rather than a top-down, authoritarian structure. Many of these attributes are exactly the traits associated with women, even if not all women exhibit them.

## In male-dominated occupations, from the military to auto sales, women are still judged less effective than men.

But there are wrinkles. Leaders face expectations that they must meet to persuade others to get behind them, and what peers and subordinates look for can vary according to circumstance. "Neither men nor women are better," Eagly says. "Effectiveness is contextual." Women are ranked higher as leaders in fields such as education, government, and social services, where there is more focus on interaction and—some say—less on the bottom line. And since women are already more numerous in the upper ranks of these fields, those on the way up have an easier time persuading others to accept them as leaders. But in male-dominated occupations, from the military to auto sales, women are still judged less effective than men.

In many industries, stereotypes about leaders are ripped from the playbook of men, and women are at a disadvantage because they don't look "usual or natural" in a leader role, Eagly says. "Women in highly masculine domains often have to contend with expectations and criticisms that they lack the toughness and competitiveness needed to succeed." When they do show grit, they are accused of being unfeminine. Just ask Hillary Clinton, who is criticized for being both too steady and controlled and not emotional *enough*.

Recalling her stint as the head of the troubled computer giant Hewlett-Packard, Carly Fiorina said in a recent interview that her enemies in the corporate and tech worlds routinely referred to her "as either a bimbo—too soft, or a bitch—too hard." She shook up the entire company, eventually laying off 36,000 people and attracting almost as much media attention as the executives who bankrupted Enron and went to jail. "It broke my heart every time we had to do it," she says of the layoffs. "It was tearing what people thought was the heart of the company. But it had to be done to save more jobs. Once I was fired, they said I didn't do enough of it." Hewlett-Packard has since gone from being a laggard to a leader, but Fiorina's successor, rightly or wrongly, has reaped much of the credit.

Barbara Krumsiek, CEO and president of the Calvert Group, a $14 billion mutual fund company, said in an interview that advancement after a certain point "is not a matter of competence; it is how you are perceived." After her first daughter was born, Krumsiek, then still climbing the corporate ladder, began hearing

# Women at the Top

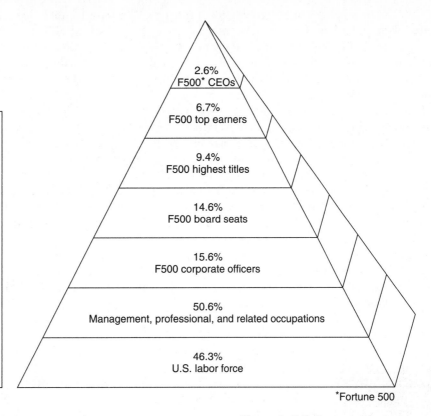

### Women CEOs by Industry

| | |
|---|---|
| Nonprofit | 29.6% |
| Health Care | 22.1% |
| Law Firms & Legal Services | 17.7% |
| Finance | 9.6% |
| Real Estate | 9.1% |
| Insurance | 8.9% |
| Pharmaceutical | 8.3% |
| Construction | 7.4% |
| Software | 7.3% |
| Manufacturing | 5.2% |
| Aerospace | 4.5% |
| Automotive | 4.2% |
| Semiconductor | 3.1% |

Pyramid:
- 2.6% F500* CEOs
- 6.7% F500 top earners
- 9.4% F500 highest titles
- 14.6% F500 board seats
- 15.6% F500 corporate officers
- 50.6% Management, professional, and related occupations
- 46.3% U.S. labor force

*Fortune 500

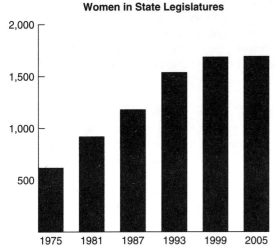

**Women in State Legislatures**

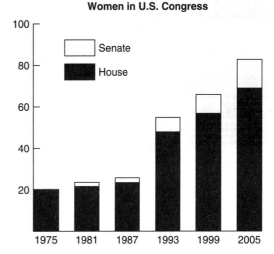

**Women in U.S. Congress**

Senate
House

Moving up: Women tend to be judged as more effective in industries where there are more of them. Female state legislators have increased five-fold since 1971, with Democrats outnumbering Republicans by more than two to one. In Congress, the party ratio is roughly the same.

Sources: (top left) *ZoomInfo Inside Report: Gender in the Executive Suite—A Quantitative View of Gender Roles in Business Leadership,* May 2007; (top right) Catalyst Research. *The Catalyst Pyramid: U.S. Women in Business,* 2007; (both bottom charts) Center for American Women and Politics, Eagleton Institute of Politics, Rutgers, The State University of New Jersey.

comments suggesting that she should step aside. A colleague flat out told her, "Women who really love their children stay home with them." Feeling that she had to produce still more signs of her commitment to work, she hired an executive coach and became active in professional organizations. Her climb resumed.

While perceptions matter a great deal, the problem with research such as Eagly's is that it only goes so far. It is one thing to ask people whether the female bosses they know are good leaders, another to find hard evidence that female leadership produces

results that are better. Scholars have been able to provide correlations, but no proof. The research group Catalyst, for example, divided the Fortune 500 companies into quartiles based on the share of top management jobs held by women, and found that the companies in the top quartile performed 35 percent better (judged by return on equity) than those in the bottom quartile. But the study didn't show that women were responsible for that success. It may be, for example, that successful companies tend to hire more women.

It is hardly surprising that scholars have not been able to identify a precise "female difference." Just consider the political agendas of these leaders: Israel's Golda Meir, Britain's Margaret Thatcher, India's Indira Gandhi, Germany's Angela Merkel. In the U.S. Senate, what common adjective could describe the leadership of California's Barbara Boxer and North Carolina's Elizabeth Dole?

In the Darwinian world of the contemporary corporation, survival of the fittest requires ambitious men and women to adapt whatever methods work, even if they are soft, "feminine" methods. Under the pressure of competition and globalization, the modern corporation has gone from fat to lean, from vertical to horizontal, and from homogeneous to diverse. Status and hierarchies are out, team building, "open innovation," and learning are in. The corporation's work force is better educated, more mobile, and more demanding than it was only a few decades ago. In this new world, the top-down leadership paradigm of the past looks only a little less outdated than a watch fob. The new mantras, propounded in books such as *Leading at a Higher Level* (2006), *Wikinomics* (2006), and *True North* (2007), are mass collaboration, "authentic" leadership, and becoming a "learning" organization through communication, vision, and shared power. And who's better at collaboration and communication than women? Well, sometimes men are, or at least they are no worse.

Analyzing the results of 50-to-80-minute interviews with male and female owners of 229 firms in the mid-1990s, management scholars Jennifer E. Cliff, Nancy Langton, and Howard E. Aldrich found striking evidence that gender had "no effect" on the organizational design and management of companies. The traditional explanation would have been that women were forced to adopt a more stereotypically masculine approach. In fact, the researchers found that "the male owners in our sample were just as likely as their female counterparts to have implemented archetypically feminine organizational arrangements and practices in their firms." Both male- and female-headed firms, for example, had reduced the levels of hierarchy and cut back on formal policies in favor of more open and informal procedures and modes of communication—actions associated with women leaders.

What was different between men and women, the authors wrote in 2005 in the journal *Organization Studies,* was the way they *talked* about leadership. Men said they wanted to be thought of "as God . . . as capable . . . as the captain of the ship who calls the shots." Women wanted to be thought of as "someone who's here to work for my employees . . . as a resource . . . [as having] their well-being at heart." But despite these contrasting self-evaluations, the management methods men and women adopted were, on the whole, "indistinguishable."

Female business leaders interviewed recently tended to stress that while gender bias often posed special challenges every step of the way, the leadership qualities needed near the top transcended gender. "We don't have a real meritocracy in this country, although we have made great progress," Fiorina says. "Women face barriers and have to work harder to get ahead. Men and women have different styles, and people focus on the style of women and the substance of men. But the fundamentals of leadership are not gender specific."

Ginger Graham, a former Arkansas state rodeo queen with a Harvard MBA, has had an unusual career. She got her first job selling herbicides to local farmers as an agricultural economics major at the University of Arkansas, rose at Eli Lilly, and eventually was named CEO of Amylin, a biopharmaceutical company. When Graham (no relation to Katharine Graham) took over at Amylin in 2003, she adopted a management style that would be unusual, perhaps inconceivable, for a man. The morning after the company's diabetes drug, Symlin, was finally approved by the federal government after 18 years of research and development, she arrived in the office in a Sleeping Beauty costume and handed out copies of the fairy tale. She wanted to inspire a company that now needed to set up a manufacturing operation and hire a sales force almost overnight. When a second drug was approved six weeks later, Graham jumped into the fountain at corporate headquarters. She punctuated company sales meetings with shouts of "whoo-hoo!"

By the time Graham stepped down, this past March, the price of Amylin's stock had nearly doubled. But while her style may have been flamboyant at times, her management moves were classic. "You stand alone in these jobs," she says. "Obviously they are well paid and very fulfilling. They call for an element of collaboration, but at some point you must make the transition from being a collaborator to a decision maker. You have to transform empathy and engagement to accountability and decisiveness."

Finally, there is the touchiest question of all: If women are such effective leaders, why aren't more of them leading? The percentage of the 500 biggest firms with women at the helm is not even close to cracking the three percent barrier, and women's advances in a number of fields have come to a standstill.

After Betty Friedan's *The Feminine Mystique* reignited feminism in 1963, women poured into politics, medicine, the clergy, and the military. Most all-male college enrollment policies crumbled within a decade. Today, more than half of all college graduates are women. They are a majority in many fields of graduate study. Affirmative action policies have helped women move into many occupations. But after early increases in the 1970s and '80s, some of the advances have stalled. The percentage of married mothers of preschool children who are in the labor force has dropped four points since 1997.

In politics, despite the emergence of stars such as Hillary Clinton, Condoleezza Rice, and Nancy Pelosi, gains are uneven. Female representation in state legislatures hasn't budged much since topping 22 percent of legislative seats in 2001. Even some advances are colored by puzzling setbacks. While young women's level of participation in college sports has soared, thanks in part to federal Title IX legislation, the number of female coaches has dropped. Coaches often travel three or four days a week and must go on many recruiting trips during the off-season, a schedule that particularly puts off women who have, or want to have, a family, according to *The Chronicle of Higher Education.*

Anxiety over this stalled progress may explain the firestorm touched off by Princeton graduate Lisa Belkin's 2003 article in *The New York Times Magazine* describing what she called an "opt-out" generation of highly educated women like herself who said, "The heck with it, I'd rather stay at home with my kids."

At first dismissed by some as a luxury confined to elite wives with well-paid husbands, the "opt-out" phenomenon has found some support in statistical evidence, notably the data that show a dip in employment among women at every income level who have younger children. (Sixty percent of these women are now in the labor force.)

"Women naturally don't like this hard-driving competitive atmosphere that is part of business and law firms," argues Phyllis Schlafly, president of the conservative Eagle Forum and a lawyer who played a prominent role in the defeat of the Equal Rights Amendment. It isn't really motherhood that makes women drop out, she says; "they just get tired of it."

Belkin's passionate critics scoff that the moms-go-home theme has been "discovered" at least four times in the last half-century by *The New York Times* alone. They say it's no surprise that women in jobs with no flexibility, forced to choose between feeling they aren't good mothers or aren't good workers, elect to stay home. "If women feel undervalued and stalled in their jobs, no wonder they opt out," says Sally J. Kenney, director of the Center on Women and Public Policy at the University of Minnesota. At the same time, many advocates surely worry that the opt-out phenomenon will reinforce the negative expectation that women won't go the distance, harming the prospects of those who remain in the race.

## Increasingly the question of whether women get to the top of the heap hinges on their own choices and actions.

For more than a hundred years, women have explained their lack of power by citing barriers: laws that bar women from certain jobs, prejudice, a pay gap that saps the incentive to keep working, the unequally shared burden of child care and housework, the "mommy track." In addition to the "glass ceiling," British writers have identified a "glass cliff"—the overrepresentation of women in nearly impossible high-level jobs in which the risk of failure is high. It is said that women are denied plum assignments because they're thought likely to opt out. They choke in emergencies. (Now making the rounds is a study of professional tennis—whose methodology has been vehemently assaulted—showing that women make more unforced errors on crucial points than on others, a difference absent in men.) They won't work as many hours as men. (A recent *Harvard Business Review* survey of "extreme jobs" found that women in these high-pressure white-collar occupations "are not matching the hours logged by their male colleagues.")

Many barriers still exist in some form, but increasingly the question of whether women get to the top of the heap hinges on their own choices and actions. It's possible that the ascension of more women will produce a tipping point, dramatically easing the way for future female leaders in every field. Perhaps the continuing transformation of the corporation and other institutions will make them more female friendly and humane. Maybe Americans three decades from now will look back on our present-day conundrums with the same disbelief with which we view "fly me" advertisements.

Yet a consistent message from women who have reached the heights is that gender does not make a big difference in conducting the essential business of leadership. Katharine Graham had to fire executives and crush unions. It was her son and successor, Donald, who added female-friendly benefits such as family leave, tax-deferred accounts for dependent care, and part-time schedules when they were needed to attract and retain talented people. For mother and son alike, the task was the same: Keep their company healthy and growing.

Just when women have the greatest opportunities in history, top jobs have become more demanding than ever. The pace of change has quickened, the rigors of competition have increased, and the scrutiny of leaders has grown more intense. The route to the top may remain even more difficult than it is for men, but the decision that women face now is whether they want to enter—and perhaps hope to alter—the demolition derby.

**JUDITH M. HAVEMANN** is senior editor of *The Wilson Quarterly.* She was a reporter and editor during a long career at *The Washington Post.*

Reprinted with permission from *The Wilson Quarterly*, Summer 2007, pp. 46–53. Copyright © 2007 by Judith M. Havemann. Reprinted by permission.

# Labor Markets, Breadwinning, and Beliefs

## How Economic Context Shapes Men's Gender Ideology

Youngjoo Cha PhD and Sarah Thébaud PhD

As women's labor force participation has rapidly increased over the past several decades, men's gender ideology has become more egalitarian (Mason and Lu 1988; Thornton and Young-DeMarco 2001). One factor contributing to this change is that men are increasingly likely to share breadwinning responsibilities with their spouse. Research has shown that men who are in dual-earner households or who experience economic dependency on their spouse are significantly more likely to endorse an egalitarian gender ideology (Gerson 1993; Wilkie 1993; Zuo 1997).

Although a wide range of findings document the positive association between men's economic dependency and gender egalitarianism, few studies have examined how macro-level conditions influence this relationship. In this article, we investigate how institutional challenges to the arrangement of men as sole breadwinners at the national level influence individual men's breadwinning experiences and how such experiences affect their normative beliefs about men's and women's behavior. To this end, we first theorize and evaluate how one institutional arrangement, labor market structure, endorses or contests individual men's gender identities as breadwinners. Then, by looking across 27 countries with varying labor market structures, we examine the extent to which this macro-level condition accounts for variability in the relationship between men's breadwinner status and gender ideology. Whereas there may be various dimensions of gender ideology depending on cultural context, we are specifically interested in how men endorse or contest normative assumptions about the separate spheres arrangement, in which men are foremost oriented to the paid labor market and women to unpaid household labor.

Among the many factors that influence norms of men's behavior, the institutional arrangements of labor markets are especially important in influencing men's ability to consistently bring resources to the family. For this reason, we focus specifically on how the level of labor market rigidity influences the effect of men's breadwinning status on their gender ideology. We define labor market rigidity as the level of formal restrictions on the hiring and firing of workers. Workers in more rigid labor markets—those with many such restrictions—are likely to stay in one job for a relatively long period of time; workers in more flexible labor markets are likely to change jobs more often. We expect that labor market rigidity influences the degree to which men are able to maintain primary breadwinner status by affecting their job security and career paths; these structural conditions in turn shape men's experiences in the household and their beliefs about how men and women should behave.

In our analysis, we use cross-national data drawn from the International Social Survey Programme (ISSP) and the World Bank's International Finance Corporation Doing Business database. We focus on men because breadwinning ability is a central component of men's masculine identity (e.g., Brines 1994; Connell 1995; Kimmel 1993). In addition, despite the widespread changes that contest the separate spheres arrangement, men have been slower than women to adopt a gender egalitarian ideology (Brewster and Padavic 2000; Mason and Lu 1988). This phenomenon may contribute to the "stalled revolution" (Hochschild and Machung 2003) by restricting men's willingness to lend ideological support for their wives' careers or contribute to household work and child care. In this sense, a focus on men will provide a key insight into the mechanisms generating or inhibiting more egalitarian gender relations.

## Gender Ideology and Breadwinning Status

The increase in women's labor force participation across most industrialized countries has produced many changes in the way men and women organize their family life and think about gender. As more people have become part of dual-earner households, they have also become more likely to approve of women's employment. This trend has been documented both in the United States (Bolzendahl and Myers 2004; Brewster and Padavic 2000; Mason and Lu 1988) and in Western European countries (Scott, Alwin, and Braun 1996). Cross-sectional comparative analyses of industrialized countries also find that despite considerable cross-national variation, ideological support for women's employment is relatively common (Alwin, Braun, and Scott 1992; Crompton and Harris 1997; Knudsen and Waerness 2001; Treas and Widmer 2000). Men are less likely than women to espouse an egalitarian ideology, however. This difference appears in various cultural contexts, such as the United States (Brewster and Padavic 2000; Mason and Lu 1988), other English-speaking countries, industrialized nations of Western Europe, postsocialist states of Central/Eastern Europe, and Japan (Baxter and Kane 1995; Panayotova and Brayfield 1997; Treas and Widmer 2000).

The most widely invoked explanation for men's slow adoption of a gender egalitarian ideology is that traditional gender norms serve men's interests. For example, having a wife who is committed to family obligations facilitates a man's ability to succeed in the workplace (Kane and Sanchez 1994). However, as women's labor force participation increases, benefits for men are being redefined by new structural arrangements with their spouses. This is most evident in the consistent finding that men who share breadwinning responsibilities with their wives espouse a more egalitarian ideology. For instance, men who make about the same amount of money as their wives, or whose wives are employed full-time, are significantly more egalitarian than are men who make the majority of the family income or whose wives are not employed (Gerson 1993; Mason and Lu 1988; Wilkie 1993; Zuo 1997).

There are two reciprocal processes that work together to produce this relationship. First, men adapt to their experience in a nontraditional household income structure. That is, men may recognize the practical benefits of being in a dual-earner situation, such as freedom from primary economic responsibilities for the family and some protection from an insecure labor market (Gerson 1993; Kane and Sanchez 1994; Kimmel 1993; Zuo 1997). Brewster and Padavic (2000, 486) argue that these men find "equilibrium with reality" by adjusting their attitudes when their wives are contributing more substantially to the family income. Also, as more men report that being involved husbands and fathers is important to them, they may come to view another income as a way to facilitate a better balance between work and family life (Coltrane 1996; Gerson 1993; Hochschild 2001). Experiencing such benefits through marital interactions and breadwinning experiences may lead men to reevaluate their own beliefs about what their primary activities should be.

A second process accounting for this relationship is that men who hold a gender egalitarian ideology before marriage may select wives with greater earning capacity. Such women may also be more likely to select a gender egalitarian man. The prevalence of this process with respect to attitudinal change has yet to be addressed with empirical data (Wilkie

1993). However, women's earning capacity is increasing on average, and dual incomes are becoming a requirement for a comfortable standard of living. As a result of these trends, men may be more likely to select a mate who has some level of earning capacity.

Although increases in women's labor force participation have reshaped many individual men's breadwinning experiences, this change has not necessarily undermined the broader cultural belief that men should be primary breadwinners. Men and women in dual-earner relationships still tend to interpret the husband's employment as providing for essential family needs, whereas the wife's earnings are "supplemental," even if she contributes the same amount to the family income as her husband does (Potuchek 1997). Similarly, if their wives are employed and earning a substantial income, men report that they feel the need to be the main providers (Gerson 1993) and often increase their work hours to maintain primary earner status (Deutsch and Saxon 1998). Men and women also report that it is important for others to perceive the man as the primary earner, even when a wife earns more (Tichenor 2005). Thus, even though men perceive an economic benefit from being in dual-earner households, their appreciation of such benefits may be limited if a central part of their masculine identity hinges on maintaining primary breadwinner status. In fact, some research suggests that when a wife is the sole or primary breadwinner, a man may reassert his gender identity by espousing a traditional gender ideology and behavior. For instance, research suggests that when men are in counternormative breadwinning situations, they often refuse to engage in traditionally feminine activities such as household work (Brines 1994; Ferree 1990).

Taken together, research suggests that living up to the norm of the male provider is important for men; however, longer-term trends suggest that men have indeed adjusted their gender ideology to be compatible with new structural arrangements in the labor market and within families. We build on this research by arguing that a man's likelihood of adopting an egalitarian ideology in a dual-earner context may be influenced by the degree to which he experiences his situation as a long-term contestation of the norm of the male provider. When this norm contestation is short-term, the deeply rooted cultural association between breadwinning and men's gender identity may serve to impede men's endorsement of an egalitarian ideology.

## The Need for a Cross-National Perspective

One useful way to uncover contextual factors that explain variability in men's attitudinal reactions to their breadwinning situations is to examine the phenomenon cross-nationally. Cross-national differences in the association between gender ideology and breadwinning has until now been examined in only one study (Baxter and Kane 1995). By comparing five countries, Baxter and Kane (1995) found that the more economically dependent women are on men in a society as a whole, the less likely men and women are to espouse egalitarian ideology. They argue that this is because men have greater access to social power, prestige, and material resources in these societies than do women and, thus, have an interest in preserving the status quo.

Baxter and Kane (1995) also hypothesize the contextual effect of gender inequality at the societal level; they argue that the influence of factors associated with dependence on a spouse, such as marriage and the spousal income gap, have a stronger effect in countries that have higher levels of gender inequality. This is because men's social dominance privileges their interpretations of gender inequality, and women's level of dependence upon them draws them toward those privileged interpretations. Although Baxter and Kane find only partial evidence for this, they do show that the number of hours men work at the individual level are negatively related to their egalitarianism in the United States, Canada, and Australia but positively related in Sweden and Norway. This suggests that there may be variations in the degree to which men's breadwinning status affects their gender ideology across countries.

Despite useful insights on the contextual effects of each country, this research leaves questions unanswered. It does not systematically evaluate which institutional factors play a role, or how these institutional factors influence men's gender beliefs. Men's ideology may vary by their micro-structural experience (for instance, if their wives are cobreadwinners or primary breadwinners), but which institutional structures account for differences in men's adaptation to nontraditional arrangements? Our study explores the answer to this question by examining the impact of labor market structure, which has significant implications for the duration of men's breadwinning experiences. Because our study is based on a larger sample (27 countries), we also provide a more robust evaluation of how gender inequality might affect the relationship between a man's economic dependency and his gender ideology.

## Breadwinning, Gender Ideology, and Labor Market Structure

To investigate how institutional structures influence the relationship between men' economic dependency and their gender ideology, we compare the contextual effects of labor markets that fall on a continuum between two ideal types: (1) labor markets where men's long-term breadwinning status is strongly endorsed by the institutional structure and (2) labor markets where men's breadwinning status is more likely to be contested by the institutional structure over the short term.

We specifically focus on the effect of the degree of legal rigidity in hiring and firing workers. The legal rigidity of the labor market is exemplified by regulations on wage protections, costs for firing employees, and the degree to which the law allows using temporary or nonstandard workers. These characteristics tend to be associated with long-term employment. The higher costs for hires and dismissals of workers in the rigid labor market reduce job mobility and contribute to the development of an internal labor market. In the internal market, promotions and transfers of workers occur within a constrained competitive market (i.e., within the firm), and mobility rates tend to be low (Doeringer and Piore 1971, 2). For this reason, firm-specific skills, which are usually evaluated based on continuous job tenure, are an important determinant of a worker's wage in rigid labor markets. This discourages workers from changing jobs. If a worker with a high level of firm-specific skills leaves a job, it is a great loss for the employer as well as for the employee because the employer loses a skilled worker and the employee loses his or her labor market value. To protect both employees and employers, institutional arrangements, such as policies that support high rates of unionization, wage protection, and dismissal protection, are common in some countries (Esping-Anderson 1990; Estévez-Abe, Iversen, and Soskice 2001). This accordingly legitimizes and enforces the rigidity of the labor market.

Although these institutional devices are intended to protect employees, they are also associated with the degree to which labor markets are gendered (Estévez-Abe, Iversen, and Soskice 2001). Valuing seniority in rigid labor markets results in the exclusion of women because many women experience career interruption during childbearing and childrearing. These interruptions are penalized more where continuous skill accumulation is important. In flexible labor markets, where returns to job tenure are smaller than in rigid markets, workers are more likely to experience fewer penalties for career interruption (Allmendinger 1989; Estévez-Abe 2005; Estévez-Abe, Iversen, and Soskice 2003). For this reason, Estévez-Abe (2005) argues that a flexible labor market is more gender-neutral than a rigid labor market. Women in rigid labor markets are more likely to be in the secondary labor market or in supplementary jobs (Rubery, Fagan, and Maier 1996) and less likely to be in high-level managerial positions than women in flexible markets (Mandel and Semyonov 2006). The overall level of occupational sex segregation is also higher in rigid labor markets than in flexible labor markets (Chang 2000; Charles and Grusky 2005; Charles et al. 2001).

These gendered characteristics of rigid labor markets consequently support a traditional male-breadwinner model of work because they provide for stable employment for men over the long term. In contrast, workers in flexible labor markets tend to have fewer legal protections and therefore experience more fluctuations in their economic status. This makes them more likely to experience nontraditional earning arrangements.

Because the rigid labor market institutionally supports the traditional separate spheres arrangement, we expect that men's gender ideology may react more dramatically to their breadwinning status in rigid labor markets than in flexible labor markets. If a man in a rigid labor market is unemployed or earns less than his partner, this dependent situation is likely to last for a long period of time due to the rigid structure of the hiring process. This structural condition provides that man with a long-term experience of nontraditional arrangements and a long-term challenge to traditional gender ideology.

By contrast, fluctuations in breadwinner status in flexible labor markets do not necessarily challenge the traditional belief that men should be primary providers in the long run. Frequent job switching in flexible labor markets produces many short transition periods when men are dependent on their partner. Even if they are economically dependent, they still can perceive themselves as primary breadwinners because job tenure is short and job loss and part-time work are more likely to be temporary, or viewed as temporary, than in rigid labor markets. For example, Winslow-Bowe (2006) finds that in the United States, while there are increasing numbers of women who out-earn their husbands, this nontraditional situation is likely to be temporary. For this reason, we expect that in flexible labor market contexts, a man's economic dependency may not strongly challenge his perception that he is the primary breadwinner. If a man still perceives himself as a breadwinner while he is economically dependent on his wife, dependency may not have as strong an impact on his gender ideology as it might in a rigid labor market, where his dependency is more likely to be long-term. Thus, labor market rigidity has different implications for the way economic dependency contests gender norms. Our central hypothesis is that men's level of economic dependency influences their gender egalitarianism more strongly in rigid labor markets than in flexible labor markets.

A second process that may contribute to this relationship is the mate-selection effect. It is possible that because rigid labor markets make workers' situations more permanent, low-earning men with an egalitarian ideology may have added incentives to choose a wife with higher earning potential. However, we believe that this would rarely be the case, given that rigid labor markets also tend to enforce a male-breadwinner model of work. Although a woman may have higher earning potential before marriage, she may also be more likely to encounter discriminatory work environments or gender-segregated occupations, which would decrease her earnings in the long run. Furthermore, men are unlikely to choose partners with higher earnings power. Deutsch and Saxon's study (1998) shows that when wives earn a higher rate of pay, men often put in more hours to regain the primary breadwinner position. This suggests that, although it is possible, it is unlikely that men would voluntarily put themselves in situations that threaten their long-term ability to be breadwinners, even if they are supportive of women's employment. This would especially be the case in the societies where the male-breadwinning norm is institutionally endorsed. Therefore, we expect that any variance in the effect of men's economic dependency according to labor market structure would be primarily due to men's responses to their structural experiences, rather than their mate selection preferences.

# Data and Variables

Because the purpose of this article is to evaluate the influence of macro-level institutional factors on individual-level outcomes, we match data from multiple sources to build multilevel models. The data for individual-level cases are drawn from the 2002 ISSP module on Family and Changing Gender Roles. The ISSP collects survey data across a wide range of nations and is made available by Zentralarchiv fur Empirische Sozialforschung, University of Cologne. The ISSP is appropriate for our study because it is one of few data sets that includes comparable information on men's gender ideology as well as measures of their individual income relative to their partners' across a wide range of countries. Our sample is composed of men aged 16 and over who have a steady life partner[1] in the form of a marital or cohabitant relationship.[2] After restricting the sample for key variables included in the analyses,[3] our total sample includes 6,184 individuals from 27 countries.[4] Countries in the sample are Australia, Brazil, Bulgaria, Chile, Czech Republic, Denmark, Finland, France, the former East and West Germany, Hungary, Ireland, Japan, Latvia, Mexico, New Zealand, Norway, Poland, Portugal, Russian Federation, Slovakia, Spain, Sweden, Switzerland, the Netherlands, the Philippines, the United Kingdom, and the United States. The sample size for each country ranges from 149 (the former East Germany) to 719 (Spain). Unlike previous cross-national comparisons of attitudes toward women's employment, which examined only Western, highly developed and/or postsocialist countries (see Treas and Widmer [2000] for a review), we broaden our analysis to include Latin American countries (Chile, Mexico, and Brazil) as well as the Philippines. This provides a more robust evaluation of our hypothesis because there is more regional and cultural variation.[5]

## Dependent Variable

Our dependent measure is an index of gender ideology indicating gender egalitarianism. It is constructed as the mean Likert-scale disagreement with statements that are supportive of a separate spheres arrangement ($\alpha = .76$): "A man's job is to earn the money; a woman's job is to look after the home and family"; "A job is alright, but what most women want is a home and children"; "All in all, family life suffers when the wife has a full-time job"; "A preschool child is likely to suffer if his or her mother works"; and "Being a housewife is just as fulfilling as working for pay." The index ranges from 1 to 5, where a score of 5 indicates strong gender egalitarianism.

## Key Independent Variables

**Economic dependency on spouse.** This indicator measures the respondent's perception of his income relative to his spouse. Participants were asked, "Who makes the higher income?" Answer choices included, "My spouse/partner has no income," "I have a much higher income," "I have a higher income," "We have about the same income," "My spouse/partner has a higher income," "My spouse/partner has a much higher income," or "I have no income." The variable ranges from 0 to 6, with higher values indicating a higher level of perceived economic dependency.

**Labor market rigidity.** Our key theoretical variable measures the degree of legal rigidity in the labor market in any given country. To construct this variable, we use data from the World Bank's International Finance Corporation Doing Business database from 2004, which provides economic statistics that are comparable across countries (World Bank Group 2004).[6] Our measure is a composite of two indicators: an index indicating the legal difficulty of hiring an employee and an index indicating the legal difficulty of firing an employee.

The difficulty of hiring index measures (1) whether term contracts can be used only for temporary tasks, (2) the maximum cumulative duration of term contracts, and (3) the ratio of the minimum wage for a trainee or first-time employee to the average value added per worker. The difficulty of firing index has eight components:(1) whether redundancy is disallowed as a basis for terminating workers, (2) whether the employer needs to notify a third party (such as a government agency) to terminate one redundant worker, (3) whether the employer needs to notify a third party to terminate a group of 25 redundant workers, (4) whether the employer needs approval from a third party to terminate one redundant worker, (5) whether the employer needs approval from a third party to terminate a group of 25 redundant workers, (6) whether the law requires the employer to consider reassignment or retraining options before redundancy termination, (7) whether priority rules apply for redundancies, and (8) whether priority rules apply for reemployment. We use standardized mean scores of these two index measures so that each variable can contribute to our measure equally. Values range from –1.35 (United States, the least rigid labor market) to 1.24 (Mexico, the most rigid labor market).

## Control Variables

We also include control variables that have been shown to affect men's gender ideology, as well as variables that might affect the way labor market structure influences the dependency effect on men's attitudes. These include the respondent's age, educational attainment, whether he has a child, labor force status, work sector, political conservatism, and religion. Educational attainment is measured by a dichotomous variable that indicates whether the respondent has a college degree.

Next, since men's work status and work hours have been shown to affect their attitudes about gender (Baxter and Kane 1995; Zuo 1997), we include measures for individuals' labor force status using a series of dummy variables for full-time and part-time employment; "not currently working" is the reference category. Additionally, particular work sectors may be associated with a gender egalitarian ideology. For example, public sectors in many Western European countries are operated by large welfare states and are often more female-dominated than private sector jobs (Borchorst 1999; Orloff, 1993), a situation that may promote more egalitarian gender ideology. Because the self-employed tend to hold more traditional gender attitudes than those in paid employment (Baxter and Kane 1995), we include dummy variables for being employed in the private sector and being self-employed (working in the public sector is the reference category). Last, we include measures of political party affiliation and religion because respondents on the political left, as well as those who are not religiously affiliated or are Jewish, are more likely to have gender egalitarian attitudes (Bolzendahl and Myers 2004; Brewster and Padavic 2000; Mason and Lu 1988; Wilkie 1993). Political conservatism is coded using respondent's party affiliation. The ISSP standardizes this measure based on the relative political positions of political parties in each country's political context. This variable ranges from 1 to 5, where 1 indicates a far left position and a 5 indicates a far right position. We use a set of dummy variables for primary religious affiliation: Roman Catholic, Protestant, Christian Orthodox, Jewish, Muslim, Buddhist, and other religion (the reference category consists of respondents who reported themselves as not affiliated with any religion).

While we are mainly interested in the impact of a country's labor market structure on the relationship between men's breadwinning status and gender ideology, we include other country-level characteristics that may explain some of the cross-national variation in the link between men's breadwinning and gender ideology. First, we adjust for the influence of gender inequality on levels of gender egalitarianism using two variables: women's labor force participation and gender wage equality. Women's labor force participation is calculated as the percentage of women among the economically active population; this is based on the most recent data available between 2002 and 2004 (World Bank Group 2006). Gender wage equality is the ratio of estimated female to male earned income published by the United Nations (United Nations Development Programme [UNDP] 2005) and is based on the most recently available data.

To account for the fact that wage inequality should be especially consequential for bargaining processes within the household (Baxter and Kane 1995), we test for the possibility that gender inequality at the country level influences the dependency effect by allowing the dependency measure to differ by levels of gender wage equality. That is, in countries with high levels of wage equality, women have more bargaining power within the household: even if they are dependent, their potential wages if they were to be in the labor market are more comparable to those of men. Thus, one would expect that the effect of economic dependency on

## Table 1 Means and Standard Deviations for Individual-Level Variables

| Variable | Mean | Standard Deviation |
|---|---|---|
| Gender Egalitarianism Index | 2.95 | 0.89 |
| Economic dependency on spouse | 1.79 | 1.30 |
| Age | 49.17 | 14.26 |
| College degree | 0.21 | |
| Child | 0.86 | |
| Work status | | |
| Currently not working | 0.27 | |
| Works full-time | 0.69 | |
| Works part-time | 0.05 | |
| Work type | | |
| Works in public sector | 0.29 | |
| Works in private sector | 0.52 | |
| Self-employed | 0.19 | |
| Religion | | |
| No religion | 0.22 | |
| Roman Catholic | 0.39 | |
| Protestant | 0.33 | |
| Christian Orthodox | 0.03 | |
| Jewish | 0.00 | |
| Muslim | 0.01 | |
| Buddhist | 0.01 | |
| Other religion | 0.03 | |
| Political conservatism | 2.92 | 1.04 |

men's gender egalitarianism would be less in countries with higher levels of wage equality.

Last, although our sample consists of countries that have high and medium levels of human development according to the UNDP (2005), there is still considerable variation with regard to levels of economic development. Because a meritocratic system is supposed to be more common than an ascriptive process in more modernized countries, gender inequality may decrease as the level of economic development increases (Jackson 1998). Economic development is also strongly correlated to women's overall levels of education and employment (Clark, Ramsbey, and Adler 1991; Klasen 2002). Thus, we adjust for heterogeneity in gender ideology that may be related to levels of economic development by including a measure of GDP. This is a scaled index calculated by the UNDP (2005).

## Method and Model

We use hierarchical linear models (HLM) to assess the impact of individual and country level variables on men's gender ideology (Raudenbush and Bryk 2002). Because the data have a nested structure such that observations for individuals within countries may be more highly correlated than those between countries, HLM provides more accurate estimations for nested data like this. In our model, we account for country-level variability by allowing each country to have their own group mean of men's egalitarianism, instead of imposing the same grand mean on all countries. We also allow the effects of men's economic dependency to differ among countries. In doing so, we expect the country-level variability in the effect of men's economic dependency to differ by the level of labor market rigidity and the level of gender pay equity of each country. By applying this modeling strategy, we can estimate how the effect of economic dependency in each country varies by labor market structure more accurately.[7]

## Results
### Descriptive Overview

Table 1 lists descriptive statistics for all individual-level variables in the study. On average, men across the 27 countries report a score of 2.95 on the gender egalitarianism index, indicating that men tend to be slightly more traditional than they are egalitarian (again, the range is 1 to 5, where 5 indicates more gender egalitarianism). The average economic dependency score is 1.79 (on a scale of 0 to 6, where 6 indicates complete dependency on partners).

Table 2 presents information on each country's average gender ideology, as well as the country-level variables used in our models. First, on average, men in Denmark are the most egalitarian, while men in Brazil are the most traditional. Overall, the average values suggest that men in Western European countries are more egalitarian than men in other countries. Second, with a score of −1.35, the United States is the country with the most flexible labor market, whereas Mexico has the most rigid labor market structure (1.24). The placement of other countries is consistent with previous research. France, known for strong legal protections for employees, has a relatively high score (1.12), as does Germany (0.42); by contrast, English-speaking countries (Australia, the United Kingdom, the United States, and New Zealand) and Central European countries have lower rigidity scores (all negative values). Japan has a low rigidity score (−0.53), even though it has historically been known for preserving long-term employment. One reason for this is that while Japanese companies value seniority for "good jobs," there are few legal prohibitions against firing employees, which makes the labor market relatively flexible.

The bivariate association between average gender egalitarianism and labor market rigidity in Figure 1 summarizes the association of these two factors. It indicates that although there is a positive association between the level of rigidity of the labor market and the overall gender egalitarianism of the country, the association is not statistically significant. This suggests that the average level of men's gender egalitarianism in a given country is not significantly affected by the level of labor market rigidity.

## Table 2 Country-Level Values on Labor Market Rigidity and Other Variables

| Country | Average Gender Egalitarianism of Men | Labor Market Rigidity Score | Gender Wage Equality | Women's Labor Force Participation | Gross Domestic Product Index |
|---|---|---|---|---|---|
| Denmark | 3.65 | −1.07 | 0.73 | 0.47 | 0.96 |
| Germany (former East) | 3.47 | 0.42 | 0.54 | 0.45 | 0.94 |
| Sweden | 3.44 | 0.09 | 0.69 | 0.47 | 0.93 |
| Norway | 3.42 | 0.65 | 0.75 | 0.47 | 0.99 |
| Ireland | 3.20 | −0.57 | 0.41 | 0.42 | 0.99 |
| Finland | 3.18 | 0.42 | 0.72 | 0.48 | 0.94 |
| New Zealand | 3.17 | −0.85 | 0.68 | 0.46 | 0.9 |
| United Kingdom | 3.08 | −0.85 | 0.62 | 0.46 | 0.94 |
| The Netherlands | 3.07 | 0.91 | 0.53 | 0.44 | 0.95 |
| France | 3.03 | 1.12 | 0.59 | 0.48 | 0.94 |
| Japan | 3.01 | −0.53 | 0.46 | 0.41 | 0.94 |
| United States | 2.97 | −1.35 | 0.62 | 0.46 | 0.99 |
| Australia | 2.94 | −1.07 | 0.72 | 0.45 | 0.95 |
| Spain | 2.93 | 1.08 | 0.44 | 0.41 | 0.9 |
| Germany (former West) | 2.93 | 0.42 | 0.54 | 0.45 | 0.94 |
| Switzerland | 2.92 | −1.07 | 0.9 | 0.46 | 0.96 |
| Czech Republic | 2.80 | −0.3 | 0.64 | 0.45 | 0.85 |
| Latvia | 2.70 | 1.08 | 0.62 | 0.49 | 0.77 |
| Poland | 2.59 | −0.03 | 0.62 | 0.46 | 0.79 |
| Portugal | 2.55 | 1.05 | 0.54 | 0.46 | 0.87 |
| Bulgaria | 2.52 | −0.72 | 0.51 | 0.46 | 0.73 |
| Chile | 2.51 | −0.12 | 0.39 | 0.35 | 0.77 |
| Slovakia | 2.48 | −0.18 | 0.65 | 0.45 | 0.82 |
| The Philippines | 2.47 | 0.63 | 0.59 | 0.39 | 0.63 |
| Russian Federation | 2.46 | 0.42 | 0.64 | 0.49 | 0.76 |
| Hungary | 2.45 | −0.85 | 0.62 | 0.45 | 0.83 |
| Mexico | 2.40 | 1.24 | 0.38 | 0.35 | 0.75 |
| Brazil | 2.25 | 0.04 | 0.43 | 0.42 | 0.73 |
| Mean | 2.95 | 0.02 | 0.60 | 0.44 | 0.90 |
| Standard deviation | 0.89 | 0.83 | 0.12 | 0.03 | 0.09 |
| Range | 1–5 | −1.35–1.24 | 0.38–0.90 | 0.35–0.49 | 0.63–0.99 |

## Modeling Men's Gender Ideology

The results from multilevel models are shown in Table 3. All variables except the economic dependency measure are centered at their mean values across countries to facilitate a meaningful interpretation of the model intercept. The intraclass correlation, as calculated from the unconditional model (not shown), is .17. This means that 17 percent of the variance in men's gender ideology can be explained by country-level variability.[8]

Model 1 presents the effects of individual-level factors that explain men's gender egalitarian ideology. First, consistent with previous research, men who are more economically dependent on their partners are more likely to demonstrate a gender egalitarian ideology. Specifically, the intercept indicates that the Taaverage scores of the gender ideology measure for breadwinning men whose spouses have no

income is 2.68 (where 5 indicates strong gender egalitarianism), holding all other variables constant at their means. The value increases by 0.10 scores per unit increase of men's economic dependency. The control variables also confirm findings of previous studies. Younger and college-educated men are more likely to endorse a gender egalitarian ideology. Having had one child or more does not significantly influence men's ideology. This is not surprising given that a positive association between men's ideology and having children has only been found in U.S. studies (Baxter and Kane 1995; Bolzendahl and Myers 2004; Mason and Lu 1988). Men who work full-time and part-time are also more egalitarian than men who are currently not working, and this is even more so the case for men who work part-time. This is a similar finding to Brines (1994), who found that men who are economically dependent do more housework than

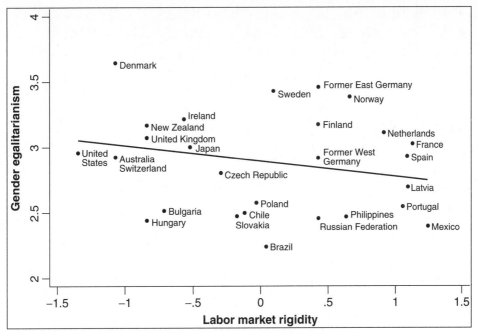

**Figure 1** Men's Gender Egalitarianism and the Labor Market Rigidity in 27 Countries.

men who are primary earners but that unemployed men do less housework than other dependent men. The work status variables included in the model may also suggest a curvilinear relationship between men's economic dependency and their ideology. Additionally, self-employed men are on average less egalitarian than men who work in the public sector. Attitudinal control measures also have strong effects on men's egalitarianism. Compared to men who report no religious affiliation, men who are religiously affiliated tend to be less egalitarian, especially those who are Roman Catholic, Protestant, Muslim, and Buddhist. Men with politically conservative attitudes are also more likely to hold traditional gender ideology.

Model 2 includes main effects for country-level variables. Not surprisingly, the coefficient for labor market rigidity is not significant, indicating that labor market structure does not influence men's gender egalitarianism on average. As suspected, the level of economic development, as measured by GDP, does significantly increase men's likelihood of endorsing gender egalitarian viewpoints, even after controlling for gender pay equity and women's overall labor force participation rate.

Next, we evaluate our main hypothesis by examining how men's economic dependency on their partners influences their gender ideology differently in countries with different levels of labor market rigidity. The interaction term in model 3 demonstrates this effect. As predicted, the positive effect of men's breadwinning status on their gender ideology is significantly stronger for men in more rigid labor markets. In particular, a one-unit increase in the measure of labor market rigidity leads to a 0.03 score increase in the effect of the economic dependency measure. This supports our hypothesis that men's economic dependency on their partners positively

affects their gender egalitarianism and that this relationship is stronger for men in more rigid labor markets: men's gender ideology is more contingent upon their breadwinning status in rigid labor markets than it is in flexible labor markets.

Figure 2 illustrates the magnitude of the coefficient of the interaction term more effectively. The $Y$-axis represents the predicted gender egalitarianism of a hypothetical respondent who has the mean characteristics across countries. Note the differences in the slopes of the lines. In Figure 2a, the upper, flatter line shows the predicted effect if the respondent is in the country with the most flexible labor market (the United States); and the lower, steeper line shows the effect for a respondent in the country with the most rigid labor market (Mexico). The upper line indicates that men who are primary breadwinners in the United States hold generally a more egalitarian ideology than men who are breadwinners in a very rigid labor market. However, the flatter slope for the United States suggests that economically dependent American men are less responsive to a nontraditional gender arrangement compared to economically dependent Mexican men. The lower line indicates that men in Mexico who are economically dependent on their wives tend to hold a considerably more gender egalitarian ideology than Mexican men who are primary providers; by contrast, American men who are dependent have only slightly more egalitarian views than American men who are primary providers.

Although the figure helps to demonstrate that economic dependency influences men's egalitarian ideology more strongly in rigid labor markets than in flexible markets, one may suspect that this effect is in part because overall egalitarianism tends to be higher in flexible labor markets than in rigid labor markets. That is, men in flexible labor markets

**Table 3:** Hierarchical Linear Models for the Effects of Labor Market Rigidity on Men's Economic Dependency and Their Gender Egalitarianism

| Independent Variable | Model 1 | | Model 2 | | Model 3 | |
|---|---|---|---|---|---|---|
| | β | SE | β | SE | β | SE |
| Intercept | 2.68*** | 0.07 | 2.75*** | 0.04 | 2.75*** | 0.05 |
| Economic dependency on spouse[a] | 0.10*** | 0.01 | 0.10*** | 0.01 | 0.10*** | 0.01 |
| Country-level effects | | | | | | |
|   Labor Market Rigidity[a] | | | 0.03 | 0.06 | 0.00 | 0.06 |
|   Gender Pay Equity[a] | | | 0.84 | 0.52 | 0.72 | 0.54 |
|   GDP [a] | | | 3.20*** | 0.49 | 3.27*** | 0.49 |
|   Women's labor force participation rate[a] | | | −2.89 | 1.78 | −2.76 | 1.78 |
| Cross-level interactions | | | | | | |
|   Dependency × Labor market rigidity | | | | | 0.03** | 0.01 |
|   Dependency × Gender pay equity | | | | | 0.06 | 0.08 |
| Other individual-level effects | | | | | | |
|   Age[a] | −0.01*** | 0.00 | −0.01*** | 0.00 | −0.01*** | 0.00 |
|   College degree | 0.31*** | 0.02 | 0.31*** | 0.02 | 0.31*** | 0.02 |
|   Child | −0.04 | 0.03 | −0.04 | 0.03 | −0.04 | 0.03 |
| Work status (omitted category = currently not working) | | | | | | |
|   Works full-time | 0.28*** | 0.03 | 0.28*** | 0.03 | 0.28*** | 0.03 |
|   Works part-time | 0.31*** | 0.05 | 0.31*** | 0.05 | 0.31*** | 0.05 |
| Work type (omitted category = works in public sector) | | | | | | |
|   Works in private sector | −0.04 | 0.02 | −0.04 | 0.02 | −0.04 | 0.02 |
|   Self-employed | −0.14*** | 0.03 | −0.14*** | 0.03 | −0.14*** | 0.03 |
| Religion (omitted category = no religion) | | | | | | |
|   Roman Catholic | −0.25*** | 0.03 | −0.25*** | 0.03 | −0.25*** | 0.03 |
|   Protestant | −0.20*** | 0.03 | −0.20*** | 0.03 | −0.20*** | 0.03 |
|   Christian Orthodox | −0.19* | 0.09 | −0.15 | 0.09 | −0.14 | 0.09 |
|   Jewish | −0.12 | 0.22 | −0.12 | 0.22 | −0.13 | 0.22 |
|   Muslim | −0.56*** | 0.13 | −0.54*** | 0.13 | −0.54*** | 0.13 |
|   Buddhist | −0.24 | 0.12 | −0.24* | 0.12 | −0.25 | 0.12 |
|   Other religion | −0.26*** | 0.06 | −0.26*** | 0.06 | −0.26*** | 0.06 |
| Political conservatism | −0.06*** | 0.01 | −0.06*** | 0.01 | −0.06*** | 0.01 |
| Variance components | | | | | | |
| Between-country | .1307*** | | .04390*** | | .04491*** | |
| Within-country | .5530*** | | .5531*** | | .5533*** | |
| Log-likelihood | 14,074.6 | | 14,043.2 | | 14,047.5 | |
| Number of countries = 28 | | | | | | |
| Number of observations = 6,184 | | | | | | |

Note. All variables except "economic dependency on spouse" are centered at the grand mean.

*p < .05. **p < .01. ***p < .001.

are already more egalitarian, and thus, the likelihood that they would become even more egalitarian is lower compared to men in rigid labor markets. Our findings rule out this possibility in two ways. First, we did not find evidence of a main effect for labor market rigidity, suggesting that men's average levels of egalitarianism are not significantly influenced by labor market rigidity (see model 2). Second,

a comparison of two countries (France and the United States) that have similar levels of gender egalitarianism (France = 3.07, United States = 3.10) but considerably different levels of labor market rigidity suggests that the difference in the effect of economic dependency is primarily driven by differences in labor market rigidity. Unlike the comparison of Mexico and the United States, the additional comparison shows that

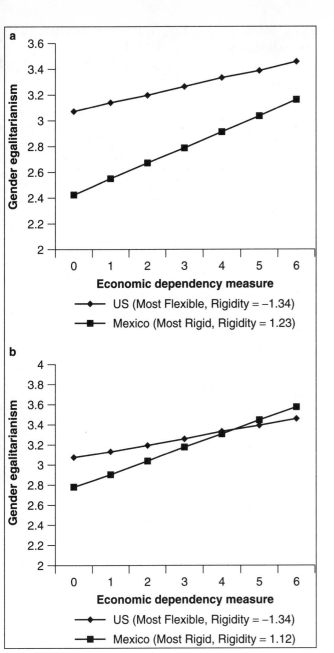

**Figure 2** The Effect of Men's Economic Dependency on Their Gender Egalitarian Ideology by Labor Market Rigidity.

Note. Estimates are derived from model 3. All the values are set to country's mean values: 0 = spouse has no income, 1 = I have much higher income, 2 = I have a higher income, 3 = we have about the same income, 4 = spouse has higher income, 5 = spouse has much higher income, and 6 = I have no income.

the lines cross at the point that men and their spouses make about the same income. This effectively demonstrates that breadwinning French men may be moderately less egalitarian than breadwinning American men, but more economically dependent French men actually hold a more egalitarian ideology than equivalent American men.

Finally, we examine whether gender equity at the societal level influences the relationship between men's economic dependency and gender ideology. We do so because previous research suggests that societal-level gender inequality may influence the bargaining process within the household

(Baxter and Kane 1995). We test this proposition by including the interaction term of the economic dependency measure and the gender wage equity measure. Our model, however, does not show support for this hypothesis because the interaction effect does not reach significance when labor market rigidity is held constant.

In sum, results presented here consistently support our central hypothesis that men's economic position relative to their partners' influences their gender egalitarianism in rigid labor markets more strongly than it does in flexible markets.

## Discussion

In this study, we sought to uncover how institutional arrangements at the country level shape the crucial role that breadwinning experiences play in influencing men's gender ideology. Consistent with previous literature, we find that labor market structure is an important determinant of gendered phenomena. Our research demonstrates that *fluctuation* matters for men's gender ideology. That is, as previous research suggests, men's breadwinning status rises and falls with changes in jobs in flexible labor markets. This fluctuation in breadwinning status can result from both men's and their spouses' employment patterns. In this study, we cannot measure changes in individual men's breadwinning status over time. However, we do find evidence that in contexts where fluctuation in bread-winning status is prevalent, it is possible to maintain the normative perception that a man's earnings are primary, whereas his spouse's are secondary, even when men earn less than their partners. We understand this to be the case because in these contexts, this situation is likely to be impermanent and does not fundamentally threaten a prescribed conception of separate spheres; cobreadwinning in a flexible labor market does not necessarily undermine traditional notions of men's main responsibility in the provider role. On the flip side, rigid labor markets provide incentives that more strongly encourage the male-breadwinner model. Because of this, men who veer away from this norm in such a context experience a more significant, more permanent structural change in their interpersonal relationships with their spouses. This may give them a stronger incentive to reconcile their ideology with their real experiences.

Additionally, our findings are robust net of more explicit forms of structural gender inequality. This implies that men's gender ideology is distinctly related to their individual breadwinning experiences, not just the degree to which women have an overall presence in the labor market. Men's ideology is not simply contingent upon seeing women in the public workplace, or in positions of management, but is negotiated through the private experience of norm contestation and resolution within the family.

While more work needs to be done on the contextual nature of men's gender ideology, this study provides implications for future work in areas beyond the scope of this research. First, our research speaks to the burgeoning literature on masculinities, which suggests that while masculinity is complex, constantly changing, and varying across cultures and demographic groups, the role of a man as a breadwinner is still a central element of masculinity in many cultures. This relationship is historically rooted; in the United States, for example, it began in the mid-nineteenth century and was reinforced by Fordist models of separate spheres and the family wage (Kimmel 1993; Potuchek 1997). As these conditions erode with the rise in female employment and flexible labor markets, a core element of dominant, or "hegemonic," masculinity comes under pressure (Connell 2005). Our research suggests that where this is the case, men's sense of masculinity as breadwinners is challenged, but only in the short term; where labor markets are rigid, this element of masculinity is challenged long-term and therefore has stronger implications for men's gender ideology.

Second, our findings provide implications, though speculative, for why men in some countries may be slower to adopt progressive gender ideology than men in other countries. To the extent that institutional arrangements endorse a traditional conception of gender in the household, men's gender ideology may change at slower rates because men have, on average, fewer opportunities to experience nontraditional arrangements. However, even if macroeconomic trends increasingly contest traditional gender beliefs, persistent normative conceptions about men's roles as breadwinners may slow their adoption of progressive gender ideology. For example, although institutional arrangements in flexible labor markets provide men frequent opportunities to contest nontraditional arrangements in the short term, this institutional arrangement is less effective in challenging a traditional gender ideology than in a more rigid labor market.

Last, cross-cultural research is essential if one is to identify the mechanisms generating many of the gendered patterns we observe. Contextualizing a gendered experience, such as breadwinning, can provide lasting insights into the importance of those experiences in contributing to people's gendered realities. Other aspects of gendered institutional structures, such as welfare states, may shed more light on the gendered connotations of breadwinning experiences at the micro-level of the family unit. For example, rigid labor markets tend to occur in larger social welfare states, whereas welfare benefits are scant in flexible labor markets (Soskice 2005). In some cases, these welfare states encourage women's employment by providing benefits for working parents, such as paid parental leave and child care assistance; in other cases, the welfare state marginalizes women's participation in the labor market by providing for long maternity leaves but not supporting working mothers with child care (Gornick and Meyers 2003; Lewis 1992; Orloff 1993). As these variations in state structures further influence the context of breadwinning for both men and women, they may help us to better understand how institutional contexts shape men's experiences and ideology.

# Notes

1. The data do not specify a respondent's sexual orientation or the gender of a respondent's "spouse/partner," though we presume that most respondents are heterosexual. The data set also includes respondents from countries that vary widely regarding cultural values about marriage. For example, in Sweden, it is much more common for couples to cohabit for their lifetimes without marrying, whereas in the United States and Japan, cohabitation is not typically a substitution for marriage.

2. We do not set an upper limit for age in our sample because the retirement age varies greatly between countries. Many men over the age of 65 in this sample reported income.

3. To address the possibility that dropping cases leads to sample bias, we also conducted the analyses after imputing missing cases. The findings from imputed data (sample size = 10,732) are consistent with nonimputed data.

4. We treat the former East Germany as a separate country-level unit in our analyses because of a great difference in gender ideology from the former West Germany. Thus, the number of countries is 27, but the number of statistical units at the country level is 28. Also, we merge Great Britain and Northern Ireland into one country (United Kingdom) because of the data availability from World Bank.

5. We conducted additional analyses to ensure that this set of countries is indeed comparable. First, we excluded countries that, according to 2002 OECD statistics, have "medium" rather than "high" levels of human development. These countries included Russia, Brazil, and the Philippines. We also conducted analyses that excluded Asian and Latin American countries. None of these analyses influenced our findings.

6. 2004 is the earliest year for which the World Bank provides these data.

7. This can be written as series of equations, as follows:

$$Y_{ij} = \beta_{0j} + \beta_{1j}I_{ij} + \beta_2 X_{ij} + R_{ij} \tag{a}$$

$Y_{ij}$ is gender egalitarianism for respondent $i$ in country $j$; $\beta_{0j}$ is the individual-level intercept; $\beta_{1j}$ indicates the coefficient of the economic dependency measure; $\beta_2$ is a vector of regression coefficients that are constant across countries; $I_{ij}$ indicates the economic dependency measure; $X_{ij}$ is a vector of covariates for individual $i$ in country $j$; and $R_{ij}$ is a random error term, which is assumed to be normally distributed with mean zero and constant variance.

The $\beta_{0j}$ and $\beta_{1j}$ takes the following forms:

$$\beta_{0j} = \gamma_{00} + \gamma_{01}(\text{RIGIDITY}_j) + \gamma_{02}(\text{EQUITY}_j) + U_{0j} \tag{b}$$

$$\beta_{1j} = \gamma_{10} + \gamma_{11}(\text{RIGIDITY}_j) + \gamma_{12}(\text{EQUITY}_j) + U_{1j} \tag{c}$$

$\text{RIGIDITY}_j$ is the level of labor market rigidity; $\text{EQUITY}_j$ is the level of gender pay equity at the country level; $\gamma_{00}$ and $\gamma_{10}$ are the country-level intercepts; $\gamma_{01}$, $\gamma_{02}$, $\gamma_{11}$, and $\gamma_{12}$ are regression coefficients; and $U_{0j}$ and $U_{1j}$ are both random effects at the country level, which are assumed to be normally distributed with mean zero.

8. $\hat{\rho}$ (intraclass correlation) $= \dfrac{\hat{\psi}}{(\hat{\psi} + \hat{\phi})}$, where $\hat{\psi}$ is the

estimate of the variance of the random intercept of countries and $\hat{\phi}$ is the estimate of the within-country variance.

# References

Allmendinger, J. 1989. Educational systems and labor market outcomes. *European Sociological Review* 5: 231–250.

Alwin, D. F., M. Braun, and J. Scott. 1992. The separation of work and family: Attitudes towards women's labour force participation in Germany, Great Britain and the United States. *European Sociological Review* 8 (1): 13–36.

Baxter, J., and E. W. Kane. 1995. Dependence and independence: A cross-national analysis of gender inequality and gender attitudes. *Gender & Society* 9: 193–215.

Bolzendahl, C. I., and D. J. Myers. 2004. Feminist attitudes and support for gender equality: opinion change in women and men, 1974–1998. *Social Forces* 83(2): 759–90.

Borchorst, A. 1999. *Feminist thinking about the welfare state. Revisioning gender.* Walnut Creek, CA: Altamira.

Brewster, K. L., and I. Padavic. 2000. Change in gender-ideology, 1977–1996: The contributions of intracohort change and population turnover. *Journal of Marriage and the Family* 62: 477–87.

Brines, J. 1994. Economic dependency, gender, and the division of labor at home. *American Journal of Sociology* 100:652–88.

Chang, M. L. 2000. The evolution of sex segregation regimes. *American Journal of Sociology* 105:1658–1701.

Charles, M., M. Buchmann, S. Halebsky, J. M. Powers, and M. M. Smith. 2001. The context of women's market careers: A cross-national study. *Work & Occupations* 28: 371.

Charles, M., and D. B. Grusky. 2005. Occupational ghettos: the worldwide segregation of women and men. *Social Forces* 84: 1311–12.

Clark, R., T. W. Ramsbey, and E. S. Adler. 1991. Culture, gender and labor force participation: A cross national study. *Gender & Society* 5 (1): 47–66.

Coltrane, S. 1996. *Family man: fatherhood, housework, and gender equity.* New York: Oxford University Press.

Connell, R. W. 1995. *Masculinities.* Berkeley: University of California Press.

Crompton, R., and F. Harris. 1997. Women's employment and gender attitudes: A comparative analysis of Britain, Norway and the Czech Republic. *Acta Sociologica* 40 (2): 183–202.

Deutsch, F. M., and S. E. Saxon. 1998. Traditional ideologies, nontraditional lives. *Sex Roles* 38 (5): 331–62.

Doeringer, P. B., and M. J. Piore. 1971. *Internal labor markets and manpower analysis.* Lexington, MA: D. C. Heath.

Esping-Anderson, G. 1990. *The three worlds of welfare capitalism.* Cambridge, UK: Polity.

Estévez-Abe, M. 2005. Gender bias in skills and social policies: The varieties of capitalism perspective on sex segregation. *Social Politics: International Studies in Gender, State & Society* 12: 180–215.

Estévez-Abe, M., T. Iversen, and D. Soskice. 2001. Social protection and the formation of skills: A reinterpretation of the welfare state. In *Varieties of capitalism: The institutional foundations of comparative advantage,* edited by P. A. Hall and D. Soskice. New York: Oxford University Press.

Ferree, M. M. 1990. Beyond separate spheres: feminism and family research. *Journal of Marriage and the Family* 52: 866–84.

Gerson, K. 1993. *No man's land: Men's changing commitments to family and work.* New York: Basic Books.

Gornick, J. C., and M. K. Meyers. 2003. *Families that work: Policies for reconciling parenthood and employment.* New York: Russell Sage Foundation.

Hochschild, A. R. 2001. *The time bind: When work becomes home and home becomes work.* New York: Metropolitan Books.

Hochschild, A. R., and A. Machung. 2003. *The second shift.* New York: Penguin.

Jackson, R. M. 1998. *Destined for equality: The inevitable rise of women's status.* Cambridge, MA: Harvard University Press.

Kane, E. W., and L. Sanchez. 1994. Family status and criticism of gender inequality at home and work. *Social Forces* 72 (4): 1079–1102.

Kimmel, M. S. 1993. What do men want? *Harvard Business Review* 71(6): 50–59.

Klasen, Stephan. 2002. Low schooling for girls, slower growth for all? Cross-country evidence on the effect of gender inequality in education on economic development. *World Bank Economic Review* 16 (3): 345–73.

Knudsen, K., and K. Waerness. 2001. National context, individual characteristics and attitudes on mothers' employment: A comparative analysis of Great Britain, Sweden and Norway. *Acta Sociologica* 44 (1): 67–79.

Lewis, J. 1992. Gender and the development of welfare regimes. *Journal of European Social Policy* 3: 159–73.

Mandel, H., and M. Semyonov. 2006. A welfare state paradox: State interventions and women's employment opportunities in 22 countries. *American Journal of Sociology* 111: 1910–49.

Oppenheimer, V. K. 1997. Women's employment and the gain to marriage: The specialization and trading model. *Annual Review of Sociology* 23: 431–53.

Orloff, A. S. 1993. Gender and the social rights of citizenship: The comparative analysis of gender relations and welfare states. *American Sociological Review* 58 (3): 303–28.

Panayotova, E., and A. Brayfield. 1997. National context and gender ideology: Attitudes toward women's employment in Hungary and the United States. *Gender & Society* 11 (5): 627–55.

Potuchek, J. L. 1997. *Who supports the family? Gender and breadwinning in dual-earner marriages.* Stanford, CA: Stanford University Press.

Raudenbush, S. W., and A. S. Bryk. 2002. *Hierarchical linear models: Applications and data analysis methods.* 2nd ed. Thousand Oaks, CA: Sage.

Rubery, J., C. Fagan, and F. Maier. 1996. Occupational segregation, discrimination and equal opportunity. In *International handbook of labour market policy and evaluation,* edited by G. Schmid, J. O'Reilly and K. Schömann. Brookfield, MA: Edward Elgar.

Scott, J., D. F. Alwin, and M. Braun. 1996. Generational changes in gender-role attitudes: Britain in a cross-national perspective. *Sociology* 30 (5): 471–92.

Soskice, David. 2005. Varieties of capitalism and cross-national gender differences. *Social Politics* 12 (2): 170–79.

Thornton, A., and L. Young-DeMarco. 2001. Four decades of trends in attitudes toward family issues in the United States: The 1960s through the 1990s. *Journal of Marriage and the Family* 63: 1009–37.

Tichenor, V. J. 2005. *Earning more and getting less: Why successful wives can't buy equality.* New Brunswick, NJ: Rutgers University Press.

Treas, J., and E. D. Widmer. 2000. Married women's employment over the life course: Attitudes in cross-national perspective. *Social Forces* 78 (4): 1409–36.

United Nations Development Programme (UNDP). 2005. *Human development report.* New York: Oxford University Press.

Wilkie, J. R. 1993. Changes in U.S. men's attitudes toward the family provider role, 1972–1989. *Gender & Society* 7 (2): 261–79.

Winslow-Bowe, S. 2006. The persistence of wives' income advantage. *Journal of Marriage and Family* 68: 824.

World Bank Group. 2004. International finance corporation: Doing business database. http://www.doingbusiness.org/MethodologySurveys/EmployingWorkers.aspx.

——. 2006. Gender stats: Database of gender statistics online. http://devdata.worldbank.org/genderstats/home.asp.

Zuo, J. 1997. The effect of men's breadwinner status on their changing gender beliefs. *Sex Roles* 37 (9/10): 799–816.

**YOUNGJOO CHA** is a PhD candidate in sociology at Cornell University. Her research examines gender, work, occupations, and social inequality. Her dissertation examines how the norm of working long hours affects men's and women's employment decisions, career mobility, and earnings differently and contributes to gender inequality. **SARAH THÉBAUD** is a PhD candidate in sociology at Cornell University. Her research focuses on gender inequality in paid and unpaid work in cross-national perspective. Her dissertation investigates how social and economic policies, together with cultural beliefs about gender in social interactions, impact gender inequality in entrepreneurship across industrialized countries.

**Authors' note**—Both authors contributed equally to the work, and their names are listed in alphabetical order. Direct correspondence to Youngjoo Cha or Sarah Thébaud at Department of Sociology, 323 Uris Hall, Cornell University, Ithaca, NY 14853. We thank Shelley Correll, Elizabeth Hirsh, Jennifer Lature, Christin Munsch, In Paik, Catherine Taylor, Jennifer Todd, Kim Weeden, and Alexa Yesukevich and the editor and Gender & Society reviewers for helpful comments on previous drafts.

From *Gender & Society*, April 1, 2009, pp. 215–243. Copyright © 2009 by Sage Publications. Reprinted by permission via Rightslink.

# A Woman's Curse?

**Why do cultures the world over treat menstruating women as taboo?
An anthropologist offers a new answer—and a challenge
to Western ideas about contraception.**

MEREDITH F. SMALL

The passage from girlhood to womanhood is marked by a flow of blood from the uterus. Without elaborate ceremony, often without discussion, girls know that when they begin to menstruate, their world is changed forever. For the next thirty years or so, they will spend much energy having babies, or trying not to, reminded at each menstruation that either way, the biology of reproduction has a major impact on their lives.

Anthropologists have underscored the universal importance of menstruation by documenting how the event is interwoven into the ideology as well as the daily activities of cultures around the world. The customs attached to menstruation take peculiarly negative forms: the so-called menstrual taboos. Those taboos may prohibit a woman from having sex with her husband or from cooking for him. They may bar her from visiting sacred places or taking part in sacred activities. They may forbid her to touch certain items used by men, such as hunting gear or weapons, or to eat certain foods or to wash at certain times. They may also require that a woman paint her face red or wear a red hip cord, or that she segregate herself in a special hut while she is menstruating. In short, the taboos set menstruating women apart from the rest of their society, marking them as impure and polluting.

Anthropologists have studied menstrual taboos for decades, focusing on the negative symbolism of the rituals as a cultural phenomenon. Perhaps, suggested one investigator, taking a Freudian perspective, such taboos reflect the anxiety that men feel about castration, an anxiety that would be prompted by women's genital bleeding. Others have suggested that the taboos serve to prevent menstrual odor from interfering with hunting, or that they protect men from microorganisms that might otherwise be transferred during sexual intercourse with a menstruating woman. Until recently, few investigators had considered the possibility that the taboos—and the very fact of menstruation—might instead exist because they conferred an evolutionary advantage.

In the mid-1980s the anthropologist Beverly I. Strassmann of the University of Michigan in Ann Arbor began to study the ways men and women have evolved to accomplish (and regulate) reproduction. Unlike traditional anthropologists, who focus on how culture affects human behavior, Strassmann was convinced that the important role played by biology was being neglected. Menstruation, she suspected, would be a key for observing and understanding the interplay of biology and culture in human reproductive behavior.

To address the issue, Strassmann decided to seek a culture in which making babies was an ongoing part of adult life. For that she had to get away from industrialized countries, with their bias toward contraception and low birthrates. In a "natural-fertility population," she reasoned, she could more clearly see the connection between the physiology of women and the strategies men and women use to exploit that physiology for their own reproductive ends.

Strassmann ended up in a remote corner of West Africa, living in close quarters with the Dogon, a traditional society whose indigenous religion of ancestor worship requires that menstruating women spend their nights at a small hut. For more than two years Strassmann kept track of the women staying at the hut, and she confirmed the menstruations by testing urine samples for the appropriate hormonal changes. In so doing, she amassed the first long-term data describing how a traditional society appropriates a physiological event—menstruation—and refracts that event through a prism of behaviors and beliefs.

What she found explicitly challenges the conclusions of earlier investigators about the cultural function of menstrual taboos. For the Dogon men, she discovered, enforcing visits to the menstrual hut serves to channel parental resources into the upbringing of their own children. But more, Strassmann, who also had training as a reproductive physiologist, proposed a new theory of why menstruation itself evolved as it did—and again, the answer is essentially a story of conserving resources. Finally, her observations pose provocative questions about women's health in industrialized societies, raising serious doubts about the tactics favored by Western medicine for developing contraceptive technology.

Menstruation is the visible stage of the ovarian cycle, orchestrated primarily by hormones secreted by the ovaries: progesterone and a family of hormones called estrogens. At the beginning of each cycle (by convention, the first day of a woman's period) the levels of the estrogens begin to rise. After about five days, as their concentrations increase, they cause the blood- and nutrient-rich inner lining of the uterus, called the endometrium, to thicken and acquire a densely branching network of blood vessels. At about the middle of the cycle, ovulation takes place, and an egg makes its way from one of the two ovaries down one of the paired fallopian tubes to the uterus. The follicle from which the egg was released in the ovary now begins to secrete progesterone as well as estrogens, and the progesterone causes the endometrium to swell and become even richer with blood vessels—in short, fully ready for a pregnancy, should conception take place and the fertilized egg become implanted.

If conception does take place, the levels of estrogens and progesterone continue to rise throughout the pregnancy. That keeps the endometrium thick enough to support the quickening life inside the uterus. When the baby is born and the new mother begins nursing, the estrogens and progesterone fall to their initial levels, and lactation hormones keep them suppressed. The uterus thus lies quiescent until frequent lactation ends, which triggers the return to ovulation.

If conception does not take place after ovulation, all the ovarian hormones also drop to their initial levels, and menstruation—the shedding of part of the uterine lining—begins. The lining is divided into three layers: a basal layer that is constantly maintained, and two superficial layers, which shed and regrow with each menstrual cycle. All mammals undergo cyclical changes in the state of the endometrium. In most mammals the sloughed-off layers are resorbed into the body if fertilization does not take place. But in some higher primates, including humans, some of the shed endometrium is not resorbed. The shed lining, along with some blood, flows from the body through the vaginal opening, a process that in humans typically lasts from three to five days.

Of course, physiological facts alone do not explain why so many human groups have infused a bodily function with symbolic meaning. And so in 1986 Strassmann found herself driving through the Sahel region of West Africa at the peak of the hot season, heading for a sandstone cliff called the Bandiagara Escarpment, in Mali. There, permanent Dogon villages of mud or stone houses dotted the rocky plateau. The menstrual huts were obvious: round, low-roofed buildings set apart from the rectangular dwellings of the rest of the village.

The Dogon are a society of millet and onion farmers who endorse polygyny, and they maintain their traditional culture despite the occasional visits of outsiders. In a few Dogon villages, in fact, tourists are fairly common, and ethnographers had frequently studied the Dogon language, religion and social structure before Strassmann's arrival. But her visit was the first time someone from the outside wanted to delve into an intimate issue in such detail.

It took Strassmann a series of hikes among villages, and long talks with male elders under the thatched-roof shelters where they typically gather, to find the appropriate sites for her research. She gained permission for her study in fourteen villages, eventually choosing two. That exceptional welcome, she thinks, emphasized the universality of her interests. "I'm working on all the things that really matter to [the Dogon]—fertility, economics—so they never questioned my motives or wondered why I would be interested in these things," she says. "It seemed obvious to them." She set up shop for the next two and a half years in a stone house in the village, with no running water or electricity. Eating the daily fare of the Dogon, millet porridge, she and a research assistant began to integrate themselves into village life, learning the language, getting to know people and tracking visits to the menstrual huts.

Following the movements of menstruating women was surprisingly easy. The menstrual huts are situated outside the walled compounds of the village, but in full view of the men's thatched-roof shelters. As the men relax under their shelters, they can readily see who leaves the huts in the morning and returns to them in the evening. And as nonmenstruating women pass the huts on their way to and from the fields or to other compounds, they too can see who is spending the night there. Strassmann found that when she left her house in the evening to take data, any of the villagers could accurately predict whom she would find in the menstrual huts.

The huts themselves are cramped, dark buildings—hardly places where a woman might go to escape the drudgery of work or to avoid an argument with her husband or a co-wife. The huts sometimes become so crowded that some occupants are forced outside—making the women even more conspicuous. Although babies and toddlers can go with their mothers to the huts, the women consigned there are not allowed to spend time with the rest of their families. They must cook with special pots, not their usual household possessions. Yet they are still expected to do their usual jobs, such as working in the fields.

Why, Strassmann wondered, would anyone put up with such conditions?

The answer, for the Dogon, is that a menstruating woman is a threat to the sanctity of religious altars, where men pray and make sacrifices for the protection of their fields, their families and their village. If menstruating women come near the altars, which are situated both indoors and outdoors, the Dogon believe that their aura of pollution will ruin the altars and bring calamities upon the village. The belief is so ingrained that the women themselves have internalized it, feeling its burden of responsibility and potential guilt. Thus violations of the taboo are rare, because a menstruating woman who breaks the rules knows that she is personally responsible if calamities occur.

Nevertheless, Strassmann still thought a more functional explanation for menstrual taboos might also exist, one closely related to reproduction. As she was well aware, even before her studies among the Dogon, people around the world have a fairly sophisticated view of how reproduction works. In general, people everywhere know full well that menstruation signals the absence of a pregnancy and the possibility of another one. More precisely, Strassmann could frame her hypothesis by reasoning as follows: Across cultures, men and women recognize that a lack of menstrual cycling in a woman implies she is either pregnant, lactating or menopausal. Moreover, at least among natural-fertility cultures that do not practice birth control, continual cycles during peak reproductive years imply to people in those cultures that a woman is sterile. Thus, even though people might not be able to pinpoint ovulation, they can easily identify whether a woman will soon be ready to conceive on the basis of whether she is menstruating. And that leads straight to Strassmann's insightful hypothesis about the role of menstrual taboos: information about menstruation can be a means of tracking paternity.

"There are two important pieces of information for assessing paternity," Strassmann notes: timing of intercourse and timing of menstruation. "By forcing women to signal menstruation, men are trying to gain equal access to one part of that critical information." Such information, she explains, is crucial to Dogon men, because they invest so many resources in their own offspring. Descent is marked through the male line; land and the food that comes from the land is passed down from fathers to sons. Information about paternity is thus crucial to a man's entire lineage. And because each man has as many as four wives, he cannot possibly track them all. So forcing women to signal their menstrual periods, or lack thereof, helps men avoid cuckoldry.

To test her hypothesis, Strassmann tracked residence in the menstrual huts for 736 consecutive days, collecting data on 477 complete cycles. She noted who was at each hut and how long each woman stayed. She also collected urine from ninety-three women over a ten-week period, to check the correlation between residence in the menstrual hut and the fact of menstruation.

The combination of ethnographic records and urinalyses showed that the Dogon women mostly play by the rules. In 86 percent of the hormonally detected menstruations, women went to the hut. Moreover, none of the tested women went to the hut when they were not menstruating. In the remaining 14 percent of the tested menstruations, women stayed home from the hut, in violation of the taboo, but some were near menopause and so not at high risk for pregnancy. More important, none of the women who violated the taboo did it twice in a row. Even they were largely willing to comply.

Thus, Strassmann concluded, the huts do indeed convey a fairly reliable signal, to men and to everyone else, about the status of a woman's fertility. When she leaves the hut, she is considered ready to conceive. When she stops going to the hut, she is evidently pregnant or menopausal. And women of prime reproductive age who visit the hut on a regular basis are clearly infertile.

It also became clear to Strassmann that the Dogon do indeed use that information to make paternity decisions. In several cases a man was forced to marry a pregnant woman, simply because everyone knew that the man had been the woman's first sexual partner after her last visit to the menstrual hut. Strassmann followed one case in which a child was being brought up by a man because he was the mother's first sexual partner after a hut visit, even though the woman soon married a different man. (The woman already knew she was pregnant by the first man at the time of her marriage, and she did not visit the menstrual hut before she married. Thus the truth was obvious to everyone, and the real father took the child.)

In general, women are cooperative players in the game because without a man, a woman has no way to support herself or her children. But women follow the taboo reluctantly. They complain about going to the hut. And if their husbands convert from the traditional religion of the Dogon to a religion that does not impose menstrual taboos, such as Islam or Christianity, the women quickly cease visiting the hut. Not that such a religious conversion quells a man's interest in his wife's fidelity: far from it. But the rules change. Perhaps the sanctions of the new religion against infidelity help keep women faithful, so the men can relax their guard. Or perhaps the men are willing to trade the reproductive advantages of the menstrual taboo for the economic benefits gained by converting to the new religion. Whatever the case, Strassmann found an almost perfect correlation between a husband's religion and his wives' attendance at the hut. In sum, the taboo is established by men, backed by supernatural forces, and internalized and accepted by women until the men release them from the belief.

But beyond the cultural machinations of men and women that Strassmann expected to find, her data show something even more fundamental—and surprising—about female biology. On average, she calculates, a woman in a natural-fertility population such as the Dogon has only about 110 menstrual periods in her lifetime. The rest of the time she will be prepubescent, pregnant, lactating or menopausal. Women in industrialized cultures, by contrast, have more than three times as many cycles: 350 to 400, on average, in a lifetime. They reach menarche (their first menstruation) earlier—at age twelve and a half, compared with the onset age of sixteen in natural-fertility cultures. They have fewer babies, and they lactate hardly at all. All those factors lead women in the industrialized world to a lifetime of nearly continuous menstrual cycling.

The big contrast in cycling profiles during the reproductive years can be traced specifically to lactation. Women in more traditional societies spend most of their reproductive years in lactation amenorrhea, the state in which the hormonal changes required for nursing suppress ovulation and inhibit menstruation. And it is not just that the Dogon bear more children (eight to nine on average); they also nurse each child on demand rather than in scheduled bouts, all through the night as well as the day, and intensely enough that ovulation simply stops for about twenty months per child. Women in industrialized societies typically do not breast-feed as intensely (or at all), and rarely breast-feed each child for as long as the Dogon women do. (The average for American women is four months.)

The Dogon experience with menstruation may be far more typical of the human condition over most of evolutionary history than is the standard menstrual experience in industrialized nations. If so, Strassmann's findings alter some of the most closely held beliefs about female biology. Contrary to what the Western medical establishment might think, it is not particularly "normal" to menstruate each month. The female body, according to Strassmann, is biologically designed to spend much more time in lactation amenorrhea than in menstrual cycling. That in itself suggests that oral contraceptives, which alter hormone levels to suppress ovulation and produce a bleeding, could be forcing a continual state of cycling for which the body is ill-prepared. Women might be better protected against reproductive cancers if their contraceptives mimicked lactation amenorrhea and depressed the female reproductive hormones, rather than forcing the continual ebb and flow of menstrual cycles.

Strassmann's data also call into question a recently popularized idea about menstruation: that regular menstrual cycles might be immunologically beneficial for women. In 1993 the controversial writer Margie Profet, whose ideas about evolutionary and reproductive biology have received vast media attention, proposed in *The Quarterly Review of Biology* that menstruation could have such an adaptive value. She noted that viruses and bacteria regularly enter the female body on the backs of sperm, and she hypothesized that the best way to get them out is to flush them out. Here, then, was a positive, adaptive role for something unpleasant, an evolutionary reason for suffering cramps each month. Menstruation, according to Profet, had evolved to rid the body of pathogens. The "anti-pathogen" theory was an exciting hypothesis, and it helped win Profet a MacArthur Foundation award. But Strassmann's work soon showed that Profet's ideas could not be supported because of one simple fact: under less-industrialized conditions, women menstruate relatively rarely.

Instead, Strassmann notes, if there is an adaptive value to menstruation, it is ultimately a strategy to conserve the body's resources. She estimates that maintaining the endometrial lining during the second half of the ovarian cycle takes substantial metabolic energy. Once the endometrium is built up and ready to receive a fertilized egg, the tissue requires a sevenfold metabolic increase to remain rich in blood and ready to support a pregnancy. Hence, if no pregnancy is forthcoming, it makes a lot of sense for the body to let part of the endometrium slough off and then regenerate itself, instead of maintaining that rather costly but unneeded tissue. Such energy conservation is common among vertebrates: male rhesus monkeys have shrunken testes during their nonbreeding season, Burmese pythons shrink

their guts when they are not digesting, and hibernating animals put their metabolisms on hold.

Strassmann also suggests that periodically ridding oneself of the endometrium could make a difference to a woman's long-term survival. Because female reproductive hormones affect the brain and other tissues, the metabolism of the entire body is involved during cycling. Strassmann estimates that by keeping hormonal low through half the cycle, a woman can save about six days' worth of energy for every four nonconceptive cycles. Such caloric conservation might have proved useful to early hominids who lived by hunting and gathering, and even today it might be helpful for women living in less affluent circumstances than the ones common in the industrialized West.

But perhaps the most provocative implications of Strassmann's work have to do with women's health. In 1994 a group of physicians and anthropologists published a paper, also in *The Quarterly Review of Biology,* suggesting that the reproductive histories and lifestyles of women in industrialized cultures are at odds with women's naturally evolved biology, and that the differences lead to greater risks of reproductive cancers. For example, the investigators estimated that women in affluent cultures may have a hundredfold greater risk of breast cancer than do women who subsist by hunting and gathering. The increased risk is probably caused not only by low levels of exercise and a high-fat diet, but also by a relatively high number of menstrual cycles over a lifetime. Repeated exposure to the hormones of the ovarian cycle—because of early menarche, late menopause, lack of pregnancy and little or no breast-feeding—is implicated in other reproductive cancers as well.

Those of us in industrialized cultures have been running an experiment on ourselves. The body evolved over millions of years to move across the landscape looking for food, to live in small kin-based groups, to make babies at intervals of four years or so and to invest heavily in each child by nursing intensely for years. How many women now follow those traditional patterns? We move little, we rely on others to get our food, and we rarely reproduce or lactate. Those culturally initiated shifts in lifestyles may pose biological risks.

Our task is not to overcome that biology, but to work with it. Now that we have a better idea of how the female body was designed, it may be time to rework our lifestyles and change some of our expectations. It may be time to borrow from our distant past or from our contemporaries in distant cultures, and treat our bodies more as nature intended.

**MEREDITH F. SMALL** is a professor of anthropology at Cornell University in Ithaca, New York. Her latest book, *Our Babies, Ourselves: How Biology And Culture Shape The Way We Parent,* was published in May 1998 [see Laurence A. Marschall's review in *Books in Brief,* November/December 1998].

This article is reprinted from *The Sciences,* January/February 1999, pp. 24–29. Copyright © 1999 by The New York Academy of Sciences. www.nyas.org. Reprinted by permission of Blackwell Publishing, Ltd. For subscription, email: publicationse@nyas.org

# Body Dissatisfaction in Adolescent Females and Males: Risk and Resilience

KATHERINE PRESNELL, PhD, SARAH KATE BEARMAN, PhD, AND MARY CLARE MADELEY, BA

One of the most remarkable and consistent research findings is the overwhelming prevalence of weight and shape-related concerns among adolescents. Estimates from community samples of adolescents suggest that as many as 46% of girls and 26% of boys report significant distress about their body size and shape, while only 12% of girls and 17% of boys indicate that they are satisfied with their body shape (Neumark-Sztainer, Story, Hannan, Perry, & Irving, 2002; Ricciardelli & McCabe, 2001). In fact, body dissatisfaction has become so commonplace in Western culture that it has been termed a "normative discontent" (Rodin, Silberstein, & Striegel-Moore, 1985). This is especially troubling because, at the upper end of the continuum, body dissatisfaction is associated with high levels of subjective distress, unhealthy weight control behaviors, and extreme methods of altering appearance, such as cosmetic surgery and steroid use (Neumark-Sztainer, Paxton, Hannan, Haines, & Story, 2006).

> **As many as 46% of girls and 26% of boys report significant distress about their body size and shape.**

Body image is a broad term comprised of an individual's internal perceptions, thoughts, and evaluation of their outward physical appearance. Body dissatisfaction is one component of body image, and refers to the subjective negative evaluation of some aspect one's physical appearance (Thompson, Heinberg, Altabe, & Tantleff-Dunn, 1999). Body dissatisfaction has been consistently shown to place adolescents at increased risk for the development and maintenance of disordered eating (Stice & Shaw, 2002), since strategies such as extreme dietary restriction or compensatory measures may be used in an attempt to alter weight and shape. Moreover, body image concerns are often resistant to change during treatment for eating disorders, and persistent body image disturbances are associated with relapse in anorexia and bulimia nervosa (Keel, Dorer, Franko, Jackson, & Herzog, 2005). Body dissatisfaction is also a strong predictor of depressed mood and low self-esteem among adolescents (Paxton, Neumark-Sztainer, Hannan, & Eisenberg, 2006). The negative impact of body dissatisfaction on a range of psychological problems underscores the need to explore factors that contribute to its development. Recent research also suggests that reducing body dissatisfaction may be successful in preventing the onset of depression and eating pathology (Bearman, Stice, & Chase, 2003).

Adolescence is a critical developmental period, bringing numerous physical changes, social challenges, and role transitions that increase vulnerability to body dissatisfaction. Theories of the development of body dissatisfaction highlight multiple contributing factors, including individual, familial, peer, and sociocultural influences. This article will highlight factors that influence the development of body dissatisfaction during adolescence, and consider protective factors that may decrease adolescents' risk of body image concerns. Understanding the mechanisms that link these factors to body dissatisfaction can help guide the development of effective prevention interventions.

## Sociocultural Influences
### Ideal-Body Internalization

Beauty standards that are sanctioned by an individual's culture are hypothesized to influence how individuals perceive and evaluate their bodies. Western culture currently endorses an ultra-thin figure for women and a lean, muscular one for men. Pressure to conform to these ideals is evident in messages from the media, parents, and peers. As these ideals become increasingly difficult to attain, a sense of dissatisfaction often develops in those who place high importance on achieving them. Historically, there has been greater sociocultural emphasis on appearance and thinness for females, and research indicates consistently higher rates of body dissatisfaction among females in relation to males (Thompson et al., 1999). However, body dissatisfaction is also a substantial concern among adolescent boys. Adolescent boys are more likely than girls to engage in behaviors to increase weight and musculature, and there is evidence that boys are divided between those who desire to lose weight and those who wish to gain weight and musculature (e.g., Neumark-Sztainer et al, 1999). Thus, there may be two pathways to body dissatisfaction among boys—weight concerns and muscularity concerns—whereas girls consistently report a desire to be thinner. Regardless of gender, however, failure to attain a highly-valued ideal has been shown to lead to body dissatisfaction (Jones, 2004).

## Differences in Ideals across Cultures

There is some evidence that beauty ideals and body dissatisfaction vary among cultural or ethnic groups. Ethnic groups that place greater emphasis on thinness tend to have higher levels of body dissatisfaction, particularly as obesity rates rise. For example, African American girls generally endorse a larger body ideal and report greater body satisfaction than Caucasian girls (Perez & Joiner, 2003). However, recent research indicates that this gap in body dissatisfaction may be decreasing, and that the most pronounced disparity occurs during the college-age years (Roberts, Cash, Feingold, & Johnson, 2006). Other research also suggests few differences in body dissatisfaction among African American, Asian American, and Hispanic women (Grabe & Hyde, 2006). Moreover, ethnic status failed to moderate the relation between body dissatisfaction and depression for girls, suggesting that regardless of ethnic identity, dissatisfaction with one's body increases the risk of depression (Siegel, 2002).

## Media Influences

Use of media that conveys messages about body ideals is consistently associated with greater body dissatisfaction, and experimental exposure to images portraying the thin-ideal result in moderate decreases in self-esteem and increases in body dissatisfaction among females (e.g., Stice & Shaw, 1994). Some evidence suggests that media and peer influences are more influential during adolescence than parental influences for girls (Shroff & Thompson, 2006), but that the effect of media may be less pronounced among boys (McCabe & Ricciardelli, 2001).

## Parent and Peer Influences

Although societal norms regarding ideal body shape and weight are transmitted in a variety of ways, messages from one's immediate subculture may be particularly salient in communicating these values. These may be transmitted through parental modeling of eating and body-related attitudes and behaviors, as well as through direct comments about weight and encouragement of weight loss. Adolescent girls perceive greater feedback from their mothers to lose weight and increase muscle tone than do boys, and this perception is greater for girls who are heavier (McCabe & Ricciardelli, 2001). Direct messages from parents encouraging their children to lose weight predict higher drive for thinness and body dissatisfaction among daughters, and appear to have a greater influence than parental modeling of dieting behaviors (Wertheim, Martin, Prior, Sanson, & Smart, 2002).

Relatedly, criticism and teasing about appearance have been associated with greater body dissatisfaction, although this may differ by gender. Boys tend to receive more messages from family and friends regarding increasing muscles and these messages decrease over time, whereas girls receive more messages regarding weight loss, and these messages increase over time (McCabe & Ricciardelli, 2005). For both adolescent boys and girls, messages from their parents and closest same-sex friend resulted in attempts to change physical size and shape.

In addition to direct pressure, lack of social support or support that is perceived as conditional on meeting appearance expectations, may promote body dissatisfaction. Indeed, deficits in social support from parents and peers predicted body dissatisfaction for both adolescent girls and boys (Bearman, Presnell, Martinez, & Stice, 2006).

# Biological Factors
## Body Mass and Pubertal Status

Biological factors may play a role in the development of body dissatisfaction when they deviate from culturally-sanctioned attractiveness ideals. Pubertal changes, including increased body fat, move girls farther from the thin-ideal. Increasing body mass is consistently associated with greater body dissatisfaction among girls, although dissatisfaction is not always associated with being objectively overweight, as many normal-weight females also express displeasure with their bodies (Presnell, Bearman, & Stice, 2004). Boys, however, may have a more complex relationship between body mass and body dissatisfaction. Overweight boys report lower self-esteem and greater self-consciousness than normal-weight boys, yet adolescent boys report nearly equal rates of wanting to lose versus gain weight, suggesting the optimal weight range may fall in the middle (Blyth et al., 1981). Indeed, research suggests that body dissatisfaction is greatest for boys who are over or underweight, with those of average weight being the most satisfied with their appearance (Presnell, Bearman, & Stice, 2004). Both types of concerns have been associated with elevated body dissatisfaction among boys, although they may employ different strategies to achieve this ideal weight, including dieting to reduce body mass, or excessive exercise and steroid use to increase size and muscularity (Ricciardelli & McCabe, 2003).

Pubertal timing may also be associated with body dissatisfaction. McCabe and Ricciardelli (2004) noted that early-maturing and on-time girls reported higher levels of body dissatisfaction than girls whose pubertal development was delayed relative to peers. Again, this may be because pubertal increases in body size move girls farther from the ideal. In contrast, boys who physically matured earlier than their same-sex peers had the highest levels of body satisfaction. However, other research suggests that pubertal status may interact with other variables, such as initiating dating, to place adolescents at risk for body dissatisfaction (Cauffman & Steinberg, 1996).

# Individual Risk Factors
## *Negative Mood*

Mood disturbances have also been implicated in the development of body dissatisfaction because depressed mood induces selective attention to negative information about oneself and the world. This may result in a focus on displeasing aspects of one's body and foster negative comparisons to others. Experimental studies indicate that temporary increases in negative mood result in temporary increases body dissatisfaction in girls, suggesting at least a short-term relation (Baker, Williamson, & Sylve, 1995).

However, prospective studies have failed to demonstrate this relationship, perhaps because the experimental studies may not represent the types of mood disturbances experienced outside of the laboratory. There is some evidence that this relation may differ by gender, with boys showing a stronger relation between negative affect and body dissatisfaction than girls (Presnell et al., 2004). Additionally, negative affect also predicted body change strategies in a sample of adolescent boys (Ricciardelli & McCabe, 2003).

# Dieting

Adolescents who believe that being thin will result in psychosocial benefits may turn to dieting as a means of altering their physique. Adolescent girls in particular may attempt to counter pubertal weight gain by restricting their caloric intake. However, research suggests that self-reported attempts to restrict caloric intake predict weight gain, rather than weight loss (Stice et al., 1999). Thus, dieting may increase frustration and reduce feelings of self-efficacy for producing weight change. Indeed, self-reported dieting attempts predict increases in body dissatisfaction among both girls and boys (Bearman et al., 2006). Despite the suggestion that boys may be more likely to strive to achieve bulk in the form of muscle rather than to lose weight, boys who express concern about weight loss and dieting are also more likely to express body dissatisfaction (Jones & Crawford, 2005). Additionally, boys with lower levels of body satisfaction are more likely to diet, and less likely to engage in activities that might increase muscle, such as physical activity (Neumark-Sztainer et al., 2006).

**Self-reported attempts to restrict caloric intake predict weight gain, rather than weight loss.**

# Potential Protective Factors

Few studies have identified factors that either enhance body image or buffer the negative effects of risk factors for body dissatisfaction. To date, this work has primarily focused on positive parental relationships. Feeling supported by one's immediate social network may serve as a protective factor from the myriad pressures that are hypothesized to foster body dissatisfaction. One prospective study found that a supportive maternal relationship was associated with increased body satisfaction (Barker & Galambos, 2003). Another found that feeling close to either parent was associated with fewer concurrent weight and eating concerns among girls, but the prospective association between parental closeness and weight concerns was not significant (Swarr & Richards, 1996). Several studies have demonstrated no impact of parental relationships or acceptance on body dissatisfaction for boys (e.g. Barker & Galambos, 2003).

It will be important for future research to consider other variables that may mitigate the impact of body dissatisfaction. Theoretically, cognitive factors such as attributional style or perceived control, which have been linked to disorders such as depression and anxiety, may be associated with body dissatisfaction. Control-related beliefs play a role in the impact of life stressors on depressed mood and perceived helplessness regarding the future (Weisz, Southam-Gerow & McCarty, 2001). It is possible that individuals who have control-related beliefs regarding their weight and shape may face less risk of body dissatisfaction because they believe they are capable of changing their appearance or adapting to those displeasing aspects. Higher levels of perceived control have been shown to act as protective factors for depression among youth (Weisz, Sweeney, Proffitt, & Carr, 1993); future research should examine the role control related beliefs play in the development of body dissatisfaction, as well as other potential buffering factors that have been implicated in research of other related disorders.

# Conclusions

Body dissatisfaction has been identified as one of the most potent and consistent risk factors for eating disorders, and contributes significantly to poor self-esteem and depression among adolescents. An understanding of the factors that increase the risk for body dissatisfaction can help guide prevention efforts for these outcomes. This article has highlighted internalization of socially-prescribed body ideals, body mass, media influences, and messages from parents and peers as key risk factors for the development of body dissatisfaction, whereas others have received less consistent support. Given the complexity of the development of body image concerns, interventions aimed at reducing body dissatisfaction will likely need to target multiple factors, including individual, familial, and sociocultural factors. Interventions that reduce sociocultural pressures to be thin and educate adolescents to more critically evaluate messages from the media hold promise in reducing body dissatisfaction. Unfortunately, there is relatively little research on protective factors that may aid youth in developing a positive body image. Additional research is needed to determine how best to foster greater body satisfaction or mitigate the effects of established risk factors.

# References

Baker, J.D., Williamson, D.A., & Sylve, C. (1995). Body image disturbance, memory bias, and body dysphoria: Effects of negative mood induction. *Behavior Therapy, 26,* 747–759.

Barker, E.T., & Galambos, N.L. (2003). Body dissatisfaction of adolescent girls and boys: Risk and resource factors. *Journal of Early Adolescence, 23,* 141–165.

Bearman, S.K., Presnell, K., Martinez, E., & Stice, E. (2006). The skinny on body dissatisfaction: A longitudinal study of adolescent girls and boys. *Journal of Youth and Adolescence, 35,* 229–241.

Bearman, S.K., Stice, E., & Chase, A. (2003). Evaluation of an intervention targeting both depressive and bulimic pathology: A randomized prevention trial. *Behavior Therapy, 34*(3), 277–293.

Blyth, D.A., Simmons, R.G., Bulcroft, R., Felt, D., Van Cleave, E.F., & Bush, D.M. (1981). The effects of physical development in self-image and satisfaction with body image for early adolescent males. *Research in Community and Mental Health, 2,* 43–73.

Cauffman, E., & Steinberg, L. (1996). Interactive effects of menarcheal status and dating on dieting and disordered eating among adolescent girls. *Developmental Psychology, 32,* 631–635.

Grabe, S. & Hyde, J.S. (2006). Ethnicity and body dissatisfaction among women in the United States: A meta-analysis. *Psychological Bulletin, 132*(4), 622–640.

Jones, D.C. (2004). Body image among adolescent girls and boys: A longitudinal study. *Developmental Psychology, 40,* 823–835.

Jones, D.C., & Crawford, J.K. (2005). Adolescent boys and body image: Weight and muscularity concerns as dual pathways to body dissatisfaction. *Journal of Youth and Adolescence, 34*(6), 629–636.

Keel, P.K., Dorer, D.J., Franko, D.L., Jackson, S.C., & Herzog, D.B. (2005). Postremission predictors of relapse in women with eating disorders. *American journal of Psychiatry, 162,* 2,263–2,268.

McCabe, M.P., & Ricciardelli, L.A. (2001). Parent, peer, and media influences on body image and strategies to both increase and decrease body size among adolescent boys and girls. *Adolescence, 36,* 225–240.

McCabe, M.P., & Ricciardelli, L.A. (2004). A longitudinal study of pubertal timing and extreme body change behaviors among adolescent boys and girls. *Adolescence, 39,* 145–166.

McCabe, M.P., & Ricciardelli, L.A., (2005). A prospective study of pressures from parents, peers, and the media on extreme weight change behaviors among adolescent boys and girls. *Behaviour Research and Therapy, 43,* 653–668.

Neumark-Sztainer, D., Paxton, S.J., Hannan, P.J., Haines, J., & Story, M. (2006). Does body satisfaction matter? Five-year longitudinal associations between body satisfaction and health behaviors in adolescent females and males. *Journal of Adolescent Health, 39,* 244–251.

Neumark-Sztainer, D., Story, M., Falkner, N.H., Beuhring, T., & Resnick, M.D. (1999). Sociodemographic and personal characteristics of adolescents engaged in weight loss and weight/muscle gain behaviors: Who is doing what? *Preventive Medicine, 28,* 40–50.

Neumark-Sztainer, D., Story, M., Hannan, P.J., Perry, C.L., & Irving, L.M. (2002). Weight-related concerns and behaviors among overweight and nonoverweight adolescents: Implications for preventing weight-related disorders. *Archives of Pediatric Adolescent Medicine, 156,* 171–178.

Paxton, S.J., Neumark-Sztainer, D., Hannan, P.J., & Eisenberg, M.E. (2006). Body dissatisfaction prospectively predicts depressive mood and low self-esteem in adolescent girls and boys. *Journal of Clinical Child and Adolescent Psychology, 35,* 539–549.

Perez, M., & Joiner, T.E. (2003). Body image dissatisfaction and disordered eating in black and white women. *International Journal of Eating Disorders, 33,* 342–350.

Presnell, K., Bearman, S.K., & Slice, E. (2004). Risk factors for body dissatisfaction in adolescent boys and girls: A prospective study. *International Journal of Eating Disorders, 36,* 389–401.

Ricciardelli, L.A., & McCabe, M.P. (2001). Dietary restraint and negative affect as mediators of body dissatisfaction and bulimic behavior in adolescent girls and boys. *Behaviour Research and Therapy, 39,* 1,317–1,328.

Ricciardelli, L.A. & McCabe, M.P. (2003). Sociocultural influences on body image and body changes among adolescent boys and girls. *Journal of Social Psychology, 143,* 5–26.

Roberts, A., Cash, T.F., Feingold, A., & Johnson, B.T. (2006). Are black-white differences in females' body dissatisfaction decreasing? A meta-analytic review. *Journal of Consulting and Clinical Psychology, 74,* 1,121–1,131.

Rodin, J., Silberstein, L., & Striegel-Moore, R. (1985). *Women and Weight: A Normative Discontent.* Nebraska Symposium on Motivation, Lincoln, Nebraska: University of Nebraska Press, 267–307.

Shroff, H., & Thompson, J.K. (2006). The tripartite influence model of body image and eating disturbance: A replication with adolescent girls. *Body Image, 3,* 17–23.

Siegel, J.M. (2002). Body image change and adolescent depressive symptoms. *Journal of Adolescent Research, 17,* 27–41.

Stice, E., Cameron, R.P., Killen, J.D. & Taylor, C.B. (1999). Naturalistic weight-reduction efforts prospectively predict growth in relative weight and onset of obesity among female adolescents. *Journal of Consulting & Clinical Psychology, 67,* 967–974.

Stice, E., & Shaw, H.E. (1994). Adverse effects of the media portrayed thin-ideal on women and linkages to bulimic symptomatology. *Journal of Social and Clinical Psychology, 13,* 288–308.

Stice, E., & Shaw, H.E. (2002). Role of body dissatisfaction in the onset and maintenance of eating pathology: A synthesis of research findings. *Journal of Psychosomatic Research, 53,* 985–993.

Swarr, A.E., & Richards, M.H. (1996). Longitudinal effects of adolescent girls' pubertal development, perceptions of pubertal timing, and parental relations on eating problems. *Developmental Psychology, 32,* 636–646.

Thompson, J.K., Heinberg, L.J., Altabe, M., & Tantleff-Dunn, S. (1999) *Exacting Beauty: Theory, Assessment, and Treatment of Body Image Disturbance.* Washington, D.C.: American Psychological Association.

Weisz, J.R., Sweeney, L., Proffitt, V. & Carr, T. (1993). Control-related beliefs and self-reported depressive symptoms in late childhood. *Journal of Abnormal Psychology, 102,* 411–418.

Weisz, J., Southam-Gerow, M.A., & McCarty, C.A. (2001). Control-related beliefs and depressive symptoms in clinic-referred children and adolescents: Developmental differences and model specificity. *Journal of Abnormal Psychology, 110,* 97–109.

Wertheim, E.H., Martin, G., Prior, M., Sanson, A., & Smart, D. (2002). Parent influences in the transmission of eating and weight-related values and behaviors. *Eating Disorders, 10,* 321–334.

**KATHERINE PRESNELL,** PhD, is an Assistant Professor in the Department of Psychology at Southern Methodist University (SMU) and Director of the Weight and Eating Disorders Research Program at SMU. Her research focuses on understanding sociocultural, psychological, and behavioral risk factors that contribute to eating disorders and obesity, as well as developing effective prevention interventions for these disorders. **SARAH KATE BEARMAN,** PhD, is a postdoctoral fellow at the Judge Baker Children's Center, Harvard Medical School. Her research interests include the etiology and prevention of youth depression and body image concerns, as well as the effectiveness of evidence-based interventions for children in real-world settings. **MARY CLARE MADELEY,** BA, is a graduate student in the Department of Psychology at Southern Methodist University. Her research interests focus on risk factors for eating disorders.

From *The Prevention Researcher,* September 2007, pp. 3–6. Copyright © 2007 by Integrated Research Services, Inc. Reprinted by permission.

# When Sex Hurts

**If lovemaking is more agony than ecstasy, the problem may be medical. Now there's help.**

LISA COLLIER COOL

Thanks to recent advances, doctors have more effective treatments than ever for sexual pain. But zeroing in on the right diagnosis may be tricky, says Susan McSherry, M.D., who is affiliated with Tulane Medical School, in New Orleans. "If the first treatment doesn't help, keep working with your doctor. Painful sex isn't something you have to grit your teeth and tolerate. It's usually very treatable." Below are some common problems—and solutions.

## Infections

Vaginal infections (collectively known as vaginitis) are so common that more than 75 percent of women can expect to develop at least one during their lifetime. The usual culprits are bacteria (bacterial vaginosis), yeast, and *Trichomonas* microorganisms, which are responsible for trichomoniasis, a sexually transmitted infection.

**Symptoms.** With some infections, you may have an unpleasant-smelling discharge, painful urination, and, in some cases, lower abdominal discomfort—plus itching and burning of the vagina and outer labia. But with other forms of vaginitis, there may be no special symptoms, says Erica V. Breneman, M.D., an obstetrician-gynecologist at Kaiser Permanente in Oakland, California.

**During sex.** The irritation may worsen when you're having intercourse or afterward.

**Diagnosis.** If itching is your main symptom and you have been diagnosed with a yeast infection in the past, try an over-the-counter medication. But if the problem doesn't clear up in a few days, see a gynecologist; left untreated, some forms of vaginitis can lead to more serious problems, including infertility. Your doctor will do a pelvic exam and examine your vaginal fluid for microorganisms.

**Treatment.** Depending on the cause, antibiotics, antifungal drugs, or medicated vaginal creams or suppositories. (For some infections, both partners need to be treated.) Symptoms should clear up—and sex should be comfortable—within several days.

## Endometriosis

This disorder occurs when cells from the uterine lining (the endometrium) migrate to other parts of the abdomen, then swell and bleed during your period but aren't discharged as the uterine lining is. Over time, this misplaced tissue often causes chronic inflammation, scars, and weblike adhesions, most commonly on the ovaries or fallopian tubes, on the outer surface of the uterus, or on the internal area between your vagina and rectum.

**Symptoms.** Pain in the abdomen or lower back, severe menstrual cramps, fatigue, diarrhea, and/or painful bowel movements during your period.

**During sex.** Often there is deep, burning pain in the pelvis, abdomen, or lower back.

**Diagnosis.** In a procedure called laparoscopy, a gynecologist examines your pelvic organs using a lighted tube inserted through a small incision in your abdomen. Small lesions can usually be removed during the same procedure.

**Treatment.** For mild or moderate endometriosis, pain medication may be enough. But if you have severe cramping, or if the condition is interfering with your ability to become pregnant, or in order to suppress further growth of the lesions, you may need surgery or hormone treatment that temporarily stops your period. Neither of these is a cure, but two thirds of women improve after surgery; for the hormone treatment, the rate is little more than half.

As for sex, you may find it's more comfortable during the week or two after your period rather than later in your cycle. And choosing a position that avoids deep penetration—side by side, for example, or with the woman on top—may help too.

**"Painful sex isn't something you have to grit your teeth and tolerate," says one expert.**

# Fibroids

An estimated 20 to 30 percent of American women are affected by these noncancerous masses of muscle and fibrous tissue that grow inside the uterus (or, occasionally, outside). No one knows why some women are more prone, but a report from the National Institute of Child Health and Development shows that women who have had two or more children are far less likely to develop fibroids than those who have never given birth.

**Symptoms.** Some women are never bothered by their fibroids. But others may have heavy and painful periods, midmonth bleeding, a feeling of fullness in the lower abdomen, frequent urination, constipation, bloating, and lower back pain.

**During sex.** Your husband's thrusting can set off deep pelvic pain, due to pressure on your uterus.

**Diagnosis.** A routine pelvic exam. If a fibroid is detected, your doctor may use ultrasound or magnetic resonance imaging to check its size and location.

**Treatment.** For mild or occasional pelvic pain—including during sex—ibuprofen or other analgesics may be enough. If your fibroids need to be treated, there are several surgical approaches, as well as a new nonsurgical technique called fibroid embolization.

# Interstitial Cystitis (IC)

Unlike "regular" cystitis, which is caused by a bacterial infection, the cause of IC is a mystery. This chronic inflammation of the bladder wall strikes women almost exclusively.

**Symptoms.** Very frequent urination (up to 30 times a day) and/or burning and pressure before urination; chronic lower abdominal pain that may intensify before your period.

**During sex.** Intercourse frequently triggers painful flare-ups, "like a severe headache all over your pelvis," says Dr. McSherry. Some women also have vaginal spasms, lower back pain, or pain that radiates down the thighs.

**Diagnosis.** First, your doctor will rule out other causes. Then she'll perform a test called cystoscopy—in which the bladder is filled with fluid and examined for tiny hemorrhages (a telltale sign of IC).

**Treatment.** Elmiron is the only oral medication specifically approved for IC. But many other drugs are available to relieve symptoms: Some women are helped by certain antidepressants that have pain-blocking effects (such as Elavil) or anti-inflammatory drugs that are inserted into the bladder. The good

---

## A Mysterious Disorder

Imagine pain so piercing you can't even tolerate panty-hose rubbing against your genitals, much less sex. That's what vulvodynia can feel like, say sufferers, who may seek help from doctor after doctor, only to be dismissed as hypochondriacs. Part of the problem is that everything usually looks normal; women have no symptoms beyond persistent pain in the vulva, the skin folds around the vagina. (In a few cases, however, there may be inflammation.)

Experts don't know for sure what causes vulvodynia, though they theorize that nerve injury may play a role. Interestingly, over-the-counter products can trigger the condition in women who are pre-disposed, says Howard Glazer, Ph.D., associate professor in the department of obstetrics and gynecology at Cornell University Medical Center in New York City and codirector of the New York Center for Vulvovaginal Pain. "Some 85 percent of my patients tell me they treated what they thought was a yeast infection with an OTC cream or douche—and then developed pain that never went away." It may be they're re-acting to an irritant in the cream, Glazer suggests.

To diagnose the condition, your doctor may do what's called a Q-Tip Test, in which a cotton swab is used to gently check the vulva and the vaginal entrance for areas of pain and hypersensitivity. You may be able to relieve symptoms with medication (antidepressants, nerve blocks, or anticonvulsant drugs that also combat pain) or with biofeedback. In severe cases, surgery to remove the affected tissue may help.

---

news is that 85 percent of patients can be successfully treated with one or more of these therapies, says Dr. McSherry. As for sex, women may find it's more comfortable side by side and when they're fully aroused.

# Vaginal Dryness

The most common reason for this annoying (though not medically serious) problem is the drop in estrogen that takes place at menopause or during perimenopause—the three to six years before your periods actually stop. Some women also experience a decrease in lubrication after having a baby or while breast-feeding. Allergies, too, can trigger dryness. Soap is probably the biggest offender, but laundry detergent, fabric softeners, bubble bath, vaginal-hygiene products, and spermicidal creams or foams can all be culprits as well.

**Symptoms.** Chafing, irritation, and itching. At menopause, falling estrogen levels also cause the walls of your vagina to become thinner and less elastic.

**During sex.** Friction may leave you quite sore. Discomfort may occur only at penetration or during thrusting.

**Diagnosis.** Fairly self-evident, but check with your doctor if you suspect an allergy.

**Treatment.** Over-the-counter lubricants, such as Replens or Astroglide. At menopause, talk to your gynecologist about hormone replacement therapy or estrogen cream. For allergic dryness, try using mild liquid bath soaps and fragrance-free or hypoallergenic brands of laundry and cosmetic products. Try different brands of spermicides until you find a nonirritating one. And ask your doctor about taking antihistamines: That might be wise until you figure out what you are allergic to.

# Pelvic Congestion Syndrome (PCS)

There's some controversy about this syndrome: Not all doctors are convinced that it is a cause of pain during sex. Those who believe it is say that the disorder is triggered by varicose veins in the pelvis, a condition similar to varicose veins in the legs (and, indeed, about half the women with PCS also have the leg problem). In both cases, valves that normally keep the blood moving forward become leaky, allowing blood to flow backward and pool. As a result of the pressure, veins become large and bulgy. Most women develop the disorder after pregnancy, says Luis Navarro, M.D., director of The Vein Treatment Center, in New York City.

**Symptoms.** Aching, heaviness, pressure, or throbbing in the pelvis; sometimes visibly protruding veins in the genital area.

**During sex.** The discomfort intensifies during or after intercourse (as well as before or during your menstrual period).

**Diagnosis.** Several noninvasive tests, including the recently developed venography. During this procedure, a thin catheter is used to inject special dye into the pelvic veins, allowing the doctor to map blood flow with X rays.

**Treatment.** Tiny metal coils or a gluelike liquid are used to block off the affected area. The procedure has a success rate of 80 to 90 percent, says Dr. Navarro. But it can take a couple of weeks for symptoms to clear up.

From *Good Housekeeping*, March 2003, pp. 67–68, 71. Copyright © 2003 by Lisa Collier Cool. Reprinted by permission of the author.

# Health Behaviors, Prostate Cancer, and Masculinities

## *A Life Course Perspective*

JOHN OLIFFE

Statistical comparisons between men's and women's health outcomes have revealed that Australian men die younger than women and suffer higher rates of injury and most illnesses (Australian Institute of Health and Welfare 2004). Predominant men's health behaviors such as the adoption of activities that risk health, denial of illness, underuse of health care services, and poor uptake of health promoting strategies are strongly linked to men's poor health results (Gibson and Denner 2000; Huggins 1998; Lee and Owens 2002a; R. White 2002). Sociological theories of gender, especially masculinities, have been used to empirically and theoretically advance understandings about men's health behaviors with the ultimate goal of reducing men's high morbidity and mortality rates (Addis and Mahalik 2003; Courtenay 1998, 2000; International Longevity Center–USA [ILC] 2004; Lee and Owens 2002a, 2002b; O'Brien, Hunt, and Hart 2005; Sabo 2005; Watson 2000).

Influential works by Watson (2000) and Courtenay (1998, 2000), among others, have described five distinct connections between masculinity and men's health behaviors. First, men's perceived sense of role, place within society, and self-esteem are influenced by dominant ideals of masculinity, which make it difficult to promote their health (Courtenay 1998, 2000; Kilmartin 2000). This is especially true of Anglo-Australian cultures, which deem it "unmanly" to publicly maintain health and voluntarily seek regular medical "check-ups" (Connell 2000; Gibson and Denner 2000; Huggins 1998; Woods 2001). Men also take enormous health risks and perform heroic feats all because they want other men to grant them or acknowledge their manhood (Courtenay 1998; Kimmel 1994; Taylor, Stewart, and Parker 1998). Second, men's denial of illness or injury and suppression of affect, particularly in relation to pain, is informed by persistent myths of masculinity—such as the perception that it is tough to hold on to symptoms of ill health in the hope they will disappear and that only weak men respond to stress (O'Hehir, Scotney, and Anderson 1997; P. White, Young, and McTeer 1995). Reactive self-care, typically including the use of some form of self treatment and asking partners for advice before finally consulting a health care professional, is

a common behavior (A. White 2001; Ziguras 1998) and health only becomes a priority for men when they are under threat of illness or injury (Jones 1996; Mansfield, Addis, and Mahalik 2003). Third, when illness occurs—such as prostate cancer—a myriad of biographical disruptions (Bury 1982) can follow. Specifically, studies about information seeking (Broom 2005), diagnostic tests (Oliffe 2004), treatment-induced impotence (Gray, Fitch, Fergus, Mykhalovskiy, and Church 2002; Oliffe 2005), hormone therapy (Chapple and Ziebland 2002; Oliffe 2006), and spousal relationships (Fergus, Gray, and Fitch 2002) have indicated that many men are at odds with dominant ideals of masculinity as a result of being diagnosed and treated for prostate cancer but eventually reformulate or redefine their masculine identities.

Fourth, competence in health-related matters is commonly expressed through visible concern for one's health and caring for the health of others. Such practices are strongly linked to feminine ideals of fragility, gentleness, and nurturing, which are the antitheses of the robustness, stoicism, and self-reliance expected of men (Courtenay 2000, 2004; Lee and Owens 2002b; Robertson 2003; Watson 2000). Fifth, men and masculinity are puzzling concepts for medical professionals (Moynihan 1998; Seymour-Smith, Wetherell, and Phoenix 2002) and men's experiences of health care institutions and interactions with professionals can dissuade them from accessing services. Specifically, men's avoidance of health services has been linked to "male unfriendly" waiting rooms (Banks 2001); health care professionals' preoccupation with changing men's behaviors (Watson 2000); and the anonymity, loss of identity, and subsequent marginalized, subordinate masculinity that can occur when men enter health care institutions (Courtenay 2000).

It is important to note that these stereotypes do not reflect all men's health behaviors but rather represent a public discourse about men's health that men have to engage with (Hunt, Ford, Harkins, and Wyke 1999; Macintyre, Ford, and Hunt 1999; Macintyre, Hunt, and Sweeting 1996). Therefore, dominant ideals of masculinity such as power relations, physical prowess, stoicism, self-reliance, competitiveness, and independence, which underpin men's health behaviors, are descriptive rather than prescriptive (Lee and Owens 2002b). At the individual level, contextual insights to men's lives show diversity as well as commonality in the way men create their social realities and identities, including their gender (Lorber 2000). The plurality of masculinities has been used to describe differences in how closely men align to the aforementioned health and illness behaviors (Connell 1995, 1997, 2000).

Many factors influence individual decisions about health behaviors, and several theories have been developed to explain men's health behaviors—including the Health Belief Model, Transtheoretical (stages of change) Model, and Theory of Reasoned Action and Planned Behavior (Nutbeam and Harris 1999; Weiss and Lonnquist 2003). All of these theories are strongly influenced by the application of health psychology to behavior change and the relationship between the perception of potential risk and self-protective behavior (Nutbeam 1998). Most theories are based on the presumption that perceived risk is a primary motivator for the adoption of self-protective behavior (Nutbeam and Harris 1999). Many researchers have critically assessed such health behavior theories because they do not take into account the social and cultural contexts of men's lives (Buchbinder 1995; Gibbs and Oliffe 2004; Huggins 1998; ILC 2004; Lambevski et al. 2001; Thorogood 2002; Watson 2000; Woods 2001). Moreover, the espoused uniformity of men's health behaviors have been challenged because of the lack of empirical data about men's health care beliefs and practices (Fletcher, Higginbotham, and Dobson 2002; Lloyd 2001; Watson 2000). Increasingly, sociologically informed research, inclusive of the broader context of men's lives, cognizant of the dynamic interplay between microfactors (personal choices) and macrofactors (social-structural conditions), is suggested as the most constructive way to understand men's health behaviors (Watson 2000). From a theoretical perspective, social learning theory—a model where behavior and social environment are considered dynamic and reciprocal—is advocated as a way to develop strategies to engage men with their health based on empirical findings about men's lives (Blair 1995; Courtenay 2004; Gibbs and Oliffe 2004; Nutbeam and Harris 1999).

The current article responds to recommendations about the need for contextual understandings of men's health and illness behaviors by making available descriptions of participants' experiences over time and a gender analysis premised on the belief that "behavior" is influenced by age, history, social class, culture, and illness, all of which intersect with masculinity (Connell 2000; Courtenay 2000; Sabo 2005). Therefore, the following section, "Historical Perspectives of Australian Masculinities," is used to provide a brief background to some of the social contexts with which participants engaged throughout their lives.

# Historical Perspectives of Australian Masculinities

Many Anglo-Australian men born in the 1920s and 1930s grew up with specific gender roles and expectations that defined men's primary focus as the family breadwinner (Crotty 2001;

Oliffe 2002). The gendered division of labor during this period was strongly influenced by government policy, which in the early 20th century, set women's wages at 54 percent of men's (Connell et al. 1999). The superior monetary worth, along with the physical demands associated with many jobs, resulted in masculine communities in industries such as mining, railway, shipping, and agriculture. Heavy manual labor and poor working conditions were common and to "keep a job," resilient, enduring male bodies were required (Donaldson 1991). A functional view of men's health was predominant—where health was measured by the ability to labor and therefore earn money and provide for one's family. Typically the female partner, as the "housewife," supported her husband by looking after the health of the men and children in her life and through the provision of meals and housework (Lee and Owens 2002b).

Working outside the home also provided men with freedom, and after the Second World War, high average wages and eight-hour working days ensured leisure time was accessible for most men (Connell et al. 1999). Sport (predominantly "Australian Rules" football) became an important arena for the display of masculinity and the yardstick by which most men were judged (Epstein 1998). Pub culture established a masculine pattern of high alcohol consumption and binge drinking, swapping yarns, laughing raucously, and literally wallowing in the rituals of Aussie mateship (Conway 1985). Men's sporting and recreational activities, as well as paid employment, were strongly linked to physical performance and prowess, thus perpetuating the superiority of a tough, durable male body (Donaldson 1991).

From the 1940s to 1970s, the therapeutic model of health care in Australia was dominant and traded on the belief "that all social problems were caused by illness and that disease had nothing to do with either working conditions or the health hazards associated with poverty" (O'Connor-Fleming and Parker 2001, 13). The focus was on individual pathology and therapies designed to cure disease, and the period saw marked weakening of departments of public health and a shift of power and resources to hospital-based services (O'Connor-Fleming and Parker 2001). In the 1970s Australian men felt the impact of feminism that challenged public and domestic patriarchy and changed work practices making men less economically autonomous (Moore 1998). Models of public health were also changing, and a shift from diagnosis and treatment to disease prevention occurred after the 1970s. Health promotion became and remains one of the key concepts in the contemporary vision of Australian public health (O'Connor-Fleming and Parker 2001) and embraces actions directed at strengthening the skills and capabilities of people and changing social, environmental, and economic conditions that create and sustain health (Nutbeam 1998). However, despite such public health policy and service changes, many men from this older generation continue to devote themselves to traditional gender roles, and previously established work, leisure, domestic, and health care behaviors often continue in later life (Lee and Owens 2002b). Although this overview relates directly to Australia, much of the information reflects similar happenings in other western countries in Europe, Canada, and the United States.

# Method

Retrospective life course methods provide an effective way to develop contextual understandings about participants' health behaviors with time (Atchley and Barush 2004; Gambling and Carr 2004; Giele and Elder 1998; Jarviluoma, Moisala, and Vikko 2003; Lambevski et al. 2001; Morse and Field 1995; Watson 2000). As older men, participants' views about health and illness were particularly important because lifetimes of gendered experiences were embedded in their health practices (Buchbinder 1995; Courtenay 2000; Huggins 1998; Lee and Owens 2002b; Thorogood 2002; Woods 2001). The examination of an individual (microhistory) within a framework of time (macrohistory) enabled the exploration of participants' current attitudes and behaviors, while giving consideration to decisions that were made at an earlier point in time and potentially in another place (Morse and Field 1995).

## *Procedure*

The three participants who were the focus of this article were recruited from prostate cancer support groups (PCSGs) and initially took part in a larger ethno-graphic study of thirty-five men that explored connections between prostate cancer and masculinity, the findings from which have been reported elsewhere (Oliffe 2004, 2005, 2006). The three men were invited to participate in the new arm of the research because of the rich stories that they shared during the original study and their willingness and general enjoyment of talking about the past, as well as the present and the future. Life course perspective emphasizes the importance of time, context, process, and meaning, and as such the small sample of three participants afforded the depth and sharing of details key to the method (Bengtson and Allen 1993). The data used for this study were drawn in part from the interviews for the original study. In addition, each of the men completed a second in-depth, semistructured interview and were observed at monthly PCSG meetings for six months.

Observations of the participants were conducted at PCSG meetings and focused on their interactions, and field notes and interpretations were documented to provide adjunct data. Participants were interviewed at their homes, and each interview averaged two hours in duration and were tape recorded and subsequently transcribed verbatim. Participants' interviews from the original study were reviewed to develop the questions, context, and focus for the second interview. The second interview began with the open-ended question, "What was it like growing up in Australia during the 1930s and 1940s?" This enabled participants to tell their stories and provide an oral history, with questions about experiences of health and illness being introduced as appropriate to the flow of the interview. Initially the interview focused on participants' experiences from childhood through to middle age and continued on chronologically to explore older age and their health behaviors since being diagnosed and treated for prostate cancer. Although specific interview questions were developed, a specialized form of dialogue in which one person asks the questions and the other gives the answers was avoided (Oakley 1981), and conversations determined how information was obtained (De Laine 1997). Occasional prompts used by the researcher in the interviews were guided by the overall research question, "How does masculinity inform and influence participants' health and illness behaviors over time?"

## *Data Analysis*

The transcripts were managed using NVivo, and data were initially fractured using time-sensitive categories of "early formative years," "middle life," and "older age." An ipsative approach to data analysis was initially used in which each participant's data were studied and transcripts read multiple times by the researcher, highlighting key phrases and noting ideas and interpretations in the margins (Gambling and Carr 2004). Data were analyzed in the ethnographic style of coding, categorizing, and clustering themes (Morse and Field 1995), and were, then, coded, organized, and reorganized several times as subcategories were developed under each time-sensitive category. Exploration of the relationships between and within subcategories was conducted, and descriptive notes for each of the subcategories were developed. A subsequent review of all the data was completed, noting the commonalities and differences (Gambling and Carr 2004), and three themes resulted from the data analysis: (a) healthy "ill" boys; (b) intersection of work, wife, and family; and (c) health following illness. The term *theme* refers to coherent behavioral and belief patterns identified in participants' accounts (both within and across transcripts; Morse and Field 1995; Stenner 1993). Analysis continued during the writing up of the study, and themes were developed into storylines and the masculinities literature interwoven with the research findings (Morse and Field 1995). Participants read their interview transcripts and formative analyses and provided comments, feedback, and additional information (Acker, Barry, and Esseveld 1983). The use of a social constructionist gendered analysis provided a lens to interpret the connections between masculinity (as it intersected with age, history, social class, culture, and illness) and health behaviors and described the commonality as well as diversity that existed within and between participants' lives.

## *Participants*

Participants had similar backgrounds; briefly, they were Anglo-Australian (defined as originating from a Welsh, English, Scottish, or Irish background, at least second-generation Australian-born), self-identified as working class, heterosexual, were diagnosed and treated for prostate cancer between 1995 and 2000, and attended PCSG meetings on a regular basis. The data were collected in 2001 and 2002, and participants had a female partner, were retired, and had lived in Melbourne, Australia, for at least forty-five years. The participants and their wives have been allocated pseudonyms and are introduced through the following vignettes.

Randwick grew up in a Victorian country town before moving to Melbourne, where he served an "eight-year apprenticeship as a baker." He later worked as a builder's laborer at a brewery and then as a truck driver. He "worked hard . . . twelve to fourteen hours a day . . . because we always seemed to need money." He and his wife had lived in the same house in a northern suburb of Melbourne for forty-five years, where they had reared their three children. He had always enjoyed "his glass of beer" and still had a couple of "great mates from the old days."

Kevin grew up in a small country town in Victoria and completed his schooling at a regional city boarding school. He moved to Melbourne and worked as "a clerk . . . at the steel works . . . and at a mill" until he "finally got a job at an oil refinery as an operator." Kevin married "early" after his partner "fell pregnant"; they had three children but later divorced. He remarried and had been with his current partner for twenty-eight years and stated that "it's the only relationship I've got and it's rat shit. . . . I sleep at one end of the house and she sleeps at the other end of the house." He "went through [his] whole working life not knowing what [he] wanted to do," and since taking an early retirement, he had been "as happy as I've ever been in my life."

Steve "knocked back a carpentry and joinery apprenticeship in [his] home town to join the railways" in the western suburbs of Melbourne. He worked for the railways for forty-three years and "was still doing night courses at fifty-five years of age"; when he retired, he "was the best in the painting field that the railways had." He married, had two children, and "lived in the same house for forty years." Being a "teetotaler," Steve was a "little bit out of it" socially and "not always invited to some social areas."

# Results and Discussion

The research findings are presented chronologically across the life course continuum under the three key themes drawn from the analysis. Commentary is balanced with data, and participants' pseudonyms are used to label their quotations.

## Early Formative Years: Healthy "Ill Boys

The theme healthy "ill" boys refers to social and self-expectations described by participants about embodying health despite experiencing episodic illnesses in childhood and adolescence.

Randwick was six years old when his father died. He was brought up by his grandmother in country Victoria while his mother lived and worked 200 kilometers away in Melbourne. Although his mother was a qualified schoolteacher, "they wouldn't let her teach so she had to wash and iron" because after the war "in special areas . . . they kept them [women] out of work." Randwick's grandmother discovered his hearing and sight difficulties in 1941, when he was fourteen years old. During a Sunday lunch at a hotel, he asked his grandmother what the notice on the table said. She told him to use his eyes to "look at it" and "read it." Randwick recalled,

> I'd squint my eyes, which I found out from school . . . you could get them to focus . . . and just through that one particular day, saying that, she [Randwick's grandmother] suddenly woke up that I couldn't see properly. Well, I'd gone through umpteen years of school, of getting up and walking down nearer to the board and then back again to do sums and things like that. In the early stages, they said it was me being lazy and the same with hearing. I had the same problem that I wasn't hearing people, and

I'd say "I didn't hear." Well, they said I was imagining it. And I began to think myself, I must be imagining that I can't hear properly and I can't see properly. Well, once it was determined that it wasn't imagination, both things were rectified. I've been using glasses and a hearing aid ever since.

Randwick's grandmother recognized and validated his sensory impairment and arranged a consultation with a Melbourne based doctor who successfully treated both his hearing and sight problems. However, for many years prior, Randwick had been uncertain about the legitimacy of what he experienced and harbored increasing self-doubt about his ability to differentiate between imaginary and real symptoms. During this time, he minimized the impact of his disabilities through trial and error problem solving that included squinting and moving closer to an object to focus.

Kevin's father fell off a lamppost in 1943 while he was working for the Electricity Commission, after which he "went on an invalid pension" and "basically never worked again." His mother went out to work, but the wages she received were "barely enough to keep the family going and what he [Kevin's father] got went on smokes and booze." Kevin had "bedwetting" (enuresis) for the first fourteen years of his life. He recalled that when it was first discovered, his mother took him to the doctor:

> I was told [by the doctor] "you'll have to eat mice if you continue wetting the bed, because that's the treatment." I didn't know at the time, but this was basically a threat. Well, I don't want to eat mice, so I'll stop wetting the bed, as if I had any control over it.

The doctor's prescribed treatment, to "eat mice," inferred Kevin's bedwetting was voluntary, which he would control with the appropriate deterrent. However, Kevin was unable to stop wetting the bed. This became particularly problematic when he was "sent to a Catholic boarding school" in a regional Victorian city, after the money "was put up by a rich uncle." At boarding school, Kevin slept in a dormitory that housed hundreds of other boys. He was wetting the bed each night and had to choose between sleeping in the smell and discomfort of his urine-soaked mattress and admitting his lack of urinary control. He initially minimized his "embarrassment about wetting the bed" by attempting to conceal it:

> I used to just pull the bed up and try and hide it, so that each night I climbed into a wet bed . . . well, it was either that or have the whole bed stripped and the sheets hung out . . . the second storey window to dry, for the whole school to see.

Christian Brothers supervised the boys in the boarding school dormitory. When they eventually discovered Kevin's soiled bed linen and mattress, they gave him "six of the best . . . for hiding it." Consequently the urine-stained sheets hung from the window each morning, and Kevin rated the four years at boarding school as the "most miserable time of my [his] life." He was unable to control or conceal his bed-wetting, and social isolation and low self-esteem followed.

Steve's mother died from cancer when he was twelve years old, and he and his three brothers were raised by his father's parents in a small Victorian country town. Steve's father was an absent provider who "spent his life as a laboring type" and although he "neglected his health" had a "good innings" before dying at age eighty-four. The entire family were "apprentice-ship-orientated" and didn't worry about health "because blokes, let's be honest, we all do neglect that sort of thing." Steve recalled that he was fit, healthy, and played Australian Rules football and cricket competitively "like my [his] uncles and brothers." On the rare occasion that he was unwell or felt "debilitated . . . the family doctor was responsible for my [his] health."

Participants' experiences showed how social expectations can implicitly and explicitly influence actions and illuminated the genesis of three commonly cited men's health behaviors. First, participant reliance on females as primary health providers was evident. This gendered practice—as has been well established by Lee and Owens (2002b)—in which females were responsible for the health of the men in their lives was established during the participant's formative years. Second, professional health services were accessed for medical problems that required the expertise of a doctor, who subsequently diagnosed and treated the ailment. This practice was reflective of the "therapeutic age" (O'Connor-Fleming and Parker 2001) in which the focus of health services was treatment rather than prevention. Third, participants were expected to be healthy and, when dysfunction or illness occurred, denial, stoicism, concealment, and private problem solving were acceptable, if not compulsory behaviors. Although economic policy preserved a gendered division of labor in which the male body was privileged, there was also pressure for those bodies to perform. The ideals of a functional, resilient, "hard" masculine body were also reinforced by the social worth ascribed to the participants' fathers, based on their ability to work. Therefore, political, social, and economic structures influenced how men lived in their bodies, which may have contributed to the labeling of imaginative or naughty rather than "disabled" or "ill" boys.

## Middle Life: Intersection of Work, Wife, and Family

Participants identified themselves as working class, and the centrality of work, wife, and family were strongly represented in discussions about their middle life. Manual labor was traded for money, which in turn enabled men to financially support their wife and family. Ownership of a family home and car were important signifiers of provider status commensurate with, and representative of, successful working-class masculinity.

Steve left home when he was fourteen years old to begin a railway apprenticeship in Melbourne. He "married a local girl" and "built locally" in the working class west of Melbourne. The family weatherboard (clapboard) home was convenient to the railways where he worked for forty-three years. Steve described the work and conditions he experienced as a painter in the railways:

> You were sort of railway fodder . . . lugging trestles and planks. In painting it was always full of fumes, oh, bloody turps and thinners . . . there was no air extrusion. In a

workshop situation, you caught everything that was going . . . hygiene was nonexistent in the railway workshops. There'd be ten or a dozen of you . . . washing with Solvol [heavy duty soap], hands all in the one bucket. When I went over there [the railway workshop] last time and saw the extruders and extraction fans and water baths . . . I said to the young people . . . you people don't know you're alive . . . in that regard.

Steve knew that as long as he kept his "nose clean" and "head down," he had a "job for life." Job security was important; Steve was newly married, had two young children and a mortgage, and was the sole breadwinner. He "had a lot of bronchial problems through spray painting" and knew "the workshop conditions weren't good but we did it that way." Steve suspected but had no proof of a connection between his persistent wheeze and the workplace, nor was there legislation to support the pursuit of improved work conditions. There was a "lot of politicking . . . like union bashing or union joining," but occupational health and safety was not legislated during the 1950s, 1960s, and 1970s at his workplace. Indeed, Steve felt fortunate to have a "permanent job, superannuation"; he was "blue collar working class . . . just above the ruck" and took pride in his physical and intellectual abilities. By his mid-forties Steve's physical prowess at work had begun to deteriorate, and he "realized those young blokes are as good, or better than me." However, he proudly recalled that, until then, he was able to do the physical work, and "all through," he had the respect of his coworkers. When Steve was unwell during his working years, he would go to the family doctor. He described a typical consultation during that period:

> What bugged me a bit, his [Doctor] actual treating surgery was only [small] . . . and my problems then were bronchial [breathing]. As soon as you got in to talk to him, he wanted to have a bloody smoke. It was just cough, cough, cough . . . that was the early 80s.

The scenario Steve described was difficult to imagine in light of current understandings of the connections between tobacco and disease. However, prior to the 1980s, tobacco was marketed in shrewd, often gendered ways, and little public health information was available to inform people about the health risks associated with smoking. Randwick smoked to be with his mates, and similarly, the work break "smoko" connected Steve with his fellow workers:

> I didn't enjoy tobacco but because my mates were smoking, to be with them . . . you had it. . . . I would wait for the first opportunity to just drop it behind me. (Randwick)

> At smoko . . . you would gather together to share a smoke and a yarn. (Steve)

For Randwick and Steve, smoking tobacco was a short-lived practice. However, Kevin began smoking at ten years of age and became addicted to cigarettes. After boarding school, he used smoking and other behaviors to express his masculinity:

> Here I am at 15 suddenly let loose. . . . I've gone from being super disciplined and whacked every day, to now . . . I've got real money in me pocket and these fancy clothes

... and women. Smokes, booze. Like the pubs never bothered about under age. They couldn't give a damn. ... I was like a dog that was let off the leash. I just went mad. A series of girlfriends and finished up getting married to this woman that somehow or another fell pregnant.

Kevin distanced himself from the Christian Brothers who "wore frocks" and "were all hung-up in one way or another." He did this by modeling himself on men who had "an axe in their hand, and a cross-cut saw" or were "truck drivers." He did what "real" Australian men did—as Kevin described, "he drank in the pub, swapped yarns with his mates, he smoked, talked about sheilas [women], didn't act on it much, and that was it." Kevin grew up with his "old man down the pub," and after leaving boarding school, he replicated his father's drinking and smoking because "it was the fast track to being a man."

Randwick and Bess married in 1948 and soon after Randwick began working as a truck driver. Eventually they saved enough money to purchase a property in an outer northern Melbourne suburb that was "a big block of land with houses built higgledy-piggledy along the way." He explained that:

There were no roads or footpaths, and we were told that a freeway was on the plans, but we wouldn't see it in our lifetime. Well, apparently we've lived too long because in 1969 they put a freeway through . . . we're about five houses from it.

Initially the noise of the freeway traffic "jumped over the wooden fence" that separated cars and houses, but in the last few years, "Citylink [the freeway construction and maintenance company] built a concrete wall, which . . . quietened it down." Randwick walked the stark iron and concrete overpass that stretched across the freeway to get his daily newspaper, but in winter "it was too cold to cross" so he would go the "long way around the creek." The eight-lane freeway, which ran underneath, connected Melbourne's major airports to the city center and carried thousands of vehicles each day. Randwick and his family endured noise and air pollution from vehicles that drove by and aircraft that flew over their house. The once serene outer suburban home of the 1950s had become a busy, almost inner-city suburb as Melbourne had grown in all directions in the past fifty years.

Randwick could not afford to sell the family home and purchase in another location after the freeway was built. He and his family had little choice but to adapt to the changing environment. Furthermore, he was proud to have "built the house" and "felt lucky . . . not to lose the house" when the freeway was built. Their home, regardless of environmental changes and potential health hazards, was important to Randwick and his family. Symbolically, the house confirmed Randwick's craftsman-ship and breadwinner status. Within the walls, a lifetime of family memories and artifacts resided and responded. Randwick and Bess would never choose to leave their home, for many challenges had been overcome in achieving the "great Australian dream"—to own your own home:

We had the car on time payment and we sold that to buy the block of land, and then we struggled to get the house done and finished . . . we only had the flooring in one room, and a small fire, we used to sit in that room with an overcoat . . . one of the kiddies got a bad flu, and the doctor said we had to line a room or she had to go to hospital. . . . I was particularly busy with the truck [working] at the time . . . Bess got a neighbor over the road . . . to line it.

Randwick explained that he subsequently "pulled out all the thin masonite [building material]" used by his neighbor to line the room in his absence so that he could rightfully claim the entire building of their family home. His late model Ford Falcon resided in the adjoining carport. Side-by-side, Randwick's two biggest investments, house and car, signified the success of a lifetime of hard work. To abandon such achievements in search of a quieter, cleaner environment would potentially negate the years of hard work. The visual representation would be lost, and the history, as well as the future, would be submerged and perhaps questioned.

The connections between social class and gender were particularly evident during middle life. Participants embodied multiple masculinities both within and between their accounts, yet the stratification in terms of class closely aligned to the ideals of working-class masculinity. Therefore these accounts reflect only certain versions of Australian masculinity, in which participants traded labor for money to establish and sustain their breadwinner role. The findings also illustrated how brief childhood could be during the 1930s and 1940s because of the imperative to take up paid employment. Health was evidenced by functionality and physical performance, and heavy manual labor and poor work conditions demanded self-sacrifice but also offered men freedom to indulge in behaviors such as smoking and binge drinking. Marriage signified a union in which the economic continuum "for richer and for poorer" was the responsibility of the working man, while the housewife assumed the primary role for the concept "in sickness and in health." Ownership of the family home and car were important signifiers of provider status. Environmental factors such as air and noise pollution were not known to have detrimental effects on health, and tobacco and alcohol consumption were marketed as valid pursuits to embody dominant ideals of Australian masculinity. The middle life was a period when participants delivered the promise of hard work but did not necessarily take control or have knowledge of factors that potentially affected their health. Furthermore "rationality" as a unified stable identity to minimize or avoid potential health risks was challenged when the material conditions, structural constraints, and human emotions in participants' lives were analyzed, as previously described by Lambevski et al. (2001) and Watson (2000).

## Older Age: Health Following Illness

The theme "health following illness" refers to participants' health behaviors in older age following prostate cancer. The diagnosis and treatment of prostate cancer provided reason to take pause, and some health behaviors were reformulated while other established practices were continued. Therefore, these thematic findings relate specifically to prostate cancer and are limited in what they can say about "older age" in other men's lives in regard to health behaviors where "health following illness" may not be relevant.

Randwick had a prostatectomy in 1995, but the cancer metastasized and he was subsequently treated with Androgen Deprivation Therapy (ADT). Bess interrupted both research interviews to give Randwick his twelve o'clock medications. I observed Randwick and Bess smiling at each other as they exchanged the pill cup and glass of water. They were content in their established roles: Randwick the "patient," taking his pills, and Bess the "caregiver," administering medications following the doctor's instructions. Randwick explained as he pointed to the medications strategically positioned on the dining room table:

It's an area of the table which [Bess] has partitioned off . . . she laid out all my pills to be taken every day, and it was a little bit of a mind-boggling thing for [Bess] to work out when and how for me to take them. . . . I wasn't any help to her. I just took what she gave me.

Randwick described the integral role Bess played in complex issues of stock control, monitoring, and administration of his medications. The designated space on the table for his medications reflected the presence of illness and treatment in their lives. Historically, the table was a site of social gatherings and family dinners at which Bess would coordinate the cooking and serve the family meals. Her role in the domestic sphere continued as a caregiver and conduit between the doctor's orders and patient's treatment. Bess continued female health care roles similar to those provided by Randwick's grandmother. Randwick proudly acknowledged the parallels "when I was growing up my grandmother saw to it that I had medication or whatever." Although cognitively and physically capable of taking his own medications, Randwick and Bess continued culturally informed gendered roles through more than forty years of marriage.

Kevin had been on ADT since his radiation therapy in 1998 because the doctor suspected the cancer had spread from the prostate gland to other parts of the body. Although the exact location of the spread was unknown, Kevin rated his prognosis as poor. He accepted that he had been responsible for his health as a younger man and regretted his subscription to what men typically did to express and prove their masculinity. Kevin's retrospective summation suggested that his understandings of health had shifted significantly over time:

My diet was the pits. Smoking and drinking, which was what you did anyhow, was all part of the deal . . . no regular exercise. You got exercise when you built something or dug the garden. So there was me in charge of me health. I made a botch of it.

Kevin described how, since being diagnosed and treated for prostate cancer, he had tried to maintain and improve his health. He took "herbal medications and alternative treatments" as "a bit of insurance" and although "you expect it's a waste of money . . . you never know." He had changed his diet and proclaimed, as he pointed to the simmering saucepan on the stove:

Eat more beans! . . . from what I've read diet has a fair bit to do with whether you cop it [prostate cancer] or not . . . to optimize your chances, the diet is . . . more beans . . . less red meat.

Kevin had established new health care practices but was determined to continue a lifelong practice of drinking beer each evening, which he perceived as contentious and perhaps contradictory to the positive lifestyle changes he had made:

I'm going to keep drinking me two bottles, because the best part of the day for me is when I'm half charged and enjoying meself with me hi-fi. If I'm gonna deny myself that, what's the point?

Although Steve had not required any further treatment since completing radiation therapy in 1999, he did not believe he was necessarily cured of cancer. He continued to meet up with "a dozen retired men" he had worked with at the railways. Five of them had been diagnosed and treated for prostate cancer. He pondered the high incidence and tentatively suggested it may have something to do with "all the manual labor." Steve described a dialogue of coded numbers shared between the men in the group who had prostate cancer. He explained,

You say "how're you managing?" "No, no, she's down on the one." You don't need to ask any more, that's the PSA readings [numerical predictive blood test for prostate gland pathology], you know. "Oh, she's up to about seven . . . I'm not doing too well at the moment I better go back again" and that's it, you don't push 'em any further.

Steve explained that numbers were used because "blokes don't talk about it" even though "we're in the same area sort of thing." The conversations were confidential because the numbers could not be understood by men who did not have prostate cancer:

. . . that's [the numbers] the secret, and the guys who don't know what you're talking about, they just look and stay quiet for a moment and then you go on to something else . . . the wife and family and footy [football] teams.

Although prostate cancer was acknowledged and discussed, it occurred only in relative privacy and with the permission of other men. Similarly, PCSG meetings provided an environment conducive to talking about prostate cancer and its treatments, as well as health-promoting activities, such as diet and exercise. Steve suggested that prior to prostate cancer "I wouldn't have talked to anyone like I do now," but at the PCSG "I can talk more openly to people, particularly in my own age group." Kevin initially went to the PCSG "hoping someone might have some sort of magical cure," and although "no one has," he continued to go because:

I can do my bit to facilitate that continuance of the group . . . where other guys can get emotional support or whatever.

Randwick had never spoken with other men about health or illness; however, the "sharing of information" at PCSGs helped him solve a posttreatment side-effect of urinary incontinence, so he continued to attend and "say your [his] little piece" as a way of helping the "different chaps that come in." Participants broke with the ideals of what men talk about and discussed their illness experiences and shared health and prostate cancer information at the support group meetings.

Speaking about illness and health with other men was new, and each of the participants interacted in specific ways and took up particular roles at the PCSG meetings. For example, many men spoke simultaneously at group meetings, and the high ceilings and echoing multivocality often isolated Randwick audibly to the buzz of the feedback from his "hearing aid." However, Randwick fulfilled a "helper" role in the quieter moments by talking one to one with men about their urinary incontinence and sharing information about how he had overcome such problems. Steve would sit forward in his chair looking over the rims of his glasses listening intensely to whoever was speaking before actively joining in with the "give 'em hell," "let's beat this cancer" catch cries that emerged from various group members. Steve was an "encourager" of other men, especially quick to reassure newly diagnosed men that they would survive. When I first spoke with Kevin at a PCSG meeting, he talked about a particular prostate cancer drug trial and asked me to search for and send him any information or results that I could find. During the meetings, Kevin's arms were generally on the fold, but occasionally his right hand would extend to his face where his thumb and forefinger would pensively massage his chin. His role was that of the "critical thinker," and he consistently discussed and critiqued specific prostate cancer research and media articles with other group members.

Interaction styles and roles varied, but all the participants discussed health and illness as a means to supporting their own as well as other men's health. As older retired men diagnosed and treated for prostate cancer, illness provided the context for health, and health was actively pursued. As Lee and Owens (2002b) predicted, participants continued some established health behaviors in later life. However, increased awareness and willingness to talk and learn about health and illness and the adoption of some "new" health-promoting behaviors were evident, especially at PCSGs. In addition, at group meetings, a process of "illness demotion" was achieved through normalizing prostate cancer and collectively hypothesizing causes, cures, and symptom controls while simultaneously sharing strategies to promote health.

# Discussion and Conclusion

This study contributes in three distinct ways to men's health research. First, empirically the findings illustrate how deeply problematic it is to think of men's health behaviors as a purely natural phenomenon, outside the influences of society and culture. Clearly health and illness behaviors are contextually bound, subject to change, and strongly influenced by individual experiences and beliefs as well as historical, political, social, and economic factors. At the individual or microlevel, diverse behaviors within, between, and across participants' lives were

described. For example, risk taking, reactive self-care, denial of illness, and the situating of females as primary health providers—all typical men's health behaviors—were taken up by the participants at various times. However, some such behaviors were abandoned and atypical practices adapted when participants actively promoted their own and other men's health while trying to understand and address the diagnosis, treatment, and recovery from their prostate cancer. The straightforward, unitary, rational perceptions about what constitutes or underpins health-enhancing or risk-taking behaviors were also consistently disrupted by the details of "what else" was occurring in and around the men's lives. For example, participants' "middle life" relationships to work, wife, and family were influenced by government policy, and the economic value ascribed to their labor strongly influenced dominant social constructions about men's breadwinner roles (despite the risk of injury and illness) at particular points in history.

Macrostructures also intersected with health and illness behaviors. For example, some health behaviors can be reasonably claimed as artifacts from the therapeutic era that spanned the 1940s through to the 1970s, however participant interactions at PCSG meetings showed how they could also engage with activities synonymous with health promotion on their own terms. The study findings did not indicate that participants were uniformly unknowing, let down by health systems, or disadvantaged by gender roles, and therefore not responsible for their health. Instead the insights and understandings about their lives revealed dynamic interplays between agency and structure and provided contextual information, the details of which could reliably inform the design of men's health services as previously suggested by Watson (2000) and Lambevski et al. (2001). That said, a significant challenge remains to raise men's awareness of the benefits of actively maintaining their health before illness occurs.

Second, theoretically this study illustrates the value of using the masculinities frameworks to provide an "act-by-act" analysis and description of how men can refashion their identities. Masculinities and health behaviors connect in unique and often contradictory ways across history and within individual lifetimes, and the study findings showed how masculine ideals are contextual and fluid across history, as are men's alliances to them. Such recognition is theoretically important because there has been a propensity to describe men's deviation from, and alignment to, a "one-size-fits-all" concept of hegemonic masculinity. In this study, reciprocity between the empirical data and the masculinities frameworks highlighted the plurality of hegemonic masculinities and the value of contextually locating gender analyses in and across specific points in history. This approach offers the opportunity for fine-grained analyses by explicitly avoiding delinked static versions of hegemonic masculinity to generate the study findings, as has previously been suggested by Connell and Messerschmidt (2006).

Third, from a methodological perspective, life course made overt the connections between health behaviors and age, history, social class, culture, and illness—all of which intersect with masculinity. The method is premised on the belief that it is helpful to remember and embed individual lives in complex and ambiguous societal and cultural relations. Epistemologically and ontologically, the capture of one truth and/or generalizability of the findings were not espoused. Instead the commitment to contextual understandings of participants' lives was the central motivation for using this method (Buchbinder 1995; Courtenay 2000; Huggins 1998; Lambevski et al. 2001; Thorogood 2002; Tierney 2000; Watson 2000; R. White 2002; Woods 2001). By making audible the experiences of individual men, the potential to empirically interrogate unitary and/or essentialized versions of what are commonly collectivized as men's health behaviors were possible. Life course methods provided a way to unearth the beliefs and experiences that inform men's health behaviors, and such information can provide the foundations for working with some rather than to change all men's health behaviors.

In summary, the lives of Randwick, Steve, and Kevin provided powerful insights about the intersections of gender and health across time. Without such approaches, there is great potential for reworking analyses that perpetuate dominant commentaries rather than inductively derive understandings about masculinity and men's health. Only by first describing behaviors and thoughtfully considering the experiences and beliefs that underpin them can the timing and content of targeted health services be effective in promoting men's health.

# References

Acker, J., K. Barry, and J. Esseveld. 1983. Objectivity and truth: Problems in doing feminist research. *Women's Studies International Forum* 6 (4): 423–89.

Addis, M., and J. Mahalik. 2003. Men, masculinity, and the contexts of help seeking. *American Psychologist* 58 (1): 5–14.

Atchley, R., and A. Barush. 2004. *Social forces and aging—An introduction to social gerontology,* 10th ed. Belmont, CA: Wadsworth/Thompson Learning.

Australian Institute of Health and Welfare. 2004. *Australia's health 2004.* Canberra, Australia: AIHW Cat. No. AUS–44.

Banks I. 2001. No man's land: men illness and the NHS. *British Medical Journal* 323: 1058–60.

Bengtson, V. L., and K. R. Allen. 1993. The life course perspective applied to families over time. In *Sourcebook of family theories and methods: A contextual approach,* edited by P. G. Boss, W. J. Doherty, R. LaRossa, W. R. Schumm, and S. K. Steinmetz, 469–504. New York: Plenum.

Blair, J. E. 1995. Social marketing: Consumer focused health promotion. *American Association of Occupational Health Nurses* 43: 527–31.

Broom, A. 2005. Virtually healthy: The impact of Internet use on disease experience and the doctor-patient relationship. *Qualitative Health Research* 15 (3): 325–45.

Buchbinder, D. 1995, August 10–11. Men's troubles: The social construction of masculinity and men's health. In *Proceedings of the National Men's Health Conference,* 39–41. Melbourne, Australia: Commonwealth Department of Human Services and Health.

Bury, M. 1982. Chronic illness as biographical disruption. *Sociology of Health and Illness* 4 (2): 167–82.

Chapple, A., and S. Ziebland. 2002. Prostate cancer: Embodied experience and perceptions of masculinity. *Sociology of Health & Illness* 24 (6): 820–41.

Connell, R. 1995. *Masculinities.* Oxford, UK: Polity.

Connell, R. 1997. Australian masculinities, health and social change. In *Proceedings of the Second National Men's Health Conference,* 1–12, in Fremantle, Western Australia.

Connell, R. 2000. *The men and the boys.* St. Leonards, New South Wales, Australia: Allen & Unwin.

Connell, R., and J. W. Messerschmidt. 2006. Hegemonic masculinity: Rethinking the concept. *Gender & Society* 19 (6): 829–59.

Connell, R., T. Schofield, L. Walker, J. Wood, D. L. Butland, J. Fisher, and J. Bowyer. 1999. *Men's health: A research agenda and background report.* Canberra, Australia: Department of Health and Aged Care.

Conway, R. 1985. *The great Australian stupor.* South Melbourne, Australia: Sun Books.

Courtenay, W. H. 1998. College men's health: An overview and a call to action. *Journal of American College Health* 46: 279–90.

Courtenay, W. H. 2000. Constructions of masculinity and their influence on men's well-being: A theory of gender and health. *Social Science and Medicine* 50: 1385–1401.

Courtenay, W. H. 2004. Making health manly: Social marketing and men's health. *The Journal of Men's Health & Gender* 1: 275–6.

Crotty, M. 2001. *Making the Australian male: Middle-class masculinity 1870–1920.* Carlton Victoria, Australia: University Press.

De Laine, M. 1997. *Ethnography theory and applications in health research.* Sydney, Australia: MacLennan and Petty.

Donaldson, M. 1991. *Time of our lives: Labour and love in the working class.* North Sydney, Australia: Allen & Unwin.

Epstein, D. 1998, August. *Stranger in the mirror: Gender, ethnicity, sexuality and nation in schooling.* Paper presented at the Multiple Marginalities: Gender Citizenship and Nationality in Education Conference at the Nordic-Baltic Research Symposium in Helsinki, Finland.

Fergus, K., R. Gray, and M. Fitch. 2002. Active consideration: Conceptualizing patient-provided support for spouse caregivers in the context of prostate cancer. *Qualitative Health Research* 12: 492–514.

Fletcher, R., N. Higginbotham, and A. Dobson. 2002. Men's perceived health needs. *Journal of Health Psychology* 7 (3): 233–41.

Gambling, L. F., and R. L. Carr. 2004. Lifelines: A life history methodology. *Nursing Research* 53 (3):207–10.

Gibbs, L., and J. L. Oliffe. 2004. Promoting men's health. In *Hands-on health promotion,* edited by R. Moodie and A. Hulme, 356–62. Melbourne, Australia: IP Communications.

Gibson, M., and B. J. Denner. 2000. *Men's health report 2000. The MAN model: Pathways to men's health.* Daylesford, Victoria, Australia: Centre for Advancement of Men's Health.

Giele, J., and G. Elder. 1998. Life course research: Development of a field. In *Methods of life course research: Qualitative and quantitative approaches,* edited by J. Giele and G. Elder, 5–28. Thousand Oaks, CA: Sage.

Gray, R., M. Fitch, K. Fergus, E. Mykhalovskiy, and K. Church. 2002. Hegemonic masculinity and the experience of prostate cancer: A narrative approach. *Journal of Aging and Identity* 7 (1): 43–62.

Huggins, A. 1998. Masculinity and self-care. In *Promoting men's health—An essential book for nurses,* edited by T. Laws, 3–14. Melbourne, Australia: Ausmed Publications.

Hunt, K., G. Ford, L. Harkins, and S. Wyke. 1999. Are women more ready to consult than men? Gender differences in family practitioner consultation for common chronic conditions. *Journal of Health Services Research & Policy* 4 (2): 96–100.

International Longevity Center–USA. 2004. *Promoting men's health: Addressing barriers to healthy lifestyle and preventative health care.* Retrieved May 22, 2005, from http://www.ilcusa.org/pub/books.htm

Jarviluoma, H., P. Moisala, and A. Vikko. 2003. *Gender and qualitative methods.* London: Sage.

Jones, J. 1996, August. *Understanding of health: The background to a study of rural men's perceptions of health.* Paper presented at the 3rd Biennial Australian Rural and Remote Health Science Conference, Toowoomba, Queensland, Australia.

Kilmartin, C. 2000. *The masculine self,* 2nd ed. Boston: McGraw-Hill.

Kimmel, M. 1994. Masculinities as homophobia: Fear, shame, and silence in the construction of gender identity. In *Theorizing masculinities,* edited by H. Brod and M. Kaufman, 119–41. Thousand Oaks, CA: Sage.

Lambevski, S., S. Kippax, J. Crawford, J. Abelson, M. Bartos, and A. Mischewski. 2001. *Living as men "it's like being in a washing machine": Masculinities in contemporary urban Australia.* Sydney, Australia: National Centre in HIV Social Research Faculty of Arts and Social Sciences, University of New South Wales, Australia.

Lee, C., and R. Owens. 2002a. Issues for a psychology of men's health. *Journal of Health Psychology* 7 (3): 209–17.

Lee, C., and R. Owens. 2002b. *The psychology of men's health series.* Philadelphia: Open University Press.

Lloyd, T. 2001. Men and health: The context for practice. In *Promoting men's health: A guide for practitioners,* edited by N. Davidson and T. Lloyd, 3–34. Edinburgh, UK: Harcourt.

Lorber, J. 2000. *Using gender to undo gender: A feminist degendering movement, feminist theory.* Retrieved June 23, 2003, from http://www.sagepub.co.uk/journals/details/issue/sample/a012013.pdf

Macintyre, S., G. Ford, and K. Hunt. 1999. Do women "over-report" morbidity? Men's and women's responses to structured prompting on a standard question on long standing illness. *Social Science and Medicine* 48 (1): 89–98.

Macintyre, S., K. Hunt, and H. Sweeting. 1996. Gender differences in health: Are things really as simple as they seem? *Social Science and Medicine* 42 (4): 617–24.

Mansfield, A., M. Addis, and J. Mahalik. 2003. "Why won't he go to the doctor?" The psychology of men's help seeking. *International Journal of Men's Health* 2 (2): 93–110.

Moore, C. 1998. Australian masculinities. *Journal of Australian Studies* 56: 1–17.

Morse, J. M., and P. A. Field. 1995. *Qualitative research methods for health professionals,* 2nd ed. Thousand Oaks, CA: Sage.

Moynihan, C. 1998. Theories in health care and research. Theories of masculinity. *British Medical Journal* 317: 1072–75.

Nutbeam, D. 1998. Promoting the health of Australians—How strong is our infrastructure support? *Australian and New Zealand Journal of Public Health* 22(Suppl. 3): 301.

Nutbeam, D., and E. Harris. 1999. *Theory in a nutshell: A guide to health promotion theory.* New York: McGraw-Hill.

Oakley, A. 1981. Interviewing women. In *Doing feminist research,* edited by H. Roberts, 30–61. London: Routledge & Kegan Paul.

O'Brien, R., K. Hunt, and G. Hart. 2005. "It's caveman stuff, but that is to a certain extent how guys still operate": Men's accounts of masculinity and help seeking. *Social Science and Medicine* 61: 503–16.

O'Connor-Fleming, M. L., and E. Parker. 2001. *Health promotion: Principles and practice in the Australian context,* 2nd ed. Crows Nest, New South Wales, Australia: Allen & Unwin.

O'Hehir, B., E. Scotney, and G. Anderson. 1997, June. *Healthy lifestyles—Are rural men getting the message?* Paper presented at the National Rural Public Health Forum: Rural Public Health in Australia, Adelaide, Australia.

Oliffe, J. L. 2002. In search of a social model of prostate cancer: Finding out about Bronch. In *Manning the next millennium: Studies in masculinities,* edited by S. Pearce & V. Muller, 69–84. Perth, Western Australia: Black Swan Press.

Oliffe, J. L. 2004. Transrectal Ultrasound Prostate Biopsy (TRUS-Bx): Patient perspectives. *Urologic Nursing* 24 (5): 395–400.

Oliffe, J. L. 2005. Constructions of masculinity following prostatectomy-induced impotence. *Social Science and Medicine* 60 (10): 2240–59.

Oliffe, J. L. 2006. Embodied masculinity and androgen deprivation therapy. *Sociology of Health and Illness* 28 (4): 410–32.

Robertson, S. 2003. Men managing health. *Men's Health Journal* 2 (4): 111–13.

Sabo, D. 2005. The study of masculinities and men's health. In *Handbook of studies on men and masculinities,* edited by M. Kimmel, J. Hearn, and R.W. Connell, 326–52. London: Sage.

Seymour-Smith, S., M. Wetherell, and A. Phoenix. 2002. "My wife ordered me to come!": A discursive analysis of doctors' and nurses' accounts of men's use of general practitioners. *Journal of Health Psychology* 7: 253–67.

Stenner, P. 1993. Discoursing jealousy. In *Discourse analytic research: Repertoires and readings of texts in action,* edited by E. Burman and I. Parker, 114–32. London: Routledge.

Taylor, C., A. Stewart, and R. Parker. 1998. "Machismo" as the barrier to health promotion in Australian males. In *Promoting men's health—An essential book for nurses,* edited by T. Laws, 15–30. Melbourne, Australia: Ausmed Publications.

Thorogood, N. 2002. What is the relevance of sociology for health promotion? In *Health promotion: Disciplines, diversity, and developments,* 2nd ed., edited by R. Bunton and G. Macdonald, 53–79. London: Routledge.

Tierney, W. 2000. Undaunted courage life history and the postmodern challenge. In *Handbook of qualitative research,* 2nd ed., edited by N. K. Denzin and Y. S. Lincoln, 537–53. Thousand Oaks, CA: Sage.

Watson, J. 2000. *Male bodies health, culture and identity.* Philadelphia: Open Press.

Weiss, G. L., and L. E. Lonnquist. 2003. *The sociology of health, healing, and illness.* London: Prentice Hall.

White, A. 2001. How men respond to illness. *Men's Health Journal* 1 (1): 18–19.

White, P., K. Young, and W. McTeer. 1995. Sports, masculinity, and the injured body. In *Men's health and illness: Gender, power and the body,* edited by D. Sabo and F. Gordon, 158–82. Thousand Oaks, CA: Sage.

White, R. 2002. Social and political aspects of men's health. *Health: An Interdisciplinary Journal for the Social Study of Health, Illness and Medicine* 6 (3): 267–85.

Woods, M. 2001. Men's use of general practitioner services. *NSW Public Health Bulletin* 12 (12): 334–35.

Ziguras, C. 1998. Masculinity and self-care. In *Promoting men's health—An essential book for nurses,* edited by T. Laws, 45–61. Melbourne, Australia: Ausmed Publications.

JOHN OLIFFE, RN, MEd, PhD, is an assistant professor at the school of nursing, University of British Columbia, Vancouver, Canada. His research program is supported by the Canadian Institutes of Health Research new investigator and the Michael Smith Foundation for Health Research scholar awards. His current research projects explore the connections between masculinity and men's health and illness in the areas of prostate cancer, immigrant health, smoking and fatherhood, and the mental health of college-age men.

**Author's Note**—Special thanks to Randwick, Steve, and Kevin, who gave so freely of their time to share the details about ordinarily private health and illness issues. This study and article were made possible through career support by the Canadian Institutes of Health Research new investigator and the Michael Smith Foundation for Health Research scholar awards. Many thanks to Joy Johnson, Michael Halpin, Maria PallottaChiarolli, and Tina Thornton for their feedback and editorial assistance on the earlier drafts of this article.

From *Men and Masculinities*, January 1, 2009. Copyright © 2009 by Sage Publications. Reprinted by permission via Rightslink.

# UNIT 5
# Genders and Sexualities

## Unit Selections

## Key Points to Consider

- Have you ever wondered what causes heterosexuality? If not, why not?

- Do our sexualities change over time? If so, how?

- What challenges do transgendered men and women face in our society today?

- What challenges do intersexed people face in our society?

- Is there such a thing as "the heterosexual lifestyle"? Or, are there multiple ways of living and different kinds of lives possible for heterosexual people? Could the same be said for lesbian, gay, bisexual, and transgendered people?

- Are the children of gay or lesbian parents significantly different from those raised by heterosexual parents?

- What social and political shifts do you anticipate with marriage over the next decade?

## Student Website
www.mhcls.com

## Internet References

**World Association for Sexology**
*http://www.tc.umn.edu/nlhome/m201/colem001/was/wasindex.htm*
**SIECUS**
*http://www.siecus.org*
**The Society for the Scientific Study of Sexuality**
*http://www.sexscience.org/*
**SexInfo**
*http://www.soc.ucsb.edu/sexinfo/*

**Teenwire.com**
*http://www.teenwire.com*
**Human Rights Campaign**
*http://www.hrc.org/*
**The Intersex Society of North America (ISNA)**
*http://www.isna.org/*
**GenderTalk**
*http://www.gendertalk.com/*

In this unit, we explore genders and sexualities as well as the diversity that we find in the world today. From intersex to transgender to heterosexualities, bisexualities, and homosexualities, there is much to learn about our gendered social realities, lived experiences, and biographies.

We cannot consider gender diversity without attempting to understand transgender experiences. For transgendered people, there is a disconnect between one's biological sex and gender identity. This can produce a very complicated life situation. Hormone therapies, sex reassignment, and related surgeries are all options for transgendered people who have the resources to pursue bringing their outside appearances in line with their gender identities. How various states and countries deal with the legalities of changing one's sex differs significantly. In some places, the form to change one's gender is easily located at the local Department of Motor Vehicles. In other locations, there may be significant obstacles, which is something to consider.

We also explore different perspectives on sexual orientations. Why we humans feel, react, respond, and behave sexually can be quite complex. This is especially true regarding sexual orientations. Although experts do not agree about what causes our sexual orientations—heterosexual, homosexual, or bisexual—growing evidence suggests many possible developmental pathways for each sexual orientation. Some factors that may contribute to sexual orientation include biological factors, sociocultural influences, and free choice. While most gay people seem to report that there is no point in time when they chose to be gay, there are some who have reported that they made a conscious choice. Whether we are heterosexual, gay, lesbian, or bisexual, who we are seems to be fixed at a very early age for most of us. For others, there may be fluidity to their sexual attractions and sexual expression. In other words, for some, sexual orientation is highly fixed, for others much less so.

In the mid-1900s, biological scientist and sex researcher Alfred Kinsey introduced his seven-point continuum of sexual orientation known as the Kinsey scale. It placed exclusive heterosexual orientation at one end, exclusive homosexual orientation at the other, and identified the middle range as where most people would fall if society and culture were unprejudiced. Since Kinsey, many others have added their research findings and theories to what is known about sexual orientation, including some apparent differences in the contributions of biological, psychological, environmental, and cultural factors. In addition, further elaboration of the "middle" on the Kinsey scale has included some distinction between bisexuality—the attraction to males

© Digital Vision/PunchStock

and females, and ambisexuality—representing individuals for whom gender is no more relevant than any other personal characteristic, such as height, hair color, or right- or left-handedness with respect to sexual attraction and/or orientation.

Research on sexual orientations has certainly come a long way since the time of Kinsey. Today, researchers examine many aspects of sexual orientation, from biological to psychological to sociocultural. Anthropological and historical evidence suggests that homosexuality has existed across cultures and times. Political scientists and sociologists have conducted research on such topics as the lesbian and gay movement, public opinion, same-sex marriage, lesbian and gay communities, among many other interesting topics.

The birth of lesbian and gay studies has been an exciting new development in academia. This multidisciplinary area of inquiry grew out of the diverse body of research conducted (especially) since the late 1960s on the lives of lesbian, gay, and bisexual, people. As this research has documented, there has been significant social change over the past several decades. There are more possibilities today than ever before for lesbian, gay, bisexual, and transgendered people to fully participate as "out" citizens with greater expectations for the same rights as their heterosexual counterparts. It will be interesting to see the social, political, and legal changes that occur over the next several decades. These changes surely will have a significant impact on the lives of many people and their families. A number of issues that are likely to continue to be important well into the future are explored in this unit.

# (Rethinking) Gender

**A growing number of Americans are taking their private struggles with their identities into the public realm. How those who believe they were born with the wrong bodies are forcing us to re-examine what it means to be male and female.**

DEBRA ROSENBERG

Growing up in Corinth, Miss., J. T. Hayes had a legacy to attend to. His dad was a well-known race-car driver and Hayes spent much of his childhood tinkering in the family's greasy garage, learning how to design and build cars. By the age of 10, he had started racing in his own right. Eventually Hayes won more than 500 regional and national championships in go-kart, midget and sprint racing, even making it to the NASCAR Winston Cup in the early '90s. But behind the trophies and the swagger of the racing circuit, Hayes was harboring a painful secret: he had always believed he was a woman. He had feminine features and a slight frame—at 5 feet 6 and 118 pounds he was downright dainty—and had always felt, psychologically, like a girl. Only his anatomy got in the way. Since childhood he'd wrestled with what to do about it. He'd slip on "girl clothes" he hid under the mattress and try his hand with makeup. But he knew he'd find little support in his conservative hometown.

In 1991, Hayes had a moment of truth. He was driving a sprint car on a dirt track in Little Rock when the car flipped end over end. "I was trapped upside down, engine throttle stuck, fuel running all over the racetrack and me," Hayes recalls. "The accident didn't scare me, but the thought that I hadn't lived life to its full potential just ran chill bumps up and down my body." That night he vowed to complete the transition to womanhood. Hayes kept racing while he sought therapy and started hormone treatments, hiding his growing breasts under an Ace bandage and baggy T shirts.

Finally, in 1994, at 30, Hayes raced on a Saturday night in Memphis, then drove to Colorado the next day for sex-reassignment surgery, selling his prized race car to pay the tab. Hayes chose the name Terri O'Connell and began a new life as a woman who figured her racing days were over. But she had no idea what else to do. Eventually, O'Connell got a job at the mall selling women's handbags for $8 an hour. O'Connell still hopes to race again, but she knows the odds are long: "Transgendered and professional motor sports just don't go together."

To most of us, gender comes as naturally as breathing. We have no quarrel with the "M" or the "F" on our birth certificates. And, crash diets aside, we've made peace with how we want the world to see us—pants or skirt, boa or blazer, spiky heels or sneakers. But to those who consider themselves transgender, there's a disconnect between the sex they were assigned at birth and the way they see or express themselves. Though their numbers are relatively few—the most generous estimate from the National Center for Transgender Equality is between 750,000 and 3 million Americans (fewer than 1 percent)—many of them are taking their intimate struggles public for the first time. In April, L.A. Times sportswriter Mike Penner announced in his column that when he returned from vacation, he would do so as a woman, Christine Daniels. Nine states plus Washington, D.C., have enacted antidiscrimination laws that protect transgender people—and an additional three states have legislation pending, according to the Human Rights Campaign. And this month the U.S. House of Representatives passed a hate-crimes prevention bill that included "gender identity." Today's transgender Americans go far beyond the old stereotypes (think "Rocky Horror Picture Show"). They are soccer moms, ministers, teachers, politicians, even young children. Their push for tolerance and acceptance is reshaping businesses, sports, schools and families. It's also raising new questions about just what makes us male or female.

**Born female, he feels male. 'I challenge the idea that all men were born with male bodies.'**

—Mykell Miller, age 20

What is gender anyway? It is certainly more than the physical details of what's between our legs. History and science suggest that gender is more subtle and more complicated than anatomy. (It's separate from sexual orientation, too, which determines which sex we're attracted to.) Gender helps us organize the world into two boxes, his and hers, and gives us a way of quickly sizing up every person we see on the street. "Gender is a way of making the world secure," says feminist scholar Judith Butler, a rhetoric professor at University of California, Berkeley. Though some scholars like Butler consider gender largely a social construct, others increasingly see it as a complex interplay of biology, genes, hormones and culture.

---

## She kept her job as a high-school teacher. 'Most people don't get this fortunate kind of ending.'

—Karen Kopriva, age 49

---

Genesis set up the initial dichotomy: "Male and female he created them." And historically, the differences between men and women in this country were thought to be distinct. Men, fueled by testosterone, were the providers, the fighters, the strong and silent types who brought home dinner. Women, hopped up on estrogen (not to mention the mothering hormone oxytocin), were the nurturers, the communicators, the soft, emotional ones who got that dinner on the table. But as society changed, the stereotypes faded. Now even discussing gender differences can be fraught. (Just ask former Harvard president Larry Summers, who unleashed a wave of criticism when he suggested, in 2005, that women might have less natural aptitude for math and science.) Still, even the most diehard feminist would likely agree that, even apart from genitalia, we are not exactly alike. In many cases, our habits, our posture, and even cultural identifiers like the way we dress set us apart.

Now, as transgender people become more visible and challenge the old boundaries, they've given voice to another debate—whether gender comes in just two flavors. "The old categories that everybody's either biologically male or female, that there are two distinct categories and there's no overlap, that's beginning to break down," says Michael Kimmel, a sociology professor at SUNY-Stony Brook. "All of those old categories seem to be more fluid." Just the terminology can get confusing. "Transsexual" is an older term that usually refers to someone who wants to use hormones or surgery to change their sex. "Transvestites," now more politely called "cross-dressers," occasionally wear clothes of the opposite sex. "Transgender" is an umbrella term that includes anyone whose gender identity or expression differs from the sex of their birth—whether they have surgery or not.

Gender identity first becomes an issue in early childhood, as any parent who's watched a toddler lunge for a truck or a doll can tell you. That's also when some kids may become aware that their bodies and brains don't quite match up. Jona Rose, a 6-year-old kindergartner in northern California, seems like a girl in nearly every way—she wears dresses, loves pink and purple, and bestowed female names on all her stuffed animals.

But Jona, who was born Jonah, also has a penis. When she was 4, her mom, Pam, offered to buy Jona a dress, and she was so excited she nearly hyperventilated. She began wearing dresses every day to preschool and no one seemed to mind. It wasn't easy at first. "We wrung our hands about this every night," says her dad, Joel. But finally he and Pam decided to let their son live as a girl. They chose a private kindergarten where Jona wouldn't have to hide the fact that he was born a boy, but could comfortably dress like a girl and even use the girls' bathroom. "She has been pretty adamant from the get-go: 'I am a girl,' " says Joel.

Male or female, we all start life looking pretty much the same. Genes determine whether a particular human embryo will develop as male or female. But each individual embryo is equipped to be either one—each possesses the Mullerian ducts that become the female reproductive system as well as the Wolffian ducts that become the male one. Around eight weeks of development, through a complex genetic relay race, the X and the male's Y chromosomes kick into gear, directing the structures to become testes or ovaries. (In most cases, the unneeded extra structures simply break down.) The ovaries and the testes are soon pumping out estrogen and testosterone, bathing the developing fetus in hormones. Meanwhile, the brain begins to form, complete with receptors—wired differently in men and women—that will later determine how both estrogen and testosterone are used in the body.

After birth, the changes keep coming. In many species, male newborns experience a hormone surge that may "organize" sexual and behavioral traits, says Nirao Shah, a neuroscientist at UCSF. In rats, testosterone given in the first week of life can cause female babies to behave more like males once they reach adulthood. "These changes are thought to be irreversible," says Shah. Between 1 and 5 months, male human babies also experience a hormone surge. It's still unclear exactly what effect that surge has on the human brain, but it happens just when parents are oohing and aahing over their new arrivals.

Here's where culture comes in. Studies have shown that parents treat boys and girls very differently—breast-feeding boys longer but talking more to girls. That's going on while the baby's brain is engaged in a massive growth spurt. "The brain doubles in size in the first five years after birth, and the connectivity between the cells goes up hundreds of orders of magnitude," says Anne Fausto-Sterling, a biologist and feminist at Brown University who is currently investigating whether subtle differences in parental behavior could influence gender identity in very young children. "The brain is interacting with culture from day one."

So what's different in transgender people? Scientists don't know for certain. Though their hormone levels seem to be the same as non-trans levels, some scientists speculate that their brains react differently to the hormones, just as men's differ from women's. But that could take decades of further research to prove. One 1997 study tantalizingly suggested structural differences between male, female and transsexual brains, but it has yet to be successfully replicated. Some transgender people blame the environment, citing studies that show pollutants have disrupted reproduction in frogs and other animals. But those links are so far not proved in humans. For now, transgender issues are classified as "Gender Identity Disorder" in the psychiatric manual DSM-IV. That's controversial, too—gay-rights activists spent years campaigning to have homosexuality removed from the manual.

Gender fluidity hasn't always seemed shocking. Cross-dressing was common in ancient Greece and Rome, as well as among Native Americans and many other indigenous societies, according to Deborah Rudacille, author of "The Riddle of Gender." Court records from the Jamestown settlement in 1629 describe the case of Thomas Hall, who claimed to be both a man and a woman. Of course, what's considered masculine or feminine has long been a moving target. Our Founding Fathers wouldn't be surprised to see men today with long hair or earrings, but they might be puzzled by women in pants.

Transgender opponents have often turned to the Bible for support. Deut. 22:5 says: "The woman shall not wear that which pertaineth unto a man, neither shall a man put on a woman's garment: for all that do so are abomination unto the Lord thy God." When word leaked in February that Steve Stanton, the Largo, Fla., city manager for 14 years, was planning to transition to life as a woman, the community erupted. At a public meeting over whether Stanton should be fired, one of many critics, Ron Sanders, pastor of the Lighthouse Baptist Church, insisted that Jesus would "want him terminated." (Stanton did lose his job and this week will appear as Susan Stanton on Capitol Hill to lobby for antidiscrimination laws.) Equating gender change with homosexuality, Sanders says that "it's an abomination, which means that it's utterly disgusting."

Not all people of faith would agree. Baptist minister John Nemecek, 56, was surfing the Web one weekend in 2003, when his wife was at a baby shower. Desperate for clues to his long-suppressed feelings of femininity, he stumbled across an article about gender-identity disorder on WebMD. The suggested remedy was sex-reassignment surgery—something Nemecek soon thought he had to do. Many families can be ripped apart by such drastic changes, but Nemecek's wife of 33 years stuck by him. His employer of 15 years, Spring Arbor University, a faith-based liberal-arts college in Michigan, did not. Nemecek says the school claimed that transgenderism violated its Christian principles, and when it renewed Nemecek's contract—by then she was taking hormones and using the name Julie—it barred her from dressing as a woman on campus or even wearing earrings. Her workload and pay were cut, too, she says. She filed a discrimination claim, which was later settled through mediation. (The university declined to comment on the case.) Nemecek says she has no trouble squaring her gender change and her faith. "Actively expressing the feminine in me has helped me grow closer to God," she says.

Others have had better luck transitioning. Karen Kopriva, now 49, kept her job teaching high school in Lake Forest, Ill., when she shaved her beard and made the switch from Ken. When Mark Stumpp, a vice president at Prudential Financial, returned to work as Margaret in 2002, she sent a memo to her colleagues (subject: Me) explaining the change. "We all joked about wearing panty hose and whether 'my condition' was contagious," she says. But "when the dust settled, everyone got back to work." Companies like IBM and Kodak now cover

trans-related medical care. And 125 Fortune 500 companies now protect transgender employees from job discrimination, up from three in 2000. Discrimination may not be the worst worry for transgender people: they are also at high risk of violence and hate crimes.

Perhaps no field has wrestled more with the issue of gender than sports. There have long been accusations about male athletes' trying to pass as women, or women's taking testosterone to gain a competitive edge. In the 1960s, would-be female Olympians were required to undergo gender-screening tests. Essentially, that meant baring all before a panel of doctors who could verify that an athlete had girl parts. That method was soon scrapped in favor of a genetic test. But that quickly led to confusion over a handful of genetic disorders that give typical-looking women chromosomes other than the usual XX. Finally, the International Olympic Committee ditched mandatory lab-based screening, too. "We found there is no scientifically sound lab-based technique that can differentiate between man and woman," says Arne Ljungqvist, chair of the IOC's medical commission.

The IOC recently waded into controversy again: in 2004 it issued regulations allowing transsexual athletes to compete in the Olympics if they've had sex-reassignment surgery and have taken hormones for two years. After convening a panel of experts, the IOC decided that the surgery and hormones would compensate for any hormonal or muscular advantage a male-to-female transsexual would have. (Female-to-male athletes would be allowed to take testosterone, but only at levels that wouldn't give them a boost.) So far, Ljungqvist doesn't know of any transsexual athletes who've competed. Ironically, Renee Richards, who won a lawsuit in 1977 for the right to play tennis as a woman after her own sex-reassignment surgery, questions the fairness of the IOC rule. She thinks decisions should be made on a case-by-case basis.

> ## 'We all joked about wearing panty hose and whether "condition" was contagious.'
> —Margaret Stumpp, age 54

Richards and other pioneers reflect the huge cultural shift over a generation of gender change. Now 70, Richards rejects the term transgender along with all the fluidity it conveys. "God didn't put us on this earth to have gender diversity," she says. "I don't like the kids that are experimenting. I didn't want to be something in between. I didn't want to be trans anything. I wanted to be a man or a woman."

But more young people are embracing something we would traditionally consider in between. Because of the expense, invasiveness and mixed results (especially for women becoming men), only 1,000 to 2,000 Americans each year get sex-reassignment surgery—a number that's on the rise, says Mara Keisling of the National Center for Transgender Equality. Mykell Miller, a Northwestern University student born female who now considers himself male, hides his breasts under a special compression vest. Though he one day wants to take hormones and get a mastectomy, he can't yet afford it. But that doesn't affect his self-image. "I challenge the idea that all men were born with male bodies," he says. "I don't go out of my way to be the biggest, strongest guy."

Nowhere is the issue more pressing at the moment than a place that helped give rise to feminist movement a generation ago: Smith College in Northampton, Mass. Though Smith was one of the original Seven Sisters women's colleges, its students have now taken to calling it a "mostly women's college," in part because of a growing number of "transmen" who decide to become male after they've enrolled. In 2004, students voted to remove pronouns from the student government constitution as a gesture to transgender students who no longer identified with "she" or "her." (Smith is also one of 70 schools that have antidiscrimination policies protecting transgender students.) For now, anyone who is enrolled at Smith may graduate, but in order to be admitted in the first place, you must have been born a female. Tobias Davis, class of '03, entered Smith as a woman, but graduated as a "transman." When he first told friends over dinner, "I think I might be a boy," they were instantly behind him, saying "Great! Have you picked a name yet?" Davis passed as male for his junior year abroad in Italy even without taking hormones; he had a mastectomy last fall. Now 25, Davis works at Smith and writes plays about the transgender experience. (His work "The Naked I: Monologues From Beyond the Binary" is a trans take on "The Vagina Monologues.")

As kids at ever-younger ages grapple with issues of gender variance, doctors, psychologists and parents are weighing how to balance immediate desires and long-term ones. Like Jona Rose, many kids begin questioning gender as toddlers, identifying with the other gender's toys and clothes. Five times as many boys as girls say their gender doesn't match their biological sex, says Dr. Edgardo Menvielle, a psychiatrist who heads a gender-variance outreach program at Children's National Medical Center. (Perhaps that's because it's easier for girls to blend in as tomboys.) Many of these children eventually move on and accept their biological sex, says Menvielle, often when they're exposed to a disapproving larger world or when they're influenced by the hormone surges of puberty. Only about 15 percent continue to show signs of gender-identity problems into adulthood, says Ken Zucker, who heads the Gender Identity Service at the Centre for Addiction and Mental Health in Toronto.

In the past, doctors often advised parents to direct their kids into more gender-appropriate clothing and behavior. Zucker still tells parents of unhappy boys to try more-neutral activities— say chess club instead of football. But now the thinking is that kids should lead the way. If a child persists in wanting to be the other gender, doctors may prescribe hormone "blockers" to keep puberty at bay. (Blockers have no permanent effects.) But they're also increasingly willing to take more lasting steps: Isaak Brown (who started life as Liza) began taking male hormones at 16; at 17 he had a mastectomy.

For parents like Colleen Vincente, 44, following a child's lead seems only natural. Her second child, M. (Vincente asked to use an initial to protect the child's privacy), was born female. But as soon as she could talk, she insisted on wearing boy's clothes. Though M. had plenty of dolls, she gravitated toward "the boy things" and soon wanted to shave off all her hair. "We went along with that," says Vincente. "We figured it was a phase." One day, when she was 2 ½, M. overheard her parents talking about her using female pronouns. "He said, 'No—I'm a him. You need to call me him,'" Vincente recalls. "We were shocked." In his California preschool, M. continued to insist he was a boy and decided to change his name. Vincente and her husband, John, consulted a therapist, who confirmed their instincts to let M. guide them. Now 9, M. lives as a boy and most people have no idea he was born otherwise. "The most important thing is to realize this is who your child is," Vincente says. That's a big step for a family, but could be an even bigger one for the rest of the world.

---

This story was written by **DEBRA ROSENBERG,** with reporting from Lorraine Ali, Mary Carmichael, Samantha Henig, Raina Kelley, Matthew Philips, Julie Scelfo, Kurt Soller, Karen Springen, and Lynn Waddell.

From *Newsweek*, May 21, 2007, pp. 50–57. Copyright © 2007 by Newsweek, Inc. All rights reserved. Used by permission and protected by the Copyright Laws of the United States. The printing, copying, redistribution, or retransmission of the Material without express written permission via PARS International Corp. is prohibited.

# Progress and Politics in the Intersex Rights Movement
## Feminist Theory in Action

ALICE D. DREGER AND APRIL M. HERNDON

Since 1990, when Suzanne Kessler published her ground-breaking feminist analysis of the understanding of gender among clinicians treating children with intersex, many academic feminists have produced important scholarly work on intersex and intersex rights.[1] A notable few have also lent their energies to actively working for intersex rights in medical and mainstream social arenas. Although the intersex rights movement and feminist scholarship on intersex have both progressed considerably since 1990, there remains theoretical and political irresolution on certain key issues, most notably those involving intersex identity and the constitution of gender.

This essay considers the progress made in intersex rights since 1990 and delineates important points of contention within feminist intersex scholarship and intersex politics. We argue that in the last fifteen years much progress has been made in improving medical and social attitudes toward people with intersex, but that significant work remains to be done to ensure that children born with sex anomalies will be treated in a way that privileges their long-term well-being over societal norms. We also argue that, while feminist scholars have been critically important in developing the theoretical underpinnings of the intersex rights movement and sometimes in carrying out the day-to-day political work of that movement, there have been intellectual and political problems with some feminists' approaches to intersex.

The authors have a foot in both camps considered here—academic feminism and intersex rights work. We are academic feminists who also worked as paid directors at the Intersex Society of North America (ISNA), the longest-running, best-funded, and historically most influential intersex advocacy group. Alice Dreger began working with ISNA in 1996 and volunteered as chair of its board of directors from 1998 to 2003 and 2004 to 2005, and as chair of the fund-raising committee in the 2003–4 interim. In 2005 she left the board to take on the paid, part-time position of director of medical education, which she completed in late 2005. April Herndon was employed full-time as director of programming for ISNA from June 2005 to May 2006, producing and updating educational and Web site materials, organizing speakers and volunteers, writing grants, and so forth.

Dreger's graduate training is in the history and philosophy of science; in academic practice she is an historian of medicine and a bioethicist. Herndon's graduate training is in American studies; in academic practice she is a women's studies and cultural studies scholar.

A word on terminology is in order here. In this essay we use the term inter-sex to refer to variations in congenital sex anatomy that are considered atypical for females or males. The definition of intersex is thus context specific. What counts as an intersex phallus, for example, depends on local standards for penises and clitorises. Similarly, as we elaborate below, a person with no obvious sex ambiguity but with "sex chromosomes" other than simply XX (female-typical) or XY (male-typical) is today considered an intersex person by some intersex advocates, medical researchers, and clinicians, but not by all.[2] Yet such a person could not have been considered intersex before the ability to diagnose "sex chromosomes." So the definition of intersex depends on the state of scientific knowledge as well as general cultural beliefs about sex.

For this reason, in practice we define a person as intersex if she or he was born with a body that someone decided isn't typical for males or females. (This is also ISNA's current definition—not a coincidence, since Dreger helped develop this definition at an ISNA board retreat around 2000.)[3] Delineating intersex ultimately depends on delineating males and females, and when you get into the nitty-gritty of biology, this is not a simple task; nature is messy and often surprising, as Vernon Rosario argues in this volume.[4] That said, there are some forms of intersex that make a person's body obviously different from what is usual—for example, when a child is born otherwise male but without a penis, or when a child is born otherwise female but with a very small vagina and a large clitoris. So when we say that intersex is context specific, we do not mean to imply that these biological variations are not real but that how many variations (and thus people) are included in the category intersex depends on time and place.

Several dozen known biological variations and conditions may be considered intersex. Some have their basis in genetic variations. Some result from nongenetically caused prenatal developmental anomalies. A few involve "ambiguous" genitalia, but not all do; some involve more subtle blends of female and male types—for example, when a person has the external appearance of one sex but internally most of the organs of the other sex. Making things rather confusing to the novice, the medical names for various intersex conditions may refer specifically to the genotype (genetic basis), or to the phenotype (body type), or to the etiology (causal pathway of the condition), or to some combination of these. So saying someone is "intersex" does not tell you anything specific about a person's genes, anatomy, physiology, developmental history, or psychology. *Intersex* functions as a blanket term for many different biological possibilities—and as we show, many different political possibilities too.

# Background History of Intersex

Historical records in the West suggest that until well into the twentieth century intersex people tended simply to blend in with the general population, living their lives as unremarkable boys, girls, men, and women. Given that notable genital ambiguity shows up once in about every two thousand births, if genital ambiguity had been considered terribly disturbing throughout Western history, there would likely exist significantly more records of legal, religious, and medical reactions.[5] Indeed, although largely ignored by medical practitioners who treat intersex today, there is in fact a body of medical literature from the nineteenth and twentieth centuries that shows that people with "ambiguous" sex anatomies lived relatively uneventful lives psychologically and socially.[6] The only reason many of these people even show up in that medical literature is that they wandered into the medical systems for some other concern, and then the physician noted their sex anomalies. Doctors often seem to have been more concerned with sex anomalies than many of their patients.

Historically the tendency in the West—in legal, medical, and religious affairs—has been to try to keep people sorted into clear male and female roles, and people with intersex seem to have generally participated in that binary sorting.[7] Lorraine Daston and Katherine Park found that in early modern France people labeled hermaphrodites were strictly required to adhere to one gender (male or female) and to partner only with someone of the other gender, to avoid the appearance of homosexual or other "deviant" sexuality.[8] Dreger, Christine Matta, and Elizabeth Reis have shown that a similar system took hold in European and American medicine by the late nineteenth century.[9] The growing specter of homosexuality—*behavioral* sexual ambiguity—drove many late-nineteenth-century physicians to insist that *physical* ambiguity—hermaphroditism—must be illusory and solvable through careful diagnosis of "true" sex. Matta, for example, shows "the connection between physicians' increased interest in preventing 'abnormal' sexual behavior and their insistence that interventionist surgeries were the most appropriate means of treating cases of hermaphroditism."[10] Reis meanwhile notes that "nineteenth century doctors insisted on certainty rather than ambiguity in gender designation. . . .

Choosing an infrangible sex (despite indefinite and contradictory markers) was mandatory."[11]

By the mid-nineteenth century, some surgeons began offering "corrective" operations for large clitorises, short vaginas, and hypospadias (wherein the urinary meatus—the "pee hole"—appears somewhere other than the tip of the penis). Occasionally such operations were requested by patients or by parents of intersex children.[12] But surgical "normalization" did not become the standard of care for intersex children until the 1950s, when the psychologists John Money, Joan Hampson, John Hampson, and their colleagues at Johns Hopkins University developed what came to be known as the "optimum gender of rearing" model, which held that *all* sexually ambiguous children should—indeed *must*—be made into unambiguous-looking boys or girls to ensure unambiguous gender identities.[13]

The optimum gender of rearing (OGR) model was based on the assumption that children are born psychosexually neutral at birth—that gender is primarily a product of nurture (upbringing), not nature (genes and prenatal hormones)—and that having a sex anatomy that appeared to match one's gender identity is necessary to a stable gender identity. Money and the Hampsons believed that children could be steered one way or the other so long as the steering began before the age of two, give or take a few months.[14] After the 1950s, surgeons at Hopkins and then at other major U.S. medical centers operated early to make children's genitals more closely approximate the typical genitals of the gender assigned. They also removed gonads that did not match the assigned gender, even if those gonads were healthy and potentially fertile. When the child reached the age of puberty, endocrinologists administered hormones to push secondary-sex development in the direction of assigned gender if the hormones produced by the child's own endocrine glands were inadequate to the task. Most children were assigned female because of the belief that it was easier to make a convincing-looking girl than a convincing-looking boy. (At least one surgeon has summed it up, "You can make a hole but you can't build a pole.")[15] Boys were expected to have reasonably sized and reasonably functional penises; girls were primarily expected to be able to be on the receiving end of penile penetration.[16]

The team at Hopkins also provided intensive psychological gender coaching, though this last aspect of treatment was less common at other medical centers, even while everyone agreed intersex represented a psychosocial concern.[17] Although defenders of the Hopkins OGR team point out that their publications include suggestions that intersex children be told their medical histories in age-appropriate ways, in practice and in print many clinicians favored deception and withholding of medical records, lest patients become confused and depressed by their intersex states.[18] By the early 1990s it was common practice for medical students and residents to be taught that their ethical duty meant deceiving women born with XY chromosomes and testes, telling them, if anything, that they had "twisted ovaries" that had to be removed.[19] The pediatric endocrinologist Jorge Daaboul remembers telling women with XY chromosomes that they had one regular X chromosome and one X chromosome with a short arm, something he knew a Y chromosome is not.[20]

# History of the Intersex Rights Movement

Kessler's 1990 *Signs* article, the first publication to provide a sustained feminist critique of the OGR model, explored the sexist and heterosexist assumptions made by clinicians working with intersex patients regarding what counts as normal for girls and boys.[21] Using published medical literature as well as original interviews with intersex clinicians, Kessler demonstrated that the medical treatment of inter-sex was directed primarily at obscuring, and when possible eliminating, apparent sex and gender ambiguity.

Anne Fausto-Sterling brought a feminist understanding of intersex to a wider audience in 1993 by simultaneously publishing "The Five Sexes" in *The Sciences* and an op-ed called "How Many Sexes Are There?" in the *New York Times*.[22] In these companion pieces Fausto-Sterling reiterated and thus publicized the existing medical taxonomy of five sex types, a division that had coalesced in the late nineteenth century.[23] These included males, females, true hermaphrodites (which Fausto-Sterling called "herms"), male pseudohermaphrodites ("merms"), and female pseudohermaphrodites ("ferms"). "Herms" were people with both ovarian and testicular tissues; "merms" were people with ambiguous or mixed-sex anatomy and testes; "ferms" were people with ambiguous or mixed sex anatomy and ovaries. Fausto-Sterling's purpose was to challenge the pervasive belief that sex (and thus, in many people's minds, gender) came in a simple dichotomy.

In response to Fausto-Sterling's article Cheryl Chase (now known as Bo Laurent) published a letter in *Sciences* announcing the formation of ISNA.[24] Cognizant of how people with intersex were treated as if they were shameful and in need of strict social discipline, Chase originally planned to call the organization "Intersex Is Not Criminal."[25] Around the time of Fausto-Sterling's articles, Chase and other intersex people, including Max Beck, Morgan Holmes, and Kiira Triea, had come to the realization that they had been wronged by the medical establishment and that they needed to agitate for the rights of children born like them.[26] Because intersex activists felt the harm that had come to them had occurred largely because of the medicalization and medical mismanagement of intersex, they focused their attentions on critiquing the OGR model. In doing so, these activists were informed by principles of feminism (particularly the right to speak for oneself and critiques of sexism), gay and lesbian rights (particularly critiques of heterosexism and homophobia), and patients' rights (especially regarding autonomy, informed consent, and truth telling).[27]

Slowly at first (from about 1993 to 1999) and more rapidly later, intersex activists found allies in academic feminism, medicine, law, and the media. Like the activists born intersex, the great majority of nonintersex allies focused their attentions on the contemporary medical standard of care for intersex. Among the problems noted with the OGR model were these: it treated children in a sexist, asymmetrical way, valuing aggressiveness and sexual potency for boys and passiveness and reproductive/sexual-receptive potential for girls; it presumed that homosexuality (apparent same-sex relations) and transgenderism (changing or blurring gender identities) constituted bad outcomes; it violated principles of informed consent by failing to tell decision-making parents about the poor evidentiary support for the approach; it violated the axioms of truth telling and "first, do no harm"; it forced children to have their bodies adapted to oppressive social norms, using surgeries and hormone treatments that sometimes resulted in irrevocable harm; it generally involved treating psychosocial issues without the active participation of psychosocial professionals such as psychologists, psychiatrists, and social workers.[28] A more recent critique questions whether there is any reason to believe nonstandard genitals constitute a psychological risk factor; in fact, the medical literature fails to support the medical establishment's foundational assumption that having inter-sex genitals significantly increases psychosocial risk.[29]

As intersex advocacy grew so did the number and prominence of activist and support organizations for people born with intersex. Partly to make up for the gap left by ISNA's move away from day-to-day support toward systematic medical reform, the Internet-based, U.S.-located Coalition for Intersex Support, Activism, and Education (CISAE), founded by Triea and Heike Boedeker, and Bodies Like Ours, founded by Janet Green and Betsy Driver, sought to provide active peer support for parents and affected adults. Emi Koyama conceived Intersex Initiative as a relatively local group, originally focused on Portland, Oregon, but she has since brought it to national prominence. Diagnosis-specific groups such as the international Androgen Insensitivity Syndrome Support Group (AISSG) thrived throughout the late 1990s and continue today. However, not all relevant patient advocacy groups agreed with ISNA, Bodies Like Ours, and Intersex Initiative that the OGR model had to go: for example, the CARES Foundation (for congenital adrenal hyperplasia) and the MAGIC Foundation (for conditions that affect children's growth, including some types of intersex), run mostly by parents and clinicians, tended to remain in agreement with the medical establishment.

Independent of advocacy organizations, some sex researchers and clinicians took a stand against the OGR, most notably Milton Diamond and his associates. Diamond and H. Keith Sigmundson reported what happened to David Reimer, the nonintersex boy whose transformation into a girl (following a circumcision accident) Money had directed.[30] Money had claimed Reimer's gender transformation worked—and that therefore the OGR system was likely to work for intersex children. But Money was lying; Money knew Reimer had not been happy as a girl, and indeed transitioned socially to a boy almost as soon as he learned of his past.[31] Knowing this and hearing the painful stories of many adults with inter-sex, Diamond called in 1998 for a moratorium on intersex genital surgeries while data was collected on outcomes.[32]

Initially the medical establishment mostly ignored critiques and calls for change, issuing only occasionally a restatement of the belief that the OGR model was necessary and effective.[33] These statements rarely answered the specific critiques noted above. When Dreger edited a 1998 special issue on intersex for the *Journal of Clinical Ethics* (which became the basis for the 1999 anthology *Intersex in the Age of Ethics*), she tried to find a clinician who would defend the OGR model, but could not. Notably, several were by that point willing to criticize it.[34] The one critique to which traditionalist clinicians did begin to respond was the lack of outcomes data in favor of the approach. The outcomes data that has recently emerged is mixed and tends to vary wildly in terms of implicit assumptions on the goal of intersex treatment.[35]

Since about 2004, there has been a marked increase in interest among clinicians to reform practice. For example, thanks to the initiative of the feminist academic sociologist Monica Casper, who served as ISNA's executive director in 2003, ISNA developed a medical advisory board of approximately twenty-five people, most of them clinicians, something that seemed a distant dream as late as 1998. In 2004, at the American Academy of Pediatrics Section on Urology meeting, many clinicians were clearly agonizing over the choice of treatment in intersex cases. Even surgeons who had historically been ardent defenders of the OGR model were publicly expressing serious reservations.[36] In October 2005 the highly influential Lawson Wilkins Pediatric Endocrine Society and the European Society for Paediatric Endocrinology held a consensus meeting in Chicago that resulted in a hopeful degree of movement toward providing more psychosocial care, peer support, truth telling, informed consent, and outcomes data.[37]

Also in 2005, a collective comprised mostly of the three stakeholder groups—intersex people, parents of intersex people, and clinicians—formed and issued new clinical guidelines and a handbook for parents based on a "patient-centered model of care," an explicit alternative to the OGR.[38] That group, known as the Consortium on the Management of Disorders of Sex Development (or DSD Consortium for short), was formed as a result of grants given to ISNA to complete, produce, and distribute drafts written several years earlier by the social workers Sallie Foley and Christine Feick. The DSD Consortium includes founders and leaders of many of the major diagnosis-specific intersex support groups as well as clinicians from all the specialties involved in intersex care. (We were members of the DSD Consortium, and Dreger led the project as coordinator and editor in chief.)

The DSD Consortium's *Clinical Guidelines* state:

Patient-centered care means remaining clearly focused on the well-being of individual patients. In the case of DSDs this specifically involves the following principles.

1. Provide *medical and surgical care when dealing with a complication that represents a real and present threat.* . . .

2. Recognize that what is normal for one individual may not be what is normal for others. . . .

3. Minimize the potential for the patient and family to feel ashamed, stigmatized, or overly obsessed with genital appearance; avoid the use of stigmatizing terminology (like "pseudo-hermaphroditism") and medical photography; *promote openness.* . . .

4. Delay elective surgical and hormonal treatments *until the patient can actively participate in decision-making.* . . .

5. *Respect parents by addressing their concerns and distress empathetically,* honestly, and directly. . . .

6. *Directly address the child's psychosocial distress* (if any) with the efforts of psychosocial professionals and peer support.

7. Always *tell the truth* to the family and the child.[39]

These principles may seem like common sense, but they are considered somewhat radical by clinicians who have long believed that the presence in a child of a trait that challenges social norms means the most basic tenets of medical ethics can (and indeed must) be set aside.[40]

The DSD Consortium's handbooks are drawing much interest and praise in medical centers around the United States and are being distributed by advocacy groups (such as the MAGIC Foundation) historically supportive of the medical establishment. Our own experience suggests that clinicians who until recently practiced the OGR model are quite receptive to the patient-centered alternative. We see this as clear evidence that the changes for which intersex activists first hoped in the early 1990s are finally happening. This is not to overlook continued delays in the implementation of a reformed model. In our experience many medical centers currently lack institutional resources—including adequately trained psychosocial professionals, leadership, cross-disciplinary relationships, and funding—needed to implement psychosocially attentive integrated team care. Some also suffer from disputes among clinicians over the best approach. But more and more are expressing interest in providing something like the patient-centered, multidisciplinary team approach recommended by the DSD Consortium.[41]

The success of the intersex rights movement is almost certainly due in part to concomitant success in the LGBT rights movement. As noted above, the treatment of intersex has historically been motivated by homophobia and transphobia—that is, fear of apparent same-sex relations and fear of people changing or blurring gender categories. Positive changes in social attitudes toward queer-identified people have thus led to positive changes in social attitudes toward people with what some have called "queer bodies."[42] Success can also be credited to the fact that intersex advocates have been extremely effective at using the power of the media to change minds.[43] Substantial Western media attention to intersex people and intersex medicine, as well as the publication in 2002 of Jeffrey Eugenides's Pulitzer Prize–winning *Middlesex: A Novel,* has helped make the existence of intersex known, believed, and understood by tens of millions more people. We should note that, although a few intersex people objected to Eugenides's portrayal of an intersex person because it was a fictional story by a nonintersex man, our experience has been that the learning engendered by his novel for doctors and laypeople alike has been generally progressive. (Both of us have been surprised at how many conservative older men and women have told us excitedly what they learned about intersex from reading *Middlesex* in book clubs, including Oprah Winfrey's.) The intersex rights movement has also benefited from several talented writers—including Martha Coventry, Esther Marguerite Morris Leidolf, and Triea—who have conveyed their personal histories with eloquence and power.[44] We see therefore many reasons to believe that the intersex rights movement will continue to make marked progress in the coming years, even while we are concerned that the skyrocketing marketing of genital cosmetic procedures—including penile enlargement and labia reduction surgeries—has the potential to produce a negative effect on intersex clinical reform, as norms for genital appearance become increasingly visible and rigid.[45]

# Intersex Identity Politics

Although people sometimes refer to "the intersex community" as they do "the lesbian community," this is somewhat misleading. There are online virtual communities of people with intersex, but large numbers of intersex people do not live together in brick-and-mortar communities, and only occasionally do they come together for meetings that are primarily about political consciousness-raising rather than about sharing information about particular medical diagnoses (like hypospadias or congenital adrenal hyperplasia). ISNA has hosted a few small invitation-only retreats, and a number of intersex people have come together at the annual Creating Change conference of America's National Gay and Lesbian Task Force, and for one-time events such as the 2002 "Rated XXXY" San Francisco fund-raiser produced by the intersex advocate, performer, and poet Thea Hillman, but such gatherings remain either irregular or infrequent.

There are sizable annual meetings of diagnosis-specific groups like the AISSG, the CARES Foundation, and the Hypospadias and Epispadias Association, but often the participants of these meetings do not consider themselves "intersex" and are in fact offended by the term being used in reference to them. Objections we have heard include that the term sexualizes them (or their children if the objector is a parent) by making the issue one of eroticism instead of biology; that it implies they have no clear sex or gender identity; and that it forces on them an identity, especially a queer identity, to which they do not relate.[46]

Historically the word *intersex* as we know it dates to the early twentieth century when it was coined by the biologist Richard Goldschmidt as a term for biological sex types that fell between male and female.[47] Throughout the twentieth century, members of the medical profession occasionally used the term to refer to what they would more typically call hermaphroditisms or pseudohermaphroditisms. Early intersex advocates chose the term because it was less confusing and stigmatizing than terms based on the root *hermaphrodite,* although occasionally they used those alternate terms for in-your-face self-empowerment. For example, ISNA's first newsletter was called *Hermaphrodites with Attitude,* and Chase's 1996 video of ten intersex people telling their own stories was called *Hermaphrodites Speak!* But today few intersex advocates call themselves "hermaphrodites" both because the irony is lost on most people and because the term makes intersex people sound like mythical figures who are simultaneously fully male and fully female—something physiologically impossible but a frequent fantasy of certain fetishists who e-mail support groups seeking "hermaphrodite" sex partners. (Such people are known contemptuously in intersex activist circles as "wannafucks.") Early in the intersex rights movement, activists, scholars, and journalists sometimes referred to

*intersexuals,* but this term has largely fallen out of favor because it can be essentializing and dehumanizing to equate people with one aspect of their physicality. Instead, many advocates and activists now prefer to use terms such as *person with intersex, intersex person,* or *person with an intersex condition,* taking a cue from the disability rights movement.[48]

As suggested above, the question of who counts as intersex remains contentious. The people who made up the early intersex rights movement tended to share a common experience: they were born with noted sexual ambiguity, surgically "corrected" as young children, subjected to continued medicalization and stigma inside and outside the clinic, and they eventually developed a queer political consciousness that allowed them to understand their plight as unjust. But as the intersex rights movement grew, the diversity of actual experiences became more obvious, and this led to internal questions of identity politics. Were people intersex who "just" had hypospadias? Were women intersex who had well-controlled congenital adrenal hyperplasia and very little genital "masculinization" (so little it was never medically "fixed")?

The movement tended to welcome all these people out of the generosity that typically marks early social movements looking for people who will help and be helped.[49] But the anxiety about who should belong is obvious in venues like *Hermaphrodites Speak!* where Tom, born with hypospadias, jokes, "I'm the real hermaphrodite here—these people are just imposters." The intersex activist David Iris Cameron took to carrying around a card that asked, "Is XXY intersex?"[50] Cameron has Klinefelter syndrome (XXY chromosomes), which the layperson prone to a simplistic algebraic understanding of "sex chromosomes" might think of as obviously intersex. But many physicians do not count Klinefelter syndrome as intersex, just as they do not count Turner's syndrome (one X with no second "sex chromosome"), because in many physicians' minds, neither results in enough external sex-atypical development to count.

In our experience some clinicians have played a sort of moving target game whereby their definition of intersex changes from venue to venue, or moment to moment. We end up spending a remarkable amount of time just trying to agree on which diagnoses (and thus which people) count in the conversation we're trying to have. This does not usually seem to be a purposeful attempt to stall or derail conversation (although that does sometimes result); rather it seems to stem from a lack of systematic consideration of what the term might mean. For example, some want to call intersex only those born with visibly ambiguous genitalia, or only those who have had a particularly unusual mix of prenatal sex hormones.

Two illustrations: the physician William Reiner, a longtime ISNA ally, has tended to insist that males born with cloacal exstrophy are not intersex because their brains are not subjected prenatally to a sex-atypical mix of hormones.[51] Yet in cases of cloacal exstrophy, because the gut wall does not form properly, males are born with no penis. Standard practice (challenged by Reiner's work) has been to assign these children as girls, castrate them, and give them feminizing hormones starting at the age of puberty. In other words, the children are *treated* as intersex. Indeed, in all other cases when a boy is born with very little or no penis, the child would fall under the category intersex. Yet Reiner—who has been a staunch advocate of both intersex rights and the well-being of children born with cloacal exstrophy—seems not to want to apply the intersex label to cloacal exstrophy males purely because they have male-typical prenatal brain development.

A second example: in a recent discussion with a clinician, the name of one particular intersex activist came up, and the clinician stopped conversation to say, "she isn't intersex, she was just progesterone-virilized." In other words, given her genotype the activist in question would have developed as a standard female, but because her mother was given progesterone during pregnancy (presumably to prevent miscarriage), the activist's genitals had been virilized to some degree in the womb. So this activist was born with ambiguous genitalia, and as a result she was sent through the OGR system. Yet because she had medically induced (rather than "naturally" occurring) genital virilization, the clinician did not think she counted as intersex.

To make matters even more confusing, sex development is complicated enough that two people who share nominally the same condition may have quite different genotypes (genetic codes) or phenotypes (body types). For example, just knowing a person has ovotestes (misleadingly called "true hermaphroditism" in the medical literature) won't reveal much about the person's chromosomes or even his or her genitalia; a person with ovotestes may appear fairly feminine, fairly masculine, or in-between in terms of genitalia and overall physique. The majority of people with ovotestes have XX (female-typical) sex chromosomes, but others have XY or some other combination. Moreover, genitals that start as "ambiguous" may become naturally less so, and vice versa. Sharon Preves notes the case of Sierra, a child born with a large clitoris. The doctors wanted to shorten the clitoris for psychosocial reasons. Her mother refused. Several weeks later Sierra's clitoris shrunk to a normal size.[52] She probably had genital engorgement—that is, blood had pooled in her genitals, causing them to temporarily swell, from her being squeezed through her mother's birth canal. Had Sierra had surgery she might now count as intersex. Because of her mother's good sense she now probably doesn't count by anyone's definition.

The definitional challenges encountered with physicians, combined with the rejection of the intersex label by many parents and affected adults, have led us to participate in a move toward using a new blanket term: *disorders of sex development* (DSDs). When we started working with the group that became the DSD Consortium, it became clear that we couldn't reach agreement on practice unless we came to agreement on terminology. Otherwise we couldn't say to whom our guidelines applied. Everyone recognized that it was critical to avoid all terms based on the misleading and stigmatizing "hermaphrodite."[53] Alternative available medical terms included *disorders of sex(ual) differentiation* and *disorders of sexual development*. Terms with *sexual* in them were rejected because of the implication that we were talking primarily about an issue of sexuality (eroticism, orientation) instead of sex (anatomy and physiology). "Differentiation" was rejected in favor of "development" because of disciplinary disagreement about what "differentiation" means.

(Endocrinologists mean one thing, geneticists another.) One participant, David Iris Cameron, suggested "variations of sex development," but this was rejected for discounting the health concerns that come with some intersex conditions—concerns like dangerous endocrine imbalances and an increased risk of gonadal cancers. Besides, "variations" would describe every human, not just the people we meant to describe, namely, those liable to be treated as problematically sex-atypical. In the end handbook contributors settled on "disorders of sex development," with many people in the group expressing enormous relief at this.

As noted above, the DSD Consortium's handbooks represented significant progress. The consortium included past and present leaders from many other critically important advocacy and support groups, including the AISSG, the CARES Foundation, ISNA, the MRKH Organization (for girls and women born with conditions including incomplete vaginal development), and Bodies Like Ours. In other words, we achieved buy-in on a clearly articulated patient-centered model of care among people who previously appeared not to agree. We know that this would have been impossible without the shift of nomenclature to DSD.

At the same time that the DSD Consortium was working in earnest, in October 2005 the Lawson Wilkins Pediatric Endocrine Society and the European Society for Paediatric Endocrinology held their consensus conference on inter-sex. One agreement reached at that meeting was to abandon the terms *intersex* and *(pseudo)hermaphroditism* in favor of *disorders of sex development,* defined as "congenital conditions in which development of chromosomal, gonadal, or anatomical sex is atypical."[54] This was not a coincidence; several clinicians from the DSD Consortium (notably the pediatric urologist and geneticist Eric Vilain, the pediatric psychiatrist and urologist Reiner, and the pediatric psychologist David Sandberg) called for the change in nomenclature. But it is worth noting that their call fell on receptive ears; clinicians were ready for this change.

Reception of the new terminology has been mixed among people with intersex. Several months after publication of the DSD Consortium's handbooks, three participating intersex adults—Cameron, Esther Morris Leidolf, and Peter Trinkl—asked that a one-sentence disclaimer be added noting that, though they support the documents, they do not support the term. Several adults with intersex also objected to the term at an October 2006 conference held by ISNA and in written responses to the Chicago consensus document.[55] It is obvious from the way we write that, as scholars and activists, we still prefer the term *intersex* even while we recognize the usefulness of using *DSD* in many contexts.[56] Understandably, many people dislike having the label of disorder applied to them. Ironically, after years of trying to demedicalize intersex to some extent, the term we're now using remedicalizes it. But we have found that the terminology accords with the experience of many intersex adults and parents; it gives them a term that feels right in that it seems simultaneously to name, scientize, and isolate what it is that has happened. It therefore makes the phenomenon seem more manageable by being less potentially all-encompassing of their identities. Moreover, the shift to this terminology clearly has allowed serious progress toward patient-centered care, in part because it has allowed alliance building across support and advocacy groups, and with clinicians. For that reason we have been pragmatists about the nomenclature change. We strongly suspect that as attitudes and behaviors among clinicians improve, it will become possible and indeed necessary to revisit the nomenclature issue. Reis's recent suggestion of "Divergence of Sex Development" might turn out to be a viable compromise.[57]

A number of transgender people who were not born with any apparent sex anomalies and were not subjected to intersex medical management believe they should count as intersex because something in their brains obviously makes them feel differently than average males and females. One transgender person wrote to us that unless one believes in a mind-brain dichotomy (which we don't), obviously there is something sex-atypical in the brains of transgender people. But it is not clear that that sex-atypicality (always) represents a neurological intersex comprising a female brain in a male body, or vice versa. Some transgendered persons' brains may be different from the average in some way other than a neurological sex inversion.

For transgender adults, there are definite advantages to counting as inter-sex. For one, people in the United States tend to be more accepting of identities that have a definitive (or at least implied) biological basis. The current *Diagnostic and Statistical Manual of Mental Disorders* (*DSM-IV*) provides another reason for transgender people to seek the intersex label. According to the *DSM-IV,* a person with atypical gender identity can be classed as having gender identity disorder only if the person is not intersex.[58] Thus being labeled with an intersex condition means avoiding the diagnosis of a "mental disorder" and possibly easier access to legal and medical sex reassignment.

Yet many intersex advocates have rejected the idea that transgender people are necessarily intersex. For one thing they (and we) have found that a few transgender adults claim specific intersex conditions (like 5-alpha-reductase deficiency or partial androgen insensitivity syndrome) they don't actually have. But even beyond that, some intersex activists argue that transgender persons have had radically different experiences from intersex persons who have been through the OGR mill. Of course many (though by no means all) transgender people have experienced significant stigma for being gender atypical since childhood. But Chase writes that some transgender advocates inappropriately imply that intersex often results in gender transition, an inaccurate implication that "facilitates the doctors' misguided perceptions that incorrect gender assignment is the only harm of OGR, and that studies documenting low transition rates are evidence of success."[59] While there is no singular intersex experience to which a singular transgender experience can be compared, we think it is important to acknowledge the concern that intersex experiences and advocacy may become muddied, co-opted, or misguided in the conflation of transgender and intersex.[60]

Still, even though there may be differences between intersex and transgender, there are also reasons for intersex and trans activists to unite. As Leslie Feinberg notes, the divisive behavior of territory marking over identities often weakens the movement for human rights. Feinberg states emphatically that "we

can never throw enough people overboard to win approval from our enemies."[61] Feinberg goes on to say that "people who don't experience common oppression *can* make history when they unite."[62] While there may be moments when intersex activists are justified in their demands that people understand the particulars of intersex and transgender, there is also reason to carefully consider whether these particulars are always important and why such lines are drawn in the first place. If the particulars of transgender and intersex are highlighted only in order to make intersex people more intelligible or acceptable, then the result might be that trans-gender people are made less intelligible or even pathologized. Thus intersex activists doing the work of cleaving intersex and transgender must diligently examine their motives and the possible outcomes of such work.

Finally, on the issue of intersex identity politics we might note for other scholars thinking about stepping into identity-centered activism that we have each been criticized and had our motives questioned for being nonintersex people working on intersex scholarship and activism. For example, we have both had our intentions interrogated in online forums, and Herndon has been attacked for daring to point out the similarities between what intersex people and fat people face in terms of stigma and medicalization.[63] But this has by no means been a frequent occurrence. In general, activists born intersex have welcomed our collaboration and have often acted as enthusiastic advisers to and supporters of our efforts.

# Intersex and the Nature of Gender

Much scholarship in science and the humanities on intersex (including our own) has been motivated by attempts to ascertain the nature of gender. Historically, feminist intersex scholarship has aligned with other feminist theoretical scholarship in that it has taken gender to be a social construct distinct from sex (anatomy and physiology). For example, Kessler's 1990 intersex work aligned with her earlier work on gender by showing how social assumptions about what it means to be a male or a female are taught, learned, and reinforced. Dreger, Fausto-Sterling, Myra Hird, Holmes, Iain Morland, and many other feminist scholars working on intersex have similarly shown how social beliefs about gender are actively imposed on people whose bodies don't fit the simplistic assumptions that gender equals sex and that sex-gender formations come in only two flavors.[64]

Indeed, until relatively recently some feminists cited the alleged success of the OGR model as proof that gender is socially constructed.[65] But the concept of gender (as distinct from sex) as it developed in intersex clinical practice was hardly meant to be progressive. As Dreger has shown, the move in the early twentieth century to assigning a "workable" gender instead of a gender that aligned with a biological "true sex" was a conservative reaction to the unrelenting messiness of sex. Doctors dealing with intersex decided they had better resort to a system of gender assignment that would allow them to socially sort everyone into two types no matter how apparently in-between they were physically.[66] As Kessler and others have shown, the work of the Hopkins team continued in this tradition.[67] So even while Money and his allies supported the idea that gender is to a large degree socially constructed, in intersex care they maintained traditionalist, sexist, and heterosexist concepts.

Nevertheless, particularly in the early years of the intersex rights movement, many intersex people found feminist writings about the social construction of gender empowering and liberating. They could use this work to see how one particular construction had been forced on them and how their lives might have been better (and could yet be better) under different social constructions.[68] Social constructivism also gave solace to those who felt their gender identities did not fit into the simplistic male-female dichotomy promoted by Western popular culture. It was especially painful, therefore, for some intersex women (particularly women with AIS) to find their self-identities as women rejected by Germaine Greer in her book *The Whole Woman* because she insisted that "it is my considered position that femaleness is conferred by the final pair of XX chromosomes. Otherwise I don't know what it is."[69] As Morland has noted, when Greer was challenged by women with AIS and family members of girls with AIS, she was "dismissive; she then used the book's second edition not to retract the claims, but to publicly mock the AIS correspondents by referring to them too as men." Morland has persuasively argued that ironically "in trying to criticize the social construction of femaleness and intersex, Greer disenfranchised precisely those people who live at the intersection of the two categories."[70] Greer's simplistic and essentialist position seemed to represent something of a rearguard action against admitting anyone who might be a male-to-female transsexual into the ranks of real womanhood. Yet, we confess to never really understanding the intellectual balancing act performed by Greer and people like the leaders of the Michigan Womyn's Music Festival (who have tried hard to keep a "womyn born womyn only" policy of admission): they seem simultaneously to condemn and employ essentialist notions of womanhood.

In fact, neither a hard-line social constructivist nor a hard-line biological essentialist theory of gender seems supportable by the real-life experiences of people with intersex. On the one hand, if gender identity were purely a matter of social construction, it would not make sense that people with certain intersex conditions tend to revert to one particular gender identity despite monumental efforts aimed at making them the other. Consider, for example, the high percentage of males born with cloacal exstrophy, castrated and raised as girls, who declare themselves to be boys.[71] Similarly, many transgender people present gender identities in contradiction with the intensive gender training they've received—or indeed identities that confound any description in gendered terms.[72]

On the other hand, a simplistic biological explanation for gender identity also fails in the face of intersex. Not all males born with cloacal exstrophy or a micropenis and raised girls decide they are really boys or men. Of course, some who retain their female gender identities may be unaware of their medical histories or have plenty of reasons to decide to stay with the gender they were assigned. Gender transition comes at significant financial, physical, and emotional costs.

Ultimately it seems illogical to have so firm a belief in either the biological determination or social construction of gender that all of us with stable gender identities amount to either biologically programmed robots or victims of false consciousness. As Diana Fuss pointed out in *Essentially Speaking,* even hard-core constructivism amounts to an essentialism itself—in this case, actually a biological essentialism that presumes everyone is born with a blank slate for a brain where gender is concerned.[73]

Chase has argued that it is the very obsession with "the gender question" that has led to so much harm for people with intersex. According to Chase, while some people (like Money and some feminists) have used intersex to sit around debating nature versus nurture, real people with intersex have been hurt by these theories and their manifestations. Chase has therefore argued that "intersex [has been] primarily a problem of stigma and trauma, not gender."[74] Clearly, most OGR clinicians—from Money through today—have disagreed, arguing instead that "problems of gender identity development are *the core concern* in the psychosocial management of medical conditions involving ambiguous genitalia."[75] Yet a close reading of intersex autobiographical writing suggests that relatively few feel that getting the "wrong" gender assignment formed the central cause of their suffering. Indeed, this is a finding supported by outcome studies by OGR clinicians, . . . who then take this as proof that they've been on the right track all along![76] This failure to see why they're on the wrong track results from believing that "successful" gender identity means success in intersex patient care. Most intersex autobiographies support Chase's argument, showing how shame (including, but not limited to, shame about gender variation), secrecy, and medical mismanagement led to significant suffering.[77]

Nevertheless, contrary to Chase's simple formulation, clearly for a significant number of intersex people, gender—in the form of gender identity and gender role expectations—*is* a central concern in their lives. It is not uncommon for people with intersex to ponder how their gender identities and histories relate to their intersex. A few, like Mani Mitchell, feel that their intersex biology explains their feelings of being bigendered or intergendered.[78] Indeed, some have claimed that ISNA's message (that intersex is mostly about shame and trauma, not gender) fails to acknowledge their socially atypical genders. In fact, ISNA has never suggested people should not have the right to express their genders however they wish. ISNA (like the DSD Consortium, Bodies Like Ours, and all the diagnosis-specific support groups) has advocated raising all children as boys or girls, providing a best-guess gender assignment based on what can be surmised (after extensive tests) about the child's biology and future psychology, including how the parents are thinking about the child's gender. The reasoning behind this is twofold: (1) raising a child in a third or no gender is not a socially feasible way to reduce shame and stigma; (2) intersex is not a discrete biological category, so someone would always be deciding who to raise as male, female, or intersex: three categories don't solve the problem any more than two or five or ten do.

ISNA argued that gender assignment should not be reinforced with surgeries—that healthy tissue should be left in place for the patient to decide herself or himself what, if anything, to do with it. Although certain members of the medical establishment erroneously believed (and some still do believe) that ISNA advocated "raising children in a third gender," this was never the case. The cause of confusion seems to come from the fact that many clinicians can't understand what it would mean to raise a child with "ambiguous" genitalia as a boy or a girl, despite plenty of historical evidence that this has worked, no doubt because sex anomalies are largely hidden by clothing.[79]

We've been asked innumerable times why ISNA did not want to get rid of gender altogether. This question typically comes not from intersex adults but from scholars and students in gender studies. As Herndon noted while she was director of programming, ISNA privileged what is known from adults with intersex, and most adults with intersex don't have any problem with having a gender as men or women, nor do most reject the gender assignments given to them as children.[80] Many enjoy publicly "doing their gender," as Judith Butler would say.[81] This is true even for those who see themselves privately as third-gendered or ungendered. As noted above, most intersex adults agree that the problem with the medical management of intersex is not gender assignment but surgical and hormonal reinforcement of the assignment and other risky—and indeed physically and emotionally *costly*—manifestations of shame and secrecy.

A few critics have suggested that a better system than ISNA's would be more like what Feinberg, Kate Bornstein, and some other transgender activists promote. But our readings of Feinberg and Bornstein do not seem to be inconsistent with the message of ISNA—that people should ultimately be allowed to express their genders as they wish. Recounting a tense moment with a lesbian friend, Feinberg notes that many people believe that gender expression can only be oppressive. She writes of her friend, "She believes that once true equality is achieved in society humankind will be genderless. . . . If we can build a more just society, people like me will cease to exist. She assumes that I am simply a product of oppression."[82] Meanwhile, Bornstein notes that her own work is received in many different ways by members of the trans community, with some people agreeing with her and others being upset by her views. Trying to explain these disparate reactions, Bornstein writes, "Every transsexual I know went through a gender transformation for different reasons, and there are as many truthful experiences of gender as there are people who think they have a gender."[83] Thus several of the most visible leaders of the trans movement express views similar to those expressed by many intersex activists—that people's gender expressions need not be read only as oppressive and that the vast majority of people will have at least some positive investment in their gender expression.

## The Future

Serious progress has been made in intersex rights in the last fifteen years, progress that we believe would have been much slower or even impossible without the philosophical and practical efforts of many academics who have devoted their energies to trying to end the oppression of intersex people. There remains much theoretical and practical work to be done in and around the intersex rights movement, and we fully expect that academic feminists will continue to be an essential part of this work. We believe there are key insights feminists interested in helping can develop from the history we have presented here. For one, feminists should seek to listen carefully to intersex people in the same way they have listened to other marginalized groups, rather than assume they know what is true or right for intersex people.[84] Additionally, they should seek to write about intersex people on their own terms rather than just appropriate intersex for talking about other issues like the social construction of gender. They may also help by doing more than theorizing—by helping with the day-to-day fund-raising and advocacy work that support the intersex rights movement. Finally, such feminist commentators should acknowledge that many intersex (and also transgender) people have suffered even more than biologically typical women from sexist and heterosexist oppression.

## References

During the publication process of this essay, ISNA closed. Its Web site content remains available, and its assets have been transferred to a new nonprofit organization, Accord Alliance (www.accordalliance. org). We are grateful to Myra Hird, Emi Koyama, Bo Laurent, Esther Morris Leidolf, Kiira Triea, and especially Iain Morland for comments on earlier drafts of this essay.

1. Suzanne J. Kessler, "The Medical Construction of Gender: Case Management of Intersexed Infants," *Signs* 16 (1990): 3–26. For examples of subsequent work, see Alice Domurat Dreger, *Hermaphrodites and the Medical Invention of Sex* (Cambridge, MA: Harvard University Press, 1998); Dreger, ed., *Intersex in the Age of Ethics* (Hagerstown, MD: University Publishing Group, 1999); Anne Fausto-Sterling, *Sexing the Body: Gender Politics and the Construction of Sexuality* (New York: Basic, 2000); Michelle Morgan LeFay Holmes, "The Doctor Will Fix Everything: Intersexuality in Contemporary Culture" (PhD diss., Concordia University, 2000); Suzanne J. Kessler, *Lessons from the Intersexed* (New Brunswick: Rutgers University Press, 1998); Iain Morland, "Narrating Intersex: On the Ethical Critique of the Medical Management of Intersexuality, 1985–2005" (PhD diss., University of London, 2005); Sharon E. Preves, *Intersex and Identity: The Contested Self* (New Brunswick: Rutgers University Press, 2003).

2. "Sex chromosomes" is misleading; the X chromosome includes genes important to nonsex traits, and genes on chromosomes other than the X and Y are necessary for sex development. See Alice Domurat Dreger, "Sex beyond the Karyotype," in *Controversies in Science and Technology,* ed. Daniel Lee Kleinman and Jo Handelsman (New Rochelle, NY: Mary Ann Leibert, 2007), 467–78.

3. Intersex Society of North America, "What Is Intersex?" www.isna.org/faq/what_is_intersex (accessed July 29, 2008).

4. Vernon A. Rosario, "Quantum Sex: Intersex and the Molecular Deconstruction of Sex," this issue.

5. Intersex Society of North America, "How Common Is Intersex?" www.isna.org/faq/frequency (accessed July 29, 2008).

6. Dreger, *Hermaphrodites;* Intersex Society of North America, "What Evidence Is There That You Can Grow Up Psychologically Healthy with Intersex Genitals?" www.isna.org/faq/healthy (accessed July 29, 2008); Christine Matta, "Ambiguous Bodies and Deviant Sexualities: Hermaphrodites, Homosexuality, and Surgery in the United States, 1850–1904," *Perspectives in Biology and Medicine* 48 (2005): 74–83;

John Money, "Hermaphroditism: An Inquiry into the Nature of a Human Paradox" (PhD diss., Harvard University, 1952); Elizabeth Reis, "Impossible Hermaphrodites: Intersex in America, 1620–1960," *Journal of American History* 92 (2005): 411–41; Elizabeth Reis, *Bodies in Doubt: An American History of Intersex* (Baltimore: Johns Hopkins University Press, 2009).

7. For an example of an exception, see the story of Thomas/ Thomasine Hall in Reis, "Impossible Hermaphrodites."

8. Lorraine Daston and Katherine Park, "The Hermaphrodite and the Order of Nature: Sexual Ambiguity in Early Modern France," *GLQ* 1 (1995): 419–38.

9. Dreger, *Hermaphrodites;* Matta, "Ambiguous Bodies"; Reis, "Impossible Hermaphrodites."

10. Matta, "Ambiguous Bodies," 74.

11. Reis, "Impossible Hermaphrodites," 412–13.

12. Dreger, *Hermaphrodites;* Matta, "Ambiguous Bodies"; Reis, "Impossible Hermaphrodites."

13. John Money, Joan G. Hampson, and John L. Hampson, "Imprinting and the Establishment of Gender Role," *Archives of Neurology and Psychiatry* 77 (1957): 333–36.

14. Money, Hampson, and Hampson, "Imprinting and the Establishment of Gender Role."

15. Melissa Hendricks, "Is It a Boy or a Girl?" *Johns Hopkins Magazine,* November 1993, 15.

16. Alice Domurat Dreger, "'Ambiguous Sex'—or Ambivalent Medicine? Ethical Problems in the Treatment of Intersexuality," *Hastings Center Report* 28, no. 3 (1998): 24–35.

17. For examples of Hopkins's gender coaching, see John Colapinto, *As Nature Made Him: The Boy Who Was Raised as a Girl* (New York: HarperCollins: 2000); and Kiira Triea, "Power, Orgasm, and the Psychohormonal Research Unit," in Dreger, *Intersex in the Age of Ethics,* 141–44.

18. For a recommendation of disclosure, see John Money, Joan G. Hampson, and John L. Hampson, "Hermaphroditism: Recommendations Concerning Assignment of Sex, Change of Sex, and Psychological Management," *Bulletin of the Johns Hopkins Hospital* 97 (1955): 284–300. On withholding, see Dreger, "Ambiguous Sex"; and Anita Natarajan, "Medical Ethics and Truth-Telling in the Case of Androgen Insensitivity Syndrome," *Canadian Medical Association Journal* 154 (1996): 568–70.

19. Sherri Groveman, "The Hanukkah Bush: Ethical Implications in the Clinical Management of Intersex," in Dreger, *Intersex in the Age of Ethics,* 23–28.

20. Jorge Daaboul, "Does the Study of History Affect Clinical Practice? Intersex as a Case Study: The Physician's View" (paper presented at the annual meeting of the American Association for the History of Medicine, Bethesda, May 2000).

21. Kessler, "Medical Construction of Gender."

22. Anne Fausto-Sterling, "The Five Sexes: Why Male and Female Are Not Enough," *Sciences* (March–April 1993): 20–25; Fausto-Sterling, "How Many Sexes Are There?" *New York Times,* March 12, 1993.

23. Dreger, *Hermaphrodites,* 139–66.

24. Cheryl Chase, letter to the editor, *Sciences* (July–August 1993): 3.

25. Cheryl Chase, pers. comm., July 9, 2004.

26. Kiira Triea, "Learning about Transsexuality from Transsexuals," Transkids, www.transkids.us/learning (accessed July 29, 2008).

27. Cheryl Chase, "Hermaphrodites with Attitude: Mapping the Emergence of Intersex Political Activism," *GLQ* 4 (1998): 189–211.

28. Kessler, "Medical Construction of Gender"; Dreger, "Ambiguous Sex"; Kessler, *Lessons from the Intersexed; Hermaphrodites Speak!* dir. Cheryl Chase, Intersex Society of North America, 1996; Julie Greenberg, "Legal Aspects of Gender Assignment," *Endocrinologist* 13 (2003): 277–86;

Groveman, "Hanukkah Bush"; Holmes, "Doctor Will Fix Everything."

29. Alice Domurat Dreger, "Intersex and Human Rights: The Long View," in *Ethics and Intersex,* ed. Sharon Sytsma (Dordrecht: Springer, 2006), 73–86; Intersex Society of North America, "What Evidence"; Peter A. Lee et al., "Consensus Statement on Management of Intersex Disorders," *Pediatrics* 118 (2006): 814–15.

30. Milton Diamond and H. Keith Sigmundson, "Sex Reassignment at Birth: A Long Term Review and Clinical Implications," *Archives of Pediatric and Adolescent Medicine* 150 (1997): 298–304.

31. Colapinto, *As Nature Made Him.*

32. Kenneth Kipnis and Milton Diamond, "Pediatric Ethics and the Surgical Assignment of Sex," *Journal of Clinical Ethics* 9 (1998): 398–410.

33. Alice Domurat Dreger, "Cultural History and Social Activism: Scholarship, Identities, and the Intersex Rights Movement," in *Locating Medical History: The Stories and Their Meaning,* ed. Frank Huisman and John Harley Warner (Baltimore: Johns Hopkins University Press, 2004), 390–409.

34. See, for example, Justine M. Schober, "A Surgeon's Response to the Intersex Controversy," in Dreger, *Intersex in the Age of Ethics,* 161–68; Bruce E. Wilson and William G. Reiner, "Management of Intersex: A Shifting Paradigm," in Dreger, *Intersex in the Age of Ethics,* 119–35.

35. See, for example, Dreger, "Cultural History and Social Activism"; Heino F. L. Meyer-Bahlburg et al., "Attitudes of Adult 46,XY Intersex Persons to Clinical Management Policies," *Journal of Urology* 171 (2004): 1615–19; Lee et al., "Consensus Statement"; Justine M. Schober, "Feminization (Surgical Aspects)," in *Pediatric Surgery and Urology: Long-Term Outcomes,* ed. Mark D. Stringer, Keith D. Oldham, and Peter D. E. Moriquand, 2nd ed. (Cambridge: Cambridge University Press, 2006), 595–610; and Schober, "Surgeon's Response."

36. Alice Domurat Dreger, "Agonize—Then Cut This Way" (2004), www.isna.org/articles/aap_urology_2004.

37. Lee et al., "Consensus Statement."

38. Consortium on the Management of Disorders of Sex Development, *Clinical Guidelines for the Management of Disorders of Sex Development in Childhood* (Rohnert Park, CA: Intersex Society of North America, 2006), and *Handbook for Parents* (Rohnert Park, CA: Intersex Society of North America, 2006). Both books can be read and downloaded from www.dsdguidelines.org.

39. Consortium, *Clinical Guidelines,* 2–3; emphases in original.

40. Dreger, "Ambiguous Sex"; Alice Domurat Dreger, *One of Us: Conjoined Twins and the Future of Normal* (Cambridge, MA: Harvard University Press, 2004).

41. See, for example, Lee et al., "Consensus Statement."

42. Morgan Holmes, "Queer Cut Bodies," in *Queer Frontiers: Millennial Geographies, Genders, and Generations,* ed. Joseph A. Boone et al. (Madison: University of Wisconsin Press, 2000), 84–110.

43. Chase, "Hermaphrodites with Attitude"; Dreger, "Cultural History and Social Activism"; Sharon E. Preves, "Out of the O.R. and into the Streets: Exploring the Impact of Intersex Media Activism," *Research in Political Sociology* 13 (2004): 179–223.

44. Martha Coventry, "Making the Cut," *Ms.,* October–November, 2000, 52–60; Esther Marguerite Morris Leidolf, "The Missing Vagina Monologue," *Sojourner* 27 (2001): 20–21, 28; Triea, "Power, Orgasm, and the Psychohormonal Research Unit."

45. Virginia Braun, "In Search of (Better) Sexual Pleasure: Female Genital 'Cosmetic' Surgery," *Sexualities* 8 (2005): 407–24.

46. April Herndon, "What Are Disorders of Sex Development?" (originally written for www.isna.org), www.alicedreger.com/herndon/DSDs (accessed June 5, 2007).

47. Elizabeth Reis, "Divergence or Disorder? The Politics of Naming Intersex," *Perspectives in Biology and Medicine* 50 (2007): 535–43.

48. Nowadays *intersex* is commonly used as both an adjective and as a noun. Previously *intersexed* had been the standard adjective.

49. Kiira Triea, pers. comm., August 31, 2006.

50. Alice Domurat Dreger, "Is XXY Intersex?" *ISNA News,* Fall 2002, 2.

51. William G. Reiner and John P. Gearhart, "Discordant Sexual Identity in Some Genetic Males with Cloacal Exstrophy Assigned to Female Sex at Birth," *New England Journal of Medicine* 350 (2004): 333–41.

52. Preves, *Intersex and Identity,* 148.

53. Alice Domurat Dreger et al., "Changing the Nomenclature/Taxonomy for Intersex: A Scientific and Clinical Rationale," *Journal of Pediatric Endocrinology and Metabolism* 18 (2005): 729–33.

54. Lee et al., "Consensus Statement."

55. Reis, "Divergence or Disorder?"

56. Herndon, "What Are Disorders?"

57. Reis, "Divergence or Disorder?"

58. For the reasoning behind this, see Heino F. L. Meyer-Bahlburg, "Intersexuality and the Diagnosis of Gender Identity Disorder," *Archives of Sexual Behavior* 23 (1994): 21–40.

59. Cheryl Chase, pers. comm., September 7, 2006.

60. Triea, "Learning about Transsexuality"; April Herndon, "What's the Difference between Being Transgender or Transsexual and Having an Intersex Condition?" Intersex Society of North America, www.isna.org/faq/transgender (accessed July 29, 2008).

61. Leslie Feinberg, *Transgender Warriors: Making History from Joan of Arc to Dennis Rodman* (New York: Beacon, 1997), 98.

62. Feinberg, *Transgender Warriors,* 99; emphasis in original.

63. April Herndon, "Fat and Intersex?" (2005), www.isna.org/node/961. This practice has also been extended to intersex people; Iain Morland, who was born intersex, has had his motives questioned online because he has also identified himself as a researcher (pers. comm., December 31, 2006).

64. Dreger, *Hermaphrodites;* Fausto-Sterling, "Five Sexes" and *Sexing the Body;* Myra J. Hird, "Gender's Nature: Intersexuals, Transsexuals, and the 'Sex'/'Gender' Binary," *Feminist Theory* 1 (2000): 347–64; Holmes, "Doctor Will Fix Everything"; Iain Morland, "Is Intersexuality Real?" *Textual Practice* 15 (2001): 527–47.

65. Judith Butler, "Doing Justice to Someone: Sex Reassignment and Allegories of Trans-sexuality," *GLQ* 7 (2001): 624–25.

66. Dreger, *Hermaphrodites.*

67. See, for example, Kessler, "Medical Construction of Gender."

68. Dreger, "Cultural History and Social Activism."

69. Germaine Greer, "Greer Replies to the Father," www.medhelp.org/www/ais/debates/letters/father.htm (accessed July 29, 2008).

70. Iain Morland, "Postmodern Intersex," in *Ethics and Intersex,* ed. Sharon E. Sytsma (Dordrecht: Springer, 2006), 328.

71. Reiner and Gearhart, "Discordant Sexual Identity."

72. Kate Bornstein, *Gender Outlaw: On Men, Women, and the Rest of Us* (New York: Routledge, 1994).

73. Diana Fuss, *Essentially Speaking: Feminism, Nature, and Difference* (New York: Routledge, 1989).

74. Cheryl Chase, "What Is the Agenda of the Intersex Patient Advocacy Movement?" *Endocrinologist* 13 (2003): 240.

75. Meyer-Bahlburg, "Intersexuality," 21; emphasis added.

76. See, for example, Meyer-Bahlburg et al., "Attitudes of Adult 46,XY Intersex Persons."

77. See, for example, the narratives of people with intersex discussed in Kessler, *Lessons from the Intersexed* and Preves, *Intersex and Identity.*

78. *Yellow for Hermaphrodite: Mani's Story,* dir. John Keir, Greenstone Pictures, 2004.

79. Intersex Society of North America, "What Evidence Is There?"

80. Intersex Society of North America, "Why Doesn't ISNA Want to Eradicate Gender?" (2006), www.isna.org/faq/not_eradicating_gender.

81. Judith Butler, *Gender Trouble: Feminism and the Subversion of Identity* (New York: Routledge, 1990), 33.

82. Feinberg, *Transgender Warriors,* 83.

83. Bornstein, *Gender Outlaw,* 7–8.

84. April Herndon, ed., *Teaching Intersex Issues* (Rohnert Park, CA: Intersex Society of North America, 2006).

From *GLQ: A Journal of Lesbian and Gay Studies,* 15(2), 2009, pp. 199–224. Copyright © 2009 by Duke University Press. Reprinted by permission.

# What Do Women Want?

Daniel Bergner

Meredith Chivers is a creator of bonobo pornography. She is a 36-year-old psychology professor at Queen's University in the small city of Kingston, Ontario, a highly regarded scientist and a member of the editorial board of the world's leading journal of sexual research, *Archives of Sexual Behavior*. The bonobo film was part of a series of related experiments she has carried out over the past several years. She found footage of bonobos, a species of ape, as they mated, and then, because the accompanying sounds were dull—"bonobos don't seem to make much noise in sex," she told me, "though the females give a kind of pleasure grin and make chirpy sounds"—she dubbed in some animated chimpanzee hooting and screeching. She showed the short movie to men and women, straight and gay. To the same subjects, she also showed clips of heterosexual sex, male and female homosexual sex, a man masturbating, a woman masturbating, a chiseled man walking naked on a beach, and a well-toned woman doing calisthenics in the nude.

While the subjects watched on a computer screen, Chivers, who favors high boots and fashionable rectangular glasses, measured their arousal in two ways, objectively and subjectively. The participants sat in a brown leatherette La-Z-Boy chair in her small lab at the Center for Addiction and Mental Health, a prestigious psychiatric teaching hospital affiliated with the University of Toronto, where Chivers was a postdoctoral fellow and where I first talked with her about her research a few years ago. The genitals of the volunteers were connected to plethysmographs—for the men, an apparatus that fits over the penis and gauges its swelling; for the women, a little plastic probe that sits in the vagina and, by bouncing light off the vaginal walls, measures genital blood flow. An engorgement of blood spurs a lubricating process called vaginal transudation: the seeping of moisture through the walls. The participants were also given a keypad so that they could rate how aroused they felt.

The men, on average, responded genitally in what Chivers terms "category specific" ways. Males who identified themselves as straight swelled while gazing at heterosexual or lesbian sex and while watching the masturbating and exercising women. They were mostly unmoved when the screen displayed only men. Gay males were aroused in the opposite categorical pattern. Any expectation that the animal sex would speak to something primitive within the men seemed to be mistaken; neither straights nor gays were stirred by the bonobos. And for the male participants, the subjective ratings on the keypad matched the readings of the plethysmograph. The men's minds and genitals were in agreement.

All was different with the women. No matter what their self-proclaimed sexual orientation, they showed, on the whole, strong and swift genital arousal when the screen offered men with men, women with women and women with men. They responded objectively much more to the exercising woman than to the strolling man, and their blood flow rose quickly—and markedly, though to a lesser degree than during all the human scenes except the footage of the ambling, strapping man—as they watched the apes. And with the women, especially the straight women, mind and genitals seemed scarcely to belong to the same person. The readings from the plethysmograph and the keypad weren't in much accord. During shots of lesbian coupling, heterosexual women reported less excitement than their vaginas indicated; watching gay men, they reported a great deal less; and viewing heterosexual intercourse, they reported much more. Among the lesbian volunteers, the two readings converged when women appeared on the screen. But when the films featured only men, the lesbians reported less engagement than the plethysmograph recorded. Whether straight or gay, the women claimed almost no arousal whatsoever while staring at the bonobos.

"I feel like a pioneer at the edge of a giant forest," Chivers said, describing her ambition to understand the workings of women's arousal and desire. "There's a path leading in, but it isn't much." She sees herself, she explained, as part of an emerging "critical mass" of female sexologists starting to make their way into those woods. These researchers and clinicians are consumed by the sexual problem Sigmund Freud posed to one of his female disciples almost a century ago: "The great question that has never been answered and which I have not yet been able to answer, despite my 30 years of research into the feminine soul, is, What does a woman want?"

Full of scientific exuberance, Chivers has struggled to make sense of her data. She struggled when we first spoke in Toronto, and she struggled, unflagging, as we sat last October in her university office in Kingston, a room she keeps spare to help her mind stay clear to contemplate the intricacies of the erotic. The cinder-block walls are unadorned except for three photographs she took of a temple in India featuring carvings of an entwined couple, an orgy and a man copulating with a horse. She has been pondering sexuality, she recalled, since the age of 5 or 6, when she ruminated over a particular kiss, one she still remembers vividly, between her parents. And she has been discussing sex without much restraint, she said, laughing, at least since the age of 15 or 16, when, for a few male classmates who hoped to please their girlfriends, she drew a picture and clarified the location of the clitoris.

In 1996, when she worked as an assistant to a sexologist at the Center for Addiction and Mental Health, then called the Clarke Institute of Psychiatry, she found herself the only woman on a floor of researchers investigating male sexual preferences and what are known as paraphilias—erotic desires that fall far outside the norm. She told me that when she asked Kurt Freund, a scientist on that floor who had developed a type of penile plethysmograph and who had been studying male homosexuality and pedophilia since the 1950s, why he never turned his attention to women, he replied: "How am I to know what it is to be a woman? Who am I to study women, when I am a man?"

Freund's words helped to focus her investigations, work that has made her a central figure among the small force of female sexologists devoted to comprehending female desire. John Bancroft, a former director of the Kinsey Institute for Research in Sex, Gender and Reproduction, traces sexological studies by women at least as far back as 1929, to a survey of the sexual experiences of 2,200 women carried out by Katharine Bement Davis, a prison reformer who once served as New York City's first female commissioner of corrections. But the discipline remains male-dominated. In the International Academy of Sex Research, the 35-year-old institution that publishes Archives of Sexual Behavior and that can claim, Bancroft said, most of the field's leading researchers among its 300 or so members, women make up just over a quarter of the organization. Yet in recent years, he continued, in the long wake of the surveys of Alfred Kinsey, the studies of William Masters and Virginia Johnson, the sexual liberation movement and the rise of feminism, there has been a surge of scientific attention, paid by women, to illuminating the realm of women's desire.

It's important to distinguish, Julia Heiman, the Kinsey Institute's current director, said as she elaborated on Bancroft's history, between behavior and what underlies it. Kinsey's data on sexuality, published in the late 1940s and early '50s in his best-selling books *Sexual Behavior in the Human Male* and *Sexual Behavior in the Human Female*, didn't reveal much about the depths of desire; Kinsey started his scientific career by cataloging species of wasps and may, Heiman went on, have been suspicious of examining emotion. Masters and Johnson, who filmed hundreds of subjects having sex in their lab, drew conclusions in their books of the late '60s and early '70s that concentrated on sexual function, not lust. Female desire, and the reasons some women feel little in the way of lust, became a focal point for sexologists, Heiman said, in the '70s, through the writing of Helen Singer Kaplan, a sex therapist who used psychoanalytic methods—though sexologists prefer to etch a line between what they see as their scientific approach to the subject and the theories of psychoanalysis. Heiman herself, whom Chivers views as one of sexology's venerable investigators, conducted, as a doctoral candidate in the '70s, some of the earliest research using the vaginal plethysmograph. But soon the AIDS epidemic engulfed the attention of the field, putting a priority on prevention and making desire not an emotion to explore but an element to be feared, a source of epidemiological disaster.

To account partly for the recent flourishing of research like Chivers's, Heiman pointed to the arrival of Viagra in the late '90s. Though aimed at men, the drug, which transformed the treatment of impotence, has dispersed a kind of collateral electric current into the area of women's sexuality, not only generating an effort—mostly futile so far—to find drugs that can foster female desire as reliably as Viagra and its chemical relatives have facilitated erections, but also helping, indirectly, to inspire the search for a full understanding of women's lust. This search may reflect, as well, a cultural and scientific trend, a stress on the deterministic role of biology, on nature's dominance over nurture—and, because of this, on innate differences between the sexes, particularly in the primal domain of sex. "Masters and Johnson saw men and women as extremely similar," Heiman said. "Now it's research on differences that gets funded, that gets published, that the public is interested in." She wondered aloud whether the trend will eventually run its course and reverse itself, but these days it may be among the factors that infuse sexology's interest in the giant forest.

"No one right now has a unifying theory," Heiman told me; the interest has brought scattered sightlines, glimpses from all sorts of angles. One study, for instance, published this month in the journal *Evolution and Human Behavior* by the Kinsey Institute psychologist Heather Rupp, uses magnetic resonance imaging to show that, during the hormonal shifts of ovulation, certain brain regions in heterosexual women are more intensely activated by male faces with especially masculine features. Intriguing glimmers have come not only from female scientists. Richard Lippa, a psychologist at California State University, Fullerton, has employed surveys of thousands of subjects to demonstrate over the past few years that while men with high sex drives report an even more polarized pattern of attraction than most males (to women for heterosexuals and to men for homosexuals), in women the opposite is generally true: the higher the drive, the greater the attraction to both sexes, though this may not be so for lesbians.

Investigating the culmination of female desire, Barry Komisaruk, a neuroscientist at Rutgers University, has subjects bring themselves to orgasm while lying with their heads in an fM.R.I. scanner—he aims to chart the activity of the female brain as subjects near and reach four types of climax: orgasms attained by touching the clitoris; by stimulating the anterior wall of the vagina or, more specifically, the G spot; by stimulating the cervix; and by "thinking off," Komisaruk said, without any touch at all. While the possibility of a purely cervical orgasm may be in considerable doubt, in 1992 Komisaruk, collaborating with the Rutgers sexologist Beverly Whipple (who established, more or less, the existence of the G spot in the '80s), carried out one of the most interesting experiments in female sexuality: by measuring heart rate, perspiration, pupil dilation and pain threshold, they proved that some rare women can think themselves to climax. And meanwhile, at the Sexual Psychophysiology Laboratory of the University of Texas, Austin, the psychologist Cindy Meston and her graduate students deliver studies with names like "Short- and long-term effects of ginkgo biloba extract on sexual dysfunction in women" and "The roles of testosterone and alpha-amylase in exercise-induced sexual arousal in women" and "Sex differences in memory for sexually relevant information" and—an Internet survey of 3,000 participants—"Why humans have sex."

Heiman questions whether the insights of science, whether they come through high-tech pictures of the hypothalamus, through Internet questionnaires or through intimate interviews, can ever produce an all-encompassing map of terrain as complex as women's desire. But Chivers, with plenty of self-doubting humor, told me that she hopes one day to develop a scientifically supported model to explain female sexual response, though she wrestles, for the moment, with the preliminary bits of perplexing evidence she has collected—with the question, first, of why women are aroused physiologically by such a wider range of stimuli than men. Are men simply more inhibited, more constrained by the bounds of culture? Chivers has tried to eliminate this explanation by including male-to-female transsexuals as subjects in one of her series of experiments (one that showed only human sex). These trans women, both those who were heterosexual and those who were homosexual, responded genitally and subjectively in categorical ways. They responded like men. This seemed to point to an inborn system of arousal. Yet it wasn't hard to argue that cultural lessons had taken permanent hold within these subjects long before their emergence as females could have altered the culture's influence. "The horrible reality of psychological research," Chivers said, "is that you can't pull apart the cultural from the biological."

Still, she spoke about a recent study by one of her mentors, Michael Bailey, a sexologist at Northwestern University: while fMRI. scans were taken of their brains, gay and straight men were shown pornographic pictures featuring men alone, women alone, men having sex with men and women with women. In straights, brain regions associated with inhibition were not triggered by images of men; in gays, such regions weren't activated by pictures of women. Inhibition, in Bailey's experiment, didn't appear to be an explanation for men's narrowly focused desires. Early results from a similar Bailey study with female subjects suggest the same absence of suppression. For Chivers, this bolsters the possibility that the distinctions in her data between men and women—including the divergence in women between objective and subjective responses, between body and mind—arise from innate factors rather than forces of culture.

Chivers has scrutinized, in a paper soon to be published in *Archives of Sexual Behavior*, the split between women's bodies and minds in 130 studies by other scientists demonstrating, in one way or another, the same enigmatic discord. One manifestation of this split has come in experimental attempts to use Viagra-like drugs to treat women who complain of deficient desire.

By some estimates, 30 percent of women fall into this category, though plenty of sexologists argue that pharmaceutical companies have managed to drive up the figures as a way of generating awareness and demand. It's a demand, in any event, that hasn't been met. In men who have trouble getting erect, the

genital engorgement aided by Viagra and its rivals is often all that's needed. The pills target genital capillaries; they don't aim at the mind. The medications may enhance male desire somewhat by granting men a feeling of power and control, but they don't, for the most part, manufacture wanting. And for men, they don't need to. Desire, it seems, is usually in steady supply. In women, though, the main difficulty appears to be in the mind, not the body, so the physiological effects of the drugs have proved irrelevant. The pills can promote blood flow and lubrication, but this doesn't do much to create a conscious sense of desire.

Chivers isn't especially interested at this point, she said, in pharmaceutical efforts in her field, though she has done a bit of consulting for Boehringer Ingelheim, a German company in the late stages of testing a female-desire drug named Flibanserin. She can't, contractually, discuss what she describes as her negligible involvement in the development of the drug, and the company isn't prepared to say much about the workings of its chemical, which it says it hopes to have approved by the Food and Drug Administration next year. The medication was originally meant to treat depression—it singles out the brain's receptors for the neurotransmitter serotonin. As with other such drugs, one worry was that it would dull the libido. Yet in early trials, while it showed little promise for relieving depression, it left female—but not male—subjects feeling increased lust. In a way that Boehringer Ingelheim either doesn't understand or doesn't yet want to explain, the chemical, which the company is currently trying out in 5,000 North American and European women, may catalyze sources of desire in the female brain.

Testosterone, so vital to male libido, appears crucial to females as well, and in drug trials involving postmenopausal women, testosterone patches have increased sexual activity. But worries about a possibly heightened risk of cancer, along with uncertainty about the extent of the treatment's advantages, have been among the reasons that the approach hasn't yet been sanctioned by the F.D.A.

Thinking not of the search for chemical aphrodisiacs but of her own quest for comprehension, Chivers said that she hopes her research and thinking will eventually have some benefit for women's sexuality. "I wanted everybody to have great sex," she told me, recalling one of her reasons for choosing her career, and laughing as she did when she recounted the lessons she once gave on the position of the clitoris. But mostly it's the aim of understanding in itself that compels her. For the discord, in women, between the body and the mind, she has deliberated over all sorts of explanations, the simplest being anatomy. The penis is external, its reactions more readily perceived and pressing upon consciousness. Women might more likely have grown up, for reasons of both bodily architecture and culture—and here was culture again, undercutting clarity—with a dimmer awareness of the erotic messages of their genitals. Chivers said she has considered, too, research suggesting that men are better able than women to perceive increases in heart rate at moments of heightened stress and that men may rely more on such physiological signals to define their emotional states, while women depend more on situational cues. So there are hints, she told me, that the disparity between the objective and the subjective might exist, for women, in areas other than sex. And this disconnection, according to yet another study she mentioned, is accentuated in women with acutely negative feelings about their own bodies.

Ultimately, though, Chivers spoke—always with a scientist's caution, a scientist's uncertainty and acknowledgment of conjecture—about female sexuality as divided between two truly separate, if inscrutably overlapping, systems, the physiological and the subjective. Lust, in this formulation, resides in the subjective, the cognitive; physiological arousal reveals little about desire. Otherwise, she said, half joking, "I would have to believe that women want to have sex with bonobos."

Besides the bonobos, a body of evidence involving rape has influenced her construction of separate systems. She has confronted clinical research reporting not only genital arousal but also the occasional occurrence of orgasm during sexual assault. And she has recalled her own experience as a therapist with victims who recounted these physical responses. She is familiar, as well, with the preliminary results of a laboratory study showing surges of vaginal blood flow as subjects listen to descriptions of rape scenes. So, in an attempt to understand arousal in the context of unwanted sex, Chivers, like a handful of other sexologists, has arrived at an evolutionary hypothesis that stresses the difference between reflexive sexual readiness and desire. Genital lubrication, she writes in her upcoming paper in *Archives of Sexual Behavior*, is necessary "to reduce discomfort, and the possibility of injury, during vaginal penetration. . . . Ancestral women who did not show an automatic vaginal response to sexual cues may have been more likely to experience injuries during unwanted vaginal penetration that resulted in illness, infertility or even death, and thus would be less likely to have passed on this trait to their offspring."

Evolution's legacy, according to this theory, is that women are prone to lubricate, if only protectively, to hints of sex in their surroundings. Thinking of her own data, Chivers speculated that bonobo coupling, or perhaps simply the sight of a male ape's erection, stimulated this reaction because apes bear a resemblance to humans—she joked about including, for comparison, a movie of mating chickens in a future study. And she wondered if the theory explained why heterosexual women responded genitally more to the exercising woman than to the ambling man. Possibly, she said, the exposure and tilt of the woman's vulva during her calisthenics was processed as a sexual signal while the man's unerect penis registered in the opposite way.

When she peers into the giant forest, Chivers told me, she considers the possibility that along with what she called a "rudderless" system of reflexive physiological arousal, women's system of desire, the cognitive domain of lust, is more receptive than aggressive. "One of the things I think about," she said, "is the dyad formed by men and women. Certainly women are very sexual and have the capacity to be even more sexual than men, but one possibility is that instead of it being a go-out-there-and-get-it kind of sexuality, it's more of a reactive process. If you have this dyad, and one part is pumped full of testosterone, is more interested in risk taking, is probably more aggressive, you've got a very strong motivational force. It wouldn't make sense to have another similar force. You need something

complementary. And I've often thought that there is something really powerful for women's sexuality about being desired. That receptivity element. At some point I'd love to do a study that would look at that."

The study Chivers is working on now tries to re-examine the results of her earlier research, to investigate, with audiotaped stories rather than filmed scenes, the apparent rudderlessness of female arousal. But it will offer too a glimpse into the role of relationships in female eros. Some of the scripts she wrote involve sex with a longtime lover, some with a friend, some with a stranger: "You meet the real estate agent outside the building. . . ." From early glances at her data, Chivers said, she guesses she will find that women are most turned on, subjectively if not objectively, by scenarios of sex with strangers.

Chivers is perpetually devising experiments to perform in the future, and one would test how tightly linked the system of arousal is to the mechanisms of desire. She would like to follow the sexual behavior of women in the days after they are exposed to stimuli in her lab. If stimuli that cause physiological response—but that do not elicit a positive rating on the keypad—lead to increased erotic fantasies, masturbation or sexual activity with a partner, then she could deduce a tight link. Though women may not want, in reality, what such stimuli present, Chivers could begin to infer that what is judged unappealing does, nevertheless, turn women on.

Lisa Diamond, a newly prominent sexologist of Chivers's generation, looks at women's erotic drives in a different way. An associate professor of psychology and gender studies at the University of Utah, with short, dark hair that seems to explode anarchically around her head, Diamond has done much of her research outside any lab, has focused a good deal of her attention outside the heterosexual dyad and has drawn conclusions that seem at odds with Chivers's data about sex with strangers.

"In 1997, the actress Anne Heche began a widely publicized romantic relationship with the openly lesbian comedian Ellen DeGeneres after having had no prior same-sex attractions or relationships. The relationship with DeGeneres ended after two years, and Heche went on to marry a man." So begins Diamond's book, *Sexual Fluidity: Understanding Women's Love and Desire*, published by Harvard University Press last winter. She continues: "Julie Cypher left a heterosexual marriage for the musician Melissa Etheridge in 1988. After 12 years together, the pair separated and Cypher—like Heche—has returned to heterosexual relationships." She catalogs the shifting sexual directions of several other somewhat notable women, then asks, "What's going on?" Among her answers, based partly on her own research and on her analysis of animal mating and women's sexuality, is that female desire may be dictated—even more than popular perception would have it—by intimacy, by emotional connection.

Diamond is a tireless researcher. The study that led to her book has been going on for more than 10 years. During that time, she has followed the erotic attractions of nearly 100 young women who, at the start of her work, identified themselves as either lesbian or bisexual or refused a label. From her analysis of the many shifts they made between sexual identities and from their detailed descriptions of their erotic lives, Diamond argues that for her participants, and quite possibly for women on the whole, desire is malleable, that it cannot be captured by asking women to categorize their attractions at any single point, that to do so is to apply a male paradigm of more fixed sexual orientation. Among the women in her group who called themselves lesbian, to take one bit of the evidence she assembles to back her ideas, just one-third reported attraction solely to women as her research unfolded. And with the other two-thirds, the explanation for their periodic attraction to men was not a cultural pressure to conform but rather a genuine desire.

"Fluidity is not a fluke," Diamond declared, when I called her, after we first met before a guest lecture she gave at Chivers's university, to ask whether it really made sense to extrapolate from the experiences of her subjects to women in general. Slightly more than half of her participants began her study in the bisexual or unlabeled categories—wasn't it to be expected that she would find a great deal of sexual flux? She acknowledged this. But she emphasized that the pattern for her group over the years, both in the changing categories they chose and in the stories they told, was toward an increased sense of malleability. If female eros found its true expression over the course of her long research, then flexibility is embedded in the nature of female desire.

Diamond doesn't claim that women are without innate sexual orientations. But she sees significance in the fact that many of her subjects agreed with the statement "I'm the kind of person who becomes physically attracted to the person rather than their gender." For her participants, for the well-known women she lists at the start of her book and for women on average, she stresses that desire often emerges so compellingly from emotional closeness that innate orientations can be overridden. This may not always affect women's behavior—the overriding may not frequently impel heterosexual women into lesbian relationships—but it can redirect erotic attraction. One reason for this phenomenon, she suggests, may be found in oxytocin, a neurotransmitter unique to mammalian brains. The chemical's release has been shown, in humans, to facilitate feelings of trust and well-being, and in female prairie voles, a monogamous species of rodent, to connect the act of sex to the formation of faithful attachments. Judging by experiments in animals, and by the transmitter's importance in human childbirth and breast feeding, the oxytocin system, which relies on estrogen, is much more extensive in the female brain. For Diamond, all of this helps to explain why, in women, the link between intimacy and desire is especially potent.

Intimacy isn't much of an aphrodisiac in the thinking of Marta Meana, a professor of psychology at the *University of Nevada* at Las Vegas. Meana, who serves with Chivers on the board of *Archives of Sexual Behavior,* entered the field of sexology in the late 1990s and began by working clinically and carrying out research on dyspareunia—women's genital pain during intercourse. She is now formulating an explanatory model of female desire that will appear later this year in *Annual Review of Sex Research.* Before discussing her overarching ideas, though, we went together to a Cirque du Soleil show called "Zumanity," a performance of very soft-core pornography that Meana mentioned to me before my visit.

On the stage of the casino's theater, a pair of dark-haired, bare-breasted women in G-strings dove backward into a giant glass bowl and swam underwater, arching their spines as they slid up the walls. Soon a lithe blonde took over the stage wearing a pleated and extremely short schoolgirl's skirt. She spun numerous Hula-Hoops around her minimal waist and was hoisted by a cable high above the audience, where she spread her legs wider than seemed humanly possible. The crowd consisted of men and women about equally, yet women far outnumbered men onstage, and when at last the show's platinum-wigged M.C. cried out, "Where's the beef?" the six-packed, long-haired man who climbed up through a trapdoor and started to strip was surrounded by 8 or 10 already almost-bare women.

A compact 51-year-old woman in a shirtdress, Meana explained the gender imbalance onstage in a way that complemented Chivers's thinking. "The female body," she said, "looks the same whether aroused or not. The male, without an erection, is announcing a lack of arousal. The female body always holds the promise, the suggestion of sex"—a suggestion that sends a charge through both men and women. And there was another way, Meana argued, by which the Cirque du Soleil's offering of more female than male acrobats helped to rivet both genders in the crowd. She, even more than Chivers, emphasized the role of being desired—and of narcissism—in women's desiring.

The critical part played by being desired, Julia Heiman observed, is an emerging theme in the current study of female sexuality. Three or four decades ago, with the sense of sexual independence brought by the birth-control pill and the women's liberation movement, she said, the predominant cultural and sexological assumption was that female lust was fueled from within, that it didn't depend on another's initiation. One reason for the shift in perspective, she speculated, is a depth of insight gathered, in recent times, through a booming of qualitative research in sexology, an embrace of analyses built on personal, detailed interviews or on clinical experience, an approach that has gained attention as a way to counter the field's infatuation with statistical surveys and laboratory measurements.

Meana made clear, during our conversations in a casino bar and on the U.N.L.V. campus, that she was speaking in general terms, that, when it comes to desire, "the variability within genders may be greater than the differences between genders," that lust is infinitely complex and idiosyncratic.

She pronounced, as well, "I consider myself a feminist." Then she added, "But political correctness isn't sexy at all." For women, "being desired is the orgasm," Meana said somewhat metaphorically—it is, in her vision, at once the thing craved and the spark of craving. About the dynamic at "Zumanity" between the audience and the acrobats, Meana said the women in the crowd gazed at the women onstage, excitedly imagining that their bodies were as desperately wanted as those of the performers.

Meana's ideas have arisen from both laboratory and qualitative research. With her graduate student Amy Lykins, she published, in *Archives of Sexual Behavior* last year, a study of visual attention in heterosexual men and women. Wearing goggles that track eye movement, her subjects looked at pictures of heterosexual foreplay. The men stared far more at the females, their faces and bodies, than at the males. The women gazed equally at the two genders, their eyes drawn to the faces of the men and to the bodies of the women—to the facial expressions, perhaps, of men in states of wanting, and to the sexual allure embodied in the female figures.

Meana has learned too from her attempts as a clinician to help patients with dyspareunia. Though she explained that the condition, which can make intercourse excruciating, is not in itself a disorder of low desire, she said that her patients reported reduced genital pain as their desire increased. The problem was how to augment desire, and despite prevailing wisdom, the answer, she told me, had "little to do with building better relationships," with fostering communication between patients and their partners. She rolled her eyes at such niceties. She recalled a patient whose lover was thoroughly empathetic and asked frequently during lovemaking, "'Is this O.K.?' Which was very unarousing to her. It was loving, but there was no oomph"—no urgency emanating from the man, no sign that his craving of the patient was beyond control.

"Female desire," Meana said, speaking broadly and not only about her dyspareunic patients, "is not governed by the relational factors that, we like to think, rule women's sexuality as opposed to men's." She finished a small qualitative study last year consisting of long interviews with 20 women in marriages that were sexually troubled. Although bad relationships often kill desire, she argued, good ones don't guarantee it. She quoted from one participant's representative response: "We kiss. We hug. I tell him, 'I don't know what it is.' We have a great relationship. It's just that one area"—the area of her bed, the place desolated by her loss of lust.

The generally accepted therapeutic notion that, for women, incubating intimacy leads to better sex is, Meana told me, often misguided. "Really," she said, "women's desire is not relational, it's narcissistic"—it is dominated by the yearnings of "self-love," by the wish to be the object of erotic admiration and sexual need. Still on the subject of narcissism, she talked about research indicating that, in comparison with men, women's erotic fantasies center less on giving pleasure and more on getting it. "When it comes to desire," she added, "women may be far less relational than men."

Like Chivers, Meana thinks of female sexuality as divided into two systems. But Meana conceives of those systems in a different way than her colleague. On the one hand, as Meana constructs things, there is the drive of sheer lust, and on the other the impetus of value. For evolutionary and cultural reasons, she said, women might set a high value on the closeness and longevity of relationships: "But it's wrong to think that because relationships are what women choose they're the primary source of women's desire."

Meana spoke about two elements that contribute to her thinking: first, a great deal of data showing that, as measured by the frequency of fantasy, masturbation and sexual activity, women have a lower sex drive than men, and second, research suggesting that within long-term relationships, women are more likely than men to lose interest in sex. Meana posits that it takes a greater jolt, a more significant stimulus, to switch on a woman's libido than a man's. "If I don't love cake as much as you," she told me, "my cake better be kick-butt to get me excited to eat it." And within a committed relationship, the crucial stimulus of being desired decreases considerably, not only because the woman's partner loses a degree of interest but also, more important, because the woman feels that her partner is trapped, that a choice—the choosing of her—is no longer being carried out.

A symbolic scene ran through Meana's talk of female lust: a woman pinned against an alley wall, being ravished. Here, in Meana's vision, was an emblem of female heat. The ravisher is so overcome by a craving focused on this particular woman that he cannot contain himself; he transgresses societal codes in order to seize her, and she, feeling herself to be the unique object of his desire, is electrified by her own reactive charge and surrenders. Meana apologized for the regressive, anti-feminist sound of the scene.

Yet while Meana minimized the role of relationships in stoking desire, she didn't dispense with the sexual relevance, for women, of being cared for and protected. "What women want is a real dilemma," she said. Earlier, she showed me, as a joke, a photograph of two control panels, one representing the workings of male desire, the second, female, the first with only a simple on-off switch, the second with countless knobs. "Women want to be thrown up against a wall but not truly endangered. Women want a caveman and caring. If I had to pick an actor who embodies all the qualities, all the contradictions, it would be Denzel Washington. He communicates that kind of power and that he is a good man."

After our discussion of the alley encounter, we talked about erotic—as opposed to aversive—fantasies of rape. According to an analysis of relevant studies published last year in *The Journal of Sex Research,* an analysis that defines rape as involving "the use of physical force, threat of force, or incapacitation through, for example, sleep or intoxication, to coerce a woman into sexual activity against her will," between one-third and more than one-half of women have entertained such fantasies, often during intercourse, with at least 1 in 10 women fantasizing about sexual assault at least once per month in a pleasurable way.

The appeal is, above all, paradoxical, Meana pointed out: rape means having no control, while fantasy is a domain manipulated by the self. She stressed the vast difference between the pleasures of the imagined and the terrors of the real. "I hate the term 'rape fantasies,'" she went on. "They're really fantasies of submission." She spoke about the thrill of being wanted so much that the aggressor is willing to overpower, to take. "But 'aggression,' 'dominance,' I have to find better words. 'Submission' isn't even a good word"—it didn't reflect the woman's imagining of an ultimately willing surrender.

Chivers, too, struggled over language about this subject. The topic arose because I had been drawn into her ceaseless puzzling, as could easily happen when we spent time together. I had been thinking about three ideas from our many talks: the power, for women, in being desired; the keen excitement stoked by descriptions of sex with strangers; and her positing of distinct systems of arousal and desire. This last concept seemed to confound a simpler truth, that women associate lubrication with being turned on. The idea of dual systems appeared, possibly, to be the product of an unscientific impulse, a wish to make comforting sense of the unsettling evidence of women's arousal during rape and during depictions of sexual assault in the lab.

As soon as I asked about rape fantasies, Chivers took my pen and wrote "semantics" in the margin of my notes before she said, "The word 'rape' comes with gargantuan amounts of baggage." She continued: "I walk a fine line, politically and personally, talking frankly about this subject. I would never, never want to deliver the message to anyone that they have the right to take away a woman's autonomy over her body. I hammer home with my students, 'Arousal is not consent.'"

We spoke, then, about the way sexual fantasies strip away the prospect of repercussions, of physical or psychological harm, and allow for unencumbered excitement, about the way they offer, in this sense, a pure glimpse into desire, without meaning—especially in the case of sexual assault—that the actual experiences are wanted.

"It's the wish to be beyond will, beyond thought," Chivers said about rape fantasies. "To be all in the midbrain."

One morning in the fall, Chivers hunched over her laptop in her sparsely decorated office. She was sifting through data from her study of genital and subjective responses to audiotaped sex scenes. She peered at a jagged red line that ran across the computer's screen, a line that traced one subject's vaginal blood flow, second by second. Before Chivers could use a computer program to analyze her data, she needed to "clean" it, as the process is called—she had to eliminate errant readings, moments when a subject's shifting in her chair caused a slight pelvic contraction that might have jarred the plethysmograph, which could generate a spike in the readings and distort the overall results. Meticulously, she scanned the line, with all its tight zigs and zags, searching for spots where the inordinate height of a peak and the pattern that surrounded it told her that arousal wasn't at work, that this particular instant was irrelevant to her experiment. She highlighted and deleted one aberrant moment, then continued peering. She would search in this way for about two hours in preparing the data of a single subject. "I'm going blind," she said, as she stared at another suspicious crest.

It was painstaking work—and difficult to watch, not only because it might be destroying Chivers's eyesight but also because it seemed so dwarfed by the vastness and intricacy of the terrain she hoped to understand. Chivers was constantly conjuring studies she wanted to carry out, but with numberless aberrant spikes to detect and cleanse, how many could she possibly complete in one lifetime? How many could be done by all the sexologists in the world who focus on female desire, whether they were wiring women with plethysmographs or mapping the activity of their brains in fM.R.I. scanners or fitting them with goggles or giving them questionnaires or following their erotic lives for years? What more could sexologists ever provide than intriguing hints and fragmented insights and contradictory conclusions? Could any conclusion encompass the erotic drives of even one woman? Didn't the sexual power of intimacy, so stressed by Diamond, commingle with Meana's forces of narcissism? Didn't a longing for erotic tenderness coexist with a yearning for alley ravishing? Weren't these but two examples of the myriad conflicting elements that create women's lust? Had Freud's question gone unanswered for nearly a century not because science had taken so long to address it but because it is unanswerable?

Chivers, perhaps precisely because her investigations are incisive and her thinking so relentless, sometimes seemed on the verge of contradicting her own provisional conclusions. Talking about how her research might help women, she said that it could "shift the way women perceive their capacity to get turned on," that as her lab results make their way into public consciousness, the noncategorical physiological responses of her subjects might get women to realize that they can be turned on by a wide array of stimuli, that the state of desire is much more easily reached than some women might think. She spoke about helping women bring their subjective sense of lust into agreement with their genital arousal as an approach to aiding those who complain that desire eludes them. But didn't such thinking, I asked, conflict with her theory of the physiological and the subjective as separate systems? She allowed that it might. The giant forest seemed, so often, too complex for comprehension.

And sometimes Chivers talked as if the actual forest wasn't visible at all, as if its complexities were an indication less of inherent intricacy than of societal efforts to regulate female eros, of cultural constraints that have left women's lust dampened, distorted, inaccessible to understanding. "So many cultures have quite strict codes governing female sexuality," she said. "If that sexuality is relatively passive, then why so many rules to control it? Why is it so frightening?" There was the implication, in her words, that she might never illuminate her subject because she could not even see it, that the data she and her colleagues collect might be deceptive, might represent only the creations of culture, and that her interpretations might be leading away from underlying truth. There was the intimation that, at its core, women's sexuality might not be passive at all. There was the chance that the long history of fear might have buried the nature of women's lust too deeply to unearth, to view.

It was possible to imagine, then, that a scientist blinded by staring at red lines on her computer screen, or blinded by peering at any accumulation of data—a scientist contemplating, in darkness, the paradoxes of female desire—would see just as well.

---

**DANIEL BERGNER** is a contributing writer for the magazine, and author of, His new book, *The Other Side of Desire: Four Journeys Into the Far Realms of Lust and Longing . . .*

From *The New York Times,* January 2009. Copyright © 2009 by The New York Times Company. Reprinted by permission via PARS International.

# Women's Sexuality as They Age
## *The More Things Change, the More They Stay the Same*

PATRICIA BARTHALOW KOCH, PhD AND PHYLLIS KERNOFF MANSFIELD, PhD

With the aging of the baby boomers and the development and hugely successful marketing of Viagra® to treat erectile dysfunction, attention from sexologists, pharmaceutical companies, and the public has become focused on the sexuality of aging women.[1]

Some of the burning questions that are currently being pursued are: Does women's sexual functioning (sexual desire, arousal, orgasm, activity, and/or satisfaction) decrease with age and/or menopausal status? And what can be done to enhance aging women's sexual functioning?

As researchers try to provide answers for women, pharmaceutical companies, and other interested parties, what is becoming crystal clear is that we (the scientific community, health care professionals, and society at large) don't understand women's sexuality as they age because we don't understand women's sexuality. Therefore, we may not even be pursuing the right questions. For example, are specific elements of sexual "functioning" the most important aspects of women's sexuality or do we need to shift our focus?

## Models of Female Sexuality: The Importance of Context

Much of the information accumulated about women's sexuality has been generated from theories, research methodologies, and interpretation of data based on male models of sexuality, sexual functioning, and scientific inquiry.

As explained by Ray Rosen, Ph.D., at a recent conference on "Emerging Concepts in Women's Health," sexology has pursued a path of treating male and female functioning as similar, as evidenced by Masters and Johnson's development of the human sexual response cycle.[2]

What has resulted is a lack of appreciation for and documentation of the unique aspects of women's sexual functioning and expression. There is a growing chorus of sexologists acknowledging that women's sexuality, including their sexual response, merits different models than those developed for men.[3]

As Leonore Tiefer, Ph.D., has advocated, what is needed is a model of women's sexuality that is more "psychologically-minded, individually variable, interpersonally oriented, and socioculturally sophisticated."[4] Such models are beginning to emerge.[5]

The new models of female sexual response have been developed from quantitative and qualitative research findings and clinical practice assessments that more accurately reflect women's actual experiences than previous male-centered models.

A key component of these models is the importance of context to women's sexual expression. Context has been defined as "the whole situation, background, or environment relevant to some happening."[6] For example, unlike men whose sexual desire often is independent of context, women's sexual desire is often a responsive reaction to the context (her partner's sexual arousal, expressions of love and intimacy) rather than a spontaneous event.[7] Jordan identified the central dynamic of female adolescent sexuality as the relational context.[8] She described young women's sexual desire as actually being "desire for the experience of joining toward and joining in something that thereby becomes greater than the separate selves."[9]

So throughout women's development and the transitions in their lives (adolescence, pregnancy, parenthood, menopause) context is a key factor in their sexual expression. Thus, the more things change (their bodies, their relationships, their circumstances), the more they stay the same (the importance of context to their sexual expression).

## Insights from the Midlife Women's Health Survey

Applying the new models of women's sexuality that emphasize the importance of context helps us to better understand women's sexuality as they age. Findings from the Midlife Women's Health Survey (MWHS), a longitudinal study of the menopausal transition that is part of the broader Tremin Trust Research Program on Women's Health, support these new models.[10]

The Tremin Trust is a longitudinal, intergenerational study focusing on menstrual health that first enrolled 2,350 university women in 1934 and a second cohort of 1,600 young women between 1961 and 1963. (See the Tremin Trust Web site at www.pop.psu.edu/tremin/). In 1990, an additional 347 mid-life women were enrolled in order to better study various aspects of the menopausal transition, including sexual changes.

All the participants complete a daily menstrual calendar recording detailed information about their menstrual health

They also complete a yearly comprehensive survey, assessing biopsychosocial information about their health and aging, life experiences, and sexuality, among other factors. These surveys collect both quantitative and qualitative data. Throughout the years, some of the women have been called upon to participate in special qualitative studies in which they have been interviewed. One hundred of the perimenopausal women who are not taking hormone replacement therapy have also supplied daily morning urine specimens so that hormonal analysis could be conducted.

The Tremin Trust participants are incredibly dedicated to the project. For example, they keep daily records throughout their lives (for some almost 70 years) and enlist participation from their daughters, granddaughters, and great-granddaughters. The study's potential for providing a greater understanding of women's sexuality throughout their lives, and the factors that affect sexual changes, is unparalleled. The greatest limitation is the lack of diversity among the participants, since over 90 percent are well-educated white women. However, data collection has been conducted with additional samples of African-American and Alaskan women as well as lesbians. More diverse cohorts may be enlisted in the future.

Analysis of the sexuality data is ongoing, with more data being collected each year. Interesting findings have emerged regarding midlife women's sexuality (ages 35 through 55 years of age) as they progress through menopausal transition. The average age of menopause is 51, with perimenopause beginning as early as the late thirties. In an open-ended question asking what they enjoyed most about their sexuality, more than two-thirds of the women referred to aspects of their relationships with their partners.[11] Most of these responses described some aspect of intimacy, including love, closeness, sharing, companionship, affection, and caring, as described below. About 15 percent of the women noted feeling comfortable and secure in their relationship, emphasizing feelings of mutual trust and honesty.

It is the most healthy relationship I've ever been in. Sex in the context of a respectful, caring, non-exploitative relationship is very wonderful.

Wow! The sexual experience is another heightened way we share the humor that comes from shared experiences such as canoeing, fine music, backyard work, scuba trips. It makes the "union" a joyous and complete one!

Many of the lesbian participants felt that the intimacy they shared in their relationships was even greater than what they had experienced or observed in male-female relationships.

Many straight women in 20-to-25-year marriages are distant and emotionally separate from their husbands. I think this is a time when lesbian women and their partners really come into their own—their best time together. There's much greater emotional intimacy with less emphasis on sex. It's very nurturing and increases the bond between us.

Another very important contextual feature that at least one in ten women enjoyed about their sexuality was a newly-found sexual freedom they experienced as they aged, either from their children leaving home or from being with a new partner.

Freedom and ability to be spontaneous with our sexual desires due to the "empty nest."

The freedom to have sex at his apartment. The growing intimacy and closeness that goes along with sex itself. The sexual playfulness and frivolity that threads itself through regular daily activities (teasing, sexual nuances, private jokes, and touches).

Approximately 20 percent of the women discussed some particular aspect to their sexual interactions, with mutual sexual satisfaction, continuing sexual interest, desire, and attraction, and lessened inhibitions and increased experimentation mentioned most often.

We seem to enjoy sex more and more as the years go by. The orgasms seem even better. We both respond well to each other sexually since we feel safe in our loving monogamous relationship.

One-third of these discussions emphasized that touching, kissing, hugging, and cuddling were the most important aspects of the sexual interactions.

You may not consider it sexual, but sleeping together in a queen-sized bed in the last year and a half. While the kids were growing up, we had twin beds. We enjoy the cuddling this provides daily.

Qualities exhibited by their sexual partners, who are most often the women's husbands, have been found to significantly impact the women's sexual responding.[12] Specifically, the more love, affection, passion, assertiveness, interest, and equality expressed by the sexual partners, the higher the women's sexual desire, arousal, frequency, and enjoyment. Women also expressed appreciation for a non-demanding partner who was responsive to their needs.

My partner is very accepting about how I feel and what I like and what I don't like even though it changes often. I also appreciate that he doesn't expect me to have an orgasm every time we make love.

## Sexual Changes as Women Age

Each year the women report many changes in their sexual responding. Some women have reported enjoying sex more (8.7 percent), easier arousal (8.7 percent), desiring sexual relations more (7 percent), easier orgasm (6.7 percent), and engaging in sexual relations more often (4.7 percent).[13] The women attribute their improved sexuality most often to changes in life circumstances (new partner, more freedom with children leaving home), improved emotional well-being, more positive feelings toward partner, and improved appearance.[14]

However, two to three times more women have reported declines in their sexual responding, including: desiring sexual relations less (23.1 percent), engaging in sexual relations less often (20.7 percent), desiring more non-genital touching (19.7 percent), more difficult arousal (19.1 percent), enjoying sexual relations less (15.4 percent), more difficult orgasm (14 percent), and more pain (10 percent).

Women are much more likely to attribute declining sexual response to physical changes of menopause than to other factors.[15] Analysis of the health data has found a statistically significant relationship between having vaginal dryness and decreased sexual desire and enjoyment.[16] However, no statistically significant relationship between menopausal status and decreased sexual desire, enjoyment, or more difficulty with orgasm was found. On the other hand, sexual desire and enjoyment were significantly related to marital status, with decreases associated with being married. The woman's age was also significantly related to her sexual enjoyment, with enjoyment decreasing as the woman became older. Further, a significant relationship has been found between poor body image and decreased sexual satisfaction.[17]

Other studies among general populations of aging women have failed to find clear associations between menopausal status and declines in sexual functioning.[18] Similar to the MWHS findings, they found psychosocial factors to be more important determinants of sexual responding among midlife (perimenopausal and menopausal) women than menopausal status.[19] The factors include sexual attitudes and knowledge; previous sexual behavior and enjoyment; length and quality of relationship; physical and mental health; body image and self-esteem; stress; and partner availability, health, and sexual functioning.

## Sexual Satisfaction and the Importance of Sex for Women

Even with many aging women in the MWHS identifying declines in their sexual desire, frequency, or functioning, about three-quarters of them reported overall sexual satisfaction (71 percent), including being physically and emotionally satisfied (72 percent).

> Even though sex is less frequent and it takes much longer to feel turned on, it is still very satisfying.

> I have been a very fortunate person. The man I married I still love dearly. We both respect each other and try to keep each other happy. We don't have sex as much as we used to but we kiss and hug and hold each other a lot.

The importance of sexual expression varied in the midlife women's lives and was affected by the circumstances in which they found themselves (married, divorced, widowed, in a same-sex relationship). Once again, women evaluated the importance of sexuality in the overall context of their lives. Some women who had lost their sexual partners to death or divorce reported missing a sexual relationship, mostly because of the lack of intimacy.

> I find being a widow at a young age to be very lonely. I find that I miss the desire to have a sexual closeness with a man. I also feel very sad and confused as my husband

---

## Half of Americans over 60 Have Sexual Relations at Least Once a Month

Nearly half of all Americans over the age of 60 have sexual relations at least once a month, and 40 percent would like to have it more often. In addition, many seniors say their sex lives are more emotionally satisfying now than when they were in their forties.

These findings were part of the latest Roper-Starch Inc. survey of 1,300 men and women over the age of 60 conducted by the National Council on the Aging.

"This study underscores the enduring importance of sex among older men and women—even among those who report infrequent sexual activity," said Neal Cutler, director of survey research for the Council. "When older people are not sexually active, it is usually because they lack a partner or because they have a medical condition."

As most people might expect, the survey found that sexual relations taper off with age, with 71 percent of men and 51 percent of women in their sixties having sex once a month or more and 27 percent of men and 18 percent of women in their eighties saying they do. Cutler said women had sex less often in part because women are more likely to be widowed.

Thirty-nine percent of people said they were happy with the amount of sexual relations they currently have—even if it is none—while another 39 percent said they would like to make love more often. Only four percent of the people surveyed said they would like to have sexual relations less frequently. The people who had sex at least once a month said it was important to their relationship.

The survey also found that 74 percent of men and 70 percent of women find their sex lives more emotionally satisfying now that they are older than when they were in their forties. As to whether it is physically better, 43 percent say it is just as good as or better than in their youth, while 43 percent say sex is less satisfying.

"When it comes to knowledge about sex, older people are not necessarily wiser than their children. A third of the respondents believed it was natural to lose interest in sex as they got older," said Cutler.

---

was the only man I have ever been with. Having lost him, I fear beginning a new relationship.

I have been alone for 18 years after a 14 year marriage and three children. I miss regular sex, but *most* of all I miss touching, cuddling, body-to-body contact, not the sex act.

Yet many women without partners had decided that having sexual relations was not worth the price if the overall relationship was not fulfilling.

I am single by choice (heterosexual) and have never wanted children. I am finding it difficult to meet men as I get older and my relationships are further apart. My sexual response is still very strong, but I am not willing to compromise what I want in a relationship just for sex. My attitude is that if that doesn't happen, I am doing fine, and am happy with my life.

I find myself wishing for a "partner" but only if he's a real friend. My celibacy is comfortable at the moment. It has become apparent to me that our culture has taught most females to sacrifice themselves to their partner's desires and not to defend themselves. I hope I don't fall in that trap again. I find that I satisfy my physical sexual desires better than my husband ever did.

On the other hand, sexual interaction is very important to many of the aging women.

I am 58 and as horny as ever. . . . The sex urge is still with me, not much different from my earlier years. Maybe I am too physically active and healthy! I can't seem to get it into my head that I am approaching a different time of life. . . . There is little or no speaking about a situation like mine in books or media. Yet women my age say the same thing: "Where are the men? Men want only younger women. The 'good men' are married or in relationships." . . . My request to you is—listen to the voice of the horny women. When we hear each other and gain our dignity, solutions will come!

# Conclusion

Results from the MWHS, some of which have been shared in this article, illustrate that women experience their sexuality as complex and holistic. Thus, it is doubtful that a particular drug or other substance or device that could improve physical functioning (increase libido or vasocongestion) would be the "magic bullet" to transform women's sexuality as they age. In order to understand and enhance women's sexuality throughout their lives, we must listen to their voices, learn from their experiences, and appreciate the importance of context to their sexual expression.

# References

1. R. Basson, J. Berman, et al., "Report on the International Consensus Development Conference on Female Sexual Dysfunction: Definitions and Classifications," *Journal of Urology,* vol. 163, pp. 888–93; J. Hitt, "The Second Sexual Revolution," *The New York Times Magazine,* February 20, 2000, pp. 34–41, 50, 62, 64, 68–69; J. Leland, "The Science of Women and Sex," *Newsweek,* May 29, 2000, pp. 48–54; P. K. Mansfield, P. B. Koch, and A. M. Voda, "Qualities Midlife Women Desire in Their Sexual Relationships and Their Changing Sexual Response," *Psychology of Women Quarterly,* vol. 22, pp. 285–303.

2. R. Rosen, *Major Issues in Contemporary Research in Women's Sexuality.* (Roundtable discussion at the Women's Health Research Symposium, Baltimore, MD.)

3. R. Basson, "The Female Sexual Response: A Different Model," *Journal of Sex and Marital Therapy,* vol. 26, pp. 51–65. S. R. Leiblum, "Definition and Classification of Female Sexual Disorders," *International Journal of Impotence Research,* vol. 10, pp. S102–S106; R. Rosen, *Major Issues in Contemporary Research in Women's Sexuality.*

4. L. Tiefer, "Historical, Scientific, Clinical and Feminist Criticisms of the Human Sexual Response Cycle," *Annual Review of Sex Research,* vol. 2, p. 2.

5. R. Basson, "The Female Sexual Response: A Different Model," pp. 51–65; L. Tiefer, "A New View of Women's Sexual Problems: Why New? Why Now?," *The Journal of Sex Research,* vol. 38, no. 2, pp. 89–96.

6. *Webster's New World Dictionary of the American Language: College Edition* (New York: The World Publishing Company, 2000).

7. R. Basson, "The Female Sexual Response: A Different Model," pp. 51–65.

8. J. Jordan, *Clarity in Connection: Empathic Knowing, Desire and Sexuality,* work in progress (Wellesley, MA: Stone Center Working Papers Series, 1987).

9. J. Jordan, *Clarity in Connection: Empathic Knowing, Desire and Sexuality.*

10. A. M. Voda and P. K. Mansfield, *The Tremin Trust and the Midlife Women's Health Survey: Two Longitudinal Studies of Women's Health and Menopause.* (Paper presented at the Society for Menstrual Cycle Research Conference, Montreal, June 1995.); A. M. Voda, J. M. Morgan, et al., "The Tremin Trust Research Program" in N. F. Taylor and D. Taylor, editors, *Menstrual Health and Illness* (New York: Hemisphere Press, 1991), pp. 5–19.

11. *Midlife Women's Health Survey,* 1992, unpublished data.

12. P. K. Mansfield, P. B. Koch, et al., "Qualities Midlife Women Desire in Their Sexual Relationships and Their Changing Sexual Response," *Psychology of Women Quarterly,* vol. 22, pp. 285–303.

13. Ibid.

14. P. K. Mansfield, P. B. Koch, et al., "Midlife Women's Attributions for Their Sexual Response Changes," *Health Care for Women International,* vol. 21, pp. 543–59.

15. Ibid.

16. P. K. Mansfield, A. Voda, et al., "Predictors of Sexual Response Changes in Heterosexual Midlife Women," *Health Values,* vol. 19, no. 1, pp. 10–20.

17. D. A. Thurau, *The Relationship between Body Image and Sexuality among Menopausal Women.* (Unpublished master's thesis, Pennsylvania State University, 1996).

18. N. E. Avis, M. A. Stellato, et al., "Is There an Association between Menopause Status and Sexual Functioning?," *Menopause,* vol. 7, no. 5, pp. 297–309; K. Hawton, D. Gaith, et al., "Sexual Function in a Community Sample of Middle-aged Women with Partners: Effects of Age, Marital, Socioeconomic, Psychiatric, Gynecological, and Menopausal Factors," *Archives of Sexual Behavior,* vol. 23, no. 4, pp. 375–95.

19. N. E. Avis, M. A. Stellato, et al., "Is There an Association between Menopause Status and Sexual Functioning?," pp. 297–309; I. Fooken, "Sexuality in the Later Years—The Impact of Health and Body-Image in a Sample of Older Women," *Patient Education and Counseling,* vol. 23, pp. 227–33; K. Hawton, D. Gaith, et al., "Sexual Function in a Community Sample of Middle-aged Women with Partners: Effects of Age, Marital, Socioeconomic, Psychiatric, Gynecological, and Menopausal Factors," *Archives of Sexual Behavior,* vol. 23, no. 4, pp. 375–95; B. K. Johnson,

"A Correlational Framework for Understanding Sexuality in Women Age 50 and Older," *Health Care for Women International,* vol. 19, pp. 553–64.

---

PATRICIA BARTHALOW KOCH, PhD is an Associate Professor, Biobehavioral Health & Women's Studies at Pennsylvania State University State College, PA. Dr. Koch is also adjunct professor of human sexuality at Widener University in West Chester, PA. PHYLLIS KERNOFF MANSFIELD, PhD is a Professor, Women's Studies & Health Education at Pennsylvania State University State College, PA. Dr. Mansfield is director of the Tremin Trust Research Program on Women's Health. Dr. Koch is assistant director.

From *SIECUS Report*, December 2001/January 2002, pp. 5–9. Copyright © 2002 by Sex Information & Education Council of the United States. Reprinted by permission.

# Peer Marriage

PEPPER SCHWARTZ

Our generation has been the first to witness the emergence of "partnership" or "peer" marriages on a large social scale. Such marriages differ from their traditional counterparts in at least four key respects: men and women in these relationships regard each other as full social equals; both pursue careers; partners share equal authority for financial and other decision making; and, not least important, husbands typically assume far greater responsibility for child-rearing than in the past. Many of us—including much of the feminist movement, of which I have been a part—tend to regard these marriages as a major social breakthrough, the culmination of an arduous, generation-long effort to redefine women's roles and to secure for women the same freedom and dignity that society has traditionally accorded to men.

Yet in recent years conservatives, particularly the adherents of the "pro-family" or "family values" movement, have increasingly called for a rejection of the peer marriage ideal and a return by society as a whole to the traditional role-differentiated model. Bolstering their case is a significant body of traditional social theory arguing for the superior stability of the role-differentiated marriage, in which the husband serves as sole provider and main figure of authority, and the wife bears the lion's share of responsibilities for child rearing and day-to-day household maintenance.

Contemporary concerns with marital and family stability are certainly warranted. In a society with a 50 percent divorce rate—in which a host of social pathologies can be traced directly to havoc in fatherless or broken homes—policymakers and theorists are right to place a high priority on measures aimed at keeping families intact. Yet it is far from self-evident that the road to greater marital stability lies in a return to tradition. Over the past generation, I would argue, broad changes in society—and in the expectations that men and women bring to the marital relationship—have undermined much of the original basis of the traditional model of marriage. In reality, as I will try to show here, peer marriage offers a new formula for family and marital stability that may be both more durable and better adapted to the demands of contemporary culture than the older form. New data from studies that I and others have conducted support the notion that peer marriages are at least as stable as traditional unions and may in the long run prove more resilient vis-à-vis the special social pressures that marriages confront today.

## Marital Stability and Marital Satisfaction

There is a close connection between marital stability and happiness or satisfaction in marriage—in both practice and theory. Even the most hard-headed theorists of the traditional model—such as sociologist Talcott Parsons or economist Gary Becker—have invariably sought to reconcile their advocacy of gender-based role differentiation with the possibility of marital satisfaction. To justify the traditional division of labor in marriage purely on the basis of men's and women's different biological aptitudes, historical experience, or cultural training is, after all, not a difficult theoretical task. But to posit happiness and mutual satisfaction as the outcome of such a union is another matter.

This is not to say that happiness was or is impossible to achieve under the traditional marital regime. Many people, especially when the larger culture supports it, find happiness in holding up their part of the marital bargain: women who like to be in charge of the kitchen, and men who want to bring home the bacon but do not want to cook it. In the past, and even today, this contract has worked for many people. Increasingly, however, it does not work as well as it used to. It did not work for me as well as it worked for my mother, and it didn't work for her all the time, either. The gender-based division of labor, so automatic for so much of history, increasingly fails to bring the promised emotional fulfillment that was supposed to be a major part of its contribution to family satisfaction and stability—emotional fulfillment which is increasingly vital to marital stability today.

We may contrast the experience of my mother's generation with that of my own. Like so many women of her era, my mother traded *service* for *support,* a transaction with which she usually seemed content. She bore almost complete responsibility for raising her children and at the same time had full charge of household upkeep: cooking, cleaning, keeping my father's closets and drawers impeccably neat, and so forth. My father, not atypical of his generation, was a man who never packed his own suitcase for a trip. In return, he provided handsomely—beyond my mother's wildest dreams, since she had grown up in poverty and was forced to drop out of high school to support her ailing mother and her youngest sisters. Having met my father as a secretary in his fledgling law office, my mother was very grateful to have been pulled from destitution into a different social class. Later she could afford to finish high school and college, raise three children, and become a docent in an art museum. Her lifestyle with my father was something secure and in a sense wonderful, exceeding all her childhood expectations.

The arrangement worked well for my father also. He was not born to privilege. The eldest of five growing up on a farm in Indiana, he put himself through law school, transferring from the University of Chicago to night school at Loyola when times got rough. He scrambled to better himself and his family. He and his wife had the same goal: to achieve the means for the good life. They entertained clients and traveled.

But my father also expected my mother to do everything he told her to do. After all, his own father had been dictatorial; it was something a woman owed a man—even though, in my grandfather's case, his wife had purchased the farm for the family. No matter. Leadership at home was owed a man as part of his birthright. When my mother—an intense, intelligent woman—would occasionally resist an order or talk back, my father's response to her was scathing and uninhibited.

What was the bargain my mother willingly made? She had a husband who loved her, who created an increasingly luxurious environment, and who ordered her around and reminded her—almost incessantly—about how lucky she was to have him. Love and what my generation of women would call patriarchal control went hand in hand. On my mother's side, gratitude, deep resentment, and anger all came in a neat package. The marriage lasted 55 years, until my mother's death. Children were launched. The marriage could be declared a success. Nevertheless, under today's circumstances, I would expect such a marriage to survive ten years at best.

Today my mother would have had a chance at her own career, at which she had the talent to excel. She would have had a new identity as a human being with core rights and her own sense of entitlement. (Surely, she promoted mine.) She would have had a different standard of equality and different ideas about equity. She would probably not have thought it enough to have been rescued from poverty. She would have felt entitled to a different style of family decision making, and she would have had the options—and the cultural support—to demand more. But if my father had remained the

same man he was when I was growing up, he would not have acquiesced. Under contemporary circumstances, the marriage most probably would have broken up—much to my own, my siblings', and probably my parents' disadvantage.

And that is one reason why I believe peer marriage—a marriage founded on the principle of equality and supported by shared roles and a greater chance of shared sensibilities—is an adaptation in the direction of greater family stability rather than instability. Indeed, in contemporary culture, a peer or partner relationship between spouses has become increasingly vital to keeping families intact. It also offers new advantages to children, to which I will return in a moment.

We must be clear, however, that the mere existence of separate careers does not guarantee a peer marriage. Such a marriage also requires a comprehensive reconceptualization of the partners' roles. Dual incomes alone are insufficient to guarantee stability.

## Money and Work

Indeed, much empirical research, some of it my own, indicates that labor force participation and achievement of high income by women destabilizes marriage. A number of studies, including the well-known Income Maintenance Study done out of the University of Michigan, found that when one raised the income of low-income women—hoping to stabilize families by reducing poverty—divorce increased substantially. Theorists have deduced that, under such circumstances, growth in income simply opens a new option for women to leave the relationship, an option that many of them exercise. Moreover, many studies show high-earning women with higher breakup rates. It is unclear whether high earnings make women less willing to tolerate unwanted behaviors or other disappointments on the part of their spouses, or whether men find women who are ambitious or aggressive (or who possess other traits consonant with career success) unsatisfying to be with in the long run. At any rate, the correlation is real enough.

Nor do couples necessarily adapt smoothly to equalization of income and status between partners. In *American Couples,* a study of 6,000 married, cohabiting, and lesbian and gay couples, Phil Blumstein and I found that a partner's power rose in relation to his or her relative income as compared with that of the spouse or live-in lover, but not necessarily in the ways we would have predicted. Women's power rose and became equal to their partners' when they had equal income—but only if they had a supportive ideology that allowed them to claim equal power. And power did not necessarily increase proportionally to the income differential. For example, more power did not release women from as much housework as one might expect. Higher-income career women did less, but not equivalently less, and their partners did not do proportionately more. (Male partners of high-earning women *did* feel their partners were entitled to do less housework, but did not feel required to do more themselves!) Feminists may be inclined to despair: Are men so resistant to participation in household labor that nothing will induce them to pitch in appropriately?

Yet—and this is the key point—it remains to be seen whether the tensions we found are the permanent consequence of change or merely transitional pains that arise as couples, and society as a whole, grope for a new definition of the marital relationship. Many men are clearly uncomfortable with the weakening of the traditional male role as sole provider. And, notably, there has been little effort—outside a small and probably unrepresentative "men's movement"—to reconceptualize the husband's role under these new economic circumstances. However, several changes are conspiring to move society as a whole beyond this sometimes painful transitional phase: transformations in the economy, in the attitudes of younger men, and in the cultural definition of marriage itself.

In the first place, in the contemporary economy female income has become an important ingredient of family prosperity (even, in many cases, a necessity). Economists have long recognized that household income has maintained stability in the United States over the past decades only through large-scale entry of women into the work force. The two-income household, once an exception, is now increasingly the norm.

Furthermore, corporate restructuring and downsizing have tended to intensify the trend. Women's labor force participation has become increasingly vital to family stability in a society where job security is, for all but a few, a thing of the past. Men are now beginning to realize that their hold on continuous employment after age 40 is, to say the least, shaky. By age 55, less than half of all men are still fully employed. Women, having many of the skills necessary for a service-oriented society, stay employable longer and more steadily. Indeed, in our society, the nonworking wife is increasingly becoming a symbol of exceptional wealth or conspicuous consumption—or of a major ideological commitment either to the patriarchal family or to a vision of the female as the primary parent.

There are signs that these new economic realities are beginning to affect attitudes among men in their 20s. Young boys today are increasingly growing up in two-parent families where females are either the chief provider or an essential contributor to family income. Moreover, they understand their own economic futures as providers to be far from secure. Partly as a result, more and more young men are seeking in marriage someone to be part of an economic team rather than an exclusive parenting specialist. Just as women have in the past sought "a good provider," so, I predict, men will increasingly want to marry (and stay married to) a woman who can provide her share of economic stability.

But possibly the most important change has come in the subtle cultural redefinition of the marital relationship itself. In a society in which divorce is prevalent and the economic independence of both spouses is the rule, marital stability depends increasingly on factors of personal satisfaction and emotional fulfillment. The glue holding marriages together today is neither economic necessity nor cultural sanction, but emotion. Marital stability in contemporary society increasingly depends on sustaining the emotional satisfaction of *both* partners. It is here that peer marriage shows its special advantages.

Under these new economic and cultural circumstances, the ability of men and women to participate in each other's lives—to build companion status—becomes essential to marital survival. Equality is a crucial ingredient of this form of intimacy. When women have validation in the outside world through career, and when couples can operate as a team on both economic and home issues, partners become more similar to each other and achieve greater emotional compatibility—or so I would hypothesize on the basis of my research with peer couples. With more outside experiences to bring to the marital community, the woman becomes a more interesting companion for the long run. Moreover, whatever competition or tensions may result from this new arrangement, women today probably need some of these career-related personality traits simply to stay competitive with the women men increasingly meet in the workplace. This was less important in a society where home and family were sacrosanct and a mother and wife—no matter how far she was from being a "soul mate"—was automatically protected from outside contenders for her spouse. However, that is not the society we live in any more, nor is it likely to return. And even though income creates independence and therefore opportunities for separation, the recognition that spouses would lose their mutually constructed lifestyle if the marriage ended has its own stabilizing effect, as I have found in my interviews with dozens of peer couples.

## Love Versus Money

Of course, even today, if one were to analyze marriage in purely economic terms, the traditional model can seem to offer certain advantages over the peer arrangement. Becker and others have contended that, at least during child-raising years, couples with the woman in a full-time mothering role tend to gain more income. And a few studies have shown that men with working wives have lower incomes than men with nonworking wives. Economically ambitious couples probably calculate correctly that one parent, usually the male, should be released from most parental duties to earn as much as he can; the payoff here will lie in enhanced family income and social status, in which both partners presumably will share.

But this approach fails to address the real problem at the base of today's shaky marital system—maintaining a high standard of emotional fulfillment. "Efficient" role allocation frequently leaves partners leading parallel and largely separate lives. Mom and Dad did that—each an expert in their separate spheres. It worked when there was less expectation that marriage should produce a soul mate, and when Mom's tolerance levels were higher for the habitual carping at dinner. While this system did and does work for some, it tends to diminish emotional partnership. People in such "parallel marriages," financially secure, look at each other ten years later and say, "Why you?"—and they divorce, often with children in primary grades.

## Secrets of Peer Success

One key to the success of peer unions lies in *joint child rearing*—the creation of a male parenting niche in day-to-day family life. Indeed, I would go so far as to say that joint child rearing constitutes the secret of successful peer unions and a new pathway to marital and family stability in contemporary life. Joint child-rearing cements a new intimacy between husband and wife and, research shows, builds a critical and difficult-to-sever tie between the two parents and the children.

Some theorists in the past have actually argued *against* a model of significant daily paternal participation in parenting, on the grounds that male involvement will erode the natural dependence of men on women and that men, resenting the extra burden, will ultimately leave. Of course, a lot of men are leaving in any case. And certainly some studies, particularly among working-class men, show child care and household labor participation to be associated with lower marital satisfaction. Still, other researchers have found large numbers of men whose perception of shared participation correlates with greater marital satisfaction.

On the woman's side, moreover, the picture is not at all ambiguous. Shared labor has a *major* impact on women's satisfaction in marriage—and since more women than men leave relationships, this is a significant finding. A 1996 study by Nancy K. Grote and others showed that the more traditional the division of labor, the lower marital satisfaction was for women (though *not* for men). However, *both* men and women reported higher erotic satisfaction and friendship with one another when household labor, including parenting, was shared more equitably.

My studies and others show several other important benefits to joint child rearing: First, the more men participate, the more attached they are to their children. Second, the more they parent, the more grateful wives are. Third, under joint parenting, it becomes harder for either the husband or the wife to consider leaving. And finally, unless the men are manifestly awful parents, children benefit from their father's attention, skills, and additional perspective. This extra parenting and contact with the father can represent a real boon for children.

While my study draws from interviews with only about one hundred couples, some research based on large data sets reinforces my findings. In *Bitter Choices: Blue Collar Women In and Out of Work,* E. I. Rosin showed that a substantial number of working-class women interpreted the husband's help with children and housework as an expression of love and caring. A very interesting study by Diane Lye at the University of Washington found, among other things, that men who had the lowest divorce rates had the highest interaction with their sons around traditionally male games—football, baseball, etc. Interestingly, the same was true of men who participated in similar activities with their daughters. Other studies have found a lower divorce rate among men who attended prenatal classes.

Still, one may argue that we are talking here about atypical men. Only a certain kind of fellow will participate in a prenatal class: peer men are born, not made. Yet that is not what I found in my own research. Most men I interviewed in egalitarian marriages did not come to them by way of ideological motivation, nor were they married to women who described themselves as feminists. The usual road to peer marriage was happenstance. The four most common routes: (1) A serious desire on the part of the husband to father more, and more effectively, than he himself had been fathered (men in these situations were frequently wrestling with significant pain left over from paternal abuse, neglect, or abandonment). (2) A job that *required* shift work or role sharing and which, over time, greatly attached the father to the parenting role. (3) A strong-willed working partner who presumed egalitarian marriage; men in these cases were mostly prepared to structure the marriage any way their wives (often not declared feminists) preferred to have it. (4) The experience of an unsatisfactory, highly traditional first marriage in which the wife was perceived as too emotionally dependent during the marriage and too economically helpless after it was over; men in these cases consciously selected a different kind of spouse and marital bargain in the second marriage.

Were they happy with their new bargain? Most of these men expressed pride in themselves, their wives, and their home life. Were these typical egalitarian marriages? It is impossible to say. But these marriages, while not invulnerable, looked more stable for their integration—in much the way traditional marriages often appear: integrated, independent, and satisfied.

## "Near Peers"

Some of the most troubled contemporary marriages, I have found, are those, in essence, caught between the old and the new paradigm—marriages that are neither fully traditional nor fully peer. I called such couples "near peers," since they professed belief in equal participation but failed to achieve it in practice. I believe the experience of such "near peers" may lie behind some of the frustrations that lead conservatives and others today to declare, in effect, that "We have tried equality and it has failed." In reality, what many couples have tried is inequality under the label of equality—an experience which has given equality, in some quarters, a bad name.

In "near peer" marriages, the wife typically devoted vastly more energy to the children while holding down a job. Although the husband made certain contributions to child rearing and household upkeep, and professed an eagerness to do more, actual male performance fell short of the intended ideal, stirring the wife's resentment. In most cases, "near peer" men still controlled the finances and exercised veto power over the wife. The wife, performing a full-time job outside the home with little or no relief inside of it, was typically caught in a "slow burn" of inward anger. Paradoxically, such women did not long for more equality, since they assumed it would bring more of the same—increased responsibilities with no substantial male contribution. These women felt trapped and overwhelmed and many of them, I found, would have been happy to leave the work force if it were financially possible. Furthermore, all their power—and much of their pleasure—continued to reside in the mothering role. They loved their children, felt compromised at the inadequacy of parenting time, and, perhaps surprisingly, rarely considered that one answer might be greater paternal participation. In truth, many such women were unwilling to surrender hegemony at home.

In such marriages, each spouse typically clings to his or her traditional powers while simultaneously craving a more partnership-oriented relationship. The result is emotional disappointment and conflict. Women in such relationships tend to view egalitarian gender roles as oppressive—seeing more respect, security, and satisfaction in the role of full-time mother. Yet they simultaneously resent the husband's low participation and quasi-autocratic behavior, since they feel they have earned equality and crave it on an emotional level.

## Roadblocks and Suggested Policy Reforms

While I have found that there are many different routes to a stable peer marriage, achievement of such a relationship is not automatic, as the experiences of the "near peers" attest. Several barriers stand in the way.

In the first place, it is often hard to avoid role differentiation, especially when partners have been strongly socialized to one or the other role. For example, it is simply not in the couple's best interests for the "bad cook" to prepare dinner while the good one does dishes. Even though cooking can be learned—quite easily, in fact—the startup costs (bad meals for a while) stop most couples in their tracks. The better the homemaker-parent and the more outstanding the provider, the less likely there is to be taste for change.

Other inhibitors to peer marriages include the gender-based organization of jobs in the outside world (which affect evaluations of each partner's career prospects), and the overall pull of the status quo. Yet in a sense, the biggest roadblock we face is our sense of the possible. Many women and men simply do not believe an egalitarian marriage is feasible—unless they happen to be in one. Even many who desire the peer model do not believe it can be achieved within ordinary working schedules. And most women expect significant male resistance and see a risk in asserting themselves, fearing that conflict with their husbands will lead to defeat and deeper resentment on their own part, or even divorce.

These are all reasonable cautions. The pleasure of sharing the day-to-day administration of home and family is not apparent to many men, especially those socialized to the older model. Nonetheless, today we find an increasing number of young men and remarried men actually yearning to be an involved parent. This represents a shift in ideology, a new view of "what is important in life."

However, women, too, need to change. Many women are used to being taken care of and are trained for submissive interaction with men. In effect, they set up during courtship many of the inequities they will complain about in marriage—and ultimately flee from. They want intimacy, yet they often establish conditions—such as maximization of male income—that subvert family time and marital closeness.

In addition, there are several public policy reforms that might assist in the formation of peer marriages and thereby help anchor families of the future. Such reforms might include classes on marriage and the family in high school, where young men and women can learn a model of partnership, equity, and friendship; more pressure on employers to offer flextime and on-site child care, so that individuals are not penalized for their parenting choices; and after-school care in the public schools (until 6 P.M.).

There also needs to be more cultural support from the larger society. Most parents do not want to see their sons in the role of primary parent, do not want their sons' careers compromised, and still view a woman's work—including care for children—as unmanly. Moreover, most women are not encouraged to think of themselves as potential providers; only recently have they come to imagine themselves as fully committed to careers. I know there is a great split of opinion over whether young mothers should work at all, much less be encouraged to be responsible for their own economic welfare. But I would suggest that too much specialization in parenting and insufficient equality of experience may be more injurious in the long run than the difficulties involved when both partners juggle work and home.

## Conclusions

We must recognize that there is no one form of marital organization appropriate for all couples. But I believe the "pro-family" or "family values" movement has been needlessly antagonistic to feminist models of marriage. After all, the two sides in this dialogue share some important goals: we do not want marriages to break up unless they absolutely have to; we want children to be loved and cherished and brought to adulthood in an intact family if there is any way it can be accomplished without punishment to either the children or the parents; we want people to want to form lasting bonds that strengthen the extended family.

The big question is how best to accomplish this. I suggest that shared parenting and increased spousal satisfaction are the most effective routes to family stability. I think that newfound feelings about equity and emotional closeness are essential to modern marital durability. Peer relationships will be good for women, children, and families—and a great benefit for men as well. Peer marriage is not a feminist or elitist vision.

It is a practical plan to lower the divorce rate. But in order to see how well it works, society needs to offer the cultural and structural support to permit both men and women to parent, to participate in each other's lives, and to have the time together that a strong relationship requires. Whether peer marriage will actually work better than traditional marriage is, at this point a matter of conjecture. We do know, however, that traditional roles have failed to ensure stability. The new model is an experiment we can ill afford to ignore.

From *The Communitarian Reader: Beyond the Essentials* by Amitai Etzioni, Andrew Volmert, and Elanit Rothschild, Rowman & Littlefield, 2004, pp. 149–160. Copyright © 2004 by Rowman & Littlefield. Reprinted by permission.

# State of Our Unions

## Marriage Promotion and the Contested Power of Heterosexuality

MELANIE HEATH

In the 2002 *Frontline* documentary "Let's Get Married," Alex Kotlowitz declared that today "everyone from the government to church leaders to intellectuals—on both the right and the left—are pushing marriage." Kotlowitz is referring to the marriage movement launched in the late 1990s by a coalition of religious and civic leaders, public officials, family therapists, educators, researchers, and others. Advocates support an array of government policies collectively known as "marriage promotion," which seek to reduce the rate of divorce and single parenting. Many of these policies were codified into federal law in the Personal Responsibility and Work Opportunity Reconciliation Act of 1996. Ending more than 60 years of federal welfare benefits to poor families, the Personal Responsibility and Work Opportunity Reconciliation Act created discretionary state block grants under the rubric of Temporary Assistance to Needy Families (TANF) and specifically designated marriage promotion as a sanctioned use of federal funds. Since the election of President George W. Bush, federal funding for marriage promotion has grown substantially. The Healthy Marriage Initiative has directed federal money to promote marriage and fatherhood programs, and in 2005, Congress passed a federal appropriations act that includes more than $500 million annually for marriage promotion.

This article explores the power dynamics of marriage promotion, particularly in terms of the enforcement of heterosexuality and hierarchies of gender, race, and class. I place the emerging field of critical heterosexuality studies in dialogue with feminist state theory to bring to light the crisis tendencies of institutionalized heterosexuality in relation to the diminishing dominance of the white, nuclear family (Connell 1995; Ingraham 1999). As marriage promotion programs have sprouted across the country, feminist and gay/lesbian scholars have offered criticisms of such policies as a form of discipline and control, particularly for poor women (Cahill 2005; Coltrane 2001; Coontz and Folbre 2002; Hardisty 2007; Mink 2003; Moon and Whitehead 2006; Polikoff 2008). Others embrace the benefits of marriage but caution against it as a panacea for poverty (Lichter, Graefe, and Brown 2003). To date, no study has examined the implementation of marriage promotion policies on the ground.

This article draws on data from the first in-depth study of marriage promotion in both state and local contexts. Examining the state's structure as forming a gendered and sexualized national identity, this study reveals the state's polycentric practices that seek to stabilize the norm of the white, middle-class, heterosexual family. At the policy level, state practices seek to secure boundaries of exclusion in the form of rhetoric on "fractured families" and inclusion through the norm of the white, middle-class family. On the ground, marriage workshops teach about gender hierarchy to rehearse an implicit ideology of marital heterosexuality. In contrast to feminist state theories that present a monolithic, top-down model of state control, this article offers a more nuanced examination of the relationship between macro and micro levels of power and their uneven consequences for social change (see Haney 1996).

## State Interest in Heterosexual Marriage

Nation-building strategies tied to the white, nuclear family have a long history in the United States. Federal and state law has shaped marriage as a form of inclusion and exclusion by determining who can marry, the rights and obligations involved in marriage, and the conditions under which a marriage can end. Historian Nancy Cott (2000, 3) identifies how in the United States the government has promoted a particular model of marriage: "lifelong, faithful monogamy, formed by the mutual consent of a man and a woman, bearing the impress of the Christian religion and the English common law in its expectations for the husband to be the family head and economic provider." The ideal of the nuclear family in the United States evolved by separating "productive labor" from the home, creating a new social category: the "housewife" (Pascale 2001). Domesticity attributed to wealthy white women became the standard for all women, and the "Cult of True Womanhood" elevated the submissive housewife as morally superior (Brown 1990; Pascale 2001). In contrast, racial ethnic women have systematically been relegated to do the "dirty work" in domestic service and industry (Duffy 2007). Protecting the family and nation has meant maintaining boundaries of racial and sexual purity. In building the nation, the federal and state government sought to "civilize" American Indians by instituting monogamous households, instilling a work ethic among men and domesticity among women (Cott 2000). Slaves were denied the right to marry, signifying their lack of civil rights that would entail the freedom to consent to marriage's obligations. Before and after slaves' emancipation, many states passed laws to ban marriage across the color line, as the specter of sexual relations between white women and African American men created moral panic. Concerns about race and morality also motivated the evolution of immigration law, which largely restricted the entry of Chinese and Japanese women.

Governmental intervention has changed over time in how it envisions protecting "the family," but the thread in this history can be traced to the need to safeguard the boundaries of the nation along the lines of race, class, gender, and sexuality (McClintock 1997). In recent years, federal and state concern has focused on "family breakdown." Sharp rises in female labor force participation, divorce, cohabitation, and single parenting have triggered a "deinstitutionalization" of marriage (Cherlin 2004). These changes, together with the growing movement to legalize same-sex marriage, call into question what constitutes "normal" family life in the United States (Stacey 1996). In the 1960s, President Lyndon Johnson drew on a report from a little-known senator, Patrick Daniel Moynihan, to address the problem of the "breakdown of the Negro family structure" (quoted in Blankenhorn 2007, 5). Controversy about the report ultimately led to a new consensus between conservative and liberal policy makers about what they viewed as the bad behavior of impoverished single mothers inherent in "welfare dependency" (Reese 2005). More recently, marriage advocate David Blankenhorn (2007, 5) has identified a united policy stance to address "the breakdown of *white* family structure" that he believes has followed the trends purportedly undermining Black families. These concerns now motivate federal and state policy to promote marriage. While race and class are visible in these policies, below the surface are anxieties about changing gender relations and the challenge to heterosexuality presented by the increased visibility of lesbian and gay families. Thus, marriage promotion offers a novel case to contribute to the development of feminist state theory as federal and state actors enact policies to reinstate the heterosexual, nuclear family in American culture.

## State Theory and Critical Heterosexuality Studies

Feminist theories of the state are relatively new (Haney 2000). Theories that emerged out of second-wave feminism often envisioned the state as the perpetuator of patriarchy, offering a monolithic conceptualization of state power over women as a homogeneous group. In recent years, feminist state theory has expanded to analyze the gendered state and its social practices that regulate the gender of its citizens along the lines of race and class (Brown 1992; Mosse 1985; Yuval-Davis 1997). Scholars doing comparative and U.S.-focused research on welfare states have demonstrated the ways that government policy and law

concerning welfare, pension, child care/education, and the labor market shapes and is shaped by ideologies of gender, race, and class while at the same time interacting with norms around family and marriage (Glauber 2008; Gordon 1994; Hays 2003; Misra 1998; Misra, Moller, and Budig 2007; O'Connor, Orloff, and Shaver 1999; Reese 2005). Feminist scholarship on the state, however, has tended to take for granted normative ideas about heterosexuality, including the presumption that heterosexual pairings define social institutions like marriage and the family. As a corrective to this presumption, I put state theory and critical heterosexuality studies in dialogue to examine the relationship of the gendered and sexualized state to normative heterosexuality (Cooper 1995, 2002).

In the 1990s, scholars began to focus a critical lens on the ways that heterosexuality serves as the standard for all "sexual-social behavior," charting a new theoretical path called critical heterosexuality studies (Ingraham 2005, 4). Contemporary theorists of sexuality have elucidated the emergence of "the homosexual" as a category of person distinct from "the heterosexual" in the later part of the nineteenth century and the subsequent amassing of medical, legal, psychological, and literary discourses based on the heterosexual/homosexual binary (Foucault 1981; Katz 1996; Sedgwick 1990). Originating in radical lesbian feminist critiques of heterosexuality as a patriarchal institution, critical heterosexuality scholarship has established heterosexuality and its exclusionary practices vis-à-vis homosexuality as an important topic of inquiry and shed light on its organizational and ritualistic practices as a set of rules and norms for behavior (Ingraham 1999). Marital heterosexuality occupies the largely invisible core of natural and desirable sexuality, and homosexuality the periphery as perverse and unnatural (Roseneil 2002). Legal marriage has consequently been a central mechanism the state has used to regulate institutionalized heterosexuality and the construct of the "natural" (white, middle-class) family.

Critical heterosexuality studies stress the coconstitution of gender and sexuality, contributing to scholarship on the performative aspects within marital heterosexuality (Butler [1990] 1999; Ingraham 1999). Valorizing the "natural" family, U.S. federal and state law attaches a considerable number of benefits to heterosexual marriage: retirement and death benefits, family leave policies, health care decision making and access, taxation, immigration, and numerous others. The power of state practice rests not only in specific law and policy but in its ability to conceal the work involved in maintaining the unitary "nature" of institutionalized heterosexuality. But beyond this, more recent, and more active, efforts to promote marriage have further institutionalized inequalities in the face of growing challenges posed by structural changes in global economies, transformation in family life, and movements for lesbian and gay rights and gender equality (Ingraham 1999). In this article, I examine the uneven outcomes of state policy efforts to implement marriage promotion on the ground.

## Studying Marriage Promotion

To study marriage promotion, I conducted ethnographic research for 10 months in 2004 in Oklahoma. Oklahoma is home to the most extensive statewide marriage initiative in the nation, and consequently its policy "extends out" and is influenced by national marriage promotion politics (Burawoy 1998). In 1999, the governor employed the marriage promotion provisions of the Personal Responsibility and Work Opportunity Reconciliation Act to pioneer the Oklahoma Marriage Initiative at a time when few states opted to exercise this option. The Oklahoma Department of Human Services (OKDHS) committed $10 million from its federal TANF block grant and contracted with Public Strategies, Inc. (a private, for-profit firm) to develop and manage the initiative. The Oklahoma Marriage Initiative trains state employees, community leaders, and other volunteers to offer marriage education workshops throughout the state. The workshops use the Prevention and Relationship Enhancement Program (PREP), a research-based curriculum created by Howard Markman and Scott Stanley that teaches communication skills, conflict management, and problem solving. The initiative also trains volunteers to offer a Christian version of the PREP curriculum in settings that are not state funded. In exchange for receiving free workshop training, volunteers pledge to provide at least four free workshops in their communities.

In addition to its groundbreaking marriage initiative, Oklahoma is also well known for being a Bible Belt state. Nearly 60 percent of registered voters say they attend church regularly, compared to the national average of 40 percent (Campbell 2002). Oklahoma's high religiosity would appear to render it exceptional with respect to wide-ranging marriage promotion activities across the nation. Indeed, Oklahoma's social and cultural environment is likely one reason that the marriage initiative was able to take root in the early years of welfare reform, as a Republican governor initiated it with little political resistance. While there are many unique aspects to the formation of the marriage initiative, Oklahoma has nevertheless served as a model for state and community marriage promotion programs across the nation. In recent years, Alabama, Georgia, North Carolina, New Mexico, New York, Ohio, Texas, and Utah have also designated portions of their TANF block grants for marriage promotion. Texas legislated $7.5 million a year.[1]

The Oklahoma Marriage Initiative blends two models of marriage promotion. On the one hand, it seeks to blanket the state with messages about marriage by providing free marriage workshops to as many Oklahomans as possible. On the other, it targets specific populations, including welfare recipients, low-income parents, high school students, the prison population, the military, and Native Americans. I conducted fieldwork on the workshops for both the general and target populations and found that the more sustained efforts were the workshops for the general population.

These included large Sweetheart Weekends that occurred every few months and offered the curriculum on a Friday evening and all day Saturday.[2] Advertised on local radio stations and in the newspaper, they drew 50 or more couples on average. Weekly smaller workshops were advertised on the Oklahoma Marriage Initiative's Web site and through local churches. By 2006, the initiative had trained 1,500 volunteers to conduct the workshops and had provided services to 37,500 people. Data for this article include fieldwork on public workshops and in-depth interviews with marriage initiative leaders and participants.

To gain access, I first met with two Oklahoma Marriage Initiative employees at the annual conference of the marriage movement held in Las Vegas in 2003. The Smart Marriages conference features presentations by more than 100 marriage experts and is attended by therapists, counselors, clergy, policy makers, educators, and the public. My two initial contacts expressed enthusiasm about my idea of doing ethnographic research on the initiative's cultural impact. When I arrived in Oklahoma in February of 2004, I contacted them about attending workshops as a single woman. Altogether, I participated in 30 workshops for the general public that were advertised on the marriage initiative's Web site, including three Sweetheart Weekends (six classes), three six-week workshops (15 classes), and 24 weekend workshops (24 classes).[3] At the beginning of each workshop, I introduced myself and my research and took detailed field notes. I also conducted participant observation of a state-sponsored PREP training weekend to discover the method for training volunteers. Finally, I conducted 20 in-depth, semistructured interviews with volunteer participants and leaders from workshops and 15 with the Oklahoma Marriage Initiative leadership and OKDHS staff that lasted between one and two hours.[4] All interviewees were given pseudonyms. The transcribed interviews and field notes were coded using a qualitative software program, Atlas.ti. In this process, I discovered a gap between the Oklahoma Marriage Initiative's stated goals and its on-the-ground practices. This article examines marriage promotion activities targeted to a general population that included predominantly white, middle-class couples.

# Rein[State]Ing White, Middle-Class Marriage

In 1999, the former Republican governor of the state of Oklahoma, responding to an economic report that linked Oklahoma's declining economy to its purportedly weakening family structure, announced a goal of reducing the state's divorce rate by one-third by the year 2010. This goal was later restated more nebulously as an initiative to strengthen healthy marriages, an objective that might, at first glance, appear benign. However, when I asked the president and the acting project manager of Public Strategies about the objective, she confirmed that it is specifically aimed to promote marriage—in and of itself—as a special and beneficial type of relationship. She stated,

> The goal of the initiative is to strengthen marriage, and we are really unwavering about that goal. We believe that marriage is a different kind of relationship with different kinds of outcomes, and so we are not in any way, shape, or form going to do anything that sells that goal short.

By "outcomes," the project manager evokes the statistical debate about social scientific research on childhood outcomes. This research has shown that, on average, children growing up in a one-parent family experience some disadvantage compared to those growing up with two parents. Although scholars are divided about the causes of these disadvantages (e.g., Blankenhorn 2007; Cherlin 2003), marriage promotion advocates recite this body of research to justify the need to promote marriage so that every child can grow up with her or his biological, married parents.

Fears about the declining significance of the nuclear family have spurred the Oklahoma Marriage Initiative to offer marriage education to the public as a mechanism to reinstitutionalize marriage. As one report puts it, the strategy of the marriage initiative is to provide marriage education services to all Oklahomans to effect "specific behavior change at the individual level" and to "restore support for the institution of marriage as a valued social good" (Dion 2006). When I interviewed the OKDHS director, he described being enlightened by reading Barbara Dafoe Whitehead's (1993, 84) *Atlantic Monthly* article "Dan Quayle Was Right," which explains "family breakup" as breeding behaviors that "damage the social ecology, threaten the public order, and impose new burdens on core institutions." Whitehead goes on to express concern that the once isolated breakup of Black families is now spreading to white ones. This implicit (and sometimes explicit) racial comparison is a common theme in the discourse of the marriage movement. Kay Hymowitz (2006, 78), the author of *Marriage and Caste in America,* argues that educating the young to be "self-reliant" members of a democratic society is "The Mission" of white, middle-class families and that poor Black parents are not "simply middle-class parents *manqué;* they have their own culture of child-rearing, and—not to mince words—that culture is a recipe for more poverty." This philosophy harks back to nation-building principles that analogize marriage and the state as a necessary form of governance to produce worthy (white, middle-class) citizens (Cott 2000).

In the national discussion, the poor Black family remains an invisible standard of deviancy. As the focus of policy has turned to family breakdown, the mostly unspoken concern of marriage promotion leaders is the norm of the white, middle-class family and the harm caused to this norm. During our interview, the OKDHS director outlined the cost of "fractured families":

> Another piece of this, when you sit back and think about it, we spend $40 million in this state to run our child support enforcement division. Every one of those faces is a fractured relationship. So, we are spending $40 million in the state to do nothing but administer the transfer of cash from non-custodial parents to custodial parents who have experienced fractured relationships. You can see the high cost of having fractured relationships. It's worth the investment.

The director's words suggest that the "deviancy" of fractured families hurts middle-class families that consist of good citizens who pay taxes and embrace Hymowitz's (2006) "Mission."

The focus on fractured families reinforces a boundary around the normalcy of the white, middle-class, nuclear family. One of the top managers of the marriage initiative, a social worker who maintains a more critical stance, offered this evaluation:

> The way Governor Keating attached lowering the divorce rate through a poverty-funded program, who are we blaming for the divorce rate? I mean that kind of message is real strong in my mind. I've got an education so I was concerned about people living in poverty being blamed for the divorce rate and the state of families and that kind of thing.

Attaching marriage promotion to TANF shifts attention away from transformations taking place among white, middle-class families and places it on poor ones. Moreover, the welfare-to-work provisions in TANF, which enforce stringent work requirements and set time limits for receiving aid, help to ensure that poor "dependent" women (most often U.S.-born and immigrant women of color) are bound to low-wage jobs in service industry.

Marriage promotion follows a long history in the United States of defending the ideal gendered family to preserve a bounded space of normalcy against "deviant" others, with attendant social consequences of race and class inequalities. While positioning fractured families as a social problem, the marriage initiative's practices on the ground predominantly focus on white, middle-class couples to promote a bounded heterosexual space to define the ideal family. In the marriage workshops, issues of race and class disappear, and the focus turns on the problematic of gender relations for heterosexual couples. Heterosexuality is the unexamined backdrop to teach about the "opposite sexes" within the ideal family.

# Teaching the Importance of Gender (and Heterosexuality)

A dominant ideology of marriage promotion, and its historical presumption in the gendered behavior of the opposite sexes, view it as form the foundation of a cohesive and stable society. Crisis tendencies, in the form of growing marriage activism by gays and lesbians, are beneath the surface of this ideology, informing the need to strengthen heterosexual relationships. When I asked the OKDHS director, for example, about the goal of the marriage initiative, he confirmed the ideal of marital heterosexuality: "In terms of the marriage initiative, it's relationships between men and women which are committed preferably for life." His use of the words "relationships between men and women" announces the kind of relationships applicable—a declaration that would have been unnecessary 20 years ago—and suggests the prohibition of nonheterosexual love.

With heterosexuality as the unquestioned footing, the marriage workshops for the general population represent a forum to teach the mostly white, middle-class couples who attend about gender as *the* visible problem. The instruction encourages self-discipline and motivation to do gender in the manner compelled by the ideology of the "natural" family (Hay 2003). PREP, the secular version of the curriculum, engages communication and problem-solving skills. One of its main features is the speaker/listener technique, which instructs the speaker, who holds the "floor"—a tile that lists the rules of communication—to make brief "I" statements and the listener to paraphrase what he or she has heard. Despite the mostly gender-neutral curriculum, the 30 workshops I attended stressed gender relations in marriage.

The three-day, state-sponsored workshop leader training of PREP and its Christian version, taught by its creators—Howard Markman and Scott Stanley—and Vice President Natalie

Jenkins, established the importance of gender to an implicit heterosexuality. Volunteers attending the training were predominantly white, many of them counselors and educators receiving continuing education units. Throughout, the three presenters focused on what men versus women do in relationships. Scott Stanley told the audience that he wanted to talk about gender differences and explained how researchers have found a pattern that involves women's pursuing an issue and men's withdrawing. He attributed this to men's tendency to be more physiologically reactive and women to be more emotionally aroused. Stanley acknowledged that these patterns of behavior are complex and that researchers have difficulty deciding what is physiological and what is not. Yet he suggested that the pattern seems to reflect a greater need for men not to argue with their mates. He conveyed that a central goal for teaching PREP is helping couples manage gender differences.

Stanley explained the impact of the decline of marriage on men and women. He argued that today, young people think that cohabiting is a good first step to test marriage but that in reality, practicing serial non-monogamy hurts women because marriage is the only means to ensure a man's commitment. Citing research, Stanley told us that a young man who lives with his girlfriend tends to think she is not the "one," while a young woman thinks just the opposite. He explained, "We have talked young people out of thinking that marriage matters, particularly young women. Women get the worse deal if men don't marry them." Although it is not clear what he meant by the "worse deal," Stanley implied that women are naturally more committed to men, whereas men need the institution of marriage to become self-disciplined practitioners of lifelong monogamy. A dominant script of marital heterosexuality is that men know to settle down—that is, no longer act on their sexual urges—after they marry.

The curriculum includes a number of videos of real couples fighting. One shows a young African American couple who argue over the amount of time the man spends watching sports. During the young man's explanation for why his sport watching is not excessive, Howard Markman stopped the video to point out the way he lifts his hands up and "gazes towards heaven." Markman called this the "beam me up Scotty response." He explained, "This really is an appeal to God. We have a special message to the women in the room. If your partner, husband, son has this response, you might mistakenly think that he is withdrawing, but he is having a spiritual moment." I laughed along with the audience, but what makes this statement funny is the cultural assumption of an embattled masculinity. Markman implied that women cannot really understand the nature of men, which leads to the kind of exasperation shown in the video. Later, Scott Stanley told us that the young man is asking for his wife to accept this important part of him—the part that lives on sports. Statements like this place the onus on the wife to understand the "nature" of men.

Throughout the training, the presenters performed gender and made jokes that drew on the innate differences between men and women, providing a message about handling gender within heterosexual relationships (Butler [1990] 1999; West and Zimmerman 1987). These performances and dialogue subtly suggest a gender hierarchy compelling women to put up with men's idiosyncrasies since ultimately men are the stronger sex. At one point, Howard Markman told a joke about how many men it takes to change the toilet paper. The punch line: There is no scientific answer because it has not happened. Underneath the humor is the suggestion that men have more important things to do than change toilet paper. Several moments later, he flipped the remote as if he were surfing television channels, distracting from Natalie Jenkin's presentation. She told him to "sit" and informed us that she forgot to take the batteries out of the men's toy. She quickly qualified that she "needed" these guys because she is not the most technologically advanced. As we watched a video of a couple fighting over the way the husband put the laundry soap in the washer, Jenkins asserted that the wife is "missing the miracle. He's doing the laundry!" Later, Jenkins discussed expectations and how, when she was first married, she wanted flowers because all her friends were getting them. She and her husband were having financial difficulties, so she found a 99-cent coupon for a dozen carnations. She put four quarters and the coupon on the fridge with a note saying, "Honey, if this coupon expires so will you."

All of this gender work solidifies the importance of the differences between men and women. Men play with toys (and are technologically advanced); women want flowers (and do laundry). The state's promotion of marriage makes visible the importance of these gendered practices, teaching men and women to monitor and accept the differences between men and women. At heart is a lesson about gender difference as the glue that keeps two people of the opposite sex together. The ideal for white, middle-class families is a configuration of gender hierarchy premised on institutionalized heterosexuality. Tying gender difference to understandings of bodies solidifies marital heterosexuality.

The union of gender differences and bodies together with institutionalized heterosexuality was even more pronounced in the breakout training session of the Christian version of PREP. Scott Stanley discussed how gender differences originate in the Genesis passage of the Bible. He explained,

> I think it is interesting that it says man [will leave his mother and father] and not man and woman. I have come to believe from science—and this is going to sound sexist—why males are called to a higher level of commitment and sacrifice, biologically and scripturally. Women are inherently made more vulnerable than men because they have babies. Males need to protect. Unfortunately, in our culture, we have gutted that, and women bear the most burden by the lack of a sacrificial ethic.

His statement makes explicit the often implicit instruction on gender difference throughout the training—men are naturally less emotional and better equipped for certain responsibilities in marriage, namely, the need to protect their families. The interaction of gender and heterosexuality is important to position men and women hierarchically as part of a social order that rewards married, heterosexual (and mostly white, middle-class) men as husbands and often as the primary breadwinner.

Linking ideas of gender and heterosexuality directly to bodies, the instructor presented the definition of marriage as a union of male and female. According to Stanley,

God meant something when he specified that there should be male and female and what to do with bodies. I don't just mean sex and physical union, but I mean oneness. They covered up where they are most obviously different. We don't cover up where we are similar. We fear rejection in relationships because of the possibility of difference. Difference symbolizes physical union, which is now apparent to them.

The heterosexual footing implied by the idea of the opposite sexes is also the ground for the performance of gender hierarchy. Through the state-sponsored instruction, potential instructors of PREP and the Christian version of PREP are taught to present ideas about gender and sexuality to encourage self-monitoring in relation to the ideal of the "natural," married family.

# Rehearsing the Power of Heterosexuality

Teaching about gender within the confines of marital hetero-sexuality enables the state to govern indirectly by encouraging self-regulation. However, success is never guaranteed. While the hierarchical heterosexual/ homosexual binary is a systematic presence in modern society, shifts within its organization can render an unproblematic heterosexuality less trouble free. Crisis tendencies motivate efforts like marriage promotion to shore up marriage's boundary while simultaneously undermining these labors. For the marriage initiative, the increasing visibility of same-sex couples troubles efforts to strengthen a clear boundary of marital heterosexuality.

In the 30 marriage promotion workshops I attended, most included heterosexual married or engaged couples and sometimes a single woman or man. In two of the six-week workshops, however, there was one lesbian couple.[5] The first of these included 14 white heterosexual couples, one interracial heterosexual couple, and three female coaches, two white and one Black. Tammy and Chris, white lesbians in their fifties, had introduced themselves as "life partners" on the first day. They had a number of issues with communication. After hearing about the workshop on the radio, Tammy enrolled herself and "a friend." They told me they were relieved they were not asked to leave. The next workshop included Amanda and Jennifer, a white lesbian couple in their late twenties, among the 18 white couples, two white single men, and two female coaches, one white and one Black. Amanda and Jennifer were less talkative, but with their severe communication problems, by their own admission, they monopolized much of the coaches' energy during the practice exercises.

Some of the workshops, especially those targeted to low-income populations, are taught by social workers or other state employees aware of and often committed to the National Association of Social Workers (NASW) code of ethics that takes a strong stand against discrimination on the basis of sexual orientation. In the first workshop, the instructors were volunteers from the community and not social workers: David, a white married professional, and Randy, a white married associate Baptist pastor at a church in town. Randy, joined by Susan, who attended his church, taught the second workshop.

Similar to the training seminar I attended, a central focus of the workshops was on gender differences within marriage. David and Randy often referenced sports to command men's attention. For example, Randy talked about the tendency for one person to withdraw in an argument and said, "This is just what men do, withdraw." He provided the analogy of playing baseball. When you get hit a few times, you tend to give up. He said this is the same with arguing; sometimes it just feels easier to give up or withdraw. Instead of giving up, he encouraged men to practice. David piped in, "Can you do the same analogy with knitting?" and Randy shot back, "I can't, but I'm sure there are those in the audience who can!" In the next six-week workshop, Randy told the participants that having "crappy experiences in marriage is a man thing, not a God thing." This is a "big boy thing," he declared. "God gives me a good picture of how I am supposed to be in a relationship. He calls you to love one person."

The focus on gender within the confines of marital heterosexuality ensured that the same-sex couples' presence remained invisible. This was true even in the case of Tammy and Chris, who were very vocal. The last class of the first six-week session on sensuality/sexuality offered one of the more poignant examples. David asked people to share how their families of origin had discussed sexuality with them when they were young. I was sitting at an end table with Tammy and Chris. David began at the table opposite us and stopped at the table next to ours to talk about his own upbringing, skipping Tammy, Chris, and myself. This omission did not deter the two from participating. When David asked about sensuality and touch, Tammy spoke up: "We assume that what we like, the other person likes." Her words drew attention to the fact that her partner is a woman and not a man. While it is probably true that heterosexuals and nonheterosexuals make this kind of assumption, her statement stood in bold relief to the dominant message of managing difference in heterosexual relationships. Comments such as this one challenge taken-for-granted assumptions of gender and sexuality.

All the participants I interviewed acknowledged awareness of the lesbian couples without my asking, and most admitted feeling a little uncomfortable due to either their disapproval of or their inexperience dealing with same-sex relationships. Tom, a white man in his mid-twenties who attended with Suzanne, said he was caught off guard by "the two girls who were there together. They were like lesbians. I was surprised, I guess." Becky, a white woman in her thirties who was married and had four children with Martin, an African American man in his early forties, answered my question about whether anything in the workshop made her uncomfortable:

Mmm. I did feel uncomfortable with the fact that there were couples in there of the same sex, just because I feel strongly about family values and what the traditional family is. But I know it is something that is happening in the United States, and there is really nothing I can do about it. And, I mean, they are human. They have needs too. It doesn't mean that I agree with them.

Norm, a white man in his sixties who attended with his third wife, moved from talking about men's responsiveness to his disapproval of homosexuality. He said,

At first, the unknown [was uncomfortable]. When you go around and there is more and more interaction, I felt like there was a quality of responses and information given by the men in that class that usually doesn't happen. [Pause] I do consider homosexuality a sin, but I'm not here to judge that. I have a lot of patients that are gay, and they have a lifestyle I do not approve of. But I thought even the gay couple had a lot of good information to toss out.

Some of the other participants expressed a subtle resentment about dealing with same-sex couples in the marriage workshop but admitted that these couples "have needs too." It is unclear what the reaction would have been if the couples had taken a more in-your-face position, were gay men instead of lesbians, or were not middle class and white. Martin articulated his desire that lesbians and gay men remain in the closet: "Be gay. Don't force it on me."

The invisibility of the same-sex couples confirms the power of heterosexuality to exclude. Nevertheless, same-sex couples in marriage workshops have the effect of troubling dominant gender prescriptions within marital heterosexuality. Bettina, a white woman in her thirties and the only self-identified feminist I interviewed among the heterosexual participants, remarked on the tension that the presence of a lesbian couple brings to gender assumptions: "I was surprised at the lesbian couple who attended. I was shocked every time we came and they were still there! I was very happy to see that, especially because I thought stereotypically everybody is going to be pigeonholed into male-female. I can't imagine what that put on them." Bettina's words reflect the tension that the presence of a same-sex couple created for normative heterosexual gender performance. The environment of these marriage workshops discouraged dealing with gender outside the confines of marital heterosexuality, as doing so might have called into question the institution itself.

One of the lesbians, Jennifer, expressed her exasperation with and resistance to the focus on gender and marital heterosexuality: "So, that was the thing I really found offensive because they kind of gender stereotyped relationships, and I don't think that is completely appropriate if you're teaching gender diverse people." Her words stress the tension of being placed outside the rigid gender binary fundamental to the training. Amanda told me that taking a class with a lesbian was important to change people's perceptions. She said,

I don't know the personal story of all these people in our class, but if they never met a lesbian before, and now they do, now they see, and hear what I say in class, and don't think we are the devil now, you know, that's a goal in itself. I mean, people are ignorant, and they don't know. So just being open and honest about stuff and talking to people or just being a good person around them and knowing you are gay, it has a positive influence.

Her words rang true. Even though most of the participants I interviewed expressed negative feelings about homosexuality, when faced with a same-sex couple, they tended to soften their stereotypic perceptions. Ultimately, the presence of lesbians in the workshops both strengthened and disrupted the power of heterosexuality; the question of same-sex relationships consistently remained in the background and sometimes came to the foreground when the couples discussed their relationships.

The (in)visibility of the lesbian couples suggests the unevenness of state efforts to reinstate the dominance of the heterosexual, white, middle-class family. On one hand, the teachings on gender and marital heterosexuality inscribe a powerful vision of the "natural" family. On the other, this prevailing image can be interrupted by the increasing diversity of families and prominence of lesbian and gay couples in American society. Even in the face of what appears a monolithic achievement to promote gender and marital heterosexuality, instances of defused power can create small opportunities for social change.

# Conclusion

In their annual report, "State of Our Unions: The Social Health of Marriage in America," Barbara Whitehead and David Popenoe (2004, 4) remark that "the pathway into marriage is changing. The meaning of marriage is changing. The institutional role of marriage is changing." Fears about the declining significance of the nuclear family have spurred national marriage promotion policies to fund programs to reinstitutionalize heterosexual marriage. For many marriage promotion advocates, concerns about the state of "our unions" center on fears for the white, middle-class (heterosexual) family. In Oklahoma, anxiety about "fractured families" and the use of TANF money to fund marriage promotion focuses attention on single-mother families—coded as women of color and their children. Yet its practices on the ground offer services predominantly to white, middle-class couples.

This research contributes to feminist theories of the state by problematizing the assumption of a male state with unidimensional control of its citizens or subjects. Instead, it reveals polycentric state practices that are structured as gendered and sexualized, and that uphold the dominance of the white, middle-class family and its importance to a cohesive national identity. In the case of marriage promotion, diverse state practices focus policy concerns on "deviant" (coded Black) single-mother families while resources are allocated to teach about gender hierarchy to predominantly white, middle-class couples. Putting feminist state theory and critical heterosexuality studies in dialogue demonstrates the importance of an unspoken heterosexuality to state control. State actors who seek to promote marriage rely on a particular, and conservative, interpretation of social scientific research on families as a noncontroversial way to focus policy concerns on the need to promote "healthy" (heterosexual) families. These policies demonstrate a perceived need on the part of the state to safeguard the health of the nation by strengthening the "mission" of white, middle-class (heterosexual) marriage. The race and class assumptions of this reasoning are largely made invisible as marriage promotion leaders use the rhetoric of health and social capital.

On the ground, marriage education becomes a tool to teach self-monitoring gendered practices within the confines of heterosexual marriage. In the workshops I attended, instruction on the "opposite" sexes signaled heterosexuality to reaffirm the sexual outsider status of same-sex couples as well as that of single-mother families. The on-the-ground practices of promoting heterosexual marriage mirror antigay countermovements, such as the ex-gay movement, which encourages individuals to police their behavior according to scripted gender and heterosexual norms (Robinson and Spivey 2007). This strategy provides states and social movements the ability to govern the behavior of citizens and members from a distance.

Marriage workshops rehearse dominant scripts on gender polarity to reinforce expectations of men's and women's "nature" to make marital heterosexuality appear instinctive and effortless. The decline of marriage and women's increased workforce participation during the past 40 years has challenged traditional norms that created social cohesion through gender hierarchy and implicit heterosexuality. Marriage workshops offer a forum to revisit ideas on hierarchical relationships between men and women. State training for workshop leaders teaches that managing gender differences is essential to a harmonious marriage. The trainers provide examples and offer gendered performances to focus on indisputable differences between men and women that cater to cultural ideas of men as rational (strong) and women as emotional (weak). These performances provide simple answers to complex negotiations that many families face as they juggle tight work schedules along with raising children and try to manage households that often bring children from previous marriages or relationships. The gendered performances teach that wives need to allow "men to be men" and that husbands need to cater to their wives' emotional needs.

State activities to implement self-monitoring practices carry an assumption that "good" citizens will act according to dominant norms; however, this assumption does not necessarily entail success. In two six-week workshops, for example, the presence of a lesbian couple challenged the ideology of marital heterosexuality. The performance of gendered binaries intrinsic to institutionalized heterosexuality, a generally seamless aspect of the marriage workshops I attended, was rendered more palpable and transparent. Even while the relationships of the lesbians were disregarded, their presence created a disruption. The assumptions underlying the workshops marked these two couples as different from other heterosexual women in the context of a marriage class, and the gendered prescriptions made them gender and sexual outsiders. Alternatively, their presence provided a rare opportunity to bring together heterosexuals and nonheterosexuals in an equalizing environment to learn communication and problem-solving skills. This was probably one of the few environments in the state, and anywhere else for that matter, that mixed together heterosexual and nonheterosexual couples in an intimate and prolonged setting, specifically in the context of enriching relationships. For heterosexuals, such exposure has the ability to challenge stereotypes about nonheterosexuals and perhaps about gender itself. Thus, while state practices seek to reestablish the hegemony of the white, middle-class, heterosexual family through rhetoric and cultural practice, marriage promotion offers insight into the way these can be destabilized on the ground by the very outsiders whom state policy seeks to outlaw.

## Notes

1. Many of these states, including Texas, have incorporated the "one percent solution," putting 1 percent of their Temporary Assistance to Needy Families money toward marriage promotion. From my calculations, Oklahoma designates roughly 5 percent of its Temporary Assistance to Needy Families block grant per year.

2. Recently, the marriage initiative changed the name from "Sweetheart Weekends" to "All about Us."

3. I was not able to attend every class in the series during the six-week and weekend workshops. Since I acted as a participant in these workshops and determined not to provide any information that would identify other participants, I did not seek individual consent except in the case of volunteers for in-depth interviews.

4. In addition to the participant observation and interviews described above, I did fieldwork in 20 marriage workshops for welfare recipients and led three focus groups; attended eight weeks of daily marriage classes for high school students and conducted in-depth interviews with the high school teachers; conducted in-depth interviews with a prisoner and the prison's chaplain; and did participant observation of a marriage workshop for the Chickasaw Nation and interviewed a Chickasaw government official. Finally, I conducted extensive fieldwork on the campaign against the initiative to ban same-sex marriage that was placed on the November ballot in 2004. For analysis of all ethnographic research in this project, see Heath (forthcoming).

5. One of the initiative leaders told me that she knew of other same-sex couples attending marriage workshops. There was no way to find out how many actually did attend since the "All about You" forms that participants fill out at the beginning of the workshops do not ask about sexual orientation or same-sex relationships.

## References

Blankenhorn, David. 2007. *The future of marriage.* New York: Encounter Books.

Brown, Gillian. 1990. *Domestic individualism: Imagining self in nineteenth-century America.* Berkeley: University of California Press.

Brown, Wendy. 1992. Finding the man in the state. *Feminist Studies* 18: 7–34.

Burawoy, Michael. 1998. The extended case method. *Sociological Theory* 16: 4–33.

Butler, Judith. [1990] 1999. *Gender trouble.* New York: Routledge.

Cahill, Sean. 2005. Welfare moms and the two grooms: The concurrent promotion and restriction of marriage in US public policy. *Sexualities* 8: 169–87.

Campbell, Kim. 2002. Can marriage be taught? *Christian Science Monitor,* July 18.

Cherlin, Andrew J. 2003. Should the government promote marriage? *Contexts* 3: 22–29.

———. 2004. The deinstitutionalization of American marriage. *Journal of Marriage and Family* 66: 848–61.

Coltrane, Scott. 2001. "Marketing the marriage solution": Misplaced simplicity in the politics of fatherhood. *Sociological Perspectives* 44: 387–418.

Connell, R. W. 1995. *Masculinities.* Berkeley: University of California Press.

Coontz, Stephanie, and Nancy Folbre. 2002. Marriage, poverty, and public policy. Discussion paper from the annual conference of the Council on Contemporary Families, New York, April 26–28.

Cooper, Davina. 1995. *Power in struggle: Feminism, sexuality and the state.* London: Open University Press/NYU Press.

———. 2002. Imagining the place of the state: Where governance and social power meet. In *Handbook of lesbian and gay studies,* edited by Diane Richardson and Steven Seidman. London: Sage.

Cott, Nancy. 2000. *Public vows: A history of marriage and the nation.* Cambridge, MA: Harvard University Press.

Dion, Robin. 2006. *The Oklahoma Marriage Initiative: An overview of the longest-running statewide marriage initiative in the U.S.* ASPE research brief. Washington, DC: Office of the Assistant Secretary for Planning and Evaluation, U.S. Department of Health and Human Services.

Duffy, Mignon. 2007. Doing the dirty work: Gender, race, and reproductive labor in historical perspective. *Gender & Society* 21: 313–36.

Foucault, Michel. 1981. *The history of sexuality.* Vol. 1, *An introduction.* Harmondsworth, UK: Penguin.

Glauber, Rebecca. 2008. Race and gender in families and at work: The fatherhood wage premium. *Gender & Society* 22: 8–30.

Gordon, Linda. 1994. *Pitied but not entitled.* Cambridge, MA: Harvard University Press.

Haney, Lynne A. 1996. Homeboys, babies, men in suits: The state and the reproduction of male dominance. *American Sociology Review* 61: 759–78.

——. 2000. Feminist state theory: Applications to jurisprudence, criminology, and the welfare state. *Annual Review of Sociology* 26: 641–66.

Hardisty, Jean. 2007. Pushed to the altar: The right wing roots of marriage promotion. Somerville, MA: Political Research Associates and the Women of Color Resource Center.

Hay, James. 2003. Unaided virtues: The (neo)liberalization of the domestic sphere and the new architecture of community. In *Foucault, cultural studies, and governmentality,* edited by Jack Z. Bratich, Jeremy Packer, and Cameron McCarthy. Albany: State University of New York Press.

Hays, Sharon. 2003. *Flat broke with children: Women in the age of welfare reform.* Oxford, UK: Oxford University Press.

Heath, Melanie. Forthcoming. *One marriage under God: Defense of marriage actions in middle America.* New York: New York University Press.

Hymowitz, Kay S. 2006. *Marriage and caste in America: Separate and unequal families in a post-marital age.* Chicago: Ivan R. Dee.

Ingraham, Chrys. 1999. *White weddings: Romancing heterosexuality in popular culture.* New York: Routledge.

——. ed. 2005. *Thinking straight: The power, the promise, and the paradox of heterosexuality.* New York: Routledge.

Katz, Jonathan Ned. 1996. *The invention of heterosexuality.* New York: Plume.

Lichter, Daniel, Deborah Roempke Graefe, and J. Brian Brown. 2003. Is marriage a panacea? Union formation among economically-disadvantaged unwed mothers. *Social Problems* 50: 60–86.

McClintock, Ann. 1997. "No longer in a future heaven": Gender, race, and nationalism. In *Dangerous liaisons: Gender, nation, and postcolonial perspectives,* edited by Anne McClintock, Aamir Mufti, and Ella Shohat. Minneapolis: University of Minnesota Press.

Mink, Gwendolyn. 2003. From welfare to wedlock: Marriage promotion and poor mothers' inequality. In *Fundamental differences: Feminists talk back to social conservatives,* edited by Cynthia Burack and Jyl J. Josephson. Lanham, MD: Rowman & Littlefield.

Misra, Joya. 1998. Mothers or workers? The value of women's labor: Women and the emergence of family allowance policy. *Gender & Society* 12: 376–99.

Misra, Joya, Stephanie Moller, and Michelle J. Budig. 2007. Work-family policies and poverty for partnered and single women in Europe and North America. *Gender & Society* 21: 804–27.

Moon, Dawne, and Jaye Cee Whitehead. 2006. Marrying for America. In *Fragile families and the marriage agenda,* edited by Lori Kowaleski-Jones and Nicholas H. Wolfinger. New York: Springer.

Mosse, George L. 1985. *Nationalism and sexuality.* New York: Howard Fertig.

O'Connor, Julia S., Ann Shola Orloff, and Sheila Shaver. 1999. *States, markets, families.* Cambridge, UK: Cambridge University Press.

Pascale, Celine-Marie. 2001. All in a day's work: A feminist analysis of class formation and social identity. *Race, Gender & Class* 8: 34–59.

Polikoff, Nancy. 2008. *Beyond (straight and gay) marriage: Valuing all families under the law.* Boston: Beacon.

Reese, Ellen. 2005. *Backlash against welfare mothers.* Berkeley: University of California Press.

Robinson, Christine M., and Sue E. Spivey. 2007. The politics of masculinity and the ex-gay movement. *Gender & Society* 21: 650–75.

Roseneil, Sasha. 2002. The heterosexual/homosexual binary: Past, present, and future. In *Handbook of lesbian and gay studies,* edited by Diane Richardson and Steven Seidman. London: Sage.

Sedgwick, Eve Kosofsky. 1990. *Epistemology of the closet.* Berkeley: University of California Press.

Stacey, Judith. 1996. *In the name of the family: Rethinking family values in the postmodern age.* Boston: Beacon.

West, Candace, and Don Zimmerman. 1987. Doing gender. *Gender & Society* 1: 125–51.

Whitehead, Barbara Dafoe. 1993. Dan Quayle was right. *Atlantic Monthly,* April, 47–84.

Whitehead, Barbara Dafoe, and David Popenoe. 2004. *The state of our unions: The social health of marriage in America.* Piscataway, NJ: National Marriage Project.

Yuval-Davis, Nira. 1997. *Gender and nation.* London: Sage.

**MELANIE HEATH** is an assistant professor of sociology at McMaster University. She studies the cultural and global politics of family and sexuality. Her research on marriage promotion politics will appear in the forthcoming book *One Marriage under God: Defense of Marriage Actions in Middle America* (New York University Press).

**Authors' Note**—Many thanks to Shari Dworkin, Celine-Marie Pascale, Kathleen Hull, Cheryl Cooky, Judith Stacey, Michael Messner, Sharon Hays, and Mary Bernstein for their invaluable feedback on theory and revisions. Also a special thanks to editor Dana Britton and to five anonymous reviewers for their incredibly helpful comments and suggestions. The research this article draws on was funded by a grant from the Center for Religion and Civic Culture at the University of Southern California.

From *Gender & Society,* February 1, 2009, pp. 27–48. Copyright © 2009 by Sage Publications. Reprinted by permission via Rightslink.

# Five Years on, Gay Marriage Debate Fades in Massachusetts

DAVID CRARY

Twenty years after he met the love of his life, nearly five years after their wedding helped make history, it took a nasty bout of pneumonia for Gary Chalmers to fully appreciate the blessings of marriage.

"I was out of work for eight weeks, spent a week in the hospital," Chalmers said. "That was the first time I really felt thankful for the sense of the security we had, with Rich there, talking with the physicians, helping make decisions. . . . It really made a difference."

At stake was the most basic recognition of marital bonds — something most spouses take for granted. But until May 17, 2004, when Chalmers and Richard Linnell were among a surge of same-sex couples marrying in Massachusetts, it was legally unavailable to American gays and lesbians.

Since that day, four other states—Connecticut in 2008, and Iowa, Vermont and Maine this year—have legalized same-sex marriage, and more may follow soon. A measure just approved by New Hampshire's legislature awaits the governor's decision on whether to sign. But Massachusetts was the first, providing a five-year record with which to gauge the consequences.

At the time of those first weddings, the debate was red-hot — protests were frequent, expectations ran high that legislators would allow a referendum on whether to overturn the court ruling ordering same-sex marriage. Now, although Roman Catholic leaders and some conservative activists remain vocally opposed, there is overwhelming political support for same-sex marriage and no prospect for a referendum.

According to the latest state figures, through September 2008, there had been 12,167 same-sex marriages in Massachusetts—64 percent of them between women—out of 170,209 marriages in all. Some consequences have been tangible—a boom for gay-friendly wedding businesses, the exit of a Roman Catholic charity from the adoption business—and some almost defy description.

"Having your committed relationships recognized—to say it's deeply meaningful is to trivialize it," said Mary Bonauto, lead lawyer in the landmark lawsuit. "I know people who'd been together 20 years who say, 'Getting married—it knocked my socks off.'"

Chalmers and Linnell were among seven gay and lesbian couples recruited by Bonauto's team to be the plaintiffs in the lawsuit.

They had been partners since meeting in Worcester in 1988, and now live nearby in Linnell's childhood house in the rural outskirts of Whitinsville with their 16-year-old daughter, Paige, whom they adopted as an infant.

The south-central town of 6,300, with no gay community to speak of, is relatively far from cosmopolitan Boston and the gay vacation mecca of Provincetown, but the family feels thoroughly comfortable.

Paige, who brims with self-confidence, is helping form a gay-straight alliance at her high school. When her fathers got married, she said, "all my friends were saying they wanted to come to the wedding."

Chalmers, an elementary school curriculum coordinator in nearby Shrewsbury, and Linnell, nurse manager at a medical center, say they didn't need the wedding to prove their commitment to one another, but they appreciate the added legal stability and the recognition they get from others.

"Before, we had wills, we had power of attorney," Chalmers said. "But the fact of the matter was, you can't make up for the thousand or so rights that are given to married couples."

They said many of the fellow townspeople they'd spoken with were unaware that gay couples—pre-2004—generally lacked these rights, ranging from income tax provisions to medical decision-making to property inheritance.

Another plus: Explanations about family ties are easier now that "husband" is an option.

"More than once," Chalmers recalled, "I was introducing Rich and said, 'This is my partner,' and they'd say, 'Oh, what kind of company do you own? What business are you in?'"

Another of the seven lawsuit couples—Gina and Heidi Nortonsmith—live in the lesbian-friendly college town of Northampton with their two sons—Quinn, 9, and Avery 12. Like their fellow plaintiffs, they married as soon as legally possible—on May 17, 2004.

Heidi, who is white, runs an emergency food pantry, while Gina, an African-American, is an elementary school classroom aide. Heidi gave birth to both sons, who are biracial, and the family name merges the moms' maiden names.

"When we were getting ready to have the kids, we wanted to cross all our T's and dot all our I's, feeling there were so many protections for heterosexual married families that just weren't available to us," Heidi said.

"When marriage finally happened, there was that emotional sigh of relief—just knowing there would be a legal framework, and a court of law would understand our family."

Heidi and Gina bridle at the contention of some gay-marriage opponents that children such as theirs will suffer from not being raised by both a mother and father.

"We have really great kids," says Gina. "It's been fun to have people see who we are."

Listening in on the conversation were Quinn—just arrived from shooting baskets outside—and Avery, both doing homework on the sofa, occasionally offering their thoughts.

Said Heidi, "Having two parents who can feel and express love for each other, and give it in abundance to their children, that's what matters. It doesn't matter what the identities of those parents are."

One of the striking developments, since 2004, is the fading away of opposition to gay marriage among elected officials in Massachusetts.

When the state's Supreme Judicial Court ruled in 2003 that banning same-sex marriage was unconstitutional, there seemed to be sufficient support in the Legislature for a ballot measure that would overturn the decision. But efforts to unseat pro-gay-marriage legislators floundered; a gay-marriage supporter, Deval Patrick, was elected governor; and a climactic push for a referendum was rejected by lawmakers in 2007 by a 151–45 vote.

Last year, lawmakers went further, repealing a 1913 law that blocked most out-of-state gays from marrying in Massachusetts. The vote in the House was 119–36.

The near-consensus now among political leaders is a far cry from 2003–04, when the debate was wrenching for legislators such as Sen. Marian Walsh. Her district, including parts of Boston and some close-in suburbs, is heavily Catholic and socially conservative, so when same-sex marriage became a public issue, "there wasn't an appetite to discuss it, let alone support it," Walsh said.

Once the high court ruled, Walsh faced intense pressure from constituents wanting to know whether she would support efforts to overturn it.

"I had hundreds of requests to meet with people on both sides," Walsh said. "Everyone wanted to know how was I going to vote."

She read up on the law, engaged in countless conversations, wrestled with her conscience, and finally decided the court was right—and there should be no referendum.

"It was a lot of hard work," she said. "I came to the decision that it really is a civil right—that the constitution was there to protect rights, not to diminish rights."

She described the reaction as a "firestorm"—embittered constituents, hate mail and death threats, rebukes from Catholic clergy, but she won re-election in 2004 and again in 2006 over challengers who opposed gay marriage.

"They said marriage is always between a man and women," Walsh mused. "I used to think that was true. I had those same premises, but those premises were false."

For all the joy and reassurance that marriage has brought to same-sex couples, it also entails periodic reminders that neither the federal government nor the vast majority of other states recognize their unions. Partly as a backlash to Massachusetts, 26 states have passed constitutional amendments since May 2004 explicitly limiting marriage to male/female unions.

Even the 2010 census, under the prevailing federal Defense of Marriage Act, likely won't record legally wed couples in Massachusetts and elsewhere as married.

"It feels like a slap in the face," said Heidi Nortonsmith.

Gay & Lesbian Advocates & Defenders, the Boston legal firm which won the same-sex marriage case, filed a new lawsuit in March challenging the portion of the act that bars the federal government from recognizing same-sex marriages.

President Barack Obama has pledged to work to repeal the act, but it hasn't been among his priorities since taking office.

"I'm so dying to meet him and have him sit down with my family," Heidi said of Obama. "He could be a leader about this."

For now, federal non-recognition can be stinging.

After Michael and Rick McManus of Charlton married in 2006, they honeymooned in Panama, and on return to the United States were told at the immigration booth that they had to go through separately because U.S. law didn't consider them married.

Michael and Rick have subsequently adopted a son, turning 2 on May 7, and a daughter, almost 1. They plan to limit international travel until the federal policy changes.

"I don't want our kids to be coming through customs and having to explain that their dads aren't married there," Michael said.

Within Massachusetts, they said, being married has been a big plus—for example in dealing with state adoption officials.

"They knew we were a family that was in it for the long haul," Michael said.

But they are frustrated at having to file two sets of tax returns, at extra cost, as a married couple in Massachusetts and as single men for the Internal Revenue Service. And they were dismayed when Arkansas voters last fall approved a ballot measure that bans gay couples from adopting.

"We're constantly reminding our friends that we still live in a world where people in another state voted that Rick and I aren't fit to parent," Michael said. "There's a sense of security for our family here—but when we leave this state, it's a very different world."

Joyce Kauffman, a Boston family-law attorney with many gay and lesbian clients, said particular hardships await same-sex couples who marry in Massachusetts and later seek to be divorced in a state that doesn't recognize the union.

"Sometimes people don't make it," she said. "What are they going to do?"

Massachusetts doesn't track same-sex divorces as a distinct category, so there are no statistics comparing how same-sex and opposite-sex couples who married since 2004 have fared in terms of breakups.

Overall, Kauffman thinks same-sex marriages—many between longtime partners—have been more stable. But she also has encountered same-sex couples who wed unwisely on impulse in 2004.

"A lot of people got caught up in the moment, for the wrong reason," she said. "But most are truly committed."

One of the couples that divorced, Julie and Hillary Goodridge, was among the plaintiffs in the landmark lawsuit, which became known as the Goodridge case.

Janet Halley, a professor at Harvard Law School who has studied same-sex divorce, said gays and lesbians will likely split at the same rate as heterosexuals, even though they face extra challenges.

"The stresses are going to be higher because of the very inconsistent ways in which different states and the federal government enforce the legal elements of marriage," she said.

Halley advised gay couples not to strive for some idealized goal of family perfection.

"In order to argue that they were entitled to marry, they thought they had to represent same-sex relationships as more committed, more loving, more altruistic than is realistic," she said.

"Holy cow, the sky hasn't fallen."

That assessment of five years of same-sex marriage came from Jennifer Chrisler, who advocates for gay and lesbian parents as head of the Boston-based Family Equality Council. It's a common refrain from many like-minded activists, and the message can be grating for those who still speak out with opposing views.

"We absolutely believe the sky is falling," said Kris Mineau, a former Air Force pilot and pastor who is president of the Massachusetts Family Institute. "But we believe it would be a generational downfall, not an overnight downfall."

Mineau and his allies say their primary concern is the welfare of children raised by same-sex couples—even though establishment groups such as the American Academy of Pediatrics say such children fare just as well as children with heterosexual parents.

"No matter how loving and how caring two women are, there's no way they can replace the role of the father," Mineau

said. "It will take a generation to prove that, but we have no reason to think otherwise."

Mineau also said religious liberty is at risk in Massachusetts, and cited the example of Catholic Charities of Boston, which stopped providing adoption services in 2006 because state law required it to consider same-sex parents when looking for adoptive homes.

At Boston College, one of the nation's leading Catholic universities, law professor Scott FitzGibbon said legalization of same-sex marriage also has created friction in the public school system and exposed students to "indoctrination".

Statewide, there is no mandate that schools teach about same-sex marriage, but FitzGibbon said he was troubled by some local districts' policies. Citing a 2004 anti-bias directive in Boston, he said a teacher there could risk his or her career "by encouraging an examination of the cons as well as the pros of same-sex marriage."

FitzGibbon also said many parents had been troubled by the Goodridge case.

"Same-sex programs lead on almost inevitably to a situation of discord and tension between teachers and school officials, on the one hand, and those numerous parents who adhere to ethical beliefs and belong to religious communities which disfavor those practices."

One such couple, David and Tonia Parker of Lexington, have withdrawn their two sons from public school and are now homeschooling them after a lengthy confrontation with school officials.

Parker objected in 2005 when his youngest son brought home a book from kindergarten that depicted a gay family. He was later arrested for refusing to leave the school after officials wouldn't agree to notify him when homosexuality was discussed in his son's class.

The Parkers filed an unsuccessful lawsuit contending that school administrators violated a state law requiring that parents get a chance to exempt their children from sex-education curriculum. School officials said the books didn't focus on sex education, and merely depicted various families.

"Parental rights lost out in a big way—the right of parents to oversee the moral upbringing of their own children," said Parker. "The judges are trying to force the government to affirm, embrace and celebrate gay marriage."

Opposition to same-sex marriage remains strong in the Roman Catholic hierarchy, though church leaders are less vocal on the issue than a few years ago when they campaigned hard for a referendum. Disappointment in the legislature for blocking a public vote is still deep.

"Why was it squelched?" asked Bishop Robert McManus of Worcester. "It seems to me, in terms of the politicians, that they have listened more intently to a well-heeled, organized political action group than they have to the will of the people."

McManus, who was installed as bishop just three days before the first same-sex weddings, says traditional husband/wife marriage already was under stress, as evidenced by the high divorce rate, and could be undermined further by the spread of same-sex marriage.

"The mantra that the sky hasn't fallen takes a short-term view," he said. "We don't know what the implications will be."

The Catholic church, he said, would welcome a civil debate, but he questioned whether this was feasible.

"The proponents of same-sex marriage argue that if you're opposed, you are exercising bigotry," the bishop said. "No one who's proud of being an American wants to be accused of being a bigot, so some people retreat into a live-and-let-live situation."

McManus insists the church won't compromise on marriage and says its views, over time, can still prevail.

Bonauto, the lead lawyer in the lawsuit, sees a different outcome as more states consider same-sex marriage or extend other recognition to gay couples.

"Goodridge set a new standard, and the standard was equality," she said. "It was a game changer. Even our opponents know it's only matter of time before there's marriage equality nationwide."

From *Associated Press*, May 9, 2009. Copyright © 2009 by Associated Press. Reprinted by permission.

# Everyone's Queer

Leila J. Rupp

When I was growing up, one of my Quaker mother's favorite expressions was "Everyone's queer except thee and me, and sometimes I think thee is a little queer, too." Even as a child, I loved both the sentiment and the language, and then later I got a special kick out of the possibilities of the word "queer." But until I sat down to write this piece, I had never thought about how appropriate the saying is to a consideration of the history of sexuality. For the most striking thing about the literature is that the vast majority of what we know about sexuality in the past is about what is "queer," in the sense of nonnormative. We assume that "normative" describes most of what happened sexually in the past, but we know very little about that. Except what the history of nonnormative sexuality—same-sex, commercial, non- or extra-marital, or in some other way deemed inappropriate—can tell us. And that, it turns out, is quite a lot.

## Like motherhood or childhood, sexuality, we once assumed, had no history. Now we know better.

Like motherhood or childhood, sexuality, we once assumed, had no history. Now we know better. Sexuality, consisting of, among other elements, sexual desires, sexual acts, love, sexual identities, and sexual communities, has not been fixed over time and differs from place to place. That is, whether and how people act on their desires, what kinds of acts they engage in and with whom, what kinds of meanings they attribute to those desires and acts, whether they think love can be sexual, whether they think of sexuality as having meaning for identities, whether they form communities with people with like desires—all of this is shaped by the societies in which people live. On the streets of New York at the turn of the nineteenth century, men engaged in sexual acts with other men without any bearing on their identity as heterosexual, as long as they took what they thought of as the "male part." Women embraced their women friends, pledged their undying love, and slept with each other without necessarily interfering with their married lives. Knowing these patterns, it begins to make more sense that Jonathan Katz wrote a wonderfully titled book. *The Invention of Heterosexuality* (1995). for it was only when certain acts and feelings came to be identified as the characteristics of a new type of person, "the homosexual."

that people began to think of "heterosexuals".[1] And what defined a heterosexual? Someone who did not, under any (or almost any) circumstances, engage in same-sex love or intimacy or sex. That this never became a hard and fast rule throughout U.S. society is suggested by the recent attention to life on "the down low," the practice of some black men who secretly engage in sex with other men but live in heterosexual relationships, or to patterns of sexuality among Latino men.[2] But the important point here is that normative heterosexuality—what scholars sometimes call "heteronormativity—can only be defined in contrast to what it is not. Which is why the history of nonnormative sexuality and the concept of "queer" is so important.

So how did people come to think of themselves as homosexual or bisexual or heterosexual or transsexual? That is one of the interesting questions that historians have explored. We now know a great deal about the development of the concepts by the sexologists, scientists, and social scientists who studied sexual behavior, but we also are learning more about the complex relationship between scientific definitions (and, in the case of transsexuality, medical techniques) and the desires and identities of individuals.[3] For example, Lisa Duggan, in her book *Sapphic Slashers* (2000), details the ways that publicity about a notorious lesbian murder in Memphis in the late nineteenth century both fed on and fed into such diverse genres as scientific case studies and French novels.[4] In his work on New York, George Chauncey opens the curtains on an early twentieth-century world in which men were not homosexual or heterosexual, despite the categorizations of the sexologists, but instead fairies or pansies, wolves or husbands, queers or "normal" men depending on their class position, ethnicity, and sexual role (the part one plays in a sexual act—generally penetrator or encloser).[5] And Joanne Meyerowitz, in *How Sex Changed* (2002), reveals that even before the publicity about Christine Jorgensen's sex-change surgery hit American newsstands, individual men and women wrote of their longings to change sex and bombarded physicians with questions and demands.[6] That is, we do not have the doctors and scientists to thank for our identities; their definitions sometimes enabled people to come to an understanding of their feelings and actions, sometimes to reject the definitions. But it was observation of individuals and communities that led the sexologists to their thinking about categories in the first place. We, as homosexuals and heterosexuals and bisexuals, were not created out of thin air.

Identities—and by identities I mean not just homosexual or gay or lesbian, but all their elaborate manifestations such as fairy, faggot, pogue, lamb, bulldagger, ladylover, butch, stud, fem—have a complex relationship to behavior, as the contemporary case of life on the down low makes clear. Over time, the sexologists came to define homosexuality not as gender inversion—effeminacy in men and masculinity in women—but as desire for someone of the same sex. By extension, heterosexuals felt no such desire. But how to explain men who identified as heterosexual but had (appropriately masculine-defined—that is, insertive rather than receptive) sex with other men? Or, in the case of women who came to be known as "political lesbians" in 1970s lesbian feminist communities, women who identified as lesbians but didn't have sex with women?[7] Identity and behavior are not always a neat fit, as the revelations of widespread same-sex sexual interactions in the famous Kinsey studies of male and female sexuality made clear to a stunned American public in the postwar decades. In response to his findings, based on interviews with individuals about their sexual behavior, Kinsey developed a scale to position people in terms of their behavior on a spectrum from exclusively heterosexual to exclusively homosexual.[8]

Another aspect of the relationship of identity to behavior is suggested by some of the labels people claimed for themselves, for many of them referred to a preference for specific kinds of sexual acts, sexual roles, or sexual partners. George Chauncey's research on the Naval investigation into "perversion" in Newport, Rhode Island, in the second decade of the twentieth century revealed the very specific terms used for those who preferred particular acts and roles.[9] In his study of the Pacific Northwest, Peter Boag describes a preference for anal or interfemoral intercourse in the intergenerational relationships between "wolves" and "punks" among transient laborers.[10] Liz Kennedy and Madeleine Davis's study of the working-class lesbian bar community in Buffalo, New York, in the 1940s and 1950s makes clear how central sexual roles were, at least in theory, to the making of butches and fems.[11] One identity, that of "stone butch," was defined by what a woman did not do, in this case desire and/or allow her lover to make love to her.

One of the things that historians' uncovering of the sexual acts that took place between people of the same sex reveals is how these changed over time. Sharon Ullman's research shows that oral sex between men was considered something new in the early twentieth century. When the police in Long Beach, California, broke up a "society of queers," they were confounded to discover that they were having oral rather than anal sex and concluded that that didn't really count as homosexual sex. The men themselves dubbed oral sex "the twentieth-century way".[12] Likewise, Kennedy and Davis found that butches and fems in Buffalo did not engage in oral sex. We know, or should know, that cultures in different times and places foster different kinds of sexual acts. Kissing, for example, is a relatively recent Western innovation as something erotic. But on the whole, as Heather Miller has pointed out, historians of sexuality have paid very little attention to the actual sexual acts in which people—and especially heterosexual people—engage.[13] One of the things that nonnormative sexuality can tell us about heteronormativity is what kinds of sexual acts are acceptable. We know, for example,

that heterosexual oral sex was something confined to prostitution—at least in theory—until the early twentieth century. What prostitutes, both male and female, were willing to do, especially for increased fees, tells us something about what "respectable" women were probably not.

In addition to interest in desire, love, sexual acts, and identities—and the complex relationships among them—historians of sexuality have concentrated on the building of communities and on struggles to make the world a better place. Martin Meeker, in his book *Contacts Desired* (2006), uncovers the communications networks that made same-sex sexuality visible and both resulted from and contributed to the building of communities and the homophile movement in the post-Second World War decades.[14] His concentration on a wide variety of media adds to incredibly rich research on different communities. In addition to Chauncey on New York, Kennedy and Davis on Buffalo, and Boag on Portland, there's Esther Newton on Cherry Grove, telling the story of the creation of a gay resort.[15] In the same vein, Karen Krahulik has detailed the ways that Provincetown became "Cape Queer".[16] Marc Stein, in *City of Sisterly and Brotherly Loves* (2000), uses the history of Philadelphia to detail, among other things, the relationship between lesbian and gay worlds in the city and in the movement.[17] Nan Alamilla Boyd, in her study of San Francisco, shows not only how the city by the Bay became a gay mecca (something Meeker addresses as well from a different perspective), but also how queer culture and the homophile movement had a more symbiotic relationship than we had thought.[18] A collection of articles on different communities, *Creating a Place for Ourselves* (1997), provides even more geographical diversity, as does John Howard's work on the vibrant networks gay men fashioned in the rural South.[19]

> **We know that, without the concept of homosexuality, there would be no heterosexuality. Without knowing which sexual desires and acts are deemed deviant, we would not know which ones passed muster. Knowing how identities are created, institutions established, communities built, and movements mobilized, we learn from the margins what the center looks like.**

What these studies collectively reveal is the way economic, political, and social forces, especially in the years since the Second World War, enhanced the possibilities for individuals with same-sex desires to find others like themselves, to build institutions and communities, to elaborate identities, and to organize in order to win basic rights: to gather, work, play, and live. This despite the crackdown following the war, which David Johnson argues in *The Lavender Scare* (2004) was more intense and long lasting than the effort to root Communists out of government.[20] These works on diverse communities have also fleshed out the story John D'Emilio tells of the rise of the homophile movement in his classic *Sexual Politics, Sexual Communities* (1983) and responded to the question of how the war shaped the experiences of gay men and women first told by Allan Bérubé in his 1990 book *Coming Out Under fire.*[21]

Increasingly, research on same-sex sexuality and other forms of nonnormative sexuality has attended to the relationship of sexual desires and identities to gender, class, race, and ethnicity. Lisa Duggan's *Sapphic Slashers,* for example, tells the story of white middle-class Alice Mitchell's murder of her lover Freda Ward intertwined with the Memphis lynching that drove Ida B. Wells from her hometown and into her anti-lynching crusade. Judy Wu and Nayan Shah attend to how ethnicity shaped sexuality in the Chinese American community.[22] John D'Emilio's biography of Bayard Rustin makes his identity as a black gay man inseparable from considering his role in the civil rights movement.[23] George Chauncey and Peter Boag detail different ways that class distinctions emerged in forms of male same-sex sexuality on opposite sides of the continent. Karen Krahulik makes ethnicity and class central to the story of the coexistence, sometimes peaceful and sometimes not, of gay and lesbian pioneers and Portuguese fishermen in Provincetown. And Kevin Mumford, in *Interzones* (1997), argues for the centrality of the areas of New York and Chicago in which racial mixing and all sorts of nonnormative sexuality took place for the shaping of both mainstream and gay culture.[24]

Which brings us back to the notion of the queerness of us all. We know that, without the concept of homosexuality, there would be no heterosexuality. Without knowing which sexual desires and acts are deemed deviant, we would not know which ones passed muster. Knowing how identities are created, institutions established, communities built, and movements mobilized, we learn from the margins what the center looks like.

What we do know more directly about normative sexuality tends to be about prescription, and we know that directives about how to act are not necessary if everyone is behaving properly. So Marilyn Hegarty has shown how the forces of government, the military, and medicine cooperated and competed both to mobilize and contain women's sexuality in the interests of victory during the Second World War.[25] Carolyn Lewis's forthcoming work on the premarital pelvic exam in the 1950s reveals the cold war anxieties that lay behind the initiative to teach women how to enjoy and reach orgasm through heterosexual vaginal intercourse.[26] To take another example, in her forthcoming book, Susan Freeman explores sex education directed at girls in the 1950s and 1960s, revealing, among other things, the ways that girls pushed to learn what they needed to know.[27] These contributions—examples from my own students or former students—add to what we know about heteronormativity from scholars such as Sharon Ullman, Beth Bailey, David Allyn, and Jeffrey Moran.[28]

So my mother was right, except she didn't go far enough. As Dennis Altman pointed out in arguing for the "homosexualization of America," and as my own work with Verta Taylor on drag queens and the responses they evoke in audience members reveals, in a wide variety of ways, from what we desire to how we love to how we make love to how we play, we are all a little queer.[29] And we have a lot to learn from the history of nonnormative sexualities.

# References

1. Jonathan Ned Katz, *The Invention of Heterosexuality* (New York: Dutton, 1995).

2. See, for example, J. L. King, On *the Down Low: A Journey Into the Lives of "Straight" Black Men Who Sleep with Men* (New York: Broadway Books, 2004); Tomás Almaguer, "Chicano Men: A Cartography of Homosexual Identity and Behavior," *differences: A Journal of Feminist Cultural Studies* 3 (Summer 1991): 75–100; Don Kulick, *Travesti: Sex, Gender, and Culture among Brazilian Transgendered Prostitutes* (Chicago: University of Chicago Press, 1998); Annick Prieur, *Mema's House, Mexico City. On Transvestites, Queens, and Machos* (Chicago: University of Chicago Press, 1998); Claibome Smith, "Gay Caballeros: Inside the Secret World of Dallas' *Mayates," Dallas Observer* (January 13, 2005).

3. On sexology, see Jennifer Terry, *An American Obsession: Science, Medicine, and Homosexuality in Modern Society* (Chicago: University of Chicago Press, 1999).

4. Lisa Duggan, *Sapphic Slashers: Sex, Violence, and American Modernity* (Durham, NC: Duke University Press, 2000).

5. George Chauncey, *Gay New York: Gender, Urban Culture, and the Making of the Gay Male World,* 1590–1940 (New York: Basic Books, 1994),

6. Joanne Meyerowitz, *How Sex Changed: A History of Transsexuality in the United States* (Cambridge, MA: Harvard University Press, 2002).

7. See Arlene Stein, *Sex and Sensibility: Stories of a Lesbian Generation* (Berkeley: University of California Press, 1997).

8. Alfred Kinsey et al., *Sexual Behavior in the Human Male* (Philadelphia: W.B. Saunders Col, 1948); Kinsey et al., *Sexual Behavior in the Human Female* (Philadelphia: W.B. Sanders Co., 1953).

9. George Chauncey Jr., "Christian Brotherhood or Sexual Perversion? Homosexual Identities and the Construction of Sexual Boundaries in the World War I Era," *Journal of Social History* 19 (1985): 189–212.

10. Peter Boag, *Same-Sex Affairs: Constructing and Controlling Homosexuality in the Pacific Northwest* (Berkeley: University of California Press. 2003).

11. Elizabeth Lapovsky Kennedy and Madeline D. Davis, *Boots of Leather, Slippers of Gold: The History of a Lesbian Community* (New York: Routledge, 1993).

12. Sharon Ullman, " 'The Twentieth Century Way:' Female Impersonation and Sexual Practice in Turn-of-the-Century America," *Journal of the History of Sexuality 5* (1995): 573–600.

13. Heather Lee Miller, "The Teeming Brothel: Sex Acts, Desires, and Sexual Identities in the United States, 1870–1940" (Ph.D. diss., Ohio State University, 2002).

14. Martin Meeker, *Contacts Desired: Gay and Lesbian Communications and Community,* 1940s–1970s (Chicago: University of Chicago Press, 2006).

15. Esther Newton, *Cherry Grove, Fire Island: Sixty Years in America's First Gay and Lesbian Town* (Boston: Beacon Press, 1993).

16. Karen Christel Krahulik, *Provincetown: From Pilgrim Landing to Gay Resort* (New York: New York University Press, 2005).

17. Marc Stein, *City of Sisterly and Brotherly Loves: Lesbian and Gay Philadelphia,* 1945–1972 (Chicago: University of Chicago Press, 2000).

18. Nan Alamilla Boyd, *Wide Open Town: A History of Queer San Francisco to 1965* (Berkeley: University of California Press, 2003).

19. Brett Beemyn, ed., *Creating a Place for Ourselves: Lesbian, Gay, and Bisexual Community Histories* (New York: Routledge, 1997); John Howard, ed., *Carryin' on in the Lesbian and Gay South* (New York: New York University Press, 1997); and Howard, *Men Like That: A Southern Queer History (Chicago:* University of Chicago Press, 1999).

20. David K. Johnson, *The Lavender Scare: The Cold War Persecution of Gays and Lesbians in the Federal Government* (Chicago: University of Chicago Press, 2004).

21. John D'Emilio, *Sexual Politics, Sexual Communities: The Making of a Homosexual Minority in the United States,* 1940–1970 (Chicago: University of Chicago Press, 1983); Allan Bérubé, *Coming Out Under Fire: The History of Gay Men and Women in World War II* (New York: Free Press, 1990).

22. Judy Tzu-Chun Wu, *Doctor Mom Chung of the Fair-Haired Bastards: The Life of a Wartime Celebrity* (Berkeley: University of California Press, 2005); Nayan Shah, *Contagious Divides: Epidemics and Race in San Francisco's Chinatown* (Berkeley: University of California Press, 2001).

23. John D'Emilio, *Lost Prophet: The Life and Times of Bayard Rustin* (New York: Free Press, 2003).

24. Kevin J. Mumford, *Interzones: Black/White Sex Districts in Chicago and New York in the Early Twentieth Century* (New York: Columbia University Press, 1997).

25. Marilyn Elizabeth Hegarty, "Patriots, Prostitutes, Patriotutes: The Mobilization and Control of Female Sexuality in the United States during World War II" (Ph.D. diss., Ohio State University, 1998). Revised version forthcoming from the University of California Press.

26. Carolyn Herbst Lewis, "Waking Sleeping Beauty: The Pelvic Exam, Heterosexuality and National Security in the Cold War," *Journal of Women's History* 17 (2005): 86–110.

27. Susan Kathleen Freeman, "Making Sense of Sex: Adolescent Girls and Sex Education in the United States, 1940–1960" (Ph. D, diss., Ohio State University, 2002). Revised version to be published by the University of Illinois Press.

28. Sharon R. Ullman, *Sex Seen: The Emergence of Modern Sexuality in America* (Berkeley; University of California Press, 1997); Beth Bailey, *Sex in the Heartland,* 1st paperback ed. (Cambridge, MA: Harvard University Press, 2002); David Allyn, *Make Love, Not War. The Sexual Revolution, An Unfettered History,* 1st paperback ed. (New York: Routledge, 2001); Jeffrey P. Moran, *Teaching Sex: The Shaping of Adolescence in the 20th Century* (Cambridge, MA: Harvard University Press, 2000).

29. Dennis Altman, *The Homosexualization of America* (New York: St. Martin's Press, 1982); Leila J. Rupp and Verta Taylor, *Drag Queens at the 801 Cabaret* (Chicago: University of Chicago Press, 2003).

**Leila J. Rupp** is Professor and Chair of Women's Studies at the University of California, Santa Barbara. She is the author of *A Desired Past: A Short History of Same-Sex Love in America* (1999) and coauthor, with Verta Taylor, of *Drag Queens at the 801 Cabaret* (2003). She is currently working on a book called "Sapphistries."

From *OAH Magazine of History,* March 2006, pp. 8–10. Copyright © 2006 by Organization of American Historians. Reprinted by permission via the Copyright Clearance Center.

# The Berdache Tradition

WALTER L. WILLIAMS

Because it is such a powerful force in the world today, the Western Judeo-Christian tradition is often accepted as the arbiter of "natural" behavior of humans. If Europeans and their descendant nations of North America accept something as normal, then anything different is seen as abnormal. Such a view ignores the great diversity of human existence.

This is the case of the study of gender. How many genders are there? To a modern Anglo-American, nothing might seem more definite than the answer that there are two: men and women. But not all societies around the world agree with Western culture's view that all humans are either women or men. The commonly accepted notion of "the opposite sex," based on anatomy, is itself an artifact of our society's rigid sex roles.

Among many cultures, there have existed different alternatives to "man" or "woman." An alternative role in many American Indian societies is referred to by anthropologists as *berdache*. . . . The role varied from one Native American culture to another, which is a reflection of the vast diversity of aboriginal New World societies. Small bands of hunter-gatherers existed in some areas, with advanced civilizations of farming peoples in other areas. With hundreds of different languages, economies, religions, and social patterns existing in North America alone, every generalization about a cultural tradition must acknowledge many exceptions.

This diversity is true for the berdache tradition as well, and must be kept in mind. My statements should be read as being specific to a particular culture, with generalizations being treated as loose patterns that might not apply to peoples even in nearby areas.

Briefly, a berdache can be defined as a morphological male who does not fill a society's standard man's role, who has a non-masculine character. This type of person is often stereotyped as effeminate, but a more accurate characterization is androgyny. Such a person has a clearly recognized and accepted social status, often based on a secure place in the tribal mythology. Berdaches have special ceremonial roles in many Native American religions, and important economic roles in their families. They will do at least some women's work, and mix together much of the behavior, dress, and social roles of women and men. Berdaches gain social prestige by their spiritual, intellectual, or craftwork/artistic contributions, and by their reputation for hard work and generosity. They serve a mediating function between women and men, precisely because their character is seen as distinct from either sex. They are not seen as men, yet they are not seen as women either. They occupy an alternative gender role that is a mixture of diverse elements.

In their erotic behavior berdaches also generally (but not always) take a nonmasculine role, either being asexual or becoming the passive partner in sex with men. In some cultures the berdache might become a wife to a man. This male-male sexual behavior became the focus of an attack on berdaches as "sodomites" by the Europeans who, early on, came into contact with them. From the first Spanish conquistadors to the Western frontiersmen and the Christian missionaries and government officials, Western culture has had a considerable impact on the berdache tradition. In the last two decades, the most recent impact on the tradition is the adaptation of a modern Western gay identity.

To Western eyes berdachism is a complex and puzzling phenomenon, mixing and redefining the very concepts of what is considered male and female. In a culture with only two recognized genders, such individuals are gender nonconformist, abnormal, deviant. But to American Indians, the institution of another gender role means that berdaches are not deviant—indeed, they do conform to the requirements of a custom in which their culture tells them they fit. Berdachism is a way for society to recognize and assimilate some atypical individuals without imposing a change on them or stigmatizing them as deviant. This cultural institution confirms their legitimacy for what they are.

Societies often bestow power upon that which does not neatly fit into the usual. Since no cultural system can explain everything, a common way that many cultures deal with these inconsistencies is to imbue them with negative power, as taboo, pollution, witchcraft, or sin. That which is not understood is seen as a threat. But an alternative method of dealing with such things, or people, is to take them out of the realm of threat and to sanctify them.[1] The berdaches' role as mediator is thus not just between women and men, but also between the physical and the spiritual. American Indian cultures have taken what Western culture calls negative, and made it a positive; they have successfully utilized the different skills and insights of a class of people that Western culture has stigmatized and whose spiritual powers have been wasted.

Many Native Americans also understood that gender roles have to do with more than just biological sex. The standard

Western view that one's sex is always a certainty, and that one's gender identity and sex role always conform to one's morphological sex is a view that dies hard. Western thought is typified by such dichotomies of groups perceived to be mutually exclusive: male and female, black and white, right and wrong, good and evil. Clearly, the world is not so simple; such clear divisions are not always realistic. Most American Indian worldviews generally are much more accepting of the ambiguities of life. Acceptance of gender variation in the berdache tradition is typical of many native cultures' approach to life in general.

Overall, these are generalizations based on those Native American societies that had an accepted role for berdaches. Not all cultures recognized such a respected status. Berdachism in aboriginal North America was most established among tribes in four areas: first, the Prairie and western Great Lakes, the northern and central Great Plains, and the lower Mississippi Valley; second, Florida and the Caribbean; third, the Southwest, the Great Basin, and California; and fourth, scattered areas of the Northwest, western Canada, and Alaska. For some reason it is not noticeable in eastern North America, with the exception of its southern rim. . . .

## American Indian Religions

Native American religions offered an explanation for human diversity by their creation stories. In some tribal religions, the Great Spiritual Being is conceived as neither male nor female but as a combination of both. Among the Kamia of the Southwest, for example, the bearer of plant seeds and the introducer of Kamia culture was a man-woman spirit named Warharmi.[2] A key episode of the Zuni creation story involves a battle between the kachina spirits of the agricultural Zunis and the enemy hunter spirits. Every four years an elaborate ceremony commemorates this myth. In the story a kachina spirit called ko'lhamana was captured by the enemy spirits and transformed in the process. This transformed spirit became a mediator between the two sides, using his peacemaking skills to merge the differing lifestyles of hunters and farmers. In the ceremony, a dramatic reenactment of the myth, the part of the transformed ko'lhamana spirit, is performed by a berdache.[3] The Zuni word for berdache is lhamana, denoting its closeness to the spiritual mediator who brought hunting and farming together.[4] The moral of this story is that the berdache was created by the deities for a special purpose, and that this creation led to the improvement of society. The continual reenactment of this story provides a justification for the Zuni berdache in each generation.

In contrast to this, the lack of spiritual justification in a creation myth could denote a lack of tolerance for gender variation. The Pimas, unlike most of their Southwestern neighbors, did not respect a berdache status. Wi-kovat, their derogatory word, means "like a girl," but it does not signify a recognized social role. Pima mythology reflects this lack of acceptance, in a folk tale that explains male androgyny as due to Papago witchcraft. Knowing that the Papagos respected berdaches, the Pimas blamed such an occurrence on an alien influence.[5] While the Pimas' condemnatory attitude is unusual, it does point out

the importance of spiritual explanations for the acceptance of gender variance in a culture.

Other Native American creation stories stand in sharp contrast to the Pima explanation. A good example is the account of the Navajos, which presents women and men as equals. The Navajo origin tale is told as a story of five worlds. The first people were First Man and First Woman, who were created equally and at the same time. The first two worlds that they lived in were bleak and unhappy, so they escaped to the third world. In the third world lived two twins, Turquoise Boy and White Shell Girl, who were the first berdaches. In the Navajo language the world for berdache is nadle, which means "changing one" or "one who is transformed." It is applied to hermaphrodites—those who are born with the genitals of both male and female—and also to "those who pretend to be nadle," who take on a social role that is distinct from either men or women.[6]

In the third world, First Man and First Woman began farming, with the help of the changing twins. One of the twins noticed some clay and, holding it in the palm of his/her hand, shaped it into the first pottery bowl. Then he/she formed a plate, a water dipper, and a pipe. The second twin observed some reeds and began to weave them, making the first basket. Together they shaped axes and grinding stones from rocks, and hoes from bone. All these new inventions made the people very happy.[7]

The message of this story is that humans are dependent for many good things on the inventiveness of nadle. Such individuals were present from the earliest eras of human existence, and their presence was never questioned. They were part of the natural order of the universe, with a special contribution to make.

Later on in the Navajo creation story, White Shell Girl entered the moon and became the Moon Bearer. Turquoise Boy, however, remained with the people. When First Man realized that Turquoise Boy could do all manner of women's work as well as women, all the men left the women and crossed a big river. The men hunted and planted crops. Turquoise Boy ground the corn, cooked the food, and weaved cloth for the men. Four years passed with the women and men separated, and the men were happy with the nadle. Later, however the women wanted to learn how to grind corn from the nadle, and both the men and women had decided that it was not good to continue living separately. So the women crossed the river and the people were reunited.[8]

They continued living happily in the third world, until one day a great flood began. The people ran to the highest mountaintop, but the water kept rising and they all feared they would be drowned. But just in time, the ever-inventive Turquoise Boy found a large reed. They climbed upward inside the tall hollow reed, and came out at the top into the fourth world. From there, White Shell Girl brought another reed, and they climbed again to the fifth world, which is the present world of the Navajos.[9]

These stories suggest that the very survival of humanity is dependent on the inventiveness of berdaches. With such a mythological belief system, it is no wonder that the Navajos held nadle in high regard. The concept of the nadle is well formulated in the creation story. As children were educated by these stories, and all Navajos believed in them, the high status accorded to gender variation was passed down from generation to generation. Such stories also provided instruction for *nadle* themselves to live by. A spiritual explanation guaranteed a special place for a person who was considered different but not deviant.

For American Indians, the important explanations of the world are spiritual ones. In their view, there is a deeper reality than the here-and-now. The real essence or wisdom occurs when one finally gives up trying to explain events in terms of "logic" and "reality." Many confusing aspects of existence can better be explained by actions of a multiplicity of spirits. Instead of a concept of a single god, there is an awareness of "that which we do not understand." In Lakota religion, for example, the term *Wakan Tanka* is often translated as "god." But a more proper translation, according to the medicine people who taught me, is "The Great Mystery."[10]

While rationality can explain much, there are limits to human capabilities of understanding. The English language is structured to account for cause and effect. For example, English speakers say, "It is raining," with the implication that there is a cause "it" that leads to rain. Many Indian languages, on the other hand, merely note what is most accurately translated as "raining" as an observable fact. Such an approach brings a freedom to stop worrying about causes of things, and merely to relax and accept that our human insights can go only so far. By not taking ourselves too seriously, or overinflating human importance, we can get beyond the logical world.

The emphasis of American Indian religions, then, is on the spiritual nature of all things. To understand the physical world, one must appreciate the underlying spiritual essence. Then one can begin to see that the physical is only a faint shadow, a partial reflection, of a supernatural and extrarational world. By the Indian view, everything that exists is spiritual. Every object—plants, rocks, water, air, the moon, animals, humans, the earth itself—has a spirit. The spirit of one thing (including a human) is not superior to the spirit of any other. Such a view promotes a sophisticated ecological awareness of the place that humans have in the larger environment. The function of religion is not to try to condemn or to change what exists, but to accept the realities of the world and to appreciate their contributions to life. Everything that exists has a purpose.[11]

One of the basic tenets of American Indian religion is the notion that everything in the universe is related. Nevertheless, things that exist are often seen as having a counterpart: sky and earth, plant and animal, water and fire. In all of these polarities, there exist mediators. The role of the mediator is to hold the polarities together, to keep the world from disintegrating. Polarities exist within human society also. The most important category within Indian society is gender. The notions of Woman and Man underlie much of social interaction and are comparable to the other major polarities. Women, with their nurtural qualities, are associated with the earth, while men are associated with the sky. Women gatherers and farmers deal with plants (of the earth), while men hunters deal with animals.

The mediator between the polarities of woman and man, in the American Indian religious explanation, is a being that combines the elements of both genders. This might be a combination in a physical sense, as in the case of hermaphrodites.

Many Native American religions accept this phenomenon in the same way that they accept other variations from the norm. But more important is their acceptance of the idea that gender can be combined in ways other than physical hermaphroditism. The physical aspects of a thing or a person, after all, are not nearly as important as its spirit. American Indians use the concept of a person's *spirit* in the way that other Americans use the concept of a person's *character*. Consequently, physical hermaphroditism is not necessary for the idea of gender mixing. A person's character, their spiritual essence, is the crucial thing.

## The Berdache's Spirit

Individuals who are physically normal might have the spirit of the other sex, might range somewhere between the two sexes, or might have a spirit that is distinct from either women or men. Whatever category they fall into, they are seen as being different from men. They are accepted spiritually as "Not Man." Whichever option is chosen, Indian religions offer spiritual explanations. Among the Arapahos of the Plains, berdaches are called *haxu'xan* and are seen to be that way as a result of a supernatural gift from birds or animals. Arapaho mythology recounts the story of Nih'a'ca, the first *haxu'xan*. He pretended to be a woman and married the mountain lion, a symbol for masculinity. The myth, as recorded by ethnographer Alfred Kroeber about 1900, recounted that "These people had the natural desire to become women, and as they grew up gradually became women. They gave up the desires of men. They were married to men. They had miraculous power and could do supernatural things. For instance, it was one of them that first made an intoxicant from rainwater."[12] Besides the theme of inventiveness, similar to the Navajo creation story, the berdache role is seen as a product of a "natural desire." Berdaches "gradually became women," which underscores the notion of woman as a social category rather than as a fixed biological entity. Physical biological sex is less important in gender classification than a person's desire—one's spirit.

They myths contain no prescriptions for trying to change berdaches who are acting out their desires of the heart. Like many other cultures' myths, the Zuni origin myths simply sanction the idea that gender can be transformed independently of biological sex.[13] Indeed, myths warn of dire consequences when interference with such a transformation is attempted. Prince Alexander Maximilian of the German state of Wied, traveling in the northern Plains in the 1830s, heard a myth about a warrior who once tried to force a berdache to avoid women's clothing. The berdache resisted, and the warrior shot him with an arrow. Immediately the berdache disappeared, and the warrior saw only a pile of stones with his arrow in them. Since then, the story concluded, no intelligent person would try to coerce a berdache.[14] Making the point even more directly, a Mandan myth told of an Indian who tried to force *mihdake* (berdaches) to give up their distinctive dress and status, which led the spirits to punish many people with death. After that, no Mandans interfered with berdaches.[15]

With this kind of attitude, reinforced by myth and history, the aboriginal view accepts human diversity. The creation story of the Mohave of the Colorado River Valley speaks of a time when people were not sexually differentiated. From this perspective, it is easy to accept that certain individuals might combine elements of masculinity and femininity.[16] A respected Mohave elder, speaking in the 1930s, stated this viewpoint simply: "From the very beginning of the world it was meant that there should be [berdaches], just as it was instituted that there should be shamans. They were intended for that purpose."[17]

This elder also explained that a child's tendencies to become a berdache are apparent early, by about age nine to twelve, before the child reaches puberty: "That is the time when young persons become initiated into the functions of their sex. . . . None but young people will become berdaches as a rule."[18] Many tribes have a public ceremony that acknowledges the acceptance of berdache status. A Mohave shaman related the ceremony for his tribe: "When the child was about ten years old his relatives would begin discussing his strange ways. Some of them disliked it, but the more intelligent began envisaging an initiation ceremony." The relatives prepare for the ceremony without letting the boy know if it. It is meant to take him by surprise, to be both an initiation and a test of his true inclinations. People from various settlements are invited to attend. The family wants the community to see it and become accustomed to accepting the boy as an *alyha*.

On the day of the ceremony, the shaman explained, the boy is led into a circle: "If the boy showed a willingness to remain standing in the circle, exposed to the public eye, it was almost certain that he would go through with the ceremony. The singer, hidden behind the crowd, began singing the songs. As soon as the sound reached the boy he began to dance as women do." If the boy is unwilling to assume *alyha* status, he would refuse to dance. But if his character—his spirit—is *alyha,* "the song goes right to his heart and he will dance with much intensity. He cannot help it. After the fourth song he is proclaimed." After the ceremony, the boy is carefully bathed and receives a woman's skirt. He is then led back to the dance ground, dressed as an *alyha,* and announces his new feminine name to the crowd. After that he would resent being called by his old male name.[19]

Among the Yuman tribes of the Southwest, the transformation is marked by a social gathering, in which the berdache prepares a meal for the friends of the family.[20] Ethnographer Ruth Underhill, doing fieldwork among the Papago Indians in the early 1930s, wrote that berdaches were common among the Papago Indians, and were usually publicly acknowledged in childhood. She recounted that a boy's parents would test him if they noticed that he preferred female pursuits. The regular pattern, mentioned by many of Underhill's Papago informants, was to build a small brush enclosure. Inside the enclosure they placed a man's bow and arrows, and also a woman's basket. At the appointed time the boy was brought to the enclosure as the adults watched from outside. The boy was told to go inside the circle of brush. Once he was inside, the adults "set fire to the enclosure. They watched what he took with him as he ran out and if it was the basketry materials, they reconciled themselves to his being a berdache."[21]

What is important to recognize in all of these practices is that the assumption of a berdache role was not forced on the boy by others. While adults might have their suspicions, it was only when the child made the proper move that he was considered a berdache. By doing woman's dancing, preparing a meal, or taking the woman's basket he was making an important symbolic gesture. Indian children were not stupid, and they knew the implications of these ceremonies beforehand. A boy in the enclosure could have left without taking anything, or could have taken both the man's and the woman's tools. With the community standing by watching, he was well aware that his choice would mark his assumption of berdache status. Rather than being seen as an involuntary test of his reflexes, this ceremony may be interpreted as a definite statement by the child to take on the berdache role.

Indians do not see the assumption of berdache status, however, as a free will choice on the part of the boy. People felt that the boy was acting out his basic character. The Lakota shaman Lame Deer explained:

> They were not like other men, but the Great Spirit made them *winktes* and we accepted them as such. . . . We think that if a woman has two little ones growing inside her, if she is going to have twins, sometimes instead of giving birth to two babies they have formed up in her womb into just one, into a half-man/half-woman kind of being. . . . To us a man is what nature, or his dreams, make him. We accept him for what he wants to be. That's up to him.[22]

While most of the sources indicate that once a person becomes a berdache it is a lifelong status, directions from the spirits determine everything. In at least one documented case, concerning a nineteenth-century Klamath berdache named Lele'ks, he later had a supernatural experience that led him to leave the berdache role. At that time Lele'ks began dressing and acting like a man, then married women, and eventually became one of the most famous Klamath chiefs.[23] What is important is that both in assuming berdache status and in leaving it, supernatural dictate is the determining factor.

## Dreams and Visions

Many tribes see the berdache role as signifying an individual's proclivities as a dreamer and a visionary. . . .

Among the northern Plains and related Great Lakes tribes, the idea of supernatural dictate through dreaming—the vision quest—had its highest development. The goal of the vision quest is to try to get beyond the rational world by sensory deprivation and fasting. By depriving one's body of nourishment, the brain could escape from logical thought and connect with the higher reality of the supernatural. The person doing the quest simply sits and waits for a vision. But a vision might not come easily; the person might have to wait for days.

The best way that I can describe the process is to refer to my own vision quest, which I experienced when I was living on a Lakota reservation in 1982. After a long series of prayers and blessings, the shaman who had prepared me for the ceremony took me out to an isolated area where a sweat lodge had been set up for my quest. As I walked to the spot, I worried that I might not be able to stand it. Would I be overcome by hunger?

Could I tolerate the thirst? What would I do if I had to go to the toilet? The shaman told me not to worry, that a whole group of holy people would be praying and singing for me while I was on my quest.

He had me remove my clothes, symbolizing my disconnection from the material would, and crawl into the sweat lodge. Before he left me I asked him, "What do I think about?" He said, "Do not think. Just pray for spiritual guidance." After a prayer he closed the flap tightly and I was left in total darkness. I still do not understand what happened to me during my vision quest, but during the day and a half that I was out there, I never once felt hungry or thirsty or the need to go to the toilet. What happened was an intensely personal experience that I cannot and do not wish to explain, a process of being that cannot be described in rational terms.

When the shaman came to get me at the end of my time, I actually resented having to end it. He did not need to ask if my vision quest was successful. He knew that it was even before seeing me, he explained, because he saw an eagle circling over me while I underwent the quest. He helped interpret the signs I had seen, then after more prayers and singing he led me back to the others. I felt relieved, cleansed, joyful, and serene. I had been through an experience that will be a part of my memories always.

If a vision quest could have such an effect on a person not even raised in Indian society, imagine its impact on a boy who from his earliest years had been waiting for the day when he could seek his vision. Gaining his spiritual power from his first vision, it would tell him what role to take in adult life. The vision might instruct him that he is going to be a great hunter, a craftsman, a warrior, or a shaman. Or it might tell him that he will be a berdache. Among the Lakotas, or Sioux, there are several symbols for various types of visions. A person becomes *wakan* (a sacred person) if she or he dreams of a bear, a wolf, thunder, a buffalo, a white buffalo calf, or Double Woman. Each dream results in a different gift, whether it is the power to cure illness or wounds, a promise of good hunting, or the exalted role of a *heyoka* (doing things backward).

A white buffalo calf is believed to be a berdache. If a person has a dream of the sacred Double Woman, this means that she or he will have the power to seduce men. Males who have a vision of Double Woman are presented with female tools. Taking such tools means that the male will become a berdache. The Lakota word *winkte* is composed of *win,* "woman," and *kte,* "would become."[24] A contemporary Lakota berdache explains, "To become a *winkte,* you have a medicine man put you up on the hill, to search for your vision. "You can become a *winkte* if you truly are by nature. You see a vision of the White Buffalo Calf Pipe. Sometimes it varies. A vision is like a scene in a movie."[25] Another way to become a *winkte* is to have a vision given by a *winkte* from the past.[26]. . .

By interpreting the result of the vision as being the work of a spirit, the vision quest frees the person from feeling responsible for his transformation. The person might even claim that the change was done against his will and without his control. Such a claim does not suggest a negative attitude about berdache status, because it is common for people to claim reluctance to fulfill their spiritual duty no matter what vision appears to them. Becoming any kind of sacred person involves taking on various social responsibilities and burdens.[27]. . .

A story was told among the Lakotas in the 1880s of a boy who tried to resist following his vision from Double Woman. But according to Lakota informants "few men succeed in this effort after having taken the strap in the dream." Having rebelled against the instructions given him by the Moon Being, he committed suicide.[28] The moral of that story is that one should not resist spiritual guidance, because it will lead only to grief. In another case, an Omaha young man told of being addressed by a spirit as "daughter," whereupon he discovered that he was unconsciously using feminine styles of speech. He tried to use male speech patterns, but could not. As a result of this vision, when he returned to his people he resolved himself to dress as a woman.[29] Such stories function to justify personal peculiarities as due to a fate over which the individual has no control.

Despite the usual pattern in Indian societies of using ridicule to enforce conformity, receiving instructions from a vision inhibits others from trying to change the berdache. Ritual explanation provides a way out. It also excuses the community from worrying about the cause of that person's difference, or the feeling that it is society's duty to try to change him.[30] Native American religions, above all else, encourage a basic respect for nature. If nature makes a person different, many Indians conclude, a mere human should not undertake to counter this spiritual dictate. Someone who is "unusual" can be accommodated without being stigmatized as "abnormal." Berdachism is thus not alien or threatening; it is a reflection of spirituality.

# References

1. Mary Douglas, *Purity and Danger* (Baltimore: Penguin, 1966), p. 52. I am grateful to Theda Perdue for convincing me that Douglas's ideas apply to berdachism. For an application of Douglas's thesis to berdaches, see James Thayer, "The Berdache of the Northern Plains: A Socioreligious Perspective," *Journal of Anthropological Research* 36 (1980): 292–93.

2. E. W. Gifford, "The Kamia of Imperial Valley," *Bureau of American Ethnology Bulletin* 97 (1931): 12.

3. By using present tense verbs in this text, I am not implying that such activities are necessarily continuing today. I sometimes use the present tense in the "ethnographic present," unless I use the past tense when I am referring to something that has not continued. Past tense implies that all such practices have disappeared. In the absence of fieldwork to prove such disappearance, I am not prepared to make that assumption, on the historic changes in the berdache tradition.

4. Elsie Clews Parsons, "The Zuni La' Mana," *American Anthropologist* 18 (1916): 521; Matilda Coxe Stevenson, "Zuni Indians," *Bureau of American Ethnology Annual Report* 23 (1903): 37; Franklin Cushing, "Zuni Creation Myths," *Bureau of American Ethnology Annual Report* 13 (1894): 401–3. Will Roscoe clarified this origin story for me.

5. W. W. Hill, "Note on the Pima Berdache," *American Anthropologist* 40 (1938): 339.

6. Aileen O'Bryan, "The Dine': Origin Myths of the Navaho Indians," *Bureau of American Ethnology Bulletin* 163 (1956): 5;

W. W. Hill, "The Status of the Hermaphrodite and Transvestite in Navaho Culture,"*American Anthropologist 37* (1935): 273.

7. Martha S. Link, *The Pollen Path: A Collection of Navajo Myths* (Stanford: Stanford University Press, 1956).

8 O'Bryan, "Dine'," pp. 5, 7, 9–10.

9. Ibid.

10. Lakota informants, July 1982. See also William Powers, *Oglala Religion* (Lincoln: University of Nebraska Press, 1977).

11. For this admittedly generalized overview of American Indian religious values, I am indebted to traditionalist informants of many tribes, but especially those of the Lakotas. For a discussion of native religions see Dennis Tedlock, *Finding the Center* (New York: Dial Press, 1972); Ruth Underhill, *Red Man's Religion* (Chicago: University of Chicago Press, 1965); and Elsi Clews Parsons, *Pueblo Indian Religion* (Chicago: University of Chicago Press, 1939).

12. Alfred Kroeber, "The Arapaho," *Bulletin of the American Museum of Natural History 18* (1902–7): 19.

13. Parsons, "Zuni La' Mana," p. 525.

14. Alexander Maximilian, *Travels in the interior of North America, 1832–1834,* vol. 22 of *Early Western Travels,* ed. Reuben Gold Thwaites, 32 vols. (Cleveland: A. H. Clark, 1906), pp. 283–84, 354. Maximilian was quoted in German in the early homosexual rights book by Ferdinand Karsch-Haack, *Das Gleichgeschlechtliche Leben der Naturvölker* (The same-sex life of nature peoples) (Munich: Verlag von Ernst Reinhardt, 1911; reprinted New York: Arno Press, 1975), pp. 314, 564.

15. Oscar Koch, *Der Indianishe Eros* (Berlin: Verlag Continent, 1925), p. 61.

16. George Devereux, "Institutionalized Homosexuality of the Mohave Indians," *Human Biology 9* (1937): 509.

17. Ibid., p. 501

18. Ibid.

19. Ibid., pp. 508–9.

20. C. Daryll Forde, "Ethnography of the Yuma Indians," *University of California Publications in American Archaeology and Ethnology 28* (1931): 157.

21. Ruth Underhill, *Social Organization of the Papago Indians* (New York: Columbia University Press, 1938), p. 186. This story is also mentioned in Ruth Underhill, ed., *The Autobiography of a Papago Woman* (Menasha, Wisc.: American Anthropological Association, 1936), p. 39.

22. John Fire and Richard Erdoes, *Lame Deer, Seeker of Visions* (New York: Simon and Schuster, 1972), pp. 117, 149.

23. Theodore Stern, *The Klamath Tribe: A People and Their Reservation* (Seattle: University of Washington Press, 1965), pp. 20, 24; Theodore Stern, "Some Sources of Variability in Klamath Mythology,"*Journal of American Folklore 69* (1956): 242ff; Leshe Spier, *Klamath Ethnography* (Berkeley: University of California Press, 1930), p. 52.

24. Clark Wissler, "Societies and Ceremonial Associations in the Oglala Division of the Teton Dakota," *Anthoropological Papers of the American Museum of Natural History 11,* pt. 1 (1916): 92; Powers, *Oglala Religion,* pp. 57–59.

25. Ronnie Loud Hawk, Lakota informant 4, July 1982.

26. Terry Calling Eagle, Lakota informant 5, July 1982.

27. James S. Thayer, "The Berdache of the Northern Plains: A Socioreligious Perspective," *Journal of Anthropological Research 36* (1980): 289.

28. Fletcher, "Elk Mystery," p. 281.

29. Alice Fletcher and Francis La Flesche, "The Omaha Tribe," *Bureau of American Ethnology Annual Report 27* (1905–6): 132.

30. Harriet Whitehead offers a valuable discussion of this element of the vision quest in "The Bow and the Burden Strap: A New Look at Institutionalized Homosexuality in Native North America," in *Sexual Meanings,* ed. Sherry Ortner and Harriet Whitehead (Cambridge: Cambridge University Press, 1981), pp. 99–102. See also Erikson, "Childhood," p. 329.

From *The Spirit and the Flesh*, Beacon Press, 1986. Copyright © 1986 by Beacon Press. Reprinted by permission of Beacon Press and Georges Borchardt Inc.

# Children of Lesbian and Gay Parents

Does parental sexual orientation affect child development, and if so, how? Studies using convenience samples, studies using samples drawn from known populations, and studies based on samples that are representative of larger populations all converge on similar conclusions. More than two decades of research has failed to reveal important differences in the adjustment or development of children or adolescents reared by same-sex couples compared to those reared by other-sex couples. Results of the research suggest that qualities of family relationships are more tightly linked with child outcomes than is parental sexual orientation.

CHARLOTTE J. PATTERSON

Does parental sexual orientation affect child development, and if so, how? This question has often been raised in the context of legal and policy proceedings relevant to children, such as those involving adoption, child custody, or visitation. Divergent views have been offered by professionals from the fields of psychology, sociology, medicine, and law (Patterson, Fulcher, & Wainright, 2002). While this question has most often been raised in legal and policy contexts, it is also relevant to theoretical issues. For example, does healthy human development require that a child grow up with parents of each gender? And if not, what would that mean for our theoretical understanding of parent–child relations? (Patterson & Hastings, in press) In this article, I describe some research designed to address these questions.

## Early Research

Research on children with lesbian and gay parents began with studies focused on cases in which children had been born in the context of a heterosexual marriage. After parental separation and divorce, many children in these families lived with divorced lesbian mothers. A number of researchers compared development among children of divorced lesbian mothers with that among children of divorced heterosexual mothers and found few significant differences (Patterson, 1997; Stacey & Biblarz, 2001).

These studies were valuable in addressing concerns of judges who were required to decide divorce and child custody cases, but they left many questions unanswered. In particular, because the children who participated in this research had been born into homes with married mothers and fathers, it was not obvious how to understand the reasons for their healthy development. The possibility that children's early exposure to apparently heterosexual male and female role models had contributed to healthy development could not be ruled out.

When lesbian or gay parents rear infants and children from birth, do their offspring grow up in typical ways and show healthy development? To address this question, it was important to study children who had never lived with heterosexual parents. In the 1990s, a number of investigators began research of this kind.

An early example was the Bay Area Families Study, in which I studied a group of 4- to 9-year-old children who had been born to or adopted early in life by lesbian mothers (Patterson, 1996, 1997). Data were collected during home visits. Results from in-home interviews and also from questionnaires showed that children had regular contact with a wide range of adults of both genders, both within and outside of their families. The children's self-concepts and preferences for same-gender playmates and activities were much like those of other children their ages. Moreover, standardized measures of social competence and of behavior problems, such as those from the Child Behavior Checklist (CBCL), showed that they scored within the range of normal variation for a representative sample of same-aged American children. It was clear from this study and others like it that it was quite possible for lesbian mothers to rear healthy children.

## Studies Based on Samples Drawn from Known Populations

Interpretation of the results from the Bay Area Families Study was, however, affected by its sampling procedures. The study had been based on a convenience sample that had been assembled by word of mouth. It was therefore impossible to rule out the possibility that families who participated in the research were especially well adjusted. Would a more representative sample yield different results?

To find out, Ray Chan, Barbara Raboy, and I conducted research in collaboration with the Sperm Bank of California

Chan, Raboy, & Patterson, 1998; Fulcher, Sutfin, Chan, Scheib, & Patterson, 2005). Over the more than 15 years of its existence, the Sperm Bank of California's clientele had included many lesbian as well as heterosexual women. For research purposes, this clientele was a finite population from which our sample could be drawn. The Sperm Bank of California also allowed a sample in which, both for lesbian and for heterosexual groups, one parent was biologically related to the child and one was not.

We invited all clients who had conceived children using the resources of the Sperm Bank of California and who had children 5 years old or older to participate in our research. The resulting sample was composed of 80 families, 55 headed by lesbian and 25 headed by heterosexual parents. Materials were mailed to participating families, with instructions to complete them privately and return them in self-addressed stamped envelopes we provided.

Results replicated and expanded upon those from earlier research. Children of lesbian and heterosexual parents showed similar, relatively high levels of social competence, as well as similar, relatively low levels of behavior problems on the parent form of the CBCL. We also asked the children's teachers to provide evaluations of children's adjustment on the Teacher Report Form of the CBCL, and their reports agreed with those of parents. Parental sexual orientation was not related to children's adaptation. Quite apart from parental sexual orientation, however, and consistent with findings from years of research on children of heterosexual parents, when parent–child relationships were marked by warmth and affection, children were more likely to be developing well. Thus, in this sample drawn from a known population, measures of children's adjustment were unrelated to parental sexual orientation (Chan et al., 1998; Fulcher et al., 2005).

Even as they provided information about children born to lesbian mothers, however, these new results also raised additional questions. Women who conceive children at sperm banks are generally both well educated and financially comfortable. It was possible that these relatively privileged women were able to protect children from many forms of discrimination. What if a more diverse group of families were to be studied? In addition, the children in this sample averaged 7 years of age, and some concerns focus on older children and adolescents. What if an older group of youngsters were to be studied? Would problems masked by youth and privilege in earlier studies emerge in an older, more diverse sample?

# Studies Based on Representative Samples

An opportunity to address these questions was presented by the availability of data from the National Longitudinal Study of Adolescent Health (Add Health). The Add Health study involved a large, ethnically diverse, and essentially representative sample of American adolescents and their parents. Data for our research were drawn from surveys and interviews completed by more than 12,000 adolescents and their parents at home and from surveys completed by adolescents at school.

Parents were not queried directly about their sexual orientation but were asked if they were involved in a "marriage, or marriage-like relationship." If parents acknowledged such a relationship, they were also asked the gender of their partner. Thus, we identified a group of 44 12- to 18-year-olds who lived with parents involved in marriage or marriage-like relationships with same-sex partners. We compared them with a matched group of adolescents living with other-sex couples. Data from the archives of the Add Health study allowed us to address many questions about adolescent development.

Consistent with earlier findings, results of this work revealed few differences in adjustment between adolescents living with same-sex parents and those living with opposite-sex parents (Wainright, Russell, & Patterson, 2004; Wainright & Patterson, 2006). There were no significant differences between teenagers living with same-sex parents and those living with other-sex parents on self-reported assessments of psychological well-being, such as self-esteem and anxiety; measures of school outcomes, such as grade point averages and trouble in school; or measures of family relationships, such as parental warmth and care from adults and peers. Adolescents in the two groups were equally likely to say that they had been involved in a romantic relationship in the last 18 months, and they were equally likely to report having engaged in sexual intercourse. The only statistically reliable difference between the two groups—that those with same-sex parents felt a greater sense of connection to people at school—favored the youngsters living with same-sex couples. There were no significant differences in self-reported substance use, delinquency, or peer victimization between those reared by same- or other-sex couples (Wainright & Patterson, 2006).

Although the gender of parents' partners was not an important predictor of adolescent well-being, other aspects of family relationships were significantly associated with teenagers' adjustment. Consistent with other findings about adolescent development, the qualities of family relationships rather than the gender of parents' partners were consistently related to adolescent outcomes. Parents who reported having close relationships with their offspring had adolescents who reported more favorable adjustment. Not only is it possible for children and adolescents who are parented by same-sex couples to develop in healthy directions, but—even when studied in an extremely diverse, representative sample of American adolescents—they generally do.

These findings have been supported by results from many other studies, both in the United States and abroad. Susan Golombok and her colleagues have reported similar results with a near-representative sample of children in the United Kingdom (Golombok et al., 2003). Others, both in Europe and in the United States, have described similar findings (e.g., Brewaeys, Ponjaert, Van Hall, & Golombok, 1997).

The fact that children of lesbian mothers generally develop in healthy ways should not be taken to suggest that they encounter no challenges. Many investigators have remarked upon the fact that children of lesbian and gay parents may encounter anti-gay sentiments in their daily lives. For example, in a study of 10-year-old children born to lesbian mothers, Gartrell, Deck, Rodas, Peyser, and Banks (2005) reported that a substantial minority had encountered anti-gay sentiments among their peers. Those who had had such encounters were likely to report having felt angry, upset, or sad about these experiences. Children of lesbian and gay parents may be exposed to prejudice against their parents in some settings, and this may be painful for them, but evidence for the idea that such encounters affect children's overall adjustment is lacking.

# Conclusions

Does parental sexual orientation have an important impact on child or adolescent development? Results of recent research provide no evidence that it does. In fact, the findings suggest that parental sexual orientation is less important than the qualities of family relationships. More important to youth than the gender of their parent's partner is the quality of daily interaction and the strength of relationships with the parents they have.

One possible approach to findings like the ones described above might be to shrug them off by reiterating the familiar adage that "one cannot prove the null hypothesis." To respond in this way, however, is to miss the central point of these studies. Whether or not any measurable impact of parental sexual orientation on children's development is ever demonstrated, the main conclusions from research to date remain clear: Whatever correlations between child outcomes and parental sexual orientation may exist, they are less important than those between child outcomes and the qualities of family relationships.

Although research to date has made important contributions, many issues relevant to children of lesbian and gay parents remain in need of study. Relatively few studies have examined the development of children adopted by lesbian or gay parents or of children born to gay fathers; further research in both areas would be welcome (Patterson, 2004). Some notable longitudinal studies have been reported, and they have found children of same-sex couples to be in good mental health. Greater understanding of family relationships and transitions over time would, however, be helpful, and longitudinal studies would be valuable. Future research could also benefit from the use of a variety of methodologies.

Meanwhile, the clarity of findings in this area has been acknowledged by a number of major professional organizations. For instance, the governing body of the American Psychological Association (APA) voted unanimously in favor of a statement that said, "Research has shown that the adjustment, development, and psychological well-being of children is unrelated to parental sexual orientation and that children of lesbian and gay parents are as likely as those of heterosexual parents to flourish" (APA, 2004). The American Bar Association, the American Medical Association, the American Academy of Pediatrics, the American Psychiatric Association, and other mainstream professional groups have issued similar statements.

The findings from research on children of lesbian and gay parents have been used to inform legal and public policy debates across the country (Patterson et al., 2002). The research literature on this subject has been cited in amicus briefs filed by the APA in cases dealing with adoption, child custody, and also in cases related to the legality of marriages between same-sex partners. Psychologists serving as expert witnesses have presented findings on these issues in many different courts (Patterson et al., 2002). Through these and other avenues, results of research on lesbian and gay parents and their children are finding their way into public discourse.

The findings are also beginning to address theoretical questions about critical issues in parenting. The importance of gender in parenting is one such issue. When children fare well in two-parent lesbian-mother or gay-father families, this suggests that the gender of one's parents cannot be a critical factor in child development. Results of research on children of lesbian and gay parents cast doubt upon the traditional assumption that gender is important in parenting. Our data suggest that it is the quality of parenting rather than the gender of parents that is significant for youngsters' development.

Research on children of lesbian and gay parents is thus located at the intersection of a number of classic and contemporary concerns. Studies of lesbian- and gay-parented families allow researchers to address theoretical questions that had previously remained difficult or impossible to answer. They also address oft-debated legal questions of fact about development of children with lesbian and gay parents. Thus, research on children of lesbian and gay parents contributes to public debate and legal decision making, as well as to theoretical understanding of human development.

# References

American Psychological Association (2004). Resolution on sexual orientation, parents, and children. Retrieved September 25, 2006, from http://www.apa.org/pi/lgbc/policy/parentschildren.pdf

Brewaeys, A., Ponjaert, I., Van Hall, E.V., & Golombok, S. (1997). Donor insemination: Child development and family functioning in lesbian mother families. *Human Reproduction, 12,* 1349–1359.

Chan, R.W., Raboy, B., & Patterson, C.J. (1998). Psychosocial adjustment among children conceived via donor insemination by lesbian and heterosexual mothers. *Child Development, 69,* 443–457.

Fulcher, M., Sutfin, E.L., Chan, R.W., Scheib, J.E., & Patterson, C.J. (2005). Lesbian mothers and their children: Findings from the Contemporary Families Study. In A. Omoto & H. Kurtzman (Eds.), *Recent research on sexual orientation, mental health, and substance abuse* (pp. 281–299). Washington, DC: American Psychological Association.

Gartrell, N., Deck., A., Rodas, C., Peyser, H., & Banks, A. (2005). The National Lesbian Family Study: 4. Interviews with the 10-year-old children. *American Journal of Orthopsychiatry, 75,* 518–524.

Golombok, S., Perry, B., Burston, A., Murray, C., Mooney-Somers, J., Stevens, M., & Golding, J. (2003). Children with lesbian parents: A community study. *Developmental Psychology, 39,* 20–33.

Patterson, C.J. (1996). Lesbian mothers and their children: Findings from the Bay Area Families Study. In J. Laird & R.J. Green (Eds.), *Lesbians and gays in couples and families: A handbook for therapists* (pp. 420–437). San Francisco: Jossey-Bass.

Patterson, C.J. (1997). Children of lesbian and gay parents. In
T. Ollendick & R. Prinz (Eds.), *Advances in clinical child
psychology* (Vol. 19, pp. 235–282). New York: Plenum Press.

Patterson, C.J. (2004). Gay fathers. In M.E. Lamb (Ed.), *The role
of the father in child development* (4th ed., pp. 397–416). New
York: Wiley.

Patterson, C.J., Fulcher, M., & Wainright, J. (2002). Children of
lesbian and gay parents: Research, law, and policy. In
B.L. Bottoms, M.B. Kovera, & B.D. McAuliff (Eds.), *Children,
social science and the law* (pp. 176–199). New York: Cambridge
University Press.

Patterson, C.J., & Hastings, P. (in press). Socialization in context of
family diversity. In J. Grusec & P. Hastings (Eds.), *Handbook of
socialization.* New York: Guilford Press.

Stacey, J., & Biblarz, T.J. (2001). (How) Does sexual orientation of
parents matter? *American Sociological Review, 65,* 159–183.

Wainright, J.L., & Patterson, C.J. (2006). Delinquency,
victimization, and substance use among adolescents
with female same-sex parents. *Journal of Family Psychology,
20,* 526–530.

Wainright, J.L., Russell, S.T., & Patterson, C.J. (2004). Psychosocial
adjustment and school outcomes of adolescents with same-sex
parents. *Child Development, 75,* 1886–1898.

Address correspondence to **CHARLOTTE J. PATTERSON,** Department
of Psychology, P.O. Box 400400, University of Virginia, Charlottesville,
VA 22904; e-mail: cjp@virginia.edu.

From *Current Directions in Psychological Science*, October 2006, pp. 241–244. Copyright © 2006 by the Association for Psychological Science. Reprinted by permission of
Wiley-Blackwell.

# UNIT 6

# Gender and Social Issues

## Unit Selections

## Key Points to Consider

- What is your view on abortion? Would you be willing to have an abortion or offer support to someone who chooses to have an abortion?

- What myths or stereotypes about rape have you personally heard?

- Does your college or university have a rape awareness/prevention program?

- Do you know how a report of an assault is supposed to be handled at your college or university? How do you think these issues should be handled on college and university campuses?

- What are your criteria for consent when two (or more) people have a sexual encounter? What age must the partners be? Why this age?

- Are sex workers and clients of sex workers dealt with equally by the criminal justice system?

- Should prostitution be legal? Why or why not?

## Student Website

www.mhcls.com

## Internet References

**Department of State: Human Rights**
*http://www.state.gov/g/drl/hr/*
**SocioSite: Feminism and Women's Issues**
*http://www.sociosite.net/topics/women.php*
**Planned Parenthood**
*http://www.plannedparenthood.org*
**Rape, Abuse and Incest National Network (RAINN)**
*http://www.rainn.org/*
**Child Rights Information Network (CRIN)**
*http://www.crin.org*
**Child Exploitation and Obscenity Section (CEOS)/U.S. Department of Justice**
*http://www.usdoj.gov/criminal/ceos/trafficking.html*

This final unit deals with several social issues that are of interest for different reasons. These topics have a common denominator—they have all taken positions of prominence in the public's awareness. All of the topics explored in this unit are controversial in today's society. The articles highlight areas of debate and disagreement in how we, as a society, should deal with these issues. Controversies are associated with almost anything having to do with sex, including sexual assault, contraception, and abortion. Indeed, sex in one way or another has been at the heart of the "culture wars" in the U.S. Although the focus of this unit is on gender and social issues, many of the articles included here (and the most controversial topics related to gender) are linked in some way to sex.

Abortion and birth control remain emotionally charged issues in U.S. society. While opinion surveys indicate that most of the public supports family planning and legal access to abortion (at least in some circumstances), there are certain individuals and groups who are strongly opposed to birth control and abortion. Voices for and against access to birth control and abortion remain passionate, and face-offs range from debates and legislative hearings to work stoppages by pharmacists and protests with or without violence. Supreme Court, legislative, and medical community efforts are at times at odds. Some seek to restrict access to abortion or the availability of birth control methods, while others seek to mandate freer access to contraceptive and reproductive choice options. Voices on both sides are raised in emotional and political debate between "we must never go back to the old days" (of illegal and unsafe back-alley abortions) and "the baby has no choice." Because abortion remains a fiercely debated topic, legislative efforts for and against it abound. This will likely continue for a very long time to come.

Other emotionally charged and difficult topics, such as sexual abuse and violence, permeate our society. For centuries, a strong code of silence surrounded sexual abuse and violence. Many now agree that silence has increased not only the likelihood of sexual abuse and violence, but the harm to the victims and survivors of these acts. Two social movements have been instrumental in the effort to break this code of silence. The child welfare/child rights movement exposed child abuse and mistreatment and sought to improve the lives of children and families. Soon after, and to a large extent fueled by the emerging women's movement, primarily grassroots organizations that became known as "rape crisis" groups or centers became catalysts for altering the way we viewed rape and sexual abuse. Research suggests that these movements have accomplished many of their initial goals and have brought about significant social change. The existence and prevalence of rape and other sexual abuse is better known today than ever before. Many of the myths previously believed (rapists are strangers that jump out of bushes, sexual abuse only occurs in poor families, all rapists are male and all victims are female, and so on) have been replaced with more accurate information. The code of silence has been recognized for the harm it can cause. Millions of friends, parents, teachers, counselors, and others have learned how to be approachable, supportive listeners to survivors disclosing their abuse experiences. Also, we have come to recognize the role that power—especially unequal power—plays in rape, sexual abuse, sexual violence, and sexual

© BananaStock/PunchStock

harassment. However, the battle is far from over, and sexual abuse continues.

As we have sought to expose and reduce abusive sex, it has become increasingly clear that all of society and each of us as individuals and potential partners must grapple with the broader issue of what constitutes consent. What is nonabusive sexual interaction? How can people communicate interest, arousal, desire, and/or propose sexual interaction, when remnants of unequal power, ignorance, misinformation, fear, adversarial sex roles, and inadequate communication skills still exist? What is (or should be) the role of employers, school personnel, or individuals who may be seen as contributing on some level to an environment that allows uncomfortable, abusive, or inappropriate sexual interactions? Conversely, is it possible that we could become so "sensitive" to the potential for abuse that combined with our discomfort, anger, and fear we could become hysterical vigilantes pushing an eager legal system to indict "offenders" who have not committed abuse or harassment?

In addition to the hot button issues above, this unit touches on a variety of other social issues. Regardless of the topic, the theme that unites all of the articles in this unit is that gender inequalities still exist and permeate society. May we someday live in a world that is characterized by true gender equality and full acceptance of gender diversity.

# Flower Grandma's Secret

**Physician Susan Wicklund had never told her grandmother about her medical specialty: reproductive health and abortion. She finally decided to divulge the truth just before appearing on a national television program that would reveal the constant harassment and danger she faced from anti-abortion fanatics. Before Wicklund could say much, Grandma offered her own heartbreaking disclosure. Here, from Wicklund's new memoir.**

SUSAN WICKLUND

When I drove into Grandma's driveway all I could think about was how she would react. I had started out to tell her many times over the last years. On so many visits I had meant to have that conversation, but had never found a way. Something had always intervened. Some other errand had always come up. I had found a way not to face her judgment.

It didn't matter that I was rock solid in my resolve and in my chosen profession. This was my grandma. My Flower Grandma. What she thought of me mattered a lot, and I had no idea how she'd take it.

It was February of 1992, a Saturday afternoon. The next day the *60 Minutes* segment I'd done with Leslie Stahl would air. Grandma never missed *60 Minutes*. I had to tell her before she saw it—before she saw her oldest granddaughter talking about the death threats and stalking and personal harassment my family and I were enduring.

The harassment wasn't the issue that mattered now. It was the fact that I was, as a physician, traveling to five clinics in three states to provide abortion services for as many as one hundred women every week, and that I had been doing this work for four years already.

I wasn't at all ashamed of my career. In fact, I always considered it an honor to be involved in reproductive choices, this most personal and intimate realm for women. I just never felt the need to make it public. Very few of my family and friends were aware of what I did.

Within a day, however, everyone I had grown up with, everyone who knew my family, and every member of my family would know the truth. Would I be isolated and ostracized? Would I get support or condemnation?

I pulled off the highway and into the drive leading to the house I'd grown up in. Mom and Dad still lived in the white, two-story wood-frame home.

Dad had worked as a precision machinist in the town of Grantsburg, 10 miles away. His love had been the gunsmithing, hunting and fishing he did in his free time. My three siblings and I had always been included. We were as competent with firearms, field dressing a deer or catching a batch of sunfish as anyone in the area. Dad was retired now and not feeling well. It was painful to watch him, the strong man who starred in my memories, struggling with simple tasks.

Mom was retired too, from her elected position as Clerk of Court for our county. She was the one everyone—especially women—turned to for advice and support. Mom had been instrumental, many years earlier, in starting a shelter for victims of domestic abuse. In her job she had seen so many situations where women and children had nowhere to go for help. It was just like Mom to tackle a need that everyone else ignored.

I grew up in the unincorporated village of Trade Lake, Wis. a small gathering of about six houses, several of which were the homes of my relatives. The only business left was one small gas station/grocery store. When I was a kid there had been a feed store and creamery and a meat market, but those had been gone for better than 30 years. Only rotten shells of buildings remained.

Even now, Trade Lake is a very rural place. People still raise chickens in backyards, drive tractors to the little grocery store. Chimneys puff wood smoke in the winter.

The small river that wound its way through our yard came into view. Behind it, the woods where I'd built forts and climbed oak trees with my sister. She and I each had a horse and spent the bulk of our summers out of doors. Grandma and Grandpa had lived just down the road. We picked mayflowers every spring with Grandma. In the summer we fished with Grandpa for sunfish and crappies with cane poles baited with worms dug out of the garden.

Mine had been a good childhood. This was a safe place. Turning in the driveway had always been a good thing—a coming home. This time was different.

I felt myself sweating under my coat. My racing heart pushed against my throat. I had to reveal something to my dear grandma that could change everything she believed and loved about me.

Grandma had moved into a trailer house in the backyard of the family home. Grandpa died 15 years earlier and Mom wanted her mother even closer—just steps across the yard. I saw the clothesline filled with rugs, the twine still strung up on the porch to hold the morning glories that filled the railings in the summer.

Flower Grandma. My daughter, Sonja, gave her the name when she was 3 and there were too many grandmas to keep track of. Sonja spent many days baking cookies with her great-grandmother and playing outside, just as I had as a young girl. She ran back and forth constantly between the houses of her two grandmothers. This grandma always had flowers growing in every nook and cranny, inside and out.

Flower Grandma she became, and Flower Grandma she stayed. Before long my entire extended family called her Flower Grandma, and even her friends at the local senior center fell into the habit.

I coasted to a stop at the bottom of the slope. I sat there long enough to take a deep breath and fight back a few unexpected tears. I didn't know where the sadness came from. The car engine ticked. I was alone, vulnerable, aching. Was I longing for those simple childhood days, whipping down the hill on my sled? How far I'd come from that.

I peeled myself out of the car, shed my coat and left it on the seat. It was unusually warm for February in Wisconsin. The hardwood forest was all bare sticks and hard lines. I knew it would soon be time to tap the maple trees and cook the wonderful syrup we all loved on Grandma's Swedish pancakes.

I turned and deliberately moved up the steps to the trailer house. I was terrified of what Grandma would say, but there was no avoiding this moment.

The big door was already open by the time I got to the top step. Out peeked her welcoming smile. She was giggling.

"Hi, Grandma!"

"Oh my goodness! What a surprise! What a sweet, sweet surprise! Did I know you were coming today?"

I hugged her in the doorway, held her tight, stepped inside.

"Did you somehow know I was making ginger snaps?" she teased as she set a plate full on the kitchen table. She poured me a glass of milk and I sat down on the wooden chair next to hers. I tried to bury myself in the smell of her place, a mixture of ginger cookies, Estée Lauder perfume (the one in the blue, hourglass bottle always on her dresser), and home permanents. She and Mom always gave each other perms, trying to get just the right curl in their hair. The smell never left the place.

I think she sensed that I had come to talk about something important. I started talking a few times about other, inconsequential things, then, finally, I plunged in.

"Grandma, you know I work as a doctor."

"Of course. And we are all so proud of you."

"Yes, but I don't think you know the whole story. I'm a doctor who works mostly for women, helping women with pregnancy problems."

Flower Grandma hesitated just a second, pushed back her chair, stood and held out her hand for me to follow. She went to sit in her rocker, the same one sitting in my living room today. The rocker I have sat in so many hours since. The rocker I sit in right now, writing this down and trembling as I do.

She seemed distant. I moved to the old leather hassock beside her. She took my hand and placed it on top of one of hers, then covered it with her other one. Our hands made a stack on the arm of the rocker—old skin, young skin. We sat in silence a minute. She turned to look directly at me. Her eyes, framed by gentle wrinkles, were full of some deep trouble.

After a moment, she stared straight ahead and started to speak. Slowly. Deliberately. In a very quiet voice. At the same time she began stroking my hand. It was as if the gentle stroking was pushing her to talk.

"When I was 16 years old my best friend got pregnant," she said. A chill went through me.

"I always believed it was her father that was using her," she went on, "but I never knew for sure. She came to my sister, Violet, and me, and asked us to help her."

While I listened, my thoughts whirled through my head. Stories I had read of women self-aborting and dying of infections when a safe, legal option was not available. The many women who came to the clinics where I worked, many of whom still had to overcome huge difficulties to end an unwanted pregnancy.

It isn't uncommon to have patients confide in me that prior to coming in for an abortion, they had used combinations of herbs to try to force a miscarriage. These home remedies can be extremely dangerous and have caused the deaths of many women.

I felt myself tighten and withdraw, anticipating what Flower Grandma was going to tell me. I wanted to see her eyes, but she kept them straight ahead. And she kept stroking my hand. So soft. I only wanted to think about those hands. Hands embracing and caressing mine—strong, gentle, soft.

"The three of us were so naive. We knew very little about these things, but we had heard that if you put something long and sharp 'up there,' in the private place, sometimes it would end the pregnancy."

In spite of myself I conjured the modest room: a dresser in the corner with a kerosene lamp and maybe a hairbrush or hand mirror beside it. I saw three young, scared girls, still children, acting on old wives' tales and whispered instructions.

My stomach turned. Was this my Grandma? Was I really here in her trailer house hearing this? I could barely breathe. She kept talking, all the while stroking the top of my hand, her eyes looking off into space, traveling back in time. Occasionally a pat-pat with her hand would break the rhythm of the stroking. Such old skin, full of brown age spots and paper thin. Stroking my hand in perfect measure with her words.

Please just stop, Grandma. Don't tell me anymore. Just hold my hand and let's talk about what you'll plant in the spring. Tell me about the oatmeal bread you baked yesterday. Are there many birds coming to the birdfeeder? I was flushed all over. And still she stroked while she talked. Pat-pat, stroke.

"We closed ourselves, the three of us, in one of the bedrooms late one morning. We didn't talk much, and she didn't ever cry out in pain. It took a few tries to make the blood come. None of us spoke. We didn't know what to expect next, or what to do when the blood kept coming. It was all over the sheets. All over us. So bright red. It was awful. It just wouldn't stop."

She was still stroking my hand. I was shaking uncontrollably. I stared at the African violets under the plant light, trying to make them the focus of my attention. Her voice was a monotone, never a pause.

"We put rags inside of her to try to stop the bleeding, but they soaked full. We all three stayed in her bed. We just didn't know what to do."

My hand was trembling so hard it was all I could do to keep it on top of hers. She grasped it briefly, held it tight, patted it a few times and then went on.

"We stayed there together, unable to move, even after she was dead. Her father found us, all three of us, in the bed. He stood in the doorway, staring. No words for a long time. When he did speak, he told my sister and me to leave and that we were never, ever to speak of this. We were not to tell anyone, ever. Ever."

She stopped stroking my hand and sat still before turning to look directly at me. "That was 72 years ago. You are the first person I have ever told that story. I am still so ashamed of what happened. We were just so young and scared. We didn't know anything."

Terrible sadness welled up inside me. And anger. I couldn't picture my Grandma as someone responsible for the death of anything, much less her best friend at the age of 16. She had carried this secret all her life, kept it inside, festering with guilt and shame.

I wondered if the pregnancy was indeed the result of incest. Would it have made a difference? What were friends and family told about the death? What had they actually used to start the bleeding? What had the doctor put on the death certificate as the cause of death?

I knew, through the patients I had met, that no one has to look very far into their family history to find these stories tucked away, hidden from view. But it didn't lessen the shock of finding it here, so close, in the heart of my own family.

Flower Grandma sighed and held my hand tight. Tears welled in her eyes.

"I know exactly what kind of work you do, and it is a good thing. People like you do it safely so that people like me don't murder their best friends. I told you how proud I am of what you do, and I meant it."

---

**SUSAN WICKLUND** has worked in the field of women's reproductive health for more than 20 years. For much of that time she has been on the front lines of the abortion war, both as a doctor and as a spokesperson for women's rights.

---

From *Ms.*, by Susan Wicklund, Fall 2007, pp. 67–69. Copyright © 2007 by Ms. Magazine. Reprinted by permission of Ms. Magazine and Susan Wicklund.

# Sexual Assault on Campus: What Colleges and Universities Are Doing about It

HEATHER M. KARJANE, PHD, BONNIE S. FISHER, PHD, AND FRANCIS T. CULLEN, PHD

Campus crime in general and sexual assault in particular have been receiving more attention than in the past, and concern has been expressed at the highest levels of government. On the Federal level, Congress responded by enacting several laws requiring institutions of higher education to notify students about crime on campus, publicize their prevention and response policies, maintain open crime logs, and ensure sexual assault victims their basic rights.[1] The Clery Act, the most notable of these laws, mandates an annual security report from each Federally funded school (see "Recent Federal Laws on Campus Crime").

In 1999, Congress asked the National Institute of Justice to find out what policies and procedures schools use to prevent and respond to reports of sexual assault.[2] The resulting study revealed that schools are making strides in some areas but must continue efforts to increase student safety and accountability. After summarizing what is known about the nature and extent of sexual assault on campus, the researchers highlighted findings regarding response policies and procedures; reporting options; barriers and facilitators; reporter training and prevention programming; victim resources; and investigation, adjudication, and campus sanctions. The study's baseline information can be used to measure progress in how institutions of higher education respond to sexual assault.

## The Scope of the Problem

Administrators want their campuses to be safe havens for students as they pursue their education and mature intellectually and socially. But institutions of higher education are by no means crime-free; women students face a high risk for sexual assault.

Just under 3 percent of all college women become victims of rape (either completed or attempted) in a given 9-month academic year. On first glance, the risk seems low, but the percentage translates into the disturbing figure of 35 such crimes for every 1,000 women students. For a campus with 10,000 women students, the number could reach 350. If the percentage is projected to a full calendar year, the proportion rises to nearly 5 percent of college women. When projected over a now-typical

---

### Recent Federal Laws on Campus Crime

Starting in 1990, Congress acted to ensure that institutions of higher education have strategies to prevent and respond to sexual assault on campus and to provide students and their parents accurate information about campus crime. The major Federal laws pertaining to this study are:

**Student Right-to-Know and Campus Security Act of 1990 (the "Clery Act"*) (20 U.S.C. § 1092).** This law, Title II of Public Law 101–542, requires that schools annually disclose information about crime, including specific sexual crime categories, in and around campus.

**Campus Sexual Assault Victims' Bill of Rights of 1992.** This amendment to the 1990 act requires that schools develop prevention policies and provide certain assurances to victims. The law was amended again in 1998 to expand requirements, including the crime categories that must be reported.

*The act was renamed in 1998 the "Jeanne Clery Disclosure of Campus Security Policy and Campus Crime Statistics Act" in honor of a student who was sexually assaulted and murdered on her campus in 1986.

---

5-year college career, one in five young women experiences rape during college.[3]

Counter to widespread stranger-rape myths, in the vast majority of these crimes—between 80 and 90 percent—victim and assailant know each other.[4] In fact, the more intimate the relationship, the more likely it is for a rape to be completed rather than attempted.[5] Half of all student victims do not label the incident "rape."[6] This is particularly true when no weapon was used, no sign of physical injury is evident, and alcohol was involved—factors commonly associated with campus acquaintance rape.[7] Given the extent of non-stranger rape on campus, it is no surprise that the majority of victimized women do not define their experience as a rape.

These reasons help explain why campus sexual assault is not well reported. Less than 5 percent of completed and attempted rapes of college students are brought to the attention of campus authorities and/or law enforcement.[8] Failure to recognize and report the crime not only may result in underestimating the extent of the problem, but also may affect whether victims seek medical care and other professional help. Thus, a special concern of the study was what schools are doing to encourage victims to come forward.

# Federal Law and the Schools' Response

Institutions of higher education vary widely in how well they comply with Clery Act mandates and respond to sexual victimization. Overall, a large proportion of the schools studied—close to 80 percent—submit the annual security report required by the Act to the U.S. Department of Education; more than two-thirds include their crime statistics in the report. Yet, according to a General Accounting Office study, schools find it difficult to consistently interpret and apply the Federal reporting requirements, such as deciding which incidents to cite in the annual report, classifying crimes, and the like.[9]

Definitions, even of such terms as "campus" and "student," are often a challenge and contribute to inconsistency in calculating the number of reported sexual assaults. Only 37 percent of the schools studied report their statistics in the required manner; for example, most schools failed to distinguish forcible and nonforcible sex offenses in their reports as required by the Clery Act.

# The Issues and the Findings

Congress specified the issues to be investigated (see "Study Design"). Key areas of concern were whether schools have a written sexual assault response policy; whether and how they define sexual misconduct; who on campus is trained to respond to reports of sexual assault; how students can report sexual victimization; what resources are available to victims; and what investigation and adjudication procedures are followed once a report is made. Researchers also examined policies that encourage or discourage reporting and some promising practices (see "Promising Practices").

# Definitions of Sexual Assault

Although the Clery Act instructs schools to use the FBI's Uniform Crime Report crime classification system as the basis for their annual statistics, schools may also define forms of "sexual misconduct" in their student code of conduct. Clear behavioral definitions—including definitions of consent and scenarios with nonstrangers—can help victims decide whether what happened to them should be reported to campus or law enforcement authorities. This strategy, used at schools with promising practices, directly challenges stranger-rape myths that disguise the problem and provide a false sense of safety.

---

## Study Design[a]

In 1999, Congress mandated investigation of nine issues concerning how colleges and universities are responding to campus sexual assault. Most of these issues are discussed in this Research for Practice.[b]

To collect the mandated information, the researchers studied a random sample of schools in the United States and Puerto Rico that receive student financial aid from the Federal Government and therefore must comply with the Clery Act. Almost 2,500 schools were in the sample, including all Historically Black Colleges and Universities and all Tribal Colleges and Universities. Schools were classified using the U.S. Department of Education's classification system. Results were reported by school type. The policy analysis was derived from almost two-thirds of the dataset of results from 4-year and 2-year public institutions and 4-year private nonprofit schools.

The researchers used three methods to study how schools are complying:

- Content analysis of the written sexual assault policies of the schools.
- A survey of campus administrators that asked about the issues mandated for study.
- Using 29 criteria, onsite examination of 8 schools found to use promising practices in addressing sexual assault on campus.

The eight schools with promising practices were:

- Central Washington University, Ellensburg, Washington.
- Lafayette College, Easton, Pennsylvania.
- Lewis & Clark College, Portland, Oregon.
- Metropolitan Community College, Omaha, Nebraska.
- Oklahoma State University, Stillwater.
- University of California at Los Angeles.
- University of California at Santa Cruz.
- West Virginia State College, Institute, West Virginia.

Response rates varied by type of institution. Overall, 1,015 schools sent their policies, and 1,001 campus administrators participated in the survey.

### Notes

a. A complete description of the study methodology is at Karjane, H.M., B.S. Fisher, and F.T. Cullen, *Campus Sexual Assault: How America's Institutions of Higher Education Respond,* final report to NIJ, Oct. 2002, NCJ 196676: chapter 2.
b. A list of the nine issues mandated for study can be found at ibid.: 12–13.

Congress asked about the prevalence and publication of school and State definitions of sexual assault. The researchers found:

- States have their own criminal codes; thus, definitions of acts that constitute sexual assault vary.
- Like State definitions, school definitions vary widely.
- A slight majority of the schools studied mentioned acquaintance rape in their sexual assault response policy.

## Sexual Assault Response Policy

A formal policy that addresses sexual assault on campus is a statement of the school's commitment to recognizing and dealing with the problem. To meet the intent of the Federal laws, the policy should be widely and easily accessible to students.

Congress asked whether the schools have and disseminate a sexual assault response policy. The researchers found:

- Traditional 4-year public and private nonprofit schools—which educate the majority of students—are the most likely to have a written sexual assault response policy.
- About half the schools studied spell out specific policy goals; for example, not tolerating sexual offenses on campus or pursuing disciplinary action against perpetrators. This is more common in 4-year institutions and Historically Black Colleges and Universities (HBCUs).

## Who Is Trained to Respond?

Students who are sexually assaulted are most likely to tell their friends first.[10] Research shows that social support from friends—and other "first responders"—can help the victim recognize what happened as a violation of the school's sexual misconduct policy and potentially a crime and encourage the victim to report it to the authorities.[11] For this reason it makes sense for schools to train students and staff in what to do if someone discloses that she or he has been sexually assaulted.

Congress wanted information about who is trained to respond to sexual assault and how much training is offered. The researchers found:

- Overall, only about 4 in 10 schools offer any sexual assault training. What training is available is usually for resident advisers and student security officers, not the general student population.
- Of the schools that provide training, about half train their faculty and staff in the school's response policies and procedures.
- Fewer than two in five schools train campus security personnel, even though formal complaints are likely to be reported to campus security. The majority of 4-year public institutions and HBCUs require this training.

## How Do Students Report an Assault?

If students know what to do in the event of a sexual assault (for example, whom to notify) and what steps the school will take, they are more likely to feel reassured and report to authorities. The probability of reporting is also linked to concerns about confidentiality. Victims may be embarrassed or fear reprisal; and victims who may have been drinking before the assault might fear sanctions for violating campus policy on alcohol use. Confidential reporting can be essential in these instances. Some victims prefer anonymous reporting, which allows the crime to be "counted," while letting the victim decide whether to file an official report.

Congress asked what on- and off-campus reporting options are available to victims and what procedures the schools follow after an assault. The researchers found:

- Although 84 percent of the schools studied offer confidential reporting, only 46 percent offer anonymous reporting.
- Contact procedures are specified in the sexual assault response policies of almost three in four schools, with campus or local police the most frequently named contact.
- Even though almost half of schools with a contact procedure listed a phone number, less than half provide service after business hours.
- Information about filing criminal charges and campus reports is included in the policies of less than half the schools, although, following the pattern, the figures for 4-year institutions are higher.

## Prevention Efforts and Resources for Victims

Services for victims are essential, but prevention is also key. Many 4-year colleges and universities offer a variety of educational programs geared to prevention, including rape awareness and self defense. Many schools also offer a combination of on- and off-campus services.

Congress asked what resources are available for victim safety, support, and health. The researchers found:

- About 6 in 10 schools offer safety-related educational programs. Of the programs offered by these schools, 6 in 10 address sexual assault.
- Of the schools that offer general educational programs, less than one-third include acquaintance rape prevention in the program. Even in 4-year public schools, less than half do so.
- Only about one-fourth of schools provide residence hall staff with safety training, have security staff on duty in the residences, or require overnight guests to register.
- For students who have been sexually assaulted, mental health crisis counseling is the most widely available service.

# What Discourages Victims from Reporting?

The small proportion of sexual assault victims who report the offense to authorities attests to the existence of multiple reporting barriers.

When schools adopt sexual assault response policies, their goal is to protect victims and the general student population by holding the perpetrator accountable while also protecting the rights of the accused. But any policy that compromises or restricts the victim's ability to make informed choices about how to proceed may deter reporting. At the individual level, some victims do not initially recognize the assault as a crime, or they have concerns about their confidentiality. Others may not want to participate in adjudication because they want to avoid public disclosure; they are not certain they can prove a crime occurred or that the perpetrator will be punished. Nonstranger rapists are rarely convicted of their crimes.[12]

Congress asked what policies and practices may prevent reporting or obstruct justice. The researchers found:

- Campus policies on drug and alcohol use have been adopted at three-fourths of the schools studied. At more than half of these schools, administrators say these policies inhibit reporting.
- A majority of campus administrators believe that requiring victims to participate in adjudication discourages reporting; about one-third of schools still have such a policy.
- Campuses may unintentionally condone victim-blaming by overemphasizing the victim's responsibility to avoid sexual assault without balancing messages stressing the perpetrator's responsibility for committing a crime and strategies bystanders can use to intervene.
- A trauma response, which may involve high levels of psychological distress, some of it triggered by shame and self-blame, inhibits reporting.
- The desire to avoid the perceived—and real—stigma of having been victimized also inhibits reporting.

# What Promotes Reporting?

Because barriers to reporting exist at many levels, a single policy or approach, such as allowing confidential reporting, is inadequate. The optimum approach to encourage reporting would be to combine a number of strategies, including making campus staff more responsive to reports of sexual assault and offering prevention education for the general student population as well as for specific groups.

Congress asked what policies aid in encouraging reporting. The researchers found:

- Services for victims, written law enforcement response protocols, coordination between campus and community, new student orientations, and campuswide publicity about past crimes are seen by administrators as facilitating reporting.
- Administrators at almost 90 percent of the schools studied believe that prevention programs targeting athletes and students in the Greek system encourage reporting. Only about one in five schools offers such programs, however, although over half of 4-year public schools have them.
- As noted earlier, most administrators believe that a policy allowing confidential and anonymous reporting encourages both victims and other students to report assaults.
- Most administrators consider sexual assault peer educators to be conducive to reporting, but only about one in five schools offers this type of program. Again, 4-year public institutions and HBCUs are more likely to have such programs.

Although campus administrators believe these policies encourage reporting, few have adopted them.

# Investigating and Punishing Victimizers

In responding to and adjudicating reports of sexual assault, schools need to balance the victim's need for justice with the rights of the accused. Bringing victimizers to justice is made more complex by the dual jurisdiction of campus administration and law enforcement. Sexual assault may be a violation of the school's sexual misconduct policy, with the accused brought before a disciplinary board or other body to determine his or her *responsibility* in violating the student code of conduct, but it is also a crime and therefore within the jurisdiction of the criminal justice system to determine *guilt*.

Congress asked what procedures schools have adopted for investigating sexual assault and disciplining and punishing perpetrators. The researchers found:

- Most reports of sexual assault on campus are dealt with through binding administrative actions, such as no-contact orders.
- An information-gathering or investigative process is used at only one-fourth of schools overall, only one-fourth of 4-year private nonprofit schools, and less than half of 4-year public schools.
- Due process for the accused is guaranteed in fewer than 40 percent of schools that have disciplinary procedures.
- In about 80 percent of schools, the body that decides whether the student code of conduct has been violated is the disciplinary board. In just over half the schools, this body also decides what sanction will be imposed.
- The most common penalty is expulsion, imposed by 84 percent of the schools. Many schools suspend offenders or place them on probation. Offenders may also be censured, required to make restitution, or lose privileges.

# Promising Practices

The researchers identified promising practices at eight schools (see "Study Design") in the areas of prevention, sexual assault policy, reporting, investigation, adjudication, and victim support services. Some examples are included here.[a]

## Prevention

A campus sexual assault education program should include comprehensive education about rape myths, common circumstances under which the crime occurs, rapist characteristics, prevention strategies, rape trauma responses and the healing process, and campus policies and support services. To reach the entire student body, these messages should be disseminated in many forms, i.e., through student orientation, curriculum infusion, resource center trainings, campus events, and public information materials. For example, Lafayette College's sexual misconduct policy is communicated to students where they live as well as where they learn, in a kind of "road show." Much larger University of California, Santa Cruz (UCSC), conducts a weekly saturation campaign of flier dissemination all over campus.

Several schools have peer educators and advocates who present programs that feature scenarios followed by facilitated discussion. Some campuses gear prevention and intervention programs to all-male groups, such as male athletes, fraternity members, and male members of ROTC. These prevention programs stress male culpability for committing the vast majority of sex crimes, men's individual and collective responsibility for helping to prevent these crimes, and the attitudes men may hold that foster the crimes. For example, UCSC supports a "Mentors in Violence Prevention" program that emphasizes the bystander's role in violence prevention, in part by using a "playbook" of strategies men can use to interrupt their peers when they believe they may be edging toward criminal behavior.[b]

## Sexual Assault Policy

A school's sexual assault policy should be a reader-friendly, easily accessible, and widely distributed statement of the school's definitions and expectations regarding sexual conduct. The policy should:

- Clearly define all forms of sexual misconduct, including operational and behavioral definitions of what acts constitute consent and what acts constitute a sexual assault.
- Discuss the prevalence of nonstranger sexual assault.
- Describe circumstances in which sexual assault most commonly occurs.
- Advise what to do if the student or someone she/he knows is sexually assaulted.
- List resources available on campus and in the local community.
- Identify a specific person or office to contact when a sexual assault occurs (preferably available 24/7) and when and where to file a complaint.
- Strongly encourage victims to report the incident to campus authorities and to the local criminal justice system.
- Provide for and list available reporting options, including a confidential option and preferably including an anonymous option.
- State the school's sanctions for violating the sexual misconduct policy.
- Provide an official statement prohibiting retaliation against individuals who report rape or sexual assault and specifying the school's disciplinary actions for retaliation attempts.
- Provide an official statement noting the separate actions available to the victim, i.e., reporting; investigating the report; informal administrative actions, such as issuing a no-contact order; formal adjudication on campus; and criminal prosecution.

## Reporting

All eight schools allow anonymous, confidential, and third-party reporting. Highly recommended are reporting and response policies that allow the victim to participate in decisionmaking, to exert some control over the pace of the process, and to be in charge of making decisions as she/he moves through the campus adjudication and/or the local law enforcement system. Written response protocols ensure a coordinated, consistent, victim-centered response.[c]

For example, Oklahoma State University counsels student victims that reporting an incident, choosing to prosecute, adjudicating a complaint through the University, and filing a civil action are separate steps. Reporting the incident does not obligate the victim to prosecute, but does allow gathering of information. The student chooses whether to move to the next step in the process and is advised of the consequences of each action, what to expect, and how confidentiality will be maintained.

## Investigation

Protocols to ensure confidentiality for the victim and the accused during the investigation are essential. Also important are protocols for shared collection and use of information to eliminate the need for the victim to retell the experience multiple times.

One of the most promising practices is providing victims access to a trained, certified Sexual Assault Nurse Examiner (SANE). SANE practitioners provide appropriate treatment and forensic examination. Their documentation of evidence can corroborate a victim's account.[d]

## Adjudication

Many schools offer a range of adjudication options, from informal administrative actions that do not require a formal complaint to a formal adjudication board hearing. Proceedings should follow an established, documented, and consistent format that balances the rights of the complainant and the accused. Sexual misconduct adjudication boards are not criminal proceedings; their purpose is to establish

*(Continued)*

## Promising Practices *(continued)*

whether the accused is responsible for violating the school's policy, not to determine the accused's guilt or innocence.[e]

### Victim Support Services

The most promising practice in this area is the formation of partnerships between the school and the community to provide student victims access to a comprehensive, coordinated network of service providers—medical, psychological, advocacy, legal, and safety. More research is needed to help schools determine which practices are best for their campus and students.

### Notes

a. A comprehensive review of promising practices is in Karjane, H., B. Fisher, and F.T. Cullen, *Campus Sexual Assault: How America's Institutions of Higher Education Respond,* final report to the National Institute of Justice, Oct. 2002, NCJ 196676.

b. See Katz, J., "Reconstructing Masculinity in the Locker Room: The Mentors in Violence Prevention Project," *Harvard Educational Review* 65(2)(1995): 163–174; also see Karjane et al., *Campus Sexual Assault:* 128.

c. See Karjane et al., *Campus Sexual Assault:* 133–134.

d. For more information about SANEs, see Littel, K., "Sexual Assault Nurse Examiner (SANE) Programs: Improving the Community Response to Sexual Assault Victims," *OVC Bulletin,* Washington, DC: U.S. Department of Justice, Office for Victims of Crime, 2001, available online at www.ojp.usdoj.gov/ovc/publications/bulletins/sane_4_2001/welcome.html. Also see Sommers, M.S., B.S. Fisher, and H.M. Karjane, "Using Colposcopy in the Rape Exam: Health Care, Forensic, and Criminal Justice Issues," *Journal of Forensic Nursing* 1(1)(2005): 28–34, 19.

e. For more about adjudication protocols and practices, see Karjane et al., *Campus Sexual Assault:* chapter 6 and 135–136.

---

- Only about half the schools keep the complainant apprised of the progress of the case; they are far more likely to notify the accused.
- Use of protocols for coordinating the responses of campus and local law enforcement agencies were found to be a promising practice, but only about one in four schools have them, most of these 4-year public institutions and HBCUs.

## Do Schools Need to Do More?

The study confirmed that there is much confusion among schools about what the Clery Act requires. The fact that only 37 percent fully comply in reporting crime statistics indicates a need for guidance. The researchers recommend development of a policy that includes explicit and behavioral definitions of consent, sexual offenses, and other terminology and practices.

Many schools either do not have a sexual assault response policy or could not provide it for the study. The larger, 4-year institutions and HBCUs tend to have policies, often available on their Web sites, but these vary in clarity and thoroughness. This suggests a model policy could be useful to the schools as a template in developing their own.

More could be done to increase reporting. Practices that are perceived by college administrators to discourage or encourage reporting need to be examined empirically.

Because underreporting may be linked to the victim's inability to recognize sexual victimization as a violation of the school's student code of conduct and, further, as a crime, more research is needed into such issues as the perpetuation of stranger-rape myths, the relationship of the victim to the assailant, use of alcohol before the assault, and other contributory factors.

## References

1. These laws affect all institutions of higher education that receive student financial aid from the Federal Government.

2. The study was mandated as part of the 1998 amendments to the Higher Education Act of 1965, Public Law 105–244.

3. Fisher et al., *The Sexual Victimization of College Women:* 10–11.

4. See ibid.: 17; also see Koss, M., C. Gidycz, and N. Wisniewski, "The Scope of Rape: Incidence and Prevalence of Sexual Aggression and Victimization in a National Sample of Higher Education Students," *Journal of Consulting and Clinical Psychology* 55(2)(1987): 162–170.

5. Fisher et al., "Extent and Nature of the Sexual Victimization of College Women": 89–90; 123–124.

6. Fisher, B.S., L.E. Daigle, F.T. Cullen, and M.G. Turner, "Acknowledging Sexual Victimization as Rape: Results From a National-Level Study," *Justice Quarterly* 20(3)(2000): 401–440. A study 13 years earlier reported that 3 in 4 women (73 percent) who had an experience that met Ohio penal code criteria for rape did not label the incident "rape." See Koss et al., "The Scope of Rape": 162–170.

7. See Bondurant, B., "University Women's Acknowledgment of Rape: Individual, Situational, and Social Factors," *Violence Against Women* 7(3)(2001): 294–314.

8. Fisher et al., *The Sexual Victimization of College Women:* 23.

9. *Campus Crime: Difficulties Meeting Federal Reporting Requirements,* Washington, DC: General Accounting Office, 1997.

10. Fisher, B.S., L.E. Daigle, F.T. Cullen, and M.G. Turner, "Reporting Sexual Victimization to the Police and Others: Results from a National-level Study of College Women," *Criminal Justice and Behavior: An International Journal* 30(1)(2003): 6–38.

11. Kahn, A., and V. Andreoli Mathie, "Understanding the Unacknowledged Rape Victim," in *Sexuality, Society and Feminism,* ed. C. Travis and J. White, Washington, DC: American Psychological Association, 2000: 337–403; Neville, H., and A. Pugh, "General and Culture-Specific Factors Influencing African American Women's Reporting Patterns and Perceived Social Support Following Sexual Assault," *Violence Against Women* 3(4)(1997): 361–381.

12. See Spohn, C., and D. Holleran, "Prosecuting Sexual Assault: A Comparison of Charging Decisions in Sexual Assault Cases Involving Strangers, Acquaintances, and Intimate Partners," *Justice Quarterly* 18(3)(2001): 651–688.

HEATHER M. KARJANE, PhD, is coordinator for gender issues at the Commonwealth of Massachusetts Administrative Office of the Trial Court. BONNIE S. FISHER, PhD, and FRANCIS T. CULLEN, PhD, are faculty in the Division of Criminal Justice at the University of Cincinnati. The Police Executive Research Forum conducted some of the field research.

From *National Institute of Justice Journal*, December 2005, pp. ii, 1–16.

# Male Rape Myths
## The Role of Gender, Violence, and Sexism

Kristine M. Chapleau MS, Debra L. Oswald, PhD, and Brenda L. Russell, PhD

More than 247,000 women and men in the United States were estimated as being raped or sexually assaulted in 2002 (U.S. Department of Justice, 2003). Most research has focused on female victims; however, 13% (31,640) of reported rape and sexual assault victims were male (U.S. Department of Justice, 2003). Although women are victimized far more often than men, the proportion of male victims compared to female victims may be skewed because of gender differences in reporting rates. While the reporting rate for women is low (e.g., Koss, Gidycz, & Wisniewski, 1987), preliminary results suggest that men are 1.5 times less likely to report a rape by a male perpetrator to the police than are women (Pino & Meier, 1999). This rate may be even lower when accounting for sexual assaults committed by women, although little is known about the effects of perpetrator gender on the likelihood that male victims will report sexual assault to the police.

Unfortunately, even when rape victims do report, the legal system often fails to punish the perpetrators. Justice for female sexual assault victims is often derailed by unsympathetic police officers (Campbell & Johnson, 1997), district attorneys (Frohmann, 1991), and juries (Koss, 2000). Similar data are not reported for male victims, which, given the lower reporting rate, suggests that perpetrators of male rape are also seldom prosecuted. Sexual assault is often emotionally devastating to men. Like female victims, men can experience vulnerability, depression, suicidal thoughts, sleep disturbances, social isolation, sexual dysfunction, and confusion about their sexual orientation if the perpetrator was male (Goyer & Eddleman, 1984; Groth & Burgess, 1980; Mezey & King, 1989). Furthermore, there is correlational evidence that male victims sexually coerce others as well. Russell and Oswald (2002) found that of college-aged men who reported using coercion to obtain sex, almost 63% reported having at least one experience of being sexually coerced themselves by a female partner. Thus, sexual coercion against men has serious consequences for the victims as well as for others.

In sum, male rape is problematic and currently understudied. Because male and female victims experience similar social sanctions and negative sequelae, it follows that similar social forces and ideologies work against rape victims of both genders. In this study, we investigate the extent to which people believe rape myths about male victims. Rape myths about female victims have been found to play a central role in the misperceptions and treatment of female rape victims. Similarly, we argue that there are myths about male victims of rape that need to be explored and understood. Given the limited research on male rape myths, we first examine the research on female rape victims to direct our study of biases toward male rape victims.

## Rape Myths about Female Victims

For female victims, past research has shown that a primary social force in their maltreatment is rape myths (e.g., Brownmiller, 1975; Burt, 1980; Campbell & Johnson, 1997; Du Mont, Miller, & Myhr, 2003). Rape myths are stereotypical or false beliefs about the culpability of victims, the innocence of rapists, and the illegitimacy of rape as a serious crime (Lonsway & Fitzgerald, 1994). For example, in the development of the Illinois Rape Myth Acceptance Scale, Payne, Lonsway, and Fitzgerald (1999) identified seven types of female rape myths: (a) "she asked for it"; (b) "it wasn't really rape"; (c) "he didn't mean to"; (d) "she wanted it"; (e) "she lied"; (f) "rape is a trivial event"; and (g) "rape is a deviant event" (p. 37). Although there seems to be agreement on the identification of rape myths (Lonsway & Fitzgerald, 1994), pinpointing the underlying ideologies that facilitate female rape myth acceptance has been more challenging.

With roots in feminist theory, most of the proposed attitudinal variables relate to sexism (for a review, see Lonsway & Fitzgerald, 1994). One of the earliest studies on this topic found that the best attitudinal predictor of rape myth acceptance was acceptance of interpersonal violence (Burt, 1980). This is the belief that "force and coercion are legitimate ways to gain compliance and specifically that they are legitimate in intimate and sexual relationships" (Burt, 1980, p. 218). Other strong predictors in Burt's study were sex role stereotyping and adversarial sexual beliefs. So participants who judged others based on rigid sex roles, thought that men and women naturally struggle for dominance, and that men should ultimately win this struggle, even if by force, were more likely to denounce female rape victims.

Updating Burt's (1980) construct of sex role stereotyping, Glick and Fiske (1996) proposed that sexism consists of two components reflecting hostile and benevolent attitudes toward women. Hostile sexism is denigrating attitudes that punish women who defy traditional gender roles (Glick, Diebold, Bailey-Werner, & Zhu, 1997). Conversely, benevolent sexism is reverent attitudes that reward women who are traditionally feminine (Glick et al., 1997). Although hostile and benevolent sexism are both stereotypical beliefs about women, they differ in prejudicial evaluations (i.e., bad and good) (Glick & Fiske, 1996). Those who have these conflicting feelings toward women resolve this conflict by categorizing individual women as either "good girls" or "bad girls" (Glick & Fiske, 1996). "Good girls" are venerated and thus worthy of chivalry; "bad girls" are denigrated and denied patriarchal protection. Glick and Fiske (1997) found that for both male and female participants, hostile sexism (but not benevolent sexism) significantly correlated with Burt's (1980) Rape Myth Acceptance Scale (using partial correlations controlling for benevolent sexism scores).

Viki and Abrams (2002), however, suggested that individuals who score higher in benevolent sexism may be more likely to blame victims of acquaintance rape for falling short of the "ladylike" standard. Consistent with this hypothesis, benevolent sexism, but not hostile sexism, was associated with blaming victims of acquaintance rape (but not stranger rape) (Abrams, Viki, Masser, & Bohner, 2003; Viki & Abrams, 2002) and recommendations for shorter prison sentences for acquaintance rapists (Viki, Abrams, & Masser, 2004). Viki and colleagues concluded that individuals who are high in benevolent sexism may blame acquaintance rape victims to protect their belief in a just world.

A consistent finding is that heterosexual men are more accepting of rape myths than are women (Lonsway & Fitzgerald, 1994). To explain this gender difference, Lonsway and Fitzgerald (1995) examined the role of hostility toward women in rape myth acceptance. They hypothesized that Burt's (1980) Acceptance of Interpersonal Violence Scale and Adversarial Sexual Beliefs Scale share a common ideology: hostility toward women. Using revised scales that were gender neutral, they found that hostility toward women accounted for almost twice the variance in rape myth acceptance scores for men than it did for women. Lonsway and Fitzgerald (1995) concluded that rape myths serve different purposes for men and women. For men, rape myths about female victims justify men's sexual domination of women; for women, rape myths mitigate fear and feelings of vulnerability.

## Rape Myths about Male Victims

Less is known about rape myths concerning male victims, but previous research has identified the following beliefs: (a) Being raped by a male attacker is synonymous with the loss of masculinity (Groth & Burgess, 1980), (b) "men who are sexually assaulted by men must be gay" (Stermac, Del Bove, & Addison, 2004, p. 901), (c) "men are incapable of functioning sexually unless they are sexually aroused" (Smith, Pine, & Hawley, 1988, p. 103), (d) "men cannot be forced to have sex against their will" (Stermac et al., 2004, p. 901), (e) "men are less affected by sexual assault than women" (Stermac et al., 2004, p. 901), (f) "men are in a constant state of readiness to accept any sexual opportunity" (Clements-Schreiber & Rempel, 1995, p. 199), and (g) "a man is expected to be able to defend himself against sexual assault" (Groth & Burgess, 1980, p. 808). For example, in Smith et al.'s (1988) study, participants perceived a male victim of a female-perpetrated assault as more likely to have encouraged the assault, enjoyed the encounter, and thus experienced little trauma. Male participants endorsed these perceptions more than women did, but this gender difference disappeared when the perpetrator was another man.

Struckman-Johnson and Struckman-Johnson (1992) first attempted to measure these myths by focusing on three general beliefs: (a) Male rape does not happen (e.g., "it is impossible to rape a man"), (b) rape is the victim's fault (e.g., "men are to blame for not escaping"), and (c) men would not be traumatized by rape (e.g., "men do not need counseling after being raped"). Each of these beliefs was presented twice to manipulate the gender of the perpetrator. Consistent with research on female rape myths, they found that men were more accepting of male rape myths than were women. Furthermore, with the exception of the myth that denies the existence of male rape, male and female participants endorsed male rape myths to a greater extent when the perpetrator was a woman instead of a man. Despite these interesting initial results, little additional research has been conducted to further understand male rape myths. Thus, it is not clear how these rape myths develop, who believes these myths, and the function these myths have in determining attitudes toward male victims of rape.

We speculate that the same attitudes that function to support rape myths about female victims may also function to support rape myths about male victims. Specifically, adversarial sexual beliefs and acceptance of interpersonal violence correlates with participants' support of female rape myths (Lonsway & Fitzgerald, 1995). It may be that individuals who accept interpersonal aggression will accept aggressive behavior in general, regardless of the victim's gender. Furthermore, many of the items on the Acceptance of Interpersonal Violence Scale depict men as the sexual aggressor. Participants who believe that men should assert themselves through violence may also be less sympathetic to male victims.

Furthermore, just as ambivalent sexism toward women is related to rape myth acceptance concerning female victims (e.g., Chapleau, Oswald, & Russell, 2007; Glick & Fiske, 1997; Viki et al., 2004), we hypothesize that Glick and Fiske's (1999) corresponding ambivalent sexism toward men (including the components of hostile and benevolent sexism toward men) will be related to support of male rape myths. Glick and Fiske state that just as sexist attitudes about women can be positive and negative, there are also ambivalent sexist attitudes toward men. Specifically, women resent men for their greater social power and aggressiveness while also admiring and needing them for these same qualities. For example, women may characterize men as being arrogant, sex starved, and domineering (hostile sexism) but also strong, resourceful, and stoic (benevolent sexism). Male participants also can hold these dual stereotypes toward men, but they typically score higher on benevolent sexism and lower on hostile sexism than do women. We expect that participants who are higher in benevolent sexism toward men will be more supportive of male rape myths, such that they will judge male rape victims harshly for not being "man enough" to escape a sexual assault and, if assaulted, expect male victims to quickly reclaim their manhood and deny that the assault was traumatic. We also expect that hostile sexism toward men will be associated with rape myth acceptance because the belief that men often use unscrupulous means to obtain sex and power may be incompatible with the idea that a man could be sexually victimized.

## Study Summary

The overall purpose of this study is to further investigate male rape myths using Struckman-Johnson and Struckman-Johnson's (1992) measure. Currently, this is the only measure of male rape myth acceptance that distinguishes between male and female assailants; however, it has not yet been examined for its psychometric properties. Therefore, the first goal is to use confirmatory factor analysis to examine the underlying structure the male rape myth measures. In their study, Struckman-Johnson and Struckman-Johnson calculated one total score for male rape myth acceptance suggesting a general, one-factor model. Yet they created their measure using three of most prevalent male rape myths in research literature (i.e., denial, blame, and trauma) suggesting a three-factor model. They also expected that the acceptance of each myth would differ depending on the gender of the perpetrator, suggesting a two-factor structure. In sum, we test three possible models of male rape myths: a three-factor solution by myth, a two-factor solution by gender of the perpetrator, or a one-factor solution of general male rape myths.

The second goal of this study is to explore the variables that might be associated with increased support of male rape myths. Specifically, we examine how acceptance of interpersonal violence, adversarial sex beliefs, and ambivalent sexism toward men relate to male rape myth acceptance, as these variables are similar to factors that support female rape myths. We also examine gender differences in the acceptance of male rape myths and compare the level of support for male rape myths versus female rape myths. We expect to replicate previous findings (Struckman-Johnson & Struckman-Johnson, 1992) that men are more supportive of male rape myths than are women.

## Method
### Participants

The participants were 423 college students from a medium-sized Midwestern, private, Catholic university (57.7%; $n = 246$) and a small Eastern public college ($n = 180$). The demographics of the combined sample were 65% female ($n = 276$), 85.2% White/Caucasian ($n = 363$), with a mean age of 19.6 ($SD = 2.74$).

### Procedure

The participants completed measures of male rape myth acceptance, female rape myth acceptance, ambivalent sexism toward men, adversarial sexual beliefs, and acceptance of interpersonal violence, as part of a larger study on sexual aggression (see Oswald & Russell, 2006). All participants received extra credit in an introductory psychology course.

### Measures
#### Male rape myths

Using Struckman-Johnson and Struckman-Johnson's (1992) measure, participants indicated how much they agreed with 12 items that reflect misconceptions about men as victims of rape. Six items refer to men victimized by another man (e.g., "it is impossible for a man to rape a man"), and six items refer to women as perpetrators (e.g., "it is impossible for a man to be raped by a woman"). This measure uses a 6-point Likert-type scale (1 = *strongly disagree, 6 = strongly agree*), with higher scores indicating more endorsement of these rape myths.

#### Illinois Rape Myth Acceptance Scale, Short Form

Participants completed Payne et al.'s (1999) scale, which uses a 5-point Likert-type scale (1 = *strongly disagree, =strongly agree*) to assess agreement with myths about women as victims of rape (e.g., "many women secretly desire to be raped"). Higher scores signify more agreement with rape myths. The coefficient alpha was .85.

#### Adversarial sexual beliefs

Burt's (1980) measure contains nine items that assess participants' belief that men and women's romantic relationships with each other are, by nature, adversarial and exploitative. This measure uses a 7-point Likert-type scale (1 = *strongly - disagree, 7 = strongly agree*), with higher scores denoting reater endorsement of this viewpoint. The coefficient alpha was .83, and the overall mean was used in the analyses.

### Acceptance of interpersonal violence

Participants completed five items from Burt's (1980) measure (e.g., "sometimes women need to be forced to have sex"). Participants responded using a 7-point Likert-type scale (1 = *strongly disagree, 7 = strongly agree*). The coefficient alpha was .51, and the overall mean was used in the analyses. Although the reliability is lower than desired, it is similar to what was reported by Burt. Despite the low reliability, this scale was used because previous research has found it to be one of the best predictors of rape myth acceptance (Burt, 1980).

### Ambivalence Toward Men Inventory

Employing Glick and Fiske's (1999) measure, participants expressed how much they agreed with items advocating hostile and benevolent stereotypes and prejudices about men (e.g., men are unwilling to share power with women; men should provide for women) using a 6-point Likert-type scale (0 = *disagree strongly, 5 = agree strongly*). Two means were extracted for analysis to assess benevolent sexism and hostile sexism (Glick & Fiske, 1999). The coefficient alphas for benevolent and hostile sexism were .85 and .81, respectively.

# Results
## Confirmatory Factor Analysis

To examine the factor structure of the male rape myth measure, we computed three alternative confirmatory factor models using EQS 5.7 (Bentler, 1998). The first model had each myth (denial, blame, and trauma) as a latent factor with four items as indicator variables. The three latent factors were allowed to covary. The second model was a two-factor model where each factor represented the myths by the gender of the perpetrator. There were six items as indicator variables to each latent factor, and the factors were allowed to covary. The third model was a general factor model in which all 12 items represented the single latent variable of male rape myth.

For identification purposes, the variance for each latent variable was set to 1. Maximum likelihood with Satorra-Bentler estimation was used to estimate the parameters and model chi-square. In interpreting the models, we examined the path estimates, standardized root mean residuals (SRMR), root mean square error of approximation (RMSEA), $\chi^2$, and several fit indices. Because the $\chi^2$ is influenced by the sample size, we also looked at the $\chi^2$ to degrees of freedom ratio, where a ratio of 2 or less indicates a good fit (Ullman, 1996). We considered the following general "rules of thumb" that an RMSEA less than .05 indicates a "good fit" and less than .08 indicates an "acceptable fit" (Hu & Bentler, 1999; McDonald

& Ho, 2002 suggest .06 for a "good fit"), the SRMR should be close to .08 or less (Hu & Bentler, 1999), and goodness of fit statistics should generally be larger than .90 (Hu & Bentler, 1999; McDonald & Ho, 2002).

The three-factor model with each latent variable representing a type of myth resulted in a Satorra-Bentler Scaled $\chi^2$ (51) = 154.53, $p < .01$ ($\chi^2/df$ ratio = 3.03, Goodness of Fit Index [GFI] = .89, Comparative Fit Index [CFI] = .83, SRMR = .07, and RMSEA = .10). All the items had statistically significant parameters on the designated factor, indicating that the items were loaded onto the correct factors. The chi-square was significant, and the fit indices were weaker than desired according to traditional "rules of thumb." However, the SRMR and relatively small residuals suggest an adequate first approximation of the data. Factor analyses for the two-factor model by gender, $\chi^2(53) = 200.42, p < .01$ ($\chi^2/df$ ratio = 3.78, GFI = .87, CFI = .80, SRMR = .08, and RMSEA = .11) and general model, $\chi^2(54) = 233.09, p < .01$ ($\chi^2/df$ ratio = 4.32, GFI = .85, CFI = .74, SRMR = .09, and RMSEA = .12) each demonstrated worse fit indices and model statistics.

Of the models tested, the three-factor model was the best fit and indicates that the myths should be examined as separate factors. The three subscales were labeled Denial (alpha = .60), Blame (alpha = .82), and Trauma (alpha = .50). The intercorrelations between the three subscales were significant. Denial positively correlated with Blame ($r = .44, p < .01$) and Trauma ($r = .50, p < .01$). Blame positively correlated with Trauma ($r = .44, p < .01$). Although the three-factor model was the best fit of the tested models, the less than ideal fit statistics, significant chi-square, and low coefficient alphas for two of the subscales suggest that this confirmatory factor model does not meet most of the traditional standards of a good scale structure. Additional scale development is needed. Thus, although we use the subscales in subsequent analyses to examine gender differences and the ideologies associated with male rape myth acceptance, these results should be considered exploratory until additional scale validation and replication of the results occur.

## Comparisons of Rape Myth Acceptance by Participant Gender

The mean for each subscale was computed and used in a 2 (Gender) × 3 (Myth) mixed model ANOVA, with myth as the within-subjects variable. The goal was to determine gender differences in male rape myth acceptance and across myth type. There was a main effect of myth type, $F(2, 416) = 32.07, p < .01, \eta^2 = .13$, such that participants were most supportive of the Blame myth ($M = 2.01, SD = 1.09$) followed by the Trauma myth ($M = 1.86, SD = .83$), and the Denial myth ($M = 1.71, SD = .79$). Post hoc analysis revealed that all mean differences were significant ($ps < .01$). Collapsing across myth type, men ($M = 2.14$) demonstrated more overall male rape myth acceptance than did women ($M = 1.71$),

$F(1, 417) = 35.51, p < .01, < \eta^2 = .08$. These main effects were qualified by the Myth Type × Gender interaction, $F(2, 416) \times 18.15, p < .01, \eta^2 = .08$, such that men were more supportive of male rape myths than were women, but the magnitude of these differences depended on the type of myth. For men, there were significant differences between all three rape myths ($ps < .01$). Men had the highest mean on the Blame subscale ($M = 2.49, SD = 1.23$), followed by the Trauma subscale ($M = 2.13, SD = .85$), and the lowest mean for the Denial subscale ($M = 1.80, SD = .84$). For women, the differences between the three rape myths (Blame: $M = 1.76, SD = .92$; Trauma: $M = 1.71, SD = .77$; Denial: $M = 1.66, SD = .76$) were nonsignificant ($ps < .10$).

## Comparisons of Male Rape Acceptance with Female Rape Acceptance

A total score on the male rape myth measure significantly correlated with the Illinois Rape Myth Acceptance Scale ($r = .58, p < .01$). Not surprisingly, men ($M = 2.01, SD = .61$), compared to women ($M = 1.72, SD = .50$), were more supportive of female rape myths, $t(247.3) = 4.89, p < .01$. To determine if there were differences in the acceptance of male versus female rape myths within genders, the raw scores on the male and female rape myth scales were transformed into $z$ scores for analysis (because they were measured using different Likert-type scales). For men, there was no difference in the level of support for male ($M = .38, SD = 1.06$) and female rape myths ($M = .34, SD = 1.10$), $t(144) = .51, p > .10$. Similarly, for women, there was also no significant difference between the acceptance of male ($M = -.21, SD = .90$) and female rape myths ($M = -.19, SD = .89$), $t(273) = -.44, p > .10$. Thus, support for rape myths did not vary by gender of the victim. and, overall, men were more supportive of all rape myths than were women.

## Regression Models for Male Rape Myth Acceptance

Separate regression models were conducted for men and women to see if the underlying ideologies supporting male rape myths differed by participant gender. All predictors were entered into regression equation simultaneously.

For the Denial myth, acceptance of interpersonal violence was the only significant predictor ($\beta = .31, t = 3.17, p < .01$) for men, $F(4, 140) = 6.76, p < .01, R^2 = .14$. For women, $F(4, 268) = 16.01, p < .01, R^2 = .18$, benevolent sexism toward men ($\beta = .30, t = 4.37, p < .01$) and acceptance of interpersonal violence ($\beta = .13, t = 2.08, p < .05$) were significant predictors, and hostile sexism was marginally significant ($\beta = .13, t = 1.78, p = .08$).

For the Blame myth, benevolent sexism toward men was the only predictor ($\beta = .35, t = 3.71, p < .01$), $F(4, 140)$ = 15.09, $p < .01, R^2 = .28$, and acceptance of interpersonal violence was marginally significant ($\beta = .16, t = 1.77, p = .08$) for men. For women, $F(4, 268) = 19.75, p < .01, R^2 = .22$ benevolent sexism ($\beta = .29, t = 4.36, p < .01$) and acceptance of interpersonal violence ($\beta = .15, t = 2.55, p < .05$) were significant predictors.

For the Trauma myth, acceptance of interpersonal violence was a significant predictor for men, $F(4, 140) = 5.14, p < .01$ $R^2 = .10$ ($\beta = .27, t = 2.65, p < .01$). For women, $F(4, 268)$ = 14.48, $p < .01, R^2 = .16$, benevolent sexism ($\beta = .24$ $t = 3.51, p < .01$) and acceptance of interpersonal violence ($\beta = .22, t = 3.63, p < .01$) were significant predictors.

## Discussion

The goal of this study was to develop a better understanding of rape myths about male victims. To date, the only measure of male rape myth acceptance that distinguishes between male and female perpetrators (Struckman-Johnson & Struckman-Johnson, 1992) has received little psychometric investigation. We found that subscales by myth type (Denial, Blame, and Trauma), rather than by the perpetrator's gender or a general model of male rape myth acceptance, was the best fit for the data. This suggests that it is beneficial to examine male rape myths separately rather than to use an overall rape myth score. Indeed, all three myths are unique and it would be important for theoretical reasons to examine them separately.

However, although breaking down the scale by myth type resulted in the best fit of the three tested models, the scale fit statistics and model chi-square did not meet the traditional standards of a good fit. Furthermore, the Denial and Trauma subscales had reliability coefficients that were lower than desired. Thus, the results suggest that the current Male Rape Myth Scale needs to be improved, and we recommend two specific changes. First, we suggest that a six-factor model that examines the three myths separated by gender of the perpetrator should be tested in future research. Research has shown that people are more likely to agree with the myths when the perpetrator is a woman than a man (Struckman-Johnson & Struckman-Johnson, 1992), and this is potentially important theoretical distinction. Furthermore, collapsing across gender of perpetrator may have resulted in the weak fit statistics and low reliability coefficients for the subscales. Second, we suggest developing and including additional items. There were not enough scale items to allow a test of a six-factor model in the current study, and additional items would allow for this test. The additional items relevant to each of the myths should also help to increase the scale reliability. In sum, we conclude that although the Struckman-Johnson and Struckman-Johnson Male Rape Myth Scale was an important step for research on male rape myths, efforts for additional scale development and improvements are warranted. We hope that this study raises the awareness of other researchers who use this scale as well as prompts future validation efforts.

The second goal of this study was to investigate the factors associated with support of male rape myths. Given the concern about the rape myth subscales, these findings should be interpreted with caution. Nonetheless, these preliminary results provide tentative insights into the ideologies associated with acceptance of male rape myths. Similar to previous research, we found that men were more supportive of the rape myths than were women. Men were most accepting of the myth that male rape victims are responsible for being raped. Men were less accepting of the myth that men would not be upset after a sexual assault and the least accepting of the idea that men simply do not get raped. Overall, acceptance of male and female rape myths was highly correlated. Consistent with previous research, men were more accepting of rape myths against both male and female victims. Past literature on female rape myths has argued that men are more accepting of female rape myths because of adversarial, antiwoman attitudes (e.g., Lonsway & Fitzgerald, 1995). If hostility toward women is the only contributing ideology, we would expect that men would endorse female rape myths to a greater extent than they endorse male rape myths. However, men's acceptance of rape myths did not significantly differ based on the gender of the victim. Women's acceptance of rape myths also did not vary based on the gender of the victim. This supports Struckman-Johnson and Struckman-Johnson's (1992) conclusion that men are more accepting of rape myths in general, not just against female victims.

In exploring the ideologies associated with each of the rape myths, we find that benevolent sexism toward men is associated with male rape myths. This is consistent with the research that benevolent sexism toward women is associated with blaming female victims of acquaintance rape (Abrams et al., 2003; Chapleau et al., 2007; Viki et al., 2004). Viki et al. (2004) concluded that benevolent sexism is associated with victim blaming to protect one's belief in a just world. Similarly, individuals high in benevolent sexism toward men may believe that men are supposed to be invincible and, if a man is raped, he must have showed some unmanly weakness to provoke or permit the assault. For female participants, agreement with benevolent sexism toward men was associated with support for all three myths; however, for men, benevolent sexism was associated with only the blame myth. Perhaps future research can shed light on this gender difference.

Surprisingly, hostile sexism toward men was not significantly associated with support for any of the male rape myths. Hostile sexism toward men is the belief that men exploit women for sex and power. It might be that hostile sexist beliefs are relevant only in the cases of heterosexual interactions and may not apply when the aggressor is male. Alternatively, Abrams et al. (2003) found that hostile sexism against women was associated with men's rape proclivity, not rape myth acceptance. Similarly, hostile sexism toward men may also predict rape proclivity against male victims. For example, Clements-Schreiber and Rempel (1995) found that women who endorsed stereotypes that men are sexually weak were more likely to coerce men into having sex. This is an interesting issue for future research.

Consistent with research on female rape myths, acceptance of interpersonal violence was a strong predictor for support of male rape myths for both male and female participants. Men and women who normalize sexual violence may not think of such acts as "real rape" (e.g., Du Mont et al., 2003). However, this finding is tentative given the low reliability coefficient for the Acceptance of Interpersonal Violence Scale. Contrary to expectations, adversarial sexual beliefs were not a predictor of male rape myths. In hindsight, this is not surprising as this scale assesses the belief that men and women are competing for dominance in a relationship (Burt, 1980), whereas the Male Rape Myth Scale includes aggressors of both genders. Future research should explore this association when the rape myth scales are broken down by perpetrator gender.

In sum, we find preliminary support that the ideologies associated with rape myths about female victims are also associated with rape myths about male victims. Because this is the first study to examine the ideologies underlying male rape myths, there may be other important attitudinal variables that were not part of this study. Continued examination of other attitudinal variables is warranted.

Although this study provides a first step toward understanding male rape myths, there are limitations to consider. The first limitation is that our findings show the Male Rape Myth Scale is in need of additional development. Thus, the subsequent analyses must be interpreted with caution until replicated. Similarly, the Acceptance of Interpersonal Violence Scale, despite being commonly used in research, displays poor internal reliability, and future research would be wise to revise this measure. The second limitation is that the attitudes of college students may not generalize to other populations. However, rape and sexual coercion is a serious problem on college campuses, and these findings are important to consider within that context. We also had a relatively small number of men compared to women, so research with additional samples is needed. A third limitation is that the mean level of support for the rape myths was below the midpoint, suggesting that people do not believe in rape myths. Struckman-Johnson and Struckman-Johnson (1992) had a similar finding and posited that by providing a definition of male rape in the instructions, they had "educated" their participants and dissipated the associated myths. Nonetheless, we found sizable proportions of men and women who agreed with the myths. Most notably, 26% of men and 16% of women agreed that a man would not be very upset after being raped by a woman, and 25% of men and nearly 10% of women agreed that a man is blameworthy for not escaping a woman. Thus, low mean values on this scale do not necessarily suggest that rape myth acceptance is not a significant problem.

This research takes a first step at systematically understanding myths about male rape and the ideologies that support these beliefs. Our results suggest that the ideologies that support male rape myths are similar to those that support female rape myths. Brownmiller (1975) discussed "rape culture" to describe how rape and the threat of rape are used to intimidate women. Although we do not disagree with her view that rape is used as a tool to keep women "in their place," we believe that this is only half of the story. We propose that rape is a weapon used to keep both women and men from straying too far from their prescribed gender roles. Although the call to study male rape sounded not long after researchers began examining female rape, this area of research is still understudied. By mapping the largely uncharted territory of male rape myths, we can refine our current understanding of sexual aggression to better serve everyone.

# References

Abrams, D., Viki, G. T., Masser, B., & Bohner, G. (2003). Perceptions of stranger and acquaintance rape: The role of benevolent and hostile sexism in victim blame and rape proclivity. *Journal of Personality and Social Psychology, 84,* 111–125.

Bentler, P. (1998). *EQS 5.7b* (Multivariate Software, Inc.). Hillsdale, NJ: Lawrence Erlbaum.

Brownmiller, S. (1975). *Against our will: Men, women, and rape.* New York: Simon & Schuster.

Burt, M. R. (1980). Cultural myths and supports for rape. *Journal of Personality and Social Psychology, 38,* 217–230.

Campbell, R., & Johnson, C. R. (1997). Police officers' perceptions of rape: Is there consistency between state law and individual beliefs? *Journal of Interpersonal Violence, 12,* 255–274.

Chapleau, K. M., Oswald, D. L., & Russell, B. L. (2007). How ambivalent sexism toward women and men support rape myth acceptance. *Sex Roles, 57,* 131–136.

Clements-Schreiber, M. E., & Rempel, J. K. (1995). Women's acceptance of stereotypes about male sexuality: Correlations with strategies to influence reluctant partners. *Canadian Journal of Human Sexuality, 4,* 223–231.

Du Mont, J., Miller, K., & Myhr, T. L. (2003). The role of "real rape" and "real victim" stereotypes in the police reporting practices of sexually assaulted women. *Violence Against Women, 9,* 466–486.

Frohmann, L. (1991). Discrediting victims' allegations of sexual assault: Prosecutorial accounts of case rejections. *Social Problems, 38,* 213–226.

Glick, P., Diebold, J., Bailey-Werner, B., & Zhu, L. (1997). The two faces of Adam: Ambivalent sexism and polarized attitudes toward women. *Personality and Social Psychology Bulletin, 23,* 1323–1334.

Glick, P., & Fiske, S. (1996). The ambivalent sexism inventory: Differentiating hostile and benevolent sexism. *Journal of Personality and Social Psychology, 70,* 491–512.

Glick, P., & Fiske, S. (1997). Hostile and benevolent sexism: Measuring ambivalent sexist attitudes toward women. *Psychology of Women Quarterly, 21,* 119–136.

Glick, P., & Fiske, S. (1999). The Ambivalence toward Men Inventory: Differentiating hostile and benevolent beliefs about men. *Psychology of Women Quarterly, 23,* 519–536.

Goyer, P. F., & Eddleman, H. C. (1984). Same-sex rape of nonincarcerated men. *American Journal of Psychiatry, 141,* 576–579.

Groth, A. N., & Burgess, A. W. (1980). Male rape: Offenders and victims. *American Journal of Psychiatry, 137,* 806–810.

Hu, L., & Bentler, P. M. (1999). Cutoff criteria for fit indexes in covariance structure analysis: Conventional criteria versus new alternatives. *Structural Equation Modeling, 6,* 1–55.

Koss, M. P. (2000). Shame, blame, and community: Justice responses to violence against women. *American Psychologist, 55,* 1332–1343.

Koss, M. P., Gidycz, C. A., & Wisniewski, N. (1987). The scope of rape: Incidence and prevalence of sexual aggression and victimization on a national sample of students in higher education. *Journal of Consulting and Clinical Psychology, 55,* 162–170.

Lonsway, K. A., & Fitzgerald, L. F. (1994). Rape myths: In review. *Psychology of Women Quarterly, 18,* 133–164.

Lonsway, K. A., & Fitzgerald, L. F. (1995). Attitudinal antecedents of rape myth acceptance: A theoretical and empirical reexamination. *Journal of Personality and Social Psychology, 68,* 704–711.

McDonald, R., & Ho, M. R. (2002). Principles and practices in reporting structural equation analyses. *Psychological Methods, 7,* 64–82.

Mezey, G., & King, M. (1989). The effects of sexual assault on men: A survey of 22 victims. *Psychological Medicine, 19,* 205–209.

Oswald, D. L., & Russell, B. L. (2006). Perceptions of sexual coercion in heterosexual dating relationships: The role of initiator gender and tactics. *Journal of Sex Research, 43,* 87–95.

Payne, D. L., Lonsway, K. A., & Fitzgerald, L. F. (1999). Rape myth acceptance: Exploration of its structure and its measurement using the Illinois rape myth acceptance scale. *Journal of Research in Personality, 33,* 27–68.

Pino, N. W., & Meier, R. F. (1999). Gender differences in rape reporting. *Sex Roles, 40,* 979–990.

Russell, B. L., & Oswald, D. L. (2002). Sexual coercion and victimization of college men: The role of love styles. *Journal of Interpersonal Violence, 17,* 273–285.

Smith, R. E., Pine, C. J., & Hawley, M. E. (1988). Social cognitions about adult male victims of female sexual assault. *Journal of Sex Research, 24,* 101–112.

Stermac, L., Del Bove, G., & Addison, M. (2004). Stranger and acquaintance sexual assault of adult males. *Journal of Interpersonal Violence, 19,* 901–915.

Struckman-Johnson, C., & Struckman-Johnson, D. (1992). Acceptance of male rape myths among college men and women. *Sex Roles, 27,* 85–100.

Ullman, J. B. (1996). Structural equation modeling. In B. Tabachnick & L. Fidell (Eds.), *Using multivariate statistics* (3rd ed., pp. 709–812). New York: HarperCollins.

U.S. Department of Justice. (2003). *2002 national crime victimization statistics.* Retrieved October 28, 2004, from http://www.ojp.usdoj.gov/abstract/cvus/index.htm

Viki, G. T., & Abrams, D. (2002). But she was unfaithful: Benevolent sexism and reactions to rape victims who violate traditional gender role expectations. *Sex Roles, 47,* 289–293.

Viki, G. T., Abrams, D., & Masser, B. (2004). Evaluating stranger and acquaintance rape: The role of benevolent sexism in perpetrator blame and recommended sentence length. *Law and Human Behavior, 28,* 295–303.

**KRISTINE M. CHAPLEAU,** MS, is a doctoral student in clinical psychology at Marquette University. Her research interests include sexual coercion and rape as well as gender and racial stereotyping and prejudice. **DEBRA L. OSWALD**, PhD, completed her doctorate in social psychology and a postdoctoral fellowship in quantitative psychology. She is currently an assistant professor at Marquette University. Her research examines social stigma, gender issues, and interpersonal relationships. **BRENDA L. RUSSELL,** PhD, completed her doctorate in social psychology. She is currently an associate professor at Pennsylvania State University—Berks. Her research interests include legal psychology, sexual coercion and rape, and program evaluation.

**Authors' Note**—This study was conducted as a first-year project for the clinical psychology graduate program at Marquette University. The results of this study were presented in a poster at the annual meeting of the Midwestern Psychological Association (May 2005). The authors would like to thank Kara Lindstedt, Angela Pirlott, and Sara Thimsen for their assistance with data collection. Please address correspondence to Kristine M. Chapleau, Marquette University, Department of Psychology, P.O. 1881, Milwaukee, WI 53201; e-mail: kristine.chapleau@marquette.edu.

From *Journal of Interpersonal Violence*, May 1, 2008, pp. 600–615. Copyright © 2008 by Sage Publications. Reprinted by permission via Rightslink.

# Effects of Sexual Assaults on Men: Physical, Mental and Sexual Consequences

Richard Tewksbury

This paper presents an overview and summary of the consequences of male sexual assault. At present there are few discussions of the physical, mental health and sexual consequences for men who are sexually assaulted (however, see Davies, 2002 for a "selective review of the . . . prevalence and effects of male sexual assault victims" [p. 203]). The present discussion presents an update to the existing literature and a more focused discussion of the health consequences than is presently available. The intent is to provide both scholars and practitioners with a concise resource for guidance on what to expect in cases of reported male sexual assault so as to facilitate formulating effective, efficient and sensitive systems for receiving and responding to reports of men's sexual victimization.

Research addressing sexual assault/rape of men did not appear until less than 30 years ago (and, most of the early literature focuses on male children rather than adults [e.g., Josephson, 1979]). Although a few studies addressing sexual assault in correctional facilities were available prior to 1980, it was not until the early 1980s that any research specifically addressing the consequences of "male rape" in the community appeared. Most of the sexual assault/rape literature that is available focuses on female victims/survivors.

The existing literature encompasses both documentation and estimates of rates of men's victimization and clinical assessments of consequences of victimization. However, public perceptions of, and education about, male sexual assault in the free community continue to lag behind that which is known about sexual assault victimization of females.

To date the most comprehensive discussion of the consequences of sexual assault for men is that provided by Davies (2002). In this overview, drawing on the research published prior to and including the year 2000, the author shows that community and service providers' reactions to male sexual assault victims are often dependent on the victim's sexual orientation and the perpetrator's gender. Also included are discussions of the difficulties such victims may experience in (and in deciding to) report their victimization, stigmas service providers may apply to reporting victims, and the importance of service providers to be cognizant of such experiences and to work to overcome or alleviate such obstacles. Davies' discussion is organized around identifying the ways such reactions are constructed and the effects of such on service provision. What Davies does not provide is a discussion organized around the varieties of consequences for male victims, specifically the physical, mental health and sexual consequences that may be experienced by victims.

In pursuit of providing both scholars and service providers with a concise overview of the diverse consequences male victims of sexual assault experience, the discussion that follows draws from a diverse body of literatures, informed by medical, health care, forensic, psychological, sociological and criminological research. This discussion is intended to provide scholars and practitioners with a comprehensive overview of the physical, mental health and sexual consequences of the sexual assault of males. Discussion begins with a review of what is known about the prevalence of male sexual assault and an overview of the likelihood of men to report their victimization (and reasons for not reporting).

## Prevalence of Male Sexual Assault

The currently available research literature on male sexual assault has a primary focus on documenting the existence of such events. The research literature suggests that a significant number of men do report at least one instance of sexual assault. One community-wide epidemiological study in Los Angeles reported 7.2 percent of men were sexually assaulted (after age 15) at least one time (Sorenson, Stein, Siegel, Golding & Burnam, 1988). Elliott, Mok, and Briere (2004) report that among a stratified random sample of the American population 3.8 percent of men report sexual assault victimization during adulthood (with 61% of these men also reporting a sexual victimization during childhood). An Australian study using data from a representative sample of more than 10,000 men shows a sexual victimization rate of 4.8 percent for adulthood and 2.8 percent for childhood. In the United States, data from the National Violence Against

Women Survey showed three percent of men had experienced some form of sexual victimization (Desai, Arias, & Thompson, 2002; Pimlott-Kubiak & Cortina, 2003). Martin and colleagues (1998) report a 6.7 percent sexual victimization rate among male members of the U.S. Army. Three clinic based studies in the United Kingdom report rates of 6.6 percent adult victimization (Keane, Young, Boyle, & Curry, 1995), 8 percent victimization during adulthood and 12 percent during childhood (Coxell, King, Mezey, & Kell, 2000) and 2.89 percent and 5.35 percent adult and childhood victimization rates (Coxell, King, Mezey, & Gordon, 1999). Also from the United Kingdom, Plant, Plant, and Miller (2005) report a sexual abuse rate of 3.2 percent for men post age 16 and 11.7 percent for victimization prior to age 16. Other research, reviewing cases in hospital emergency rooms or rape crisis centers suggests between four percent and 12 percent of sexual assault victims are male (Forman, 1983; Frazier, 1993; Grossin, Sibille, Grandmaison, Banasr, Brion, & Derigon, 2003; Kaufman, Divasto, Jackson, Voorhees, & Christy, 1980; Pesola, Westfal, & Kuffner, 1999; Riggs, Houry, Long, Markovchick, & Feldhaus, 2000; Scarce, 1997; Stermac, Sheridan, Davidson, & Dunn, 1996).

Research with college student samples has reported rates of victimization suggesting between one in five and one in eleven males being victims of some form of sexual victimization. Struckman-Johnson (1988) reported 16 percent of a sample of male undergraduates had been pressured or forced to have sex at some point in life. Tewksbury and Mustaine (2001) reported 22.2 percent of male undergraduates at 12 universities had been victimized by some form of sexual assault and 8.3 percent had been a victim of a "serious sexual assault" at some point in time. Similar results (14%) have also been reported with a British sample of college students (Davies, Pollard, & Archer, 2001).

Others (Hickson, Davies, Hunt Weatherburn, McManus, & Coxon, 1994; Island & Letellier, 1991; Krahe, Schutze, Fritscher, & Waizenhofer, 2000; Waterman, Dawson, & Bologna, 1989) have reported sexual assault victimizations among gay/bisexual men dating or in relationships with other men. These studies have reported rates of victimization ranging from 12 percent to 27.6 percent.

It is important to acknowledge, however, that most researchers believe that male sexual assault (perpetrated by any variety of assailant) is severely under-reported, perhaps even more so than sexual assaults of women (see discussion below).

Stermac, del Bove, and Addison (2004) report that few differences are seen between men sexually assaulted by a stranger and those assaulted by an acquaintance, with the exception that those who are victimized by strangers are more likely to be single, to be assaulted in an outdoor location, and, if the assault is reported, it is so in a shorter period of time (Stermac et al., 1996). Some scholars (and other observers), however, believe that male sexual assault is primarily an occurrence between homosexual men, similar to either heterosexual date rape or marital rape. Support for this view comes from the research that suggests that gay and bisexual men are over-represented among male victims (Keane et al., 1995; Mezey & King, 1989) and others who also report that either current or former intimate partners are responsible for 65 percent of sexual assaults on gay/bisexual men (Hickson et al., 1994).

One commonly reported correlate of men's sexual victimization as adults is the high rate of these men to have also been sexually victimized during childhood. Two major studies, drawing on data from both the United Kingdom (Coxell et al., 1999) and the United States (Desai et al., 2002) have shown a strong correlation between childhood sexual victimization and subsequent adult sexual victimization. Coxell et al. (1999) report that consensual childhood sexual experiences are also statistically related to men's adult sexual victimization. Additionally, Elliott et al. (2004) report that among a representative community sample, 61 percent of men who report a sexual victimization during adulthood also report having been sexually victimized as a child.

# Reporting and Seeking of Services

Throughout the literature there is both frequent discussion of what scholars believe to be under-reporting of male sexual assault victimization and documentation of research subjects that have never reported their victimization (to law enforcement, health care, mental health, or social services providers). Numerous reports suggest that male sexual assault victims (both adult and child) are far less likely to report their victimization than are female victims (Calderwood, 1987; Hodge & Cantor, 1998; Kaufman et al., 1980; McLean, Balding, & White, 2005). However, this differential rate of reporting may be dissipating or disappearing (McLean et al., 2005). Individuals sexually assaulted during childhood, however, are more likely than those assaulted as adults to subsequently seek mental health services (Golding, Stein, Siegel, Burnam, & Sorenson, 1988). Often, but not universally, implicit is the belief that victims anticipate rejection and authorities not to believe them if they should report. Central to the discouragement to report are issues of stigma, shame, fear, and a belief victims may have their sexuality questioned (Anderson, 1982; Scarce, 1997).

Several sets of researchers (King & Woollett, 1997; Lacey & Roberts, 1991; Walker, Archer, & Davies, 2005) have reported that men who are sexually assaulted and seek mental health services frequently do not do so for lengthy periods of time. King and Woollett (1997), drawing on data from 115 men sexually assaulted in the community, show a mean of 16.4 years between victimization and seeking of mental health services. Lacey and Roberts (1991) report fewer than one-half of victims reported the incident or sought services within 6 months, and an average of approximately 2.5 years passed between occurrence and seeking of services. Walker et al. (2005) reported that 12.5 percent of victimized men never disclosed their victimization to anyone, and among those who did disclose, 54 percent did not do so for at least one year. However, Pesola et al. (1999) report that among male sexual assault victims seeking services in a New York City (Greenwich Village) hospital emergency department, 94 percent do so within 36 hours.

It is not uncommon, especially for victims who do not have serious physical injuries, for male sexual assault victims to deny victimization (Kaufman et al., 1980; Scarce, 1997). Denial directly links to a low likelihood of reporting or seeking services (medical and/or mental health) following victimization. Or, when seeking medical or mental health services victims may do so by claiming an alternative reason or need, or will do so and be very vague in explaining injuries and requests for services.

One major problem identified in the research literature, however, is that many rape crisis centers either explicitly refuse services to male victims, or are highly insensitive to male victims needs (Donnelly & Kenyon, 1996). Furthermore, when services are offered for men they are rarely designed specifically for men; one study of service availability reports that only five percent of programs that serve male victims have any programs or services specifically designed for men (Washington, 1999). It is not surprising, then, that male sexual assault may be severely under-reported.

# Physical Consequences of the Sexual Assault of Men

At the baseline level, men who report having been sexually assaulted as adults (post age 16) report poorer physical health statuses than men who do not report adult sexual victimization (Plant et al., 2005).

Most research suggests that the sexual assault of men is more likely to be violent, and accompanied by more and greater corollary injuries, than sexual assaults of women (however, also see Kimberling, Rellini, Kelly, Judson, & Learman, 2002; and McLean et al., 2005). Here it is important to acknowledge that not all sexual assaults are violent, and often center on coercion of victims. However, "rapes" in the traditional sense of the word have been shown to be more violent when perpetrated against male victims. King (1995) reported that when men are raped in almost all instances some form of physical force is used against the victim, and weapons are commonly involved. Weapons are most likely to be involved when men are sexually assaulted by a stranger (Stermac et al., 2004). Kaufman et al. (1980), describing data drawn from male rape survivors seen in hospital emergency rooms, report men who are sexually assaulted are more likely than women to have nongenital injuries (see also Hillman, Tomlinson, McMillan, French, & Harris, 1990). However, they also conclude that men who are sexually assaulted are not likely to seek medical attention, unless they suffer significant physical injuries.

Only one study to date (Lipscomb, Muram, Speck, & Mercer, 1992) compares the experiences and consequences of men sexually assaulted in the community ($n = 19$) with those sexually assaulted while incarcerated ($n = 80$). This study suggests that men sexually assaulted while incarcerated are less likely to be assaulted with a weapon (67.5% vs. 31.6% report no weapon involved), and to have their assault be either only oral or a combination of oral and anal penetration (62.5% vs. 52.6%). And, although not a statistically significant difference, men sexually assaulted while incarcerated may be more likely to exhibit an absence of physical trauma resulting from their assault (75% vs. 58% having no physical trauma observed by examining health care professionals). Hodge and Canter (1998) reporting on cases in the community report that gay male sexual assault victims are more likely than heterosexual male victims to sustain serious injuries.

Studies of the incidence of physical trauma or injuries of male sexual assault victims suggest that while some victims do experience significant physical injuries, a majority of victims do not. Five studies in hospital emergency rooms report disparate results for the presence of injuries. Genital or rectal trauma is reported in 35 percent of male victims in a Denver-based study (Riggs et al., 2000). However, "general body trauma occurred more often than genital trauma" (p. 360) with approximately two-thirds of victims having some form of general injury. A second study, in a NYC hospital emergency room reports 25 percent of male sexual assault victims have some form of "documented trauma or physical injury" (Pesola et al., 1999). Stermac et al. (2004) report that 45 percent of male sexual assault victims seen in a large, urban Canadian hospital-based sexual assault care center present with some type of physical injuries. The most common type of injury was some form of soft tissue injury (approximately 25% of male victims), most frequently seen in the perineal and anal areas. Also, 20 percent present with lacerations. Grossin et al. (2003), however, report that only 5.6 percent of male sexual assault victims seen in a French medical clinic suffered any type of genital trauma. And McLean, Balding, and White (2004) report that 66 percent of a sample of 376 cases of male sexual assault victimizations in Manchester, UK are rapes, with 18 percent of the sample presenting with anal injuries. However, these researchers also report that fewer male than female sexual assault victims present with non-genital injuries.

Among men who are anally penetrated during sexual assault, a majority (63%) who present to health care professionals do exhibit at least one form of rectal injury (Ernst, Green, Ferguson, Weiss, & Green, 2000; Hillman et al., 1990; however, also see McLean et al., 2004). The types of injuries seen include tears of the anus, abrasions, bleeding, erythema, hematoma, discoloration with tenderness, fissures, the presence of dirt, vegetation or hair in the anus, engorgement, and friability. It is important to note that no male victim had "gross active bleeding on examination of the external genitalia" (p. 434), although fully 18 percent of victims reported such had occurred prior to seeking medical care (Ernst et al., 2000).

Injuries to victims may also come as a result of assailants' means of controlling victims. One-third of victims in Struckman-Johnson et al.'s (1996) Nebraska study reported having been restrained during their assault. Not infrequently the act of restraint itself can lead to injuries. Also, abrasions to the throat and abdomen may be common, as these are consequences of victims being held down and attempting to resist (Schiff, 1980). Bruises, broken bones and black eyes may be found, as these can be indications of "submissive injuries" (striking the victim in a way that will quickly and effectively subdue them) (Schiff, p. 1499). Stermac et al. (2004) reported that in addition to perineal/anal area injuries, other common locations for injuries are head/neck/face (16% of victims), leg/knee/feet (10%), and arm/hands (15%).

Male sexual assault victims also report somatic symptoms, including tension headaches, nausea, ulcers, and colitis (Anderson, 1982; Rentoul & Appleboom, 1997). In some cases male sexual assault victims have also been identified as hypochondriacal (Anderson, 1982).

A number of symptoms have been reported by male sexual assault victims, although few are unique to this population, and no constellation of symptoms has yet to be identified as indicative of sexual assault victimization. Included among the symptoms reported have been decreased appetite and weight loss (Anderson, 1982; Huckle, 1995; Mezey & King, 1989), nausea and vomiting (Huckle, 1995; Mezey & King, 1989), constipation and abdominal pain (Goyer & Eddleman, 1984; Mezey & King, 1989) and fecal incontinence (Schiff, 1980). One study of long-term consequences of sexual victimization among adolescents suggests that for boys there is a relationship between sexual assault victimization and sleep difficulties, depression, somatic complaints, alcohol, drug and tobacco use, suicide attempts, and violence (Choquet, Darves-Bornoz, Ledoux, Manfredi, & Hassler, 1997).

There is also evidence in the literature of the transmission of sexually transmitted diseases as a result of male rape (Hillman et al., 1990, 1991). However, while instances of STDs being transmitted during a sexual assault have been documented, they are also infrequent and involved only a very small proportion of sexually assaulted men (Lacey & Roberts, 1991). Others have documented that men with a history of sexual victimization are more likely to (at some point in time) acquire a sexually transmitted disease (deVisser et al., 2003).

While some identification of symptoms and physical markers/consequences have been identified, there is very little guidance provided in the research literature regarding prevalence of encountered injuries, what clinicians can/should expect to encounter with "typical" male sexual assault victims or other consequences that may be reported. Similarly, while some medical literature (Josephson, 1979; Schiff, 1980; Wiwanitkit, 2005) purports to present guidance on how to conduct examinations of male victims, and where examinations should focus, these discussions are brief and lacking in specifics and details. Finally, readers are cautioned that the findings of studies conducted in clinical settings need to be viewed as representing only a subset of the population of male sexual assault victims; as reported above, most male sexual assault victims do not seek services, therefore studies based on those who do seek services need to be viewed and generalized with caution.

# Mental Health Consequences of the Sexual Assault of Men

Scarce (1997) reports that in his review of the available research on male rape there is no "typical" emotional/psychological response. Rather, responses range from apparent calm and composure to near complete emotional breakdown. However, men who are sexually victimized are more likely than non-victimized men to display psychological disturbances. Male children who are sexually victimized are more likely than victimized adults to report mental health problems. King, Coxell, and Mezey (2002) report that men victimized during childhood have a 2.4 times greater likelihood of reporting psychological disturbance and men victimized as adults have a 1.7 times greater likelihood of psychological disturbance than non-victimized men. Similarly, Burnam et al. (1988) report that among a cross-sectional probability sample of more than 3,000 adults in two Los Angeles communities, not only is sexual assault victimization related to later onset of depression, anxiety

disorders and substance abuse, but the likelihood of such consequences are greater for men victimized as children, rather that for those first victimized as adults. And, the presences of such consequences are also statistically significant predictors of subsequent sexual assault victimization.

More specifically, drawing on a stratified random sample of the American population, Elliott et al. (2004) report higher scores on the Trauma Symptom Inventory for sexually assaulted men than women. On eight of the ten scales of the Inventory, sexually assaulted men report higher levels of distress than sexually assaulted women. Depression also frequently leads to attempts to self-medicate (Burnam et al., 1988; Choquet et al., 1997; Coxell et al., 1999; Iseley & Gehrenbeck-Shim, 1997; Plant, Miller, & Plant, 2004; Ratner et al., 2002; Walker et al., 2005) in efforts to block out memories or overcome feelings of low self-worth (Scarce, 1997). Self-medication includes use/abuse of alcohol, illicit drugs and licit (both prescription and over-the-counter) medications. Male sexual assault victims are more likely than female sexual assault victims to report subsequent alcohol abuse problems, although abuse of illicit drugs does not show a gender difference (Burnam et al., 1988). Additionally, researchers in both England (Plant et al., 2004) and Australia (deVisser et al., 2003) report that sexually assaulted men are more likely than other men to smoke tobacco.

The most common emotional response of men to sexual assault victimization is a sense of stigma, shame, and embarrassment, and, at least in part, because of such perceptions male sexual assault victims more often than not "cope" while displaying a "calm, composed and subdued demeanor" (Rentoul & Appleboom, 1997, p. 270). King et al. (2002) also report that subsequent self-harming behaviors are more likely for males victimized as children (as compared with adult victims). Compared with non-victimized men, rates of self-harm are 3.7 times higher for men sexually victimized as children and more than twice as likely to be seen in men victimized as adults. Clearly, shame is directly tied to frequent expressions of self-blame from victims and importantly serves to inhibit reporting or seeking of medical or mental health services.

Men who are sexually assaulted commonly present a high degree of depression and hostility (Iseley & Gehrenbeck-Shim, 1997; Walker et al., 2005). Several community-based studies have shown that male sexual assault victims are, in the short run at least, more likely than female victims to present with greater degrees of depression and hostility (Carmen, Ricker, & Mills, 1984; Frazier, 1993; Goyer & Eddleman, 1984). Depression often includes shame, questions of one's efficacy in general, sexually and in regards to constructions/presentation of masculinity, and changes toward a more negative body image. Not infrequently sleep disturbances (Anderson, 1982; Goyer & Eddleman, 1984), and/or thoughts and attempts at suicide may result (Choquet et al., 1997; Isely & Gehrenbeck-Shim, 1997; Lockwood, 1980; Ratner et al., 2002; Scarce, 1997; Struckman-Johnson et al., 1996; Walker et al., 2005). Suicidal attempts are most likely among adolescent and young adult victims (Calderwood, 1987). And, as reported in numerous studies (see Rentoul & Appleboom, 1997) male rape victims also frequently report heightened levels of anxiety, both related to fears of re-victimization and free-floating. Decreased levels of self esteem among male sexual assault victims is common (Ratner et al., 2002; Walker et al., 2005). Some observers (Calderwood, 1987) have suggested that men's emotional reactions are at least in part a result of shock as men are not socialized (as are women) to fear and be aware of the risk of rape.

Male sexual assault victims have also been shown to be more ready to acknowledge and express anger and hostility following victimization than female victims (Groth & Burgess, 1980). Expressions of anger and hostility may be directed/focused on nearly any others in the immediate environment, including one's assailant, support system members or caretakers (Anderson, 1982). Withdrawal from social settings and social contacts also commonly occur among male sexual assault victims (Walker et al., 2005).

Victims may also experience rape trauma syndrome (a form of posttraumatic stress disorder). Rape trauma syndrome (RTS) is conceptualized as composed of two phases: acute and long term (however, others [Calderwood, 1987] have conceptualized RTS as a three stage process: acute, re-organization, and latent phases). The acute phase is characterized by a period of extreme disorganization and chaos in the victim's life. The acute phase also is frequently accompanied by physical symptoms, including skeletal muscular tension and pain, gastrointestinal irritability, genitourinary disturbances, impotence and extreme emotional expressions. The long term phase is typically characterized by efforts to re-organize one's life and some form of avoidance/withdrawal behaviors. Long term symptoms of RTS also include nightmares/flashbacks, fear of places similar to where victimization occurred, fear of crowds, and fear/avoidance of consensual sexual activities. Additionally, while RTS is not a universally accepted diagnosis (especially in the judicial system), there are also multiple researchers who have reported male sexual assault survivors near-universally experience some form of post-traumatic stress disorder (Huckle, 1995; Isely & Gehrenbeck-Shim, 1997; Mezey, 1992; Mezey & King, 1989; Myers, 1989; Rogers, 1997).

## Effects on Sexuality and Identity

In addition to physical and mental health consequences many sexually assaulted men also report effects on their sexuality and sexual activities. These effects include consequences for how sexually assaulted men think of themselves sexually, as gendered beings and how men construct and manage a sexual identity.

The most common sexual consequence reported in the literature for sexually assaulted men are questions about one's "true" sexuality (Forman, 1983; Huckle, 1995; Iseley & Gehrenbeck-Shim, 1997; King & Woollett, 1997; Mezey & King, 1989; Scarce, 1997; Struckman-Johnson & Struckman-Johnson, 1994; Walker et al., 2005). Victims often question whether being raped "makes" them gay and may question whether there is something about them that leads others to perceive them as gay. Perhaps the most serious and significant questions and concerns arise related to sexually assaulted men questioning their "true" sexuality if and when during the course of being assaulted men experience any form of sexual arousal. However, erections are a common involuntary response for many men in times of intense pain, anxiety, panic and/or fear (see Redmond, Kosten, & Reiser, 1983).

Relatedly, men who are sexually victimized (especially those perpetrated against by males) may be expected to question their gender and gender role presentations. Walker et al. (2005) report that 70 percent of a sample of male sexual assault victims report long-term crises with their sexual orientation and 68 percent with their sense of masculinity. These reactions may be most acute for men who hold traditional or stereotypical views about sexuality and gender; to be put into a "homosexual" or "feminine" role may lead to questions about whether one is "sufficiently" masculine. This type of reaction is found among both heterosexual and gay/bisexual men (Garnets & Herek, 1990). Similarly (see Struckman-Johnson & Struckman-Johnson, 1994) men who are victimized by female assailants may question how they could be victimized by a "weaker" female. This too may contribute to questions about gender role fulfillment.

Male sexual assault victims also are likely to report sexual anxieties (deVisser et al., 2003), sexual dysfunction, and possibly impotence, following victimization (Huckle, 1995; Lacey & Roberts, 1991; Walker et al., 2005). For other men periods of frequent sexual activity, including with a number of different partners, is common following victimization (Plant et al., 2005; Walker). Some heterosexual men may also begin to engage in consensual same-sex sexual behaviors following victimization (Walker). Plant et al. report that male sexual assault victims (whether victimized as children or adults) are more likely than their non-victimized peers to report that sexual activity has "interfered with" their everyday lives.

Sexual identity questions and sexual dysfunction are commonly reported consequences of sexual assault for victimized men. While often overlooked, or not recognized for extended periods of time, they may, in fact, be among the most severe and longest lasting consequences for victimized men.

## Summary

In sum, the existing literature suggests that men who are sexually assaulted are highly unlikely to report their victimization or to seek medical or mental health services. Among those who do seek services, it is frequently a long time (perhaps one year or longer) after victimization when medical or mental health services are accessed, except in cases where significant injuries are suffered during the assault and immediate care is necessary. When services are sought, those presenting with health care needs often present either due to suffering significant injuries that cannot be ignored or with myriad different symptoms or problems, most of which will either be non-sexual/non-genital in nature or vague and difficult to initially connect to sexual victimization. Because many sexual assaults on men do not involve anal penetration (Hickson et al., 1994; Lacey & Roberts, 1991; Lipscomb et al., 1992; Ratner et al., 2002; Stermac et al., 2004) it may be extremely difficult to identify physical markers of an assault. The mental health status of men who are sexual assault victims can vary quite widely, ranging from highly emotional responses that inhibit normal functioning to very calm and subdued approaches where victims are highly introspective and would not likely be perceived to have suffered trauma. However, depression, anxiety, anger/hostility and on occasional suicidal ideations/attempts are common. Sexually assaulted men also commonly suffer from sexual dysfunction and questions about their sexuality.

There are no universal signs, symptoms, consequences or markers of sexual assault victimization for men. Some sexually assaulted men will experience some forms of physical injuries, some will experience some forms of psychological/emotional disturbance, and some may experience sexual dysfunction or identity questions. Many sexually assaulted men, however, will not exhibit physical or mental health indications, or will present themselves to service providers under false pretenses or so long after being victimized that connecting symptoms/injuries to sexual assault victimization may not be likely/possible.

In the end, it is important to understand that some sexually assaulted men may not exhibit any visible or identifiable consequences of sexual assault victimization, and that men reporting (or suspected of having experienced) a victimization need to be viewed with an eye toward questioning the cause of any physical or mental health issues that are presented. Because of the nature of many male sexual assaults and the socialized expectations for how men manage and cope with victimization(s), this may continue to be both one of the most under-reported and misunderstood forms of violence and health problems in our society.

# References

Anderson, C. L. (1982). Males as sexual assault victims: Multiple levels of trauma. *Journal of Homosexuality, 7,* 145–162.

Burnam, M. A., Stein, J. A., Golding, J. M, Siegel, J. M., Sorenson, S. B., Forsythe, A. B., et al. (1988). Sexual assault and mental disorders in a community population. *Journal of Consulting and Clinical Psychology, 56,* 843–850.

Calderwood, D. (1987). The male rape victim. *Medical Aspects of Human Sexuality, 21*(5), 53–55.

Carmen, E., Ricker, P. R., & Mills, T. (1984). Victims of violence and psychiatric illness. *American Journal of Psychiatry, 141,* 378–383.

Choquet, M., Darves-Bornoz, J. M., Ledoux, S., Manfredi, R., & Hassler, C. (1997). Self-reported health and behavioral problems among adolescent victims of rape in France: Results of a cross-sectional survey. *Child Abuse and Neglect, 21,* 823–832.

Coxell, A., King, M. B., Mezey, G. C., & Gordon, D. (1999). Lifetime prevalence, characteristics, and associated problems of non-consensual sex in men: Cross sectional survey. *British Medical Journal, 318,* 846–850.

Coxell, A., King, M. B., Mezey, G. C., & Kell, P. (2000). Sexual molestation of men: Interviews with 224 men attending a genitourinary medicine service. *International Journal of STD and AIDS, 11,* 574–578.

Davies, M. (2002). Male sexual assault victims: A selective review of the literature and implications for support services. *Aggression and Violent Behavior, 7,* 203–214.

Davies, M., Pollard, P., & Archer, J. (2001). The influence of victim gender and sexual orientation on blame towards the victim in a depicted stranger rape. *Violence and Victims, 16,* 607–619.

Desai, S., Arias, I., & Thompson, M. P. (2002). Childhood victimization and subsequent adult revictimization assessed in a nationally-representative sample of women and men. *Violence and Victims, 17,* 639–653.

deVisser, R. O., Smith, A. M., Rissel, C. E., Richters, J., & Grulich, A. E. (2003). Sex in Australia: Experiences of sexual coercion among a representative sample of adults. *Australian and New Zealand Journal of Public Health, 27,* 198–203.

Donnelly, D., & Kenyon, S. (1996). "Honey, we don't do men." Gender stereotypes and the provision of services to sexually assaulted males. *Journal of Interpersonal Violence, 11,* 441–448.

Elliott, D. M., Mok, D. S., & Briere, J. (2004). Adult sexual assault: prevalence, symptomatology, and sex differences in the general population. *Journal of Traumatic Stress, 17,* 203–211.

Ernst, A. A., Green, E., Ferguson, M. T., Weiss, S. J., & Green, W. M. (2000). The utility of anoscopy and colposcopy in the evaluation of male sexual assault victims. *Annals of Emergency Medicine, 36,* 432–437.

Forman, B. D. (1983). Reported male rape. *Victimology, 7,* 235–236.

Frazier, P. (1993). A comparative study of male and female rape victims seen at a hospital based rape crisis program. *Journal of Interpersonal Violence, 8,* 65–76.

Garnets, L., & Herek, G. (1990). Violence and victimization of lesbians and gay men: Mental health consequences. *Journal of Interpersonal Violence, 5,* 366–383.

Golding, J. M., Stein, J. A., Siegel, J. M., Burnam, M. A., & Sorenson, S. B. (1988). Sexual assault history and use of health and mental health services. *American Journal of Community Psychology, 16,* 625–644.

Goyer, P., & Eddleman, H. (1984). Same-sex rape of nonincarcerated men. *American Journal of Psychiatry, 141,* 576–579.

Grossin, C., Sibille, I., de la Grandmaison, G. L., Banasr, A., Brion, F., & Durigon, M. (2003). Analysis of 418 cases of sexual Assault. *Forensic Science International, 131,* 125–130.

Groth, N., & Burgess, A. W. (1980). Male rape: Offenders and victims. *American Journal of Psychiatry, 137,* 806–810.

Hickson, F. C. I., Davies, P. M., Hunt, A. J., Weatherburn, P., McManus, T. J., & Coxon, A. P. M. (1994). Gay men as victims of non-consensual sex. *Archives of Sexual Behavior, 23,* 281–294.

Hillman, R., O'Mara, N., Tomlinson, D., & Harris, J. R. W. (1991). Adult male victims of sexual assault: An underdiagnosed condition. *International Journal of STD and AIDS, 2,* 22–24.

Hillman, R., Tomlinson, D., McMillan, A., French P. D., & Harris, J. R. (1990). Sexual assault of men: A series. *Genitourinary Medicine, 66,* 247–250.

Hodge, S., & Cantor, D. (1998). Victims and perpetrators of male sexual assault. *Journal of Interpersonal Violence, 13,* 222–239.

Huckle, P. L. (1995). Male rape victims referred to a forensic psychiatric service. *Medicine, Science, and the Law, 35*(3), 187–192.

Iseley, P. J., & Gehrenbeck-Shim, D. (1997). Sexual assault of men in the community. *Journal of Community Psychology, 25,* 159–166.

Island, D., & Letellier, P. (1991). *Men who beat the men who love them.* New York: Harrington Park Press.

Josephson, G. W. (1979) The male rape victim: Evaluation and treatment. *Journal of the American College of Emergency Physicians, 8,* 13–15.

Kaufman, A., Divasto, P. Jackson, R, Voorhees, R., & Christy, J. (1980). Male rape victims: Non-institutionalized assault. *American Journal of Psychiatry, 137,* 221–223.

Keane, F. E., Young, S. M., Boyle, H. M., & Curry, K. M. (1995). Prior sexual assault reported by male attenders at a department of genitourinary medicine. *International Journal of STD and AIDS, 6,* 95–100.

Kimberling, R., Rellini, A., Kelly, V., Judson, P. L., & Learnman, L. A. (2002). Gender differences in victim and crime characteristics of sexual assaults. *Journal of Interpersonal Violence, 17,* 526–532.

King, M. (1995). Sexual assaults on men: Assessment and management. *British Journal of Hospital Medicine, 53,* 245–246.

King, M., Coxell, A., & Mezey, G. (2002). Sexual molestation of males: Associations with psychological disturbance. *British Journal of Psychiatry, 181,* 153–157.

King, M., & Woollett, E. (1997). Sexually assaulted males: 115 men consulting a counseling service. *Archives of Sexual Behavior, 26,* 579–588.

Krahe, B., Schutze, S., Fritscher, I., & Waizenhofer, E. (2000). The prevalence of sexual aggression and victimization among homosexual men. *Journal of Sex Research, 37*(2), 142–150.

Lacey, H. G., & Roberts, R. (1991). Sexual assault on men. *International Journal of STD and AIDS, 2,* 258–260.

Lipscomb, G. H., Muram, D., Speck, P. M., & Mercer, B. M. (1992). Male victims of sexual assault. *Journal of the American Medical Association, 267,* 3064–3066.

Lockwood, D. (1980). *Prison sexual violence.* New York: Elsevier.

Martin, L., Rosen, L. N., Durand, D. B., Stretch, R. H., & Knudson, K. H. (1998). Prevalence and timing of sexual assaults in a sample of male and female U.S. Army soldiers. *Military Medicine, 163,* 213–216.

McLean, I. A., Balding, V., & White, C. (2004). Forensic medical aspects of male-on-male rape and sexual assault in greater Manchester. *Medicine, Science and the Law, 44,* 165–169.

McLean, I. A., Balding, V., & White, C. (2005). Further aspects of male-on-male rape and sexual assault in greater Manchester. *Medicine, Science and the Law, 45,* 225–232.

Mezey, G. C. (1992). Treatment for male victims of rape. In G. C. Mezey & M. B. King (Eds.), *Male victims of sexual assault* (pp. 131–144). Oxford: Oxford University Press.

Mezey, G. C., & King, M. (1989). The effects of sexual assault on men: A survey of 22 victims. *Psychological Medicine, 19,* 205–209.

Myers, M. F. (1989). Men sexually assaulted as adults and sexually abused as boys. *Archives of Sexual Behavior, 18,* 203–215.

Pesola, G. R., Westfal, R. E., & Kuffner, C. A. (1999). Emergency department characteristics of male sexual assault. *Academic Emergency Medicine, 6,* 792–798.

Pimlott-Kubiak, S., & Cortina, L. M. (2003). Gender, victimization and outcomes: Reconceptualizing risk. *Journal of Consulting and Clinical Psychology, 71,* 528–539.

Plant, M., Miller, P., & Plant, M. (2004). Childhood and adult sexual abuse: Relationships with alcohol and other psychoactive drug use. *Child Abuse Review, 13,* 200–214.

Plant, M., Plant, M., & Miller, P. (2005). Childhood and adult sexual abuse: Relationships with "addictive" or "problem" behaviours and health. *Journal of Addictive Diseases, 21,* 25–38.

Ratner, P. A., Johnson, J. L., Shoveller, J. A., Chan, K., Martindale, S. L., Schilder, A. J., et al. (2002). Non-consensual sex experienced by men who have sex with men: Prevalence and association with mental health. *Patient Education and Counseling, 49,* 67–74.

Redmond, D. E. Jr., Kosten, T. R., & Reiser, M. F. (1983). Spontaneous ejaculation associated with anxiety: Psychophysiological considerations. *American Journal of Psychiatry, 140,* 1163–1166.

Rentoul, L., & Appleboom, N. (1997). Understanding the psychological impact of rape and serious sexual assault of men: A literature review. *Journal of Psychiatric and Mental Health Nursing, 4,* 267–274.

Riggs, N., Houry, D., Long, G., Markovchick, V., & Feldhaus, K. M. (2000). Analysis of 1,076 cases of sexual assault. *Annals of Emergency Medicine, 35,* 358–360.

Rogers, P. (1997). Post traumatic stress disorder following male rape. *Journal of Mental Health, 6,* 5–10.

Scarce, M. (1997). *Male on male rape: The hidden toll of stigma and shame.* New York: Insight Books.

Schiff, A. (1980). Examination and treatment of the male rape victim. *Southern Medical Journal, 73,* 1498–1502.

Sorenson, S. B., Stein, J. A., Siegel, J. M., Golding, J., & Burnam, M. (1988). The prevalence of adult sexual assault. *Journal of Sex Research, 24,* 101–112.

Stermac, L., del Bove, G., & Addison, M. (2004). Stranger and acquaintance sexual assault of adult males. *Journal of Interpersonal Violence, 19,* 901–915.

Stermac, L., Sheridan, P., Davidson, A., & Dunn, S. (1996). Sexual assault of adult males. *Journal of Interpersonal Violence, 11,* 52–64.

Struckman-Johnson, C. (1988). Forced sex on dates: It happens to men too. *Journal of Sex Research, 24,* 234–241.

Struckman-Johnson, C., & Struckman-Johnson, D. (1994). Men pressured and forced into sexual experience. *Archives of Sexual Behavior, 23,* 93–114.

Struckman-Johnson, C., Struckman-Johnson, D., Rucker, L., Bumby, K., & Donaldson, S. (1996). Sexual coercion reported by men and women in prison. *Journal of Sex Research, 33,* 67–76.

Tewksbury, R., & Mustaine, E. E. (2001). Lifestyle factors associated with the sexual assault of men: A routine activity theory analysis. *The Journal of Men's Studies, 9,* 153–182.

Walker, J., Archer, J., & Davies, M. (2005). Effects of rape on men: A descriptive analysis. *Archives of Sexual Behavior, 34,* 69–80.

Washington, P. A. (1999). Second assault of male survivors of sexual violence. *Journal of Interpersonal Violence, 14,* 713–730.

Waterman, C. K., Dawson, L. J., & Bologna, M. J. (1989). Sexual coercion in gay male and lesbian relationships: Predictors and implications for support services. *Journal of Sex Research, 26,* 118–124.

Wiwanitkit, V. (2005). Male rape, some notes on the laboratory investigation. *Sexuality and Disability, 23*(1), 41–46.

**RICHARD TEWKSBURY,** Department of Justice Administration, University of Louisville. Correspondence concerning this article should be addressed to Richard Tewksbury, Department of Justice Administration, University of Louisville, Louisville, KY 40292. Electronic mail: tewks@louisville.edu

From *International Journal of Men's Health,* Spring 2007, pp. 22–35. Copyright © 2007 by Men's Studies Press. Reprinted by permission.

# Human Rights, Sex Trafficking, and Prostitution

ALICE LEUCHTAG

Despite laws against slavery in practically every country, an estimated twenty-seven million people live as slaves. Kevin Bales, in his book *Disposable People: New Slavery in the Global Economy* (University of California Press, Berkeley, 1999), describes those who endure modern forms of slavery. These include indentured servants, persons held in hereditary bondage, child slaves who pick plantation crops, child soldiers, and adults and children trafficked and sold into sex slavery.

## A Life Narrative

Of all forms of slavery, sex slavery is one of the most exploitative and lucrative with some 200,000 sex slaves worldwide bringing their slaveholders an annual profit of $10.5 billion. Although the great preponderance of sex slaves are women and girls, a smaller but significant number of males—both adult and children—are enslaved for homosexual prostitution.

The life narrative of a Thai girl named Siri, as told to Bales, illustrates how sex slavery happens to vulnerable girls and women. Siri is born in northeastern Thailand to a poor family that farms a small plot of land, barely eking out a living. Economic policies of structural adjustment pursued by the Thai government under the aegis of the World Bank and the International Monetary Fund have taken former government subsidies away from rice farmers, leaving them to compete against imported, subsidized rice that keeps the market price artificially depressed.

Siri attends four years of school, then is kept at home to help care for her three younger siblings. When Siri is fourteen, a well-dressed woman visits her village. She offers to find Siri a "good job," advancing her parents $2,000 against future earnings. This represents at least a year's income for the family. In a town in another province the woman, a trafficker, "sells" Siri to a brothel for $4,000. Owned by an "investment club" whose members are business and professional men—government bureaucrats and local politicians—the brothel is extremely profitable. In a typical thirty-day period it nets its investors $88,000.

To maintain the appearance that their hands are clean, members of the club's board of directors leave the management of the brothel to a pimp and a bookkeeper. Siri is initiated into prostitution by the pimp who rapes her. After being abused by her first "customer," Siri escapes, but a policeman—who gets a percentage of the brothel profits—brings her back, whereupon the pimp beats her up. As further punishment, her "debt" is doubled from $4,000 to $8,000. She must now repay this, along with her monthly rent and food, all from her earnings of $4 per customer. She will have to have sex with three hundred men a month just to pay her rent. Realizing she will never be able to get out of debt, Siri tries to build a relationship with the pimp simply in order to survive.

The pimp uses culture and religion to reinforce his control over Siri. He tells her she must have committed terrible sins in a past life to have been born a female; she must have accumulated a karmic debt to deserve the enslavement and abuse to which she must reconcile herself. Gradually Siri begins to see herself from the point of view of the slaveholder—as someone unworthy and deserving of punishment. By age fifteen she no longer protests or runs away. Her physical enslavement has become psychological as well, a common occurrence in chronic abuse.

Siri is administered regular injections of the contraceptive drug Depo-Provera for which she is charged. As the same needle is used for all the girls, there is a high risk of HIV and other sexual diseases from the injections. Siri knows that a serious illness threatens her and she prays to Buddha at the little shrine in her room, hoping to earn merit so he will protect her from dreaded disease. Once a month she and the others, at their own expense, are tested for HIV. So far Siri's tests have been negative. When Siri tries to get the male customers to wear condoms—distributed free to brothels by the Thai Ministry of Health—some resist wearing them and she can't make them do so.

As one of an estimated 35,000 women working as brothel slaves in Thailand—a country where 500,000 to one million prostituted women and girls work in conditions of degradation and exploitation short of brothel slavery—Siri faces at least a 40 percent chance of contracting the HIV virus. If she is lucky, she can look forward to live more years before she becomes too ill to work and is pushed out into the street.

## Thailand's Sex Tourism

Though the Thai government denies it, the World Health Organization finds that HIV is epidemic in Thailand, with the largest segment of new cases among wives and girlfriends of men who buy prostitute sex. Viewing its women as a cash crop to be exploited, and depending on sex tourism for foreign exchange dollars to help pay interest on the foreign debt, the Thai government can't acknowledge the epidemic without contradicting the continued promotion of sex tourism and prostitution.

By encouraging investment in the sex industry, sex tourism creates a business climate conducive to the trafficking and enslavement of vulnerable girls such as Siri. In 1996 nearly five million sex tourists from the United States, Western Europe, Australia, and Japan visited Thailand. These transactions brought in about $26.2 billion—thirteen times more than Thailand earned by building and exporting computers.

In her 1999 report *Pimps and Predators on the Internet: Globalizing the Sexual Exploitation of Women and Children,* published by the Coalition Against Trafficking in Women (CATW), Donna Hughes quotes from postings on an Internet site where sex tourists share experiences and advise one another. The following is one man's description of having sex with a fourteen-year-old prostituted girl in Bangkok:

> "Even though I've had a lot of better massages . . . after fifteen minutes, I was much more relaxed . . . Then I asked for a condom and I fucked her for another thirty minutes. Her face looked like she was feeling a lot of pain. . . . She blocked my way when I wanted to leave the room and she asked for a tip. I gave her 600 bath. Altogether, not a good experience."

Hughes says, "To the men who buy sex, a 'bad experience' evidently means not getting their money's worth, or that the prostituted woman or girl didn't keep up the act of enjoying what she had to do . . . one glimpses the humiliation and physical pain most girls and women in prostitution endure."

Nor are the men oblivious to the existence of sexual slavery. One customer states, "Girls in Bangkok virtually get sold by their families into the industry; they work against their will." His knowledge of their sexual slavery and lack of sensitivity thereof is evident in that he then names the hotels in which girls are kept and describes how much they cost!

As Hughes observes, sex tourists apparently feel they have a right to prostitute sex, perceiving prostitution only from a self-interested perspective in which they commodify and objectify women of other cultures, nationalities, and ethnic groups. Their awareness of racism, colonialism, global economic inequalities, and sexism seems limited to the way these realities benefit them as sex consumers.

## Sex Traffickers Cast Their Nets

According to the *Guide to the New UN Trafficking Protocol* by Janice Raymond, published by the CATW in 2001, the United Nations estimates that sex trafficking in human beings is a $5 billion to $7 billion operation annually. Four million persons are moved illegally from one country to another and within countries each year, a large proportion of them women and girls being trafficked into prostitution. The United Nations International Children's Emergency Fund (UNICEF) estimates that some 30 percent of women being trafficked are minors, many

under age thirteen. The International Organization on Migration estimates that some 500,000 women per year are trafficked into Western Europe from poorer regions of the world. According to *Sex Trafficking of Women in the United States: International and Domestic Trends,* also published by the CATW in 2001, some 50,000 women and children are trafficked into the United States each year, mainly from Asia and Latin America.

Because prostitution as a system of organized sexual exploitation depends on a continuous supply of new "recruits," trafficking is essential to its continued existence. When the pool of available women and girls dries up, new women must be procured. Traffickers cast their nets ever wide and become ever more sophisticated. The Italian Camorra, Chinese Triads, Russian Mafia, and Japanese Yakuza are powerful criminal syndicates consisting of traffickers, pimps, brothel keepers, forced labor lords, and gangs which operate globally.

After the breakdown of the Soviet Union, an estimated five thousand criminal groups formed the Russian Mafia, which operates in thirty countries. The Russian Mafia traffics women from African countries, the Ukraine, the Russian Federation, and Eastern Europe into Western Europe, the United States, and Israel. The Triads traffick women from China, Korea, Thailand, and other Southeast Asian countries into the United States and Europe. The Camorra traffics women from Latin America into Europe. The Yakuza traffics women from the Philipines, Thailand, Burma, Cambodia, Korea, Nepal, and Laos into Japan.

## A Global Problem Meets a Global Response

Despite these appalling facts, until recently no generally agreed upon definition of trafficking in human beings was written into international law. In Vienna, Austria, during 1999 and 2000, 120 countries participated in debates over a definition of trafficking. A few nongovernmental organizations (NGOs) and a minority of governments—including Australia, Canada, Denmark, Germany, Ireland, Japan, the Netherlands, Spain, Switzerland, Thailand, and the United Kingdom—wanted to separate issues of trafficking from issues of prostitution. They argued that persons being trafficked should be divided into those who are forced and those who give their consent, with the burden of proof being placed on persons being trafficked. They also urged that the less explicit means of control over trafficked persons—such as abuse of a victim's vulnerability—not be included in the definition of trafficking and that the word *exploitation* not be used. Generally supporters of this position were wealthier countries where large numbers of women were being trafficked and countries in which prostitution was legalized or sex tourism encouraged.

**People being trafficked shouldn't be divided into those who are forced and those who give their consent because trafficked persons are in no position to give meaningful consent.**

The CATW—140 other NGOs that make up the International Human Rights Network plus many governments (including those of Algeria, Bangladesh, Belgium, China, Colombia, Cuba, Egypt, Finland, France, India, Mexico, Norway, Pakistan, the Philippines, Sweden, Syria, Venezuela, and Vietnam)—maintains that trafficking can't be separated from prostitution. Persons being trafficked shouldn't be divided into those who are forced and those who give their consent because trafficked persons are in no position to give meaningful consent. The subtler methods used by traffickers, such as abuse of a victim's vulnerability, should be included in the definition of trafficking and the word *exploitation* be an essential part of the definition. Generally supporters of this majority view were poorer countries from which large numbers of women were being trafficked or countries in which strong feminist, anti-colonialist, or socialist influences existed. The United States, though initially critical of the majority position, agreed to support a definition of trafficking that would be agreed upon by consensus.

The struggle—led by the CATW to create a definition of trafficking that would penalize traffickers while ensuring that all victims of trafficking would be protected—succeeded when a compromise proposal by Sweden was agreed to. A strongly worded and inclusive *UN Protocol to Prevent, Suppress, and Punish Trafficking in Persons*—especially women and children—was drafted by an ad hoc committee of the UN as a supplement to the Convention Against Transnational Organized Crime. The UN protocol specifically addresses the trade in human beings for purposes of prostitution and other forms of sexual exploitation, forced labor or services, slavery or practices similar to slavery, servitude, and the removal of organs. The protocol defines trafficking as:

> The recruitment, transportation, transfer, harboring or receipt of persons, by means of the threat or use of force or other forms of coercion, of abduction, of fraud, of deception, of the abuse of power or of a position of vulnerability or of the giving or receiving of payments or benefits to achieve the consent of a person having control over another person, for the purpose of exploitation.

While recognizing that the largest amount of trafficking involves women and children, the wording of the UN protocol clearly is gender and age neutral, inclusive of trafficking in both males and females, adults and children.

In 2000 the UN General Assembly adopted this convention and its supplementary protocol; 121 countries signed the convention and eighty countries signed the protocol. For the convention and protocol to become international law, forty countries must ratify them.

## Highlights

Some highlights of the new convention and protocol are: For the first time there is an accepted international definition of trafficking and an agreed-upon set of prosecution, protection, and prevention mechanisms on which countries can base their national legislation.

- The various criminal means by which trafficking takes place, including indirect and subtle forms of coercion, are covered.
- Trafficked persons, especially women in prostitution and child laborers, are no longer viewed as illegal migrants but as victims of a crime.

**For the first time there is an accepted international definition of trafficking and an agreed-upon set of prosecution, protection, and prevention mechanisms on which countries can base their national legislation.**

- The convention doesn't limit its scope to criminal syndicates but defines an organized criminal group as "any structured group of three or more persons which engages in criminal activities such as trafficking and pimping."
- All victims of trafficking in persons are protected, not just those who can prove that force was used against them.
- The consent of a victim of trafficking is meaningless and irrelevant.
- Victims of trafficking won't have to bear the burden of proof.
- Trafficking and sexual exploitation are intrinsically connected and not to be separated.
- Because women trafficked domestically into local sex industries suffer harmful effects similar to those experienced by women trafficked transnationally, these women also come under the protections of the protocol.
- The key element in trafficking is the exploitative purpose rather than the movement across a border.

The protocol is the first UN instrument to address the demand for prostitution sex, a demand that results in the human rights abuses of women and children being trafficked. The protocol recognizes an urgent need for governments to put the buyers of prostitution sex on their policy and legislative agendas, and it calls upon countries to take or strengthen legislative or other measures to discourage demand, which fosters all the forms of sexual exploitation of women and children.

As Raymond says in the *Guide to the New UN Trafficking Protocol*:

> "The least discussed part of the prostitution and trafficking chain has been the men who buy women for sexual exploitation in prostitution. . . . If we are to find a permanent path to ending these human rights abuses, then we cannot just shrug our shoulders and say, "men are like this," or "boys will be boys," or "prostitution has always been around." Or tell women and girls in prostitution that they must continue to do what they do because

prostitution is inevitable. Rather, our responsibility is to make men change their behavior, by all means available—educational, cultural and legal."

Two U.S. feminist, human rights organizations—Captive Daughters and Equality Now—have been working toward that goal. Surita Sandosham of Equality Now says that when her organization asked women's groups in Thailand and the Philippines how it could assist them, the answer came back, "Do something about the demand." Since then the two organizations have legally challenged sex tours originating in the United States and have succeeded in closing down at least one operation.

# Refugees, Not Illegal Aliens

In October 2000 the U.S. Congress passed a bill, the Victims of Trafficking and Violence Protection Act of 2000, introduced by New Jersey republican representative Chris Smith. Under this law penalties for traffickers are raised and protections for victims increased. Reasoning that desperate women are unable to give meaningful consent to their own sexual exploitation, the law adopts a broad definition of sex trafficking so as not to exclude so-called consensual prostitution or trafficking that occurs solely within the United States. In these respects the new federal law conforms to the UN protocol.

Two features of the law are particularly noteworthy:

- In order to pressure other countries to end sex trafficking, the U.S. State Department is to make a yearly assessment of other countries' anti-trafficking efforts and to rank them according to how well they discourage trafficking. After two years of failing to meet even minimal standards, countries are subject to sanctions, although not sanctions on humanitarian aid. "Tier 3" countries—those failing to meet even minimal standards—include Greece, Indonesia, Israel, Pakistan, Russia, Saudi Arabia, South Korea, and Thailand.
- Among persons being trafficked into the United States, special T-visas will be provided to those who meet the criteria for having suffered the most serious trafficking abuses. These visas will protect them from deportation so they can testify against their traffickers. T-non immigrant status allows eligible aliens to remain in the United States temporarily and grants specific non-immigrant benefits. Those acquiring T-1 non-immigrant status will be able to remain for a period of three years and will be eligible to receive certain kinds of public assistance—to the same extent as refugees. They will also be issued employment authorization to "assist them in finding safe, legal employment while they attempt to retake control of their lives."

# A Debate Rages

A worldwide debate rages about legalization of prostitution fueled by a 1998 International Labor Organization (ILO) report entitled *The Sex Sector: The Economic and Social Bases of*

*Prostitution in Southeast Asia.* The report follows years of lobbying by the sex industry for recognition of prostitution as "sex work." Citing the sex industry's unrecognized contribution to the gross domestic product of four countries in Southeast Asia, the ILO urges governments to officially recognize the "sex sector" and "extend taxation nets to cover many of the lucrative activities connected with it." Though the ILO report says it stops short of calling for legalization of prostitution, official recognition of the sex industry would be impossible without it.

Raymond points out that the ILO's push to redefine prostitution as sex work ignores legislation demonstrating that countries can reduce organized sexual exploitation rather than capitulate to it. For example, Sweden prohibits the purchase of sexual services with punishments of still fines or imprisonment, thus declaring that prostitution isn't a desirable economic and labor sector. The government also helps women getting out of prostitution to rebuild their lives. Venezuela's Ministry of Labor has ruled that prostitution can't be considered work because it lacks the basic elements of dignity and social justice. The Socialist Republic of Vietnam punishes pimps, traffickers, brothel owners, and buyers—sometimes publishing buyer's names in the mass media. For women in prostitution, the government finances medical, educational, and economic rehabilitation.

**Instead of transforming the male buyer into a legitmate customer, the ILO should give thought to innovative programs that make the buyer accountable for his sexual exploitation.**

Raymond suggests that instead of transforming the male buyer into a legitimate customer, the ILO should give thought to innovative programs that make the buyer accountable for his sexual exploitation. She cites the Sage Project, Inc. (SAGE) program in San Francisco, California, which educates men arrested for soliciting women in prostitution about the risks and impacts of their behavior.

Legalization advocates argue that the violence, exploitation, and health effects suffered by women in prostitution aren't inherent to prostitution but simply result from the random behaviors of bad pimps or buyers, and that if prostitution were regulated by the state these harms would diminish. But examples show these arguments to be false.

**Prostituted women are even more marginalized and tightly locked into the system of organized sexual exploitation while the state, now an official party to the exploitation, has become the biggest pimp of all.**

In the pamphlet entitled *Legalizing Prostitution Is Not the Answer: The Example of Victoria, Australia,* published by the CATW in 2001, Mary Sullivan and Sheila Jeffreys describe the way legalization in Australia has perpetuated and strengthened the culture of violence and exploitation inherent in prostitution. Under legalization, legal and illegal brothels have proliferated, and trafficking in women has accelerated to meet the increased demand. Pimps, having even more power, continue threatening and brutalizing the women they control. Buyers continue to abuse women, refuse to wear condoms, and spread the HIV virus—and other sexually transmitted diseases—to their wives and girlfriends. Stigmatized by identity cards and medical inspections, prostituted women are even more marginalized and tightly locked into the system of organized sexual exploitation while the state, now an official party to the exploitation, has become the biggest pimp of all.

The government of the Netherlands has legalized prostitution, doesn't enforce laws against pimping, and virtually lives off taxes from the earnings of prostituted women. In the book *Making the Harm Visible* (published by the CATW in 1999), Marie-Victoire Louis describes the effects on prostituted women of municipal regulation of brothels in Amsterdam and other Dutch cities. Her article entitled "Legalizing Pimping, Dutch Style" explains the way immigration policies in the Netherlands are shaped to fit the needs of the prostitution industry so that traffickers are seldom prosecuted and a continuous supply of women is guaranteed. In Amsterdam's 250 officially listed brothels, 80 percent of the prostitutes have been trafficked in from other countries and 70 percent possess no legal papers. Without money, papers, or contact with the outside world, these immigrant women live in terror instead of being protected by the regulations governing brothels, prostituted women are frequently beaten up and raped by pimps. These "prostitution managers" have practically been given a free hand by the state and by buyers who, as "consumers of prostitution," feel themselves entitled to abuse the women they buy. Sadly and ironically the "Amsterdam model" of legalization and regulation is touted by the Netherlands and Germany as "self-determination and empowerment for women." In reality it simply legitimizes the "right" to buy, sexually use, and profit from the sexual exploitation of someone else's body.

# A Human Rights Approach

As part of a system of organized sexual exploitation, prostitution can be visualized along a continuum of abuse with brothel slavery at the furthest extreme. All along the continuum, fine lines divide the degrees of harm done to those caught up in the system. At the core lies a great social injustice no cosmetic reforms can right: the setting aside of a segment of people whose bodies can be purchased for sexual use by others. When this basic injustice is legitimized and regulated by the state and when the state profits from it, that injustice is compounded.

In her book *The Prostitution of Sexuality* (New York University Press, 1995), Kathleen Barry details a feminist human rights approach to prostitution that points the way to the future. Ethically it recognizes prostitution, sex trafficking, and the globalized industrialization of sex as massive violations of women's human rights. Sociologically it considers how and to what extent prostitution promotes sex discrimination against individual women, against different racial categories of women, and against women as a group. Politically it calls for decriminalizing prostitutes while penalizing pimps, traffickers, brothel owners, and buyers.

Understanding that human rights and restorative justice go hand in hand, the feminist human rights approach to prostitution addresses the harm and the need to repair the damage. As Barry says:

> "Legal proposals to criminalize customers, based on the recognition that prostitution violates and harms women, must . . . include social-service, health and counseling and job retraining programs. Where states would be closing down brothels if customers were criminalized, the economic resources poured into the former prostitution areas could be turned toward producing gainful employment for women."

With the help of women's projects in many countries—such as Buklod in the Philippines and the Council for Prostitution Alternatives in the United States—some women have begun to confront their condition by leaving prostitution, speaking out against it, revealing their experiences, and helping other women leave the sex industry.

Ending the sexual exploitation of trafficking and prostitution will mean the beginning of a new chapter in building a humanist future—a more peaceful and just future in which men and women can join together in love and respect, recognizing one another's essential dignity and humanity. Humanity's sexuality then will no longer be hijacked and distorted.

Freelance writer **ALICE LEUCHTAG** has worked as a social worker, counselor, college instructor, and researcher. Active in the civil rights, peace, socialist, feminist, and humanist movements, she has helped organize women in Houston to oppose sex trafficking.

From *The Humanist*, January/February 2003. Copyright © 2003 by Alice Leuchtag. Reprinted by permission of the author.

# Fall Girls

**The "D.C. Madam" took a prostitution rap, then took her own life. But her alleged johns—including sanctimonious U.S. senator David Vitter—walked away uncensured and unscathed.**

MARK BENJAMIN

Louisiana Republican Sen. David Vitter strolled about his business under the snow-white U.S. Capitol dome on May 1, 2008—a routine, even mundane day for the staunch social conservative. He mostly slogged through negotiations about an expansion of the National Flood Insurance Program.

That isn't the kind of red-meat issue that fueled Vitter's meteoric ascent into the Senate in 2004, just four years after he was elected to the House. Vitter campaigned as a man who best represents "mainstream Louisiana values." Verging on holier-than-thou, Vitter is one of the most moralistic, "pro-family" elected officials walking the Capitol's polished hall-ways. He reserves most of his fire and brimstone for the defense of traditional heterosexual marriage, an institution Vitter has described passionately as a precious tenet of Western civilization, even a panacea that "goes to the core of so many of the deep social problems."

At about the same time that Thursday, some 800 miles to the south, Deborah Jeane Palfrey, known as the D.C. Madam, was taking her last breaths. She walked out of her mother's trailer home in Tarpon Springs, Fla., into a shed out back. According to police, she then hung herself. The suicide note she wrote to her mother, dated five days earlier, described the ordeal of her very public trial on charges related to the prostitution ring she operated as a "modern-day lynching." She had been convicted two weeks earlier of money laundering, using the mail for illegal purposes and racketeering, and faced a maximum of 55 years in prison. In simpler terms, she had been busted for arranging sexual liaisons for powerful men.

Vitter may have been one of those powerful men.

Last summer, it was revealed that Vitter's Washington phone number had shown up five times in Palfrey's 1999–2000 call-girl service phone records. Larry Flynt's *Hustler* magazine had obtained the records from a journalist working with Palfrey on a book, then contacted Vitter's office. At a hastily called press conference, the senator admitted to a "very serious sin in my past." He added, "Several years ago,

I asked for and received forgiveness from God and from my wife in confession and marriage counseling." As have other wives of politicians who strayed, Vitter's wife, Wendy—a woman who implied rather saltily in 2000 that if her husband committed adultery she'd behave more like Lorena Bobbitt, the woman who severed her husband's penis, than Hillary Clinton—stood faithfully by her man.

Even by the most jaded Washington standards, Vitter's indiscretions smack of hypocrisy. The Christian Coalition has rated Vitter 100 percent on his voting record for their key issues. He supports abstinence-only education, and earmarked $100,000 (later withdrawn) to the Louisiana Family Forum for promoting "better science education"—in other words, so-called intelligent design. He is a staunch and reliable opponent of gun control, abortion, gambling, immigrants' rights and particularly gay marriage.

With Vitter, it has never just been that gay marriage is so wrong, but that a wholesome heterosexual marriage is a sacred institution. Vitter sponsored a 1999 House resolution "recognizing the importance of strong marriages" and fought for the Marriage Protection Act of 2007 (designed to prevent federal courts from hearing any challenges to the anti-gay-marriage Defense of Marriage Act). In 2006, he argued in favor of a constitutional amendment that would define marriage as a union reserved only for heterosexual couples. Vitter—who himself is married with four children—claimed at the time that traditional marriage would precipitate ethical behavior.

"Marriage is truly the most fundamental social institution in human history," he said in a speech on the Senate floor on June 6, 2006. "Let's take time to remember and focus on truly significant, enduring social institutions which are the greatest predictors, the greatest factors in terms of encouraging good behavior and success [and] discouraging bad behavior and failure." He called alternatives to traditional heterosexual marriage a "threat" and a "problem."

For a man who had so much to say about the benefits of conventional matrimony and such vitriol for consensual behavior he considers immoral, Vitter's "serious sin" confession last summer was just about all he has said about his own transgressions. The silence is particularly deafening given the numerous questions he has faced from reporters who wanted to know if his calls to the D.C. Madam represented an anomaly or reflected a habit.

Indeed, shortly after dropping his unsuccessful 2002 bid to be Louisiana's governor, Vitter had been accused by a member of his own party's state central committee, Victor Bruno, of carrying on an affair with a French Quarter prostitute in his hometown of New Orleans. Others in the New Orleans sex industry have also come forward, claiming that despite all of Vitter's lofty rhetoric about morality, Palfrey wasn't the only madam taking his calls. Within days of the news breaking about Vitter and Palfrey last summer, former prostitute Wendy Yow Ellis charged that Vitter had been a client, and Jeanette Maier, known in New Orleans as the "Canal Street Madam," told reporters that Vitter used *her* service as well. Vitter has denied all the allegations.

In an interview with *Ms.*, Maier chuckled incredulously at Vitter's denial and claimed that her business had dispatched prostitutes to his home years ago, before Vitter was elected to the Senate. Maier added that in her 30 years of experience in the sex industry, men who visit prostitutes are often regular customers. "Once a trick, always a trick," she said. (Vitter's office did not return phone calls from *Ms.* requesting his response to any of these issues.)

Maier, 49, claims she doesn't harbor any ill feelings toward Vitter, but described as unfair the fact that prosecutors tend to target the women in prostitution cases but show little appetite for hauling in their male clients. And a New Orleans judge seemed to agree: At Maier's 2002 sentencing for running a Canal Street brothel, Judge Ivan Lemelle questioned why federal authorities pursued the case in the first place. He added that the idea of prosecuting madams and prostitutes—but not their clients—was a "disparity of justice." Nonetheless, Maier was fined $10,000 and sentenced to six months in a halfway house and three years' probation.

Palfrey's prosecution was an even more depressing and destructive affair. While the trial ultimately led to Palfrey's suicide, it was also a humiliating spectacle for some of her former employees. They included women who seemed like they were, by the time of the trial, simply moving on with their lives and trying to leave prostitution behind.

Navy Lt. Cmdr. Rebecca Dickinson, 38, had an exemplary service record, a raft of commendation medals and had helped teach a leadership course at the Naval Academy in Annapolis, Md. The divorced mother of three, so nervous when she took the stand in April that the judge had to remind her to take deep breaths, testified that she simply "needed the money" when she first contacted Palfrey for work. Palfrey said during the trial that Dickinson was struggling to provide child care for her kids, and did in fact need the $130 she made on each assignation (out of a total fee of $275).

Dickinson hadn't worked as a prostitute for two years before her testimony, but the revelation of her previous employ sank her military career. A Navy spokesman told reporters at the time that Dickinson's actions "will prevent her from wearing this uniform again in the service of our country."

---

## The Abramoff Connection

David Vitter was yet another of the multitude who had fishy dealings with the disgraced Republican lobbyist.

Sen. David Vitter is a longtime crusader against gambling.

As part of that crusade, he added language to the 2004 Department of the Interior appropriations bill to discourage the development of an off-reservation casino in Vinton, La., by the Jena Band of Choctaws. Subsequently, Ralph Reed, former leader of the Christian Coalition, sent thousands of postcards from his Committee Against Gambling Expansion praising Vitter to voters, and Vitter was given permission to use Reed's group's name in a phone bank.

But behind both men's antigambling moralizing larked a money-making scheme run by Jack Abramoff, the former Republican lobbyist now serving a jail term for fraud, tax evasion and conspiracy. Abramoff was actually being paid millions of dollars by a *different* casino-operating Indian tribe, the Lousiana Coushattas, to block the Jena casino strictly on economic grounds (it would cut into the Coushattas' revenues). Indeed, Reed's organization received as much as $4 million from Abramoff and his associate Michael Scanion that had been contributed through a nonprofit by the Coushatta tribe—a fact both Reed and Vitter insisted they were unaware of.

Moreover, just prior to Vitter filing the Indian gaming rider, Jack Abramoff held a September, 2003 fundraiser for Vitter at a Washington, D.C., restaurant that he co-owned. Vitter's response to this revelation was that only 10 people showed up at the event, and Abramoff was absent.

"I've never met with Jack Abramoff on any Indian gaming issue, never," said Vitter in a statement he issued. "To my knowledge, I have only met him once briefly in passing, and to this day I couldn't pick him out of a crowd." Later, though, Vitter admitted that his staff worked with Abramoff's law firm to help draft language for the appropriations rider.

In February, Vitter introduced his "Common Sense Indian Gambling Reform Act of 2008," which was similar to legislation he offered before. It would make it much harder for Indian tribes to open casinos off their reservation lands.

—Michele Kort

---

There were other women casualties even before the trial began. In January 2007, Brandy Britton, 43—a Ph.D. and former University of Maryland at Baltimore professor of sociology and anthropology (she had done her dissertation on battered women) who had lost her job and allegedly turned to prostitution—committed suicide just days before she was scheduled to stand trial. Before her death, Palfrey had named Britton as one of her employees. Ironically, Palfrey had claimed to be made of "tougher material" than Britton, yet both died, severely depressed, by hanging.

# Broken Pledge

AIDS czar Randall L. Tobias forced countries receiving U.S. aid to sign a document condemning prostitution. Too bad he didn't sign it himself before calling the D.C. Madam.

When George W. Bush went looking for his first "AIDS czar" in 2003—someone who could implement his ambitious program to address the global pandemic—he settled on an upstanding Republican businessman.

Randall L. Tobias had been vice chairman of AT&T, then chairman and CEO of pharmaceutical giant Eli Lilly. He was a member of numerous corporate boards, a trustee of Duke University, and a large donor to Republican candidates and political committees. He was a married man.

As AIDS czar—or, more formally, ambassador for the President's Emergency Plan for AIDS Relief (PEPFAR)—Tobias was charged with distributing the $15 billion fund. Much of the budget went to the purchase of antiretroviral drugs, but critics have charged that Tobias, with his Big Pharma background, helped block the use of lower-cost generic medication in favor of name brands. Yusuf Hamied, chairman of the Indian generic pharmaceutical company Cipla, said in 2006 that Tobias "put in a lot of hurdles [to ensure] that the PEPFAR money wouldn't go to the generics," according to the Center for Public Integrity.

Moreover, Tobias administered the moralistic guidelines of U.S. funding, which included teaching the "ABCs" to countries desperate for AIDS monies. This was the Bush administration's AIDS strategy: emphasize **A**bstinence first, then **B**eing Faithful, then, last and least, **C**ondoms—which had previously been considered the *first* line of defense against AIDS transmission. "Statistics show that condoms really have not been very effective," insisted Tobias at a 2004 news conference.

There was one more element of the Bush plan that Tobias willingly promoted: the antiprostitution and sex trafficking pledge. Although no one would disagree with a stance against trafficking, the antiprostitution pledge was another matter: Successful AIDS prevention programs depend on partnerships with sex workers, who can carry the disease to and from their clients and on to their children and others.

When the Brazilian government offered a compromise—it would distance its support programs for sex workers from

its U.S.-supported AIDS programs—Tobias wouldn't have it. "Any organization receiving U.S. global AIDS funding will have to agree to our policy," he told *The Guardian* in 2005.

The impact of this decision was drastic and immediate. Brazil turned down the restricted funds. Clinics staffed by and serving prostitutes and their children were summarily closed. Halfway houses, schools and shelters were shuttered; the distribution of free condoms dropped by half at the prostitutes' union in Rio. Sex workers in Bangladesh thronged the streets, sobbing and pleading for condoms, their only protection from disease.

But President Bush was pleased with Tobias' work. In 2006, Tobias was promoted to administrator of the U.S. Agency for International Development (USAID), which distributes family-planning funds to developing nations, as well as U.S. director of foreign assistance. He was given the rank of a deputy secretary of state.

That all ended in April of 2007, when Tobias' cell phone number was found in a list of clients of Deborah Jeane Palfrey's "sexual fantasy" service. The deputy secretary was stunned, and in a private phone conversation told Brian Ross of ABC News that the "gals" came over to "the condo" only to give him "massages." He claimed it was an innocent transaction, "like ordering pizza." In any case, he no longer used the services of Palfrey: He'd switched to another "massage" agency and now used "Central Americans."

Tobias resigned the next day. Palfrey was prosecuted; Tobias was never charged, or even called as a witness.

Instead, he went back to Indianapolis, where Mayor Greg Ballard, another alum of Big Pharma (he worked for Bayer), believes "in second chances." He named Tobias director of the Indianapolis Airport Authority: no salary, but control of contracts worth more than $95 million. His secretary still answers his phone "Ambassador Tobias," from what sounds like a nice office. Leather, dark wood, glass perhaps.

A far cry from the mobile home in a Florida bayou town where Deborah Jeane Palfrey's mother found her after she'd been convicted, hanging from a nylon rope.

—Vicky Shorr

Vitter, meanwhile, will remain comfortably ensconced in the Senate until at least 2010. He was never called to the witness stand during Palfrey's trial. Neither was Randall L. Tobias—the U.S. AIDS czar who refused to direct U.S. funds to countries who wouldn't sign an antiprostitution pledge—although Tobias did step down from his post once his name surfaced. Another client never forced to testify was Harlan K. Ullman, the retired U.S. Navy commander who developed the "shock and awe" combat strategy used by the Pentagon at the start of the Iraq war.

"The thing that I find that is so up-setting about Vitter is how sexist the whole thing has been," says Melanie Sloan, executive director of the non-partisan watchdog group Citizens

for Responsibility and Ethics in Washington (CREW—see *Ms.*, Winter 2007). "To me it is like the Salem witch trials. The men walk free while women were burned," she laments. "All of these women suffered enormously."

Sloan's group filed a complaint about Vitter with the Senate Select Committee on Ethics, a body unfortunately considered an anemic enforcer at best—reflecting the fact that there is no great appetite on Capitol Hill for investigating one's fellow senators. Still, wrote Sloan in her complaint, "at the very least . . . the committee should issue a public statement criticizing the senator's conduct." She pointed out that it's against the law to solicit for prostitution in Washington, D.C., as well as in Louisiana.

Nonetheless, the committee dismissed the matter in a May 8, 2008, letter to Vitter. The "conduct at issue" occurred before Vitter got to the Senate, the committee wrote, and he was never charged with a crime. Also, Vitter's alleged transgressions "did not involve use of public office or status for improper uses." But the letter to Vitter did include this pointed statement: "The committee reserves the right to reopen an investigation should new allegations or evidence be brought to our attention."

Vitter has returned to the Senate, where he's still working on flooding, as he helps shepherd along initiatives to deal with the lingering aftermath of Hurricane Katrina. And of course he still cares deeply about family issues. Vitter has even established an initiative to deal with a special constituency of his: women.

According to his website, Vitter's Women's Leadership Forum includes meetings that are "designed to help me focus on the views and needs of women and families." Topics for discussion include breast cancer and domestic violence. Vitter says the meetings with women "have produced an ongoing dialogue about the initiatives you want me to address in the Senate as well as specific work we can pursue together in the community."

---

**MARK BENJAMIN** is an investigative reporter based in Washington, D.C. He specializes in national security issues and politic.

From *Ms.*, Summer 2008. Copyright © 2008 by Ms. Magazine. Reprinted by permission of Ms. Magazine and the author.

# Women, Citizens, Muslims

Amy Zalman

On December 13, 2003, 502 members of Afghanistan's constitutional Grand Council, or loya jirga, met in the capital, Kabul, to begin writing the document that would henceforth shape governance of an Islamic, representative democracy. Three weeks later, after at least two rocket attacks near the council's meeting place and even more explosive politicking among the council's members, the council emerged with a new constitution.

Among those who watched the process with attention were Afghan women and their activist partisans in other parts of the world, who wanted the new constitution explicitly to reflect the rights and needs of women. They had particular reason to worry that the assembly gathered in Kabul would be hijacked by conservative extremists who would interpret women's rights narrowly using religion as an excuse, or who might eliminate mentions of women's human rights altogether.

The Grand Council met just two years after the United States toppled the Taliban, the extremist party that had been in control of Afghanistan's capital since 1996. The American objective was to destabilize a regime that had given refuge to Osama bin Laden and the leaders of Al Qaeda, whose bases were in Afghanistan. At that time, the United States linked its military agenda in Afghanistan with the need to liberate Afghan women from oppression. As First Lady Laura Bush put the matter in a national radio address in November 2001, "The brutal oppression of women is a central goal of the terrorists. Long before the current war began, the Taliban and its terrorist allies were making the lives of children and women in Afghanistan miserable." The first lady went on to assert that the removal of the Taliban from power would mean the liberation of Afghan women. For the next year, Afghan women were big news: There were books and reports, and pictures on the front pages of newspapers showing formerly illiterate women learning to read. Women began the work of reconstructing their lives by returning to the streets, to school, to work. Then the war in Iraq began, and Afghan women, and Afghanistan's reconstruction, became old news.

By the beginning of 2003, warlords in provinces who had been allies of the United States when it went to war against the Taliban were instituting measures themselves that were reminiscent of the Taliban era. Human Rights Watch reported in January 2003 that in the Western province of Herat, girls and boys would no longer be permitted to go to school together. Because most teachers are men, the ruling effectively shut girls

and women out of an education. Other restrictions against interactions between the sexes were imposed; girls or women seen in public with a male might be taken against their will to a hospital to check for their "chastity." These alarming trends coincided with a sharp drop in international scrutiny, although Afghan women themselves continued to seek access to good health, higher education, and equal pay for their work.

Their experience in the last two years has made it clear that simply removing a dictatorial regime and installing a democracy does not automatically guarantee women's rights. Indeed, the challenges facing women's effort to make sure their rights are legally enforceable in the future highlight broad conflicts in Afghanistan between conservative and liberalizing factions of the future government and between forces competing to control interpretations of Islam in the public sphere. Islam is the prism through which human rights are articulated in Afghanistan, and it is it is therefore crucial for women that their rights to education, work, and freely chosen marriages be articulated in its terms. The importance of the relationship between Islam and rights is one supported by women. Indeed, "Ninety-nine percent of Afghan women are Muslims, and their faith is extremely important to them. Most feel their rights are available to them through Islam," says Masuda Sultan, the spokesperson for Women for Afghan Women (WAW), a New York City-based grassroots organization of Afghan women and their supporters. Sultan explains that the number of women who frame their rights in secular terms is much smaller.

The process of shaping a new women's rights doctrine that would take Islam into account was in evidence in the making of the "Women's Bill of Rights," authored in September 2003 by a representative group of 45 women who found ways to interpret relevant Islamic edicts in ways that amplified their human rights. The bill of rights was the achievement of a unique conference on women and the constitution sponsored by WAW. Organized with the help of the Afghan Women's Network and Afghans for Civil Society, the Kandahar conference brought women together to deliberate over how their rights could best be reflected in the constitution. Kandahar, unlike the more liberal capital, is one of Afghanistan's most conservative provinces, and it was unclear until the day of the conference whether it would be secure enough for the gathering to take place. It was, but only under heavily armed guard. The conference participants comprised elite female decision-makers as well as largely illiterate everyday women from all over the country. For some, simply completing the trip, whether alone or in the company of a male relative, was itself a triumph.

Over the course of three days, these women reviewed the 1964 constitution on which the 2003 draft was based and began composing the 16-point bill of rights, framed by the demand that the rights be not simply "secured in the constitution but implemented." Some of the demands are basics on the menu of modern human rights: women require mandatory education, equal pay for equal work, freedom of speech, and the freedom to vote and run for office and to be represented equally in Parliament and the judiciary.

But other points are specific to the situation of Afghan Muslim women and responsive to the recent forms of deprivation imposed by the Taliban and long-standing excesses based on tribal convention. There is, for example, the demand that women and children be protected against sexual abuse, domestic violence, and bad-blood price—when one family compensates a second for a crime by giving them one of the family's women. There is a request for "the provision of up-to-date heath services for women with special attention to reproductive rights." Under the Taliban women were denied healthcare by male doctors, who were not allowed to touch the bodies of women to whom they were not related, and severe restrictions on women's movements made it difficult for female doctors to supply healthcare. Women made it clear they wanted the right to marry and divorce according to Islamic law.

At the end of the conference, the document was presented publicly to President Hamed Karzai, and women were promised that their rights would be incorporated explicitly into the new constitution. However, when the draft constitution was released in November 2003, there was no explicit mention of women's rights. Instead, the constitution granted rights to all Afghan citizens. As Rim Sharma, the co-founder and executive director of the Women's Edge Coalition and Afifa Azim, the director of the Afghan Women's Network, argued in a joint editorial on the eve of the council's meeting, lumping together men and women in the text of the constitution, rather than clearly designating rights for women as well as men is "an important distinction because Afghan women are not issued the identification cards given to men. Therefore, some men argue, women are not citizens and entitled to equality." A crucial question at the Grand Council was whether women would be identified separately from men in the final constitution. It was a triumph when the constitution that was released contained an article stating that "The citizens of Afghanistan—whether man or woman—have equal rights and duties before the law."

At the same time, other challenges remain. The introduction of women's rights to the national political agenda cannot itself be taken for granted while control of the country is still in question. Although it is true that on paper, the government of Afghanistan is headed by President Karzai and moving toward democracy along well established lines such as the creation of a constitution, the actual situation in many parts of the country do not reflect this shift in power. The Taliban have reasserted power in Southern and Eastern parts of the country. Indeed, in the few days leading up to the meeting of the constitutional Grand Council, coalition forces waged their largest attacks to date on Taliban members who threatened violence against the proceedings. As a recent Amnesty International report also noted, Northern Alliance commanders who committed human rights abuses under the Taliban government now hold government positions themselves (the October 2003 report, Afghanistan: "No one listens to us and no one treats us as human beings" Justice denied to women, can be found at www.web.amnesty.org/library/index/engasa110232003). Where these commanders govern, women's movements remain as restricted, or nearly as restricted, as they did before they were "liberated."

So, one of the threats to women's rights is related to the ongoing danger to the entire nation's stability as well as to the ability of the most conservative or militant actors in Afghanistan to influence the political process. Extremists exploit claims to Islam to intimidate women. This means that although women themselves frame their rights in terms of Islam, they can also be intimidated into making claims for interpretations that don't serve their needs at all. Sultan explains:

> Security is still a huge issue, and regional warlords and extremists are around. A woman who doesn't speak in terms that acknowledge Islam will face trouble. The affirmation of being Muslim is important because otherwise they'll be called infidels or be threatened or seen as secular or non-Muslim.

The proper response to this situation, in the view of Sultan and others who work closely with Afghan women, is to promote the education of women in Islamic law and history so that they can express their own rights as well as refute interpretations that do not serve them. As the legal system begins to hammer out laws that confirm the bases of the constitution, such knowledge will be increasingly important. Jurists are qualified in Afghanistan through higher education or training in Islamic law. As Sultan notes, these qualifications "leave open the door" for those trained informally by radical Islamist clerics to shape law. Women's education in the language, tradition, and law through which they understand their rights and themselves is a practical and necessary step in this context. This may appear counterintuitive to onlookers in the United States and Europe, whose recent revolutions in rights have often taken place in social and political contexts that opposed democracy to religion. Enhancing the rights of women by encouraging their access to religious education may also seem counterintuitive in the present media environment, which is saturated by the idea that Islam is inherently undemocratic. But women working for their rights in Afghanistan make it clear that both Islam and democracy are evolving practices that permit competing interpretations. It is their right to shape both in ways that confirm their identities as women, Afghan citizens, and Muslims.

From *The Women's Review of Books*, February 1, 2004. Copyright © 2004 by Amy Zalman. Reprinted by permission of the author.

# Beyond Hillary
## Strength in Numbers

**The focus this primary season has been on the ambitions and achievements of one woman, but women won't claim their share of political power until they achieve critical mass at all levels of government.**

Ann Friedman

In 1992, the much-vaunted "Year of the Woman" when 27 women were elected to Congress, Sen. Barbara Mikulski of Maryland said, "Calling 1992 the Year of the Woman makes it sound like the Year of the Caribou or the Year of the Asparagus. We're not a fad, a fancy, or a year."

To a certain degree, Mikulski was right. It wasn't just a fad; the numbers of women in Congress have slowly and steadily increased since then. But there has never since been an election like 1992, with a sizable class of incoming women legislators. And, needless to say, women have yet to achieve anything close to parity at the highest levels of government.

Hillary Clinton's historic campaign for president has inspired some important conversations about women in politics, mostly focused on how sexism has played out in her campaign, or how voters have responded to a female candidate for such a high office. But it's time for us to look down the pipeline. Progressives have a vested interest in getting more women into office—and not only because it's good to have our elected bodies better reflect the population. Nearly 30 percent of women in Congress are members of the Progressive Caucus, while only 10 percent of men in Congress are. As blogger Matt Stoller put it, "The more women in office, the more progressives in office." (For a look at some up-and-coming progressive women in politics, see the chart on page 249.)

For all the progress made in electing women over the past 16 years, however, the glass ceiling remains stubbornly in place. None of the remarkable individual women who have risen to the highest ranks of our political system—Nancy Pelosi, Hillary Clinton—has been more than a crack in the glass. To be sure, they are inspirational pioneers who give us a first glimpse of a better, more equitable future. But the glass ceiling won't truly be shattered until women have achieved a critical mass in government.

Despite the drama and excitement that have accompanied Clinton's campaign, we're not at a high point for women in politics. The high-water mark came nearly two decades ago.

The biggest shifts toward a more woman-friendly political culture all happened between 1991 and 1993. Those years saw not only the largest group of women elected to Congress but to state legislatures and as governors. That's also when Democratic women came together to form the Women's Leadership Forum to get more women involved in the party. Whether it was the Anita Hill hearings (which some women have cited as the reason they chose to run for office) or simply an unusual number of open seats, a record-breaking number of women seized the moment and, for the first time as a group, got a foothold in national politics.

Those days feel a long way away. Since the Year of the Woman, the number of women in national office has leveled off. Today, women are still less than 25 percent of senators, representatives, governors, and state legislators. The 2008 election isn't shaping up to be much different. In 1992, 11 women were candidates in Senate races. So far this year, only two women have won Senate primaries. We currently have eight women governors (including Democrat Janet Napolitano, whom Dana Goldstein profiles in this issue), and this election year will see 11 gubernatorial races. Thus far, only two women have won primaries. Compare that to the record-setting year for women governors, 1994, which saw 34 women file for races and 10 win their primaries. It's clear we aren't going anywhere fast.

Those numbers mirror the situation for women in other careers. In almost every professional field, women are stuck at the 25 percent barrier. We're less than 25 percent of corporate officers, law partners, writers for major magazines, and Wall Street execs. And I would argue it's the same set of factors (partners unwilling to shoulder their share of the child-care burden, inflexible workplace policies, straight-up sexism) that keep women from rising through the ranks of both corporations and Congress. Outliers like Pelosi and Clinton—and Fortune 500 CEOs like Xerox's Ann Mulcahy—do not in themselves amount to the shift necessary to make lasting change. When a magazine hires a female editor-in-chief, the number of women's bylines does not automatically increase. I would argue that the reason sweeping change doesn't occur is not because these remarkable women aren't doing enough. It's simply that one woman at the top cannot change an entire culture. Looking at these numbers across the board, it's clear that the real ceiling is not limiting individual women's ambitions. It's keeping women as a group from breaking the 25 percent barrier.

## We need to change our political culture, not just have one woman triumph over it.

If we want to cross that threshold, we need to look at the system. We're never going to successfully implement quotas as other countries have, and it takes time to change the traditional views about a woman's proper place in society that persist in certain U.S. regions. But those who would agree with the statement, "We need more women in positions of political power"—most of the Democratic Party leadership and most readers of this magazine, I'd guess—need to take a step back in the wake of Clinton's candidacy and, rather than examine what went wrong in the Clinton example, look at how to ensure we don't have to rely on outliers like Clinton in elections for the next 30 years. The real goal should be to identify significant numbers of female candidates as future leaders and promote them through the ranks in a far more conventional manner. In other words, to change our very political culture—not just have one woman triumph over it.

That's why the Year of the Woman was actually important, despite the fact that it did not usher in a new, woman-friendly era of politics. It showed us how a group of women in politics could support each other and rise through the ranks together, rather than a single woman simply trying to play the game with the boys. The four Democratic women senators elected in 1992 held meetings as a group once they had made it to Capitol Hill (they were joined by Mikulski, who was already serving in the Senate), and discussed the problems they were facing in the boys'-club culture. At times they issued joint statements that began with, "We, the women of the Senate." The women in the House demanded equal access to the main gym and fitness facilities, because the women's gym had fallen into disrepair. The Democratic women also consistently voted together—including lending crucial support to President Bill Clinton during the 1993 budget battle. All this amounted to a subtle shift in the culture of the U.S. Congress—not a sea change but a bigger step toward breaking the 25 percent barrier (and thus the glass ceiling) than Hillary Clinton's candidacy.

Our recent political history offers many examples of women in national politics who boosted each other's careers. One key way to get more women into office is to ask them to run (as Ezra Klein points out in this issue), and women are often the ones doing the asking. Pelosi was elected to Congress in part because

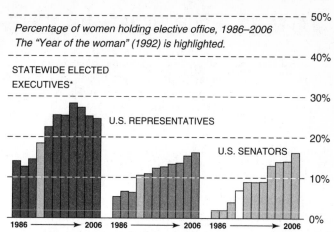

Percentage of women holding elective office, 1986–2006
The "Year of the woman" (1992) is highlighted.

STATEWIDE ELECTED EXECUTIVES*

U.S. REPRESENTATIVES

U.S. SENATORS

1986 ——➤ 2006   1986 ——➤ 2006   1986 ——➤ 2006

*Elected executive positions vary by state, but can include governors, lieutenant governors, attorneys general, secretaries of state, treasurers, and auditors.

she was handpicked in 1987 by the dying Rep. Sala Burton to be her successor. Louisiana's Mary Landrieu was pushed to enter politics by Gov. Ann Richards of Texas—Landrieu lost her 1995 gubernatorial bid but was elected to the Senate the following year. And once they're elected, women are more likely to turn to other women for mentorship. Sen. Barbara Mikulski made how-to manuals for the Democratic women who joined the Senate in 1992, Eleanor Clift and Tom Brazaitis note in their 2003 book, *Madam President*. Mikulski's guidebook, titled "Getting Started in the Senate," contained tips on everything from responding to constituent mail to getting a good committee appointment.

Of course, women can increase their political prominence in ways besides winning electoral office. The Democratic Party has long anointed its rising stars by designating them to give speeches at the Democratic National Convention or the official response to the president's State of the Union address. There are also cabinet positions, which carry great political power. (Only 37 women have ever been cabinet members.) Using these appointments to elevate more women in politics is something we should demand of all elected progressives.

Until a critical mass is reached, this sort of concerted effort to promote women in politics is crucial. In an ideal world, such efforts would start with party apparatuses like the Democratic campaign committees taking pains to encourage women to run for office—and then supporting their campaigns. They would continue with donations from groups like EMILY's List and, after women are elected, with additional support and mentoring from their colleagues in Congress. Mikulski, for her part, was shepherded through her first year in the Senate by her Democratic colleagues Paul Sarbanes of Maryland and Ted Kennedy of Massachusetts. She called them her "Galahads."

The goal, though, is to shift the political culture enough so that newly elected women don't need Galahads. Since the 1970s, many women, in politics and business, have "broken the glass ceiling" alone. But until women are lined up behind (and next to) that one woman who busts through, it's going to be hard for us to move beyond the exceptions like Hillary Clinton.

From *The American Prospect*, July/August 2008. Copyright © 2008. Reprinted with permission from Ann Friedman and The American Prospect, 11 Beacon Street, Suite 1120, Boston, MA 02108. All rights reserved.

# Test-Your-Knowledge Form

We encourage you to photocopy and use this page as a tool to assess how the articles in *Annual Editions* expand on the information in your textbook. By reflecting on the articles you will gain enhanced text information. You can also access this useful form on a product's book support website at *http://www.mhcls.com*.

NAME:                                                    DATE:
_____

TITLE AND NUMBER OF ARTICLE:
_____

BRIEFLY STATE THE MAIN IDEA OF THIS ARTICLE:


_____

LIST THREE IMPORTANT FACTS THAT THE AUTHOR USES TO SUPPORT THE MAIN IDEA:




_____

WHAT INFORMATION OR IDEAS DISCUSSED IN THIS ARTICLE ARE ALSO DISCUSSED IN YOUR TEXTBOOK OR OTHER READINGS THAT YOU HAVE DONE? LIST THE TEXTBOOK CHAPTERS AND PAGE NUMBERS:




_____

LIST ANY EXAMPLES OF BIAS OR FAULTY REASONING THAT YOU FOUND IN THE ARTICLE:




_____

LIST ANY NEW TERMS/CONCEPTS THAT WERE DISCUSSED IN THE ARTICLE, AND WRITE A SHORT DEFINITION:

# We Want Your Advice

ANNUAL EDITIONS revisions depend on two major opinion sources: one is our Advisory Board, listed in the front of this volume, which works with us in scanning the thousands of articles published in the public press each year; the other is you—the person actually using the book. Please help us and the users of the next edition by completing the prepaid article rating form on this page and returning it to us. Thank you for your help!

## ANNUAL EDITIONS: Gender 10/11

### ARTICLE RATING FORM

Here is an opportunity for you to have direct input into the next revision of this volume.
We would like you to rate each of the articles listed below, using the following scale:

1. **Excellent: should definitely be retained**
2. **Above average: should probably be retained**
3. **Below average: should probably be deleted**
4. **Poor: should definitely be deleted**

Your ratings will play a vital part in the next revision.
Please mail this prepaid form to us as soon as possible.
Thanks for your help!

| RATING | ARTICLE | RATING | ARTICLE |
|--------|---------|--------|---------|
| | 1. The Social Construction of Gender | | 24. A Woman's Curse? |
| | 2. Framed before We Know It: How Gender Shapes Social Relations | | 25. Body Dissatisfaction in Adolescent Females and Males: Risk and Resilience |
| | 3. Gender Is Powerful: The Long Reach of Feminism | | 26. When Sex Hurts |
| | 4. The World, the Flesh and the Devil | | 27. Health Behaviors, Prostate Cancer, and Masculinities: A Life Course Perspective |
| | 5. A Case for Angry Men and Happy Women | | 28. (Rethinking) Gender |
| | 6. Beauty, Gender and Stereotypes: Evidence from Laboratory Experiments | | 29. Progress and Politics in the Intersex Rights Movement: Feminist Theory in Action |
| | 7. I'm Not a Very Manly Man: Qualitative Insights into Young Men's Masculine Subjectivity | | 30. What Do Women Want? |
| | 8. Gender and Group Process: A Developmental Perspective | | 31. Women's Sexuality as They Age: The More Things Change, the More They Stay the Same |
| | 9. Gender Bender | | 32. Peer Marriage |
| | 10. The Secret Lives of Single Women | | 33. State of Our Unions: Marriage Promotion and the Contested Power of Heterosexuality |
| | 11. Goodbye to Girlhood | | 34. Five Years on, Gay Marriage Debate Fades in Massachusetts |
| | 12. Teenage Fatherhood and Involvement in Delinquent Behavior | | 35. Everyone's Queer |
| | 13. How Many Fathers Are Best for a Child? | | 36. The Berdache Tradition |
| | 14. What Autistic Girls Are Made Of | | 37. Children of Lesbian and Gay Parents |
| | 15. Learning and Gender | | 38. Flower Grandma's Secret |
| | 16. Educating Girls, Unlocking Development | | 39. Sexual Assault on Campus: What Colleges and Universities Are Doing about It |
| | 17. Boys and Girls Together: A Case for Creating Gender-Friendly Middle School Classrooms | | 40. Male Rape Myths: The Role of Gender, Violence, and Sexism |
| | 18. Female Faculty in Male-Dominated Fields: Law, Medicine, and Engineering | | 41. Effects of Sexual Assaults on Men: Physical, Mental, and Sexual Consequences |
| | 19. Scaling the Ivory Towers | | 42. Human Rights, Sex Trafficking, and Prostitution |
| | 20. The Emperor's New Woes | | 43. Fall Girls |
| | 21. The Media Depiction of Women Who Opt Out | | 44. Women, Citizens, Muslims |
| | 22. Great Expectations | | 45. Beyond Hillary: Strength in Numbers |
| | 23. Labor Markets, Breadwinning, and Beliefs: How Economic Context Shapes Men's Gender Ideology | | |

NO POSTAGE
NECESSARY
IF MAILED
IN THE
UNITED STATES

## BUSINESS REPLY MAIL
FIRST CLASS MAIL PERMIT NO. 551 DUBUQUE IA

POSTAGE WILL BE PAID BY ADDRESSEE

**McGraw-Hill Contemporary Learning Series**
501 BELL STREET
DUBUQUE, IA 52001

## ABOUT YOU

Name

Date

Are you a teacher? ❑ A student? ❑
Your school's name

Department

Address                City                State                Zip

School telephone #

## YOUR COMMENTS ARE IMPORTANT TO US!

Please fill in the following information:
For which course did you use this book?

Did you use a text with this ANNUAL EDITION? ❑ yes ❑ no
What was the title of the text?

What are your general reactions to the Annual Editions concept?

Have you read any pertinent articles recently that you think should be included in the next edition? Explain.

Are there any articles that you feel should be replaced in the next edition? Why?

Are there any World Wide Websites that you feel should be included in the next edition? Please annotate.

May we contact you for editorial input? ❑ yes ❑ no
May we quote your comments? ❑ yes ❑ no